Industrial Organization

The International Library of Critical Writings in Economics

Series Editor: Mark Blaug

Professor Emeritus, University of London
Consultant Professor, University of Buckingham
Visiting Professor, University of Exeter

Industrial Organization

Edited by

Oliver E. Williamson

Edgar F. Kaiser Professor of Business Administration
Professor of Economics, Professor of Law
University of California at Berkeley, US

An Elgar Critical Writings Reader
Cheltenham, UK ● Brookfield, US

Published by
Edward Elgar Publishing Limited
8 Lansdown Place
Cheltenham
Glos GL50 2HU
UK

Edward Elgar Publishing Company
Old Post Road
Brookfield
Vermont 05036
US

Paperback edition 1996

A CIP catalogue record for this book is available from the British Library

ISBN 1 85898 488 2

Printed in Great Britain by Galliard (Printers) Ltd, Great Yarmouth

Contents

Acknowledgements

The editor and publishers wish to thank the authors and the following publishers who have kindly given permission for the use of copyright material.

Academic Press, Inc. for article: D. Kreps and R. Wilson (1982), 'Reputation and Imperfect Information', *Journal of Economic Theory*, **27** (2), August, 253–79.

American Economic Association for articles: K. Arrow (1963), 'Uncertainty and the Welfare Economics of Medical Care', *American Economic Review*, **53** (5), December, 941–73; G. Akerlof (1983), 'Loyalty Filters', *American Economic Review*, **73** (1), March, 54–63; D. Fudenberg and J. Tirole (1984), 'The Fat-Cat Effect, The Puppy-Dog Ploy, and the Lean and Hungry Look', *American Economic Review*, **74** (2), May 361–6; P. Aghion and P. Bolton (1987), 'Contracts as a Barrier to Entry', *American Economic Review*, **77** (3), June, 388–401.

American Philosophical Society for article: H. Simon (1962), 'The Architecture of Complexity', *Proceedings of the American Philosophical Society*, **106** (6), December, 467–82.

Blackwell Publishers Ltd for articles: R. Coase (1937), 'The Nature of the Firm', *Economica*, **4**, November, 386–405; L. McKenzie (1951), 'Ideal Output and the Interdependence of Firms', *Economic Journal*, **61**, December, 785–803; A. Dixit (1980), 'The Role of Investment in Entry-Deterrence', *Economic Journal*, **90**, March 95–106.

Econometric Society for article: P. Milgrom and J. Roberts (1982), 'Limit Pricing and Entry Under Incomplete Information: An Equilibrium Analysis', *Econometrica*, **50** (2), March, 443–59.

Journal of Law, Economics and Organization for articles: P. Joskow (1985), 'Vertical Integration and Long-term Contracts: The Case of Coal-burning Electric Generating Plants', *Journal of Law, Economics and Organization*, **1** (1), Fall, 33–80; J. Tirole (1986), 'Hierarchies and Bureaucracies: On the Role of Collusion in Organizations', *Journal of Law, Economics and Organization*, **2** (2), Fall, 181–214.

Little, Brown and Company Publishers for excerpt: H. Demsetz (1974), 'Two Systems of Belief about Monopoly', in H. Goldschmid, H.M. Mann and J.F. Weston (eds), *Industrial Concentration: The New Learning*, 164–84.

Macmillan Press Ltd for excerpt: W. Baumol, J. Panzar and R. Willig (1986), 'On the Theory of Perfectly-Contestable Markets', in J. Stiglitz and F. Mathewson (eds), *New Developments in the Analysis of Market Structure*, 339–65.

M.I.T. Press Journals for article: M. Rothschild and J. Stiglitz (1976), 'Equilibrium in Competitive Insurance Markets: An Essay on the Economics of Imperfect Information', *Quarterly Journal of Economics*, **90** (4), November, 629–49.

RAND for articles: S. Salop (1979), 'Monopolies Competition with Outside Goods', *Bell Journal of Economics*, **10** (1), Spring, 141–56; B. Holmstrom (1982), 'Moral Hazard in Teams', *Bell Journal of Economics*, **13** (2), Autumn, 324–40.

University of Chicago Press for articles: A. Alchian (1950), 'Uncertainty, Evolution and Economic Theory', *Journal of Political Economy*, **58**, February–December, 211–21; F. Modigliani (1958), 'New Developments on the Oligopoly Front', *Journal of Political Economy*, **66**, June, 215–32; G. Stigler (1964), 'A Theory of Oligopoly', *Journal of Political Economy*, **72**, February, 44–61; O. Williamson (1979), 'Transaction-Cost Economics: The Governance of Contractual Relations', *Journal of Law and Economics*, **22** (2), October, 233–61; B. Klein and K. Leffler (1981), 'The Role of Market Forces in Assuring Contractual Performance', *Journal of Political Economy*, **89** (4), August, 615–41; S. Grossman and O. Hart (1986), 'The Costs and Benefits of Ownership: A Theory of Vertical and Lateral Integration', *Journal of Political Economy*, **94** (4), August, 691–719.

In addition the publishers wish to thank the Library of the London School of Economics and Political Science for their assistance in obtaining these articles.

Introduction

Whither industrial organization? Victor Fuchs posed that query in 1972 and answered it as follows: 'all is not well in this once flourishing field' (1972, p. xv). The answer to that same query is entirely different in 1990: industrial economics is alive and well and is the queen of applied microeconomics.

If both Fuchs and I are right, as I think that we are, then the intervening years have witnessed a remarkable transformation. The articles reprinted as Parts II and III of this book, which deal, respectively, with 'The New Economics of Organization' and 'Strategic Behaviour and Competition' helped to effect that transformation.

These new developments had distinguished antecedents. The articles reprinted in Part I, many of which were written by economists from outside of the field of industrial economics, supplied the foundations upon which Parts II and III – the new economics of organization and a revitalized theory of strategic behaviour and competition – were built. Albeit perhaps still premature, I submit that a new science of organization is taking shape to which industrial economics has been both a principal contributor and beneficiary.

This chapter is organized in three parts. Section 1 provides an overview of the field of industrial economics, section 2 provides a short introduction to each of the articles reprinted in this volume, and section 3 contrasts the state of industrial economics today with that of the field 25 years ago.

1. An Overview

That industrial economics has had distinguished antecedents is evident from the articles reprinted in Part I of this volume. These are not my concern here. Rather, what I want to emphasize are

1. the centrality of industrial economics within applied microeconomics,
2. the growing importance of the economics of organization, and
3. the nature of the new developments in the area of strategic behaviour and competition.

1.1   Centrality

Viewed strategically, it is hard to identify another field within applied microeconomics that is as centrally located as industrial economics. That is partly because industrial economics is the natural arena in which to do work on the theory of the firm. Inasmuch as the theory of the firm and the theory of consumer behaviour form the twin pillars of microeconomics, industrial economics deals with core issues.

The main concern of industrial economics has been less with the firm itself than with the behaviour of the firm in relation to other firms. Joe Bain, whose important work has had a lasting impact on the field, approached the subject in the following way:

Being concerned in the main with the market behavior of enterprises, I have given major emphasis to the relative incidence of competitive and monopolistic tendencies in various industries or markets. Correspondingly, my primary unit for analysis is the industry or competing group of firms (Bain 1959, p. vii).

The theory of the firm that informed such industry analysis held that the 'firm is a technical unit in which commodities are produced. [It] transforms inputs into outputs, subject to the technical rules specified by [the] production function' (Henderson and Quandt 1971, p. 52). Although the adequacy of that construction was challenged many years ago (Commons 1934; Coase 1937), the production function approach prevailed. That is because it takes a theory to beat a theory (or to join a theory), whence a rival (or complementary) conception of the firm needed to be fashioned. The new economics of organization has attempted precisely that.

Directly or indirectly, many of the articles reprinted in Part II, which deals with the new economics of organization, have had that purpose and effect. These efforts were driven by a growing perception that many firm-as-production-function explanations for puzzling firm and market practices did not satisfy weak plausibility tests. Feeble 'existence' arguments (many of which appealed to price discrimination as the explanation for nonstandard or unfamiliar business practices) elicited increasing scepticism. Demands for new theory mounted.

1.2 The new economics of organization

Bain relegated the study of 'how enterprises do and should behave' to the field of management science (1959, p. vii). This division of labour was widely felt to be appropriate, as a consequence of which the theory of the firm to which industrial economics appealed was essentially that 'of the category of the individual agent' (Kreps 1984, p. 8). It being the usual practice to describe individual agents by utility functions and consumption sets, profit functions and production possibility sets were evidently the appropriate terms with which to describe firms.

Albeit instructive, viewing the firm as a production function is seriously delimiting. It encourages the view that technology is determinative of economic organization, whence the allocation of economic activity as between firm and market is unproblematic. The study of economic organization 'on its own terms' was discouraged as a consequence.

An alternative view – which, however, was very slow to take hold – is to attempt a unified theory of market, hierarchy, and hybrid modes of organization. This was accomplished by regarding the firm and the market as alternative forms of contracting. Although the rudiments of such a unified theory can be variously described, I focus here on three features:

1. microanalytics (which includes choice of a unit of analysis),
2. behavioural assumptions, and
3. an economizing orientation.

As indicated, the unit of analysis with which Bain worked was 'the industry or competing group of firms'. Although this composite level of aggregation is useful for purposes of describing the economic context within which competition takes place, it incompletely engages the organizational/institutional structures within which economic *activity* takes place. The new economics of organization is preoccupied with this latter class of issues. Knowledge of the details of alternative forms of organization has become vital to an assessment of competition.

A rather cautious version of the micro-forces argument is as follows (Kreps and Spence 1985, pp. 374–5):

> ... if one wishes to model the behaviour of organizations such as firms, then study of the firm as an organization ought to be high on one's agenda. This study is not strictly speaking, necessary: one can hope to divine the correct 'reduced form' for the behaviour of the organization for the behaviour of the organization without considering the micro-forces within the organization. But the study of the organization is likely to help in the design of reduced forms that stress the important variables.

There are at least two ways to read this statement. One is to regard the last sentence as an afterthought or throw-away, in which case the basic message is that economists can continue the past practice of 'divining' reduced forms. That is the business-as-usual interpretation. The other possibility is that the last sentence carries the freight – in which event past practice is no longer viable (if ever it was) and needs to give way to a more microanalytic treatment of the details of organization.

The first interpretation would relegate the study of microanalytics to noneconomists or, alternatively, turns on the hope that economists will be lucky. The main risks with the first of these are that those to whom the study of the details are relegated will either take the wrong observations or will report the right observations in ways that mask their economic significance. Since hoping to get lucky is even more problematic, the evident need is for economists to take the study of organization seriously.

Herbert Simon's contrast between the physical sciences and economics in microanalytic respects is instructive. As he observes (1984, p. 40):

> In the physical sciences, when errors of measurement and other noise are found to be of the same order of magnitude as the phenomena under study, the response is not to try to squeeze more information out of the data by statistical means; it is instead to find techniques for observing the phenomena at a higher level of resolution. The corresponding strategy for economics is obvious: to secure new kinds of data at the micro level.

But while the strategy may be obvious, its implementation is not. How micro is micro? One possibility is to become very micro, in which event Simon's proposal that the 'decision premise' be made the basic unit of analysis (1956, p. xxxii) warrants consideration. Albeit useful for purposes of psychology (Newell and Simon, 1972), the decision premise has yet to find widespread application to economics.

An alternative unit, proposed earlier by John R. Commons, has proved more promising. Thus Commons described the problem of economic organization as that of dealing simultaneously with conflict, mutual dependence, and order, whereupon the criterion for the 'ultimate unit of economic activity... [should] contain in itself the three principles of conflict, mutuality and order', (Commons 1925, p. 4). The transaction, in his view, was responsive to these principles and he proposed that the transaction be made the basic unit of analysis

(Commons 1925, p. 4; 1934, pp. 4–8). The obvious next steps – to identify the principal dimensions with respect to which transactions differ, and to ascertain the (comparative) organizational implications that accrue thereto – were a long time in coming, however.

The second rudimentary feature to which I referred are the behavioural assumptions. Of special importance are choices of (1) a cognitive assumption and (2) a self-interest seeking assumption. Directly or indirectly, much of the new economics of organization assumes that economic agents are boundedly rational. Moreover, all of this literature assumes that economic agents are given to opportunism – where this is expansively defined as self-interest seeking with guile and includes both moral hazard and adverse selection.

Herbert Simon has defined bounded rationality as behaviour that is '*intendedly* rational, but only *limitedly* so' (1957, p. xxiv). Although the latter part of the definition has attracted more attention and has elicited great resistance among economists, the intended rationality part of the definition deserves equal weight. Intendedly rational agents are attempting effectively to cope, which is in the 'rational spirit' tradition that Kenneth Arrow associates with economics (1974, p. 16). Intendedly rational agents who perceive their limited cognitive competence will presumably treat mind like any other scarce resource. *Ceteris paribus*, forms of organization that economize on bounded rationality are favoured.

As Simon remarks, it is 'only because individual human beings are limited in knowledge, foresight, skill, and time that organizations are useful instruments for the achievement of human purpose' (1957, p. 199). More generally, and more importantly, *all complex contracts are unavoidably incomplete* in a regime of bounded rationality. Accordingly, comprehensive contracting models, of both Arrow–Debreu and mechanism design kinds, give way to models of incomplete contracting.

The second behavioural assumption to which I referred – that of self-interest seeking – is also pertinent. If parties to a contract would self-enforce promises, then incomplete contracting could be saved by introducing a general clause, whereby each party pledged to cooperate – in a joint profit maximizing manner – during contract execution and at contract renewal intervals. If, however, economic agents will sometimes break their covenants, and if court ordering is costly, then 'contract as promise' is not reliably efficacious. To the contrary, if economic agents are given to opportunism – which is a subtle form of self-interest seeking that includes a willingness to make self-disbelieved promises – then contract as promise is naive and safeguarding contracts against the hazards of opportunism becomes the source of added value.

An economizing orientation is the last of the three key features that I ascribe to the new economics of organization. Note in this connection that the economizing to which I refer is broader and more rudimentary than is customary. Frank Knight's characterization of the economic problem is pertinent (1941, p. 252; emphasis added):

> . . . . men in general, and within limits, wish to behave economically, to make their activities *and their organization* 'efficient rather than wasteful.' This fact does deserve the utmost emphasis; and an adequate definition of the science of economics . . . might well make it explicit that the main relevance of the discussion is found in its relation to social policy, assumed to be directed toward the end indicated, of increasing economic efficiency, of reducing waste.

This conception of economizing is broader than is customary in that it goes beyond technology to include organization. The efficiency condition referred to, moreover, is rudimentary: the reduction of waste. Moves toward rather than along an efficiency frontier are thus contemplated.

Note in this connection that the standard for judging efficiency is not of an abstract Pareto optimality kind but instead is one of remediability. If all feasible forms of organization are flawed, then the relevant test with which to judge a 'condition of inefficiency' is whether a move to an alternative mode can be orchestrated which yields net social gains. The costs of the move as well as the defects associated with the proposed mode are thus entered into the calculus (Coase 1964).

The new economics of organization works out of this general framework and attempts to answer some of the most nettlesome problems in economics. Why do we have firms? What are the factors that are responsible for limits to firm size? Is the modern corporation well-described by a production function, or does the appearance of hierarchy and do the uses of internal incentive and control apparatus really require that the corporation be conceived as a governance structure? Is a unified approach to the study of contract feasible, and if so what are the regularities or themes out of which a unified contractual theory works? New microanalytic concepts, new theory, and new empirical work have all taken shape as efforts to answer these and related questions of economic organization have taken their place on the research agenda. The essays in Part II elaborate.

1.3 Strategic behaviour and competition

Several types of strategic behaviour can be distinguished. First, there is nonstrategic behaviour. This would obtain if prices in product and factor markets are parameters. More generally, optimizing behaviour that does not entail conscious efforts to preposition in relation to actual or potential rivals and/or to discipline or otherwise respond punitively to rivalry is nonstrategic. *Ex ante* positioning and *ex post* contingent responsiveness, especially in combination, are appropriately regarded as strategic.

Some contend that the recent literature on strategic behaviour merely dresses up and warms over the entry barrier analysis that appeared in the 1950s and dominated industrial economics through the early 1970s. But there is a great deal more to it than that.

The systematic analysis of entry barriers made its appearance with the publication of books by Paolo Sylos-Labini (1956) and Joe Bain (1956) and by Franco Modigliani's interpretation and presentation of the central arguments (1958). It quickly made headway and became a core concept in the structure–conduct–performance paradigm. Dissent nevertheless appeared as entry barrier arguments came to be used uncritically.

Objections of three kinds were registered: logic, mechanics, and irremediability. The first of these is that many entry barrier arguments were static and focused on *ex post* outcomes when the condition that needed to be assessed was the competitive process *in its entirety*. Pertinent in this connection is that competition is an intertemporal process, while many entry barrier arguments were of an atemporal kind.

Secondly, entry barrier models purported to deal with oligopoly without ever asking how the mechanics of collective action were to be realized. More generally, whole classes of activity were described as entry barriers without reference to cost effectiveness. If, however, the efficacy, say, of advertising as a barrier to entry is conditional on customer, firm, and market attributes, then critiques of a generic activity (advertising) ought to be supplanted by focused critiques in which the requisite preconditions are satisfied. Regrettably, that was not done but sweeping indictments against broad classes of activities – to include virtually all vertical market restrictions – were registered instead.

The third objection is the remediability criterion to which I referred earlier. If all feasible forms of organization are flawed, then the mere existence of an entry impediment does not, without more, warrant public policy intervention. Instead, intervention is warranted only upon a showing of prospective net social gains.

Mistaken treatments of economies of scale are illustrative of this last. To describe economies as a barrier to entry invites the conclusion that this is an antisocial outcome. Public policy hostility towards economies easily could and did result. Only upon displaying the tradeoffs implicit in moving from the (supposedly) less preferred market structure, in which larger firms enjoyed greater economies of scale, to the (supposedly) more preferred market structure, in which all firms were small and on a parity in scale *dis*economy respects, was this convoluted application of entry barriers reasoning reversed.

That entry barrier analysis was incomplete and/or overreaching does not, however, establish that there was nothing there. Much of what has been in progress during the past decade is an effort to put the analysis of strategic behaviour on more secure foundations. At first implicitly and later explicitly, the concepts and apparatus of noncooperative game theory have become the prevailing techniques of analysis.

The critical need in dealing with strategic behaviour was first to recognize and then to operationalize the distinction between credible and noncredible threats. That many firms and individuals (executives, lawyers, and even economists) bluster, cajole, threaten, and fulminate is easy to document. But it is also true that many of these claims are idle threats – in that to carry out the threat would leave the maker of the threat worse off as a consequence. It is elementary that idle threats will not serve as deterrents if they are seen through by others.

To be sure, 'bogey-man' economics can be good fun – and antitrust cases are replete with solemn pronouncements by lawyers and expert witnesses that firms are intimidated by idle threats made by rivals. The credible threat literature insists, however, that business behaviour be viewed in a more hardheaded way. Only those threats that satisfy credibility conditions are ones to which real economic consequences are appropriately ascribed.

Although industrial economists backed into the literature on noncooperative games and even self-discovered subgame perfection, it was not long before the relation between the needs to explicate and analyse strategic behaviour and the extant literature on noncooperative games was correctly discerned. Indeed, not only has industrial economics drawn on this literature, but the study of strategic behaviour became the source of a number of extensions to and elaborations or clarifications of the underlying game theoretic framework that John Harsanyi (1967; 1973) and Reinhard Selten (1965; 1975) had pioneered. The logic of small numbers rivalry in the context of interdependent sequential decisions with varying information structures is now well advanced.

These advances notwithstanding, there are good reasons to be discomfited by the current state of strategic analysis. The assumptions of the models are heroic in ascribing a very high level of sophistication (tantamount to hyperrationality) to the actors. Also, strong common knowledge assumptions regarding key parameters and probability distributions are needed.

The sensitivity of the results to what appear to be small changes in the assumptions is disconcerting.

But there has been real progress. The purported 'illogic' of strategic behaviour has given way to disputes over realism, predictive content, and remediability. That our understanding of the issues has greatly benefitted from this literature and that continuing advances are in prospect are broadly conceded. Industrial economics has definitely become more cautious and qualified in public policy respects as a consequence. But if the world of competition is very complicated, then excesses of simplification are to be avoided. Industrial economics has simply moved beyond an 'oversimplification' threshold from which there is no returning.

2. The Essays

As indicated, the articles selected for reprinting in this volume are organized in three clusters. The first group is classic antecedents. The second deals with the new economics of organization. Strategic business behaviour is the main focus of group three.

2.1 Antecedents

The first essay in the book is fittingly the influential 1937 article by Ronald Coase on 'The Nature of the Firm'. Coase in that article squarely faced the matter of firm and market as alternative modes of organization. Thus although it had been customary to take the allocation of economic activity as between firm and market (or, in more mundane terms, the decision to make-or-buy) as given, Coase observed that this needs to be derived. He further urged that a symmetrical approach to firm and market organization be adopted in which differential transaction costs are made the cutting edge. Albeit plausible, the economic import of this line of analysis became evident only upon subsequent operationalization.

Armen Alchian's provocative paper on 'Uncertainty, Evolution, and Economic Theory' (1950) is the second essay (and interestingly, is the only article to appear in both the *Readings in Industrial Organization and Public Policy* (Heflebower and Stocking 1958) and in this volume). The Alchian article is significant in several respects. For one thing, selection arguments play a large (albeit often unacknowledged) role in virtually all forms of long-run competitive analysis. Second, the use of simplifying assumptions of an 'as if' hyperrationality kind can sometimes be justified by invoking selection arguments. And third, Alchian's treatment of evolutionary issues is insightful and is carefully nuanced (more so than many of those who rely on Alchian for authority). Significant subsequent contributions to evolutionary economics notwithstanding (Nelson and Winter, 1982), there is no other single article that covers the material as well as Alchian.

The third article is somewhat of an outlier. This is Lionel McKenzie's treatment of 'Ideal Output and the Interdependence of Firms' (1951). The issue of vertical integration is examined in circumstances where the upstream supplier possesses monopoly power and inputs are used in either fixed or variable proportions. Although subsequent work addresses efficiency and monopoly consequences more completely and symmetrically, McKenzie's early treatment is still illuminating.

The fourth essay is Franco Modigliani's review article, 'New Developments on the Oligopoly

Front' (1958). Modigliani summarizes and interprets the two books – one by Sylos-Labini (1956), the other by Bain (1956) – in which the basic barriers to entry framework was first advanced. But there is more to this article than summary and interpretation. Modigliani clarifies, unifies, and introduces added apparatus. Entry barrier analysis was off to an auspicious start.

George Stigler's famous paper on 'A Theory of Oligopoly' (1964) appears next. This article is one of a series of applications that work off of 'The Economics of Information' (1961) approach that Stigler had developed earlier (and which has inspired a great deal of work in the information economics field). Accordingly, Stigler approaches oligopoly by posing it as a problem in the theory of information, with special emphasis on the factors that influence the ease of policing a collusive agreement.

Although the immediate concern in Kenneth Arrow's article on 'Uncertainty and the Welfare Economics of Medical Care' (1963) is with the provision of medical care, the more general purposes of this article are

1. to show that 'market failure' is a more subtle and pervasive condition than had been hitherto realized and
2. to advance the proposition that nonmarket forms of organization often arise as a means by which to mitigate market failures.

In opposition, therefore, to prevailing views that nonstandard forms of contracting (by firms or physicians) had monopoly purpose and effect and that market failures ought to be rectified by realigning property rights, Arrow advanced a rival interpretation in which the hypothesis that nonmarket forms of organization often serve to relieve market failures was introduced.

The final article in this background section is Herbert Simon's 'The Architecture of Complexity' (1962). Simon maintains that hierarchy is one of the central structural schemes that the architect of complexity uses and shows wherein hierarchy is a recurrent organizing theme in complex biological, physical, and social systems. Simon observes that most complex systems are supported by stable subsystems; and he associates a condition of 'near-decomposability', which is a rudimentary form of hierarchy, with many of them. Many heated controversies over complex economic organization are needlessly confused because of a failure to appreciate the uncontrived appearance of and the instrumental purposes served by hierarchy.

The section on 'The New Economics of Organization' opens with the article by Michael Rothschild and Joseph Stiglitz on 'Equilibrium in Competitive Insurance Markets: An Essay on the Economics of Imperfect Information' (1976). This insightful treatment of information asymmetries – mainly in the form of adverse selection – shows that a pooling equilibrium with customers from two risk classes is impossible. Because, moreover, high-risk individuals impose a negative externality on low-risk individuals, a separating equilibrium always comes at a cost. The upshot is that insurance markets (and other markets beset by information asymmetries and information impactedness) pose novel and difficult problems – to which, however, new methods of economic analysis can be brought productively to bear. Applications of this general approach to other areas (such as the organization of work, where ability differentials are the concern) have since been made.

Bengt Holmstrom's article, 'Moral Hazard in Teams' (1982), is in the information economics tradition. Holmstrom extends earlier work of a principal/single-agent kind to include relations between multiple agents in teams. Whereas the main role that had previously been ascribed to principals in a team production context was monitoring, the primary role of the principal in Holmstrom's setup is to administer incentive schemes for which budget balancing is not required. His treatment of incentives in teams also relates to the tournament literature. He develops a sufficient statistic condition on relative performance evaluation according to which competition among agents is not valued because it induces added effort but rather because it is a device to extract information optimally.

Jean Tirole's examination of 'Hierarchies and Bureaucracies: On the Role of Collusion in Organizations' (1986) works out of a three-tier agency theory setup. Rather than treat contracting between successive interfaces within a firm in dyadic terms, Tirole investigates the contracting ramifications of a principal–supervisor–agent setup in which collusion between supervisor and agent (vis-à-vis the principal) is permitted. A farsighted principal will foresee these effects and factor them into the incentive scheme. Although in this model collusion is responsible for added inefficiency, the approach invites further analysis in which social benefits to collusion are admitted.

George Akerlof's essay on 'Loyalty Filters' (1983) is related to, but different from, Kenneth Arrow's essay on medical care. A fundamental hypothesis advanced by Arrow is that nonmarket forms of organization often have the purpose and effect of mitigating market failures. In the absence, for example, of 'ideal insurance', a variety of nonstandard contracting and organizational practices with trust-infusing consequences may be created. Akerlof, however, takes this argument off in another direction: various forms of nonmarket behaviour can have the purpose and effect of advantaging one group in relation to another. Broadly speaking, the loyalty filters examined by Akerlof favour the haves in relation to the have-nots. Welfare losses, rather than welfare gains, arguably result.

My paper, 'Transaction-Cost Economics: The Governance of Contractual Relations' (1979), is also in the spirit of crafting nonmarket (or market-assisted) responses to market failures. It relates both to Coase's early article on 'The Nature of the Firm' and to the Arrow essay referred to above. If transactions differ in their attributes, if alternative governance structures (firms, markets, hybrid modes) differ in their costs and competencies, and if economizing on transaction costs is taken to be a leading purpose of economic organization, then transactions will presumably be aligned with governance structures in a discriminating way. The view of the firm as production function makes way for the view of the firm as governance structure in the process.

Sanford Grossman and Oliver Hart's paper on 'The Costs and Benefits of Ownership: A Theory of Vertical and Lateral Integration' (1986) embraces the transaction cost economics argument that all complex contracts are unavoidably incomplete, as a consequence of which (and contrary to agency theory) it is impossible to concentrate all of the relevant contracting action in the *ex ante* incentive alignment. Although the formal modelling of incomplete contracting is formidably difficult, Grossman and Hart develop a model in which both *ex ante* alignment and *ex post* adaptation differences between market and hierarchical modes of organization are recognized. The paper invites further efforts to model and thereby assess the properties of discrete structural contracting alternatives, which is precisely what has materialized.

Although Paul Joskow's paper, 'Vertical Integration and Long-term Contracts: The Case of Coal-burning Electric Generating Plants' (1985), is mainly an empirical contribution, it provides added conceptual framework for understanding issues of comparative institutional analysis as well. Assessing the efficacy of alternative modes of economic organization is a more microanalytic undertaking than has been characteristic of empirical microeconomics in the past. Joskow's imaginative approach to these issues demonstrates that the added empirical burdens of transaction cost economics can be met. Subsequent empirical work (by Joskow and others) is corroborative.

The last paper in this section is by Benjamin Klein and Keith Leffler, 'The Role of Market Forces in Assuring Contractual Performance' (1981). This paper adopts a very stringent self-enforcing contract orientation. If manufacturers are unable to appeal to the courts to enforce contractual covenants that require distributors to behave 'responsibly', and if there are free-riding and other contractual hazards, then how will contracts be designed to mitigate these effects? Klein and Leffler show that, in relation to a first-best optimum, inefficient production techniques will appear and that distributors will be paid a premium, the prospective loss of which, through contract cancellation, will deter cheating. The use of rents for deterrence purposes has general application, as witnessed by the extensive literature on 'efficiency wages'.

Strategic behaviour is a fascinating subject and has attracted considerable attention from those who do theoretical industrial economics. It is perhaps surprising, therefore, that the first article in Part III is an empirical one. The provocatively titled paper by Harold Demsetz, 'Two Systems of Belief About Monopoly' (1974), is also provocatively written. The main target of the paper was the then widespread view that many large firms enjoyed monopoly power by reason of contrived entry barriers. Demsetz took exception with the arguments and evidence that supported this view and provided arguments and evidence to the contrary. Further theoretical and especially empirical work on these matters has resulted.

As previously remarked, the logic of entry barrier analysis was held to be defective. A new and more rigorous logic was evidently needed and began to take shape (Spence, 1977). The duopoly model used by Avinash Dixit in his paper, 'The Role of Investment in Entry-Deterrence' (1980), sets out the basic logic and demonstrates the critical importance of investments in durable, nonredeployable assets to effect entry deterrence. Albeit without expressly invoking subgame perfection, this is the spirit of the Dixit analysis nonetheless. Given credible pre-entry commitments, the logic of entry barriers was made secure. But inasmuch as a duopoly setup is highly specialized, the empirical significance and antitrust enforcement ramifications of the argument can be questioned.

Philippe Aghion and Patrick Bolton examine the use of 'Contracts as a Barrier to Entry' (1987). Credible threats remain the focus. What Aghion and Bolton examine is whether an incumbent supplier can fashion a penalty clause, the effects of which penalty make the incumbent better off. While leaving the buyer indifferent between a simple contract (with no penalty) and a contract with a penalty that is paid only in the event of entry (in which event the buyer would switch his purchases to the entrant). They show that penalties can be devised such that lower cost entrants can be deterred – although not necessarily precluded – from entering. Extensions are proposed and a possible rationale for the hitherto puzzling legal prohibition against 'unreasonable' liquidated damages clauses in contracts is suggested.

A further significant development in the strategic behaviour literature is the paper by Paul Milgrom and John Roberts, 'Limit Pricing and Entry Under Incomplete Information: An Equilibrium Analysis' (1982). The use of limit pricing here turns on an information asymmetry between the sitting monopolist (or incumbent) and the potential entrant. Whereas the incumbent knows its costs, the potential entrant can only infer them. The incumbent would like to signal to the potential entrant that it has low costs, thereby to deter entry. Although it can do this by setting a low price, the entrant is alert to the strategic nature of the game and recognizes that signaling can be used for strategic purpose. Milgrom and Roberts formulate the resulting dynamic game of incomplete information as one of 'perfect Bayesian equilibrium'. As hitherto remarked, such a complex formulation involves heroic assumptions about cognitive competence. That is where an examination of deep game theoretic subtleties takes the analysis nonetheless.

The paper by David Kreps and Robert Wilson on 'Reputation and Imperfect Information' (1982) deals with related gaming considerations. They address the chain-store paradox posed by Selten (1978), the issue being whether or not a sitting monopolist should contest entry to a succession of N entrants. By a logic of unravelling, Selten showed that the rational monopolist would everywhere accede to entry. This defies experience and intuition. Kreps and Wilson show that the introduction of a small amount of imperfect or incomplete information can transform such a game into one whereby monopolists strategically contest entry. The logic of unravelling gives way to a logic of reputation in an intertemporal framework into which imperfect information has been introduced. The argument enriches the concept of credible threat beyond that previously employed – since, if appearances count, predation may be undertaken for its deterrence effects even where, in a Dixit-type setup, predation would fail the test of *ex post* (objective) optimality.

Drew Fudenberg and Jean Tirole's paper 'The Fat-Cat Effect, The Puppy-Dog Ploy, and the Lean and Hungry Look' (1984), examines strategic behaviour in conjunction with investment in plant and equipment, advertising, and research and development. The manner in which investments of these kinds influence (1) the slope of the entrant's reaction curve and (2) the incumbent firm's output are shown to be the critical features. As compared with a nonstrategic equilibrium, either an under- or over-investment result can obtain – depending on how these reaction functions play out. Plainly, strategic behaviour has become much more cautious, qualified, and conditional than earlier entry models had revealed or suggested.

The article by William Baumol, John Panzar, and Robert Willig, 'On the Theory of Perfectly-Contestable Markets' (1986), is of the nature of a survey. It summarizes the central arguments of their influential book and advances the argument that the perfectly contestable market – that in which asset-specificity is negligible, whence assets are easily redeployable to alternative uses and by alternative users – is usefully regarded as an analytical and public policy benchmark. This has been a controversial approach – in that the lessons for antitrust and regulation are contested (Shepherd 1984) and because the relation between this work and related literature are sometimes obscured (Stigler 1988, p. 1735).

The last essay in this book is by Steven Salop, 'Monopolistic Competition with Outside Goods' (1979). Salop uses a spatial competition model (akin to that of William Vickrey (1964)) to investigate monopolistic competition. Monopolistic competition in economics shares two critical attributes with the concept of power in the social sciences: both power and monopolistic competition are intriguing concepts; but just as power has been a disappointing concept in the social sciences (March 1966, p. 70), so has monopolistic competition failed to deliver on early promises in economics. A need in each case is to *delimit* the use of the concept to a plainly pertinent subset. That is rarely done. Be that as it may, Salop's treatment nicely displays the key features of a monopolistically competitive contest in a spatial equilibrium setting.

3. A Retrospective

One way to judge the changes that have occurred within a field are to compare the selections
in a current readings book with those in predecessor readings volumes. Also current textbooks
in industrial economics can be contrasted with earlier textbooks. A comparison of this book
with the selections made by Richard Heflebower and George Stocking in the 1958 publication
of *Readings in Industrial Organization and Public Policy* is thus germane. A comparison
of Jean Tirole's recently published *The Theory of Industrial Organization* (1988) with Joe
Bain's *Industrial Organization* (1959) is likewise instructive.

Interestingly, Heflebower and Stocking compared their volume with *Readings in the Social
Control of Industry*, which appeared in 1942. As they point out, 'The latter volume was
concerned almost exclusively with policy issues. Several of the articles dealt with the
governmental problem of regulating prices, a topic omitted entirely from the present volume'
(Heflebower and Stocking 1958, p. v). As they saw it, their 1958 volume was much more
concerned with analysis.

Analysis has taken a quantum leap since. As compared with the selections in this volume,
the Heflebower and Stocking book has fewer classics; relies extensively on the structure-
conduct-performance paradigm (in theoretical, empirical, and public policy respects); and
is much more preoccupied with antitrust.

The first of these differences is understandable: since industrial economics is now only
50 years old, it was, perforce, very young in 1958. That the present volume includes only
two articles that are expressly in the structure–conduct–performance tradition (one dealing
with the theory (by Franco Modigliani); the other dealing with the evidence (by Harold
Demsetz)) is because industrial economics has moved beyond this paradigm in the intervening
years. Perhaps the most dramatic difference, however, is that none of the articles in this book
has antitrust as the main focus – whereas at least 10 of the 21 articles reprinted in the
Heflebower and Stocking volume deal significantly if not preponderantly with antitrust. That
is a further reflection of the enormous growth of the theory of industrial economics (and
of need for antitrust to be informed thereby).

The differences between Bain's influential text, *Industrial Organization*, and Tirole's recent
text, *The Theory of Industrial Organization*, also reflect this condition. As Bain indicates
in his Preface, industrial organization as a field owed its origins to the work of Edward Mason
and his colleagues at Harvard in the late 1930s. To a large extent, the work of the Mason
group relied on and was an outgrowth of Edward Chamberlin's *Theory of Monopolistic
Competition* (1933), Joan Robinson's *The Economics of Imperfect Competition* (1933), Adolph
Berle and George Means's *The Modern Corporation and Private Property* (1932), and a series
of studies by the Temporary National Economic Committee.

Mason was continuously interested in public policy, with special reference to antitrust,
and the field of industrial organization in the United States became preoccupied with the
monopoly problem. Rather than study anatomy and physiology of industrial economics,
attention became focused on pathology instead. As Coase put it (1972, p. 67):

> The ways in which [antitrust] was viewed by the lawyers (judges and advocates) were
> accepted as the ways in which [economists] should approach the problem. The opinions

of the judges often became the starting point of the analysis, and an attempt was made to make sense of what they had said....

One important result of this preoccupation with the monopoly problem is that if an economist finds something – a business practice of one sort or other – that he does not understand, he looks for a monopoly explanation. And as in this field we are very ignorant, the number of ununderstandable practices tends to be rather large, and the reliance on a monopoly explanation, frequent.

Fanciful antitrust arguments invited and were facilitated by fanciful economic reasoning. Antitrust enforcement excesses predictably resulted. Miniscule mergers were held to be anticompetitive. Vertical contractual restraints were held to be wholly without redeeming purpose. Economies by larger firms which put smaller rivals at a 'disadvantage' were even regarded as antisocial. Heads of antitrust enforcement agencies that attempted to rein-in convoluted enforcement efforts were criticized on all sides – by the career staff, Congressional committees, the press, and by populist 'public interest' advocates.

The pressing need was for economists concerned with industrial economics to give up their role as supporters/rationalizers for expansionist antitrust and adopt the role of analysts. That is the orientation that Tirole adopts in his new book, which he introduces with the observation that 'Theoretical industrial organization has made substantial progress since the early 1970s and has become a central element of the culture of microeconomics' (1988, p. xi). A much more highly nuanced theory of firms, markets, interfirm relations, and hybrid modes of contracting and organization is the result.

Industrial economics has not only made great strides in reconceptualizing and advancing its own agenda but has had widespread influence throughout applied microeconomics, to a number of related fields in business administration, and to the contiguous social sciences. Other applied microeconomics fields to which industrial economics can be or has been applied include labour economics, international trade, comparative systems, economic development, and economic history. Also, some of the issues first posed in industrial economics have stimulated new work in microeconomic theory.

Fields of business administration with which industrial economics makes contact include marketing, manufacturing, business strategy, and international business as well as aspects of accounting and finance. Organization theory, moreover, both informs and is informed by the new economics of organization.

The study of law and economics has been massively influenced by the work in industrial economics, much of it reported in this volume. Effects on sociology and political science have been less extensive but are growing. A rich and rewarding dialogue – within industrial economics and with related fields – is developing.

This brings me back to the proposition with which this introductory chapter began: industrial economics is both alive and well. Having said that, however, I quickly add that a great deal remains to be done. Significant accomplishments notwithstanding, industrial economics has not earned for itself a quiet life. I fully anticipate that the next decade will witness continuing vitality. Industrial economics is in for an exciting future.

Oliver Williamson
March 1990

References

Arrow, Kenneth J. (1974), *The Limits of Organization*, New York: W.W. Norton.

Bain, Joe (1956), *Barriers to New Competition*, Cambridge, MA: Harvard University Press.

_____ (1959), *Industrial Organization*, New York, John Wiley and Sons.

Berle, A. and G. C. Means, Jr (1932), *The Modern Corporation and Private Property*, New York: Macmillan.

Chamberlin, E. (1933), *Theory of Monopolistic Competition*, Cambridge, MA: Harvard University Press.

Coase, Ronald H. (1937), 'The Nature of the Firm', *Economica N.S.*, **4**, 386–405.

Coase, R. H. (1964), 'The Regulated Industries: Discussion', *American Economic Review*, **54** (May), 194–7.

_____ (1972), 'Industrial Organization: A Proposal for Research', in V. R. Fuchs, ed., *Policy Issues and Research Opportunities in Industrial Organization*, New York: National Bureau of Economic Research, 59–73.

Commons, John R. (1925), 'Law and Economics', *Yale Law Journal*, **34**, 371–82.

_____ (1934), *Institutional Economics*, Madison: University of Wisconsin Press.

Fuchs, V. (ed.) (1972), *Policy Issues and Research Opportunities in Industrial Organization*, New York: Columbia University Press.

Harsanyi, J. (1967), 'Games With Incomplete Information Played by Bayesian Players', *Management Science*, **14**, 159–82, 320–34, 486–502.

_____ (1973), 'Games With Randomly Disturbed Payoffs: A New Rationale for Mixed Strategy Equilibrium Points', *International Journal of Game Theory*, **2**, 1–23.

Heflebower, R. and G. Stocking (eds) (1958), *Readings in Industrial Organization and Public Policy*, Homewood, IL: Richard D. Irwin, Inc.

Henderson, James M. and Richard E. Quandt (1971), *Microeconomic Theory*, 2nd ed., New York: McGraw-Hill.

Knight, Frank (1941), 'Anthropology and Economics', *Journal of Political Economy* (April), 247–68.

Kreps, David (1984), 'Corporate Culture', Unpublished manuscript.

_____ and Michael Spence (1985), 'Modelling the Role of History in Industrial Organization and Competition', in George Feiwel (ed.), *Issues in Contemporary Microeconomics and Welfare*, London: Macmillan, 340–79.

March, James (1966), 'The Power of Power', in David Easton (ed.), *Varieties of Political Theory*, Englewood Cliffs, NJ: Prentice-Hall, 39–70.

Modigliani, Franco (1958), 'New Developments on the Oligopoly Front', *Journal of Political Economy*, **66**, June, 215–32.

Nelson, Richard and Sidney Winter (1982), *An Evolutionary Theory of Economic Change*, Cambridge, MA: Harvard University Press.

Newell, A. and H. Simon (1972), *Human Problem Solving*, Englewood Cliffs, NJ: Prentice-Hall, Inc.

Robinson, J. (1933), *The Economics of Imperfect Competition*, London: Macmillan.

Selten, R. (1965), 'Spieltheoretische Behandlunjeines Oligopolmodeles mit Nachfragetragheit', *Zeitschrift für die gesante Staatswissenschaft*, **12**, 301–24.

_____ (1975), Reexamination of the Perfectness Concept for Equilibrium Points in Extensive Games', *International Journal of Game Theory*, **4**, 25–55.

_____ (1978), 'The Chain-Store Paradox', *Theory and Decision*, **9**, 127–59.

Shepherd, W. G. (1984), '"Contestability" vs Competition', *American Economic Review*, **74**, September, 572–87.

Simon, Herbert (1957), *Administrative Behavior*, 2nd edn, New York: Macmillan.

_____ (1984), 'On the Behavioral and Rational Foundations of Economic Dynamics', *Journal of Economic Behavior and Organization*, **5**, March, 35–56.

Spence, A. M. (1977), 'Entry, Capacity Investment, and Oligopolistic Pricing', *Bell Journal of Economics*, **8**, Autumn, 534–44.

Stigler, George (1961), 'The Economics of Information', *Journal of Political Economy*, **69**, June, 213–25.

_____ (1988), 'Palgrave's Dictionary of Economics', *Journal of Economic Literature*, **26**, December, 1729–36.

Sylos-Labini, P. (1956), *Oligopoly and Technical Progress*, (Trans. Elizabeth Henderson), Cambridge, MA: Harvard University Press, 1962.
Tirole, Jean (1988), *The Theory of Industrial Organization*, Cambridge, MA: MIT Press.
Vickrey, W. (1964), *Microstatics*, New York: Harcourt, Brace, and World, Inc.

Part I
Antecedents

[1]

The Nature of the Firm

By R. H. Coase

ECONOMIC theory has suffered in the past from a failure to state clearly its assumptions. Economists in building up a theory have often omitted to examine the foundations on which it was erected. This examination is, however, essential not only to prevent the misunderstanding and needless controversy which arise from a lack of knowledge of the assumptions on which a theory is based, but also because of the extreme importance for economics of good judgment in choosing between rival sets of assumptions. For instance, it is suggested that the use of the word "firm" in economics may be different from the use of the term by the "plain man."[1] Since there is apparently a trend in economic theory towards starting analysis with the individual firm and not with the industry,[2] it is all the more necessary not only that a clear definition of the word "firm" should be given but that its difference from a firm in the "real world," if it exists, should be made clear. Mrs. Robinson has said that "the two questions to be asked of a set of assumptions in economics are : Are they tractable ? and : Do they correspond with the real world ? "[3] Though, as Mrs. Robinson points out, "more often one set will be manageable and the other realistic," yet there may well be branches of theory where assumptions may be both manageable and realistic. It is hoped to show in the following paper that a definition of a firm may be obtained which is not only realistic in that it corresponds to what is meant by a firm in the real world, but is tractable by two of the most powerful instruments of economic analysis developed by Marshall, the idea of the margin and that of substitution, together giving the idea of substitution at

[1] Joan Robinson, *Economics is a Serious Subject*, p. 12.
[2] See N. Kaldor, "The Equilibrium of the Firm," *Economic Journal*, March, 1934.
[3] Op. cit., p. 6.

the margin.[1] Our definition must, of course, " relate to formal relations which are capable of being *conceived* exactly."[2]

I

It is convenient if, in searching for a definition of a firm, we first consider the economic system as it is normally treated by the economist. Let us consider the description of the economic system given by Sir Arthur Salter.[3] " The normal economic system works itself. For its current operation it is under no central control, it needs no central survey. Over the whole range of human activity and human need, supply is adjusted to demand, and production to consumption, by a process that is automatic, elastic and responsive." An economist thinks of the economic system as being co-ordinated by the price mechanism and society becomes not an organisation but an organism.[4] The economic system " works itself." This does not mean that there is no planning by individuals. These exercise foresight and choose between alternatives. This is necessarily so if there is to be order in the system. But this theory assumes that the direction of resources is dependent directly on the price mechanism. Indeed, it is often considered to be an objection to economic planning that it merely tries to do what is already done by the price mechanism.[5] Sir Arthur Salter's description, however, gives a very incomplete picture of our economic system. Within a firm, the description does not fit at all. For instance, in economic theory we find that the allocation of factors of production between different uses is determined by the price mechanism. The price of factor A becomes higher in X than in Y. As a result, A moves from Y to X until the difference between the prices in X and Y, except in so far as it compensates for other differential advantages, disappears. Yet in the real world, we find that there are many areas where this does not apply. If a workman moves from department Y to department X, he does not go because of a change in relative prices, but because he is ordered to do so. Those who

[1] J. M. Keynes, *Essays in Biography*, pp. 223–4.
[2] L. Robbins, *Nature and Significance of Economic Science*, p. 63.
[3] This description is quoted with approval by D. H. Robertson, *Control of Industry*, p. 85, and by Professor Arnold Plant, " Trends in Business Administration," ECONOMICA, February, 1932. It appears in *Allied Shipping Control*, pp. 16-17.
[4] See F. A. Hayek, " The Trend of Economic Thinking," ECONOMICA, May, 1933.
[5] See F. A. Hayek, op. cit.

object to economic planning on the grounds that the problem is solved by price movements can be answered by pointing out that there is planning within our economic system which is quite different from the individual planning mentioned above and which is akin to what is normally called economic planning. The example given above is typical of a large sphere in our modern economic system. Of course, this fact has not been ignored by economists. Marshall introduces organisation as a fourth factor of production; J. B. Clark gives the co-ordinating function to the entrepreneur; Professor Knight introduces managers who co-ordinate. As D. H. Robertson points out, we find " islands of conscious power in this ocean of unconscious co-operation like lumps of butter coagulating in a pail of buttermilk."[1]. But in view of the fact that it is usually argued that co-ordination will be done by the price mechanism, why is such organisation necessary? Why are there these " islands of conscious power "? Outside the firm, price movements direct production, which is co-ordinated through a series of exchange transactions on the market. Within a firm, these market transactions are eliminated and in place of the complicated market structure with exchange transactions is substituted the entrepreneur-co-crdinator, who directs production.[2] It is clear that these are alternative methods of co-ordinating production. Yet, having regard to the fact that if production is regulated by price movements, production could be carried on without any organisation at all, well might we ask, why is there any organisation?

Of course, the degree to which the price mechanism is superseded varies greatly. In a department store, the allocation of the different sections to the various locations in the building may be done by the controlling authority or it may be the result of competitive price bidding for space. In the Lancashire cotton industry, a weaver can rent power and shop-room and can obtain looms and yarn on credit.[3] This co-ordination of the various factors of production is, however, normally carried out without the intervention of the price mechanism. As is evident, the amount of " vertical " integration, involving as it does

[1] Op. cit., p. 85.
[2] In the rest of this paper I shall use the term entrepreneur to refer to the person or persons who, in a competitive system, take the place of the price mechanism in the direction of resources.
[3] *Survey of Textile Industries*, p. 26.

the supersession of the price mechanism, varies greatly from industry to industry and from firm to firm.

It can, I think, be assumed that the distinguishing mark of the firm is the supersession of the price mechanism. It is, of course, as Professor Robbins points out, " related to an outside network of relative prices and costs,"[1] but it is important to discover the exact nature of this relationship. This distinction between the allocation of resources in a firm and the allocation in the economic system has been very vividly described by Mr. Maurice Dobb when discussing Adam Smith's conception of the capitalist : " It began to be seen that there was something more important than the relations inside each factory or unit captained by an undertaker ; there were the relations of the undertaker with the rest of the economic world outside his immediate sphere . . . . the undertaker busies himself with the division of labour inside each firm and he plans and organises consciously," but " he is related to the much larger economic specialisation, of which he himself is merely one specialised unit. Here, he plays his part as a single cell in a larger organism, mainly unconscious of the wider rôle he fills."[2]

In view of the fact that while economists treat the price mechanism as a co-ordinating instrument, they also admit the co-ordinating function of the " entrepreneur," it is surely important to enquire why co-ordination is the work of the price mechanism in one case and of the entrepreneur in another. The purpose of this paper is to bridge what appears to be a gap in economic theory between the assumption (made for some purposes) that resources are allocated by means of the price mechanism and the assumption (made for other purposes) that this allocation is dependent on the entrepreneur-co-ordinator. We have to explain the basis on which, in practice, this choice between alternatives is effected.[3]

[1] Op. cit., p. 71.

[2] *Capitalist Enterprise and Social Progress*, p. 20. Cf., also, Henderson, *Supply and Demand*, pp. 3–5.

[3] It is easy to see when the State takes over the direction of an industry that, in planning it, it is doing something which was previously done by the price mechanism. What is usually not realised is that any business man in organising the relations between his departments is also doing something which could be organised through the price mechanism. There is therefore point in Mr. Durbin's answer to those who emphasise the problems involved in economic planning that the same problems have to be solved by business men in the competitive system. (See " Economic Calculus in a Planned Economy," *Economic Journal*, December, 1936.) The important difference between these two cases is that economic planning is imposed on industry while firms arise voluntarily because they represent a more efficient method of organising production. In a competitive system, there is an " optimum " amount of planning !

II

Our task is to attempt to discover why a firm emerges at all in a specialised exchange economy. The price mechanism (considered purely from the side of the direction of resources) might be superseded if the relationship which replaced it was desired for its own sake. This would be the case, for example, if some people preferred to work under the direction of some other person. Such individuals would accept less in order to work under someone, and firms would arise naturally from this. But it would appear that this cannot be a very important reason, for it would rather seem that the opposite tendency is operating if one judges from the stress normally laid on the advantage of " being one's own master."[1] Of course, if the desire was not to be controlled but to control, to exercise power over others, then people might be willing to give up something in order to direct others ; that is, they would be willing to pay others more than they could get under the price mechanism in order to be able to direct them. But this implies that those who direct pay in order to be able to do this and are not paid to direct, which is clearly not true in the majority of cases.[2] Firms might also exist if purchasers preferred commodities which are produced by firms to those not so produced ; but even in spheres where one would expect such preferences (if they exist) to be of negligible importance, firms are to be found in the real world.[3] Therefore there must be other elements involved.

The main reason why it is profitable to establish a firm would seem to be that there is a cost of using the price mechanism. The most obvious cost of " organising " production through the price mechanism is that of discovering what the relevant prices are.[4] This cost may be reduced but it will not be eliminated by the emergence of specialists who will sell this information. The costs of negotiating and

---

[1] Cf. Harry Dawes, "Labour Mobility in the Steel Industry," *Economic Journal*, March, 1934, who instances " the trek to retail shopkeeping and insurance work by the better paid of skilled men due to the desire (often the main aim in life of a worker) to be independent " (p. 86).

[2] None the less, this is not altogether fanciful. Some small shopkeepers are said to earn less than their assistants.

[3] G. F. Shove, " The Imperfection of the Market : a Further Note," *Economic Journal*, March, 1933, p. 116, note 1, points out that such preferences may exist, although the example he gives is almost the reverse of the instance given in the text.

[4] According to N. Kaldor, " A Classificatory Note on the Determinateness of Equilibrium," *Review of Economic Studies*, February, 1934, it is one of the assumptions of static theory that " All the relevant prices are known to all individuals." But this is clearly not true of the real world.

concluding a separate contract for each exchange transaction which takes place on a market must also be taken into account.[1] Again, in certain markets, e.g., produce exchanges, a technique is devised for minimising these contract costs ; but they are not eliminated. It is true that contracts are not eliminated when there is a firm but they are greatly reduced. A factor of production (or the owner thereof) does not have to make a series of contracts with the factors with whom he is co-operating within the firm, as would be necessary, of course, if this co-operation were as a direct result of the working of the price mechanism. For this series of contracts is substituted one. At this stage, it is important to note the character of the contract into which a factor enters that is employed within a firm. The contract is one whereby the factor, for a certain remuneration (which may be fixed or fluctuating), agrees to obey the directions of an entrepreneur *within certain limits*.[2] The essence of the contract is that it should only state the limits to the powers of the entrepreneur. Within these limits, he can therefore direct the other factors of production.

There are, however, other disadvantages—or costs—of using the price mechanism. It may be desired to make a long-term contract for the supply of some article or service. This may be due to the fact that if one contract is made for a longer period, instead of several shorter ones, then certain costs of making each contract will be avoided. Or, owing to the risk attitude of the people concerned, they may prefer to make a long rather than a short-term contract. Now, owing to the difficulty of forecasting, the longer the period of the contract is for the supply of the commodity or service, the less possible, and indeed, the less desirable it is for the person purchasing to specify what the other contracting party is expected to do. It may well be a matter of indifference to the person supplying the service or commodity which of several courses of action is taken, but not to the purchaser of that service or commodity. But the purchaser will not know which of these several courses he will want the supplier to take. Therefore,

---

[1] This influence was noted by Professor Usher when discussing the development of capitalism. He says : "The successive buying and selling of partly finished products were sheer waste of energy." (*Introduction to the Industrial History of England*, p. 13). But he does not develop the idea nor consider why it is that buying and selling operations still exist.

[2] It would be possible for no limits to the powers of the entrepreneur to be fixed. This would be voluntary slavery. According to Professor Batt, *The Law of Master and Servant*, p. 18, such a contract would be void and unenforceable.

the service which is being provided is expressed in general terms, the exact details being left until a later date. All that is stated in the contract is the limits to what the persons supplying the commodity or service is expected to do. The details of what the supplier is expected to do is not stated in the contract but is decided later by the purchaser. When the direction of resources (within the limits of the contract) becomes dependent on the buyer in this way, that relationship which I term a " firm " may be obtained.[1] A firm is likely therefore to emerge in those cases where a very short term contract would be unsatisfactory. It is obviously of more importance in the case of services— labour—than it is in the case of the buying of commodities. In the case of commodities, the main items can be stated in advance and the details which will be decided later will be of minor significance.

We may sum up this section of the argument by saying that the operation of a market costs something and by forming an organisation and allowing some authority (an " entrepreneur ") to direct the resources, certain marketing costs are saved. The entrepreneur has to carry out his function at less cost, taking into account the fact that he may get factors of production at a lower price than the market transactions which he supersedes, because it is always possible to revert to the open market if he fails to do this.

The question of uncertainty is one which is often considered to be very relevant to the study of the equilibrium of the firm. It seems improbable that a firm would emerge without the existence of uncertainty. But those, for instance, Professor Knight, who make the *mode of payment* the distinguishing mark of the firm—fixed incomes being guaranteed to some of those engaged in production by a person who takes the residual, and fluctuating, income— would appear to be introducing a point which is irrelevant to the problem we are considering. One entrepreneur may sell his services to another for a certain sum of money, while the payment to his employees may be mainly or wholly a share in profits.[2] The significant question would

---

[1] Of course, it is not possible to draw a hard and fast line which determines whether there is a firm or not. There may be more or less direction. It is similar to the legal question of whether there is the relationship of master and servant or principal and agent. See the discussion of this problem below.

[2] The views of Professor Knight are examined below in more detail.

appear to be why the allocation of resources is not done directly by the price mechanism.

Another factor that should be noted is that exchange transactions on a market and the same transactions organised within a firm are often treated differently by Governments or other bodies with regulatory powers. If we consider the operation of a sales tax, it is clear that it is a tax on market transactions and not on the same transactions organised within the firm. Now since these are alternative methods of " organisation "—by the price mechanism or by the entrepreneur—such a regulation would bring into existence firms which otherwise would have no *raison d'être*. It would furnish a reason for the emergence of a firm in a specialised exchange economy. Of course, to the extent that firms already exist, such a measure as a sales tax would merely tend to make them larger than they would otherwise be. Similarly, quota schemes, and methods of price control which imply that there is rationing, and which do not apply to firms producing such products for themselves, by allowing advantages to those who organise within the firm and not through the market, necessarily encourage the growth of firms. But it is difficult to believe that it is measures such as have been mentioned in this paragraph which have brought firms into existence. Such measures would, however, tend to have this result if they did not exist for other reasons.

These, then, are the reasons why organisations such as firms exist in a specialised exchange economy in which it is generally assumed that the distribution of resources is " organised " by the price mechanism. A firm, therefore, consists of the system of relationships which comes into existence when the direction of resources is dependent on an entrepreneur.

The approach which has just been sketched would appear to offer an advantage in that it is possible to give a scientific meaning to what is meant by saying that a firm gets larger or smaller. A firm becomes larger as additional transactions (which could be exchange transactions co-ordinated through the price mechanism) are organised by the entrepreneur and becomes smaller as he abandons the organisation of such transactions. The question which arises is whether it is possible to study the forces which determine the size of the firm. Why does the entrepreneur not organise one less transaction or one more ? It is interesting to note that Professor Knight considers that :

" the relation between efficiency and size is one of the most serious problems of theory, being, in contrast with the relation for a plant, largely a matter of personality and historical accident rather than of intelligible general principles. But the question is peculiarly vital because the possibility of monopoly gain offers a powerful incentive to *continuous and unlimited* expansion of the firm, which force must be offset by some equally powerful one making for decreased efficiency (in the production of money income) with growth in size, if even boundary competition is to exist."[1]

Professor Knight would appear to consider that it is impossible to treat scientifically the determinants of the size of the firm. On the basis of the concept of the firm developed above, this task will now be attempted.

It was suggested that the introduction of the firm was due primarily to the existence of marketing costs. A pertinent question to ask would appear to be (quite apart from the monopoly considerations raised by Professor Knight), why, if by organising one can eliminate certain costs and in fact reduce the cost of production, are there any market transactions at all ?[2] Why is not all production carried on by one big firm ? There would appear to be certain possible explanations.

First, as a firm gets larger, there may be decreasing returns to the entrepreneur function, that is, the costs of organising additional transactions within the firm may rise.[3] Naturally, a point must be reached where the costs of organising an extra transaction within the firm are equal to the costs involved in carrying out the transaction in the open market, or, to the costs of organising by another entrepreneur. Secondly, it may be that as the transactions which are organised increase, the entrepreneur fails to place the factors of production in the uses where their value

---

[1] *Risk, Uncertainty and Profit*, Preface to the Re-issue, London School of Economics Series of Reprints, No. 16, 1933.

[2] There are certain marketing costs which could only be eliminated by the abolition of " consumers' choice " and these are the costs of retailing. It is conceivable that these costs might be so high that people would be willing to accept rations because the extra product obtained was worth the loss of their choice.

[3] This argument assumes that exchange transactions on a market can be considered as homogeneous ; which is clearly untrue in fact. This complication is taken into account below.

is greatest, that is, fails to make the best use of the factors
of production. Again, a point must be reached where the
loss through the waste of resources is equal to the marketing
costs of the exchange transaction in the open market or
to the loss if the transaction was organised by another
entrepreneur. Finally, the supply price of one or more of
the factors of production may rise, because the " other
advantages " of a small firm are greater than those of a
large firm.[1] Of course, the actual point where the expansion
of the firm ceases might be determined by a combination
of the factors mentioned above. The first two reasons
given most probably correspond to the economists' phrase
of " diminishing returns to management."[2]

The point has been made in the previous paragraph that
a firm will tend to expand until the costs of organising an
extra transaction within the firm become equal to the costs
of carrying out the same transaction by means of an exchange
on the open market or the costs of organising in another
firm. But if the firm stops its expansion at a point below
the costs of marketing in the open market and at a point
equal to the costs of organising in another firm, in most
cases (excluding the case of " combination "[3]), this will
imply that there is a market transaction between these
two producers, each of whom could organise it at less than
the actual marketing costs. How is the paradox to be
resolved ? If we consider an example the reason for this
will become clear. Suppose *A* is buying a product from
B and that both *A* and *B* could organise this marketing
transaction at less than its present cost. *B*, we can assume,
is not organising one process or stage of production, but
several. If *A* therefore wishes to avoid a market transaction,
he will have to take over all the processes of production
controlled by *B*. Unless *A* takes over all the processes of

[1] For a discussion of the variation of the supply price of factors of production to firms
of varying size, see E. A. G. Robinson, *The Structure of Competitive Industry*. It is sometimes said that the supply price of organising ability increases as the size of the firm increases
because men prefer to be the heads of small independent businesses rather than the heads
of departments in a large business. See Jones, *The Trust Problem*, p. 531, and Macgregor,
Industrial Combination, p. 63. This is a common argument of those who advocate Rationalisation. It is said that larger units would be more efficient, but owing to the individualistic
spirit of the smaller entrepreneurs, they prefer to remain independent, apparently in spite
of the higher income which their increased efficiency under Rationalisation makes possible.

[2] This discussion is, of course, brief and incomplete. For a more thorough discussion
of this particular problem, see N. Kaldor, " The Equilibrium of the Firm," *Economic Journal*,
March, 1934, and E. A. G. Robinson, "The Problem of Management and the Size of the
Firm," *Economic Journal*, June, 1934.

[3] A definition of this term is given below.

production, a market transaction will still remain, although it is a different product that is bought. But we have previously assumed that as each producer expands he becomes less efficient ; the additional costs of organising extra transactions increase. It is probable that A's cost of organising the transactions previously organised by B will be greater than B's cost of doing the same thing. A therefore will take over the whole of B's organisation only if his cost of organising B's work is not greater than B's cost by an amount equal to the costs of carrying out an exchange transaction on the open market. But once it becomes economical to have a market transaction, it also pays to divide production in such a way that the cost of organising an extra transaction in each firm is the same.

Up to now it has been assumed that the exchange transactions which take place through the price mechanism are homogeneous. In fact, nothing could be more diverse than the actual transactions which take place in our modern world. This would seem to imply that the costs of carrying out exchange transactions through the price mechanism will vary considerably as will also the costs of organising these transactions within the firm. It seems therefore possible that quite apart from the question of diminishing returns the costs of organising certain transactions within the firm may be greater than the costs of carrying out the exchange transactions in the open market. This would necessarily imply that there were exchange transactions carried out through the price mechanism, but would it mean that there would have to be more than one firm ? Clearly not, for all those areas in the economic system where the direction of resources was not dependent directly on the price mechanism could be organised within one firm. The factors which were discussed earlier would seem to be the important ones, though it is difficult to say whether " diminishing returns to management " or the rising supply price of factors is likely to be the more important.

Other things being equal, therefore, a firm will tend to be larger :

(*a*) the less the costs of organising and the slower these costs rise with an increase in the transactions organised.

(*b*) the less likely the entrepreneur is to make mistakes and the smaller the increase in mistakes with an increase in the transactions organised.

(*c*) the greater the lowering (or the less the rise) in the supply price of factors of production to firms of larger size.

Apart from variations in the supply price of factors of production to firms of different sizes, it would appear that the costs of organising and the losses through mistakes will increase with an increase in the spatial distribution of the transactions organised, in the dissimilarity of the transactions, and in the probability of changes in the relevant prices.[1] As more transactions are organised by an entrepreneur, it would appear that the transactions would tend to be either different in kind or in different places. This furnishes an additional reason why efficiency will tend to decrease as the firm gets larger. Inventions which tend to bring factors of production nearer together, by lessening spatial distribution, tend to increase the size of the firm.[2] Changes like the telephone and the telegraph which tend to reduce the cost of organising spatially will tend to increase the size of the firm. All changes which improve managerial technique will tend to increase the size of the firm.[3-4]

It should be noted that the definition of a firm which was given above can be used to give more precise meanings to the terms " combination " and " integration."[5] There is a combination when transactions which were previously

[1] This aspect of the problem is emphasised by N. Kaldor, op. cit. Its importance in this connection had been previously noted by E. A. G. Robinson, *The Structure of Competitive Industry*, pp. 83–106. This assumes that an increase in the probability of price movements increases the costs of organising within a firm more than it increases the cost of carrying out an exchange transaction on the market—which is probable.

[2] This would appear to be the importance of the treatment of the technical unit by E. A. G. Robinson, op. cit., pp. 27–33. The larger the technical unit, the greater the concentration of factors and therefore the firm is likely to be larger.

[3] It should be noted that most inventions will change both the costs of organising and the costs of using the price mechanism. In such cases, whether the invention tends to make firms larger or smaller will depend on the relative effect on these two sets of costs. For instance, if the telephone reduces the costs of using the price.mechanism more than it reduces the costs of organising, then it will have the effect of reducing the size of the firm.

[4] An illustration of these dynamic forces is furnished by Maurice Dobb, *Russian Economic Development*, p. 68. " With the passing of bonded labour the factory, as an establishment where work was organised under the whip of the overseer, lost its *raison d'être* until this was restored to it with the introduction of power machinery after 1846." It seems important to realise that the passage from the domestic system to the factory system is not a mere historical accident, but is conditioned by economic forces. This is shown by the fact that it is possible to move from the factory system to the domestic system, as in the Russian example, as well as *vice versa*. It is the essence of serfdom that the price mechanism is not allowed to operate. Therefore, there has to be direction from some organiser. When, however, serfdom passed, the price mechanism was allowed to operate. It was not until machinery drew workers into one locality that it paid to supersede the price mechanism and the firm again emerged.

[5] This is often called " vertical integration," combination being termed " lateral integration."

organised by two or more entrepreneurs become organised by one. This becomes integration when it involves the organisation of transactions which were previously carried out between the entrepreneurs on a market. A firm can expand in either or both of these two ways. The whole of the " structure of competitive industry " becomes tractable by the ordinary technique of economic analysis.

III

The problem which has been investigated in the previous section has not been entirely neglected by economists and it is now necessary to consider why the reasons given above for the emergence of a firm in a specialised exchange economy are to be preferred to the other explanations which have been offered.

It is sometimes said that the reason for the existence of a firm is to be found in the division of labour. This is the view of Professor Usher, a view which has been adopted and expanded by Mr. Maurice Dobb. The firm becomes " the result of an increasing complexity of the division of labour . . . . The growth of this economic differentiation creates the need for some integrating force without which differentiation would collapse into chaos ; and it is as the integrating force in a differentiated economy that industrial forms are chiefly significant."[1] The answer to this argument is an obvious one. The " integrating force in a differentiated economy " already exists in the form of the price mechanism. It is perhaps the main achievement of economic science that it has shown that there is no reason to suppose that specialisation must lead to chaos.[2] The reason given by Mr. Maurice Dobb is therefore inadmissible. What has to be explained is why one integrating force (the entrepreneur) should be substituted for another integrating force (the price mechanism).

The most interesting reasons (and probably the most widely accepted) which have been given to explain this fact are those to be found in Professor Knight's *Risk, Uncertainty and Profit*. His views will be examined in some detail.

[1] Op. cit., p. 10. Professor Usher's views are to be found in his *Introduction to the Industrial History of England*, pp. 1-18.

[2] Cf. J. B. Clark, *Distribution of Wealth*, p. 19, who speaks of the theory of exchange as being the " theory of the organisation of industrial society."

Professor Knight starts with a system in which there is no uncertainty :

" acting as individuals under absolute freedom but without collusion men are supposed to have organised economic life with the primary and secondary division of labour, the use of capital, etc., developed to the point familiar in present-day America. The principal fact which calls for the exercise of the imagination is the internal organisation of the productive groups or establishments. With uncertainty entirely absent, every individual being in possession of perfect knowledge of the situation, there would be no occasion for anything of the nature of responsible management or control of productive activity. Even marketing transactions in any realistic sense would not be found. The flow of raw materials and productive services to the consumer would be entirely automatic."[1]

Professor Knight says that we can imagine this adjustment as being " the result of a long process of experimentation worked out by trial-and-error methods alone," while it is not necessary " to imagine every worker doing exactly the right thing at the right time in a sort of ' pre-established harmony ' with the work of others. There might be managers, superintendents, etc., for the purpose of co-ordinating the activities of individuals," though these managers would be performing a purely routine function, " without responsibility of any sort."[2]

Professor Knight then continues :

" With the introduction of uncertainty—the fact of ignorance and the necessity of acting upon opinion rather than knowledge—into this Eden-like situation, its character is entirely changed . . . . With uncertainty present doing things, the actual execution of activity, becomes in a real sense a secondary part of life ; the primary problem or function is deciding what to do and how to do it."[3]

This fact of uncertainty brings about the two most important characteristics of social organisation.

" In the first place, goods are produced for a market, on the basis of entirely impersonal prediction of wants, not for the satisfaction of the wants of the producers themselves. The producer takes the responsibility of

---

[1] *Risk, Uncertainty and Profit*, p. 267.
[2] Op. cit., pp. 267–8.   [3] Op. cit., p. 268.

forecasting the consumers' wants. In the second place, the work of forecasting and at the same time a large part of the technological direction and control of production are still further concentrated upon a very narrow class of the producers, and we meet with a new economic functionary, the entrepreneur. . . . . When uncertainty is present and the task of deciding what to do and how to do it takes the ascendancy over that of execution the internal organisation of the productive groups is no longer a matter of indifference or a mechanical detail. Centralisation of this deciding and controlling function is imperative, a process of ' cephalisation ' is inevitable."[1] The most fundamental change is :

" the system under which the confident and venturesome assume the risk or insure the doubtful and timid by guaranteeing to the latter a specified income in return for an assignment of the actual results. . . . With human nature as we know it it would be impracticable or very unusual for one man to guarantee to another a definite result of the latter's actions without being given power to direct his work. And on the other hand the second party would not place himself under the direction of the first without such a guarantee. . . . The result of this manifold specialisation of function is the enterprise and wage system of industry. Its existence in the world is the direct result of the fact of uncertainty."[2]

These quotations give the essence of Professor Knight's theory. The fact of uncertainty means that people have to forecast future wants. Therefore, you get a special class springing up who direct the activities of others to whom they give guaranteed wages. It acts because good judgment is generally associated with confidence in one's judgment.[3]

Professor Knight would appear to leave himself open to criticism on several grounds. First of all, as he himself points out, the fact that certain people have better judgment or better knowledge does not mean that they can only get an income from it by themselves actively taking part in production. They can sell advice or knowledge. Every business buys the services of a host of advisers. We can imagine a system where all advice or knowledge was bought

[1] Op. cit., pp. 268–95. [2] Op. cit., pp. 269–70.
[3] Op. cit., p. 270.

as required. Again, it is possible to get a reward from
better knowledge or judgment not by actively taking part
in production but by making contracts with people who
are producing. A merchant buying for future delivery
represents an example of this. But this merely illustrates
the point that it is quite possible to give a guaranteed
reward providing that certain acts are performed without
directing the performance of those acts. Professor Knight
says that " with human nature as we know it it would be
impracticable or very unusual for one man to guarantee
to another a definite result of the latter's actions without
being given power to direct his work." This is surely
incorrect. A large proportion of jobs are done to contract,
that is, the contractor is guaranteed a certain sum providing
he performs certain acts. But this does not involve any
direction. It does mean, however, that the system of
relative prices has been changed and that there will be a
new arrangement of the factors of production.[1] The fact
that Professor Knight mentions that the " second party
would not place himself under the direction of the first
without such a guarantee " is irrelevant to the problem
we are considering. Finally, it seems important to notice
that even in the case of an economic system where there
is no uncertainty Professor Knight considers that there
would be co-ordinators, though they would perform only
a routine function. He immediately adds that they would
be " without responsibility of any sort," which raises the
question by whom are they paid and why ? It seems that
nowhere does Professor Knight give a reason why the price
mechanism should be superseded.

IV

It would seem important to examine one further point
and that is to consider the relevance of this discussion to
the general question of the " cost-curve of the firm."

It has sometimes been assumed that a firm is limited
in size under perfect competition if its cost curve slopes
upward,[2] while under imperfect competition, it is limited

---

[1] This shows that it is possible to have a private enterprise system without the existence
of firms. Though, in practice, the two functions of enterprise, which actually influences
the system of relative prices by forecasting wants and acting in accordance with such fore-
casts, and management, which accepts the system of relative prices as being given, are
normally carried out by the same persons, yet it seems important to keep them separate
in theory. This point is further discussed below.

[2] See Kaldor, op. cit., and Robinson, *The Problem of Management and the Size of the Firm.*

in size because it will not pay to produce more than the output at which marginal cost is equal to marginal revenue.[1] But it is clear that a firm may produce more than one product and, therefore, there appears to be no *prima facie* reason why this upward slope of the cost curve in the case of perfect competition or the fact that marginal cost will not always be below marginal revenue in the case of imperfect competition should limit the size of the firm.[2] Mrs. Robinson[3] makes the simplifying assumption that only one product is being produced. But it is clearly important to investigate how the number of products produced by a firm is determined, while no theory which assumes that only one product is in fact produced can have very great practical significance.

It might be replied that under perfect competition, since everything that is produced can be sold at the prevailing price, then there is no need for any other product to be produced. But this argument ignores the fact that there may be a point where it is less costly to organise the exchange transactions of a new product than to organise further exchange transactions of the old product. This point can be illustrated in the following way. Imagine, following von Thunen, that there is a town, the consuming centre, and that industries are located around this central point in rings. These conditions are illustrated in the following diagram in which *A*, *B* and *C* represent different industries.

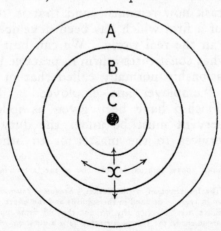

[1] Mr. Robinson calls this the Imperfect Competition solution for the survival of the small firm.

[2] Mr. Robinson's conclusion, op. cit., p. 249, note 1, would appear to be definitely wrong. He is followed by Horace J. White, Jr., "Monopolistic and Perfect Competition," *American Economic Review*, December, 1936, p. 645, note 27. Mr. White states "It is obvious that the size of the firm is limited in conditions of monopolistic competition."

[3] *Economics of Imperfect Competition*.

Imagine an entrepreneur who starts controlling exchange
transactions from x. Now as he extends his activities in
the same product (B), the cost of organising increases until
at some point it becomes equal to that of a dissimilar product
which is nearer. As the firm expands, it will therefore
from this point include more than one product (A and C).
This treatment of the problem is obviously incomplete,[1]
but it is necessary to show that merely proving that the
cost curve turns upwards does not give a limitation to the
size of the firm. So far we have only considered the case
of perfect competition ; the case of imperfect competition
would appear to be obvious.

To determine the size of the firm, we have to consider
the marketing costs (that is, the costs of using the price
mechanism), and the costs of organising of different entrepreneurs and then we can determine how many products
will be produced by each firm and how much of each it
will produce. It would, therefore, appear that Mr. Shove[2]
in his article on " Imperfect Competition " was asking
questions which Mrs. Robinson's cost curve apparatus
cannot answer. The factors mentioned above would seem
to be the relevant ones.

V

Only one task now remains ; and that is, to see whether
the concept of a firm which has been developed fits in with
that existing in the real world. We can best approach the
question of what constitutes a firm in practice by considering
the legal relationship normally called that of " master and
servant " or " employer and employee."[3] The essentials
of this relationship have been given as follows :

" (1) the servant must be under the duty of rendering
personal services to the master or to others on behalf

---

[1] As has been shown above, location is only one of the factors influencing the cost of
organising.
[2] G. F. Shove, " The Imperfection of the Market," *Economic Journal*, March, 1933, p. 115.
In connection with an increase in demand in the suburbs and the effect on the price charged
by suppliers, Mr. Shove asks " . . . . why do not the old firms open branches in the
suburbs ? " If the argument in the text is correct, this is a question which Mrs. Robinson's
apparatus cannot answer.
[3] The legal concept of " employer and employee " and the economic concept of a firm
are not identical, in that the firm may imply control over another person's property as well
as over their labour. But the identity of these two concepts is sufficiently close for an
examination of the legal concept to be of value in appraising the worth of the economic
concept.

of the master, otherwise the contract is a contract for sale of goods or the like.

(2) The master must have the right to control the servant's work, either personally or by another servant or agent. It is this right of control or interference, of being entitled to tell the servant when to work (within the hours of service) and when not to work, and what work to do and how to do it (within the terms of such service) which is the dominant characteristic in this relation and marks off the servant from an independent contractor, or from one employed merely to give to his employer the fruits of his labour. In the latter case, the contractor or performer is not under the employer's control in doing the work or effecting the service ; he has to shape and manage his work so as to give the result he has contracted to effect."[1]

We thus see that it is the fact of direction which is the essence of the legal concept of " employer and employee," just as it was in the economic concept which was developed above. It is interesting to note that Professor Batt says further :

" That which distinguishes an agent from a servant is not the absence or presence of a fixed wage or the payment only of commission on business done, but rather the freedom with which an agent may carry out his employment."[2]

We can therefore conclude that the definition we have given is one which approximates closely to the firm as it is considered in the real world.

Our definition is, therefore, realistic. Is it manageable ? This ought to be clear. When we are considering how large a firm will be the principle of marginalism works smoothly. The question always is, will it pay to bring an extra exchange transaction under the organising authority ? At the margin, the costs of organising within the firm will be equal either to the costs of organising in another firm or to the costs involved in leaving the transaction to be " organised " by the price mechanism. Business men will be constantly experimenting, controlling more or less, and in this way, equilibrium will be maintained. This gives the position of equilibrium for static analysis. But

---

[1] Batt, *The Law of Master and Servant*, p. 6.
[2] Op. cit., p. 7.

it is clear that the dynamic factors are also of considerable importance, and an investigation of the effect changes have on the cost of organising within the firm and on marketing costs generally will enable one to explain why firms get larger and smaller. We thus have a theory of moving equilibrium. The above analysis would also appear to have clarified the relationship between initiative or enterprise and management. Initiative means forecasting and operates through the price mechanism by the making of new contracts. Management proper merely reacts to price changes, rearranging the factors of production under its control. That the business man normally combines both functions is an obvious result of the marketing costs which were discussed above. Finally, this analysis enables us to state more exactly what is meant by the " marginal product " of the entrepreneur. But an elaboration of this point would take us far from our comparatively simple task of definition and clarification.

[2]

UNCERTAINTY, EVOLUTION, AND ECONOMIC THEORY

ARMEN A. ALCHIAN[1]

University of California at Los Angeles

A MODIFICATION of economic analysis to incorporate incomplete information and uncertain foresight as axioms is suggested here. This approach dispenses with "profit maximization"; and it does not rely on the predictable, individual behavior that is usually assumed, as a first approximation, in standard textbook treatments. Despite these changes, the analytical concepts usually associated with such behavior are retained because they are not dependent upon such motivation or foresight. The suggested approach embodies the principles of biological evolution and natural selection by interpreting the economic system as an adoptive mechanism which chooses among exploratory actions generated by the adaptive pursuit of "success" or "profits." The resulting analysis is applicable to actions usually regarded as aberrations from standard economic behavior as well as to behavior covered by the customary analysis. This wider applicability and the removal of the unrealistic postulates of accurate anticipations and fixed states of knowledge have provided motivation for the study.

The exposition is ordered as follows: First, to clear the ground, a brief statement is given of a generally ignored aspect of "profit maximization," that is, where foresight is uncertain, "profit maximization" is *meaningless* as a guide to specifiable action. The constructive development then begins with an intro-

duction of the element of environmental adoption by the economic system of a posteriori most appropriate action according to the criterion of "realized positive profits." This is illustrated in an extreme, random-behavior model without any individual rationality, foresight, or motivation whatsoever. Even in this extreme type of model, it is shown that the economist can predict and explain events with a modified use of his conventional analytical tools.

This phenomenon—environmental adoption—is then fused with a type of individual motivated behavior based on the pervasiveness of uncertainty and incomplete information. Adaptive, imitative, and trial-and-error behavior in the pursuit of "positive profits" is utilized rather than its sharp contrast, the pursuit of "maximized profits." A final section discusses some implications and conjectures.

I. "PROFIT MAXIMIZATION" NOT A GUIDE TO ACTION

Current economic analysis of economic behavior relies heavily on decisions made by rational units customarily assumed to be seeking perfectly optimal situations.[2] Two criteria are well known—profit maximization and utility maximiza-

[1] I am indebted to Dr. Stephen Enke for criticism and stimulation leading to improvements in both content and exposition.

[2] See, e.g., J. Robinson, *Economics of Imperfect Competition* (London: Macmillan), p. 6, for a strong statement of the necessity of such optimal behavior. Standard textbooks expound essentially the same idea. See also P. Samuelson, *Foundations of Economic Analysis* (Cambridge: Harvard University Press, 1946).

tion.[3] According to these criteria, appropriate types of action are indicated by marginal or neighborhood inequalities which, if satisfied, yield an optimum. But the standard qualification usually added is that nobody is able really to optimize his situation according to these diagrams and concepts because of uncertainty about the position and, sometimes, even the slopes of the demand and supply functions. Nevertheless, the economist interprets and predicts the decisions of individuals in terms of these diagrams, since it is alleged that individuals use these concepts implicitly, if not explicitly.

Attacks on this methodology are widespread, but only one attack has been really damaging, that of G. Tintner.[4] He denies that profit maximization even makes any sense where there is uncertainty. Uncertainty arises from at least two sources: imperfect foresight and human inability to solve complex problems containing a host of variables even when an optimum is definable. Tintner's proof is simple. Under uncertainty, by definition, each action that may be chosen is identified with a *distribution* of potential outcomes, not with a unique outcome. Implicit in uncertainty is the consequence that these distributions of potential outcomes are overlapping.[5] It is worth emphasis that each possible action has a *distribution* of potential out-

comes, only one of which will materialize if the action is taken, and that one outcome cannot be foreseen. Essentially, the task is converted into making a decision (selecting an action) whose potential outcome *distribution* is preferable, that is, choosing the action with the *optimum distribution*, since there is no such thing as a *maximizing* distribution.

For example, let each of two possible choices be characterized by its subjective distribution of potential outcomes. Suppose one has the higher "mean" but a larger spread, so that it might result in larger profits or losses, and the other has a smaller "mean" and a smaller spread. Which one is the maximum? This is a nonsensical question; but to ask for the optimum distribution is not nonsense. In the presence of uncertainty—a necessary condition for the existence of profits—there is no meaningful criterion for selecting the decision that will "maximize profits." The maximum-profit criterion is not meaningful as a basis *for selecting* the action which will, in fact, result in an outcome with higher profits than any other action would have, unless one assumes nonoverlapping potential outcome distributions. It must be noticed that the meaningfulness of "maximum profits—a realized outcome which is the largest that could have been realized from the available actions"—is perfectly consistent with the meaninglessness of "profit maximization"—a criterion for selecting among alternative lines of action, the potential outcomes of which are describable only as distributions and not as unique amounts.

This crucial difficulty would be avoided by using a preference function as a criterion for selecting most preferred distributions of potential outcomes, but the search for a criterion of rationality and choice in terms of pref-

[3] In the following we shall discuss only profit maximization, although everything said is applicable equally to utility maximization by consumers.

[4] "The Theory of Choice under Subjective Risk and Uncertainty," *Econometrica*, IX (1941), 298–304; "The Pure Theory of Production under Technological Risk and Uncertainty," *ibid.*, pp. 305–11; and "A Contribution to the Nonstatic Theory of Production," *Studies in Mathematical Economics and Econometrics* (Chicago: University of Chicago Press, 1942), pp. 92–109.

[5] Thus uncertainty is defined here to be the phenomenon that produces overlapping distributions of potential outcomes.

UNCERTAINTY AND ECONOMIC THEORY 213

erence functions still continues. For example, the use of the mean, or expectation, completely begs the question of uncertainty by disregarding the variance of the distribution, while a "certainty equivalent" assumes the answer. The only way to make "profit maximization" a specifically meaningful action is to postulate a model containing certainty. Then the question of the predictive and explanatory reliability of the model must be faced.[6]

II. SUCCESS IS BASED ON RESULTS, NOT MOTIVATION

There is an alternative method which treats the decisions and criteria dictated by the economic *system* as more important than those made by the individuals in it. By backing away from the trees—the optimization calculus by individual units—we can better discern the forest of impersonal market forces.[7] This approach directs attention to the interrelationships of the environment and the prevailing types of economic behavior which appear through a process of economic natural selection. Yet it does not imply that individual foresight and action do not affect the nature of the existing state of affairs.

In an economic system the realization of profits is the criterion according to which successful and surviving firms are selected. This decision criterion is applied primarily by an impersonal market system in the United States and may be completely independent of the decision processes of individual units, of the variety of inconsistent motives and abilities, and even of the individual's awareness of the criterion. The reason is simple. Realized positive profits, not *maximum* profits, are the mark of success and viability. It does not matter through what process of reasoning or motivation such success was achieved. The fact of its accomplishment is sufficient. This is the criterion by which the economic system selects survivors: those who realize *positive profits* are the survivors; those who suffer losses disappear.

The pertinent requirement—positive profits through relative efficiency—is weaker than "maximized profits," with which, unfortunately, it has been confused. Positive profits accrue to those who are better than their actual competitors, even if the participants are ignorant, intelligent, skilful, etc. The crucial element is one's aggregate position relative to actual competitors, not some hypothetically perfect competitors. As in a race, the award goes to the relatively fastest, even if all the competitors loaf. Even in a world of stupid men there would still be profits. Also, the greater the uncertainties of the world, the greater is the possibility that profits would go to venturesome and lucky rather than to logical, careful, fact-gathering individuals.

The preceding interpretation suggests two ideas. First, success (survival) accompanies relative superiority; and, second, it does not require proper motivation but may rather be the result of fortuitous circumstances. Among all competitors, those whose particular conditions happen to be the most appropriate of those offered to the economic system for testing and adoption will be "se-

[6] Analytical models in all sciences postulate models abstracting from some realities in the belief that derived predictions will still be relevant. Simplifications are necessary, but continued attempts should be made to introduce more realistic assumptions into a workable model with an increase in generality and detail (see M. Friedman and L. Savage, "The Utility Analysis of Choices Involving Risks," *Journal of Political Economy*, LVI, No. 4 [1948], 279).

[7] In effect, we shall be reverting to a Marshallian type of analysis combined with the essentials of Darwinian evolutionary natural selection.

lected" as survivors. Just how such an approach can be used and how individuals happen to offer these appropriate forms for testing are problems to which we now turn.[8]

III. CHANCE OR LUCK IS ONE METHOD OF ACHIEVING SUCCESS

Sheer chance is a substantial element in determining the situation selected and also in determining its appropriateness or viability. A second element is the ability to adapt one's self by various methods to an appropriate situation. In order to indicate clearly the respective roles of luck and conscious adapting, the adaptive calculus will, for the moment, be completely removed. All individual rationality, motivation, and foresight will be temporarily abandoned in order to concentrate upon the ability of the environment to *adopt* "appropriate" survivors even in the absence of any adaptive behavior. This is an apparently unrealistic, but nevertheless very useful, expository approach in establishing the attenuation between the ex post survival criterion and the role of the individual's adaptive decision criterion. It also aids in assessing the role of luck and chance in the operation of our economic system.

Consider, first, the simplest type of biological evolution. Plants "grow" to the sunny side of buildings not because they "want to" in awareness of the fact that optimum or better conditions prevail there but rather because the leaves that happen to have more sunlight grow

[8] Also suggested is another way to divide the general problem discussed here. The process and rationale by which a unit chooses its actions so as to optimize its situation is one part of the problem. The other is the relationship between changes in the environment and the consequent observable results, i.e., the decision process of the economic *society*. The classification used in the text is closely related to this but differs in emphasizing the degree of knowledge and foresight.

faster and their feeding systems become stronger. Similarly, animals with configurations and habits more appropriate for survival under prevailing conditions have an enhanced viability and will with higher probability be typical survivors. Less appropriately acting organisms of the same general class having lower probabilities of survival will find survival difficult. More common types, the survivors, may appear to be those having *adapted* themselves to the environment, whereas the truth may well be that the environment has *adopted* them. There may have been no motivated individual adapting but, instead, only environmental adopting.

A useful, but unreal, example in which individuals act without any foresight indicates the type of analysis available to the economist and also the ability of the system to "direct" resources despite individual ignorance. Assume that thousands of travelers set out from Chicago, selecting their roads completely at random and without foresight. Only our "economist" knows that on but one road are there any gasoline stations. He can state categorically that travelers will *continue* to travel only on that road; those on other roads will soon run out of gas. Even though each one selected his route at random, we might have called those travelers who were so fortunate as to have picked the right road wise, efficient, foresighted, etc. Of course, we would consider them the lucky ones. If gasoline supplies were now moved to a new road, some formerly luckless travelers again would be able to move; and a new pattern of travel would be observed, although none of the travelers had changed his particular path. The really possible paths have changed with the changing environment. All that is needed is a set of varied, risk-taking

UNCERTAINTY AND ECONOMIC THEORY

(adoptable) travelers. The correct direction of travel will be established. As circumstances (economic environment) change, the analyst (economist) can select the types of participants (firms) that will now become successful; he may also be able to diagnose the conditions most conducive to a greater probability of survival.[9]

IV. CHANCE DOES NOT IMPLY NONDIRECTED, RANDOM ALLOCATION OF RESOURCES

These two examples do not constitute an attempt to base all analysis on adoptive models dominated by chance. But they do indicate that collective and individual random behavior does not per se imply a nihilistic theory incapable of yielding reliable predictions and explanations; nor does it imply a world lacking in order and apparent direction. It might, however, be argued that the facts of life deny even a substantial role to the element of chance and the associated adoption principle in the economic system. For example, the long lives and disparate sizes of business firms and hereditary fortunes may seem to be reliable evidence of consistent foresighted motivation and nonrandom behavior. In order to demonstrate that consistent success cannot be treated as prima facie evidence against pure luck, the following chance model of Borél, the famous French mathematician, is presented.

Suppose two million Parisians were paired off and set to tossing coins in a game of matching. Each pair plays until the winner on the first toss is again

brought to equality with the other player. Assuming one toss per second for each eight-hour day, at the end of ten years there would still be, on the average, about a hundred-odd pairs; and if the players assign the game to their heirs, a dozen or so will still be playing at the end of a thousand years! The implications are obvious. Suppose that some business had been operating for one hundred years. Should one rule out luck and chance as the essence of the factors producing the long-term survival of the enterprise? No inference whatever can be drawn until the number of original participants is known; and even then one must know the size, risk, and frequency of each commitment. One can see from the Borél illustration the danger in concluding that there are too many firms with long lives in the real world to admit an important role to chance. On the contrary, one might insist that there are actually too few!

The chance postulate was directed to two problems. On the one hand, there is the actual way in which a substantial fraction of economic behavior and activity is effected. On the other, there is the method of analysis which economists may use in their predictions and diagnoses. Before modifying the extreme chance model by adding adaptive behavior, some connotations and implications of the incorporation of chance elements will be elaborated in order to reveal the richness which is really inherent in chance. First, even if each and every individual acted in a haphazard and nonmotivated manner, it is possible that the variety of actions would be so great that the resulting collective set would contain actions that are best, in the sense of perfect foresight. For example, at a horse race with enough bettors wagering strictly at random, someone will win

[9] The undiscerning person who sees survivors corresponding to changes in environment claims to have evidence for the "Lysenko" doctrine. In truth, all he may have is evidence for the doctrine that the environment, by competitive conditions, selects the most viable of the various phenotypic characteristics for perpetuation. Economists should beware of economic "Lysenkois m."

216   ARMEN A. ALCHIAN

on all eight races. Thus individual random behavior does not eliminate the likelihood of observing "appropriate" decisions.[10]

Second, and conversely, individual behavior according to some foresight and motivation does not necessarily imply a collective pattern of behavior that is different from the collective variety of actions associated with a random selection of actions. Where there is uncertainty, people's judgments and opinions, even when based on the best available evidence, will differ; no one of them may be making his choice by tossing coins; yet the aggregate *set* of actions of the entire group of participants may be indistinguishable from a set of individual actions, each selected at random.[11]

Third, and fortunately, a chance-dominated model does not mean that an economist cannot predict or explain or diagnose. With a knowledge of the economy's realized requisites for survival and by a comparison of alternative conditions, he can state what types of firms or behavior relative to other possible types will be more viable, even though the firms themselves may not know the conditions or even try to achieve them by readjusting to the changed situation if they do know the conditions. It is sufficient if all firms are slightly different so that in the new environmental situation those who have their fixed internal conditions closer to the new, but unknown, optimum position now have a greater probability of survival and growth. They will grow relative to other firms and become the prevailing type, since survival conditions may push the observed characteristics of the set of survivors toward the unknowable optimum by either (1) repeated trials or (2) survival of more of those who happened to be near the optimum—determined ex post. If these new conditions last "very long," the dominant firms will be different ones from those which prevailed or would have prevailed under other conditions. Even if environmental conditions cannot be forecast, the economist can compare for given alternative potential situations the types of behavior that would have higher probability of viability or adoption. If explanation of past results rather than prediction is the task, the economist can diagnose the particular attributes which were critical in facilitating survival, even though individual participants were not aware of them.[12]

Fourth, the bases of prediction have been indicated in the preceding paragraph, but its character should be made explicit. The prediction will not assert that every—or, indeed, any—firm necessarily changes its characteristics. It asserts, instead, that the characteristics of the new *set* of firms, or possibly a set of new firms, will change. This may be

---

[10] The Borél gamblers analogue is pertinent to a host of everyday situations.

[11] Of course, the economic units may be going through a period of soul-searching, management training, and research activity. We cannot yet identify mental and physical activity with a process that results in sufficient information and foresight to yield uniquely determinate choices. To do so would be to beg the whole question.

[12] It is not even necessary to suppose that each firm acts as if it possessed the conventional diagrams and knew the analytical principles employed by economists in deriving optimum and equilibrium conditions. The atoms and electrons do not know the laws of nature; the physicist does not impart to each atom a wilful scheme of action based on laws of conservation of energy, etc. The fact that an economist deals with human beings who have sense and ambitions does not *automatically* warrant imparting to these humans the great degree of foresight and motivations which the economist may require for his customary analysis as an outside observer or "oracle." The similarity between this argument and Gibbsian statistical mechanics, as well as biological evolution, is *not* mere coincidence.

characterized by the "representative firm," a purely statistical concept—a vector of "averages," one dimension for each of the several qualities of the population of firms. A "representative firm" is not typical of any one producer but, instead, is a set of statistics summarizing the various "modal" characteristics of the population. Surely, this was an intended use of Marshall's "representative firm."

Fifth, a final implication drawn from consideration of this extreme approach is that empirical investigations via questionnaire methods, so far used, are incapable of evaluating the validity of marginal productivity analysis. This is true because productivity and demand analyses are essential in evaluating relative viability, even though uncertainty eliminates "profit maximization" and even if price and technological changes were to have no consciously redirecting effect on the firms. To illustrate, suppose that, in attempting to predict the effects of higher real wage rates, it is discovered that every businessman says he does not adjust his labor force. Nevertheless, firms with a lower labor-capital ratio will have relatively lower cost positions and, to that extent, a higher probability of survival. The force of competitive survival, by eliminating higher-cost firms, reveals a population of remaining firms with a new average labor-capital ratio. The essential point is that individual motivation and foresight, while sufficient, are not necessary. Of course, it is not argued here that therefore it is absent. All that is needed by economists is their own awareness of the survival conditions and criteria of the economic system and a group of participants who submit various combinations and organizations for the system's selection and adoption. Both these conditions are satisfied.[13]

As a consequence, only the method of use, rather than the usefulness, of economic tools and concepts is affected by the approach suggested here; in fact, they are made more powerful if they are not pretentiously assumed to be necessarily associated with, and dependent upon, individual foresight and adjustment. They are tools for, at least, the diagnosis of the operation of an economic system, even if not also for the internal business behavior of each firm.

V. INDIVIDUAL ADAPTING VIA IMITATION AND TRIAL AND ERROR

Let it again be noted that the preceding extreme model was designed to present in purest form only one element of the suggested approach. It is not argued that there is no purposive, foresighted behavior present in reality. In adding this realistic element—adaptation by individuals with some foresight and purposive motivation—we are expanding the preceding extreme model. We are not abandoning any part of it or futilely trying to merge it with the opposite extreme of perfect foresight and "profit maximization."

Varying and conflicting objectives motivate economic activity, yet we shall here direct attention to only one particular objective—the sufficient condition of realized positive profits. There are no implications of "profit maximization," and this difference is important. Although the latter is a far more extreme objective when definable, only the former is the sine qua non of survival and success. To argue that, with perfect competition, the two would come to the same thing is to conceal an important difference by means of a very implausible as-

[13] This approach reveals how the "facts" of Lester's dispute with Machlup can be handled with standard economic tools.

sumption. The pursuit of profits, and not some hypothetical undefinable perfect situation, is the relevant objective whose *fulfilment* is rewarded with survival. Unfortunately, even this proximate objective is too high. Neither perfect knowledge of the past nor complete awareness of the current state of the arts gives sufficient foresight to indicate profitable action. Even for this more restricted objective, the pervasive effects of uncertainty prevent the ascertainment of actions which are supposed to be optimal in achieving profits. Now the consequence of this is that modes of behavior replace optimum equilibrium conditions as guiding rules of action. Therefore, in the following sections two forms of conscious adaptive behavior are emphasized.

First, wherever successful enterprises are observed, the elements common to these observable successes will be associated with success and copied by others in their pursuit of profits or success. "Nothing succeeds like success." Thus the urge for "rough-and-ready" imitative rules of behavior is accounted for. What would otherwise appear to be merely customary "orthodox," nonrational rules of behavior turns out to be codified imitations of observed success, e.g., "conventional" markup, price "followship," "orthodox" accounting and operating ratios, "proper" advertising policy, etc. A conventionally employed type of behavior pattern is consistent with the postulates of the analysis employed, even though the reasons and justifications for the particular conventions are not.[14]

Many factors cause this motive to imitate patterns of action observable in past successes. Among these are: (1) the absence of an identifiable criterion for decision-making, (2) the variability of the environment, (3) the multiplicity of

factors that call for attention and choice, (4) the uncertainty attaching to all these factors and outcomes, (5) the awareness that superiority relative to one's competitors is crucial, and (6) the nonavailability of a trial-and-error process converging to an optimum position.

In addition, imitation affords relief from the necessity of really making decisions and conscious innovations, which, if wrong, become "inexcusable." Unfortunately, failure or success often reflects the willingness to depart from rules when conditions have changed; what counts, then, is not only imitative behavior but the willingness to abandon it at the "right" time and circumstances. Those who are different and successful "become" innovators, while those who fail "become" reckless violators of tried-and-true rules. Although one may deny the absolute appropriateness of such rules, one cannot doubt the existence of a strong urge to create conventions and rules (based on observed success) and a willingness to use them for action as well as for rationalizations of inaction. If another untried host of actions might have been even more successful, so much the worse for the participants who failed, and even for those who missed "perfect success."

Even innovation is accounted for by imitation. While there certainly are those who consciously innovate, there are those who, in their imperfect attempts

[14] These constructed rules of behavior should be distinguished from "rules" which, in effect, do no more than define the objective being sought. Confusion between objectives which motivate one and rules of behavior are commonplace. For example, "full-cost pricing" is a "rule" that one cannot really follow. He can try to, but whether he succeeds or fails in his objective of survival is not controllable by following the "rule of full-cost pricing." If he fails in his objective, he must, of necessity, fail to have followed the "rule." The situation is parallel to trying to control the speed of a car by simply setting by hand the indicator on the speedometer.

UNCERTAINTY AND ECONOMIC THEORY

to imitate others, unconsciously innovate by unwittingly acquiring some unexpected or unsought unique attributes which under the prevailing circumstances prove partly responsible for the success. Others, in turn, will attempt to copy the uniqueness, and the imitation-innovation process continues. Innovation is assured, and the notable aspects of it here are the possibility of unconscious pioneering and leadership.

The second type of conscious adaptive behavior, in addition to imitation, is "trial and error." This has been used with "profit maximization," wherein, by trial and ensuing success or failure, more appropriate actions are selected in a process presumed to converge to a limit of "profit maximization" equilibrium. Unfortunately, at least two conditions are necessary for convergence via a trial-and-error process, even if one admits an equilibrium situation as an admissible limit. First, a trial must be classifiable as a success or failure. The position achieved must be comparable with results of other potential actions. In a static environment, if one improves his position relative to his former position, then the action taken is better than the former one, and presumably one could continue by small increments to advance to a local optimum. An analogy is pertinent. A nearsighted grasshopper on a mound of rocks can crawl to the top of a particular rock. But there is no assurance that he can also get to the top of the mound, for he might have to descend for a while or hop to new rocks. The second condition, then, for the convergence via trial and error is the continual rising toward some *optimum optimorum* without intervening descents. Whether decisions and actions in economic life satisfy these two conditions cannot be proved or disproved here,

but the available evidence seems overwhelmingly unfavorable.

The above convergence conditions do not apply to a changing environment, for there can be no observable comparison of the result of an action with any other. Comparability of resulting situations is destroyed by the changing environment. As a consequence, the measure of goodness of actions in anything except a tolerable-intolerable sense is lost, and the possibility of an individual's converging to the optimum activity via a trial-and-error process disappears. Trial and error becomes survival or death. It cannot serve as a basis of the *individual's* method of convergence to a "maximum" or optimum position. Success is discovered by the economic system through a blanketing shotgun process, not by the individual through a converging search.

In general, uncertainty provides an excellent reason for imitation of observed success. Likewise, it accounts for observed uniformity among the survivors, derived from an evolutionary, adopting, competitive system employing a criterion of survival, which can operate independently of individual motivations. Adapting behavior via imitation and venturesome innovation enlarges the model. Imperfect imitators provide opportunity for innovation, and the survival criterion of the economy determines the successful, possibly because imperfect, imitators. Innovation is provided also by conscious wilful action, whatever the ultimate motivation may be, since drastic action is motivated by the hope of great success as well as by the desire to avoid impending failure.

All the preceding arguments leave the individual economic participant with imitative, venturesome, innovative, trial-and-error adaptive behavior. Most conventional economic tools and concepts are still useful, although in a vastly different analytical framework—one which is closely akin to the theory of biological evolution. The economic counterparts of genetic heredity, mutations, and natural selection are imitation, innovation, and positive profits.

VI. CONCLUSIONS AND SUMMARY

I shall conclude with a brief reference to some implications and conjectures.

Observable patterns of behavior and organization are predictable in terms of their relative probabilities of success or viability *if* they are tried. The observed prevalence of a type of behavior depends upon both this probability of viability and the probability of the different types being submitted to the economic system for testing and selecting. One is the probability of appearance of a certain type of organization (mutation), and the other is the probability of its survival or viability, once it appears (natural selection). There is much evidence for believing that these two probabilities are interrelated. But is there reason to suppose that a high probability of viability implies a high probability of an action's being taken, as would be implied in a system of analysis involving some "inner directed urge toward perfection"? If these two probabilities are not highly correlated, what predictions of types of action can the economist make? An answer has been suggested in this paper.

While it is true that the economist can define a profit maximization behavior by assuming *specific* cost and revenue conditions, is there any assurance that the conditions and conclusions so derivable are not too perfect and absolute? If profit maximization (certainty) is not ascertainable, the confidence about the predicted effects of changes, e.g., higher taxes or minimum wages, will be depend-

ent upon how close the formerly existing arrangement was to the formerly "optimal" (certainty) situation. What really counts is the various actions actually tried, for it is from these that "success" is selected, not from some set of perfect actions. The economist may be pushing his luck too far in arguing that actions in response to changes in environment and changes in satisfaction with the existing state of affairs will converge as a result of adaptation or adoption toward the optimum action that should have been selected, if foresight had been perfect.[15]

In summary, I have asserted that the economist, using the present analytical tools developed in the analysis of the firm under certainty, can predict the more adoptable or viable types of economic interrelationships that will be induced by environmental change even if individuals themselves are unable to ascertain them. That is, although individual participants may not know their cost and revenue situations, the economist can predict the consequences of higher wage rates, taxes, government policy, etc. Like the biologist, the economist predicts the effects of

---

[15] An anomalous aspect of the assumption of perfect foresight is that it nearly results in tautological and empty statements. One cannot know everything, and this is recognized by the addendum that one acts within a "given state and distribution of the arts." But this is perilously close, if not equivalent, to saying either that action is taken only where the outcome is accurately foreseen or that information is always limited. The qualification is inserted because one might contend that it is the *"constancy* of the state and distribution of arts" that is necessary as a *ceteris paribus.* But even the latter is no solution. A large fraction of behavior in a world of incomplete information and uncertainty is necessarily directed at increasing the state of arts and venturing into an unknown sphere. While it is probably permissible to start with a prescribed "distribution of the knowledge of the arts," holding it constant is too restrictive, since a large class of important and frequent actions necessarily involves changes in the state and distribution of knowledge. The modification suggested here incorporates this search for more knowledge as an essential foundation.

UNCERTAINTY AND ECONOMIC THEORY

environmental changes on the surviving class of living organisms; the economist need not assume that each participant is aware of, or acts according to, his cost and demand situation. These are concepts for the economist's use and not necessarily for the individual participant's, who may have other analytic or customary devices which, while of interest to the economist, serve as data and not as analytic methods.

An alternative to the rationale of individual profit maximization has been presented without exorcising uncertainty. Lest isolated arguments be misinterpreted, let it be clearly stated that this paper does not argue that purposive objective-seeking behavior is absent from reality, nor, on the other hand, does it indorse the familiar thesis that action of economic units cannot be expressed within the marginal analysis. Rather, the contention is that the precise role and nature of purposive behavior in the presence of uncertainty and incomplete information have not been clearly understood or analyzed.

It is straightforward, if not heuristic, to start with complete uncertainty and nonmotivation and then to add elements of foresight and motivation in the process of building an analytical model. The opposite approach, which starts with certainty and unique motivation, must abandon its basic principles as soon as uncertainty and mixed motivations are recognized.[16] The approach suggested here is intellectually more modest and realistic, without sacrificing generality. It does not regard uncertainty as an aberrational exogenous disturbance, as does the usual approach from the opposite extreme of accurate foresight. The existence of uncertainty and incomplete information is the foundation of the suggested type of analysis; the importance of the concept of a class of "chance" decisions rests upon it; it permits of various conflicting objectives; it motivates and rationalizes a type of adaptive imitative behavior; yet it does not destroy the basis of prediction, explanation, or diagnosis. It does not base its aggregate description on individual optimal action; yet it is capable of incorporating such activity where justified. The formalization of this approach awaits the marriage of the theory of stochastic processes and economics—two fields of thought admirably suited for union. It is conjectured that the suggested modification is applicable to a wide class of events and is worth attempts at empirical verification.[17]

[16] If one prefers, he may believe that the suggestions here contain reasons why the model based on certainty may predict outcomes, although individuals really cannot try to maximize profits. But the dangers of this have been indicated.

[17] Preliminary study in this direction has been very convincing, and, in addition, the suggested approach appears to contain important implications relative to general economic policy; but discussions of these are reserved for a later date.

[3]

IDEAL OUTPUT AND THE INTERDEPENDENCE OF FIRMS

I SHALL examine the question of how it may be possible to increase the value of final output at current prices in an un-rationed market, when the supplies of ultimate productive services are assumed to be constant. I am particularly concerned to emphasise the inherent complexity of the task and to refute certain theories on the subject which have received some acceptance. My discussion will be conducted under the general rubric of Ideal Output, out of deference to tradition, but it may be kept in mind what the criterion is. In any case, whatever " Foundations " may be laid, the practical suggestions of welfare theorists are usually guided perforce by the value of output at current prices, with, depending on the timidity or circumspection of the author, much or little hedging about with particular reservations to assuage common sense.

The prevalent error which has led to false theories on Ideal Output is to pay inadequate attention to the fact, which is a commonplace, that firms (and industries, however delimited) sell goods to each other and not merely to consumers. As a result many writers have adopted what I shall refer to as the Proportionality Thesis. We may accept as a typical statement of the thesis the following sentence from an article by A. M. Henderson : " The ideal distribution of resources between industries will be obtained if the ratio of prices to marginal cost is the same in all industries." [1] This thesis and its allied rule for making improvements I hope to prove erroneous. The suggestions which I shall offer toward a more adequate theory cannot assume quite the same air of precision that theories have claimed hitherto.

It is not part of my program to be too much concerned with certain vexatious fine points which might, each one, occupy an article. It will be convenient to avoid the problem of how to deal with new investment by assuming that changes in stocks of goods and productive facilities held by firms are given, while the final output the value of which we wish to maximise includes only those goods sold to consumers. I shall also ignore the fact that it is rather difficult to subsume the activities of government either in the consuming or in the producing sphere. To the reader who is interested in these and other fine points (I do not wish to minimise

[1] A. M. Henderson, " The Pricing of Public Utility Undertakings," *The Manchester School*, September 1947, p. 242.

their importance), I recommend the recent book by I. M. D. Little, *A Critique of Welfare Economics*.[1]

I also leave the reader free to make whatever special quali-fications, in the time-hallowed manner, to the principle of maxi-mising the value of output which he wishes, to keep little children from being exploited and the like. Perhaps of more immediate moment is the possibility that when output changes by a large amount the criterion of increasing the value of output may be indecisive, because prices may be so altered that the contrary change is prescribed. This dilemma may be avoided, if we refuse to apply the criterion to changes which are large enough for it to arise. In small (enough) changes price effects will be of the second order of smallness, and may be disregarded.

I

There have been approaches to the problem of allocating productive factors, which might be termed Utopian since they essay to describe certain necessary conditions for an optimum situation which is most unlikely to be reached. Another approach, however, which is of more immediate interest here, rather seeks to define a program which gives probability of an improvement even when the optimum remains unattained. It is this school which has proposed a Proportionality Rule as a guide to piecemeal reform. This Rule is a companion piece to the Proportionality Thesis, which I have cited and which itself has the Utopian ring.

By the Proportionality Rule, " it is socially desirable to expand those industries in which competition is more imperfect than the industries with which they compete for their factors of production and to contract those in which the opposite condition prevails." [2]

If it is assumed that each industry competes with " industry in general " for factors of production, then the industries should be expanded where the degree of imperfection is above the average and contracted where the degree of imperfection is below the average. The expansions and contractions are presumed to take place through shifts of the hired factors of production and not through changes in the number of firms. By definition, the degree of imperfection varies directly with the proportion price bears to marginal cost.

Sometimes the Proportionality Thesis and Rule are put in terms of more fundamental variables. The foregoing statements have tacitly assumed the absence of price discrimination in the

[1] Oxford, 1950.

[2] R. F. Kahn, " Some Notes on Ideal Output," Economic Journal, March 1935, p. 21.

sale of productive factors and the absence of monopsony in their
purchase. These assumptions are avoided if we say that "factors
should shift from industries in which the values of their marginal
products are lower than the average to industries in which the
values of their marginal products are higher than the average." [1]
Of course, the Proportionality Rule is not really a sufficient rule
for getting improvements except in the sense of increasing the
money value of output. For no account is taken of the redistribution of income, nor of numerous other significant accompani-
ments of changes in outputs. Yet it gives more promise of usefulness than the Utopian Rules which would probably never
become relevant.

From time to time exception has been taken to the Proportionality Thesis. Lerner shows that the argument is defective
if some productive factors are put to use outside the firms.[2] He
seems to be concerned principally with the use of productive
services directly by the households, which would affect the supply
of services to the firms. Reder says that the Thesis requires the
equality of price and marginal cost when products may be transformed into one another.[3] However, he seems to be using
marginal cost to mean the value of any alternative final product
sacrificed from the social output, rather than the cost of productive factors to the firm. Finally, I. M. D. Little points out
that the theory must be wrong whenever some goods serve at the
same time as consumer goods and productive factors.[4] But no
one appears to have stated the thoroughgoing wrongness of the
Thesis (and its accompanying Rule) which results from the fact
that firms are not completely integrated but sell to one another
in a complex pattern of transactions. Indeed, the Thesis is
wrong even though no goods are both consumer goods and
productive factors.

II

Let us directly face the problem of describing changes in the
allocation of resources which are in accord with the criterion of
increasing the value of final output. I assume the supply of
productive services from labour, natural resources and capital to
remain constant. The current flow of intermediate products, on
the other hand, may vary in composition and in amount. By a
constant supply of services from capital I shall mean that the

[1] J. E. Meade, *An Introduction to Economic Analysis and Policy*, Oxford,
1937, p. 177.
　　[2] Abba P. Lerner, *The Economics of Control*, New York, 1947, pp. 102–5.
　　[3] Melvin Warner Reder, *Studies in the Theory of Welfare Economics*, New
York, 1947, p. 42 n.　　　[4] *Op. cit.*, p. 136.

resources used to increase the producers' stocks of some goods and productive facilities will be provided directly or indirectly by their failure to maintain the stocks of some other goods and productive facilities.

Actually it is probably not possible to shift productive services without affecting their supplies. Therefore, one may always ask whether the measures which are suggested by an analysis of this sort would be likely to influence the supply of productive services in a way regarded as undesirable. Moreover, we shall ignore the presence of external economies in production, other than those which arise from the divergences within firms between marginal costs and prices.

Let us first consider the allocation of a fixed supply of resources among firms whose only transactions are with individuals, as consumers and as owners of resources. The firms are then completely integrated. This, as it happens, is the one case where the Proportionality Rule is likely to prove adequate. The arguments of Kahn, Meade, Henderson, as well as numerous others, imply, however, that this case is typical of the real world, although they show clearly enough by their references to industries which produce intermediate products, that they know it is not. We shall also suppose, for the sake of simplicity, that there is no price discrimination or rationing and that neither firms nor households exercise monopoly powers in the market for resources.

Under these conditions the cost to a firm of an additional unit of any productive service will be the price of the productive service. And the cost of an additional unit of output will be the cost at constant prices of the additional productive services needed to produce it. If the proportions in which productive services are combined can vary, the cost of another unit of output may be found in terms of any one of the productive services, and for total cost to be a minimum at a given output, the marginal cost must be the same whichever productive service is used in larger quantity to produce the additional output. Therefore, if price exceeds marginal cost, the value of the marginal product of any productive factor used by the firm will also exceed the price of that factor in the same ratio. If a productive service is removed from a firm where this ratio is small and placed in a firm, which also uses this type of productive factor, where the ratio is large, the value of final output will be increased by the difference between the values of the marginal products.[1] This result

---

[1] Cf. Kahn, *op. cit.*, pp. 20–1. He speaks in terms of marginal revenue, assuming it to be equal to marginal cost.

depends upon the fact that the outputs of the firms are final outputs.

Therefore, in general, productive services should be encouraged to shift from the firms where the divergences of price and marginal cost are small to firms where they are large. Were these shifts continued long enough, the firms would finally have the same ratio of price to marginal cost, and no further shifts would be advantageous. Then the allocation of resources, among existing firms, would be ideal (from the restricted point of view of the criterion which prevails in these discussions).

Kahn and Meade suggest that the desired movement of resources could be brought about by taxing the employment of " hired factors " in the industries where the proportion of price to marginal cost is lower than the average (degree of competition above the average) and subsidising the employment of " hired factors " in industries where this proportion is above the average (degree of competition below the average).[1] We may substitute for this the somewhat simpler plan of taxing and subsidising their respective outputs. Obviously this type of program would not be feasible unless the firms were so numerous in each industry that they were not led to try to influence the rate of tax or subsidy when setting their outputs. But if firms are grouped together, they will not have the same ratios of price to marginal cost. Kahn recognises the difficulty, but assumes for the purposes of his discussion that each industry is composed of firms for whom such ratios are the same.[2] It seems clear, however, that any possibility of employing a tax and subsidy policy depends upon the validity of grouping together firms for which this is not true. Then the taxes would be imposed on all firms in an industry where the average ratio is low, and subsidies would be granted on the outputs of all firms in an industry where the average ratio is high, regardless of the ratio in the individual firm.

III

We may make a further approach to reality by recognising that final outputs are not produced in fully integrated firms. The simplest model which introduces a structure of production is perhaps that where lines of production are isolated from one another but are built up of industries arranged in successive stages. In each stage of production we may suppose that the

---

[1] Meade, *op. cit.*, p. 177; Kahn, *op. cit.*, p. 29. They also propose lump-sum taxes, and subsidies to regulate the number of firms in an industry on the assumption, however, that the firms of an industry are of the same size.

[2] Kahn, *op. cit.*, p. 21 n.

firms buy productive services from households and intermediate products from the preceding stage. Let us continue to assume that the factors of production, including intermediate products, may be used in variable proportions.

The allocation problem now falls naturally into three parts, allocation among lines of production, among the industries in successive stages of a given line of production and among the firms of a single industry. The reallocation within a single industry proceeds in exactly the same manner as we have described for fully integrated firms, except that the product need not be a final product (however, the increased value of the intermediate products would make a larger final product possible). Clearly the movement of factors of all types, including intermediate products, from firms where the degree of monopoly is low to those where it is high should continue until the divergences between prices and marginal costs are, in this industry, everywhere the same. The other reallocations are more interesting. They show immediately the two fatal defects of the Proportionality arguments, that prices to consumers are not brought into line with ratios of substitution among final outputs and that prices to firms are not made consonant with substitution ratios between factors of production, in this case ultimate factors and intermediate products.

As we have observed, when the combination of factors is variable, the value of the marginal product of any factor bears the same proportion to the price of the factor that the price of the product bears to the marginal cost. Let us symbolise the average ratio of price to marginal cost in a particular stage of production by r_i, where i denotes the stage. Then the withdrawal of a small quantity of a productive service from the ith stage may be expected to reduce the value of the output of that stage by r_i times the cost of the services withdrawn. Symbolising the cost of services withdrawn by w, the expected loss is $r_i \times w$. This deprives the succeeding stage of intermediate product valued at $r_i \times w$. Then by the same argument the decline in output in the $(i + 1)$th stage will be $r_{i+1} \times r_i \times w$. Therefore, if price exceeds marginal cost in the subsequent stages of production, the loss in the value of output at successive stages will be cumulatively larger, until the largest loss of all is experienced in the stage producing the final product.[1]

---

[1] The accumulation of monopolistic effects was briefly noted by Lerner in 1934. The example he gave corresponds to our present model. See A. P. Lerner, " The Concept of Monopoly and the Measurement of Monopoly Power," *The Review of Economic Studies*, June 1934, p. 172. Since then little use has been made of his observation.

From this accumulation of the divergence between the price
of the productive service and the value of the marginal product
at later stages, it follows, given variable proportions, that the
final product will be larger if productive services are taken out
of later stages and ultilised in earlier stages. Because the factors
may be substituted the loss resulting from the removal of productive services will be overbalanced by the gain from an increased
supply of intermediate products. For example, the removal of
productive services from the $(i + 1)$th stage will reduce the value
of that stage's output by $r_{i+1} \times w$. But the employment of these
services in the preceding stage will increase the value of that
stage's output by $r_i \times w$, and the employment of this intermediate product in the $(i + 1)$th stage will increase its output
by $r_{i+1} \times r_i \times w$. The gain then exceeds the loss, $r_{i+1} \times w$,
whenever r_i is larger than one, in other words, whenever price
exceeds marginal cost in the ith stage.

Admittedly the assumption that the combination of factors
is continuously variable is not realistic. However, it can be
relaxed. The essential fact is that the intermediate product is
inflated in price above the cost of the productive services needed
to produce additional quantities of it. Therefore, it is always
possible that some group of productive services in the later stage
could produce in the earlier stage more of some type of intermediate product than is required to restore the level of output in
the later stage, but that this exchange is prevented by the inflated price of the intermediate product. Whenever such an
exchange would be advantageous, the presence of monopoly (in
the sense of a divergence between price and marginal cost) leads
to an improper allocation of productive services among the stages
of production. Furthermore, it is probable that a measure which
reduces the degree of price inflation will cause some favourable
exchanges to be made.

It is significant that this type of misallocation will not be
prevented when all industries have equally imperfect markets and
equal rates of indirect taxation. Nor need an approach to
equality provide any improvement. Only the reduction of the
divergences between price and marginal cost will be effective in
reducing the excessive prices of intermediate products compared
with productive services and thus preventing the tendency for
productive services to be applied in unjustifiably late stages of
production. This result will be preserved in the more general
model.

If the productive services allotted to each line of production, composed of industries in successive stages, are to be allocated most effectively, the shift of productive services to early stages must continue until there is *no* divergence between price and marginal cost in any stage of production save that producing the final output. Otherwise, the structure of production will be distorted. Then we are once again in the Kahn–Meade world, where the industries producing the final outputs may be regarded as if they were completely integrated, since their suppliers are " perfectly competitive." Then the Kahn prescription applies, and ideal allocation (of given productive services) is achieved when the industries in these final stages show the same ratio of price to marginal cost. Furthermore, an approach to this equality will probably raise the value of output. Therefore, productive services should be taken from the more competitive final stages and used in the less competitive.

The improper allocation of productive services among the stages of a line of production is in the stricter meaning a departure from efficiency, since by a re-arrangement within this line of production alone, without affecting production elsewhere, a larger final output is obtainable in physical units. On the other hand, the subsequent movement of productive services between the final stages of lines of production, while it increases output in value terms, must reduce some output in physical units. It might be regarded as an adaptation of the output mixture to consumer tastes. These same distinctions can be drawn in the more realistic model which I shall present in conclusion, though they assume a more complicated appearance there.

When imperfection is prevalent, the movement of productive services between lines of production must take account of the stages involved. Losses and gains must be calculated by accumulating monopoly effects up to the final products. In general, lines of production should receive services whose industries are more monopolistic and whose stages are more numerous, and the inflow should occur in the earliest stages which show divergences of prices and marginal costs. But these principles can be appropriately compromised only where definite degrees of monopoly are assigned.[1]

---

[1] The common opinion that an excessive supply of productive services are used in the extractive industries seems to be contradicted by the foregoing analysis. However, it should be recalled that we are assuming perfectly competitive markets in productive services which actually do not exist. In fact, they are largely confined to the extractive industries, especially agriculture, and both worker monopolies in manufacturing and transport and the greater fertility of rural populations tend to provide many extractive industries with excessive

IV

The model of production with disjunct lines of production is far from realistic. Although it already exposes the basic faults of the Proportionality arguments, it does not present these faults in quite the form that they assume in a complexly interdependent economy. Nor has the discussion of this model been oriented toward the development of a remedial program which might conceivably be applied and which would include the necessary amendments to the program of Kahn and Meade. It is these deficiencies which I now propose to remedy so far as this is, in any case, possible.

The true complexity of economic relationships is seen in the existence of industries, such as transportation, power and communication, which sell their outputs to nearly all firms and households, in the prevalence of merchants dealing in wide varieties of products and in the fact that the same raw materials enter into products of very diverse kinds.

Let us first consider the limiting case of interdependent industries in which the production functions are linear and homogeneous.[1] In each industry the production function will include both the productive services of households and intermediate products as factors of production. Because of the prevalence of intermediate products the cost of an output in terms of the ultimate factors supplied by households cannot be determined within the purlieus of a single industry. Indeed, the system may be so tightly bound together by the web of intermediate products that production coefficients in virtually all industries will influence the cost of a single output in terms of productive services, or the ratios of substitution between a set of outputs. However, if there are no divergences anywhere between prices and costs, that is, if the *r*s are uniformly equal to one, we can be sure without explicit computations that the prices of the products are just equal to the costs of the productive factors, including, of course, the services of capital, required to produce them. This will be true

---

supplies of, at least, labour services. This may not be true, however, of other productive services, nor may it hold for the distribution of productive services among the stages of the urban industries themselves. For example, even though retail trades were as well organised by workers as manufacturing, it seems doubtful if a proper social husbandry would lead to a shift of workers out of manufacturing into trade, more clerks handling less goods in more elaborate shops.

[1] Tjalling C. Koopmans has suggested that a model of this type, but allowing choice between productive techniques, might be useful in problems of welfare economics. See "A Mathematical Model of Production," *Econometrica*, January 1949, pp. 74–5.

in the sense that to produce an additional value of any product without encroaching on another will require an increase in the supply of ultimate productive services having an equal value at given prices.[1] However, the group of services which are increased, and the proportions in which they are increased, will generally not be unique.

It is then evident that when the supply of ultimate productive services is fixed the production of an additional value of some outputs will be managed through reductions in some other outputs of an equal value. For the substitution of outputs may be regarded as taking place in two steps. First, certain outputs are reduced and directly or indirectly productive services are released. Then, these productive services are used, directly or indirectly, to expand certain other outputs. As we have seen, values will be equated in each step. However, not every two outputs, nor every two groups of outputs, need be substitutable, for it may be that the factors which can be released in the reduction of the first output are not appropriate for producing the second output, either directly or indirectly. But whatever substitutions occur will exchange equal values of goods.

On the other hand, if in some of the industries there are divergences between prices and costs, the equality is lost. This results immediately from the fact that the production possi-

---

[1] This statement may be given a formal derivation. Set up a system of equations each of which relates the total supply of a productive service or output to the amounts consumed by the households and the industries, where the amounts consumed by the industries are in proportion to their outputs. The equations will be of the form :

$$y_i = -a_{1i}x_1 - \ldots - a_{mi}x_m \qquad \ldots \qquad (1)$$

where the xs are outputs. For i less than $m + 1$, y_i is the amount of a good consumed by households and $a_{ii} = -1$. For i larger than m, y_i is the negative of the amount of a productive service supplied by households. The equations must be consistent. This puts a restriction on the variation of the final outputs y_i.

Set up a second system of equations, each of which relates the price of an output to the amounts spent on the intermediate products and productive services used in its production. These equations will be of the form :

$$p_i = a_{i1}p_1 + \ldots + a_{in}p_n \qquad \ldots \qquad (2)$$

where the coefficients are the ones appearing in the first set of equations with the same subscripts (they are the coefficients of production). The ps are the prices. This system of equations may be solved for the prices of the outputs in terms of the prices of the productive services.

A comparison will show that any change in the ys in the first set of equations, which is permitted by the condition that the equations remain consistent, is such that the value of the decrements, at prices satisfying the second set of equations, equals the value of the increments. This result holds whether the decrements and increments are outputs or productive services.

For a study of equations of this sort see Wassily Leontiev, *The Structure of the American Economy 1919–1929*, Cambridge (Mass.), 1939.

bilities are unaffected by the change, while price relations are not.[1] Moreover, if the industries whose rs rise above unity include some which produce intermediate products the effects are likely to reverberate throughout the entire system. If we take the prices of the ultimate productive services as a basis, we may compare the prices of the outputs in the resulting system with the " competitive " prices which would be consistent with all rs equal to unity. If will be useful to refer to the ratios between the actual and the " competitive " prices as degrees of inflation.[2] If monopoly and marginal taxation are at all widespread, nearly all outputs will bear prices inflated to some degree. On the other hand, in equilibrium there will not be degrees of inflation less than unity, since there will be no degrees of monopoly less than unity (rs less than one). An exception might arise in an industry which enjoys a Government subsidy, but presumably such a subsidy would correspond to a service performed for the community, which should be regarded as an output of the industry.[3]

Where prices are inflated, it would become possible to cause an increase in the value of output at existing prices. It would only be necessary to increase the outputs of the goods bearing the more inflated prices at the expense of the goods bearing the less inflated prices. The degree of inflation need, however, bear only a distant relation to the degree of monopoly in the industries producing the final output. Moreover, when an output serves as an intermediate product, the fact that the industry producing it is exceptionally monopolistic is not a sure warrant that its output should be expanded, since the price still may not be greatly inflated, and even though its price is greatly inflated, the final outputs in which it eventuates may yet not bear the most highly inflated prices.

If the orthodox fiscal nostrums are to be applied, it seems

---

[1] Equation (1) will be the same as before, while equation (2) will now appear as

$$\frac{1}{r_i} p_i = a_{i}p_i + \ldots + a_{in}p_n \ . \ \ \ \ \ \ (2')$$

where r_i is the ratio of price to marginal cost (= average cost here) for the ith industry. A comparison of the consistency conditions for (1) and the solutions for the ps in (2') will show that they no longer correspond as before, but substitution will increase or reduce values depending on its direction.

[2] The competitive prices are found by solving equations (2) for output prices in terms of the prices of productive services. The degree of inflation of the jth output is then the actual price $\div p_j$, where p_j is obtained from the solution of (2).

[3] Similarly, some indirect taxes may represent costs imposed on the community by the industry, and therefore should not be allowed to contribute to degrees of inflation.

appropriate to levy taxes on the retail sale of outputs the prices of which are inflated less than some type of average and to provide a subsidy out of the proceeds on the retail purchase of outputs the prices of which are inflated above this average. It would not be necessary to apply any measures to intermediate products except where the taxation or subsidy of final products proved inexpedient for administrative reasons. Then, it might be expected that consumers of the final outputs would, on the whole, substitute subsidised for taxed outputs, which would mean an increase in the value of output at initial prices, and, if the program is modest enough, also at subsequent prices. Let i_1 represent the degree of inflation in price of an output which declines and i_2 the degree of inflation in price of the output which substitutes for it. Then the value of output at initial prices will be increased by $\frac{i_2}{i_1}$ times the value of the decrement in the first output. $\frac{1}{i_1}$ may be thought of as the value of the ultimate productive services which are devoted to the production of one unit, in value, of the first output. Then i_2 is the ratio of this cost in ultimate productive services to the value of the second type of output which they can alternatively contribute. The same principles apply when more than two goods are involved. It is not implied, however, that any unique bundle of productive services will underlie the substitution.

The interdependent model which has now been described is less special than may appear at first glance. Let us introduce variable coefficients of production while continuing to regard the production functions as homogeneous of the first degree. This means that increasing all productive factors in any industry in a given ratio will always permit an increase of output in the same ratio. Then the observed coefficients of production are those which firms find most economical at existing prices. The definition of the degree of inflation may be retained, and it remains meaningful.[1] A certain group of substitutions are, just as formerly, consistent with unchanged coefficients of production, and the value of output will be unaffected only if competitive prices prevail everywhere, in the sense that all the rs equal one.

The analysis is parallel to that for fixed coefficients, except that now when the prices are not competitive there will also be the possibility of advantageous substitutions in the use by producers of intermediate products. The prices of intermediate

---

[1] Equations (1), (2) and (2') are just as before. It may be noted that the xs and ys may be regarded as increments.

products will fail to reflect the rates at which substitutions are possible in the economic system, and therefore the coefficients of production selected by producers will not be socially efficient. Where proportions are variable equal values of intermediate products will have equal value products (as a condition of profit maximisation), but if their prices are inflated in different proportions it will *not* be equal values of the intermediate products which with the existing production coefficients can be substituted as outputs.[1] Rather, just as before, a unit value of one intermediate product can be exchanged (in the output of the economy) for $\frac{i_2}{i_1}$ units of value of a second. If we suppose that i_2 exceeds i_1, and that prices are made to reflect the substitution ratio, the output of the industry making a marginal substitution will show a gain in value of $\frac{i_2}{i_1}$ times the value of the intermediate product displaced times r for that industry. What the ultimate effect on final output will be would depend on the use made of the industry's increased output. In the more likely case prices would not be brought into full alignment with substitution ratios. Then the industry making the initial substitution would not receive the full benefit of the change, but productive factors would be released elsewhere which would permit expansions of other outputs.

In the general case where homogeneity of the first degree cannot be assumed, it is still possible to distinguish a definite way of varying outputs. We may consider the marginal batches of (non-specific) factors which would be used at current prices to expand outputs. These give rise to a system exactly analogous to that for linear homogeneous production functions except that it refers only to marginal increments of output, and the constants of the system are marginal rather than average coefficients of production.[2] There will be certain substitutions which are

[1] In equations (1), where the *x*s and *y*s may be read as increments, the *y*s may be regarded as increments which may be used either to make changes in consumption or, in the case of an intermediate product, to make changes in production coefficients. It is still proper to use fixed *a*s for a small change, since a marginal substitution will cause only small changes in production coefficients, which in turn will have effects on the output increments of the second order of smallness.

[2] This means that in equations (1) the *x*s and *y*s should be interpreted as increments and in equations (1), (2) and (2′) the *a*s must now refer to marginal rather than average coefficients of production. By a marginal coefficient, a_{ij}, is meant the quantity of the *j*th output or productive service used in producing a marginal unit of the *i*th output. This coefficient would not in general be unique, unless it is specified how the industry is led to produce the additional output. We are chiefly interested in output changes induced by changes in demand which are small enough to leave prices nearly constant.

consistent with output variations carried out with these marginal batches. They are reversible, and, just as formerly, if the *r*s do not equal one, the non-neutral substitutions when performed in the proper direction can increase the value of final output. The increase may come directly when such a substitution is made between final outputs, or indirectly when it is intermediate products that are exchanged. With fixed coefficients the second method of increasing the value of output, which reflects inefficiency in the strong sense that some final outputs can be expanded without infringing on others, did not arise.

The degrees of inflation may be defined in the same way as before. That is, existing prices should be compared with a set of competitive prices which are formed by setting prices everywhere equal to the cost of the marginal batches of productive factors. However, once we admit variable proportions, even with homogeneity the degree of inflation does not retain the same significance that it had for the fixed proportions. For there is no longer a definite way in which substitutions must be carried out. Innumerable patterns of factor movements would be able to effect substitutions between given outputs, and what is worse, some of these ways may be far superior to others, though they will not be chosen in a free market. Therefore, it is no longer accurate simply to say that certain outputs should be expanded and certain others curtailed, but the way in which these changes will be carried out should be specified. A substitution carried out in one manner may reduce the value of output, while carried out differently it would increase the value of output.

It may be argued, however, that these degrees of inflation are the appropriate guide posts for public policy in the absence of the virtual omniscience which would be needed to estimate the precise reactions of the economic system to stimuli. That is to say, it may be thought that an appropriate policy for getting substitutions which will increase the value of final output is to subsidise the purchase by consumers of goods which bear prices inflated above some figure and to tax the purchase of goods by consumers which bear prices inflated less than this. Although substitutions are not likely to occur in just the way these estimates of inflation assume, yet they may be close enough to these ways not to upset the probability of an improvement. We may note in particular that variations in the proportions in which that part of marginal expenditure devoted to the ultimate productive services is divided between these productive services do not affect the degrees of inflation. They are dependent entirely on the patterns of flow of intermediate products. Some stability in these patterns, however, must be assumed, at least for small variations.

Furthermore, since producers will not choose their combinations of productive factors according to " competitive " prices, which correspond to the ratios of substitution in this type of marginal variation, presumably the same argument can be extended to intermediate products as well. Only then, added caution is needed, since the subsidies and taxes will accumulate through the system in just the same way as the original divergences.

V

I wish now to ask whether it is possible for degrees of inflation to replace degrees of monopoly in the statement of the Proportionality arguments. In the first place, can rs be devised which result in equal degrees of inflation throughout the system ? And secondly, does this result, equal degrees of inflation for the prices of all outputs, mean the attainment of an ideal distribution of resources ? It should not be surprising that my answer to the latter question will be in the negative.

The problem of arranging equal degrees of inflation turns upon a very simple relation. Let the proportion of marginal expenditure that is devoted to buying ultimate productive services for the jth output be p. Let i denote the common degree of inflation of all output prices. The proportion of marginal expenditure devoted to intermediate products, the prices of which are inflated in the ratio i, is $1 - p$. Recalling definitions, we have the identities : $\frac{1}{i} \times$ price $=$ competitive price, and competitive price $=$ marginal cost, taken at competitive prices. But applying the first identity to the prices of intermediate products, marginal cost at competitive prices $= \left(p + \frac{1-p}{i}\right) \times$ marginal cost (actual). Therefore, the following equation must be identically true for the jth output :

$$\frac{1}{i} \times \text{price} = \left(p + \frac{1-p}{i}\right) \times \text{marginal cost}$$

Since $r_i \times$ marginal cost $=$ price, this reduces to

$$r_j = 1 + p(i - 1)$$

Thus we see immediately that when $i = 1$ (prices uninflated), $r_j = 1$. Not even the possibility of rs less than 1 would remove the necessity of this result. Furthermore, if all rs are equal, it would only be possible to have equal degrees of inflation if every industry had the same p, that is, spent the same part of marginal outlays on ultimate productive services. Such an eventuality is too unlikely to deserve the slightest attention. However, we also find that if the rs are allowed to be unequal, any common degree of inflation is feasible provided the rs be properly set. We must now inquire whether a common degree of inflation leads to an ideal distribution of a fixed supply of ultimate productive services.

It is true, indeed, that once the degrees of inflation are equal, it is no longer possible to encourage the production of goods with more inflated prices at the expense of those with less inflated prices. But this merely means that measures which are adapted to the substitutions with marginal coefficients based on current prices will be neutral. It does not follow that all other methods of substitution will be neutral. It might be thought that taxes on the use of the ultimate productive services would be in order, since their prices are not inflated. Such taxes, however, would be ineffectual, since the prices of all intermediate products would rise proportionately.

To discover measures, in the spirit of the interventions we have been considering, which would be appropriate, we must look at the source of non-neutral change. This lies in the inefficiency of methods of production where intermediate products are supplied by monopolistic firms (or firms subject to taxes which impinge on the margin of production). Inefficiency is present in the strong sense, because there will be a tendency to use factors of all kinds directly when the products resulting from their application elsewhere would have been more effective in their places. This is the analogue to the allocation of productive services to unjustifiably late stages of production in the model with disjunct lines of production. Only now, since intermediate products are not constrained to independent channels, other factors than ultimate productive services are involved in the distorted productive structures. The problem is not, in particular, bound up with the " uninflated " prices of the ultimate productive services. The crux of the matter is that intermediate products are not used which could be produced out of a smaller value of intermediate products and productive services, which *are* used, were these strategically disposed in other industries. Interposed between this smaller value, of the latter factors, and their product, in terms of the former, are the divergences of prices and marginal costs in intervening industries. One expression of the resulting tendency, which has attracted attention, is an encouragement to the integration of firms in successive stages of production,[1] but similar effects will occur when no merger of firms is apparent.

A fiscal policy which might tend to ameliorate this condition is the imposition of taxes and the disbursement of subsidies on a discriminatory basis. For any given output taxes should be heavier, or subsidies lower, on that part of the output which is sold to consumers or to producers who are close to the final outputs. The ultimate aim of these measures, at least, can be seen. Eventually, all taxes would be concentrated on output sales to consumers, and the proceeds used to produce competitive prices on all sales to firms. The taxes on sales to consumers would be such that the degrees of inflation to them were equal for all outputs which they purchase. Since the inflation is now concentrated in the industry making the sales to households, the tax rate there will be $\frac{i}{r_j}$ for the jth industry, where i is the common degree of inflation achieved and r_j is the ratio of price to marginal cost for the jth industry. It is conceivable that r_j should sometimes be large enough to justify a subsidy even here.

Two difficulties for even an incipient program aimed at equalising degrees of inflation for consumers and reducing the average degree of inflation for firms leap immediately to the eye. First, the taxes, falling more heavily upon the more competitive industries, would probably succeed more handily in raising prices than subsidies in reducing them. Hence the average degree of inflation to consumers would no doubt increase, which might not be favourable to an ideal adjustment of supplies of ultimate productive services (a problem which we ignore by assumption). Moreover, accompanying the fiscal measures which subsidise monopolists will be a shift in income distribution in favor of monopolists, in particular, and property owners, in general, which may not be desired. Of course, the taxes on consumer purchases could be reduced, on the average, indefinitely and subsidies met with progressive income taxes, thus removing very largely this objection. However, the supplies of productive services might then be even worse affected. A measure which Kahn suggested of levying a lump-sum tax on the firms in an

[1] J. J. Spengler has pointed out that to prevent integration in these circumstances may be to the disadvantage of the consumer. See " Vertical Integration and Antitrust Policy," *The Journal of Political Economy*, August 1950. However, to permit integration still does not reach the ideal solution, since it will tend to go too far.

industry to pay subsidies on its output was premised on firms of equal size and hardly seems realistic.

One may add that the payments could not be attuned to the situation of single firms, or even small groups of them, for fear of collusion. Hence divergences of price and marginal cost would have to be rather broadly averaged. This would reduce the efficacy of the program. Actually even when firms produce identical products they may have quite different marginal costs. An average might be taken weighting marginal costs by the sizes of firms as an approximation to their contributions to an increase of output. Finally, such a program ought to be undertaken with great caution, because the marginal-factor requirements may change quite rapidly, and also because the subsidies would accumulate in the same way as degrees of monopoly, and thus price changes may not in any case be closely related to the immediate subsidies.

VI

There are a great many further qualifications which might be discussed if more space were available, some of which have doubtless already disturbed the percipient reader. There is, for example, the fact that few if any " ultimate resources " will be available independently of the use of outputs to facilitate their supply, so that prices for them too will be distorted. This will hold even for the services of labour, but it will be particularly significant for the services of capital, and, of course, of natural resources. Enough has been said already, however, to deprive the Proportionality Thesis and its associated Rule of much of their charm. We have found that proportionality, so far as it has significance, must refer to the degrees of inflation, not to the degrees of monopoly in individual industries. And we have seen that even so, proportionality of the degrees of inflation of all output prices does *not* lead to an *ideal* distribution of resources, though an approach to such proportionality probably corresponds to an improvement by the definition of improvement in terms of the money value of output. It is necessary in addition that divergences of marginal costs and prices for intermediate products be completely eliminated.

A final word may be said on four special points, which could merit an extended discussion. First, it will make a great difference to the divergence between price and marginal cost whether an extension in output is provided by existing firms or by a new firm. The presumption is that the cost per unit of additional output will be much closer to price when the output is supplied by a new firm, though where there are special impediments to entry this need not necessarily be the case.   Second, in programs of partial nature, in addition to all that has been said heretofore, there will be the danger that the induced shifts in demand will be on the whole perverse even when the object selected for tax or subsidy has a price inflated very little or very much respectively. Particular relations of complementarity and competitiveness would need to be estimated.   Third, in all estimates of degrees of inflation the excess of the distributive margins over the marginal costs of distribution are likely to be important, and may in many cases quite obliterate the patterns of inflation as they are found at the manufacturer's gates.   Fourth, we have assumed throughout that productive services were sold in a perfectly competitive market, which is far from the case.   Often the monopoly effects in these markets will be most important and seriously impair the validity of a program drafted on other assumptions.   These strictures, however, only confirm the inadequacy of Proportionality arguments.

LIONEL W. MCKENZIE

Duke University.

[4]

NEW DEVELOPMENTS ON THE OLIGOPOLY FRONT[1]

FRANCO MODIGLIANI

Carnegie Institute of Technology

I

IN MY opinion the two books reviewed in this article represent a welcome major breakthrough on the oligopoly front. These two contributions, which appeared almost simultaneously, though clearly quite independently, have much in common in their basic models and method of approach to the problem. But, fortunately, they do not significantly repeat each other; for, having started from the same point of departure, the authors have followed divergent paths, exploring different implications of the same basic model.

Sylos deals almost exclusively with *homogeneous* oligopoly defined as a situation in which all producers, actual and potential, are able to supply the identical commodity (more generally, commodities that are perfect substitutes for each other) and have access to the very same long-run cost function. He thus focuses on barriers to entry resulting from economies of scale. Bain, on the other hand, also analyzes the effect of competitors being altogether unable to produce perfect substitutes—that is, product-differentiation barriers—or being able to do so only at higher costs—absolute cost-advantage barriers. Furthermore, Bain's book is greatly enriched by fascinating empirical data, painstakingly collected

through a variety of means, and by a courageous attempt at an empirical verification of the implications of his model. However, Bain is concerned primarily with the analysis of long-run market equilibrium, while Sylos devotes more than half of his book to examining the implications of his model for many other issues, such as (1) the effect of short-run or cyclical variations in demand and costs, (2) the validity of the so-called full-cost pricing model, (3) the effect of technological progress, and (4) the impact of oligopolistic structures on the formation and reabsorption of unemployment. His analysis is primarily theoretical and does not purport to provide new empirical evidence, with one rather significant exception. In an appendix to the introductory chapter Sylos presents indexes of concentration for various sectors of the American economy, based on the Gini coefficient.[2] Sylos finds that, according to this measure, concentration has tended to increase appreciably over the period considered—generally from the first decade of the century to the end of the 1940's—for all but one of the distributions analyzed. These include the distribution of plants by value added and by value of sales for manufacturing as a whole and by size of labor force for all manufacturing and for selected industries[3] and the distribution of cor-

---

[1] A review article of Paolo Sylos Labini, *Oligopolio e progresso tecnico* ("Oligopoly and Technical Progress"). Milan: Giuffrè, 1957. Pp. 207. L. 1,000. Joe S. Bain, *Barriers to New Competition*. Cambridge, Mass.: Harvard University Press, 1956. Pp. xi+329. $5.50. A preliminary edition of Sylos' book was published in 1956 for limited circulation. References in this article are to the final edition.

[2] The Gini coefficient is a measure of the area lying between the actual Lorenz curve and the equi-distribution Lorenz curve.

[3] The individual industries, chosen on the ground that their definition has remained reasonably stable over time, are: (1) steel works and rolling mills;

216 FRANCO MODIGLIANI

porations by size of assets. These findings are rather striking, since they run counter to widely accepted views based on well-known studies of the share of the market of the four or eight largest firms. They will undoubtedly deserve close scrutiny by the experts on the subject.

It would be impossible within the scope of a review article to summarize adequately the content of both books and take a good look at the promising new horizons they open. Under these conditions it appears wise to devote primary attention to Sylos' work. The reader can do full justice to Bain's contribution by reading the original, while in the case of Sylos this possibility is open only to the "happy few." With respect to Bain's book, therefore, my only goal will be to whet the reader's appetite.

II

Until quite recently little systematic attention has been paid in the analysis of monopoly and oligopoly to the role of entry, that is, to the behavior of potential competitors. This neglect is justified for monopoly, which is generally defined as the case of a single actual as well as potential producer whose demand curve is not significantly influenced, either in the short or in the long run, by his price policy. Oligopoly could also be defined to exclude entry, fewness being then the result of the impossibility, for firms not now in the group, of producing the commodity—whether for physical or legal reasons. And, undoubtedly, the impossibility of entry is frequently

at least implicitly assumed in the analysis of oligopoly, following the venerable example of Cournot, with his owners of mineral wells. But such a narrow definition leaves out the far more interesting case where fewness is the result of purely economic forces, entry being prevented by—and within the limits of—certain price-output policies of existing producers. This is precisely the essence of homogeneous oligopoly analyzed by both Sylos and Bain.

One might suppose that, as long as potential entrants have access to a long-run cost function identical in all respects to that of existing firms, entry must tend to occur whenever the market price is higher than the minimum long-run average cost. (Cost is used hereafter in the sense of opportunity cost, including therefore an appropriate allowance for "normal" profits.) But then long-run market equilibrium would have to involve a price equal to minimum average cost and a corresponding output[4] and would be undistinguishable from perfectly competitive equilibrium. This supposition is, however, invalid whenever the output of an optimum size firm represents a "non-insignificant" fraction of pre-entry output. The price that is relevant to the potential entrant is the price *after* entry. Even if the pre-entry price is above the lowest achievable cost, the additional output he proposes to sell may drive the price below cost, making the entry unprofitable.

Unfortunately for the theorist, the exact anticipated effect of the entry on

_____

(2) electrical machinery; (3) petroleum refining; (4) lumber and timber products; and (5) shipbuilding and iron and steel. For these industries indexes are given for 1914 and 1947. The distribution for lumber is the single instance in which concentration has decreased.

[4] This is, in fact, the conclusion reached by H. R. Edwards, "Price Formation in Manufacturing Industry and Excess Capacity," *Oxford Economic Papers*, VII, No. 1 (February, 1955), 194–218, sec. 4.2, which is, in turn, an elaboration of the model developed by P. W. S. Andrews in *Manufacturing Business* (London: Macmillan & Co., 1949). In other respects Edwards' stimulating analysis anticipates many of the conclusions of Sylos and Bain.

NEW DEVELOPMENTS ON THE OLIGOPOLY FRONT 217

price is not independent of the (anticipated) reaction of existing producers. The more they are willing to contract their output in response to the entry, the smaller will be the fall in price; in the limiting case the price may even be completely unaffected. Both authors have wisely refused to be stopped by this difficulty. They have instead proceeded to explore systematically the implications of the following well-defined assumption: that potential entrants behave as though they expected existing firms to adopt the policy most unfavorable to them, namely, the policy of maintaining output while reducing the price (or accepting reductions) to the extent required to enforce such an output policy. I shall refer to this assumption as "Sylos' postulate" because it underlies, more or less explicitly, most of his analysis, whereas Bain has also paid some attention to the possibility of potential entrants, assuming a less belligerent behavior on the part of existing firms.

The significance of Sylos' postulate lies in the fact that it enables us to find a definite solution to the problem of long-run equilibrium price and output under homogeneous oligopoly, or at least a definite upper limit to the price, to be denoted by P_0 and a corresponding lower limit to aggregate output, say, X_0. Both authors have essentially reached this conclusion, though through somewhat different routes.

I shall not attempt to reproduce faithfully their respective arguments, but shall instead concentrate on developing the logical essence of their approach. To this end, let $X = D(P)$ denote the market demand curve for the product and let P' denote the pre-entry price, $X' = D(P')$ being then the corresponding aggregate output. Under Sylos' postulate the prospective entrant is confronted not by an infinitely elastic demand at the price P' but by a sloping demand curve which is simply *the segment of the demand curve to the right of* P'. I shall refer to this segment as the marginal demand curve. Note that it is uniquely determined by the original demand curve and the pre-entry price P'. Suppose P' to be such that the corresponding marginal demand curve is *everywhere* below *the* long-run average cost function. Clearly, under these conditions, entry will not be profitable; that is, such a P' is an *entry-preventing price*. The critical price P_0 is then simply the *highest* entry-preventing price, and the critical output X_0 is the corresponding aggregate demand, $D(P_0)$. Under perfect competition, where the output of an optimum size firm is negligible relative to market demand, the marginal demand curve is itself infinitely elastic *in the relevant range;* hence the familiar conclusion that the long-run equilibrium price cannot exceed minimum average cost. But, where the output of an optimum plant is not negligible, P_0 will exceed minimum cost to an extent which depends on the nature of the demand and the long-run cost function.

In order to explore the factors controlling P_0, let us denote by $\bar{x}$ the optimum scale of output, that is, the scale corresponding to the lowest point of the long-run average cost curve. (If this scale is not unique, $\bar{x}$ will mean the smallest scale consistent with minimum cost.) If k denotes the corresponding minimum average cost, then the perfectly competitive equilibrium price is $P_c = k$, and the corresponding equilibrium output is $X_c = D(P_c) = D(k)$. Finally, let us define the size of the market, S, as the ratio of the competitive output to the optimum scale; $S = X_c / \bar{x}$. (This definition is not the same as that of either

Sylos or Bain; it appears, however, to be the most convenient for theoretical purposes, even though it may have drawbacks for empirical investigations.)

Now, following Bain, consider first the simplest case in which the technology of the industry is such that, at a scale less than $\bar{x}$, costs are prohibitively high, so that an entrant can come in only at a scale $\bar{x}$ or larger. In this case the entry-preventing output X_0 is readily found to be

$$X_0 = X_c - \bar{x} = X_c\left(1 - \frac{\bar{x}}{X_c}\right)$$

$$= X_c\left(1 - \frac{1}{S}\right),\tag{1}$$

or $(100/S)$ per cent below the competitive output. Suppose in fact that aggregate output were smaller; it would then be profitable for a firm of scale $\bar{x}$ to enter. Indeed, the post-entry output would then still be smaller than X_c, and hence the post-entry price would be larger than P_c, which is in turn equal to the entrant's average cost. By the same reasoning an output X_0 (or larger) would make entry unattractive. The critical price P_0 corresponding to X_0 can be read from the demand curve or found by solving for P the equation $X_0 = D(P)$. The relation between P_0 and the competitive equilibrium price P_c can be stated (approximately) in terms of the elasticity of demand in the neighborhood of P_c; if we denote this elasticity by η, we have

$$P_0 \simeq P_c\left(1 + \frac{1}{\eta S}\right),$$

or $100/\eta S$ per cent above P_c.[5]

We can now replace the very special

cost function assumed so far with the more conventional one, falling, more or less gradually, at least up to $\bar{x}$. In this general case the critical output may be somewhat larger, and the critical price may be lower, than indicated in the previous paragraph. Indeed, while at the output X_0 given by (1) it is not profitable to enter at the scale $\bar{x}$, it *may* still be profitable to come in at a *smaller* scale.

This possibility and its implications can be conveniently analyzed by means of the graphical apparatus presented in Figure 1. (This graphical device is not to be found in either of the books under review, but I believe that it is quite helpful in bringing out the essence of the authors' arguments.)[6] In panels IA and IIA, the light lines falling from left to right are the (relevant portions of the) market demand curve. For the sake of generality it is convenient to take $\bar{x}$ (the optimum scale) as the unit of measurement for output X and to take k (the corresponding minimum cost) as the unit of measurement for price, P. It follows that the competitive equilibrium price is, by definition, unity, while the corresponding output is precisely the size of the market S. Thus panel IA of Figure 1 relates to an industry of size 2 and panel IIA to an industry of size 10. The two demand curves have constant unit elasticity in the range shown, but, as will become apparent, the effect of different assumptions about the elasticity of demand can readily be handled.

The two heavy lines in each of the two panels represent alternative cost curves, graphed on the same scale as the demand curve, for outputs up to $\bar{x}$ (that is, for values of X up to 1). Because of the choice of units, each curve shows the

[5] This approximation will not be very satisfactory for small values of S. In particular, if the demand curve has constant elasticity, then, for small values of S, the extent of price rise will be significantly underestimated.

[6] In the case of Sylos, I am less sure of my ground, since his argument rests almost entirely on a detailed analysis of two numerical examples.

NEW DEVELOPMENTS ON THE OLIGOPOLY FRONT 219

behavior of costs, in percentage of minimum cost, as a function of plant scale, expressed in percentage of optimum scale. The steeper of the two curves is the kind of traditional, well-behaved cost function that underlies Bain's analysis and involves marked economies of scale. It is, in fact, based on the information reported by him for the cement industry, which appears to have more marked economies of scale than any other of the twenty industries analyzed in his book. It is obtained by joining with a smooth curve the data provided there for discrete scale sizes. The other cost curve, involving less pronounced economies of scale, depicts the kind of cost function that underlies Sylos' numerical examples. Sylos explicitly assumes, on grounds of presumed realism, the existence of very pronounced discontinuities in the available technologies. Plants can thus have only sizes that are very specific and far apart—only three sizes in his examples and in my graph. The rounded

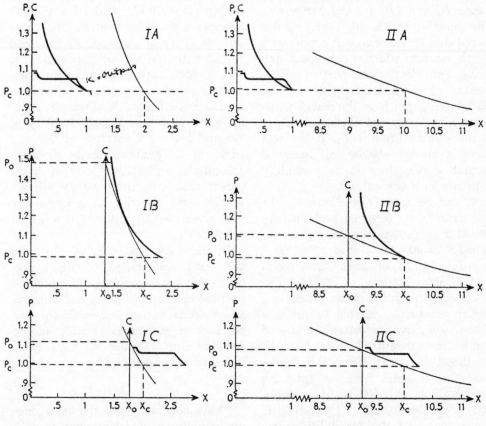

FIG. 1

ported by him for the cement industry, which appears to have more marked economies of scale than any other of the twenty industries analyzed in his book. It is obtained by joining with a smooth curve the data provided there for discrete scale sizes. The other cost curve, involving less pronounced economies of scale, depicts the kind of cost portions of the curve result from the fact that, beyond certain critical outputs, it pays to shift to a plant of a larger size, even though such a plant could not be utilized to capacity.[7]

[7] If Sylos' assumption is taken literally, the portions of the curves shown as straight lines parallel to the X-axis should really have a scalloped shape. This refinement can, however, be ignored, since it does not affect the results.

The critical price and output, P_0 and X_0, for a given cost curve can now be readily located by means of the following simple device. Slide the cost curve to the right parallel to itself, together with its co-ordinate axis, until no point of this curve lies inside the demand curve. This step is illustrated in panels IB and IIB for the steeper cost curve and in panels IC and IIC for the flatter one. The point at which the Y-axis so displaced cuts the demand curve represents P_0; the point at which it cuts the X-axis is X_0. For, clearly, the portion of the demand curve to the right of the displaced axis is precisely the marginal demand curve when the aggregate output of the existing firms is X_0. If the cost curve is nowhere below this marginal demand curve, there is no possibility of profits for a new entrant.

As can be seen from Figure 1, the cost curve in its terminal position may be either tangent to the demand curve, as in IB, or may touch it at a "corner," as in IC and IIC, or, finally, may touch it at its lower extreme, as in IIB.[8] The X co-ordinate of the point where the two curves touch, referred to the axis of the cost curve, indicates the size of firm which represents the most immediate threat of entry. Where this immediate threat comes from an optimum size plant, as in IIB, X_0 is precisely that given by formula (1) above; it is now seen that this possibility represents a limiting case—and that, in general, the formula provides only a lower bound to X_0.

With the help of Figure 1 we can also establish several interesting propositions in comparative statics. First, by comparing panel IB with IC and IIB

with IIC, we see that, for given market size, P_0 will tend to be higher the steeper the cost curve, that is, the greater the economies of scale. The common sense of this result is apparent: when economies of scale are important, the effective threat will tend to come from large-scale plants, which must widen the gap between X_0 and X_c. Similarly, by comparing IB with IIB and IC with IIC, it appears that, for a given cost curve and elasticity of demand, P_0 will tend to fall with the size of the market; it will, in fact, approach unity (the competitive price) as the size of the market approaches infinity. Furthermore, since, for given size S, a higher elasticity of demand implies a rotation of the cost curve in a counterclockwise direction around the competitive point, it is apparent that a higher elasticity will act in the same direction as a larger size with given elasticity; that is, it will tend to lower P_0.

In summary, under Sylos' postulate there is a well-defined, maximum premium that the oligopolists can command over the competitive price, and this premium tends to increase with the importance of economies of scale and to decrease with the size of market and the elasticity of demand.[9]

III

I have now laid down the basic long-run equilibrium model common to both Bain and Sylos. Hereafter, their roads part, and I shall first follow Sylos in his explorations of some of the fascinating implications of the model.

The first of these implications refers to the size distribution of firms (or, more

---

[8] It may, of course, also have several discrete points of contact with the demand curve or overlap a portion of it.

[9] As Bain points out, it is conceivable, though not likely, that P_0 will be higher than the price that "maximizes the profit" of the existing firms, in which case it will have no bearing on long-run equilibrium. See below, Sec. VIII.

NEW DEVELOPMENTS ON THE OLIGOPOLY FRONT 221

precisely, of plants) within the group—its *internal structure*, as I shall call it. If we look, for example, at panel *IC*, we see that the price P_0 is considerably above the average cost of the medium-size firms and even slightly above that of the smallest. If then any such firm *happened* to be a member of the group—Sylos here, in good Walrasian tradition, speaks of the initial structure as "criée par hasard"—it could survive and even prosper.

But would it not be profitable for the larger firms to expand, eliminating the smaller ones and securing for themselves the small firms' share of the market? In Sylos' model this possibility can be largely dismissed, thanks to his assumption of sharp technological discontinuities. Suppose, for instance, that there are only two possible scales: (*a*) large plants, producing 10,000 units, and (*b*) small plants, producing 500 units. Suppose further that X_0 is 15,000 and that this output is initially produced by one large firm and ten small ones. There is, then, no real incentive for the large firm to drive the small ones out of the market, for, in order to produce the extra 5,000 units, it would, in fact, have to operate ten small plants (at least as long as the average cost of a small plant is less than the average incremental cost of producing an extra 5,000 units by operating two large plants at 75 per cent of capacity). But the cost of a small firm must be such as to yield very little, if any, abnormal profit at the price P_0. In fact, this price must be such as not to give an inducement to enter the market with a small plant. Hence there will generally be no incentive for the large firm to undertake the price war necessary to eliminate the smaller firms.

If there existed a technology of inter-mediate size, say, size 5,000, the situation might look somewhat different, since at price P_0 such a plant would make some profits. However, even in this case the elimination of small firms would involve a costly price war. The price would have to be kept below prime cost of the small firms for a time long enough to induce them to fold up or below their average cost until their fixed plant wears out. Sylos suggests that usually the war will not be worth the prize and that it will be preferable for the larger firms not to disturb the delicate balance that always prevails in a homogeneous oligopoly structure.

Are we then to conclude that any structure, "criée par hasard," will tend to perpetuate itself as long as it is consistent with a price not higher than P_0? Sylos does not investigate this issue systematically, confining himself to illustrating various possibilities on the basis of his specific numerical examples. I suggest, however, that with the help of Sylos' model it is possible to throw some interesting light on this question. To this end I shall first introduce a definition. Consider any two structures A and B consistent with no inducement to entry: let us say that A is more rational than B if the total profits accruing to the members of the group are larger under structure A than under B.[10] It follows from this definition and our previous analysis that there exists a *most rational* structure, namely, that structure (not necessarily unique) which produces at the smallest total cost the output X_0 that can be sold at price P_0.[11] This

[10] It is apparent that this notion bears a close affinity to that of *dominance* in the theory of games.

[11] This statement is valid only to a first approximation. It is possible that the output X_0 cannot be produced with an integral number of plants of various sizes working at capacity, in which case profit maximization may involve an output somewhat

most rational structure has two features worth mentioning. (1) From a welfare point of view, it has certain optimal properties in that X_0 is being produced at the smallest (social) cost; but it still involves a departure from the usual conditions of Pareto optimality in that the output X_0 is, generally, too small and P_0 too high. (2) From a technological point of view, it has the property that the total capacity of the plants of a given size must necessarily be no larger than the capacity of one plant of the next larger size.

It seems reasonable to suppose that, if a structure B is less rational than a structure A, it will be less likely to be observed. For there is some incentive to a shift from B to A, since such a shift is accompanied by a net gain; that is, losses, if any, are more than compensated by gains. But there will be no corresponding incentive to move back from A to B. It does not follow, however, that structures other than the most rational have no chance at all of ever existing or surviving. As Sylos rightly points out, moving from one structure to another generally involves costs—at best, the cost of reaching an agreement; at worst, that of war—and the potential gain may not be worth the cost, especially when the gain, and even more the cost, may be problematic and uncertain.

The conclusions to which we are led are therefore, as it were, of a probabilistic nature. Less rational structures are less likely to be observed than more rational ones, and very irrational structures are unlikely to maintain themselves for any length of time. But certainly structures

other than the most rational can exist and survive, especially in a world that is moving and in which the most rational structure is itself continuously changing. Similar considerations apply to the price; while we should not expect prices higher that P_0 to be long maintainable, lower prices may have a certain degree of permanence. But, again, a gap between P and P_0 will provide a stimulus to reorganization of the structure, and this stimulus will be more powerful, and hence more likely to produce a response, the greater the gap.

By drawing together the analysis of market equilibrium and that of internal structure, we may venture some tentative conclusions about the factors which, according to Sylos' model, tend to control the degree of scatter in the size distributions of firms. We already know that only those sizes can survive whose average cost is no larger than P_0. From an analysis of the figure it can therefore be inferred that the possible range of the scatter of sizes will tend to be greater the smaller (a) the economies of scale, (b) the size of the markets, and (c) the elasticity of demand.

These implications, as well as those relating to P_0, are in principle testable. Indeed, it is to both Bain's and Sylos' credit that, by moving us away from conjectural variations and similar subjective notions and focusing instead on objective market and technological data, they have provided us with theories rich in empirical content and capable of being disproved by the evidence. To be sure, such tests may not be easy to carry out, especially with the information presently available, as is amply attested by Bain's gallant efforts in this direction. But, with a clear theoretical framework available as a guide in the collection of data, one may hope that more reliable

---

above X_0. However, the departure from X_0 will tend to be negligible, at least as long as the output of the smallest size consistent with P_0 represents a minor fraction of X_0.

and abundant evidence will sooner or later accumulate.

Even at this stage, ingenuity can do much to remedy inadequacies of the data. For instance, in order to compute the actual value of P for a given industry, one would need to know not only the market price but also the minimum average cost of an optimal plant. Bain ingeniously suggests that, even in the absence of precise information on this point, some notion of the relative height of P for various industries may be gotten by ranking them in terms of the rate of profits of the largest firms in each industry, since the average cost of such firms will presumably tend to be reasonably close to the minimum.[12] It should be noted, however, that, contrary to what Bain seems to imply in some of his empirical tests, there is no reason to expect any simple association between P_0 (or its proxy, the rate of profit) and the degree of scatter in plant sizes, at least within Sylos' model. While it is true that a large scatter is not to be

[12] In his book and in earlier contributions Bain measures the rate of profit as the rate of return, net of taxes, on the book value of equity. It would seem preferable to use the rate of return before taxes and interest on the book value of assets, since such a measure is not affected by financial structure. Perhaps a still more relevant measure, for the purpose of testing the model, could be derived from the rate of profit on sales. In fact, letting p denote the market price, we have

$$P = \frac{p}{k} = \frac{px}{kx} = \frac{\text{Sales}}{\text{Sales} - \text{Profit}} = \frac{1}{1 - \dfrac{\text{Profit}}{\text{Sales}}}.$$

By profit I mean here earnings over and above a "normal" rate of return on the book value of assets, which may not be easy to estimate in practice. One may also have some reservations about the assumption that minimum long-run average cost can be approximated from the actual average cost of the dominant firms in the industry. Franklyn Fisher has suggested that a better approximation may be obtained by utilizing, at least as supplementary evidence, the rate of profit on sales of the most profitable firms.

expected when P_0 is very close to unity—for then only firms of near-optimum size can survive—it does not follow that there is a positive association between P_0 and scatter. The only safe statement we can make is that, for given P_0, the scatter should tend to be smaller the steeper the cost curve and that, for given cost curve, the association between P_0 and scatter should be positive, both variables tending to decline as the size of the market and the elasticity of demand increase. A cursory examination of Bain's data for those industries in which product-differentiation and absolute-cost advantages are not supposed to be dominant does not seem to contradict this inference conspicuously. Unfortunately, the data in question provide no information on the elasticity of demand and, what is more serious, leave too much room for personal judgment in ranking industries in terms of any variable.

IV

It is tempting to explore the extent to which the implications we have derived from Sylos' model would be affected if we relaxed some of his very rigid assumptions. This question is especially pressing with respect to his assumption of technological discontinuities. Indeed, Bain has emerged from his empirical investigation with a strong conviction that, although there exists a fairly definite scale $\bar{x}$ at which average cost reaches its minimum, costs do not generally tend to rise for scales larger than $\bar{x}$. This possibility in no way affects our analysis of long-run equilibrium price and output but has considerable bearing on the conclusions concerning the size structure. Clearly, under a Bain-type cost function, the "most rational structure" must be such that all the output X_0 is produced by plants of size $\bar{x}$ or larger. It would follow that structures involving smaller plant sizes would tend to be unstable, especially where the cost function is steep in the range of (relative) costs from 1 to P_0.

The reader can decide for himself just how serious this conclusion is for Sylos' construction.[13] I shall limit myself to suggesting that Sylos' case may be considerably strengthened when we recognize the existence of product differentiation of a type not altogether inconsistent with the notion of homogeneous oligopoly, such as spatial differentiation or modifications in product design to meet customers' specifications. Under these conditions the area of the market supplied by smaller firms may be such that the dominant firms would have little to gain by capturing it, either because they have no cost advantage or because this would require an unprofitable price policy on other lines of product.

Consider, for example, the case of spatial differentiation. Suppose the large firm has a cost of 10 and the cost of transportation to a given distant market is 1. Suppose further that the highest f.o.b. price preventing entry that the large firm can charge is 12. The delivered price in the given market is then 13, and it may well be that, at this price, the market can be profitably supplied by a small local firm at, say, a cost of 12.5. In order to capture that relatively small market, the large firm would have to keep the price well below 11.5 for some considerable length of time and then keep it no higher than 11.5 in-

definitely—a policy which may well be unprofitable.[14] There is thus room for smaller firms in the industry, but this room is generated by market "exploitation" on the part of the large firm, and all customers are paying a higher price (by 2 per unit) than under competitive equilibrium.

Consider next the case of product modifications. It may well be that a class of customers is willing to pay an extra premium of 1 for a specific variation of the standard product. If the large firm charges 12 for the standard line, even though it has a cost of 10, these customers are therefore willing to pay 13. Now, suppose that, given the size of the market for the specialty, the average cost of the product is again, say, 12.5, whether it is produced by the larger firm or by a smaller one specializing in that line. If such a smaller firm exists, it is not worthwhile for the large firm to try to capture the market. But note once more that the existence of the smaller firm is made possible by the larger firm's oligopoly power. Under competitive conditions the small firm could not exist, since, if customers could get the standard product for 10, they would not be willing to pay enough for the specialty to cover its production cost of 12.5.

In short, in many situations the presence of a variety of sizes may be rendered reasonably stable by the fact that the larger firms find it advantageous to skim the fattest segment of the market, leav-

---

[13] Rosenstein-Rodan has pointed out to me that Bain's long-run cost function may not be too relevant where plant is very long lived. For, even though it may be possible to design a plant having cost k at sizes larger than $\bar{x}$, nonetheless an existing firm wishing to undertake a moderate expansion may have to utilize a smaller-scale technique with higher costs.

[14] It is assumed that the alternative, and more profitable, course of quoting a delivered price of 12.5 is not available. It is interesting to note in this connection that the prohibition of freight absorption as an antitrust measure will have a desirable effect if it induces the producer to choose a lower price in order not to lose distant markets to smaller local firms but that it will have an undesirable outcome if the producer finds it more advantageous to abandon those markets, in which case the demand will be supplied at a higher social cost.

NEW DEVELOPMENTS ON THE OLIGOPOLY FRONT 225

ing it for smaller firms to supply less profitable pockets. Nor should one forget altogether, even within the realm of pure theory, the public relations advantages that tend to accrue to the large firms from the coexistence of smaller and weaker partners. The argument that prices cannot be lowered without playing havoc with large numbers of honest and industrious small enterprises is always one of great public appeal. And, where antitrust laws are a potential threat, the advantages of having smaller competitors is even more evident.[15]

V

Before closing the subject of long-run static analysis, I must report one more observation on which Sylos lays a great deal of stress and which has to do with the effects of technological progress. While improvements in technology that are applicable to all scales must necessarily tend to depress price and expand output, he argues that improvements applicable only at, or near, the largest scale will not affect the critical price and hence will tend to result in higher profits for the larger firms. Furthermore, Sylos seems to feel that technological changes are very commonly of

this type, and he is inclined to account in this fashion for a presumed tendency of the profit margin of large firms to grow over time. Here, however, I cannot avoid feeling that Sylos is going too far. For, in the first place, even a change that affects only the largest scale may well lower P_0 when the immediate threat is, in fact, from firms of size $\bar{x}$; and, in the second place, any innovation that affects only plants of suboptimal size (and such innovations are by no means inconceivable) will also result in a fall in the critical price and thus will reduce the profit of the largest firms whose costs have remained unchanged. There is therefore serious doubt whether Sylos' argument can account for a long-run relative rise in large firms' profits, not to mention the equally serious doubt whether such a relative rise has in fact occurred. The model does suggest, however, that changes in technology may cause radical changes in the most rational structure and thus eventually may lead to pervasive changes in the actual structure, including the possible elimination of whole layers of small-scale plants.

VI

I now proceed to consider with Sylos some implications of the model for the effect of short-run changes in demand and cost conditions. Note, first, that in the analysis of market equilibrium I have made no mention of the standard categories of monopolistic competition theories, namely, marginal cost and marginal revenue. To be sure, with sufficient ingenuity, the analysis could be forced into that cast,[16] but such an undertaking would be merely an exercise in semantics

[15] The considerations of this section clearly point to the importance of factors other than those discussed in Sec. III above in controlling the scatter of the size distribution of firms and plants. In particular, under a Bain-type cost function, the model has nothing to say about the size distribution of firms above the optimum size $\bar{x}$. Here one may have to fall back on stochastic models of the type advanced, for example, by H. Simon in *Models of Man* (New York: John Wiley & Sons, 1957), chap. ix. In any event the analysis presented casts most serious doubts on the argument advanced by some authors and well exemplified by the following quotation: "Actually, we find that in most industries firms of very different sizes survive, and we may infer that commonly there is no large advantage or disadvantage to size over a very considerable range of outputs" (George Stigler, *The Theory of Price* [New York: Macmillan Co., 1952], p. 144).

[16] For such an attempt see, for example, J. R. Hicks, "The Process of Imperfect Competition." *Oxford Economic Papers*, VI (February, 1954), 41–54.

and formal logic and would in no way increase our understanding of what is involved. On the other hand, our result can readily be recast in the framework of the so-called full-cost pricing principle. According to this principle, prices are determined by adding to prime cost a markup to cover overhead per unit and by adding further an "appropriate" profit margin. So far, however, it has never been convincingly explained just at what level of output the overhead charge is computed or what determines the "appropriate" profit margin. Sylos' and Bain's models do provide answers to both questions. The large firms, which typically set the pace in the market, must base their price on long-run average cost (so that the overhead must normally be computed at capacity operation, with due allowance for normal seasonal and cyclical variations in the rate of utilization) and apply to this cost the largest profit markup that "the traffic will bear," namely, the markup P_0—for P_0, it will be recalled, is precisely the ratio of the highest possible price to average cost.

The usefulness of translating the result of the static analysis into the language of full-cost pricing becomes fully apparent when we proceed to examine the effects of a variation, say, an increase, in some element of prime cost. Such a change will generally affect all firms and hence will raise the long-run cost curve more or less uniformly. This development in turn will raise the level of the critical price and make it profitable to raise the actual price to this new level. Now it can be verified that, at least for moderate variations in costs and well-behaved demand functions, a good approximation of the new critical price can be obtained precisely by adding to the new average cost the very same profit margin that prevailed before the change; and nearly as good an approximation can be obtained by applying to the new prime cost the original total percentage markup. Thus full-cost pricing may well represent a very useful rule of thumb in reacting to cost changes affecting the entire industry, at least as long as such changes are not too drastic.

Now that we have a solid rationale for the full-cost principle, we need not have qualms about acknowledging two other sets of factors that tend to give it further sanction. (1) In an oligopolistic situation, with its precarious internal equilibrium, there is much to be gained from simple and widely understood rules of thumb, which minimize the danger of behavior intended to be peaceful and co-operative being misunderstood as predatory or retaliatory.[17] (2) The experience of those who, like myself, have conducted extensive personal interviews with executives suggests that these respondents have a strong propensity to explain their behavior in terms of simple mechanical principles, especially when they feel that these principles are blessed by general respectability.

So much about the effect of variations in costs. Let us now turn to the effect of cyclical variations in demand. For the sake of concreteness, let us start out from the prosperity phase, in which plants are being operated at, or near, capacity rates. If the demand curve now shifts to the left as a result of a fall in aggregate income, our model suggests that the optimum markup may have a slight tendency to increase. There are two main reasons for this contention:

[17] See, for example, A. Henderson, "The Theory of Duopoly," *Quarterly Journal of Economics*, LXVIII (November, 1954), 576–79, Sec. VII, and T. C. Schelling "Bargaining, Communication, and Limited War," *Conflict Resolution*, I (March, 1957), 19–36.

NEW DEVELOPMENTS ON THE OLIGOPOLY FRONT 227

(1) the critical price P_0 tends to rise when the size of the market falls and (2), with substantial idle capacity and sharply reduced profits, or even losses, prevailing in the industry, even a price somewhat higher than P_0 is not likely to encourage entry, especially where the effective threat is from plants large enough to require a substantial investment. This tendency for the critical markup to rise may partly be offset or even more than offset if, as the demand shifts, its elasticity increases; it will be reinforced if the elasticity falls—a case which Sylos regards as more typical, though, in our view, not very convincingly.

On the whole, then, the critical price P_0 may have some mild tendency to rise; but this does not mean that the actual markup will necessarily rise, for, with much idle capacity, the temptation for individual members of the oligopolistic group to secure a larger share of the shrunken business is very strong. Thus the self-discipline of the group may well tend to break down, with a resultant fall in the effective price if not in the officially quoted one.

In the course of the recovery the markup will of course tend to retrace the path followed in the contraction. But here some new interesting possibilities arise which Sylos himself has not considered. In an expanding economy the recovery will tend to push demand to levels higher than previous peaks. As a result of a rise in demand that is rapid and larger than expected, or as a result of circumstances beyond its control, such as war, the industry may be caught with capacity inadequate to satisfy the demand at the critical price P_0. In terms of traditional patterns of thinking, one would expect firms in the industry to be eager to exploit the situation by charging higher prices. But such

a price policy may not be so appealing to the larger firms whose long-run interest is to secure for themselves as much as possible of the additional demand at the profitable price P_0. A higher price may tend to encourage entry, which would not only reduce their share but possibly also threaten the maintenance of self-discipline in periods of depressed demand. Thus the dominant firms may have an incentive to "hold the price line" by such devices as lengthening delivery schedules and informal rationing (even at the risk of gray markets), while at the same time expanding capacity—but only to an extent that seems warranted by the anticipated long-run demand at the price P_0. These considerations may help to explain the otherwise rather puzzling behavior of certain important sectors of the economy in the early postwar period.[18]

On the whole it would appear that no very definite general conclusion can be reached about the cyclical behavior of the markup, although the model may have a good deal to say for well-defined classes of situations. One might, however, go along with Sylos on the following two tentative generalizations: (1) on the average, the markup is not likely to change much in the course of the cycle, but one should expect some scatter around this central tendency, and (2)

[18] A similar explanation is advanced in Edwards, *op. cit.*, and in Kuh and Meyer, *The Investment Decision* (Cambridge, Mass.: Harvard University Press, 1957), esp. chap. xii. It has also been suggested that the price policies in question may be explained by the concern that higher prices and consequent higher profits would have led to irresistible pressure for wage concessions, difficult to reverse. By contrast, the abnormally high profits of dealers or gray-market operators could be counted on to disappear automatically as the supply gradually caught up with demand. I am indebted to Albert G. Hart and Richard Cyert for stimulating discussions on the relevance of Sylos' model to the explanation of the postwar experience.

prices should tend on the average to fluctuate more in relation to prime cost where there is more chance for the discipline of the group to break down, and this chance presumably should tend to increase with the size of the group and decrease with degree of concentration (in Sylos' sense). These generalizations appear to be consistent with the evidence assembled by Stigler in his well-known criticism of the kinky demand curve,[19] though they may be less easy to reconcile with certain empirical studies of price flexibility.[20]

Sylos attempts to dispose of the latter evidence by an ingenious argument which is not entirely convincing in this context but which is of interest on its own merit. Specifically, he suggests that, where the full-cost principle is widely adhered to, it may be in the interest of the larger firms to sustain the prices of factors entering into prime cost; in fact, provided that the shifted demand curve has a sufficiently low elasticity, such a policy will increase the over-all profit of the industry. Where the large firms are themselves important producers of some critical raw materials, they may best achieve this purpose by sustaining these particular prices; where this is not possible, they may acquiesce to an increase in real wages.[21] However, the advantage of an increase in prime costs is realized only where full-cost pricing is adhered to in spite of widespread excess capacity. Hence this policy can be sensi-

ble only where discipline is maintained, which, as suggested earlier, may be related to small number and heavy concentration. Sylos suggests that these considerations may help to explain certain empirical results indicating a positive association between cyclical wage rigidity and degree of concentration.[22]

VII

The last two parts of Sylos' book expound the thesis that monopolistic and oligopolistic market structures are an important factor contributing to the development of unemployment, especially technological unemployment. In spite of the importance of the subject, this part will be reviewed in very sketchy form, both for lack of space and because Sylos' argument is not so convincing as his partial equilibrium analysis.

The main thread of his argument in Part II seems to run as follows. Starting from a stationary situation with full employment, a labor-saving innovation initially displaces labor. The reabsorption of this unemployment requires some net saving to be invested in the equipment necessary to outfit the displaced workers. (The alternative possibility of a fall in real wages leading to an appropriate change in capital coefficients is excluded by assumption.) Under perfectly competitive market structures, the fall in cost would lead to higher real income for all those who have not lost their

---

[19] George Stigler, "The Kinky Oligopoly Demand Curve and Rigid Prices," *Journal of Political Economy*, LV (October, 1947), 432–49.

[20] Richard Ruggles, "The Nature of Price Flexibility and Determinants of Relative Price Changes in the Economy," in *Business Concentration and Price Policy* (A Conference of the Universities–National Bureau Committee for Economic Research [Princeton, N.J.: Princeton University Press; 1955]), pp. 441–505.

[21] Note that this argument is applicable even to long-run equilibrium analysis. That is, when the market demand is sufficiently inelastic, an increase in wage rates may increase the total excess of receipts over (opportunity) costs accruing to the group. It may then be profitable for existing firms to tolerate high wages, as long as these are enforced by a trade union strong enough to impose the same wage scale on any potential entrant.

[22] The major piece of evidence quoted in this connection is J. W. Garbarino, "A Theory of Interindustry Wage Structure Variation," *Quarterly Journal of Economics*, LXIV (May, 1950), 282–305.

NEW DEVELOPMENTS ON THE OLIGOPOLY FRONT 229

employment, and this rise in real income, especially profits, supposedly produces the saving and investment necessary for the reabsorption. On the other hand, under oligopolistic structures, the fall in cost will frequently not be accompanied by a proportionate fall in prices and will thus result in an increase in the value added of the sector where costs have fallen. (I have already expressed some doubt about the validity of this conclusion in Sec. V above.) To the extent that the increase in value added is absorbed by higher wages, the necessary saving will not be forthcoming, since, by an assumption which is particularly unpalatable to me, workers have a marginal propensity to consume equal to 1. To the extent that the increase in value added results in higher profits—and even if these profits give rise to savings—there may still be difficulties. Sylos suggests in fact that the entrepreneurs to whom the profits accrue will be disinclined to invest outside their own industry, whereas the investment required should be spread throughout the economy.

The conclusion Sylos draws is that, with widespread oligopolistic market structures, the forces making for reabsorption, though not entirely absent, will be lagging and weak. In a world of continous technological change this weakness is sufficient, in his view, to account for a substantial permanent pool of unemployment, whose continuing existence is therefore an essentially dynamic phenomenon. He further argues that the kind of innovations the larger firms in the oligopolistic group will be inclined to adopt are likely to aggravate the technological displacement of labor. He maintains in fact that, though these firms will tend to be quite progressive in searching for, and adopting, innovations that cut

costs at current level of output, they will nonetheless shun improvements that would cut costs only at a large scale of operation. But this argument is not quite consistent with his own model, since the new, larger-scale, and cheaper technique may itself become the immediate threat to entry. Nor is it clearly relevant—for it does not per se establish a bias in favor of labor-saving innovations.

Part III purports to explore the implications of the previous analysis for the standard Keynesian theory of effective demand. This part again contains many interesting observations but also has its shortcomings. In particular, the author does not seem to be sufficiently aware that the implications of the analysis of Part III are profoundly different for an economy poor in capital and savings like the Italian economy and for one in which the main threat to unemployment springs from a lack of effective demand. In the former case, labor-saving innovations may indeed tend to aggravate the problem of unemployment, especially when coupled with powerful unions and downward wage rigidity. But, in the latter case, such innovations are, as it were, a blessing, since they increase the required stock of capital and thus make possible the absorption of full-employment saving.

This sketch of Parts III and IV may well fail to do justice to Sylos' argument. But such a failure would serve to confirm the earlier statement that these final chapters do not quite match the high level of performance that characterizes the rest of this remarkable book.

VIII

Let us now look briefly at that part of Bain's analysis that does not overlap Sylos'.

230   FRANCO MODIGLIANI

Still with respect to barriers from economies of scale, Bain makes a halfhearted attempt to explore the consequences of dropping Sylos' postulate (see Sec. II). Unfortunately, as long as we are dealing with homogeneous oligopoly, it is hard to find a well-defined sensible alternative. Certainly, the diametrically opposite assumption that existing firms will adopt a policy of maintaining price, by contracting their output, would generally be a rather foolish one for the entrant to make. It implies that established firms will graciously allow the entrant to carve out for himself whatever slice of the market he pleases, while suffering losses on two accounts: (1) by losing sales and (2) by incurring a higher average cost, at least in the short run and possibly even in the long run, if their original plant was of no more than optimal size. Furthermore, such a policy, if consistently followed, would unavoidably result in the original members' being gradually squeezed out of the market.

The only alternative systematically explored by Bain is for the entrant to assume that price will be maintained but only provided he is contented with a share of the market no larger than that of the existing firms—which are conveniently assumed, for this purpose, to be all of equal size. There is, then, in general, a well-defined critical price (and corresponding output) such that entry is unprofitable even if a prospective entrant proceeds on the stated "optimistic" assumption.[23]

As Bain is well aware, this alternative assumption is but one of a large class of assumptions that could be constructed and explored. But he has wisely refrained from following this line, which is rather unpromising at this stage. For the moment, at least, we must be satisfied with the conclusion that there exists a well-defined upper limit to the price that can be maintained under oligopoly in the long run, and this upper limit is P_0, obtained under Sylos' postulate. It is the upper limit because, at a price higher than this, entry will be profitable even if the existing firms are bent on doing the entrant as much damage as they possibly can.[24] But a price lower than P_0 cannot be excluded a priori, even in the long run, especially where P_0 would cover the cost at a scale of output which represents a small fraction of X_0 and where a plant of such scale would require a relatively small investment. But, broadly speaking, these are precisely the conditions under which P_0 is close to 1, and the classical competitive model may provide a reasonable approximation. Conversely, Sylos' postulate may well provide a reasonable approximation precisely where it makes a real difference —where it implies a value of P_0 appreciably above unity.

Dropping the assumption that all producers, actual and potential, have access

---

[23] It is easy to verify that the stated critical price, say, p_0, and corresponding output are given by the simultaneous solution of the following two equations:

$$X = D(p) \qquad (1)$$

$$p = c\,\frac{X}{(n+1)}, \qquad (2)$$

where $c(q)$ denotes the minimum long-run average cost of producing the quantity q, and n is the number of plants. In general, p_0 is an increasing function of n and is larger than the competitive price, at least as long as n is larger than S. Furthermore, for sufficiently large n, each firm is of less than optimal size, and the equilibrium bears a close resemblance to that described by Chamberlin in *Monopolistic Competition*, chap. v, sec. 5.

[24] A somewhat higher price could conceivably be maintained if the industry produced an output smaller than X_0, but had enough capacity to produce X_0 or more and a record of readiness to exploit the extra capacity to *expand* output in the face of entry. Such behavior would presumably require more or less open collusion, of a nature likely only with a very small and well-disciplined group.

NEW DEVELOPMENTS ON THE OLIGOPOLY FRONT 231

to identical cost functions enables us to analyze another set of forces which can account for a long-run excess of price over cost, and which Bain labels "absolute cost advantages." Such differential costs, arising from factors like control of scarce resources, patents and trade secrets, and generally superior technical and managerial know-how, have already been extensively analyzed and understood in the received body of theory. They underlie the traditional theory of monopoly, oligopoly without entry, and rents. Of course, with cost differential in the picture, there is no longer a specific entry-forestalling price, even under Sylos' postulate. Rather the critical price depends on the cost of the most efficient potential entrant and, hence, on just which firms are already in the group. It may then not be in the interest of existing firms to try to prevent the entry of very efficient producers, since this might require an unprofitably low price. When the price-output policy of existing firms is not intended to discourage potential entrants, Bain speaks of "ineffectively impeded" entry, in contrast to "effectively impeded" entry, in which price and output policy is designed to make entry unprofitable, and to "blockaded entry," in which the price and output policy that is most advantageous to the group, without regard to entry, happens to make entry unattractive.

But Bain's most significant finding about absolute cost barriers is probably at the empirical level. He finds in fact that, at least for his sample of twenty industries, such barriers are generally not important. Natural scarcity appears to be a significant factor in at most two industries—copper and possibly steel. In only three other cases do patents and/or technical know-how possibly play some role and apparently not a major one.

Bain also provides a valuable tabulation of available information on the size of the investment required by a new entrant (with an optimum scale plant). These capital requirements represent a somewhat special type of barrier to entry whose possible significance has been repeatedly mentioned earlier.

The remaining barrier to entry—resulting from the inability of potential competitors to produce a commodity that is a perfect substitute for the product of existing firms—is again one that has received considerable attention in the past. Bain's new contribution in this area consists of a penetrating empirical investigation of the specific barriers that impede the production of perfect or near-perfect substitutes for each industry and their consequences. The main factors may be classified roughly as follows: (1) Allegiance to brands, supported by large advertising outlays, and possibly also, by a long record of reliability; this factor is found to provide the main barrier, and a significant one, almost only in the case of inexpensive durable or non-durable consumers' goods such as cigarettes, liquor, and soap. (2) Control by the manufacturer of an extensive and exclusive dealers' organization attending to the sale and the servicing of the product; as one might expect, this phenomenon is of major importance for expensive durable goods, such as automobiles, typewriters, and tractors and other farm machinery, but it is apparently also of some significance for other commodities, such as petroleum and rubber tires. (3) Patents protecting some feature of the product or related auxiliary services. (4) Special services provided to customers. These last two factors are rarely mentioned and generally do not seem to offer very effective protection.

FRANCO MODIGLIANI

It is worth noting that factors (2) and (3), and in part also factor (1), could be largely treated as economies of scale in marketing. Both Bain and Sylos are aware of this possibility; in fact, the latter—though he pays only passing attention to product differentiation fostered by advertising—hints that the effect of this type of barrier could be analyzed along lines similar to those utilized in the homogeneous oligopoly model. That is, a new entrant could hope to match the profit performance of the successful large firms only by securing a market of the same absolute size. But, given the over-all size of the market, even if the entrant succeeded in capturing a share comparable to that of existing firms, each member would be left with too small a market, so that the final result of the entry would be to make the business unattractive for all.

After evaluating for his twenty industries the over-all barriers to entry resulting from the joint effect of economies of scale, absolute cost advantages, and product differentiation and after summarizing the effects that these over-all barriers should have on various aspects of market performance on the basis of his theoretical analysis, Bain proceeds to check his deductions against available evidence on actual performance. To be sure, the present evidence on barriers to entry as well as on market performance is frequently far from adequate, and one may have reservations about the details of some of the test procedures. Nonetheless, Bain's courageous attempt at systematic testing and his candid admission of occasional failures of his predictions is a highly welcome novelty and one whose importance can hardly be overestimated.

Finally, the implications of the analysis for public policy designed to foster workable competition are set forth in a very cautious and restrained spirit in the concluding chapter viii. On the whole, the outlook for effective public policy is not too optimistic, although it is by no means as gloomy as that of Sylos. But, then, Sylos' gloom is understandable. His inspiration comes from the Italian economy, where markets are naturally small and are made still smaller by tariffs and other artificial restrictions. According to his own model, the tendency to oligopolistic structures, and their power of market exploitation, will tend to be greater the smaller the size of the market.

I hope I have succeeded in justifying the glowing statement with which this review begins and in showing how well the two books complement each other. To be sure, much work still remains to be done in the area of oligopolistic market structures. In particular, the analysis of both authors is still largely limited to a static framework, and there is reason to believe that certain aspects of oligopolistic behavior can be adequately accounted for only by explicitly introducing dynamic elements into the analysis.[25] In my view, the real significance of Bain's and Sylos' contributions lies not merely in the results that they have already reached but at least as much in their having provided us with a framework capable of promising further developments and leading to operationally testable propositions. In addition, Bain deserves high credit for having led the way on the path of empirical testing.

[25] Some promising beginnings in this direction are already to be found in Sylos and, even more, in Bain. The latter's notion of ineffectively impeded entry, for example, is an essentially dynamic one. Similarly, Sylos hints that, where demand is growing, existing firms, to discourage entry, may have to keep their capacity somewhat larger than X_0 and their markup somewhat below P_0. Needless to say, the mere emphasis on the problem of entry is, per se, a significant movement in the direction of a dynamic analysis.

[5]

A THEORY OF OLIGOPOLY

GEORGE J. STIGLER[1]
University of Chicago

No one has the right, and few the ability, to lure economists into reading another article on oligopoly theory without some advance indication of its alleged contribution. The present paper accepts the hypothesis that oligopolists wish to collude to maximize joint profits. It seeks to reconcile this wish with facts, such as that collusion is impossible for many firms and collusion is much more effective in some circumstances than in others. The reconciliation is found in the problem of policing a collusive agreement, which proves to be a problem in the theory of information. A considerable number of implications of the theory are discussed, and a modest amount of empirical evidence is presented.

I. THE TASK OF COLLUSION

A satisfactory theory of oligopoly cannot begin with assumptions concerning the way in which each firm views its interdependence with its rivals. If we adhere to the traditional theory of profit-maximizing enterprises, then behavior is no longer something to be assumed but rather something to be deduced. The firms in an industry will behave in such a way, given the demand-and-supply functions (including those of rivals), that their profits will be maximized.

The combined profits of the entire set of firms in an industry are maximized when they act together as a monopolist. At

least in the traditional formulation of the oligopoly problem, in which there are no major uncertainties as to the profit-maximizing output and price at any time, this familiar conclusion seems inescapable. Moreover, the result holds for any number of firms.

Our modification of this theory consists simply in presenting a systematic account of the factors governing the feasibility of collusion, which like most things in this world is not free. Before we do so, it is desirable to look somewhat critically at the concept of homogeneity of products, and what it implies for profit-maximizing. We shall show that collusion normally involves much more than "the" price.

Homogeneity is commonly defined in terms of identity of products or of (what is presumed to be equivalent) pairs of products between which the elasticity of substitution is infinite. On either definition it is the behavior of buyers that is decisive. Yet it should be obvious that products may be identical to any or every buyer while buyers may be quite different from the viewpoint of sellers.

This fact that every transaction involves two parties is something that economists do not easily forget. One would therefore expect a definition of homogeneity also to be two-sided: if the products are what sellers offer, and the purchase commitments are what the buyers offer, full homogeneity clearly involves infinite elasticities of substitution between both products and purchase

[1] I am indebted to Claire Friedland for the statistical work and to Harry Johnson for helpful criticisms.

44

A THEORY OF OLIGOPOLY   45

commitments. In other words, two products are homogeneous to a buyer if he is indifferent between all combinations of x of one and (say) $20 - x$ of the other, at a common price. Two purchase commitments are homogeneous to a seller if he is indifferent between all combinations of y of one and (say) $20 - y$ of the other, at a common price. Full homogeneity is then defined as homogeneity both in products (sellers) and purchase commitments (buyers).

The heterogeneity of purchase commitments (buyers), however, is surely often at least as large as that of products within an industry, and sometimes vastly larger. There is the same sort of personal differentia of buyers as of sellers—ease in making sales, promptness of payment, penchant for returning goods, likelihood of buying again (or buying other products). In addition there are two differences among buyers which are pervasive and well recognized in economics:

1. The size of purchase, with large differences in costs of providing lots of different size.
2. The urgency of purchase, with possibly sufficient differences in elasticity of demand to invite price discrimination.

It is one thing to assert that no important market has homogeneous transactions, and quite another to measure the extent of the heterogeneity. In a regime of perfect knowledge, it would be possible to measure heterogeneity by the variance of prices in transactions; in a regime of imperfect knowledge, there will be dispersion of prices even with transaction homogeneity.[2]

The relevance of heterogeneity to collusion is this: It is part of the task of maximizing industry profits to employ a price structure that takes account of the larger differences in the costs of various classes of transactions. Even with a single, physically homogeneous product the profits will be reduced if differences among buyers are ignored. A simple illustration of this fact is given in the Appendix; disregard of differences among buyers proves to be equivalent to imposing an excise tax upon them, but one which is not collected by the monopolist. A price structure of some complexity will usually be the goal of collusive oligopolists.

II. THE METHODS OF COLLUSION

Collusion of firms can take many forms, of which the most comprehensive is outright merger. Often merger will be inappropriate, however, because of diseconomies of scale,[3] and at certain times and places it may be forbidden by law. Only less comprehensive is the cartel with a joint sales agency, which again has economic limitations—it is ill suited to custom work and creates serious administrative costs in achieving quality standards, cost reductions, product innovations, etc. In deference to American antitrust policy, we shall assume that the collusion takes the form of joint determination of outputs and prices by ostensibly independent firms, but we shall not take account of the effects of the legal prohibitions until later. Oligopoly existed before 1890, and has existed in countries that have never had an antitrust policy.

The colluding firms must agree upon the price structure appropriate to the transaction classes which they are prepared to recognize. A complete profit-maximizing price structure may have

[2] Unless one defines heterogeneity of transactions to include also differences in luck in finding low price sellers; see my "Economics of Information," *Journal of Political Economy*, June, 1961.

[3] If the firms are multiproduct, with different product structures, the diseconomies of merger are not strictly those of scale (in any output) but of firm size measured either absolutely or in terms of variety of products.

46   GEORGE J. STIGLER

almost infinitely numerous price classes: the firms will have to decide upon the number of price classes in the light of the costs and returns from tailoring prices to the diversity of transactions. We have already indicated by hypothetical example (see Appendix) that there are net profits to be obtained by catering to differences in transactions. The level of collusive prices will also depend upon the conditions of entry into the industry as well as upon the elasticities of demand.

Let us assume that the collusion has been effected, and a price structure agreed upon. It is a well-established proposition that if any member of the agreement can secretly violate it, he will gain larger profits than by conforming to it.[4] It is, moreover, surely one of the axioms of human behavior that all agreements whose violation would be profitable to the violator must be enforced. The literature of collusive agreements, ranging from the pools of the 1880's to the electrical conspiracies of recent times, is replete with instances of the collapse of conspiracies because of "secret" price-cutting. This literature is biased: conspiracies that are successful in avoiding an amount of price-cutting which leads to collapse of the agreement are less likely to be reported or detected. But no conspiracy can neglect the problem of enforcement.

Enforcement consists basically of detecting significant deviations from the agreed-upon prices. Once detected, the deviations will tend to disappear because they are no longer secret and will be matched by fellow conspirators if they are not withdrawn. If the enforcement is weak, however—if price-cutting is detected only slowly and incompletely—

the conspiracy must recognize its weakness: it must set prices not much above the competitive level so the inducements to price-cutting are small, or it must restrict the conspiracy to areas in which enforcement can be made efficient.

Fixing market shares is probably the most efficient of all methods of combating secret price reductions. No one can profit from price-cutting if he is moving along the industry demand curve,[5] once a maximum profit price has been chosen. With inspection of output and an appropriate formula for redistribution of gains and losses from departures from quotas, the incentive to secret price-cutting is eliminated. Unless inspection of output is costly or ineffective (as with services), this is the ideal method of enforcement, and is widely used by legal cartels. Unfortunately for oligopolists, it is usually an easy form of collusion to detect, for it may require side payments among firms and it leaves indelible traces in the output records.

Almost as efficient a method of eliminating secret price-cutting is to assign each buyer to a single seller. If this can be done for all buyers, short-run price-cutting no longer has any purpose. Long-run price-cutting will still be a serious possibility if the buyers are in competition: lower prices to one's own customers can then lead to an expansion of their share of their market, so the price-cutter's long-run demand curve will be more elastic than that of the industry. Long-run price-cutting is likely to be important, however, only where sellers are providing a major cost component to the buyer.

There are real difficulties of other sorts

---

[4] If price is above marginal cost, marginal revenue will be only slightly less than price (and hence above marginal cost) for price cuts by this one seller.

[5] More precisely, he is moving along a demand curve which is a fixed share of the industry demand, and hence has the same elasticity as the industry curve at every price.

A THEORY OF OLIGOPOLY 47

to the sellers in the assignment of buyers. In general the fortunes of the various sellers will differ greatly over time: one seller's customers may grow threefold, while another seller's customers shrink by half. If the customers have uncorrelated fluctuations in demand, the various sellers will experience large changes in relative outputs in the short run.[6] Where the turnover of buyers is large, the method is simply impracticable.

Nevertheless, the conditions appropriate to the assignment of customers will exist in certain industries, and in particular the geographical division of the market has often been employed. Since an allocation of buyers is an obvious and easily detectible violation of the Sherman Act, we may again infer that an efficient method of enforcing a price agreement is excluded by the antitrust laws. We therefore turn to other techniques of enforcement, but we shall find that the analysis returns to allocation of buyers.

In general the policing of a price agreement involves an audit of the transactions prices. In the absence or violation of antitrust laws, actual inspection of the accounting records of sellers has been employed by some colluding groups, but even this inspection gives only limited assurance that the price agreement is adhered to.[7] Ultimately there is no substitute for obtaining the transaction prices from the buyers.

An oligopolist will not consider making secret price cuts to buyers whose purchases fall below a certain size relative to his aggregate sales. The ease with which price-cutting is detected by rivals is decisive in this case. If p is the probability that some rival will hear of one such price reduction, $1 - (1 - p)^n$ is the probability that a rival will learn of at least one reduction if it is given to n customers. Even if p is as small as 0.01, when n equals 100 the probability of detection is .634, and when n equals 1000 it is .99996. No one has yet invented a way to advertise price reductions which brings them to the attention of numerous customers but not to that of any rival.[8]

It follows that oligopolistic collusion will often be effective against small buyers even when it is ineffective against large buyers. When the oligopolists sell to numerous small retailers, for example, they will adhere to the agreed-upon price, even though they are cutting prices to larger chain stores and industrial buyers. This is a first empirical implication of our theory. Let us henceforth exclude small buyers from consideration.

The detection of secret price-cutting will of course be as difficult as interested people can make it. The price-cutter will certainly protest his innocence, or, if this would tax credulity beyond its taxable capacity, blame a disobedient subordinate. The price cut will often take the indirect form of modifying some nonprice dimension of the transaction. The customer may, and often will, divulge price reductions, in order to have them matched by others, but he will learn from experience if each disclosure is followed by the withdrawal of the lower price offer. Indeed the buyer will frequently

[6] When the relative outputs of the firms change, the minimum cost condition of equal marginal costs for all sellers is likely to be violated. Hence industry profits are not maximized.

[7] The literature and cases on "open-price associations" contain numerous references to the collection of prices from sellers (see Federal Trade Commission, *Open-Price Trade Associations* [Washington, 1929], and cases cited).

[8] This argument applies to size of buyer relative to the individual seller. One can also explain the absence of higgling in small transactions because of the costs of bargaining, but this latter argument turns on the absolute size of the typical transaction, not its size relative to the seller.

fabricate wholly fictitious price offers to test the rivals. Policing the collusion sounds very much like the subtle and complex problem presented in a good detective story.

There is a difference: In our case the man who murders the collusive price will receive the bequest of patronage. The basic method of detection of a price-cutter must be the fact that he is getting business he would otherwise not obtain. No promises of lower prices that fail to shift some business can be really effective—either the promised price is still too high or it is simply not believed.

Our definition of perfect collusion, indeed, must be that no buyer changes sellers voluntarily. There is no competitive price-cutting if there are no shifts of buyers among sellers.

To this rule that price-cutting must be inferred from shifts of buyers there is one partial exception, but that an important one. There is one type of buyer who usually reveals the price he pays, and does not accept secret benefices: the government. The system of sealed bids, publicly opened with full identification of each bidder's price and specifications, is the ideal instrument for the detection of price-cutting. There exists no alternative method of secretly cutting prices (bribery of purchasing agents aside). Our second empirical prediction, then, is that collusion will always be more effective against buyers who report correctly and fully the prices tendered to them.[9]

It follows from the test of the absence of price competition by buyer loyalty— and this is our third major empirical prediction—that collusion is severely limited (under present assumptions excluding

[9] The problem implicitly raised by these remarks is why all sales to the government are not at collusive prices. Part of the answer is that the government is usually not a sufficiently large buyer of a commodity to remunerate the costs of collusion.

market-sharing) when the significant buyers constantly change identity. There exist important markets in which the (substantial) buyers do change identity continuously, namely, in the construction industries. The building of a plant or an office building, for example, is an essentially non-repetitive event, and rivals cannot determine whether the successful bidder has been a price-cutter unless there is open bidding to specification.

The normal market, however, contains both stability and change. There may be a small rate of entry of new buyers. There will be some shifting of customers even in a regime of effective collusion, for a variety of minor reasons we can lump together as "random factors." There will often be some sharing of buyers by several sellers—a device commending itself to buyers to increase the difficulty of policing price agreements. We move then to the world of circumstantial evidence, or, as it is sometimes called, of probability.

III. THE CONDITIONS FOR DETECTING SECRET PRICE REDUCTIONS

We shall investigate the problem of detecting secret price-cutting with a simplified model, in which all buyers and all sellers are initially of equal size. The number of buyers per seller—recalling that we exclude from consideration all buyers who take less than (say) 0.33 per cent of a seller's output—will range from 300 down to perhaps 10 or 20 (since we wish to avoid the horrors of full bilateral oligopoly). A few of these buyers are new, but over moderate periods of time most are "old," although some of these old customers will shift among suppliers. A potential secret price-cutter has then three groups of customers who would increase their patronage if given secret price cuts: the old customers of rivals;

A THEORY OF OLIGOPOLY   49

the old customers who would normally leave him; and new customers.

Most old buyers will deal regularly with one or a few sellers, in the absence of secret price-cutting. There may be no secret price-cutting because a collusive price is adhered to, or because only an essentially competitive price can be obtained. We shall show that the loyalty of customers is a crucial variable in determining which price is approached. We need to know the probability that an old customer will buy again from his regular supplier at the collusive price, in the absence of secret price-cutting.

The buyer will set the economies of repetitive purchase (which include smaller transaction costs and less product-testing) against the increased probability of secret price-cutting that comes from shifting among suppliers. From the viewpoint of any one buyer, this gain will be larger the larger the number of sellers and the smaller the number of buyers, as we shall show below. The costs of shifting among suppliers will be smaller the more homogeneous the goods and the larger the purchases of the buyer (again an inverse function of his size). Let us label this probability of repeat purchases p. We shall indicate later how this probability could be determined in a more general approach.

The second component of sales of a firm will be its sales to new buyers and to the floating old customers of rivals. Here we assume that each seller is equally likely to make a sale, in the absence of price competition.

Let us proceed to the analysis. There are n_0 "old" buyers and n_n new customers, with $n_n = \lambda n_0$ and n_s sellers. A firm may look to three kinds of evidence on secret price-cutting, and therefore by symmetry to three potential areas to practice secret price-cutting.

1. *The behavior of its own old customers.*—It has, on average, n_0/n_s such customers, and expects to sell to $m_1 = pn_0/n_s$ of them in a given round of transactions, in the absence of price cutting. The variance of this number of customers is

$$\sigma_1^2 = \frac{(1-p)pn_0}{n_s}.$$

The probability of the firm losing more old customers than

$$\frac{(1-p)n_0}{n_s} + k\sigma_1$$

is given by the probability of values greater than k. The expected number of these old customers who will shift to any one rival is, say,

$$m_2 = \frac{1}{n_s - 1}\left[\frac{(1-p)n_0}{n_s} + k\sigma_1\right],$$

with a variance

$$\sigma_2^2 = \frac{n_s - 2}{(n_s - 1)^2}\left[\frac{(1-p)n_0}{n_s} + k\sigma_1\right].$$

The probability that any rival will obtain more than $m_2 + r\sigma_2$ of these customers is determined by r. We could now choose those combinations of k and r that fix a level of probability for the loss of a given number of old customers to any one rival beyond which secret price-cutting by this rival will be inferred. This is heavy arithmetic, however, so we proceed along a less elegant route.

Let us assume that the firm's critical value for the loss of old customers, beyond which it infers secret price-cutting, is

$$\frac{(1-p)n_0}{n_s} + \sigma_1$$

$$= \frac{(1-p)n_0}{n_s}\left[1 + \sqrt{\left(\frac{p}{1-p}\frac{n_s}{n_0}\right)}\right]$$

$$= \frac{(1-p)n_0}{n_s}(1+\theta),$$

that is, one standard deviation above the mean. Any one rival will on average attract

$$m_2 = \frac{1}{n_s - 1}\left[\frac{(1-p)n_0}{n_s} + \sigma_1\right]$$

of these customers, with a variance of

$$\sigma_2^2 = \frac{n_s - 2}{(n_s - 1)^2}\left[\frac{(1-p)n_0}{n_s} + \sigma_1\right].$$

Let the rival be suspected of price-cutting if he obtains more than $(m_2 + \sigma_2)$ customers, that is, if the probability of any larger number is less than about 30 per cent. The joint probability of losing one standard deviation more than the average number of old customers and a rival obtaining one standard deviation more than his average share is about 10 per cent. The average sales of a rival are n_0/n_s, ignoring new customers. The maximum number of buyers any seller can obtain from one rival without exciting suspicion, minus the number he will on average get without price-cutting ($[1 - p]n_0/n_s$ $[n_s - 1]$), expressed as a ratio to his average sales, is

$$\frac{[\theta(1-p)n_0/(n_s-1)n_s + \sigma_2]}{n_0/n_s}.$$

This criterion is tabulated in Table 1.

TABLE 1

PERCENTAGE GAINS IN SALES FROM UNDETECTED PRICE-CUTTING BY A FIRM

Criterion I: $\dfrac{1}{(n_s - 1)}\left[\theta(1-p) + \sqrt{\dfrac{n_s(n_s-2)(1-p)(1+\theta)}{n_0}}\right]$ $\qquad \theta = \sqrt{\dfrac{p}{1-p}\dfrac{n_s}{n_0}}$

PROBABILITY OF REPEAT SALES (p)	No. OF BUYERS (n_0)	No. OF SELLERS					
		2	3	4	5	10	20
$p = 0.95$	20	6.9	11.3	11.3	11.4	11.8	12.7
	30	5.6	8.9	8.8	8.8	9.0	9.6
	40	4.9	7.5	7.4	7.4	7.5	7.9
	50	4.4	6.6	6.5	6.4	6.5	6.8
	100	3.1	4.4	4.3	4.3	4.2	4.4
	200	2.2	3.0	2.9	2.8	2.8	2.8
	400	1.5	2.1	2.0	1.9	1.8	1.8
$p = 0.90$	20	9.5	14.8	14.7	14.6	14.8	15.7
	30	7.8	11.7	11.5	11.4	11.4	12.0
	40	6.7	10.0	9.7	9.6	9.5	9.9
	50	6.0	8.8	8.6	8.4	8.3	8.6
	100	4.2	6.0	5.8	5.6	5.4	5.5
	200	3.0	4.1	3.9	3.8	3.6	3.6
	400	2.1	2.8	2.7	2.6	2.4	2.4
$p = 0.80$	20	12.6	19.3	18.9	18.7	18.6	19.4
	30	10.3	15.4	15.0	14.7	14.5	15.0
	40	8.9	13.1	12.7	12.5	12.2	12.5
	50	8.0	11.6	11.2	11.0	10.6	10.8
	100	5.7	8.0	7.7	7.4	7.1	7.1
	200	4.0	5.5	5.3	5.1	4.8	4.7
	400	2.8	3.8	3.6	3.5	3.2	3.2
$p = 0.70$	20	14.5	22.3	21.8	21.5	21.2	21.9
	30	11.8	17.8	17.3	17.0	16.6	16.9
	40	10.2	15.2	14.8	14.5	14.0	14.2
	50	9.2	13.5	13.1	12.8	12.3	12.4
	100	6.5	9.3	9.0	8.7	8.2	8.2
	200	4.6	6.5	6.2	6.0	5.6	5.5
	400	3.2	4.5	4.3	4.2	3.8	3.7

A THEORY OF OLIGOPOLY   51

The entries in Table 1 are measures of the maximum additional sales obtainable by secret price-cutting (expressed as a percentage of average sales) from any one rival beyond which that rival will infer that the price-cutting is taking place. Since the profitability of secret price-cutting depends upon the amount of business one can obtain (as well as upon the excess of price over marginal cost), we may also view these numbers as the measures of the incentive to engage in secret price-cutting. Three features of the tabulation are noteworthy:

a) The gain in sales from any one rival by secret price-cutting is not very sensitive to the number of rivals, given the number of customers and the probability of repeat sales. The aggregate gain in sales of a firm from price-cutting—its total incentive to secret price-cutting— is the sum of the gains from each rival, and therefore increases roughly in proportion to the number of rivals.

b) The incentive to secret price-cutting falls as the number of customers per seller increases—and falls roughly in inverse proportion to the square root of the number of buyers.

c) The incentive to secret price-cutting rises as the probability of repeat purchases falls, but at a decreasing rate.

We have said that the gain to old buyers from shifting their patronage among sellers will be that it encourages secret price-cutting by making it more difficult to detect. Table 1 indicates that there are diminishing returns to increased shifting: The entries increase at a decreasing rate as p falls. In a fuller model we could introduce the costs of shifting among suppliers and determine p to maximize expected buyer gains. The larger the purchases of a buyer, when buyers are of unequal size, however, the greater is the prospect that his shifts will induce price-cutting.

In addition it is clear that, when the number of sellers exceeds two, it is possible for two or more firms to pool information and thus to detect less extreme cases of price-cutting. For example, at the given probability levels, the number of old customers that any one rival should be able to take from a firm was shown to be at most

$$(1-p)\frac{n_0(1+\theta)}{n_s-1},$$

with variance

$$\frac{(n_s-2)(1-p)(1+\theta)}{(n_s-1)^2}\,n_0.$$

At the same probability level, the average number of old customers that one rival should be able to take from T firms is at most

$$\frac{T(1-p)n_0}{n_s-T}\left(1+\frac{\theta}{\sqrt{T}}\right),$$

with the variance

$$\frac{(n_s-T-1)}{(n_s-T)^2}(1-p)\left(1+\frac{\theta}{\sqrt{T}}\right)n_0T.$$

Each of these is smaller than the corresponding expression for one seller when expressed as a fraction of the customers lost by each of the firms pooling information.

There are of course limits to such pooling of information: not only does it become expensive as the number of firms increases, but also it produces less reliable information, since one of the members of the pool may himself be secretly cutting prices. Some numbers illustrative of the effect of pooling will be given at a later point.

2. *The attraction of old customers of other firms is a second source of evidence of price-cutting.*—If a given rival has not cut prices, he will on average lose $(1-p)$ (n_0/n_s) customers, with a variance of σ_1^2. The number of customers he will retain with secret price-cutting cannot exceed

a level at which the rivals suspect the price-cutting. Any one rival will have little basis for judging whether he is getting a fair share of this firm's old customers, but they can pool their information and then in the aggregate they will expect the firm to lose at least $(1 - p)$ $(n_0/n_s) - 2\sigma_1$ customers, at the 5 per cent probability level. Hence the secret price-cutter can retain at most $2\sigma_1$ of his old customers (beyond his average num-

TABLE 2

OLD CUSTOMERS THAT A SECRET PRICE-CUTTER CAN RETAIN, AS A PERCENTAGE OF AVERAGE SALES

$$\text{Criterion II: } 2\sqrt{\frac{p(1-p)}{2}\frac{n_s}{n_0}}$$

PROBABILITY THAT OLD CUSTOMER WILL REMAIN LOYAL (p)	No. of Old Customers per Seller (n_0/n_s)			
	10	20	50	100
0.95.......	13.8	9.7	6.2	4.4
.90.......	19.0	13.4	8.5	6.0
.85.......	22.6	16.0	10.1	7.1
.80.......	25.3	17.9	11.3	8.0
.75.......	27.4	19.4	12.2	8.7
.70.......	29.0	20.5	13.0	9.2
.65.......	30.2	21.3	13.5	9.5
.60.......	31.0	21.9	13.9	9.8
.55.......	31.5	22.2	14.1	10.0
0.50.......	31.6	22.4	14.1	10.0

ber), which as a fraction of his average sales (ignoring new customers) is

$$\frac{2\sigma_1}{n_0/n_s} = 2\sqrt{\frac{(1-p)pn_s}{n_0}}.$$

This is tabulated as Table 2.

If the entries in Table 2 are compared with those in Table 1,[10] it is found that a price-cutter is easier to detect by his gains at the expense of any one rival than by his unusual proportion of repeat sales. This second criterion will therefore seldom be useful.

3. *The behavior of new customers is a third source of information on price-cutting.*—There are n_n new customers per period,[11] equal to λn_0. A firm expects, in the absence of price-cutting, to sell to

$$m_3 = \frac{1}{n_s}\lambda n_0$$

of these customers, with a variance of

$$\sigma_3{}^2 = \left(1 - \frac{1}{n_s}\right)\frac{\lambda n_0}{n_s}.$$

If the rivals pool information (without pooling, this area could not be policed effectively), this firm cannot obtain more than $m_3 + 2\sigma_3$ customers without being deemed a price-cutter, using again a 5 per cent probability criterion. As a percentage of the firm's total sales, the maximum sales above the expected number in the absence of price cutting are then

$$\frac{2\sigma_3}{n_0(1+\lambda)/n_s} = \frac{2}{1+\lambda}\sqrt{\frac{(n_s-1)\lambda}{n_0}}.$$

We tabulate this criterion as Table 3.

Two aspects of the incentive to cut prices (or equivalently the difficulty of detecting price cuts) to new customers are apparent: the incentive increases rapidly with the number of sellers[12] and the

[10] For example, take $p = .95$. The entry for 10 customers per seller is 13.8 in Table 2—this is the maximum percentage of average sales that can be obtained by price reductions to old customers. The corresponding entries in Table 1 are 6.9 (2 sellers, 20 buyers), 8.9 (3 and 30), 7.4 (4 and 40), 6.4 (5 and 50), 4.2 (10 and 100), etc. Multiplying each entry in Table 1 by $(n_s - 1)$, we get the maximum gain in sales (without detection) by attracting customers of rivals, and beyond 2 sellers the gains are larger by this latter route. Since Table 1 is based upon a 10 per cent probability level, strict comparability requires that we use 1.6 σ, instead of 2 σ, in Table 2, which would reduce the entries by one-fifth.

[11] Unlike old customers, whose behavior is better studied in a round of transactions, the new customers are a flow whose magnitude depends much more crucially on the time period considered. The annual flow of new customers is here taken (relative to the number of old customers) as the unit.

[12] And slowly with the number of sellers if customers per seller are held constant.

A THEORY OF OLIGOPOLY   53

incentive increases with the rate of entry of new customers. As usual the incentive falls as the absolute number of customers per seller rises. If the rate of entry of new buyers is 10 per cent or more, price-cutting to new customers allows larger sales increases without detection that can be obtained by attracting customers of rivals (compare Tables 1 and 3).

Of the considerable number of directions in which this model could be enlarged, two will be presented briefly.

The first is inequality in the size of firms. In effect this complication has already been introduced by the equivalent device of pooling information. If we tabulate the effects of pooling of information by K firms, the results are equivalent to having a firm K times as large as the other firms. The number of old customers this large firm can lose to any one small rival (all of whom are equal in size) is given, in Table 4, as a percentage of the average number of old customers of the small firm; the column labeled $K = 1$ is of course the case analyzed in Table 1.

The effects of pooling on the detection of price-cutting are best analyzed by

TABLE 3

MAXIMUM ADDITIONAL NEW CUSTOMERS (AS A PERCENTAGE OF AVERAGE SALES) OBTAINABLE BY SECRET PRICE-CUTTING

$$Criterion\ III: \frac{2}{1+\lambda} \sqrt{\frac{\lambda(n_s-1)}{n_0}}$$

RATE OF APPEARANCE OF NEW BUYERS (λ)	No. OF OLD BUYERS (n_0)	No. OF SELLERS					
		2	3	4	5	10	20
1/100	20	4.4	6.3	7.7	8.9	13.3	19.3
	30	3.6	5.1	6.3	7.2	10.8	15.8
	40	3.1	4.4	5.4	6.3	9.4	13.6
	50	2.8	4.0	4.8	5.6	8.4	12.2
	100	2.0	2.8	3.4	4.0	5.9	8.6
	200	1.4	2.0	2.4	2.8	4.2	6.1
	400	1.0	1.4	1.7	2.0	3.0	4.3
1/10	20	12.9	18.2	22.3	25.7	38.6	56.0
	30	10.5	14.8	18.2	21.0	31.5	45.8
	40	9.1	12.9	15.8	18.2	27.3	39.6
	50	8.1	11.5	14.1	16.3	24.4	35.4
	100	5.8	8.1	10.0	11.5	17.2	25.1
	200	4.1	5.8	7.0	8.1	12.2	17.7
	400	2.9	4.1	5.0	5.8	8.6	12.5
1/5	20	16.7	23.6	28.9	33.3	50.0	72.6
	30	13.6	19.2	23.6	27.2	40.8	59.3
	40	11.8	16.7	20.4	23.6	35.4	51.4
	50	10.5	14.9	18.3	21.1	31.6	46.0
	100	7.4	10.5	12.9	14.9	22.4	32.5
	200	5.3	7.4	9.1	10.5	15.8	23.0
	400	3.7	5.3	6.4	7.4	11.2	16.2
1/4	20	17.9	25.3	31.0	35.8	53.7	78.0
	30	14.6	20.7	25.3	29.2	43.8	63.7
	40	12.6	17.9	21.9	25.3	38.0	55.1
	50	11.3	16.0	19.6	22.6	33.9	49.3
	100	8.0	11.3	13.9	16.0	24.0	34.9
	200	5.7	8.0	9.8	11.3	17.0	24.7
	400	4.0	5.7	6.9	8.0	12.0	17.4

comparing Table 4 with Table 1. If there are 100 customers and 10 firms (and $p = 0.9$), a single firm can increase sales by 5.4 per cent by poaching on one rival, or about 50 per cent against all rivals (Table 1). If 9 firms combine, the maximum amount the single firm can gain by secret price-cutting is 28.9 per cent (Table 4). With 20 firms and 200 customers, a single firm can gain 3.6 per cent from each rival, or about 30 per cent from 9

rivals; if these rivals merge, the corresponding figure falls to 14.0 per cent. The pooling of information therefore reduces substantially the scope for secret price-cutting.

This table exaggerates the effect of inequality of firm size because it fails to take account of the fact that the number of customers varies with firm size, on our argument that only customers above a certain size relative to the seller are a

TABLE 4

PERCENTAGE GAINS IN SALES FROM UNDETECTED PRICE-CUTTING BY A SMALL FIRM

Criterion IV:

$$\frac{1}{n_s - K}\left[\theta(1 - p)\sqrt{K} + \sqrt{\frac{n_s K(1-p)(n_s - K - 1)(1 + \theta/\sqrt{K})}{n_0}}\right]$$

$$\theta = \sqrt{\frac{p}{1-p}\frac{n_s}{n_0}}$$

PROBABILITY OF REPEAT SALES (p)	NO. OF FIRMS ($n_s - K + 1$)	BUYERS PER SMALL SELLER (n_0/n_s)	SIZE OF LARGE FIRM (K)			
			1	2	5	9
$p=0.9$	2	10	9.5	13.4	21.2	28.5
		30	5.5	7.7	12.2	16.4
		50	4.2	6.0	9.5	12.7
	3	10	11.7	15.8	23.9	31.4
		30	6.3	8.7	13.3	17.6
		50	4.8	6.6	10.2	13.5
	4	10	9.7	13.1	19.7	25.7
		30	5.2	7.1	10.9	14.4
		50	4.0	5.4	8.3	11.0
	10	10	5.4	7.2	10.7	14.0
		30	2.9	3.9	5.9	7.7
		50	2.2	2.9	4.5	5.9
$p=0.8$	2	10	12.6	17.9	28.3	37.9
		30	7.3	10.3	16.3	21.9
		50	5.7	8.0	12.6	17.0
	3	10	15.4	21.0	32.1	42.3
		30	8.4	11.6	18.0	23.9
		50	6.4	8.9	13.8	18.4
	4	10	12.7	17.3	26.3	34.7
		30	6.9	9.5	14.7	19.5
		50	5.3	7.3	11.3	15.0
	10	10	7.1	9.5	14.4	18.9
		30	3.8	5.2	8.0	10.6
		50	2.9	4.0	6.1	8.1

A THEORY OF OLIGOPOLY   55

feasible group for secret price-cutting. The small firm can find it attractive to cut prices to buyers which are not large enough to be potential customers by price-cutting for the large seller.

The temporal pattern of buyers' behavior provides another kind of information: What is possibly due to random fluctuation in the short run cannot with equal probability be due to chance if repeated. Thus the maximum expected loss of old customers to a rival in one round of transactions is (at the 1σ level)

$$\frac{n_0}{(n_s - 1)n_s}(1 - p)(1 + \theta),$$

but for T consecutive periods the maximum expected loss is (over T periods)

$$\frac{T}{n_s - 1}(1 - p)\frac{n_0}{n_s}[1 + \theta\sqrt{T}],$$

with a variance of

$$\sigma_b^2 = \frac{(n_s - 2)}{(n_s - 1)^2}T(1 - p)\frac{n_0}{n_s}[1 + \theta\sqrt{T}].$$

This source of information is of minor efficacy in detecting price-cutting unless the rounds of successive transactions are numerous—that is, unless buyers purchase (enter contracts) frequently.

Our approach has certain implications for the measurement of concentration, if we wish concentration to measure likelihood of effective collusion. In the case of new customers, for example, let the probability of attracting a customer be proportional to the firm's share of industry output (s). Then the variance of the firm's share of sales to new customers will be $n_n s(1 - s)$, and the aggregate for the industry will be

$$C = n_n \sum_1^r s(1 - s)$$

for r firms. This expression equals $n_n (1 - H)$, where

$$H = \Sigma s^2$$

is the Herfindahl index of concentration. The same index holds, as an approximation, for potential price-cutting to attract old customers.[13]

The foregoing analysis can be extended to non-price variables, subject to two modifications. The first modification is that there be a definite joint profit-maximizing policy upon which the rivals can agree. Here we may expect to encounter a spectrum of possibilities, ranging from a clearly defined optimum policy (say, on favorable legislation) to a nebulous set of alternatives (say, directions of research).[14] Collusion is less feasible, the less clear the basis on which it should proceed. The second modification is that

[13] A similar argument leads to a measure of concentration appropriate to potential price-cutting for old customers. Firm i will lose

$$(1 - p)n_0 s_i$$

old customers, and firm j will gain

$$(1 - p)n_0\frac{s_i s_j}{1 - s_i}$$

of them, with a variance

$$(1 - p)n_0\frac{s_i s_j}{1 - s_i}\left(1 - \frac{s_j}{1 - s_i}\right).$$

If we sum over all i ($\neq j$), we obtain the variance of firm j's sales to old customers of rivals

$$(1 - p)n_0 s_j(1 + H - 2s_j),$$

to an approximation, and summing over all j, we have the concentration measure,

$$(1 - p)n_0(1 - H).$$

The agreement of this measure with that for new customers is superficial: that for new customers implicitly assumes pooling of information and that for old customers does not.

[14] Of course, price itself usually falls somewhere in this range rather than at the pole. The traditional assumption of stationary conditions conceals this fact.

the competitive moves of any one firm will differ widely among non-price variables in their detectability by rivals. Some forms of non-price competition will be easier to detect than price-cutting because they leave visible traces (advertising, product quality, servicing, etc.) but some variants will be elusive (reciprocity in purchasing, patent licensing arrangements). The common belief that non-price competition is more common than

TABLE 5

RESIDUALS FROM REGRESSION OF ADVERTISING RATES ON CIRCULATION*

No. of Evening Papers	n	Mean Residual (Logarithm)	Standard Deviation of Mean
One..................	23	0.0211	0.0210
With morning paper.	10	− .0174	.0324
Without morning paper.............	13	.0507	.0233
Two.................	30	−0.0213	0.0135

* The regression equation is

$$\log R = 5.194 - 1.688 \log c + .139 (\log c)^2 ,$$
$$\quad\quad (.620) \quad\quad (.063)$$

where R is the 5 M milline rate and c is circulation.

Source: American Association of Advertising Agencies, *Market and Newspaper Statistics*, Vol. VIIIa (1939).

price competition is therefore not wholly in keeping with the present theory. Those forms that are suitable areas for collusion will have less competition; those which are not suitable will have more competition.

IV. SOME FRAGMENTS OF EVIDENCE

Before we seek empirical evidence on our theory, it is useful to report two investigations of the influence of numbers of sellers on price. These investigations have an intrinsic interest because, so far as I know, no systematic analysis of the effect of numbers has hitherto been made.

The first investigation was of newspaper advertising rates, as a function of the number of evening newspapers in a city. Advertising rates on a milline basis are closely (and negatively) related to circulation, so a regression of rates on circulation was made for fifty-three cities in 1939. The residuals (in logarithmic form) from this regression equation are tabulated in Table 5. It will be observed that rates are 5 per cent above the average in one-newspaper towns and 5 per cent below the average in two-newspaper towns, and the towns with one evening paper but also an independent morning paper fall nearly midway between these points. Unfortunately there were too few cities with more than two evening newspapers to yield results for larger numbers of firms.

The second investigation is of spot commercial rates on AM radio stations in the four states of Ohio, Indiana, Michigan, and Illinois. The basic equation introduces, along with number of rivals, a series of other factors (power of station, population of the county in which the station is located, etc.). Unfortunately the number of stations is rather closely correlated with population ($r^2 = .796$ in the logarithms). The general result, shown in Table 6, is similar to that for newspapers: the elasticity of price with respect to number of rivals is quite small ($-.07$). Here the range of stations in a county was from 1 to 13.

Both studies suggest that the level of prices is not very responsive to the actual number of rivals. This is in keeping with the expectations based upon our model, for that model argues that the number of buyers, the proportion of new buyers, and the relative sizes of firms are as important as the number of rivals.

To turn to the present theory, the only test covering numerous industries so far

A THEORY OF OLIGOPOLY 57

devised has been one based upon profitability. This necessarily rests upon company data, and it has led to the exclusion of a large number of industries for which the companies do not operate in a well-defined industry. For example, the larger steel and chemical firms operate in a series of markets in which their position ranges from monopolistic to competitive. We have required of each industry that the earnings of a substantial fraction of the companies in the industry (measured by output) be determined by the profit-

given in Table 8. The various concentration measures, on the one hand, and the various measures of profitability, on the other hand, are tolerably well correlated.[15] All show the expected positive relationship. In general the data suggest that there is no relationship between profitability and concentration if H is less than 0.250 or the share of the four largest firms is less than about 80 per cent. These data, like those on advertising rates, confirm our theory only in the sense that they support theories which

TABLE 6

REGRESSION OF AM SPOT COMMERCIAL RATES (26 TIMES)
AND STATION CHARACTERISTICS, 1961

$(n = 345)$

Independent Variables*	Regression Coefficient	Standard Error
1. Logarithm of population of county, 1960..........	.238	0.026
2. Logarithm of kilowatt power of station...........	.206	.015
3. Dummy variables of period of broadcasting:		
a) Sunrise to sunset.........................	−.114	.025
b) More than (*a*), less than 18 hours.............	−.086	.027
c) 18–21 hours..............................	−.053	.028
4. Logarithm of number of stations in county........	−.074	0.046
	$R^2 = .743$	

* Dependent variable: logarithm of average rate, May 1, 1961 (dollars).

Source: "Spot Radio Rates and Data," *Standard Rate and Data Service, Inc.*, Vol. XLIII, No. 5 (May 1961).

ability of that industry's products, that is, that we have a fair share of the industry and the industry's product is the dominant product of the firms.

Three measures of profitability are given in Table 7: (1) the rate of return on all capital (including debt), (2) the rate of return on net worth (stockholders' equity); (3) the ratio of market value to book value of the common stock.

In addition, two measures of concentration are presented: (1) the conventional measure, the share of output produced by the four leading firms; and (2) the Herfindahl index, H.

The various rank correlations are

assert that competition increases with number of firms.

Our last evidence is a study of the prices paid by buyers of steel products in 1939, measured relative to the quoted prices (Table 9). The figure of 8.3 for hot-

[15] The concentration measures have a rank correlation of .903. The profitability measures have the following rank correlations:

	Return on All Assets	Ratio of Market to Book Value
Return on net worth......	.866	.872
Ratio of market to book value.................	.733	....

TABLE 7

PROFITABILITY AND CONCENTRATION DATA

INDUSTRY*	CONCENTRATION (1954)		AVERAGE RATE OF RETURN (1953–57)		RATIO OF MARKET VALUE TO BOOK VALUE (1953–57)
	Share of Top 4	H†	All Assets	Net Worth	
Sulfur mining (4)...................	98	0.407	19.03	23.85	3.02
Automobiles (3)......................	98	.369	11.71	20.26	2.30
Flat glass (3)........................	90	.296	11.79	16.17	2.22
Gypsum products (2).................	90	.280	12.16	20.26	1.83
Primary aluminum (4)...............	98	.277	6.87	13.46	2.48
Metal cans (4).......................	80	.260	7.27	13.90	1.60
Chewing gum (2).....................	86	.254	13.50	17.06	2.46
Hard-surface floor coverings (3)........	87	.233	6.56	7.59	0.98
Cigarettes (5)........................	83	.213	7.23	11.18	1.29
Industrial gases (3)..................	84	.202	8.25	11.53	1.33
Corn wet milling (3).................	75	.201	9.17	11.55	1.48
Typewriters (3)......................	83	.198	3.55	5.39	0.84
Domestic laundry equipment (2).......	68	.174	9.97	17.76	1.66
Rubber tires (9).....................	79	.171	7.86	14.02	1.70
Rayon fiber (4)......................	76	.169	5.64	6.62	0.84
Carbon black (2).....................	73	.152	8.29	9.97	1.40
Distilled liquors (6).................	64	0.118	6.94	7.55	0.77

* The number of firms is given in parentheses after the industry title. Only those industries are included for which a substantial share (35 per cent or more) of the industry's sales is accounted for by the firms in the sample, and these firms derive their chief revenues (50 per cent or more) from the industry in question.

† H is Herfindahl index.

TABLE 8

RANK CORRELATIONS OF MEASURES OF PROFITABILITY AND MEASURES OF CONCENTRATION

MEASURE OF CONCENTRATION	MEASURE OF PROFITABILITY		
	Rate of Return on All Assets	Rate of Return on Net Worth	Ratio of Market Value to Book Value
Share of output produced by four largest firms........	.322	.507	.642
Herfindahl index (H).......	.524	.692	.730

TABLE 9

PRICES OF STEEL PRODUCTS, 1939, AND INDUSTRY STRUCTURE, 1938

PRODUCT CLASS	PRICES, 2D QUARTER, 1939 (PER CENT)		HERFINDAHL INDEX	OUTPUT IN 1939 RELATIVE TO 1937
	Average Discount from List Price	Standard Deviation		
Hot-rolled sheets........	8.3	7.3	0.0902	1.14
Merchant bars..........	1.2	4.5	.1517	0.84
Hot-rolled strip.........	8.5	8.3	.1069	0.56
Plates.................	2.6	4.8	.1740	0.85
Structural shapes........	3.2	4.3	.3280	0.92
Cold-rolled strip.........	8.8	9.8	.0549	0.88
Cold-rolled sheets.......	5.8	5.0	.0963	1.14
Cold-finished bars.......	0.9	3.4	0.0964	0.83

Source: Prices: "Labor Department Examines Consumers' Prices of Steel Products," *Iron Age*, April 25, 1946; industry structure: 1938 capacity data from *Directory of Iron and Steel Works of the United States and Canada;* output: *Annual Statistical Report, American Iron and Steel Institute* (New York, 1938, 1942).

A THEORY OF OLIGOPOLY   59

rolled sheets, for example, represents an average of 8.3 per cent reduction from quoted prices, *paid by buyers*, with a standard deviation of 7.3 per cent of quoted prices. The rate of price-cutting is almost perfectly correlated with the standard deviation of transaction prices, as we should expect: the less perfect the market knowledge, the more extensive the price-cutting.

In general, the more concentrated the industry structure (measured by the Herfindahl index), the larger were the price reductions. Although there were no extreme departures from this relationship, structural shapes and hot-rolled strip had prices somewhat lower than the average relationship, and cold finished bars prices somewhat higher than expected, and the deviations are not accounted for by the level of demand (measured by 1939 sales relative to 1937 sales). The number of buyers could not be taken into account, but the BLS study states:

The extent of price concessions shown by this study is probably understated because certain very large consumers in the automobile and container industries were excluded from the survey. This omission was at the request of the OPA which contemplated obtaining this information in connection with other studies. Since a small percentage of steel consumers, including these

companies, accounts for a large percentage of steel purchased, prices paid by a relatively few large consumers have an important influence upon the entire steel price structure. Very large steel consumers get greater reductions from published prices than smaller consumers, often the result of competitive bidding by the mills for the large volume of steel involved. One very large steel consumer, a firm that purchased over 2 pct of the total consumption of hot and cold-rolled sheets in 1940, refused to give purchase prices. This firm wished to protect its suppliers, fearing that "certain transactions might be revealed which would break confidence" with the steel mills. However, this company did furnish percent changes of prices paid for several steel products which showed that for some products prices advanced markedly, and in one case, nearly 50 pct. The great price advances for this company indicate that it was receiving much larger concessions than smaller buyers.[16]

These various bits of evidence are fairly favorable to the theory, but they do not constitute strong support. More powerful tests will be feasible when the electrical equipment triple-damage suits are tried.[17] The great merit of our theory, in fact, is that it has numerous testable hypotheses, unlike the immortal theories that have been traditional in this area.

[16] See "Labor Department Examines Consumers' Prices of Steel Products," *op. cit.*, p. 133.

[17] For example, it will be possible to test the prediction that prices will be higher and less dispersed in sales on public bids than in privately negotiated sales, and the prediction that price-cutting increases as the number of buyers diminishes.

APPENDIX

The importance of product heterogeneity for profit-maximizing behavior cannot well be established by an a priori argument. Nevertheless, the following simple exposition of the implications for profitability of disregarding heterogeneity may have some heuristic value. The analysis, it will be observed, is formally equivalent to that of the effects of an excise tax on a monopolist.

Assume that a monopolist makes men's suits, and that he makes only one size of suit. This is absurd behavior, but the picture of the

sadistic monopolist who disregards consumer desires has often made fugitive appearances in the literature so the problem has some interest of its own. The demand curve of a consumer for suits that fit, $f(p)$, would now be reduced because he would have to incur some alteration cost a in order to wear the suit. His effective demand would therefore decline to $f(p + a)$. Assume further that the marginal cost of suits is constant (m), and that it would be the same if the monopolist were to make suits of various sizes.

60   GEORGE J. STIGLER

The effect on profits of a uniform product—uniform is an especially appropriate word here—can be shown graphically (Fig. 1). The decrease in quantity sold, with a linear demand curve, is

$$MB = \tfrac{1}{2} a f'(p) \ .$$

The decrease in the price received by the monopolist is

$$DN = \frac{MB}{f'(p)} - a = -\frac{a}{2},$$

so if π is profit per unit, and q is output, the relative decline in total profit is approximately

$$\frac{\Delta \pi}{\pi} + \frac{\Delta q}{q},$$

or

$$\frac{MB}{OB} + \frac{ND}{AD}.$$

Since

$$OB = \frac{f(m)}{2}$$

$$AD = -\frac{p}{\eta},$$

where η is the elasticity of demand, the relative decline of profits with a uniform product is

$$\frac{a f'(p)}{f(m)} + \frac{a\eta}{2p} = \frac{a\eta}{2p} + \frac{a\eta}{2p}$$

$$= \frac{a\eta}{p}.$$

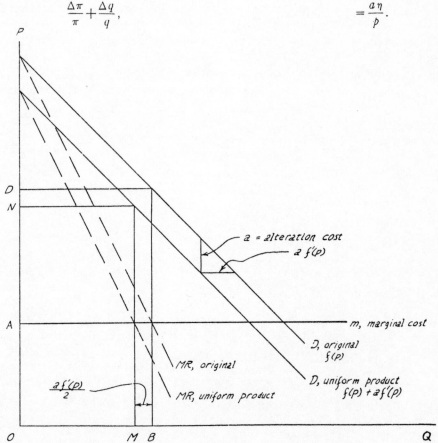

SIMPLE MONOPOLY
Price = OD
Quantity = OB
Profits = OB × AD

UNIFORM PRODUCT MONOPOLY
Price = ON
Quantity = OM
Profits = OM × AN

Fig. 1

The loss from imposed uniformity is therefore proportional to the ratio of alteration costs to price.

Our example is sufficiently unrealistic to make any quantitative estimate uninteresting. In general one would expect an upper limit to the ratio a/p, because it becomes cheaper to resort to other goods (custom tailoring in our example), or to abandon the attempt to find appropriate goods. The loss of profits of the monopolist will be proportional to the aver

age value of a/p, and this will be smaller, the smaller the variation in buyers' circumstances.

Still, monopolists are lucky if their long-run demand curves have an elasticity only as large as -5, and then even a ratio of a to p of $1/40$ will reduce their profits by 12 per cent. The general conclusion I wish to draw is that a monopolist who does not cater to the diversities of his buyers' desires will suffer a substantial decline in his profits.

[6]

THE AMERICAN ECONOMIC REVIEW

VOLUME LIII   DECEMBER 1963   NUMBER 5

UNCERTAINTY AND THE WELFARE
ECONOMICS OF MEDICAL CARE

By KENNETH J. ARROW*

I. *Introduction: Scope and Method*

This paper is an exploratory and tentative study of the specific differentia of medical care as the object of normative economics. It is contended here, on the basis of comparison of obvious characteristics of the medical-care industry with the norms of welfare economics, that the special economic problems of medical care can be explained as adaptations to the existence of uncertainty in the incidence of disease and in the efficacy of treatment.

It should be noted that the subject is the *medical-care industry,* not *health.* The causal factors in health are many, and the provision of medical care is only one. Particularly at low levels of income, other commodities such as nutrition, shelter, clothing, and sanitation may be much more significant. It is the complex of services that center about the physician, private and group practice, hospitals, and public health, which I propose to discuss.

The focus of discussion will be on the way the operation of the medical-care industry and the efficacy with which it satisfies the needs of society differ from a norm, if at all. The "norm" that the economist usually uses for the purposes of such comparisons is the operation of a competitive model, that is, the flows of services that would be

* The author is professor of economics at Stanford University. He wishes to express his thanks for useful comments to F. Bator, R. Dorfman, V. Fuchs, Dr. S. Gilson, R. Kessel, S. Mushkin, and C. R. Rorem. This paper was prepared under the sponsorship of the Ford Foundation as part of a series of papers on the economics of health, education, and welfare.

offered and purchased and the prices that would be paid for them if
each individual in the market offered or purchased services at the going
prices as if his decisions had no influence over them, and the going
prices were such that the amounts of services which were available
equalled the total amounts which other individuals were willing to
purchase, with no imposed restrictions on supply or demand.

The interest in the competitive model stems partly from its presumed descriptive power and partly from its implications for economic
efficiency. In particular, we can state the following well-known proposition (First Optimality Theorem). If a competitive equilibrium
exists at all, and if all commodities relevant to costs or utilities are in
fact priced in the market, then the equilibrium is necessarily *optimal*
in the following precise sense (due to V. Pareto): There is no other
allocation of resources to services which will make all participants in
the market better off.

Both the conditions of this optimality theorem and the definition of
optimality call for comment. A definition is just a definition, but when
the *definiendum* is a word already in common use with highly favorable connotations, it is clear that we are really trying to be persuasive;
we are implicitly recommending the achievement of optimal states.[1] It
is reasonable enough to assert that a change in allocation which makes
all participants better off is one that certainly should be made; this is
a value judgment, not a descriptive proposition, but it is a very weak
one. From this it follows that it is not desirable to put up with a nonoptimal allocation. But it does not follow that if we are at an allocation which is optimal in the Pareto sense, we should not change to any
other. We cannot indeed make a change that does not hurt someone;
but we can still desire to change to another allocation if the change
makes enough participants better off and by so much that we feel that
the injury to others is not enough to offset the benefits. Such inter-
personal comparisons are, of course, value judgments. The change,
however, by the previous argument ought to be an optimal state; of
course there are many possible states, each of which is optimal in the
sense here used.

However, a value judgment on the desirability of each possible new
distribution of benefits and costs corresponding to each possible reallocation of resources is not, in general, necessary. Judgments about
the distribution can be made separately, in one sense, from those about
allocation if certain conditions are fulfilled. Before stating the relevant
proposition, it is necessary to remark that the competitive equilibrium
achieved depends in good measure on the initial distribution of purchasing power, which consists of ownership of assets and skills that

[1] This point has been stressed by I. M. D. Little [19, pp. 71-74]. For the concept of a
"persuasive definition," see C. L. Stevenson [27, pp. 210-17].

command a price on the market. A transfer of assets among individuals will, in general, change the final supplies of goods and services and the prices paid for them. Thus, a transfer of purchasing power from the well to the ill will increase the demand for medical services. This will manifest itself in the short run in an increase in the price of medical services and in the long run in an increase in the amount supplied.

With this in mind, the following statement can be made (Second Optimality Theorem): If there are no increasing returns in production, and if certain other minor conditions are satisfied, then every optimal state is a competitive equilibrium corresponding to some initial distribution of purchasing power. Operationally, the significance of this proposition is that if the conditions of the two optimality theorems are satisfied, and if the allocation mechanism in the real world satisfies the conditions for a competitive model, then social policy can confine itself to steps taken to alter the distribution of purchasing power. For any given distribution of purchasing power, the market will, under the assumptions made, achieve a competitive equilibrium which is necessarily optimal; and any optimal state is a competitive equilibrium corresponding to some distribution of purchasing power, so that any desired optimal state can be achieved.

The redistribution of purchasing power among individuals most simply takes the form of money: taxes and subsidies. The implications of such a transfer for individual satisfactions are, in general, not known in advance. But we can assume that society can *ex post* judge the distribution of satisfactions and, if deemed unsatisfactory, take steps to correct it by subsequent transfers. Thus, by successive approximations, a most preferred social state can be achieved, with resource allocation being handled by the market and public policy confined to the redistribution of money income.[2]

If, on the contrary, the actual market differs significantly from the competitive model, or if the assumptions of the two optimality theorems are not fulfilled, the separation of allocative and distributional procedures becomes, in most cases, impossible.[3]

The first step then in the analysis of the medical-care market is the

[2] The separation between allocation and distribution even under the above assumptions has glossed over problems in the execution of any desired redistribution policy; in practice, it is virtually impossible to find a set of taxes and subsidies that will not have an adverse effect on the achievement of an optimal state. But this discussion would take us even further afield than we have already gone.

[3] The basic theorems of welfare economics alluded to so briefly above have been the subject of voluminous literature, but no thoroughly satisfactory statement covering both the theorems themselves and the significance of exceptions to them exists. The positive assertions of welfare economics and their relation to the theory of competitive equilibrium are admirably covered in Koopmans [18]. The best summary of the various ways in which the theorems can fail to hold is probably Bator's [6].

comparison between the actual market and the competitive model. The methodology of this comparison has been a recurrent subject of controversy in economics for over a century. Recently, M. Friedman [15] has vigorously argued that the competitive or any other model should be tested solely by its ability to predict. In the context of competition, he comes close to arguing that prices and quantities are the only relevant data. This point of view is valuable in stressing that a certain amount of lack of realism in the assumptions of a model is no argument against its value. But the price-quantity implications of the competitive model for pricing are not easy to derive without major—and, in many cases, impossible—econometric efforts.

In this paper, the institutional organization and the observable mores of the medical profession are included among the data to be used in assessing the competitiveness of the medical-care market. I shall also examine the presence or absence of the preconditions for the equivalence of competitive equilibria and optimal states. The major competitive preconditions, in the sense used here, are three: the *existence* of competitive equilibrium, the *marketability* of all goods and services relevant to costs and utilities, and *nonincreasing returns*. The first two, as we have seen, insure that competitive equilibrium is necessarily optimal; the third insures that every optimal state is the competitive equilibrium corresponding to some distribution of income.[4] The first and third conditions are interrelated; indeed, nonincreasing returns plus some additional conditions not restrictive in a modern economy imply the existence of a competitive equilibrium, i.e., imply that there will be some set of prices which will clear all markets.[5]

The concept of marketability is somewhat broader than the traditional divergence between private and social costs and benefits. The latter concept refers to cases in which the organization of the market does not require an individual to pay for costs that he imposes on others as the result of his actions or does not permit him to receive compensation for benefits he confers. In the medical field, the obvious example is the spread of communicable diseases. An individual who fails to be immunized not only risks his own health, a disutility which presumably he has weighed against the utility of avoiding the procedure, but also that of others. In an ideal price system, there would be a price which he would have to pay to anyone whose health is endangered, a price sufficiently high so that the others would feel compensated; or, alternatively, there would be a price which would be paid to him by others to induce him to undergo the immunization procedure.

---

[4] There are further minor conditions, for which see Koopmans [18, pp. 50-55].

[5] For a more precise statement of the existence conditions, see Koopmans [18, pp. 56-60] or Debreu [12, Ch. 5].

Either system would lead to an optimal state, though the distributional implications would be different. It is, of course, not hard to see that such price systems could not, in fact, be practical; to approximate an optimal state it would be necessary to have collective intervention in the form of subsidy or tax or compulsion.

By the absence of marketability for an action which is identifiable, technologically possible, and capable of influencing some individual's welfare, for better or for worse, is meant here the failure of the existing market to provide a means whereby the services can be both offered and demanded upon payment of a price. Nonmarketability may be due to intrinsic technological characteristics of the product which prevent a suitable price from being enforced, as in the case of communicable diseases, or it may be due to social or historical controls, such as those prohibiting an individual from selling himself into slavery. This distinction is, in fact, difficult to make precise, though it is obviously of importance for policy; for the present purposes, it will be sufficient to identify nonmarketability with the observed absence of markets.

The instance of nonmarketability with which we shall be most concerned is that of risk-bearing. The relevance of risk-bearing to medical care seems obvious; illness is to a considerable extent an unpredictable phenomenon. The ability to shift the risks of illness to others is worth a price which many are willing to pay. Because of pooling and of superior willingness and ability, others are willing to bear the risks. Nevertheless, as we shall see in greater detail, a great many risks are not covered, and indeed the markets for the services of risk-coverage are poorly developed or nonexistent. Why this should be so is explained in more detail in Section IV.C below; briefly, it is impossible to draw up insurance policies which will sufficiently distinguish among risks, particularly since observation of the results will be incapable of distinguishing between avoidable and unavoidable risks, so that incentives to avoid losses are diluted.

The optimality theorems discussed above are usually presented in the literature as referring only to conditions of certainty, but there is no difficulty in extending them to the case of risks, provided the additional services of risk-bearing are included with other commodities.[6]

However, the variety of possible risks in the world is really staggering. The relevant commodities include, in effect, bets on all possible occurrences in the world which impinge upon utilities. In fact, many of these "commodities," i.e., desired protection against many risks, are

---

[6] The theory, in variant forms, seems to have been first worked out by Allais [2], Arrow [5], and Baudier [7]. For further generalization, see Debreu [11] and [12, Ch. 7].

simply not available. Thus, a wide class of commodities is nonmarket-able, and a basic competitive precondition is not satisfied.[7]

There is a still more subtle consequence of the introduction of risk-bearing considerations. When there is uncertainty, information or knowledge becomes a commodity. Like other commodities, it has a cost of production and a cost of transmission, and so it is naturally not spread out over the entire population but concentrated among those who can profit most from it. (These costs may be measured in time or disutility as well as money.) But the demand for information is diffi-cult to discuss in the rational terms usually employed. The value of information is frequently not known in any meaningful sense to the buyer; if, indeed, he knew enough to measure the value of informa-tion, he would know the information itself. But information, in the form of skilled care, is precisely what is being bought from most physi-cians, and, indeed, from most professionals. The elusive character of information as a commodity suggests that it departs considerably from the usual marketability assumptions about commodities.[8]

That risk and uncertainty are, in fact, significant elements in medi-cal care hardly needs argument. I will hold that virtually all the special features of this industry, in fact, stem from the prevalence of uncer-tainty.

The nonexistence of markets for the bearing of some risks in the first instance reduces welfare for those who wish to transfer those risks to others for a certain price, as well as for those who would find it profit-able to take on the risk at such prices. But it also reduces the desire to render or consume services which have risky consequences; in techni-cal language, these commodities are complementary to risk-bearing. Conversely, the production and consumption of commodities and serv-ices with little risk attached act as substitutes for risk-bearing and are encouraged by market failure there with respect to risk-bearing. Thus the observed commodity pattern will be affected by the nonexistence of other markets.

---

[7] It should also be remarked that in the presence of uncertainty, indivisibilities that are sufficiently small to create little difficulty for the existence and viability of competitive equilibrium may nevertheless give rise to a considerable range of increasing returns be-cause of the operation of the law of large numbers. Since most objects of insurance (lives, fire hazards, etc.) have some element of indivisibility, insurance companies have to be above a certain size. But it is not clear that this effect is sufficiently great to create serious obstacles to the existence and viability of competitive equilibrium in practice.

[8] One form of production of information is research. Not only does the product have unconventional aspects as a commodity, but it is also subject to increasing returns in use, since new ideas, once developed, can be used over and over without being consumed, and to difficulties of market control, since the cost of reproduction is usually much less than that of production. Hence, it is not surprising that a free enterprise economy will tend to underinvest in research; see Nelson [21] and Arrow [4].

The failure of one or more of the competitive preconditions has as its most immediate and obvious consequence a reduction in welfare below that obtainable from existing resources and technology, in the sense of a failure to reach an optimal state in the sense of Pareto. But more can be said. I propose here the view that, when the market fails to achieve an optimal state, society will, to some extent at least, recognize the gap, and nonmarket social institutions will arise attempting to bridge it.[9] Certainly this process is not necessarily conscious; nor is it uniformly successful in approaching more closely to optimality when the entire range of consequences is considered. It has always been a favorite activity of economists to point out that actions which on their face achieve a desirable goal may have less obvious consequences, particularly over time, which more than offset the original gains.

But it is contended here that the special structural characteristics of the medical-care market are largely attempts to overcome the lack of optimality due to the nonmarketability of the bearing of suitable risks and the imperfect marketability of information. These compensatory institutional changes, with some reinforcement from usual profit motives, largely explain the observed noncompetitive behavior of the medical-care market, behavior which, in itself, interferes with optimality. The social adjustment towards optimality thus puts obstacles in its own path.

The doctrine that society will seek to achieve optimality by nonmarket means if it cannot achieve them in the market is not novel. Certainly, the government, at least in its economic activities, is usually implicitly or explicitly held to function as the agency which substitutes for the market's failure.[10] I am arguing here that in some circumstances other social institutions will step into the optimality gap, and that the medical-care industry, with its variety of special institutions, some ancient, some modern, exemplifies this tendency.

It may be useful to remark here that a good part of the preference for redistribution expressed in government taxation and expenditure policies and private charity can be reinterpreted as desire for insurance. It is noteworthy that virtually nowhere is there a system of subsidies that has as its aim simply an equalization of income. The subsidies or other governmental help go to those who are disadvantaged in life by events the incidence of which is popularly regarded as unpre-

[9] An important current situation in which normal market relations have had to be greatly modified in the presence of great risks is the production and procurement of modern weapons; see Peck and Scherer [23, pp. 581-82] (I am indebted for this reference to V. Fuchs) and [1, pp. 71-75].

[10] For an explicit statement of this view, see Baumol [8]. But I believe this position is implicit in most discussions of the functions of government.

dictable: the blind, dependent children, the medically indigent. Thus, optimality, in a context which includes risk-bearing, includes much that appears to be motivated by distributional value judgments when looked at in a narrower context.[11]

This methodological background gives rise to the following plan for this paper. Section II is a catalogue of stylized generalizations about the medical-care market which differentiate it from the usual commodity markets. In Section III the behavior of the market is compared with that of the competitive model which disregards the fact of uncertainty. In Section IV, the medical-care market is compared, both as to behavior and as to preconditions, with the ideal competitive market that takes account of uncertainty; an attempt will be made to demonstrate that the characteristics outlined in Section II can be explained either as the result of deviations from the competitive preconditions or as attempts to compensate by other institutions for these failures. The discussion is not designed to be definitive, but provocative. In particular, I have been chary about drawing policy inferences; to a considerable extent, they depend on further research, for which the present paper is intended to provide a framework.

II. *A Survey of the Special Characteristics of the Medical-Care Market*[12]

This section will list selectively some characteristics of medical care which distinguish it from the usual commodity of economics textbooks. The list is not exhaustive, and it is not claimed that the characteristics listed are individually unique to this market. But, taken together, they do establish a special place for medical care in economic analysis.

A. *The Nature of Demand*

The most obvious distinguishing characteristics of an individual's demand for medical services is that it is not steady in origin as, for example, for food or clothing, but irregular and unpredictable. Medical services, apart from preventive services, afford satisfaction only in the event of illness, a departure from the normal state of affairs. It is hard, indeed, to think of another commodity of significance in the average budget of which this is true. A portion of legal services, devoted to defense in criminal trials or to lawsuits, might fall in this category but the incidence is surely very much lower (and, of course, there

---

[11] Since writing the above, I find that Buchanan and Tullock [10, Ch. 13] have argued that all redistribution can be interpreted as "income insurance."

[12] For an illuminating survey to which I am much indebted, see S. Mushkin [20].

are, in fact, strong institutional similarities between the legal and medical-care markets.)[13]

In addition, the demand for medical services is associated, with a considerable probability, with an assault on personal integrity. There is some risk of death and a more considerable risk of impairment of full functioning. In particular, there is a major potential for loss or reduction of earning ability. The risks are not by themselves unique; food is also a necessity, but avoidance of deprivation of food can be guaranteed with sufficient income, where the same cannot be said of avoidance of illness. Illness is, thus, not only risky but a costly risk in itself, apart from the cost of medical care.

B. *Expected Behavior of the Physician*

It is clear from everyday observation that the behavior expected of sellers of medical care is different from that of business men in general. These expectations are relevant because medical care belongs to the category of commodities for which the product and the activity of production are identical. In all such cases, the customer cannot test the product before consuming it, and there is an element of trust in the relation.[14] But the ethically understood restrictions on the activities of a physician are much more severe than on those of, say, a barber. His behavior is supposed to be governed by a concern for the customer's welfare which would not be expected of a salesman. In Talcott Parsons's terms, there is a "collectivity-orientation," which distinguishes medicine and other professions from business, where self-interest on the part of participants is the accepted norm.[15]

A few illustrations will indicate the degree of difference between the behavior expected of physicians and that expected of the typical businessman.[16] (1) Advertising and overt price competition are virtually eliminated among physicians. (2) Advice given by physicians as to further treatment by himself or others is supposed to be completely

[13] In governmental demand, military power is an example of a service used only irregularly and unpredictably. Here too, special institutional and professional relations have emerged, though the precise social structure is different for reasons that are not hard to analyze.

[14] Even with material commodities, testing is never so adequate that all elements of implicit trust can be eliminated. Of course, over the long run, experience with the quality of product of a given seller provides a check on the possibility of trust.

[15] See [22, p. 463]. The whole of [22, Ch. 10] is a most illuminating analysis of the social role of medical practice; though Parsons' interest lies in different areas from mine, I must acknowledge here my indebtedness to his work.

[16] I am indebted to Herbert Klarman of Johns Hopkins University for some of the points discussed in this and the following paragraph.

divorced from self-interest. (3) It is at least claimed that treatment is dictated by the objective needs of the case and not limited by financial considerations.[17] While the ethical compulsion is surely not as absolute in fact as it is in theory, we can hardly suppose that it has no influence over resource allocation in this area. Charity treatment in one form or another does exist because of this tradition about human rights to adequate medical care.[18] (4) The physician is relied on as an expert in certifying to the existence of illnesses and injuries for various legal and other purposes. It is socially expected that his concern for the correct conveying of information will, when appropriate, outweigh his desire to please his customers.[19]

Departure from the profit motive is strikingly manifested by the overwhelming predominance of nonprofit over proprietary hospitals.[20] The hospital per se offers services not too different from those of a hotel, and it is certainly not obvious that the profit motive will not lead to a more efficient supply. The explanation may lie either on the supply side or on that of demand. The simplest explanation is that public and private subsidies decrease the cost to the patient in nonprofit hospitals. A second possibility is that the association of profit-making with the supply of medical services arouses suspicion and antagonism on the part of patients and referring physicians, so they do prefer nonprofit institutions. Either explanation implies a preference on the part of some group, whether donors or patients, against the profit motive in the supply of hospital services.[21]

[17] The belief that the ethics of medicine demands treatment independent of the patient's ability to pay is strongly ingrained. Such a perceptive observer as René Dubos has made the remark that the high cost of anticoagulants restricts their use and may contradict classical medical ethics, as though this were an unprecedented phenomenon. See [13, p. 419]. "A time *may come* when medical ethics will have to be considered in the harsh light of economics" (emphasis added). Of course, this expectation amounts to ignoring the scarcity of medical resources; one has only to have been poor to realize the error. We may confidently assume that price and income do have some consequences for medical expenditures.

[18] A needed piece of research is a study of the exact nature of the variations of medical care received and medical care paid for as income rises. (The relevant income concept also needs study.) For this purpose, some disaggregation is needed; differences in hospital care which are essentially matters of comfort should, in the above view, be much more responsive to income than, e.g., drugs.

[19] This role is enhanced in a socialist society, where the state itself is actively concerned with illness in relation to work; see Field [14, Ch. 9].

[20] About 3 per cent of beds were in proprietary hospitals in 1958, against 30 per cent in voluntary nonprofit, and the remainder in federal, state, and local hospitals; see [26, Chart 4-2, p. 60].

[21] C. R. Rorem has pointed out to me some further factors in this analysis. (1) Given the social intention of helping all patients without regard to immediate ability to pay, economies of scale would dictate a predominance of community-sponsored hospitals. (2)

Conformity to collectivity-oriented behavior is especially important since it is a commonplace that the physician-patient relation affects the quality of the medical care product. A pure cash nexus would be inadequate; if nothing else, the patient expects that the same physician will normally treat him on successive occasions. This expectation is strong enough to persist even in the Soviet Union, where medical care is nominally removed from the market place [14, pp. 194-96]. That purely psychic interactions between physician and patient have effects which are objectively indistinguishable in kind from the effects of medication is evidenced by the use of the placebo as a control in medical experimentation; see Shapiro [25].

C. *Product Uncertainty*

Uncertainty as to the quality of the product is perhaps more intense here than in any other important commodity. Recovery from disease is as unpredictable as is its incidence. In most commodities, the possibility of learning from one's own experience or that of others is strong because there is an adequate number of trials. In the case of severe illness, that is, in general, not true; the uncertainty due to inexperience is added to the intrinsic difficulty of prediction. Further, the amount of uncertainty, measured in terms of utility variability, is certainly much greater for medical care in severe cases than for, say, houses or automobiles, even though these are also expenditures sufficiently infrequent so that there may be considerable residual uncertainty.

Further, there is a special quality to the uncertainty; it is very different on the two sides of the transaction. Because medical knowledge is so complicated, the information possessed by the physician as to the consequences and possibilities of treatment is necessarily very much greater than that of the patient, or at least so it is believed by both parties.[22] Further, both parties are aware of this informational inequality, and their relation is colored by this knowledge.

To avoid misunderstanding, observe that the difference in information relevant here is a difference in information as to the consequence of a purchase of medical care. There is always an inequality of information as to production methods between the producer and the purchaser of any commodity, but in most cases the customer may well

Some proprietary hospitals will tend to control total costs to the patient more closely, including the fees of physicians, who will therefore tend to prefer community-sponsored hospitals.

[22] Without trying to assess the present situation, it is clear in retrospect that at some point in the past the actual differential knowledge possessed by physicians may not have been much. But from the economic point of view, it is the subjective belief of both parties, as manifested in their market behavior, that is relevant.

have as good or nearly as good an understanding of the utility of the product as the producer.

D. *Supply Conditions*

In competitive theory, the supply of a commodity is governed by the net return from its production compared with the return derivable from the use of the same resources elsewhere. There are several significant departures from this theory in the case of medical care.

Most obviously, entry to the profession is restricted by licensing. Licensing, of course, restricts supply and therefore increases the cost of medical care. It is defended as guaranteeing a minimum of quality. Restriction of entry by licensing occurs in most professions, including barbering and undertaking.

A second feature is perhaps even more remarkable. The cost of medical education today is high and, according to the usual figures, is borne only to a minor extent by the student. Thus, the private benefits to the entering student considerably exceed the costs. (It is, however, possible that research costs, not properly chargeable to education, swell the apparent difference.) This subsidy should, in principle, cause a fall in the price of medical services, which, however, is offset by rationing through limited entry to schools and through elimination of students during the medical-school career. These restrictions basically render superfluous the licensing, except in regard to graduates of foreign schools.

The special role of educational institutions in simultaneously subsidizing and rationing entry is common to all professions requiring advanced training.[23] It is a striking and insufficiently remarked phenomenon that such an important part of resource allocation should be performed by nonprofit-oriented agencies.

Since this last phenomenon goes well beyond the purely medical aspect, we will not dwell on it longer here except to note that the anomaly is most striking in the medical field. Educational costs tend to be far higher there than in any other branch of professional training. While tuition is the same, or only slightly higher, so that the subsidy is much greater, at the same time the earnings of physicians rank highest among professional groups, so there would not at first blush seem to be any necessity for special inducements to enter the profession. Even if we grant that, for reasons unexamined here, there is a social interest in subsidized professional education, it is not clear why the rate of subsidization should differ among professions. One might ex-

---

[23] The degree of subsidy in different branches of professional education is worthy of a major research effort.

pect that the tuition of medical students would be higher than that of other students.

The high cost of medical education in the United States is itself a reflection of the quality standards imposed by the American Medical Association since the Flexner Report, and it is, I believe, only since then that the subsidy element in medical education has become significant. Previously, many medical schools paid their way or even yielded a profit.

Another interesting feature of limitation on entry to subsidized education is the extent of individual preferences concerning the social welfare, as manifested by contributions to private universities. But whether support is public or private, the important point is that both the quality and the quantity of the supply of medical care are being strongly influenced by social nonmarket forces.[24, 25]

One striking consequence of the control of quality is the restriction on the range offered. If many qualities of a commodity are possible, it would usually happen in a competitive market that many qualities will be offered on the market, at suitably varying prices, to appeal to different tastes and incomes. Both the licensing laws and the standards of medical-school training have limited the possibilities of alternative qualities of medical care. The declining ratio of physicians to total employees in the medical-care industry shows that substitution of less trained personnel, technicians, and the like, is not prevented completely, but the central role of the highly trained physician is not affected at all.[26]

E. *Pricing Practices*

The unusual pricing practices and attitudes of the medical profession are well known: extensive price discrimination by income (with an extreme of zero prices for sufficiently indigent patients) and, formerly, a strong insistence on fee for services as against such alternatives as prepayment.

[24] Strictly speaking, there are four variables in the market for physicians: price, quality of entering students, quality of education, and quantity. The basic market forces, demand for medical services and supply of entering students, determine two relations among the four variables. Hence, if the nonmarket forces determine the last two, market forces will determine price and quality of entrants.

[25] The supply of Ph.D.'s is similarly governed, but there are other conditions in the market which are much different, especially on the demand side.

[26] Today only the Soviet Union offers an alternative lower level of medical personnel, the feldshers, who practice primarily in the rural districts (the institution dates back to the 18th century). According to Field [14, pp. 98-100, 132-33], there is clear evidence of strain in the relations between physicians and feldshers, but it is not certain that the feldshers will gradually disappear as physicians grow in numbers.

The opposition to prepayment is closely related to an even stronger opposition to closed-panel practice (contractual arrangements which bind the patient to a particular group of physicians). Again these attitudes seem to differentiate professions from business. Prepayment and closed-panel plans are virtually nonexistent in the legal profession. In ordinary business, on the other hand, there exists a wide variety of exclusive service contracts involving sharing of risks; it is assumed that competition will select those which satisfy needs best.[27]

The problems of implicit and explicit price-fixing should also be mentioned. Price competition is frowned on. Arrangements of this type are not uncommon in service industries, and they have not been subjected to antitrust action. How important this is is hard to assess. It has been pointed out many times that the apparent rigidity of so-called administered prices considerably understates the actual flexibility. Here, too, if physicians find themselves with unoccupied time, rates are likely to go down, openly or covertly; if there is insufficient time for the demand, rates will surely rise. The "ethics" of price competition may decrease the flexibility of price responses, but probably that is all.

III. *Comparisons with the Competitive Model under Certainty*

A. *Nonmarketable Commodities*

As already noted, the diffusion of communicable diseases provides an obvious example of nonmarket interactions. But from a theoretical viewpoint, the issues are well understood, and there is little point in expanding on this theme. (This should not be interpreted as minimizing the contribution of public health to welfare; there is every reason to suppose that it is considerably more important than all other aspects of medical care.)

Beyond this special area there is a more general interdependence, the concern of individuals for the health of others. The economic manifestations of this taste are to be found in individual donations to hospitals and to medical education, as well as in the widely accepted responsibilities of government in this area. The taste for improving the health of others appears to be stronger than for improving other aspects of their welfare.[28]

In interdependencies generated by concern for the welfare of others there is always a theoretical case for collective action if each participant derives satisfaction from the contributions of all.

---

[27] The law does impose some limits on risk-shifting in contracts, for example, its general refusal to honor exculpatory clauses.

[28] There may be an identification problem in this observation. If the failure of the market system is, or appears to be, greater in medical care than in, say, food an individual otherwise equally concerned about the two aspects of others' welfare may prefer to help in the first.

B. *Increasing Returns*

Problems associated with increasing returns play some role in allocation of resources in the medical field, particularly in areas of low density or low income. Hospitals show increasing returns up to a point; specialists and some medical equipment constitute significant indivisibilities. In many parts of the world the individual physician may be a large unit relative to demand. In such cases it can be socially desirable to subsidize the appropriate medical-care unit. The appropriate mode of analysis is much the same as for water-resource projects. Increasing returns are hardly apt to be a significant problem in general practice in large cities in the United States, and improved transportation to some extent reduces their importance elsewhere.

C. *Entry*

The most striking departure from competitive behavior is restriction on entry to the field, as discussed in II.D above. Friedman and Kuznets, in a detailed examination of the pre-World War II data, have argued that the higher income of physicians could be attributed to this restriction.[29]

There is some evidence that the demand for admission to medical school has dropped (as indicated by the number of applicants per place and the quality of those admitted), so that the number of medical-school places is not as significant a barrier to entry as in the early 1950's [28, pp. 14-15]. But it certainly has operated over the past and it is still operating to a considerable extent today. It has, of course, constituted a direct and unsubtle restriction on the supply of medical care.

There are several considerations that must be added to help evaluate the importance of entry restrictions: (1) Additional entrants would be, in general, of lower quality; hence, the addition to the supply of medical care, properly adjusted for quality, is less than purely quantitative calculations would show.[30] (2) To achieve genuinely competitive conditions, it would be necessary not only to remove numerical restrictions on entry but also to remove the subsidy in medical education. Like any other producer, the physician should bear all the costs of production,

[29] See [16, pp. 118-37]. The calculations involve many assumptions and must be regarded as tenuous; see the comments by C. Reinold Noyes in [16, pp. 407-10].

[30] It might be argued that the existence of racial discrimination in entrance has meant that some of the rejected applicants are superior to some accepted. However, there is no necessary connection between an increase in the number of entrants and a reduction in racial discrimination; so long as there is excess demand for entry, discrimination can continue unabated and new entrants will be inferior to those previously accepted.

including, in this case, education.[31] It is not so clear that this change would not keep even unrestricted entry down below the present level. (3) To some extent, the effect of making tuition carry the full cost of education will be to create too few entrants, rather than too many. Given the imperfections of the capital market, loans for this purpose to those who do not have the cash are difficult to obtain. The lender really has no security. The obvious answer is some form of insured loans, as has frequently been argued; not too much ingenuity would be needed to create a credit system for medical (and other branches of higher) education. Under these conditions the cost would still constitute a deterrent, but one to be compared with the high future incomes to be obtained.

If entry were governed by ideal competitive conditions, it may be that the quantity on balance would be increased, though this conclusion is not obvious. The average quality would probably fall, even under an ideal credit system, since subsidy plus selected entry draw some highly qualified individuals who would otherwise get into other fields. The decline in quality is not an over-all social loss, since it is accompanied by increase in quality in other fields of endeavor; indeed, if demands accurately reflected utilities, there would be a net social gain through a switch to competitive entry.[32]

There is a second aspect of entry in which the contrast with competitive behavior is, in many respects, even sharper. It is the exclusion of many imperfect substitutes for physicians. The licensing laws, though they do not effectively limit the number of physicians, do exclude all others from engaging in any one of the activities known as medical practice. As a result, costly physician time may be employed at specific tasks for which only a small fraction of their training is needed, and which could be performed by others less well trained and therefore less expensive. One might expect immunization centers, privately operated, but not necessarily requiring the services of doctors.

In the competitive model without uncertainty, consumers are presumed to be able to distinguish qualities of the commodities they buy. Under this hypothesis, licensing would be, at best, superfluous and exclude those from whom consumers would not buy anyway; but it might exclude too many.

D. *Pricing*

The pricing practices of the medical industry (see II.E above) de-

---

[31] One problem here is that the tax laws do not permit depreciation of professional education, so that there is a discrimination against this form of investment.

[32] To anticipate later discussion, this condition is not necessarily fulfilled. When it comes to quality choices, the market may be inaccurate.

part sharply from the competitive norm. As Kessel [17] has pointed out with great vigor, not only is price discrimination incompatible with the competitive model, but its preservation in the face of the large number of physicians is equivalent to a collective monopoly. In the past, the opposition to prepayment plans has taken distinctly coercive forms, certainly transcending market pressures, to say the least.

Kessel has argued that price discrimination is designed to maximize profits along the classic lines of discriminating monopoly and that organized medical opposition to prepayment was motivated by the desire to protect these profits. In principle, prepayment schemes are compatible with discrimination, but in practice they do not usually discriminate. I do not believe the evidence that the actual scale of discrimination is profit-maximizing is convincing. In particular, note that for any monopoly, discriminating or otherwise, the elasticity of demand in each market at the point of maximum profits is greater than one. But it is almost surely true for medical care that the price elasticity of demand for all income levels is less than one. That price discrimination by income is not completely profit-maximizing is obvious in the extreme case of charity; Kessel argues that this represents an appeasement of public opinion. But this already shows the incompleteness of the model and suggests the relevance and importance of social and ethical factors.

Certainly one important part of the opposition to prepayment was its close relation to closed-panel plans. Prepayment is a form of insurance, and naturally the individual physician did not wish to assume the risks. Pooling was intrinsically involved, and this strongly motivates, as we shall discuss further in Section IV below, control over prices and benefits. The simplest administrative form is the closed panel; physicians involved are, in effect, the insuring agent. From this point of view, Blue Cross solved the prepayment problem by universalizing the closed panel.

The case that price discrimination by income is a form of profit maximization which was zealously defended by opposition to fees for service seems far from proven. But it remains true that this price discrimination, for whatever cause, is a source of nonoptimality. Hypothetically, it means everyone would be better off if prices were made equal for all, and the rich compensated the poor for the changes in the relative positions. The importance of this welfare loss depends on the actual amount of discrimination and on the elasticities of demand for medical services by the different income groups. If the discussion is simplified by considering only two income levels, rich and poor, and if the elasticity of demand by either one is zero, then no reallocation of medical services will take place and the initial situation is optimal. The only effect of a change in price will be the redistribution of income as between the medical profession and the group with the zero elasticity of demand. With low elasticities of demand, the gain will be small. To illustrate, suppose the price of medical care to the rich is double that to the poor, the medical expenditures by the rich are 20 per cent of those by the poor, and the elasticity of demand for both classes is .5; then the net social gain due to the abolition of discrimination is slightly over 1 per cent of previous medical expenditures.[33]

The issues involved in the opposition to prepayment, the other major anomaly in medical pricing, are not meaningful in the world of certainty and will be discussed below.

IV. *Comparison with the Ideal Competitive Model under Uncertainty*
A. *Introduction*

In this section we will compare the operations of the actual medical-care market with those of an ideal system in which not only the usual commodities and services but also insurance policies against all conceivable risks are available.[34] Departures consist for the most part of

[33] It is assumed that there are two classes, rich and poor; the price of medical services to the rich is twice that to the poor, medical expenditures by the rich are 20 per cent of those by the poor, and the elasticity of demand for medical services is .5 for both classes. Let us choose our quantity and monetary units so that the quantity of medical services consumed by the poor and the price they pay are both 1. Then the rich purchase .1 units of medical services at a price of 2. Given the assumption about the elasticities of demand, the demand function of the rich is $D_R(p) = .14 \ p^{-.5}$ and that of the poor is $D_P(p) = p^{-.5}$. The supply of medical services is assumed fixed and therefore must equal 1.1. If price discrimination were abolished, the equilibrium price, $\bar{p}$, must satisfy the relation,

$$D_R(\bar{p}) + D_P(\bar{p}) = 1.1,$$

and therefore $\bar{p} = 1.07$. The quantities of medical care purchased by the rich and poor, respectively, would be $D_R(\bar{p}) = .135$ and $D_P(\bar{p}) = .965$.

The inverse demand functions, the price to be paid corresponding to any given quantity are $d_R(q) = .02/q^2$, and $d_P(q) = 1/q^2$. Therefore, the consumers' surplus to the rich generated by the change is:

$$(1) \qquad \int_{.1}^{.135} (.02/q^2)dq - \bar{p}(.135 - .1),$$

and similarly the loss in consumers' surplus by the poor is:

$$(2) \qquad \int_{.965}^{1} (1/q^2)dq - \bar{p}(1 - .965)$$

If (2) is subtracted from (1), the second terms cancel, and the aggregate increase in consumers' surplus is .0156, or a little over 1 per cent of the initial expenditures.

[34] A striking illustration of the desire for security in medical care is provided by the expressed preferences of *émigrés* from the Soviet Union as between Soviet medical practice and German or American practice; see Field [14, Ch. 12]. Those in Germany preferred the German system to the Soviet, but those in the United States preferred (in a ratio of 3 to 1) the Soviet system. The reasons given boil down to the certainty of medical care, independent of income or health fluctuations.

ARROW: UNCERTAINTY AND MEDICAL CARE 959

insurance policies that might conceivably be written, but are in fact not. Whether these potential commodities are nonmarketable, or, merely because of some imperfection in the market, are not actually marketed, is a somewhat fine point.

To recall what has already been said in Section I, there are two kinds of risks involved in medical care: the risk of becoming ill, and the risk of total or incomplete or delayed recovery. The loss due to illness is only partially the cost of medical care. It also consists of discomfort and loss of productive time during illness, and, in more serious cases, death or prolonged deprivation of normal function. From the point of view of the welfare economics of uncertainty, both losses are risks against which individuals would like to insure. The nonexistence of suitable insurance policies for either risk implies a loss of welfare.

B. *The Theory of Ideal Insurance*

In this section, the basic principles of an optimal regime for risk-bearing will be presented. For illustration, reference will usually be made to the case of insurance against cost in medical care. The principles are equally applicable to any of the risks. There is no single source to which the reader can be easily referred, though I think the principles are at least reasonably well understood.

As a basis for the analysis, the assumption is made that each individual acts so as to maximize the expected value of a utility function. If we think of utility as attached to income, then the costs of medical care act as a random deduction from this income, and it is the expected value of the utility of income after medical costs that we are concerned with. (Income after medical costs is the ability to spend money on other objects which give satisfaction. We presuppose that illness is not a source of satisfaction in itself; to the extent that it is a source of dissatisfaction, the illness should enter into the utility function as a separate variable.) The expected-utility hypothesis, due originally to Daniel Bernoulli (1738), is plausible and is the most analytically manageable of all hypotheses that have been proposed to explain behavior under uncertainty. In any case, the results to follow probably would not be significantly affected by moving to another mode of analysis.

It is further assumed that individuals are normally risk-averters. In utility terms, this means that they have a diminishing marginal utility of income. This assumption may reasonably be taken to hold for most of the significant affairs of life for a majority of people, but the presence of gambling provides some difficulty in the full application of this view. It follows from the assumption of risk aversion that if an individual is given a choice between a probability distribution of income, with a given mean m, and the certainty of the income m, he would prefer the latter. Suppose, therefore, an agency, a large insurance company plan, or the government, stands ready to offer insurance against medical costs on an actuarially fair basis; that is, if the costs of medical care are a random variable with mean m, the company will charge a premium m, and agree to indemnify the individual for all medical costs. Under these circumstances, the individual will certainly prefer to take out a policy and will have a welfare gain thereby.

Will this be a social gain? Obviously yes, if the insurance agent is suffering no social loss. Under the assumption that medical risks on different individuals are basically independent, the pooling of them reduces the risk involved to the insurer to relatively small proportions. In the limit, the welfare loss, even assuming risk aversion on the part of the insurer, would vanish and there is a net social gain which may be of quite substantial magnitude. In fact, of course, the pooling of risks does not go to the limit; there is only a finite number of them and there may be some interdependence among the risks due to epidemics and the like. But then a premium, perhaps slightly above the actuarial level, would be sufficient to offset this welfare loss. From the point of view of the individual, since he has a strict preference for the actuarially fair policy over assuming the risks himself, he will still have a preference for an actuarially unfair policy, provided, of course, that it is not too unfair.

In addition to a residual degree of risk aversion by insurers, there are other reasons for the loading of the premium (i.e., an excess of premium over the actuarial value). Insurance involves administrative costs. Also, because of the irregularity of payments there is likely to be a cost of capital tied up. Suppose, to take a simple case, the insurance company is not willing to sell any insurance policy that a consumer wants but will charge a fixed-percentage loading above the actuarial value for its premium. Then it can be shown that the most preferred policy from the point of view of an individual is a coverage with a deductible amount; that is, the insurance policy provides 100 per cent coverage for all medical costs in excess of some fixed-dollar limit. If, however, the insurance company has some degree of risk aversion, its loading may also depend on the degree of uncertainty of the risk. In that case, the Pareto optimal policy will involve some element of co-insurance, i.e., the coverage for costs over the minimum limit will be some fraction less than 100 per cent (for proofs of these statements, see Appendix).

These results can also be applied to the hypothetical concept of insurance against failure to recover from illness. For simplicity, let us assume that the cost of failure to recover is regarded purely as a money cost, either simply productive opportunities foregone or, more gener-

ARROW: UNCERTAINTY AND MEDICAL CARE 961

ally, the money equivalent of all dissatisfactions. Suppose further that, given that a person is ill, the expected value of medical care is greater than its cost; that is, the expected money value attributable to recovery with medical help is greater than resources devoted to medical help. However, the recovery, though on the average beneficial, is uncertain; in the absence of insurance a risk-averter may well prefer not to take a chance on further impoverishment by buying medical care. A suitable insurance policy would, however, mean that he paid nothing if he doesn't benefit; since the expected value is greater than the cost, there would be a net social gain.[35]

C. *Problems of Insurance*

1. *The moral hazard.* The welfare case for insurance policies of all sorts is overwhelming. It follows that the government should undertake insurance in those cases where this market, for whatever reason, has failed to emerge. Nevertheless, there are a number of significant practical limitations on the use of insurance. It is important to understand them, though I do not believe that they alter the case for the creation of a much wider class of insurance policies than now exists.

One of the limits which has been much stressed in insurance literature is the effect of insurance on incentives. What is desired in the case of insurance is that the event against which insurance is taken be out of the control of the individual. Unfortunately, in real life this separation can never be made perfectly. The outbreak of fire in one's house or business may be largely uncontrollable by the individual, but the probability of fire is somewhat influenced by carelessness, and of course arson is a possibility, if an extreme one. Similarly, in medical policies the cost of medical care is not completely determined by the illness suffered by the individual but depends on the choice of a doctor and his willingness to use medical services. It is frequently observed that widespread medical insurance increases the demand for medical care. Coinsurance provisions have been introduced into many major medical policies to meet this contingency as well as the risk aversion of the insurance companies.

To some extent the professional relationship between physician and patient limits the normal hazard in various forms of medical insurance. By certifying to the necessity of given treatment or the lack thereof, the physician acts as a controlling agent on behalf of the insurance companies. Needless to say, it is a far from perfect check; the physicians themselves are not under any control and it may be convenient for them or pleasing to their patients to prescribe more expensive medi-

---

[35] It is a popular belief that the Chinese, at one time, paid their physicians when well but not when sick.

cation, private nurses, more frequent treatments, and other marginal variations of care. It is probably true that hospitalization and surgery are more under the casual inspection of others than is general practice and therefore less subject to moral hazard; this may be one reason why insurance policies in those fields have been more widespread.

2. *Alternative methods of insurance payment.* It is interesting that no less than three different methods of coverage of the costs of medical care have arisen: prepayment, indemnities according to a fixed schedule, and insurance against costs, whatever they may be. In prepayment plans, insurance in effect is paid in kind—that is, directly in medical services. The other two forms both involve cash payments to the beneficiary, but in the one case the amounts to be paid involving a medical contingency are fixed in advance, while in the other the insurance carrier pays all the costs, whatever they may be, subject, of course, to provisions like deductibles and coinsurance.

In hypothetically perfect markets these three forms of insurance would be equivalent. The indemnities stipulated would, in fact, equal the market price of the services, so that value to the insured would be the same if he were to be paid the fixed sum or the market price or were given the services free. In fact, of course, insurance against full costs and prepayment plans both offer insurance against uncertainty as to the price of medical services, in addition to uncertainty about their needs. Further, by their mode of compensation to the physician, prepayment plans are inevitably bound up with closed panels so that the freedom of choice of the physician by the patient is less than it would be under a scheme more strictly confined to the provision of insurance. These remarks are tentative, and the question of coexistence of the different schemes should be a fruitful subject for investigation.

3. *Third-party control over payments.* The moral hazard in physicians' control noted in paragraph 1 above shows itself in those insurance schemes where the physician has the greatest control, namely, major medical insurance. Here there has been a marked rise in expenditures over time. In prepayment plans, where the insurance and medical service are supplied by the same group, the incentive to keep medical costs to a minimum is strongest. In plans of the Blue Cross group, there has developed a conflict of interest between the insurance carrier and the medical-service supplier, in this case particularly the hospital.

The need for third-party control is reinforced by another aspect of the moral hazard. Insurance removes the incentive on the part of individuals, patients, and physicians to shop around for better prices for hospitalization and surgical care. The market forces, therefore, tend to be replaced by direct institutional control.

4. *Administrative costs.* The pure theory of insurance sketched in Section B above omits one very important consideration: the costs of operating an insurance company. There are several types of operating costs, but one of the most important categories includes commissions and acquisition costs, selling costs in usual economic terminology. Not only does this mean that insurance policies must be sold for considerably more than their actuarial value, but it also means there is a great differential among different types of insurance. It is very striking to observe that among health insurance policies of insurance companies in 1958, expenses of one sort or another constitute 51.6 per cent of total premium income for individual policies, and only 9.5 per cent for group policies [26, Table 14-1, p. 272]. This striking differential would seem to imply enormous economies of scale in the provision of insurance, quite apart from the coverage of the risks themselves. Obviously, this provides a very strong argument for widespread plans, including, in particular, compulsory ones.

5. *Predictability and insurance.* Clearly, from the risk-aversion point of view, insurance is more valuable, the greater the uncertainty in the risk being insured against. This is usually used as an argument for putting greater emphasis on insurance against hospitalization and surgery than other forms of medical care. The empirical assumption has been challenged by O. W. Anderson and others [3, pp. 53-54], who asserted that out-of-hospital expenses were equally as unpredictable as in-hospital costs. What was in fact shown was that the probability of costs exceeding $200 is about the same for the two categories, but this is not, of course, a correct measure of predictability, and a quick glance at the supporting evidence shows that in relation to the average cost the variability is much lower for ordinary medical expenses. Thus, for the city of Birmingham, the mean expenditure on surgery was $7, as opposed to $20 for other medical expenses, but of those who paid something for surgery the average bill was $99, as against $36 for those with some ordinary medical cost. Eighty-two per cent of those interviewed had no surgery, and only 20 per cent had no ordinary medical expenses [3, Tables A-13, A-18, and A-19 on pp. 72, 77, and 79, respectively].

The issue of predictability also has bearing on the merits of insurance against chronic illness or maternity. On a lifetime insurance basis, insurance against chronic illness makes sense, since this is both highly unpredictable and highly significant in costs. Among people who already have chronic illness, or symptoms which reliably indicate it, insurance in the strict sense is probably pointless.

6. *Pooling of unequal risks.* Hypothetically, insurance requires for its full social benefit a maximum possible discrimination of risks. Those

in groups of higher incidences of illness should pay higher premiums. In fact, however, there is a tendency to equalize, rather than to differentiate, premiums, especially in the Blue Cross and similar widespread schemes. This constitutes, in effect, a redistribution of income from those with a low propensity to illness to those with a high propensity. The equalization, of course, could not in fact be carried through if the market were genuinely competitive. Under those circumsances, insurance plans could arise which charged lower premiums to preferred risks and draw them off, leaving the plan which does not discriminate among risks with only an adverse selection of them.

As we have already seen in the case of income redistribution, some of this may be thought of as insurance with a longer time perspective. If a plan guarantees to everybody a premium that corresponds to total experience but not to experience as it might be segregated by smaller subgroups, everybody is, in effect, insured against a change in his basic state of health which would lead to a reclassification. This corresponds precisely to the use of a level premium in life insurance instead of a premium varying by age, as would be the case for term insurance.

7. *Gaps and coverage*. We may briefly note that, at any rate to date, insurances against the cost of medical care are far from universal. Certain groups—the unemployed, the institutionalized, and the aged—are almost completely uncovered. Of total expenditures, between one-fifth and one-fourth are covered by insurance. It should be noted, however, that over half of all hospital expenses and about 35 per cent of the medical payments of those with bills of $1,000 a year and over, are included [26, p. 376]. Thus, the coverage on the more variable parts of medical expenditure is somewhat better than the over-all figures would indicate, but it must be assumed that the insurance mechanism is still very far from achieving the full coverage of which it is capable.

D. *Uncertainty of Effects of Treatment*

1. There are really two major aspects of uncertainty for an individual already suffering from an illness. He is uncertain about the effectiveness of medical treatment, and his uncertainty may be quite different from that of his physician, based on the presumably quite different medical knowledges.

2. *Ideal insurance*. This will necessarily involve insurance against a failure to benefit from medical care, whether through recovery, relief of pain, or arrest of further deterioration. One form would be a system in which the payment to the physician is made in accordance with the degree of benefit. Since this would involve transferring the risks from the patient to the physician, who might certainly have an aversion to bearing them, there is room for insurance carriers to pool the risks,

either by contract with physicians or by contract with the potential patients. Under ideal insurance, medical care will always be undertaken in any case in which the expected utility, taking account of the probabilities, exceeds the expected medical cost. This prescription would lead to an economic optimum. If we think of the failure to recover mainly in terms of lost working time, then this policy would, in fact, maximize economic welfare as ordinarily measured.

3. *The concepts of trust and delegation.* In the absence of ideal insurance, there arise institutions which offer some sort of substitute guarantees. Under ideal insurance the patient would actually have no concern with the informational inequality between himself and the physician, since he would only be paying by results anyway, and his utility position would in fact be thoroughly guaranteed. In its absence he wants to have some guarantee that at least the physician is using his knowledge to the best advantage. This leads to the setting up of a relationship of trust and confidence, one which the physician has a social obligation to live up to. Since the patient does not, at least in his belief, know as much as the physician, he cannot completely enforce standards of care. In part, he replaces direct observation by generalized belief in the ability of the physician.[36] To put it another way, the social obligation for best practice is part of the commodity the physician sells, even though it is a part that is not subject to thorough inspection by the buyer.

One consequence of such trust relations is that the physician cannot act, or at least appear to act, as if he is maximizing his income at every moment of time. As a signal to the buyer of his intentions to act as thoroughly in the buyer's behalf as possible, the physician avoids the obvious stigmata of profit-maximizing. Purely arms-length bargaining behavior would be incompatible, not logically, but surely psychologically, with the trust relations. From these special relations come the various forms of ethical behavior discussed above, and so also, I suggest, the relative unimportance of profit-making in hospitals. The very word, "profit," is a signal that denies the trust relations.

Price discrimination and its extreme, free treatment for the indigent, also follow. If the obligation of the physician is understood to be first of all to the welfare of the patient, then in particular it takes precedence over financial difficulties.

As a second consequence of informational inequality between physician and patient and the lack of insurance of a suitable type, the patient must delegate to the physician much of his freedom of choice.

---

[36] Francis Bator points out to me that some protection can be achieved, at a price, by securing additional opinions.

He does not have the knowledge to make decisions on treatment, referral, or hospitalization. To justify this delegation, the physician finds himself somewhat limited, just as any agent would in similar circumstances. The safest course to take to avoid not being a true agent is to give the socially prescribed "best" treatment of the day. Compromise in quality, even for the purpose of saving the patient money, is to risk an imputation of failure to live up to the social bond.

The special trust relation of physicians (and allied occúptions, such as priests) extends to third parties so that the certifications of physicians as to illness and injury are accepted as especially reliable (see Section II.B above). The social value to all concerned of such presumptively reliable sources of information is obvious.

Notice the general principle here. Because there are barriers to the information flow and because there is no market in which the risks involved can be insured, coordination of purchase and sales must take place through convergent expectations, but these are greatly assisted by having clear and prominent signals, and these, in turn, force patterns of behavior which are not in themselves logical necessities for optimality.[37]

4. *Licensing and educational standards.* Delegation and trust are the social institutions designed to obviate the problem of informational inequality. The general uncertainty about the prospects of medical treatment is socially handled by rigid entry requirements. These are designed to reduce the uncertainty in the mind of the consumer as to the quality of product insofar as this is possible.[38] I think this explanation, which is perhaps the naive one, is much more tenable than any idea of a monopoly seeking to increase incomes. No doubt restriction on entry is desirable from the point of view of the existing physicians, but the public pressure needed to achieve the restriction must come from deeper causes.

The social demand for guaranteed quality can be met in more than one way, however. At least three attitudes can be taken by the state or other social institutions toward entry into an occupation or toward the production of commodities in general; examples of all three types exist. (1) The occupation can be licensed, nonqualified entrants being simply excluded. The licensing may be more complex than it is in medicine; individuals could be licensed for some, but not all, medical activities, for example. Indeed, the present all-or-none approach could

---

[37] The situation is very reminiscent of the crucial role of the focal point in Schelling's theory of tacit games, in which two parties have to find a common course of action without being able to communicate; see [24, esp. pp. 225 ff.].

[38] How well they achieve this end is another matter. R. Kessel points out to me that they merely guarantee training, not continued good performance as medical technology changes.

be criticized as being insufficient with regard to complicated specialist treatment, as well as excessive with regard to minor medical skills. Graded licensing may, however, be much harder to enforce. Controls could be exercised analogous to those for foods; they can be excluded as being dangerous, or they can be permitted for animals but not for humans. (2) The state or other agency can certify or label, without compulsory exclusion. The category of Certified Psychologist is now under active discussion; canned goods are graded. Certification can be done by nongovernmental agencies, as in the medical-board examinations for specialists. (3) Nothing at all may be done; consumers make their own choices.

The choice among these alternatives in any given case depends on the degree of difficulty consumers have in making the choice unaided, and on the consequences of errors of judgment. It is the general social consensus, clearly, that the *laissez-faire* solution for medicine is intolerable. The certification proposal never seems to have been discussed seriously. It is beyond the scope of this paper to discuss these proposals in detail. I wish simply to point out that they should be judged in terms of the ability to relieve the uncertainty of the patient in regard to the quality of the commodity he is purchasing, and that entry restrictions are the consequences of an apparent inability to devise a system in which the risks of gaps in medical knowledge and skill are borne primarily by the patient, not the physician.

Postscript

I wish to repeat here what has been suggested above in several places: that the failure of the market to insure against uncertainties has created many social institutions in which the usual assumptions of the market are to some extent contradicted. The medical profession is only one example, though in many respects an extreme one. All professions share some of the same properties. The economic importance of personal and especially family relationships, though declining, is by no means trivial in the most advanced economies; it is based on nonmarket relations that create guarantees of behavior which would otherwise be afflicted with excessive uncertainty. Many other examples can be given. The logic and limitations of ideal competitive behavior under uncertainty force us to recognize the incomplete description of reality supplied by the impersonal price system.

REFERENCES

1. A. A. ALCHIAN, K. J. ARROW, AND W. M. CAPRON, *An Economic Analysis of the Market for Scientists and Engineers,* RAND RM-2190-RC. Santa Monica 1958.

968 THE AMERICAN ECONOMIC REVIEW

2. M. ALLAIS, "Géneralisation des théories de l'équilibre économique général et du rendement social au cas du risque," in Centre National de la Recherche Scientifique, *Econometrie*, Paris 1953, pp. 1-20.
3. O. W. ANDERSON AND STAFF OF THE NATIONAL OPINION RESEARCH CENTER, *Voluntary Health Insurance in Two Cities*. Cambridge, Mass. 1957.
4. K. J. ARROW, "Economic Welfare and the Allocation of Resources for Invention," in Nat. Bur. Econ. Research, *The Role and Direction of Inventive Activity: Economic and Social Factors*, Princeton 1962, pp. 609-25.
5. ———, "Les rôle des valeurs boursières pour la répartition la meilleure des risques," in Centre National de la Recherche Scientifique, *Econometrie*, Paris 1953, pp. 41-46.
6. F. M. BATOR, "The Anatomy of Market Failure," *Quart. Jour. Econ.* Aug. 1958, *72*, 351-79.
7. E. BAUDIER, "L'introduction du temps dans la théorie de l'équilibre général," *Les Cahiers Economiques*, Dec. 1959, 9-16.
8. W. J. BAUMOL, *Welfare Economics and the Theory of the State*. Cambridge, Mass. 1952.
9. K. BORCH, "The Safety Loading of Reinsurance Premiums," *Skandinavisk Aktuariehdskrift*, 1960, pp. 163-84.
10. J. M. BUCHANAN AND G. TULLOCK, *The Calculus of Consent*. Ann Arbor 1962.
11. G. DEBREU, "Une économique de l'incertain," *Economie Appliquée*, 1960, *13*, 111-16.
12. ———, *Theory of Values*. New York 1959.
13. R. DUBOS, "Medical Utopias," *Daedalus*, 1959, *88*, 410-24.
14. M. G. FIELD, *Doctor and Patient in Soviet Russia*. Cambridge, Mass. 1957.
15. MILTON FRIEDMAN, "The Methodology of Positive Economics," in *Essays in Positive Economics*, Chicago 1953, pp. 3-43.
16. ——— AND S. S. KUZNETS, *Income from Independent Professional Practice*. Nat. Bur. Econ. Research, New York 1945.
17. R. A. KESSEL, "Price Discrimination in Medicine," *Jour. Law and Econ.*, 1958, *1*, 20-53.
18. T. C. KOOPMANS, "Allocation of Resources and the Price System," in *Three Essays on the State of Economic Science*, New York 1957, pp. 1-120.
19. I. M. D. LITTLE, *A Critique of Welfare Economics*. Oxford 1950.
20. SELMA MUSHKIN, "Towards a Definition of Health Economics," *Public Health Reports*, 1958, *73*, 785-93.
21. R. R. NELSON, "The Simple Economics of Basic Scientific Research," *Jour. Pol. Econ.*, June 1959, *67*, 297-306.
22. T. PARSONS, *The Social System*. Glencoe 1951.
23. M. J. PECK AND F. M. SCHERER, *The Weapons Acquisition Process: An Economic Analysis*. Div. of Research, Graduate School of Business, Harvard University, Boston 1962.

24. T. C. SCHELLING, *The Strategy of Conflict*. Cambridge, Mass. 1960.
25. A. K. SHAPIRO, "A Contribution to a History of the Placebo Effect," *Behavioral Science*, 1960, *5*, 109-35.
26. H. M. SOMERS AND A. R. SOMERS, *Doctors, Patients, and Health Insurance*. The Brookings Institution, Washington 1961.
27. C. L. STEVENSON, *Ethics and Language*. New Haven 1945.
28. U. S. DEPARTMENT OF HEALTH, EDUCATION AND WELFARE, *Physicians for a Growing America*, Public Health Service Publication No. 709, Oct. 1959.

APPENDIX

On Optimal Insurance Policies

The two propositions about the nature of optimal insurance policies asserted in Section IV.B above will be proved here.

Proposition 1. If an insurance company is willing to offer any insurance policy against loss desired by the buyer at a premium which depends only on the policy's actuarial value, then the policy chosen by a risk-averting buyer will take the form of 100 per cent coverage above a deductible minimum.

Note: The premium will, in general, exceed the actuarial value; it is only required that two policies with the same actuarial value will be offered by the company for the same premium.

Proof: Let W be the initial wealth of the individual, X his loss, a random variable, $I(X)$ the amount of insurance paid if loss X occurs, P the premium, and $Y(X)$ the wealth of the individual after paying the premium, incurring the loss, and receiving the insurance benefit.

$$(1) \qquad Y(X) = W - P - X + I(X).$$

The individual values alternative policies by the expected utility of his final wealth position, $Y(X)$. Let $U(y)$ be the utility of final wealth, y; then his aim is to maximize,

$$(2) \qquad E\{U[Y(X)]\},$$

where the symbol, E, denotes mathematical expectation.

An insurance payment is necessarily nonnegative, so the insurance policy must satisfy the condition,

$$(3) \qquad I(X) \geq 0 \quad \text{for all} \quad X.$$

If a policy is optimal, it must in particular be better in the sense of the criterion (2), than any other policy with the same actuarial expectation, $E[I(X)]$. Consider a policy that pays some positive amount of insurance at one level of loss, say X_1, but which permits the final wealth at some other loss level, say X_2, to be lower than that corresponding to X_1. Then, it is intuitively obvious that a risk-averter would prefer an alternative policy with the same actuarial value which would offer slightly less protection for losses in the neighborhood of X_1 and slightly higher protection for those in the neighborhood of X_2, since risk aversion implies that the marginal utility of $Y(X)$ is greater when $Y(X)$ is smaller: hence, the original policy cannot be optimal.

To prove this formally, let $I_1(X)$ be the original policy, with $I_1(X) > 0$ and $Y_1(X_1) > Y_2(X_2)$, where $Y_1(X)$ is defined in terms of $I_1(X)$ by (I). Choose δ sufficiently small so that,

(4) $I_1(X) > 0$ for $X_1 \leq X \leq X_1 + \delta$,

(5) $Y_1(X') < Y_1(X)$ for $X_2 \leq X' \leq X_2 + \delta$, $X_1 \leq X \leq X_1 + \delta$.

(This choice of δ is possible if the functions $I_1(X)$, $Y_1(X)$ are continuous; this can be proved to be true for the optimal policy, and therefore we need only consider this case.)

Let π_1 be the probability that the loss, X, lies in the interval $\langle X_1, X_1 + \delta \rangle$, π_2 the probability that X lies in the interval $\langle X_2, X_2 + \delta \rangle$. From (4) and (5) we can choose $\epsilon > 0$ and sufficiently small so that,

(6) $I_1(X) - \pi_2\epsilon \geq 0$ for $X_1 \leq X \leq X_1 + \delta$,

(7) $Y_1(X') + \pi_1\epsilon < Y_1(X) - \pi_2\epsilon$

$$\text{for } X_2 \leq X' \leq X_2 + \delta, \quad X_1 \leq X \leq X_1 + \delta.$$

Now define a new insurance policy, $I_2(X)$, which is the same as $I_1(X)$ except that it is smaller by $\pi_2\epsilon$ in the interval from X_1 to $X_1 + \delta$ and larger by $\pi_1\epsilon$ in the interval from X_2 to $X_2 + \delta$. From (6), $I_2(X) \geq 0$ everywhere, so that (3) is satisfied. We will show that $E[I_1(X)] = E[I_2(X)]$ and that $I_2(X)$ yields the higher expected utility, so that $I_1(X)$ is not optimal.

Note that $I_2(X) - I_1(X)$ equals $-\pi_2\epsilon$ for $X_1 \leq X \leq X_1 + \delta$, $\pi_1\epsilon$ for $X_2 \leq X \leq X_2 + \delta$, and 0 elsewhere. Let $\phi(X)$ be the density of the random variable X. Then,

$$E[I_2(X) - I_1(X)] = \int_{X_1}^{X_1+\delta} [I_2(X) - I_1(X)]\phi(X)dX$$

$$+ \int_{X_2}^{X_2+\delta} [I_2(X) - I_1(X)]dX$$

$$= (-\pi_2\epsilon) \int_{X_1}^{X_1+\delta} \phi(X)dX + (\pi_1\epsilon) \int_{X_2}^{X_2+\delta} \phi(X)dX$$

$$= -(\pi_2\epsilon)\pi_1 + (\pi_1\epsilon)\pi_2 = 0,$$

so that the two policies have the same actuarial value and, by assumption, the same premium.

Define $Y_2(X)$ in terms of $I_2(X)$ by (1). Then $Y_2(X) - Y_1(X) = I_2(X) - I_1(X)$. From (7),

(8) $Y_1(X') < Y_2(X') < Y_2(X) < Y_1(X)$

$$\text{for } X_2 \leq X' \leq X_2 + \delta, \quad X_1 \leq X \leq X_1 + \delta.$$

Since $Y_1(X) - Y_2(X) = 0$ outside the intervals $\langle X_1, X_1 + \delta \rangle$, $\langle X_2, X_2 + \delta \rangle$, we

ARROW: UNCERTAINTY AND MEDICAL CARE 971

can write,

$$(9) \quad E\{U[Y_2(X)] - U[Y_1(X)]\} = \int_{X_1}^{X_1+\delta} \{U[Y_2(X)] - U[Y_1(X)]\}\phi(X)dX$$

$$+ \int_{X_2}^{X_2+\delta} \{U[Y_2(X)] - U[Y_1(X)]\}\phi(X)dX.$$

By the Mean Value Theorem, for any given value of X,

$$(10) \quad U[Y_2(X)] - U[Y_1(X)] = U'[Y(X)][Y_2(X) - Y_1(X)]$$
$$= U'[Y(X)][I_2(X) - I_1(X)],$$

where $Y(X)$ lies between $Y_1(X)$ and $Y_2(X)$. From (8),

$$Y(X') < Y(X) \quad \text{for} \quad X_2 \le X' \le X_2 + \delta, \quad X_1 \le X \le X_1 + \delta,$$

and, since $U'(y)$ is a diminishing function of y for a risk-averter,

$$U'[Y(X')] > U'[Y(X)]$$

or, equivalently, for some number u,

$$(11) \quad \begin{aligned} U'[Y(X')] > u \quad \text{for} \quad X_2 \le X' \le X_2 + \delta, \\ U'[Y(X)] < u \quad \text{for} \quad X_1 \le X \le X_1 + \delta. \end{aligned}$$

Now substitute (10) into (9),

$$E\{U[Y_2(X)] - U[Y_1(X)]\} = -\pi_2\epsilon \int_{X_1}^{X_1+\delta} U'[Y(X)]\phi(X)dX$$

$$+ \pi_1\epsilon \int_{X_2}^{X_2+\delta} U'[Y(X)]\phi(X)dX.$$

From (11), it follows that,

$$E\{U[Y_2(X)] - U[Y_1(X)]\} > -\pi_2\epsilon u\pi_1 + \pi_1\epsilon u\pi_2 = 0,$$

so that the second policy is preferred.

It has thus been shown that a policy cannot be optimal if, for some X_1 and X_2, $I(X_1) > 0$, $Y(X_1) > Y(X_2)$. This may be put in a different form: Let Y_{min} be the minimum value taken on by $Y(X)$ under the optimal policy; then we must have $I(X) = 0$ if $Y(X) > Y_{min}$. In other words, a minimum final wealth level is set; if the loss would not bring wealth below this level, no benefit is paid, but if it would, then the benefit is sufficient to bring up the final wealth position to the stipulated minimum. This is, of course, precisely a description of 100 per cent coverage for loss above a deductible.

We turn to the second proposition. It is now supposed that the insurance company, as well as the insured, is a risk-averter; however, there are no administrative or other costs to be covered beyond protection against loss.

Proposition 2. If the insured and the insurer are both risk-averters and there are no costs other than coverage of losses, then any nontrivial Pareto-optimal policy, $I(X)$, as a function of the loss, X, must have the property, $0 < dI/dX < 1$.

That is, any increment in loss will be partly but not wholly compensated by the insurance company; this type of provision is known as coinsurance. Proposition 2 is due to Borch [9, Sec. 2]; we give here a somewhat simpler proof.

Proof: Let $U(y)$ be the utility function of the insured, $V(z)$ that of the insurer. Let W_0 and W_1 be the initial wealths of the two, respectively. In this case, we let $I(X)$ be the insurance benefits less the premium; for the present purpose, this is the only significant magnitude (since the premium is independent of X, this definition does not change the value of dI/dX). The final wealth positions of the insured and insurer are:

(12)
$$Y(X) = W_0 - X + I(X),$$
$$Z(X) = W_1 - I(X),$$

respectively. Any given insurance policy then defines expected utilities, $u = E\{U[Y(X)]\}$ and $v = E\{V[Z(X)]\}$, for the insured and insurer, respectively. If we plot all points (u, v) obtained by considering all possible insurance policies, the resulting expected-utility-possibility set has a boundary that is convex to the northeast. To see this, let $I_1(X)$ and $I_2(X)$ be any two policies, and let (u_1, v_1) and (u_2, v_2) be the corresponding points in the two-dimensional expected-utility-possibility set. Let a third insurance policy, $I(X)$, be defined as the average of the two given ones,

$$I(X) = (\tfrac{1}{2})I_1(X) + (\tfrac{1}{2})I_2(X),$$

for each X. Then, if $Y(X)$, $Y_1(X)$, and $Y_2(X)$ are the final wealth positions of the insured, and $Z(X)$, $Z_1(X)$, and $Z_2(X)$ those of the insurer for each of the three policies, $I(X)$, $I_1(X)$, and $I_2(X)$, respectively,

$$Y(X) = (\tfrac{1}{2})Y_1(X) + (\tfrac{1}{2})Y_2(X),$$
$$Z(X) = (\tfrac{1}{2})Z_1(X) + (\tfrac{1}{2})Z_2(X),$$

and, because both parties have diminishing marginal utility,

$$U[Y(X)] \geq (\tfrac{1}{2})U[Y_1(X)] + (\tfrac{1}{2})U[Y_2(X)],$$
$$V[Z(X)] \geq (\tfrac{1}{2})V[Z_1(X)] + (\tfrac{1}{2})V[Z_2(X)].$$

Since these statements hold for all X, they also hold when expectations are taken. Hence, there is a point (u, v) in the expected-utility-possibility set for which $u \geq (\tfrac{1}{2})u_1 + (\tfrac{1}{2})u_2$, $v \geq (\tfrac{1}{2})v_1 + (\tfrac{1}{2})v_2$. Since this statement holds for every pair of points (u_1, y_1) and (u_2, v_2) in the expected-utility-possibility set, and in particular for pairs of points on the northeast boundary, it follows that the boundary must be convex to the northeast.

From this, in turn, it follows that any given Pareto-optimal point (i.e., any point on the northeast boundary) can be obtained by maximizing a linear function, $\alpha u + \beta v$, with suitably chosen α and β nonnegative and at least one positive, over the expected-utility-possibility set. In other words, a Pareto-optimal insurance policy, $I(X)$, is one which maximizes,

$$\alpha E\{U[Y(X)]\} + \beta E\{V[Z(X)]\} = E\{\alpha U[Y(X)] + \beta V[Z(X)]\},$$

for some $\alpha \geq 0$, $\beta \geq 0$, $\alpha > 0$ or $\beta > 0$. To maximize this expectation, it is obviously sufficient to maximize:

$$(13) \qquad \alpha U[Y(X)] + \beta V[Z(X)],$$

with respect to $I(X)$, for each X. Since, for given X, it follows from (12) that,

$$dY(X)/dI(X) = 1, \qquad dZ(X)/dI(X) = -1,$$

it follows by differentiation of (13) that $I(X)$ is the solution of the equation,

$$(14) \qquad \alpha U'[Y(X)] - \beta V'[Z(X)] = 0.$$

The cases $\alpha = 0$ or $\beta = 0$ lead to obvious trivialities (one party simply hands over all his wealth to the other), so we assume $\alpha > 0, \beta > 0$. Now differentiate (14) with respect to X and use the relations, derived from (12),

$$dY/dX = (dI/dX) - 1, \qquad dZ/dX = -(dI/dX).$$

$$\alpha U''[Y(X)][(dI/dX) - 1] + \beta V''[Z(X)](dI/dX) = 0,$$

or

$$dI/dX = \alpha U''[Y(X)]/\{\alpha U''[Y(X)] + \beta V''[Z(X)]\}.$$

Since $U''[Y(X)] < 0$, $V''[Z(X)] < 0$ by the hypothesis that both parties are risk-averters, Proposition 2 follows.

[7]

THE ARCHITECTURE OF COMPLEXITY

HERBERT A. SIMON*

Professor of Administration, Carnegie Institute of Technology

(*Read April 26, 1962*)

A NUMBER of proposals have been advanced in recent years for the development of "general systems theory" which, abstracting from properties peculiar to physical, biological, or social systems, would be applicable to all of them.[1] We might well feel that, while the goal is laudable, systems of such diverse kinds could hardly be expected to have any nontrivial properties in common. Metaphor and analogy can be helpful, or they can be misleading. All depends on whether the similarities the metaphor captures are significant or superficial.

It may not be entirely vain, however, to search for common properties among diverse kinds of complex systems. The ideas that go by the name of cybernetics constitute, if not a theory, at least a point of view that has been proving fruitful over a wide range of applications.[2] It has been useful to look at the behavior of adaptive systems in terms of the concepts of feedback and homeostasis, and to analyze adaptiveness in terms of the theory of selective information.[3] The ideas of feedback and information provide a frame of reference for viewing a wide range of situations, just as do the ideas of evolution, of relativism, of axiomatic method, and of operationalism.

In this paper I should like to report on some things we have been learning about particular kinds of complex systems encountered in the behavioral sciences. The developments I shall discuss arose in the context of specific phenomena, but the theoretical formulations themselves make little reference to details of structure. Instead they refer primarily to the complexity of the systems under view without specifying the exact content of that complexity. Because of their abstractness, the theories may have relevance—application would be too strong a term—to other kinds of complex systems that are observed in the social, biological, and physical sciences.

In recounting these developments, I shall avoid technical detail, which can generally be found elsewhere. I shall describe each theory in the particular context in which it arose. Then, I shall cite some examples of complex systems, from areas of science other than the initial application, to which the theoretical framework appears relevant. In doing so, I shall make reference to areas of knowledge where I am not expert—perhaps not even literate. I feel quite comfortable in doing so before the members of this society, representing as it does the whole span of the scientific and scholarly endeavor. Collectively you will have little difficulty, I am sure, in distinguishing instances based on idle fancy or sheer ignorance from instances that cast some light on the ways in which complexity exhibits itself wherever it is found in nature. I shall leave to you the final judgment of relevance in your respective fields.

I shall not undertake a formal definition of

* The ideas in this paper have been the topic of many conversations with my colleague, Allen Newell. George W. Corner suggested important improvements in biological content as well as editorial form. I am also indebted, for valuable comments on the manuscript, to Richard H. Meier, John R. Platt, and Warren Weaver. Some of the conjectures about the nearly decomposable structure of the nucleus-atom-molecule hierarchy were checked against the available quantitative data by Andrew Schoene and William Wise. My work in this area has been supported by a Ford Foundation grant for research in organizations and a Carnegie Corporation grant for research on cognitive processes. To all of the above, my warm thanks, and the usual absolution.

[1] See especially the yearbooks of the Society for General Systems Research. Prominent among the exponents of general systems theory are L. von Bertalanffy, K. Boulding, R. W. Gerard, and J. G. Miller. For a more skeptical view—perhaps too skeptical in the light of the present discussion—see H. A. Simon and A. Newell, Models: their uses and limitations, *in* L. D. White, ed., *The state of the social sciences*, 66–83, Chicago, Univ. of Chicago Press, 1956.

[2] N. Wiener, *Cybernetics*, New York, John Wiley & Sons, 1948. For an imaginative forerunner, see A. J. Lotka, *Elements of mathematical biology*, New York, Dover Publications, 1951, first published in 1924 as *Elements of physical biology*.

[3] C. Shannon and W. Weaver, *The mathematical theory of communication*, Urbana, Univ. of Illinois Press, 1949; W. R. Ashby, *Design for a brain*, New York, John Wiley & Sons, 1952.

"complex systems."[4] Roughly, by a complex system I mean one made up of a large number of parts that interact in a nonsimple way. In such systems, the whole is more than the sum of the parts, not in an ultimate, metaphysical sense, but in the important pragmatic sense that, given the properties of the parts and the laws of their interaction, it is not a trivial matter to infer the properties of the whole. In the face of complexity, an in-principle reductionist may be at the same time a pragmatic holist.[5]

The four sections that follow discuss four aspects of complexity. The first offers some comments on the frequency with which complexity takes the form of hierarchy—the complex system being composed of subsystems that, in turn, have their own subsystems, and so on. The second section theorizes about the relation between the structure of a complex system and the time required for it to emerge through evolutionary processes: specifically, it argues that hierarchic systems will evolve far more quickly than non-hierarchic systems of comparable size. The third section explores the dynamic properties of hierarchically-organized systems, and shows how they can be decomposed into subsystems in order to analyze their behavior. The fourth section examines the relation between complex systems and their descriptions.

Thus, the central theme that runs through my remarks is that complexity frequently takes the form of hierarchy, and that hierarchic systems have some common properties that are independent of their specific content. Hierarchy, I shall argue, is one of the central structural schemes that the architect of complexity uses.

[4] W. Weaver, in: Science and complexity, *American Scientist* 36: 536, 1948, has distinguished two kinds of complexity, disorganized and organized. We shall be primarily concerned with organized complexity.

[5] See also John R. Platt, Properties of large molecules that go beyond the properties of their chemical sub-groups, *Jour. Theoret. Biol.* 1: 342–358, 1961. Since the reductionism-holism issue is a major *cause de guerre* between scientists and humanists, perhaps we might even hope that peace could be negotiated between the two cultures along the lines of the compromise just suggested. As I go along, I shall have a little to say about complexity in the arts as well as in the natural sciences. I must emphasize the pragmatism of my holism to distinguish it sharply from the position taken by W. M. Elsasser in *The physical foundation of biology*, New York, Pergamon Press, 1958.

HIERARCHIC SYSTEMS

By a *hierarchic system,* or hierarchy, I mean a system that is composed of interrelated subsystems, each of the latter being, in turn, hierarchic in structure until we reach some lowest level of elementary subsystem. In most systems in nature, it is somewhat arbitrary as to where we leave off the partitioning, and what subsystems we take as elementary. Physics makes much use of the concept of "elementary particle" although particles have a disconcerting tendency not to remain elementary very long. Only a couple of generations ago, the atoms themselves were elementary particles; today, to the nuclear physicist they are complex systems. For certain purposes of astronomy, whole stars, or even galaxies, can be regarded as elementary subsystems. In one kind of biological research, a cell may be treated as an elementary subsystem; in another, a protein molecule; in still another, an amino acid residue.

Just why a scientist has a right to treat as elementary a subsystem that is in fact exceedingly complex is one of the questions we shall take up. For the moment, we shall accept the fact that scientists do this all the time, and that if they are careful scientists they usually get away with it.

Etymologically, the word "hierarchy" has had a narrower meaning than I am giving it here. The term has generally been used to refer to a complex system in which each of the subsystems is subordinated by an authority relation to the system it belongs to. More exactly, in a hierarchic formal organization, each system consists of a "boss" and a set of subordinate subsystems. Each of the subsystems has a "boss" who is the immediate subordinate of the boss of the system. We shall want to consider systems in which the relations among subsystems are more complex than in the formal organizational hierarchy just described. We shall want to include systems in which there is no relation of subordination among subsystems. (In fact, even in human organizations, the formal hierarchy exists only on paper; the real flesh-and-blood organization has many inter-part relations other than the lines of formal authority.) For lack of a better term, I shall use hierarchy in the broader sense introduced in the previous paragraphs, to refer to all complex systems analyzable into successive sets of subsystems, and speak of "formal hierarchy" when I want to refer to the more specialized concept.[6]

[6] The mathematical term "partitioning" will not do for what I call here a hierarchy; for the set of subsystems,

SOCIAL SYSTEMS

I have already given an example of one kind of hierarchy that is frequently encountered in the social sciences: a formal organization. Business firms, governments, universities all have a clearly visible parts-within-parts structure. But formal organizations are not the only, or even the most common, kind of social hierarchy. Almost all societies have elementary units called families, which may be grouped into villages or tribes, and these into larger groupings, and so on. If we make a chart of social interactions, of who talks to whom, the clusters of dense interaction in the chart will identify a rather well-defined hierarchic structure. The groupings in this structure may be defined operationally by some measure of frequency of interaction in this sociometric matrix.

BIOLOGICAL AND PHYSICAL SYSTEMS

The hierarchical structure of biological systems is a familiar fact. Taking the cell as the building block, we find cells organized into tissues, tissues into organs, organs into systems. Moving downward from the cell, well-defined subsystems—for example, nucleus, cell membrane, microsomes, mitochondria, and so on—have been identified in animal cells.

The hierarchic structure of many physical systems is equally clear-cut. I have already mentioned the two main series. At the microscopic level we have elementary particles, atoms, molecules, macromolecules. At the macroscopic level we have satellite systems, planetary systems, galaxies. Matter is distributed throughout space in a strikingly non-uniform fashion. The most nearly random distributions we find, gases, are not random distributions of elementary particles but random distributions of complex systems, i.e. molecules.

A considerable range of structural types is subsumed under the term hierarchy as I have defined it. By this definition, a diamond is hierarchic, for it is a crystal structure of carbon atoms that can be further decomposed into protons, neutrons, and electrons. However, it is a very "flat" hierarchy, in which the number of first-order subsystems belonging to the crystal can be indefinitely large. A volume of molecular gas is a flat hierarchy in the same sense. In ordinary usage, we and the successive subsets in each of these defines the partitioning, independently of any systems of relations among the subsets. By hierarchy I mean the partitioning in conjunction with the relations that hold among its parts.

tend to reserve the word hierarchy for a system that is divided into a *small or moderate number* of subsystems, each of which may be further subdivided. Hence, we do not ordinarily think of or refer to a diamond or a gas as a hierarchic structure. Similarly, a linear polymer is simply a chain, which may be very long, of identical subparts, the monomers. At the molecular level it is a very flat hierarchy.

In discussing formal organizations, the number of subordinates who report directly to a single boss is called his *span of control*. I will speak analogously of the *span* of a system, by which I shall mean the number of subsystems into which it is partitioned. Thus, a hierarchic system is flat at a given level if it has a wide span at that level. A diamond has a wide span at the crystal level, but not at the next level down, the molecular level.

In most of our theory construction in the following sections we shall focus our attention on hierarchies of moderate span, but from time to time I shall comment on the extent to which the theories might or might not be expected to apply to very flat hierarchies.

There is one important difference between the physical and biological hierarchies, on the one hand, and social hierarchies, on the other. Most physical and biological hierarchies are described in spatial terms. We detect the organelles in a cell in the way we detect the raisins in a cake—they are "visibly" differentiated substructures localized spatially in the larger structure. On the other hand, we propose to identify social hierarchies not by observing who lives close to whom but by observing who interacts with whom. These two points of view can be reconciled by defining hierarchy in terms of intensity of interaction, but observing that in most biological and physical systems relatively intense interaction implies relative spatial propinquity. One of the interesting characteristics of nerve cells and telephone wires is that they permit very specific strong interactions at great distances. To the extent that interactions are channeled through specialized communications and transportation systems, spatial propinquity becomes less determinative of structure.

SYMBOLIC SYSTEMS

One very important class of systems has been omitted from my examples thus far: systems of human symbolic production. A book is a hierarchy in the sense in which I am using that term. It is generally divided into chapters, the chapters

470   HERBERT A. SIMON   [PROC. AMER. PHIL. SOC.

into sections, the sections into paragraphs, the paragraphs into sentences, the sentences into clauses and phrases, the clauses and phrases into words. We may take the words as our elementary units, or further subdivide them, as the linguist often does, into smaller units. If the book is narrative in character, it may divide into "episodes" instead of sections, but divisions there will be.

The hierarchic structure of music, based on such units as movements, parts, themes, phrases, is well known. The hierarchic structure of products of the pictorial arts is more difficult to characterize, but I shall have something to say about it later.

THE EVOLUTION OF COMPLEX SYSTEMS

Let me introduce the topic of evolution with a parable. There once were two watchmakers, named Hora and Tempus, who manufactured very fine watches. Both of them were highly regarded, and the phones in their workshops rang frequently —new customers were constantly calling them. However, Hora prospered, while Tempus became poorer and poorer and finally lost his shop. What was the reason?

The watches the men made consisted of about 1,000 parts each. Tempus had so constructed his that if he had one partly assembled and had to put it down—to answer the phone say—it immediately fell to pieces and had to be reassembled from the elements. The better the customers liked his watches, the more they phoned him, the more difficult it became for him to find enough uninterrupted time to finish a watch.

The watches that Hora made were no less complex than those of Tempus. But he had designed them so that he could put together subassemblies of about ten elements each. Ten of these subassemblies, again, could be put together into a larger subassembly; and a system of ten of the latter subassemblies constituted the whole watch. Hence, when Hora had to put down a partly assembled watch in order to answer the phone, he lost only a small part of his work, and he assembled his watches in only a fraction of the man-hours it took Tempus.

It is rather easy to make a quantitative analysis of the relative difficulty of the tasks of Tempus and Hora: Suppose the probability that an interruption will occur while a part is being added to an incomplete assembly is p. Then the probability that Tempus can complete a watch he has started without interruption is $(1-p)^{1000}$—a very small number unless p is .001 or less. Each interruption will cost, on the average, the time to assemble $1/p$ parts (the expected number assembled before interruption). On the other hand, Hora has to complete one hundred eleven sub-assemblies of ten parts each. The probability that he will not be interrupted while completing any one of these is $(1-p)^{10}$, and each interruption will cost only about the time required to assemble five parts.[7]

Now if p is about .01—that is, there is one chance in a hundred that either watchmaker will be interrupted while adding any one part to an assembly—then a straightforward calculation shows that it will take Tempus, on the average, about four thousand times as long to assemble a watch as Hora.

We arrive at the estimate as follows:

1. Hora must make 111 times as many complete assemblies per watch as Tempus; but,

2. Tempus will lose on the average 20 times as much work for each interrupted assembly as Hora [100 parts, on the average, as against 5]; and,

3. Tempus will complete an assembly only 44 times per million attempts ($.99^{1000} = 44 \times 10^{-6}$), while Hora will complete nine out of ten ($.99^{10} = 9 \times 10^{-1}$). Hence Tempus will have to make 20,000 as many attempts per completed assembly as Hora. $(9 \times 10^{-1})/(44 \times 10^{-6}) = 2 \times 10^4$. Multiplying these three ratios, we get:

$$1/111 \times 100/5 \times .99^{10}/.99^{1000}$$
$$= 1/111 \times 20 \times 20,000 \sim 4,000.$$

---

[7] The speculations on speed of evolution were first suggested by H. Jacobson's application of information theory to estimating the time required for biological evolution. See his paper, Information, reproduction, and the origin of life, in *American Scientist* 43: 119–127, January, 1955. From thermodynamic considerations it is possible to estimate the amount of increase in entropy that occurs when a complex system decomposes into its elements. (See, for example, R. B. Setlow and E. C. Pollard, *Molecular biophysics*, 63–65, Reading, Mass., Addison-Wesley Publishing Co., 1962, and references cited there.) But entropy is the logarithm of a probability, hence information, the negative of entropy, can be interpreted as the logarithm of the reciprocal of the probability—the "improbability," so to speak. The essential idea in Jacobson's model is that the expected time required for the system to reach a particular state is inversely proportional to the probability of the state—hence increases exponentially with the amount of information (negentropy) of the state.

Following this line of argument, but not introducing the notion of levels and stable subassemblies, Jacobson arrived at estimates of the time required for evolution so large as to make the event rather improbable. Our analysis, carried through in the same way, but with attention to the stable intermediate forms, produces very much smaller estimates.

BIOLOGICAL EVOLUTION

What lessons can we draw from our parable for biological evolution? Let us interpret a partially completed subassembly of k elementary parts as the coexistence of k parts in a small volume—ignoring their relative orientations. The model assumes that parts are entering the volume at a constant rate, but that there is a constant probability, p, that the part will be dispersed before another is added, unless the assembly reaches a stable state. These assumptions are not particularly realistic. They undoubtedly underestimate the decrease in probability of achieving the assembly with increase in the size of the assembly. Hence the assumptions understate—probably by a large factor—the relative advantage of a hierarchic structure.

Although we cannot, therefore, take the numerical estimate seriously the lesson for biological evolution is quite clear and direct. The time required for the evolution of a complex form from simple elements depends critically on the numbers and distribution of potential intermediate stable forms. In particular, if there exists a hierarchy of potential stable "subassemblies," with about the same span, s, at each level of the hierarchy, then the time required for a subassembly can be expected to be about the same at each level—that is proportional to $1/(1-p)^s$. The time required for the assembly of a system of n elements will be proportional to $\log_s n$, that is, to the number of levels in the system. One would say—with more illustrative than literal intent—that the time required for the evolution of multi-celled organisms from single-celled organisms might be of the same order of magnitude as the time required for the evolution of single-celled organisms from macromolecules. The same argument could be applied to the evolution of proteins from amino acids, of molecules from atoms, of atoms from elementary particles.

A whole host of objections to this oversimplified scheme will occur, I am sure, to every working biologist, chemist, and physicist. Before turning to matters I know more about, I shall mention three of these problems, leaving the rest to the attention of the specialists.

First, in spite of the overtones of the watchmaker parable, the theory assumes no teleological mechanism. The complex forms can arise from the simple ones by purely random processes. (I shall propose another model in a moment that shows this clearly.) Direction is provided to the scheme by the stability of the complex forms, once these come into existence. But this is nothing more than survival of the fittest—i.e., of the stable.

Second, not all large systems appear hierarchical. For example, most polymers—e.g., nylon—are simply linear chains of large numbers of identical components, the monomers. However, for present purposes we can simply regard such a structure as a hierarchy with a span of one—the limiting case. For a chain of any length represents a state of relative equilibrium.[8]

Third, the evolution of complex systems from simple elements implies nothing, one way or the other, about the change in entropy of the entire system. If the process absorbs free energy, the complex system will have a smaller entropy than the elements; if it releases free energy, the opposite will be true. The former alternative is the one that holds for most biological systems, and the net inflow of free energy has to be supplied from the sun or some other source if the second law of thermodynamics is not to be violated. For the evolutionary process we are describing, the equilibria of the intermediate states need have only local and not global stability, and they may be stable only in the steady state—that is, as long as there is an external source of free energy that may be drawn upon.[9]

Because organisms are not energetically closed systems, there is no way to deduce the direction, much less the rate, of evolution from classical thermodynamic considerations. All estimates indicate that the amount of entropy, measured in physical units, involved in the formation of a one-celled biological organism is trivially small—about -10^{-11} cal/degree.[10] The "improbability" of evolution has nothing to do with this quantity of entropy, which is produced by every bacterial cell every generation. The irrelevance of quantity of

---

[8] There is a well-developed theory of polymer size, based on models of random assembly. See for example P. J. Flory, *Principles of polymer chemistry*, ch. 8, Ithaca, Cornell Univ. Press, 1953. Since *all* subassemblies in the polymerization theory are stable, limitation of molecular growth depends on "poisoning" of terminal groups by impurities or formation of cycles rather than upon disruption of partially-formed chains.

[9] This point has been made many times before, but it cannot be emphasized too strongly. For further discussion, see Setlow and Pollard, *op. cit.*, 49–64; E. Schrodinger, *What is life?* Cambridge Univ. Press, 1945; and H. Linschitz, The information content of a bacterial cell, in H. Questler, ed., *Information theory in biology*, 251–262, Urbana, Univ. of Illinois Press, 1953.

[10] See Linschitz, *op. cit.* This quantity, 10^{-11} cal/degree, corresponds to obout 10^{13} bits of information.

information, in this sense, to speed of evolution can also be seen from the fact that exactly as much information is required to "copy" a cell through the reproductive process as to produce the first cell through evolution.

The effect of the existence of stable intermediate forms exercises a powerful effect on the evolution of complex forms that may be likened to the dramatic effect of catalysts upon reaction rates and steady state distribution of reaction products in open systems.[11] In neither case does the entropy change provide us with a guide to system behavior.

PROBLEM SOLVING AS NATURAL SELECTION

Let us turn now to some phenomena that have no obvious connection with biological evolution: human problem-solving processes. Consider, for example, the task of discovering the proof for a difficult theorem. The process can be—and often has been—described as a search through a maze. Starting with the axioms and previously proved theorems, various transformations allowed by the rules of the mathematical systems are attempted, to obtain new expressions. These are modified in turn until, with persistence and good fortune, a sequence or path of transformations is discovered that leads to the goal.

The process usually involves a great deal of trial and error. Various paths are tried; some are abandoned, others are pushed further. Before a solution is found, a great many paths of the maze may be explored. The more difficult and novel the problem, the greater is likely to be the amount of trial and error required to find a solution. At the same time, the trial and error is not completely random or blind; it is, in fact, rather highly selective. The new expressions that are obtained by transforming given ones are examined to see whether they represent progress toward the goal. Indications of progress spur further search in the same direction; lack of progress signals the abandonment of a line of search. Problem solving requires *selective* trial and error.[12]

A little reflection reveals that cues signaling progress play the same role in the problem-solving process that stable intermediate forms play in the biological evolutionary process. In fact, we can take over the watchmaker parable and apply it also to problem solving. In problem solving, a partial result that represents recognizable progress toward the goal plays the role of a stable subassembly.

Suppose that the task is to open a safe whose lock has ten dials, each with one hundred possible settings, numbered from 0 to 99. How long will it take to open the safe by a blind trial-and-error search for the correct setting? Since there are 100^{10} possible settings, we may expect to examine about one-half of these, on the average, before finding the correct one—that is, fifty billion billion settings. Suppose, however, that the safe is defective, so that a click can be heard when any one dial is turned to the correct setting. Now each dial can be adjusted independently, and does not need to be touched again while the others are being set. The total number of settings that has to be tried is only 10×50, or five hundred. The task of opening the safe has been altered, by the cues the clicks provide, from a practically impossible one to a trivial one.[13]

A considerable amount has been learned in the past five years about the nature of the mazes that represent common human problem-solving tasks—proving theorems, solving puzzles, playing chess, making investments, balancing assembly lines, to mention a few. All that we have learned about these mazes points to the same conclusion: that human problem solving, from the most blundering to the most insightful, involves nothing more than varying mixtures of trial and error and selectivity. The selectivity derives from various rules of

[11] See H. Kacser, Some physico-chemical aspects of biological organization, Appendix, pp. 191–249 in C. H. Waddington, *The strategy of the genes*, London, George Allen & Unwin, 1957.

[12] See A. Newell, J. C. Shaw, and H. A. Simon, Empirical explorations of the logic theory machine, *Proceedings of the 1957 Western Joint Computer Conference*, February, 1957, New York: Institute of Radio Engineers; Chess-playing programs and the problem of complexity, *IBM Journal of Research and Development* 2: 320–335, October, 1958; and for a similar view of problem solving, W. R. Ashby, Design for an intelligence

amplifier, 215–233 in C. E. Shannon and J. McCarthy, *Automata studies*, Princeton, Princeton Univ. Press, 1956.

[13] The clicking safe example was supplied by D. P. Simon. Ashby, *op. cit.*, 230, has called the selectivity involved in situations of this kind "selection by components." The even greater reduction in time produced by hierarchization in the clicking safe example, as compared with the watchmaker's metaphor, is due to the fact that a random *search* for the correct combination is involved in the former case, while in the latter the parts come together in the right order. It is not clear which of these metaphors provides the better model for biological evolution, but we may be sure that the watchmaker's metaphor gives an exceedingly conservative estimate of the savings due to hierarchization. The safe may give an excessively high estimate because it assumes all possible arrangements of the elements to be equally probable.

thumb, or heuristics, that suggest which paths should be tried first and which leads are promising. We do not need to postulate processes more sophisticated than those involved in organic evolution to explain how enormous problem mazes are cut down to quite reasonable size.[14]

THE SOURCES OF SELECTIVITY

When we examine the sources from which the problem-solving system, or the evolving system, as the case may be, derives its selectivity, we discover that selectivity can always be equated with some kind of feedback of information from the environment.

Let us consider the case of problem solving first. There are two basic kinds of selectivity. One we have already noted: various paths are tried out, the consequences of following them are noted, and this information is used to guide further search. In the same way, in organic evolution, various complexes come into being, at least evanescently, and those that are stable provide new building blocks for further construction. It is this information about stable configurations, and not free energy or negentropy from the sun, that guides the process of evolution and provides the selectivity that is essential to account for its rapidity.

The second source of selectivity in problem solving is previous experience. We see this particularly clearly when the problem to be solved is similar to one that has been solved before. Then, by simply trying again the paths that led to the earlier solution, or their analogues, trial-and-error search is greatly reduced or altogether eliminated.

What corresponds to this latter kind of information in organic evolution? The closest analogue is reproduction. Once we reach the level of self-reproducing systems, a complex system, when it has once been achieved, can be multiplied indefinitely. Reproduction in fact allows the inheritance of acquired characteristics, but at the level of genetic material, of course; i.e., only characteristics acquired by the genes can be inherited. We shall return to the topic of reproduction in the final section of this paper.

ON EMPIRES AND EMPIRE-BUILDING

We have not exhausted the categories of complex systems to which the watchmaker argument can reasonably be applied. Philip assembled his

[14] A. Newell and H. A. Simon, Computer simulation of human thinking, *Science* 134: 2011–2017, December 22, 1961.

Macedonian empire and gave it to his son, to be later combined with the Persian subassembly and others into Alexander's greater system. On Alexander's death, his empire did not crumble to dust, but fragmented into some of the major subsystems that had composed it.

The watchmaker argument implies that if one would be Alexander, one should be born into a world where large stable political systems already exist. Where this condition was not fulfilled, as on the Scythian and Indian frontiers, Alexander found empire building a slippery business. So too, T. E. Lawrence's organizing of the Arabian revolt against the Turks was limited by the character of his largest stable building blocks, the separate, suspicious desert tribes.

The profession of history places a greater value upon the validated particular fact than upon tendentious generalization. I shall not elaborate upon my fancy, therefore, but will leave it to historians to decide whether anything can be learned for the interpretation of history from an abstract theory of hierarchic complex systems.

CONCLUSION: THE EVOLUTIONARY EXPLANATION OF HIERARCHY

We have shown thus far that complex systems will evolve from simple systems much more rapidly if there are stable intermediate forms than if there are not. The resulting complex forms in the former case will be hierarchic. We have only to turn the argument around to explain the observed predominance of hierarchies among the complex systems nature presents to us. Among possible complex forms, hierarchies are the ones that have the time to evolve. The hypothesis that complexity will be hierarchic makes no distinction among very flat hierarchies, like crystals, and tissues, and polymers, and the intermediate forms. Indeed, in the complex systems we encounter in nature, examples of both forms are prominent. A more complete theory than the one we have developed here would presumably have something to say about the determinants of width of span in these systems.

NEARLY DECOMPOSABLE SYSTEMS

In hierarchic systems, we can distinguish between the interactions *among* subsystems, on the one hand, and the interactions *within* subsystems —i.e., among the parts of those subsystems—on the other. The interactions at the different levels may be, and often will be, of different orders of

474   HERBERT A. SIMON   [PROC. AMER. PHIL. SOC.

	A1	A2	A3	B1	B2	C1	C2	C3
A1	—	100	—	2	—	—	—	—
A2	100	—	100	1	1	—	—	—
A3	—	100	—	—	2	—	—	—
B1	2	1	—	—	100	2	1	—
B2	—	1	2	100	—	—	1	2
C1	—	—	—	2	—	—	100	—
C2	—	—	—	1	—	100	—	100
C3	—	—	—	—	2	—	100	—

FIG. 1. A hypothetical nearly-decomposable system. In terms of the heat-exchange example of the text, A1, A2, and A3 may be interpreted as cubicles in one room, B1 and B2 as cubicles in a second room, and C1, C2, and C3 as cubicles in a third. The matrix entries then are the heat diffusion coefficients between cubicles.

A1	B1	C1
A2		C2
A3	B2	C3

magnitude. In a formal organization there will generally be more interaction, on the average, between two employees who are members of the same department than between two employees from different departments. In organic substances, intermolecular forces will generally be weaker than molecular forces, and molecular forces than nuclear forces.

In a rare gas, the intermolecular forces will be negligible compared to those binding the molecules—we can treat the individual particles, for many purposes, as if they were independent of each other. We can describe such a system as *decomposable* into the subsystems comprised of the individual particles. As the gas becomes denser, molecular interactions become more significant. But over some range, we can treat the decomposable case as a limit, and as a first approximation. We can use a theory of perfect gases, for example, to describe approximately the behavior of actual gases if they are not too dense. As a second approximation, we may move to a theory of *nearly decomposable* systems, in which the interactions among the subsystems are weak, but not negligible.

At least some kinds of hierarchic systems can be approximated successfully as nearly decomposable systems. The main theoretical findings from the approach can be summed up in two propositions:

(*a*) in a nearly decomposable system, the short-run behavior of each of the component subsystems is approximately independent of the short-run behavior of the other components; (*b*) in the long run, the behavior of any one of the components depends in only an aggregate way on the behavior of the other components.

Let me provide a very concrete simple example of a nearly decomposable system.[15] Consider a building whose outside walls provide perfect thermal insulation from the environment. We shall take these walls as the boundary of our system. The building is divided into a large number of rooms, the walls between them being good, but not perfect, insulators. The walls between rooms are the boundaries of our major subsystems. Each room is divided by partitions into a number of cubicles, but the partitions are poor insulators. A thermometer hangs in each cubicle. Suppose that at the time of our first observation of the system there is a wide variation in temperature from cubicle to cubicle and from room to room—the various cubicles within the building are in a state of thermal disequilibrium. When we take new temperature readings several hours later, what shall we find? There will be very little variation in temperature among the cubicles within each single room, but there may still be large temperature variations *among* rooms. When we take readings again several days later, we find an almost uniform temperature throughout the building; the temperature differences among rooms have virtually disappeared.

We can describe the process of equilibration formally by setting up the usual equations of heat flow. The equations can be represented by the matrix of their coefficients, r_{ij}, where r_{ij} is the rate at which heat flows from the ith cubicle to the jth cubicle per degree difference in their temperatures. If cubicles i and j do not have a common wall, r_{ij} will be zero. If cubicles i and j have a common wall, and are in the same room, r_{ij} will be large. If cubicles i and j are separated by the wall of a

[15] This discussion of near-decomposability is based upon H. A. Simon and A. Ando, Aggregation of variables in dynamic systems, *Econometrica* 29: 111–138, April, 1961. The example is drawn from the same source, 117–118. The theory has been further developed and applied to a variety of economic and political phenomena by Ando and F. M. Fisher. See F. M. Fisher, On the cost of approximate specification in simultaneous equation estimation, *Econometrica* 29: 139–170, April, 1961, and F. M. Fisher and A. Ando, Two theorems on *Ceteris Paribus* in the analysis of dynamic systems, *American Political Science Review* 61: 103–113, March, 1962.

room, r_{ij} will be nonzero but small. Hence, by grouping all the cubicles together that are in the same room, we can arrange the matrix of coefficients so that all its large elements lie inside a string of square submatrices along the main diagonal. All the elements outside these diagonal squares will be either zero or small (see figure 1). We may take some small number, ϵ, as the upper bound of the extradiagonal elements. We shall call a matrix having these properties a *nearly decomposable matrix*.

Now it has been proved that a dynamic system that can be described by a nearly decomposable matrix has the properties, stated above, of a nearly decomposable system. In our simple example of heat flow this means that in the short run each room will reach an equilibrium temperature (an average of the initial temperatures of its offices) nearly independently of the others; and that each room will remain approximately in a state of equilibrium over the longer period during which an over-all temperature equilibrium is being established throughout the building. After the intra-room short-run equilibria have been reached, a single thermometer in each room will be adequate to describe the dynamic behavior of the entire system—separate thermometers in each cubicle will be superfluous.

NEAR DECOMPOSABILITY OF SOCIAL SYSTEMS

As a glance at figure 1 shows, near decomposability is a rather strong property for a matrix to possess, and the matrices that have this property will describe very special dynamic systems—vanishingly few systems out of all those that are thinkable. How few they will be depends, of course, on how good an approximation we insist upon. If we demand that epsilon be very small, correspondingly few dynamic systems will fit the definition. But we have already seen that in the natural world nearly decomposable systems are far from rare. On the contrary, systems in which each variable is linked with almost equal strength with almost all other parts of the system are far rarer and less typical.

In economic dynamics, the main variables are the prices and quantities of commodities. It is empirically true that the price of any given commodity and the rate at which it is exchanged depend to a significant extent only on the prices and quantities of a few other commodities, together with a few other aggregate magnitudes, like the average price level or some over-all measure of

economic activity. The large linkage coefficients are associated, in general, with the main flows of raw materials and semi-finished products within and between industries. An input-output matrix of the economy, giving the magnitudes of these flows, reveals the nearly decomposable structure of the system—with one qualification. There is a consumption subsystem of the economy that is linked strongly to variables in most of the other subsystems. Hence, we have to modify our notions of decomposability slightly to accommodate the special role of the consumption subsystem in our analysis of the dynamic behavior of the economy.

In the dynamics of social systems, where members of a system communicate with and influence other members, near decomposability is generally very prominent. This is most obvious in formal organizations, where the formal authority relation connects each member of the organization with one immediate superior and with a small number of subordinates. Of course many communications in organizations follow other channels than the lines of formal authority. But most of these channels lead from any particular individual to a very limited number of his superiors, subordinates, and associates. Hence, departmental boundaries play very much the same role as the walls in our heat example.

PHYSICO-CHEMICAL SYSTEMS

In the complex systems familiar in biological chemistry, a similar structure is clearly visible. Take the atomic nuclei in such a system as the elementary parts of the system, and construct a matrix of bond strengths between elements. There will be matrix elements of quite different orders of magnitude. The largest will generally correspond to the covalent bonds, the next to the ionic bonds, the third group to hydrogen bonds, still smaller linkages to van der Waals forces.[16] If we select an epsilon just a little smaller than the magnitude of a covalent bond, the system will decompose into subsystems—the constituent molecules. The smaller linkages will correspond to the intermolecular bonds.

It is well known that high-energy, high-fre-

[16] For a survey of the several classes of molecular and inter-molecular forces, and their dissociation energies see Setlow and Pollard, *op. cit.*, chapter 6. The energies of typical covalent bonds are of the order of 80–100 k cal/mole, of the hydrogen bonds, 10 k cal/mole. Ionic bonds generally lie between these two levels, the bonds due to van der Waals forces are lower in energy.

quency vibrations are associated with the smaller physical subsystems, low-frequency vibrations with the larger systems into which the subsystems are assembled. For example, the radiation frequencies associated with molecular vibrations are much lower than those associated with the vibrations of the planetary electrons of the atoms; the latter, in turn, are lower than those associated with nuclear processes.[17] Molecular systems are nearly decomposable systems, the short-run dynamics relating to the internal structures of the subsystems; the long-run dynamics to the interactions of these subsystems.

A number of the important approximations employed in physics depend for their validity on the near-decomposability of the systems studied. The theory of the thermodynamics of irreversible processes, for example, requires the assumption of macroscopic disequilibrium but microscopic equilibrium,[18] exactly the situation described in our heat-exchange example. Similarly computations in quantum mechanics are often handled by treating weak interactions as producing perturbations on a system of strong interactions.

SOME OBSERVATIONS ON HIERARCHIC SPAN

To understand why the span of hierarchies is sometimes very broad—as in crystals—sometimes narrow, we need to examine more detail of the interactions. In general, the critical consideration is the extent to which interaction between two (or a few) subsystems excludes interaction of these subsystems with the others. Let us examine first some physical examples.

Consider a gas of identical molecules, each of which can form covalent bonds, in certain ways, with others. Let us suppose that we can associate with each atom a specific number of bonds that it is capable of maintaining simultaneously. (This number is obviously related to the number we usually call its valence.) Now suppose that two atoms join, and that we can also associate with the combination a specific number of external bonds it is capable of maintaining. If this number is the same

as the number associated with the individual atoms, the bonding process can go on indefinitely—the atoms can form crystals or polymers of indefinite extent. If the number of bonds of which the composite is capable is less than the number associated with each of the parts, then the process of agglomeration must come to a halt.

We need only mention some elementary examples. Ordinary gases show no tendency to agglomerate because the multiple bonding of atoms "uses up" their capacity to interact. While each oxygen atom has a valence of two, the O_2 molecules have a zero valence. Contrariwise, indefinite chains of single-bonded carbon atoms can be built up because a chain of any number of such atoms, each with two side groups, has a valence of exactly two.

Now what happens if we have a system of elements that possess both strong and weak interaction capacities, and whose strong bonds are exhaustible through combination? Subsystems will form, until all the capacity for strong interaction is utilized in their construction. Then these subsystems will be linked by the weaker second-order bonds into larger systems. For example, a water molecule has essentially a valence of zero—all the potential covalent bonds are fully occupied by the interaction of hydrogen and oxygen molecules. But the geometry of the molecule creates an electric dipole that permits weak interaction between the water and salts dissolved in it—whence such phenomena as its electrolytic conductivity.[19]

Similarly, it has been observed that, although electrical forces are much stronger than gravitational forces, the latter are far more important than the former for systems on an astronomical scale. The explanation, of course, is that the electrical forces, being bipolar, are all "used up" in the linkages of the smaller subsystems, and that significant net balances of positive or negative charges are not generally found in regions of macroscopic size.

In social as in physical systems there are generally limits on the simultaneous interaction of large numbers of subsystems. In the social case, these limits are related to the fact that a human being is more nearly a serial than a parallel information-processing system. He can carry on only one conversation at a time, and although this does not limit the size of the audience to which a mass communication can be addressed, it does

---

[17] Typical wave numbers for vibrations associated with various systems (the wave number is the reciprocal of wave length hence proportional to frequency):
  steel wire under tension—10^{-10} to 10^{-8} cm^{-1}
  molecular rotations—10^0 to 10^2 cm^{-1}
  molecular vibrations—10^3 to 10^5 cm^{-1}
  planetary electrons—10^4 to 10^6 cm^{-1}
  nuclear rotations—10^9 to 10^{10} cm^{-1}
  nuclear surface vibrations—10^{11} to 10^{12} cm^{-1}.

[18] S. R. de Groot, *Thermodynamics of irreversible processes*, 11–12, New York, Interscience Publishers, 1951.

[19] See, for example, L. Pauling, *General chemistry*, ch. 15.

limit the number of people simultaneously involved in most other forms of social interaction. Apart from requirements of direct interaction, most roles impose tasks and responsibilities that are time consuming. One cannot, for example, enact the role of "friend" with large numbers of other people.

It is probably true that in social as in physical systems, the higher frequency dynamics are associated with the subsystems, the lower frequency dynamics with the larger systems. It is generally believed, for example, that the relevant planning horizon of executives is longer the higher their location in the organizational hierarchy. It is probably also true that both the average duration of an interaction between executives and the average interval between interactions is greater at higher than at lower levels.

SUMMARY: NEAR DECOMPOSABILITY

We have seen that hierarchies have the property of near-decomposability. Intra-component linkages are generally stronger than intercomponent linkages. This fact has the effect of separating the high-frequency dynamics of a hierarchy—involving the internal structure of the components—from the low frequency dynamics—involving interaction among components. We shall turn next to some important consequences of this separation for the description and comprehension of complex systems.

THE DESCRIPTION OF COMPLEXITY

If you ask a person to draw a complex object—e.g., a human face—he will almost always proceed in a hierarchic fashion.[20] First he will outline the face. Then he will add or insert features: eyes, nose, mouth, ears, hair. If asked to elaborate, he will begin to develop details for each of the features—pupils, eyelids, lashes for the eyes, and so on—until he reaches the limits of his anatomical knowledge. His information about the object is arranged hierarchicly in memory, like a topical outline.

When information is put in outline form, it is easy to include information about the relations among the major parts and information about the internal relations of parts in each of the suboutlines. Detailed information about the relations of subparts belonging to different parts has no place

[20] George A. Miller has collected protocols from subjects who were given the task of drawing faces, and finds that they behave in the manner described here (private communication). See also E. H. Gombrich, *Art and illusion*, 291–296, New York, Pantheon Books, 1960.

in the outline and is likely to be lost. The loss of such information and the preservation mainly of information about hierarchic order is a salient characteristic that distinguishes the drawings of a child or someone untrained in representation from the drawing of a trained artist. (I am speaking of an artist who is striving for representation.)

NEAR DECOMPOSABILITY AND COMPREHENSIBILITY

From our discussion of the dynamic properties of nearly decomposable systems, we have seen that comparatively little information is lost by representing them as hierarchies. Subparts belonging to different parts only interact in an aggregative fashion—the detail of their interaction can be ignored. In studying the interaction of two large molecules, generally we do not need to consider in detail the interactions of nuclei of the atoms belonging to the one molecule with the nuclei of the atoms belonging to the other. In studying the interaction of two nations, we do not need to study in detail the interactions of each citizen of the first with each citizen of the second.

The fact, then, that many complex systems have a nearly decomposable, hierarchic structure is a major facilitating factor enabling us to understand, to describe, and even to "see" such systems and their parts. Or perhaps the proposition should be put the other way round. If there are important systems in the world that are complex without being hierarchic, they may to a considerable extent escape our observation and our understanding. Analysis of their behavior would involve such detailed knowledge and calculation of the interactions of their elementary parts that it would be beyond our capacities of memory or computation.[21]

[21] I believe the fallacy in the central thesis of W. M. Elsasser's *The physical foundation of biology*, mentioned earlier, lies in his ignoring the simplification in description of complex systems that derives from their hierarchic structure. Thus (p. 155): "If we now apply similar arguments to the coupling of enzymatic reactions with the substratum of protein molecules, we see that over a sufficient period of time, the information corresponding to the structural details of these molecules will be communicated to the dynamics of the cell, to higher levels of organization as it were, and may influence such dynamics. While this reasoning is only qualitative, it lends credence to the assumption that in the living organism, unlike the inorganic crystal, the effects of microscopic structure cannot be simply averaged out; as time goes on this influence will pervade the behavior of the cell 'at all levels.'"
But from our discussion of near-decomposability it would appear that those aspects of microstructure that control the slow developmental aspects of organismic

I shall not try to settle which is chicken and which is egg: whether we are able to understand the world because it is hierarchic, or whether it appears hierarchic because those aspects of it which are not elude our understanding and observation. I have already given some reasons for supposing that the former is at least half the truth—that evolving complexity would tend to be hierarchic—but it may not be the whole truth.

SIMPLE DESCRIPTIONS OF COMPLEX SYSTEMS

One might suppose that the description of a complex system would itself be a complex structure of symbols—and indeed, it may be just that. But there is no conservation law that requires that the description be as cumbersome as the object described. A trivial example will show how a system can be described economically. Suppose the system is a two-dimensional array like this:

$$
\begin{array}{cccccccc}
A & B & M & N & R & S & H & I \\
C & D & O & P & T & U & J & K \\
M & N & A & B & H & I & R & S \\
O & P & C & D & J & K & T & U \\
R & S & H & I & A & B & M & N \\
T & U & J & K & C & D & O & P \\
H & I & R & S & M & N & A & B \\
J & K & T & U & O & P & C & D
\end{array}
$$

Let us call the array $\begin{vmatrix} AB \\ CD \end{vmatrix}$ a, the array $\begin{vmatrix} MN \\ OP \end{vmatrix}$ m, the array $\begin{vmatrix} RS \\ TU \end{vmatrix}$ r, and the array $\begin{vmatrix} HI \\ JK \end{vmatrix}$ h. Let us call the array $\begin{vmatrix} am \\ ma \end{vmatrix}$ w, and the array $\begin{vmatrix} rh \\ hr \end{vmatrix}$ x. Then the entire array is simply $\begin{vmatrix} wx \\ xw \end{vmatrix}$. While the original structure consisted of 64 symbols, it requires only 35 to write down its description:

$$ S = \frac{wx}{xw} $$

$$ w = \frac{am}{ma} \qquad\qquad x = \frac{rh}{hr} $$

$$ a = \frac{AB}{CD} \qquad m = \frac{MN}{OP} \qquad r = \frac{RS}{TU} \qquad h = \frac{HI}{JK} $$

We achieve the abbreviation by making use of the redundancy in the original structure. Since

the pattern $\frac{AB}{CD}$, for example, occurs four times in the total pattern, it is economical to represent it by the single symbol, a.

If a complex structure is completely unredundant—if no aspect of its structure can be inferred from any other—then it is its own simplest description. We can exhibit it, but we cannot describe it by a simpler structure. The hierarchic structures we have been discussing have a high degree of redundancy, hence can often be described in economical terms. The redundancy takes a number of forms, of which I shall mention three:

1. Hierarchic systems are usually composed of only a few different kinds of subsystems, in various combinations and arrangements. A familiar example is the proteins, their multitudinous variety arising from arrangements of only twenty different amino acids. Similarly, the ninety-odd elements provide all the kinds of building blocks needed for an infinite variety of molecules. Hence, we can construct our description from a restricted alphabet of elementary terms corresponding to the basic set of elementary subsystems from which the complex system is generated.

2. Hierarchic systems are, as we have seen, often nearly decomposable. Hence only aggregative properties of their parts enter into the description of the interactions of those parts. A generalization of the notion of near-decomposability might be called the "empty world hypothesis"—most things are. only weakly connected with most other things; for a tolerable description of reality only a tiny fraction of all possible interactions needs to be taken into account. By adopting a descriptive language that allows the absence of something to go unmentioned, a nearly empty world can be described quite concisely. Mother Hubbard did not have to check off the list of possible contents to say that her cupboard was bare.

3. By appropriate "recoding," the redundancy that is present but unobvious in the structure of a complex system can often be made patent. The most common recoding of descriptions of dynamic systems consists in replacing a description of the time path with a description of a differential law that generates that path. The simplicity, that is, resides in a constant relation between the state of the system at any given time and the state of the system a short time later. Thus, the structure of the sequence, 1 3 5 7 9 11 . . ., is most simply expressed by observing that each member is obtained by adding 2 to the previous one. But

---

dynamics can be separated out from the aspects that control the more rapid cellular metabolic processes. For this reason we should not despair of unravelling the web of causes. See also J. R. Platt's review of Elsasser's book in *Perspectives in biology and medicine* 2: 243–245, 1959.

this is the sequence that Galileo found to describe the velocity at the end of successive time intervals of a ball rolling down an inclined plane.

It is a familiar proposition that the task of science is to make use of the world's redundancy to describe that world simply. I shall not pursue the general methodological point here, but shall instead take a closer look at two main types of description that seem to be available to us in seeking an understanding of complex systems. I shall call these *state description* and *process description*, respectively.

STATE DESCRIPTIONS AND PROCESS DESCRIPTIONS

"A circle is the locus of all points equidistant from a given point." "To construct a circle, rotate a compass with one arm fixed until the other arm has returned to its starting point." It is implicit in Euclid that if you carry out the process specified in the second sentence, you will produce an object that satisfies the definition of the first. The first sentence is a state description of a circle, the second a process description.

These two modes of apprehending structure are the warp and weft of our experience. Pictures, blueprints, most diagrams, chemical structural formulae are state descriptions. Recipes, differential equations, equations for chemical reactions are process descriptions. The former characterize the world as sensed; they provide the criteria for identifying objects, often by modeling the objects themselves. The latter characterize the world as acted upon; they provide the means for producing or generating objects having the desired characteristics.

The distinction between the world as sensed and the world as acted upon defines the basic condition for the survival of adaptive organisms. The organism must develop correlations between goals in the sensed world and actions in the world of process. When they are made conscious and verbalized, these correlations correspond to what we usually call means-end analysis. Given a desired state of affairs and an existing state of affairs, the task of an adaptive organism is to find the difference between these two states, and then to find the correlating process that will erase the difference.[22]

Thus, problem solving requires continual trans-

lation between the state and process descriptions of the same complex reality. Plato, in the *Meno*, argued that all learning is remembering. He could not otherwise explain how we can discover or recognize the answer to a problem unless we already know the answer.[23] Our dual relation to the world is the source and solution of the paradox. We pose a problem by giving the state description of the solution. The task is to discover a sequence of processes that will produce the goal state from an initial state. Translation from the process description to the state description enables us to recognize when we have succeeded. The solution is genuinely new to us—and we do not need Plato's theory of remembering to explain how we recognize it.

There is now a growing body of evidence that the activity called human problem solving is basically a form of means-end analysis that aims at discovering a process description of the path that leads to a desired goal. The general paradigm is: given a blueprint, to find the corresponding recipe. Much of the activity of science is an application of that paradigm: given the description of some natural phenomena, to find the differential equations for processes that will produce the phenomena.

THE DESCRIPTION OF COMPLEXITY IN SELF-REPRODUCING SYSTEMS

The problem of finding relatively simple descriptions for complex systems is of interest not only for an understanding of human knowledge of the world but also for an explanation of how a complex system can reproduce itself. In my discussion of the evolution of complex systems, I touched only briefly on the role of self-reproduction.

Atoms of high atomic weight and complex inorganic molecules are witnesses to the fact that the evolution of complexity does not imply self-reproduction. If evolution of complexity from simplicity is sufficiently probable, it will occur repeatedly; the statistical equilibrium of the system will find a large fraction of the elementary particles participating in complex systems.

If, however, the existence of a particular complex form increased the probability of the creation of another form just like it, the equilibrium between complexes and components could be greatly altered in favor of the former. If we have a description of an object that is sufficiently clear and

---

[22] See H. A. Simon and A. Newell, Simulation of human thinking, *in* M. Greenberger (ed.), *Management and the computer of the future*, 95–114, esp. pp 110 ff., New York, Wiley, 1962.

[23] *The works of Plato*, B. Jowett, trans., 3: 26–35, New York, Dial Press.

complete, we can reproduce the object from the description. Whatever the exact mechanism of reproduction, the description provides us with the necessary information.

Now we have seen that the descriptions of complex systems can take many forms. In particular, we can have state descriptions or we can have process descriptions; blueprints or recipes. Reproductive processes could be built around either of these sources of information. Perhaps the simplest possibility is for the complex system to serve as a description of itself—a template on which a copy can be formed. One of the most plausible current theories, for example, of the reproduction of deoxyribonucleic acid (DNA) proposes that a DNA molecule, in the form of a double helix of matching parts (each essentially a "negative" of the other), unwinds to allow each half of the helix to serve as a template on which a new matching half can form.

On the other hand, our current knowledge of how DNA controls the metabolism of the organism suggests that reproduction by template is only one of the processes involved. According to the prevailing theory, DNA serves as a template both for itself and for the related substance ribonucleic acid (RNA). RNA, in turn, serves as a template for protein. But proteins—according to current knowledge—guide the organism's metabolism not by the template method but by serving as catalysts to govern reaction rates in the cell. While RNA is a blueprint for protein, protein is a recipe for metabolism.[24]

ONTOGENY RECAPITULATES PHYLOGENY

The DNA in the chromosomes of an organism contains some, and perhaps most, of the information that is needed to determine its development and activity. We have seen that, if current theories are even approximately correct, the information is recorded not as a state description of the organism but as a series of "instructions" for the construction and maintenance of the organism from nutrient materials. I have already used the metaphor of a recipe; I could equally well compare it with a computer program, which is also a sequence of instructions, governing the construction

[24] C. B. Anfinsen, *The molecular basis of evolution*, chs. 3 and 10, New York, Wiley, 1959, will qualify this sketchy, oversimplified account. For an imaginative discussion of some mechanisms of process description that could govern molecular structure, see H. H. Pattee, On the origin of macromolecular sequences, *Biophysical Journal* 1: 683–710, 1961.

of symbolic structures. Let me spin out some of the consequences of the latter comparison.

If genetic material is a program—viewed in its relation to the organism—it is a program with special and peculiar properties. First, it is a self-reproducing program; we have already considered its possible copying mechanism. Second, it is a program that has developed by Darwinian evolution. On the basis of our watchmaker's argument, we may assert that many of its ancestors were also viable programs—programs for the subassemblies.

Are there any other conjectures we can make about the structure of this program? There is a well-known generalization in biology that is verbally so neat that we would be reluctant to give it up even if the facts did not support it: ontogeny recapitulates phylogeny. The individual organism, in its development, goes through stages that resemble some of its ancestral forms. The fact that the human embryo develops gill bars and then modifies them for other purposes is a familiar particular belonging to the generalization. Biologists today like to emphasize the qualifications of the principle—that ontogeny recapitulates only the grossest aspects of phylogeny, and these only crudely. These qualifications should not make us lose sight of the fact that the generalization does hold in rough approximation—it does summarize a very significant set of facts about the organism's development. How can we interpret these facts?

One way to solve a complex problem is to reduce it to a problem previously solved—to show what steps lead from the earlier solution to a solution of the new problem. If, around the turn of the century, we wanted to instruct a workman to make an automobile, perhaps the simplest way would have been to tell him how to modify a wagon by removing the singletree and adding a motor and transmission. Similarly, a genetic program could be altered in the course of evolution by adding new processes that would modify a simpler form into a more complex one—to construct a gastrula, take a blastula and alter it!

The genetic description of a single cell may, therefore, take a quite different form from the genetic description that assembles cells into a multi-celled organism. Multiplication by cell division would require, as a minimum, a state description (the DNA, say), and a simple "interpretive process"—to use the term from computer language—that copies this description as a part of the larger copying process of cell division. But such a mechanism clearly would not suffice for the differentiation of cells in development. It appears more natural to conceptualize that mechanism as based on a process description, and a somewhat more complex interpretive process that produces the adult organism in a sequence of stages, each new stage in development representing the effect of an operator upon the previous one.

It is harder to conceptualize the interrelation of these two descriptions. Interrelated they must be, for enough has been learned of gene-enzyme mechanisms to show that these play a major role in development as in cell metabolism. The single clue we obtain from our earlier discussion is that the description may itself be hierarchical, or nearly decomposable, in structure, the lower levels governing the fast, "high-frequency" dynamics of the individual cell, the higher level interactions governing the slow, "low-frequency" dynamics of the developing multi-cellular organism.

There are only bits of evidence, apart from the facts of recapitulation, that the genetic program is organized in this way, but such evidence as exists is compatible with this notion.[25] To the extent that we can differentiate the genetic information that governs cell metabolism from the genetic information that governs the development of differentiated cells in the multi-cellular organization, we simplify enormously—as we have already seen —our task of theoretical description. But I have perhaps pressed this speculation far enough.

The generalization that in evolving systems whose descriptions are stored in a process language, we might expect ontogeny partially to recapitulate phylogeny has applications outside the

---

[25] There is considerable evidence that successive genes along a chromosome often determine enzymes controlling successive stages of protein syntheses. For a review of some of this evidence, see P. E. Hartman, Transduction: a comparative review, *in* W. D. McElroy and B. Glass (eds.), *The chemical basis of heredity*, Baltimore, Johns Hopkins Press, 1957, at pp. 442–454. Evidence for differential activity of genes in different tissues and at different stages of development is discussed by J. G. Gall, Chromosomal Differentiation, *in* W. D. McElroy and B. Glass (eds.), *The chemical basis of development*, Baltimore, Johns Hopkins Press, 1958, at pp. 103–135. Finally, a model very like that proposed here has been independently, and far more fully, outlined by J. R. Platt, A 'book model' of genetic information transfer in cells and tissues, *in* Kasha and Pullman (eds.), *Horizons in biochemistry*, New York, Academic Press, forthcoming. Of course, this kind of mechanism is not the only one in which development could be controlled by a process description. Induction, in the form envisaged in Spemann's organizer theory, is based on process description, in which metabolites in already formed tissue control the next stages of development.

realm of biology. It can be applied as readily, for example, to the transmission of knowledge in the educational process. In most subjects, particularly in the rapidly advancing sciences, the progress from elementary to advanced courses is to a considerable extent a progress through the conceptual history of the science itself. Fortunately, the recapitulation is seldom literal—any more than it is in the biological case. We do not teach the phlogiston theory in chemistry in order later to correct it. (I am not sure I could not cite examples in other subjects where we do exactly that.) But curriculum revisions that rid us of the accumulations of the past are infrequent and painful. Nor are they always desirable—partial recapitulation may, in many instances, provide the most expeditious route to advanced knowledge.

SUMMARY: THE DESCRIPTION OF COMPLEXITY

How complex or simple a structure is depends critically upon the way in which we describe it. Most of the complex structures found in the world are enormously redundant, and we can use this redundancy to simplify their description. But to use it, to achieve the simplification, we must find the right representation.

The notion of substituting a process description for a state description of nature has played a central role in the development of modern science. Dynamic laws, expressed in the form of systems of differential or difference equations, have in a large number of cases provided the clue for the simple description of the complex. In the preceding paragraphs I have tried to show that this characteristic of scientific inquiry is not accidental or superficial. The correlation between state description and process description is basic to the functioning of any adaptive organism, to its capacity for acting purposefully upon its environment. Our present-day understanding of genetic mechanisms suggests that even in describing itself the multi-cellular organism finds a process description—a genetically encoded program—to be the parsimonious and useful representation.

CONCLUSION

Our speculations have carried us over a rather alarming array of topics, but that is the price we must pay if we wish to seek properties common to many sorts of complex systems. My thesis has been that one path to the construction of a nontrivial theory of complex systems is by way of a theory of hierarchy. Empirically, a large proportion of the complex systems we observe in nature

HERBERT A. SIMON [PROC. AMER. PHIL. SOC.

exhibit hierarchic structure. On theoretical grounds we could expect complex systems to be hierarchies in a world in which complexity had to evolve from simplicity. In their dynamics, hierarchies have a property, near-decomposability, that greatly simplifies their behavior. Near-decomposability also simplifies the description of a complex system, and makes it easier to understand how the information needed for the development or reproduction of the system can be stored in reasonable compass.

In both science and engineering, the study of "systems" is an increasingly popular activity. Its popularity is more a response to a pressing need for synthesizing and analyzing complexity than it is to any large development of a body of knowledge and technique for dealing with complexity. If this popularity is to be more than a fad, necessity will have to mother invention and provide substance to go with the name. The explorations reviewed here represent one particular direction of search for such substance.

Part II
The New Economics of Organization

[8]

EQUILIBRIUM IN COMPETITIVE INSURANCE MARKETS: AN ESSAY ON THE ECONOMICS OF IMPERFECT INFORMATION*

MICHAEL ROTHSCHILD AND JOSEPH STIGLITZ

INTRODUCTION

Economic theorists traditionally banish discussions of information to footnotes. Serious consideration of costs of communication, imperfect knowledge, and the like would, it is believed, complicate without informing. This paper, which analyzes competitive markets in which the characteristics of the commodities exchanged are not fully known to at least one of the parties to the transaction, suggests that this comforting myth is false. Some of the most important conclusions of economic theory are not robust to considerations of imperfect information.

We are able to show that not only may a competitive equilibrium not exist, but when equilibria do exist, they may have strange properties. In the insurance market, upon which we focus much of our discussion, sales offers, at least those that survive the competitive process, do not specify a price at which customers can buy all the insurance they want, but instead consist of both a price and a quantity—a particular amount of insurance that the individual can buy at that price. Furthermore, if individuals were willing or able to reveal their information, everybody could be made better off. By their very being, high-risk individuals cause an externality: the low-risk individuals are worse off than they would be in the absence of the high-risk individuals. However, the high-risk individuals are no better off than they would be in the absence of the low-risk individuals.

These points are made in the next section by analysis of a simple model of a competitive insurance market. We believe that the lessons gleaned from our highly stylized model are of general interest, and attempt to establish this by showing in Section II that our model is robust and by hinting (space constraints prevent more) in the conclusion that our analysis applies to many other situations.

* This work was supported by National Science Foundation Grants SOC 74-22182 at the Institute for Mathematical Studies in the Social Sciences, Stanford University and SOC 73-05510 at Princeton University. The authors are indebted to Steve Salop, Frank Hahn, and Charles Wilson for helpful comments, and to the participants in the seminars at the several universities at which these ideas were presented.

I. THE BASIC MODEL

Most of our argument can be made by analysis of a very simple example. Consider an individual who will have an income of size W if he is lucky enough to avoid accident. In the event an accident occurs, his income will be only $W - d$. The individual can insure himself against this accident by paying to an insurance company a premium α_1, in return for which he will be paid $\hat{\alpha}_2$ if an accident occurs. Without insurance his income in the two states, "accident," "no accident," was $(W, W - d)$; with insurance it is now $(W - \alpha_1, W - d + \alpha_2)$, where $\alpha_2 = \hat{\alpha}_2 - \alpha_1$. The vector $\alpha = (\alpha_1, \alpha_2)$ completely describes the insurance contract.[1]

I.1 Demand for Insurance Contracts

On an insurance market, insurance contracts (the α's) are traded. To describe how the market works, it is necessary to describe the supply and demand functions of the participants in the market. There are only two kinds of participants, individuals who buy insurance and companies that sell it. Determining individual demand for insurance contracts is straightforward. An individual purchases an insurance contract so as to alter his pattern of income across states of nature. Let W_1 denote his income if there is no accident and W_2 his income if an accident occurs; the expected utility theorem states that under relatively mild assumptions his preferences for income in these two states of nature are described by a function of the form,

$$(1) \qquad \hat{V}(p, W_1, W_2) = (1 - p)U(W_1) + pU(W_2),$$

where $U(\ )$ represents the utility of money income[2] and p the probability of an accident. Individual demands may be derived from (1). A contract α is worth $V(p, \alpha) = \hat{V}(p, W - \alpha_1, W - d + \alpha_2)$. From

---

1. Actual insurance contracts are more complicated because a single contract will offer coverage against many potential losses. A formal generalization of the scheme above to cover this case is straightforward. Suppose that an individual will, in the absence of insurance, have an income of W_i if state i occurs. An insurance contract is simply an n-tuple $(\alpha_1, \ldots, \alpha_n)$ whose i-th coordinate describes the net payment of the individual to the insurance company if state i occurs. We confine our discussion to the simple case mentioned in the text, although it could be trivially extended to this more complicated case.

Many insurance contracts are not as complicated as the n-tuples described above—Blue Cross schedules listing maximum payments for specific illnesses and operations are an isolated example—but are instead resolvable into a fixed premium and a payment schedule that is in general a simple function of the size of the loss such as $F(L) = \text{Max } [0, c(L\text{-}D)]$, where $c \times 100\%$ is the co-insurance rate and D is the deductible. With such a contract when a loss occurs, determining its size is often a serious problem. In other words, finding out exactly what state of the world has occurred is not always easy. We ignore these problems. A large literature analyzes optimal insurance contracts. See, for example, Arrow (1971) and Borch (1968).

2. We assume that preferences are not state-dependent.

all the contracts the individual is offered, he chooses the one that maximizes $V(p, \alpha)$. Since he always has the option of buying no insurance, an individual will purchase a contract α only if $V(p, \alpha) \geq V(p, 0) = \hat{V}(p, W, W - d)$. We assume that persons are identical in all respects save their probability of having an accident and that they are risk-averse ($U'' < 0$); thus $V(p, \alpha)$ is quasi-concave.

1.2 Supply of Insurance Contracts

It is less straightforward to describe how insurance companies decide which contracts they should offer for sale and to which people. The return from an insurance contract is a random variable. We assume that companies are risk-neutral, that they are concerned only with expected profits, so that contract α when sold to an individual who has a probability of incurring an accident of p, is worth

$$(2) \qquad \pi(p, \alpha) = (1 - p)\alpha_1 - p\alpha_2 = \alpha_1 - p(\alpha_1 + \alpha_2).$$

Even if firms are not expected profit maximizers, on a well-organized competitive market they are likely to behave as if they maximized (2).[3]

Insurance companies have financial resources such that they are willing and able to sell any number of contracts that they think will make an expected profit.[4] The market is competitive in that there is free entry. Together these assumptions guarantee that any contract that is demanded and that is expected to be profitable will be supplied.

3. Since the theory of the firm behavior under uncertainty is one of the more unsettled areas of economic theory, we cannot look to it for the sort of support of any assumption we might make, which the large body of literature devoted to the expected utility theorem provides for equation (1) above. Nonetheless, two arguments (and the absence of a remotely as attractive distinguishable alternative) justify (2): the first is the rather vaguely supported but widely held proposition that companies owned by stockholders who themselves hold diversified portfolios ought to maximize their expected profits; management that does not follow this policy will be displaced. The second supposes that insurance companies are held by a large number of small shareholders each of whom receives a small share of the firm's profits. If the risks insured against are independent or otherwise diversifiable, then the law of large numbers guarantees that each shareholder's return will be approximately constant and any individual insurance contract contributes to his profits only through its expected value. In this case stockholders' interests will be well served if, and only if, management maximizes expected profits.

A variant of the second argument is obtained by considering the case in which shareholders and policyholders are the same people, or in more familiar terms, when the insurance company is a mutual company. In this case the insurance company is just a mechanism for risk pooling. Under conditions where diversification is possible, each contract's contribution to the company's dividend (or loss) is proportional to its expected value.

4. The same kinds of arguments used to justify (2)—in particular the appeal to the law of large numbers—can be used to justify this assumption. Weaker conditions than independence will suffice. See Revesz (1960), p. 190, for a theorem that states roughly that, if insurance contracts can be arranged in space so that even though con-

632   *QUARTERLY JOURNAL OF ECONOMICS*

I.3 Information about Accident Probabilities

We have not so far discussed how customers and companies come
to know or estimate the parameter p, which plays such a crucial role
in the valuation formulae (1) and (2). We make the bald assumption
that individuals know their accident probabilities, while companies
do not. Since insurance purchasers are identical in all respects save
their propensity to have accidents, the force of this assumption is that
companies cannot discriminate among their potential customers on
the basis of their characteristics. This assumption is defended and
modified in subsection II.1.

A firm may use its customers' market behavior to make inferences about their accident probabilities. Other things equal, those with
high accident probabilities will demand more insurance than those
who are less accident-prone. Although possibly accurate, this is not
a profitable way of finding out about customer characteristics. Insurance companies want to know their customers' characteristics in
order to decide on what terms they should offer to let them buy insurance. Information that accrues after purchase may be used only
to lock the barn after the horse has been stolen.

It is often possible to force customers to make market choices in
such a way that they both reveal their characteristics and make the
choices the firm would have wanted them to make had their characteristics been publicly known. In their contribution to this symposium,
Salop and Salop call a market device with these characteristics a
self-selection mechanism. Analysis of the functioning of self-selection
mechanisms on competitive markets is a major focus of this paper.

I.4 Definition of Equilibrium

We assume that customers can buy only one insurance contract.
This is an objectionable assumption. It implies, in effect, that the seller
of insurance specifies both the prices and quantities of insurance
purchased. In most competitive markets, sellers determine only price
and have no control over the amount their customers buy. Nonetheless, we believe that what we call price and quantity competition is
more appropriate for our model of the insurance market than tradi-

---

tracts that are close to one another are not independent, those that are far apart are
approximately independent, then the average return from all contracts is equal to its
expected value with probability one. Thus, an insurance company that holds a large
number of health policies should be risk-neutral, even though the fact that propinquity
carries illness implies that not all insured risks are independent. Some risks that cannot
be diversified; i.e., the risk of nuclear war (or of a flood or a plague) cannot be spread
by appeal to the law of large numbers. Our model applies to diversifiable risks. This
class of risks is considerably larger than the independent ones.

tional price competition. We defend this proposition at length in subsection II.2 below.

Equilibrium in a competitive insurance market is a set of contracts such that, when customers choose contracts to maximize expected utility, (i) no contract in the equilibrium set makes negative expected profits; and (ii) there is no contract outside the equilibrium set that, if offered, will make a nonnegative profit. This notion of equilibrium is of the Cournot-Nash type; each firm assumes that the contracts its competitors offer are independent of its own actions.

I.5 Equilibrium with Identical Customers

Only when customers have different accident probabilities, will insurance companies have imperfect information. We examine this case below. To illustrate our, mainly graphical, procedure, we first analyze the equilibrium of a competitive insurance market with identical customers.[5]

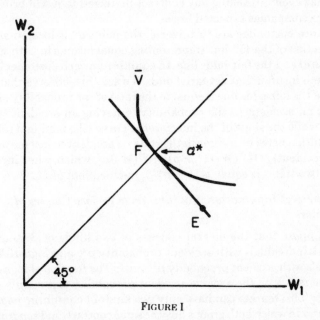

FIGURE I

In Figure I the horizontal and vertical axes represent income in

5. The analysis is identical if individuals have different p's, but companies know the accident probabilities of their customers. The market splits into several submarkets—one for each different p represented. Each submarket has the equilibrium described here.

the states: no accident, accident, respectively. The point E with coordinates $(\hat{W}_1, \hat{W}_2)$ is the typical customer's uninsured state. Indifference curves are level sets of the function of equation (1). Purchasing the insurance policy $\alpha = (\alpha_1, \alpha_2)$ moves the individual from E to the point $(\hat{W}_1 - \alpha_1, \hat{W}_2 + \alpha_2)$.

Free entry and perfect competition will ensure that policies bought in competitive equilibrium make zero expected profits, so that if α is purchased,

$$(3) \qquad\qquad \alpha_1(1 - p) - \alpha_2 p = 0.$$

The set of all policies that break even is given analytically by (3) and diagrammatically by the line EF in Figure I, which is sometimes referred to as the fair-odds line. The equilibrium policy α^* maximizes the individual's (expected) utility and just breaks even. Purchasing α^* locates the customer at the tangency of the indifference curve with the fair-odds line. α^* satisfies the two conditions of equilibrium: (i) it breaks even; (ii) selling any contract preferred to it will bring insurance companies expected losses.

Since customers are risk-averse, the point α^* is located at the intersection of the 45°-line (representing equal income in both states of nature) and the fair-odds line. In equilibrium each customer buys complete insurance at actuarial odds. To see this, observe that the slope of the fair-odds line is equal to the ratio of the probability of not having an accident to the probability of having an accident ($(1 - p)/p$), while the slope of the indifference curve (the marginal rate of substitution between income in the state no accident to income in the state accident) is $[U'(W_1) (1 - p)]/[U'(W_2)p]$, which, when income in the two states is equal, is $(1 - p)/p$, independent of U.

I.6 Imperfect Information: Equilibrium with Two Classes of Customers

Suppose that the market consists of two kinds of customers: low-risk individuals with accident probability p^L, and high-risk individuals with accident probability $p^H > p^L$. The fraction of high-risk customers is λ, so the average accident probability is $\bar{p} = \lambda p^H + (1 - \lambda)p^L$. This market can have only two kinds of equilibria: *pooling equilibria* in which both groups buy the same contract, and *separating equilibria* in which different types purchase different contracts.

A simple argument establishes that *there cannot be a pooling equilibrium*. The point E in Figure II is again the initial endowment of all customers. Suppose that α is a pooling equilibrium and consider $\pi(\bar{p}, \alpha)$. If $\pi(\bar{p}, \alpha) < 0$, then firms offering α lose money, contradicting

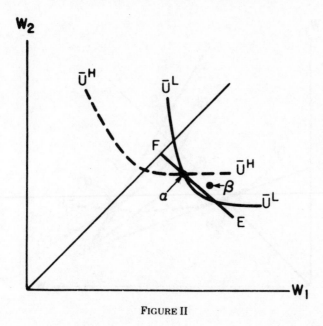

FIGURE II

the definition of equilibrium. If $\pi(\bar{p}, \alpha) > 0$, then there is a contract that offers slightly more consumption in each state of nature, which still will make a profit when all individuals buy it. All will prefer this contract to α, so α cannot be an equilibrium. Thus, $\pi(\bar{p}, \alpha) = 0$, and α lies on the market odds line EF (with slope $(1 - \bar{p})/\bar{p}$).

It follows from (1) that at α the slope of the high-risk indifference curve through α, $\bar{U}^H$, is $(p^L/1 - p^L)(1 - p^H/p^H)$ times the slope of $\bar{U}^L$, the low-risk indifference curve through α. In this figure $\bar{U}^H$ is a broken line, and $\bar{U}^L$ a solid line. The curves intersect at α; thus there is a contract, β in Figure II, near α, which low-risk types prefer to α. The high risk prefer α to β. Since β is near α, it makes a profit when the less risky buy it, $(\pi(p^L, \beta) \simeq \pi(p^L, \alpha) > \pi(\bar{p}, \alpha) = 0)$. The existence of β contradicts the second part of the definition of equilibrium; α cannot be an equilibrium.

If there is an equilibrium, each type must purchase a separate contract. Arguments, which are, we hope, by now familiar, demonstrate that each contract in the equilibrium set makes zero profits. In Figure III the low-risk contract lies on line EL (with slope $(1 - p^L)/p^L)$, and the high-risk contract on line EH (with slope $(1 - p^H)/p^H)$. As was shown in the previous subsection, the contract on EH most preferred by high-risk customers gives complete insurance.

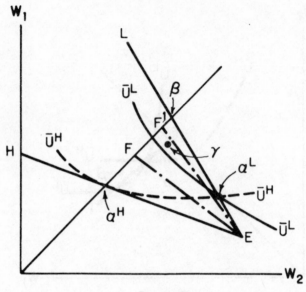

FIGURE III

This is α^H in Figure III; it must be part of any equilibrium. Low-risk customers would, of all contracts on EL, most prefer contract β which, like α^H, provides complete insurance. However, β offers more consumption in each state than α^H, and high-risk types will prefer it to α^H. If β and α^H are marketed, both high- and low-risk types will purchase β. The nature of imperfect information in this model is that insurance companies are unable to distinguish among their customers. All who demand β must be sold β. Profits will be negative; (α^H, β) is not an equilibrium set of contracts.

An equilibrium contract for low-risk types must not be more attractive to high-risk types than α^H; it must lie on the southeast side of U^H, the high-risk indifference curve through α^H. We leave it to the reader to demonstrate that of all such contracts, the one that low-risk types most prefer is α^l, the contract at the intersection of EL and U^H in Figure III. This establishes that *the set (α^H, α^L) is the only possible equilibrium for a market with low- and high-risk customers.*[6] However, (α^H, α^l) may not be an equilibrium. Consider the contract γ in Figure III. It lies above U^L, the low-risk indifference curve through α^l and also above U^H. If γ is offered, both low- and high-risk types

6. This largely heuristic argument can be made completely rigorous. See Wilson (1976).

will purchase it in preference to either α^H or α^L. If it makes a profit when both groups buy it, γ will upset the potential equilibrium of (α^H, α^L). γ's profitability depends on the composition of the market. If there are sufficiently many high-risk people that EF represents market odds, then γ will lose money. If market odds are given by EF' (as they will be if there are relatively few high-risk insurance customers), then γ will make a profit. Since (α^H, α^L) is the only possible equilibrium, in this case the competitive insurance market will have no equilibrium.

This establishes that *a competitive insurance market may have no equilibrium.*

We have not found a simple intuitive explanation for this nonexistence; but the following observations, prompted by Frank Hahn's note (1974), may be suggestive. The information that is revealed by an individual's choice of an insurance contract depends on all the other insurance policies offered; there is thus a fundamental informational externality that each company, when deciding on which contract it will offer, fails to take into account. Given any set of contracts that breaks even, a firm may enter the market using the informational structure implicit in the availability of that set of contracts to make a profit; at the same time it forces the original contracts to make a loss. But as in any Nash equilibrium, the firm fails to take account of the consequences of its actions, and in particular, the fact that when those policies are no longer offered, the informational structure will have changed and it can no longer make a profit.

We can characterize the conditions under which an equilibrium does not exist. An equilibrium will not exist if the costs to the low-risk individual of pooling are low (because there are relatively few of the high-risk individuals who have to be subsidized, or because the subsidy per individual is low, i.e., when the probabilities of the two groups are not too different), or if their costs of separating are high. The costs of separating arise from the individual's inability to obtain complete insurance. Thus, the costs of separating are related to the individuals' attitudes toward risk. Certain polar cases make these propositions clear. If $p^L = 0$, it never pays the low-risk individuals to pool, and by continuity, for sufficiently small p^L it does not pay to pool. Similarly, if individuals are risk-neutral, it never pays to pool; if they are infinitely risk averse with utility functions

$$(1') \qquad \bar{V}(p, W_1, W_2) = \text{Min}\ (W_1, W_2),$$

it always pays to pool.

I.7 Welfare Economics of Equilibrium

One of the interesting properties of the equilibrium is that the presence of the high-risk individuals exerts a negative externality on the low-risk individuals. The externality is completely dissipative; there are losses to the low-risk individuals, but the high-risk individuals are no better off than they would be in isolation.

If only the high-risk individuals would admit to their having high accident probabilities, all individuals would be made better off without anyone being worse off.

The separating equilibrium we have described may not be Pareto optimal even relative to the information that is available. As we show in subsection II.3 below, there may exist a pair of policies that break even together and that make both groups better off.

II. Robustness

The analysis of Section I had three principal conclusions: First, competition on markets with imperfect information is more complex than in standard models. Perfect competitors may limit the quantities their customers can buy, not from any desire to exploit monopoly power, but simply in order to improve their information. Second, equilibrium may not exist. Finally, competitive equilibria are not Pareto optimal. It is natural to ask whether these conclusions (particularly the first, which was an assumption rather than a result of the analysis) can be laid to the special and possibly strained assumptions of our model. We think not. Our conclusions (or ones very like) must follow from a serious attempt to comprehend the workings of competition with imperfect and asymmetric information. We have analyzed the effect of changing our model in many ways. The results were always essentially the same.

Our attempts to establish robustness took two tacks. First, we showed that our results did not depend on the simple technical specifications of the model. This was tedious, and we have excised most of the details from the present version. The reader interested in analysis of the effects (distinctly minor) of changing our assumptions that individuals are alike in all respects save their accident probabilities, that there are only two kinds of customers, and that the insurance market lasts but a single period, is referred to earlier versions of this paper.[7] An assessment of the importance of the as-

7. See Rothschild and Stiglitz (1975). One curious result of these investigations should be mentioned. In other areas of economic theory where existence of equilibrium has been a problem, smoothing things by introducing a continuum of individuals of

sumption that individuals know their accident probabilities, while insurance companies do not (which raises more interesting issues), is given in subsection II.1 below.

Another approach to the question of robustness is the subject of the next three subsections. In them we question the behavioral assumptions and the equilibrium concepts used in Section I.

II.1 Information Assumptions

Suppose that there are two groups of customers and that not all individuals within each group have the same accident probability. The average accident probability of one group is greater than that of the other; individuals within each group know the mean accident probability for members of their group, but do not know their own accident probabilities. As before, the insurance company cannot tell directly the accident probability of any particular individual, or even the group to which he belongs. For example, suppose that some persons occasionally drink too much, while the others almost never drink. Insurance firms cannot discover who drinks and who does not. Individuals know that drinking affects accident probabilities, but it affects different people differently. Each individual does not know how it will affect him.

In such a situation the expected utility theorem states that individuals make (and behave according to) estimates of their accident probabilities; if these estimates are unbiased in the sense that the average accident probability of those who estimate their accident probability to be p actually is p, then the analysis goes through as before.

Unbiasedness seems a reasonable assumption (what is a more attractive alternative?). However, not even this low level of correctness of beliefs is required for our conclusions. Suppose, for example, that individuals differ both with respect to their accident probabilities and to their risk aversion, but they all assume that their own accident probabilities are $\bar{p}$. If low-risk individuals are less risk-averse on average, then there will not exist a pooling equilibrium; there may exist no equilibrium at all; and if there does exist an equilibrium, it will entail partial insurance for both groups. Figure IV shows that there

different types can insure existence. Not so here. If there is a continuous distribution of accident probabilities (but customers are otherwise identical), then equilibrium never exists. There is an intuitive explanation for this striking result. We argued above that, if accident probabilities were close together, then equilibrium would not exist. When there is a continuum of probabilities, there always are individuals with close probabilities with whom it pays to "pool." For a proof of this result, which is not elementary, see Riley (1976).

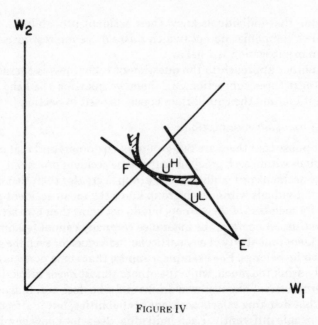

FIGURE IV

will not exist a pooling equilibrium. If there were a pooling equilibrium, it would clearly be with complete insurance at the market odds,
since both groups' indifference curves have the slope of the market
odds line there. If the low-risk individuals are less risk-averse, then
the two indifference curves are tangent at F, but elsewhere the
high-risk individuals' indifference curve lies above the low-risk individuals' indifference curve. Thus, any policy in the shaded area
between the two curves will be purchased by the low-risk individuals
in preference to the pooling contract at F.

    Other such cases can be analyzed, but we trust that the general
principle is clear. Our pathological conclusions do not require that
people have particularly good information about their accident
probabilities. They will occur under a wide variety of circumstances,
including the appealing case of unbiasedness. Neither insurance firms
nor their customers have to be perfectly informed about the differences in risk properties that exist among individuals: What is required
is that individuals with different risk properties differ in some characteristic that can be linked with the purchase of insurance and that,
somehow, insurance firms discover this link.

II.2 Price Competition Versus Quantity Competition

    One can imagine our model of the insurance market operating
in two distinct modes. The first, price competition, is familiar to all

THE ECONOMICS OF IMPERFECT INFORMATION   641

students of competitive markets. Associated with any insurance contract α is a number $q(\alpha) = \alpha_1/\alpha_2$, which, since it is the cost per unit coverage, is called the price of insurance. Under price competition, insurance firms establish a price of insurance and allow their customers to buy as much or as little insurance as they want at that price. Thus, if contract α is available from a company, so are the contracts 2α and $(\frac{1}{2})\alpha$; the former pays twice as much benefits (and costs twice as much in premiums) as α; the latter is half as expensive and provides half as much coverage.

Opposed to price competition is what we call price and quantity competition. In this regime companies may offer a number of different contracts, say $\alpha^1, \alpha^2, \dots, \alpha^n$. Individuals may buy at most one contract. They are not allowed to buy arbitrary multipies of contracts offered, but must instead settle for one of the contracts explicitly put up for sale. A particular contract specifies both a price and a quantity of insurance. Under price and quantity competition it is conceivable that insurance contracts with different prices of insurance will exist in equilibrium; people who want more insurance may be willing to pay a higher price for it (accept less favorable odds) than those who make do with shallower coverage. Under price competition customers will buy insurance only at the lowest price quoted in the market.

The argument of Section I depends heavily on our assumption that price and quantity competition, and not simply price competition, characterizes the competitive insurance market. This assumption is defended here. The argument is basically quite simple. Price competition is a special case of price and quantity competition. Nothing in the definition of price and quantity competition prevents firms from offering for sale a set of contracts with the same price of insurance. Since the argument above characterized all equilibria under price and quantity competition, it also characterized all equilibria when some firms set prices and others set prices and quantities. Thus, it must be that price competition cannot compete with price and quantity competition.[8]

This argument hinges on one crucial assumption: regardless of the form of competition, customers purchase but a single insurance contract or equivalently that the total amount of insurance purchased

8. We leave to the reader a detailed proof. A sketch follows. Suppose that there are two groups in the population. If the price of insurance is q, high- and low-risk customers will buy $\alpha^H(q)$ and $\alpha^L(q)$, respectively. It is easy to figure out what total insurance company profits, $P(q)$, are. The equilibrium price q^* is the smallest q such that $P(q) = 0$. Since $P(q)$ is continuous in q and it is easy to find q such that $P(q) > 0$ and $P(q) < 0$, such a q^* exists. To show that price competition will not survive, it is only necessary to show that $(\alpha^H(q^*), \alpha^L(q^*))$ is not an equilibrium set of contracts as defined in subsection I.4 above.

by any one customer is known to all companies that sell to him. We think that this is an accurate description of procedures on at least some insurance markets. Many insurance policies specify either that they are not in force if there is another policy or that they insure against only the first, say, $1,000 of losses suffered. That is, instead of being a simple bet for or against the occurrence of a particular event, an insurance policy is a commitment on the part of the company to restore at least partially the losses brought about by the occurrence of that event. The person who buys two $1,000 accident insurance policies does not have $2,000 worth of protection. If an accident occurs, all he gets from his second policy is the privilege of watching his companies squabble over the division of the $1,000 payment. There is no point in buying more than one policy.

Why should insurance markets operate in this way? One simple and obvious explanation is moral hazard. Because the insured can often bring about, or at least make more likely, the event being insured against, insurance companies want to limit the amount of insurance their customers buy. Companies want to see that their customers do not purchase so much insurance that they have an interest in an accident occurring. Thus, companies will want to monitor the purchases of their customers. Issuing contracts of the sort described above is the obvious way to do so.

A subtler explanation for this practice is provided by our argument that price and quantity competition can dominate price competition. If the market is in equilibrium under price competition, a firm can offer a contract, specifying price and quantity, that will attract the low-risk customers away from the companies offering contracts specifying price alone. Left with only high-risk customers, these firms will lose money. This competitive gambit will successfully upset the price competition equilibria if the entering firm can be assured that those who buy its contracts hold no other insurance. Offering insurance that pays off only for losses not otherwise insured is a way to guarantee this.

It is sometimes suggested that the term "competitive" can be applied only to markets where there is a single price of a commodity and each firm is a price taker. This seems an unnecessarily restrictive use of the term competitive. The basic idea underlying competitive markets involves free entry and noncollusive behavior among the participants in the market. In some economic environments price taking without quantity restrictions is a natural result of such markets. In the situations described in this paper, this is not so.

II.3 Restrictions on Firm Behavior and Optimal Subsidies

An important simplification of the analysis of Section I was the assumption that each insurance company issued but a single contract. We once thought this constraint would not affect the nature of equilibrium. We argued that in equilibrium firms must make nonnegative profits. Suppose that a firm offers two contracts, one of which makes an expected profit of say, S, per contract sold, the other an expected loss of L per contract. The firm can make nonnegative expected profits if the ratio of the profitable to the unprofitable contracts sold is at least μ, where $\mu = L/S$. However, the firm can clearly make more profits if it sells only the contracts on which it makes a profit. It and its competitors have no reason to offer the losing contracts, and in competitive equilibrium, they will not be offered. Since only contracts that make nonnegative profits will be offered, it does not matter, given our assumptions about entry, that firms are assumed to issue only a single contract. If there is a contract that could make a profit, a firm will offer it.

This argument is not correct. The possibility of offering more than one contract is important to firms, and to the nature and existence of equilibrium. Firms that offer several contracts are not dependent on the policies offered by other firms for the information generated by the choices of individuals. By offering a menu of policies, insurance firms may be able to obtain information about the accident probabilities of particular individuals. Furthermore, although there may not be an equilibrium in which the profits from one contract subsidize the losses of another contract, it does not follow that such a pair of contracts cannot break what would otherwise be an equilibrium.

Such a case is illustrated in Figure V. *EF* is again the market odds line. A separating equilibrium exists ($\bar{\alpha}^H$, $\bar{\alpha}^L$). Suppose that a firm offered the two contracts, $\alpha^{H\prime}$ and $\alpha^{L\prime}$; $\alpha^{H\prime}$ makes a loss, $\alpha^{L\prime}$ makes a profit. High-risk types prefer $\alpha^{H\prime}$ to $\bar{\alpha}^H$, and low-risk types prefer $\alpha^{L\prime}$ to $\bar{\alpha}^L$. These two contracts, if offered by a single firm together, do not make losses. The profits from $\alpha^{L\prime}$ subsidize the losses of $\alpha^{H\prime}$. Thus, ($\alpha^{H\prime}$, $\alpha^{L\prime}$) upsets the equilibrium ($\bar{\alpha}^H$, $\bar{\alpha}^L$).

This example points up another possible inefficiency of separating equilibria. Consider the problem of choosing two contracts (α^H, α^L) such that α^L maximizes the utility of the low-risk individual subject to the constraints that (a) the high-risk individual prefers α^H to α^L and (b) the pair of contracts α^H and α^L break even when bought by high- and low-risk types, respectively, in the ratio λ to $(1 - \lambda)$. This

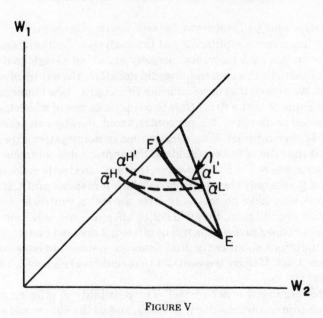

FIGURE V

is a kind of optimal subsidy problem. If the separating equilibrium, when it exists, does not solve this problem, it is inefficient. Figure V shows that the separating equilibrium can be inefficient in this sense. We now show that if there are enough high-risk people, then the separating equilibrium can be efficient.

The optimal subsidy problem always has a solution $(\alpha^{H*}, \alpha^{L*})$. The optimal high-risk contract α^{H*} will always entail complete insurance so that $V(p^H, \alpha^{H*}) = U(W - p^H d + a)$, where a is the per capita subsidy of the high risk by the low risk. This subsidy decreases income for each low-risk person by γa (where $\gamma = \lambda/(1 - \lambda)$) in each state. Net of this charge α^{L*} breaks even when low-risk individuals buy it. Thus, $\alpha^{L*} = (\alpha_1 + \gamma a, \alpha_2 - \gamma a)$, where $\alpha_1 = \alpha_2 p^L/(1 - p^L)$.

To find the optimal contract, one solves the following problem: Choose a and α_2 to maximize

$$U(X)(1 - p^L) + U(Z)p^L,$$

subject to

$$U(Y) \geq U(X)(1 - p^H) + U(Z)p^H$$

$$a \geq 0,$$

where

$$X = W_0 - \gamma a - \alpha_2 p^L/(1 - p^L),$$
$$Y = W_0 - p^H d + a,$$

and

$$Z = W_0 - d - \gamma a + \alpha_2.$$

The solution to this problem can be analyzed by standard Kuhn-Tucker techniques. If the constraint $a \geq 0$ is binding at the optimum, then the solution involves no subsidy to the high-risk persons; $(\alpha^{H*}, \alpha^{L*})$ is the separating equilibrium. It is straightforward but tedious to show that a sufficient condition for this is that

(4)
$$\frac{(p^H - p^L)\gamma}{p^L(1 - p)^L)} > \frac{U'(Y)[U'(Z) - U'(X)]}{U'(X)U'(Z)}$$

where X, Y, and Z are determined by the optimal a^*, α_2^*. The right-hand side of (4) is always less than

$$\frac{U'(W_0 - d)[U'(W_0 - d) - U'(W_0)]}{U'(W_0)^2}$$

so that there exist values of γ (and thus of λ) large enough to satisfy (4).

II.4 Alternative Equilibrium Concepts

There are a number of other concepts of equilibrium that we might have employed. These concepts differ with respect to assumptions concerning the behavior of the firms in the market. In our model the firm assumes that its actions do not affect the market—the set of policies offered by other firms was independent of its own offering.

In this subsection we consider several other equilibrium concepts, implying either less or more rationality in the market. We could, for instance, call any set of policies that just break even given the set of individuals who purchase them an *informationally consistent equilibrium*. This assumes that the forces for the creation of new contracts are relatively weak (in the absence of profits). Thus, in Figure III, α^H and any contract along the line EL below α^L is a set of informationally consistent separating equilibrium contracts; any single contract along the line EF is an informationally consistent pooling equilibrium contract. This is the notion of equilibrium that Spence (1973) has employed in most of his work. The longer the lags in the system, the greater the difficulty of competing by offering different contracts, the more stable is an informationally consistent equilibrium. Thus, while

this seems to us a reasonable equilibrium concept for the models of
educational signaling on which Spence focused, it is less compelling
when applied to insurance or credit markets (see Jaffee and Russell's
contribution to this symposium).

A *local* equilibrium is a set of contracts such that there do not
exist any contracts in the vicinity of the equilibrium contracts that
will be chosen and make a positive profit. If we rule out the subsidies
of the last subsection, then the set of separating contracts, which
maximizes the welfare of low-risk individuals, is a local equilibrium.

The notion that firms experiment with contracts similar to those
already on the market motivates the idea of a local equilibrium. Even
if firms have little knowledge about the shape of utility functions, and
about the proportions of population in different accident probabilities,
one would expect that competition would lead to small perturbations
around the equilibrium. A stable equilibrium requires that such
perturbations not lead to firms making large profits, as would be the
case with some perturbations around a pooling point.

These two concepts of equilibrium imply that firms act less ra-
tionally than we assumed they did in Section I. It is possible that firms
exhibit a greater degree of rationality; that is, firms ought not to take
the set of contracts offered by other firms as given, but ought to assume that other firms will act as they do, or at least will respond in
some way to the new contract offered by the firm. Hence, in those
cases where in our definition there was no equilibrium, because for
any set of contracts there is a contract that will break even and be
chosen by a subset of the population, given that the contracts offered
by the other firms remain unchanged, those contracts that break the
equilibrium may not break even if the other firms also change their
contracts. The peculiar provision of many insurance contracts, that
the effective premium is not determined until the *end* of the period
(when the individual obtains what is called a dividend), is perhaps
a reflection of the uncertainty associated with who will purchase the
policy, which in turn is associated with the uncertainty about what
contracts other insurance firms will offer.

Wilson (1976) introduced and analyzed one such nonmyopic
equilibrium concept. A Wilson equilibrium is a set of contracts such
that, when customers choose among them so as to maximize profits,
(a) all contracts make nonnegative profits and (b) there does not exist
a new contract (or set of contracts), which, if offered, makes positive
profits even when all contracts that lose money as a result of this entry
are withdrawn. In the simple model of Section I, such equilibria always

exist. Comparing this definition with the one of subsection I.4 above makes it clear that, when it exists, our separating equilibrium is also a Wilson equilibrium. When this does not exist, the Wilson equilibrium is the pooling contract that maximizes the utility of the low-risk customers. This is β in Figure VI. β dominates the separating pair (α^L, α^H). Consider a contract like γ, which the low risk prefer to β. Under our definition of equilibrium it upsets β. Under Wilson's it does not. When the low risk desert β for γ, it loses money and is withdrawn. Then the high risk also buy γ. When both groups buy γ, it loses money. Thus, γ does not successfully compete against β.

Although this equilibrium concept is appealing, it is not without its difficulties. It seems a peculiar halfway house; firms respond to competitive entry by dropping policies, but not by adding new policies. Furthermore, although counterexamples are very complicated to construct, it appears that a Wilson equilibrium may not exist if groups differ in their attitudes towards risk. Finally, in the absence of collusion or regulation, in a competitive insurance market, it is hard to see how or why any single firm should take into account the consequences of its offering a new policy. On balance, it seems to us that nonmyopic equilibrium concepts are more appropriate for models of monopoly (or oligopoly) than for models of competition.

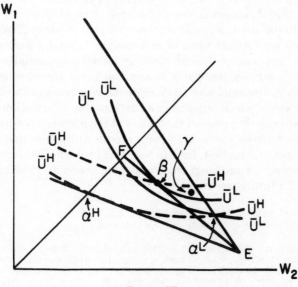

FIGURE VI

III. Conclusion

We began this research with the hope of showing that even a small amount of imperfect information could have a significant effect on competitive markets. Our results were more striking than we had hoped: the single price equilibrium of conventional competitive analysis was shown to be no longer viable; market equilibrium, when it existed, consisted of contracts which specified both prices and quantities; the high-risk (low ability, etc.) individuals exerted a dissipative externality on the low-risk (high ability) individuals; the structure of the equilibrium as well as its existence depended on a number of assumptions that, with perfect information, were inconsequential; and finally, and in some ways most disturbing, under quite plausible conditions equilibrium did not exist.

Our analysis, and our conclusions, extend beyond the simple insurance market described above. The models of educational screening and signaling studied by, among others, Arrow (1973), Riley (1975), Spence (1973, 1974), and Stiglitz (1971, 1972, 1974a, 1975b), are obvious examples. The other papers in this symposium describe models that can be profitably studied using our techniques and our concepts. Models in which communities choose the level of public goods and individuals choose among communities on the basis of the menu of public goods and taxes that the different communities offer, provide a less obvious but, we think, important case.[9]

Do these theoretical speculations tell us anything about the real world? In the absence of empirical work it is hard to say. The market on which we focused most of our analysis, that for insurance, is probably not competitive; whether our model may partially explain this fact is almost impossible to say. But there are other markets, particularly financial and labor markets, which appear to be competitive and in which imperfect and asymmetric information play an important role. We suspect that many of the peculiar institutions of these labor markets arise as responses to the difficulties that they, or any competitive market, have in handling problems of information. Establishing (or refuting) this conjecture seems to provide a rich agenda for future research.

University of Wisconsin, Madison
Stanford University and All Souls College, Oxford

9. See F. Westhoff's dissertation (1974), and Stiglitz (1974b). A more complete discussion of these is in our earlier working paper referred to in footnote 7 above. Salop and Salop (1972) demonstrated, in an early draft of their symposium paper, that contingent loan plans for repayment of tuition, and their possible defects, can be analyzed along these lines.

THE ECONOMICS OF IMPERFECT INFORMATION 649

REFERENCES

Arrow, K. J., *Essays in the Theory of Risk Bearing* (Chicago: Markham, 1971).

——, "Higher Education as a Filter," *Journal of Public Economics, II* (July 1973), 193–216.

Borch, K., *The Economics of Uncertainty* (Princeton, N.J.: Princeton University Press, 1968).

Hahn, F. H., "Notes on R-S Models of Insurance Markets," mimeo, Cambridge University, 1974.

Riley, J., "Competitive Signaling," *Journal of Economic Theory,* X (April 1975), 174–86.

——, "Informational Equilibrium," mimeo, Rand Corporation, 1976.

Revesz, P., *Laws of Large Numbers* (New York: Academic Press, 1960).

Rothschild, M., and J. E. Stiglitz, "Equilibrium in Competitive Insurance Markets," Technical Report No. 170, IMSSS Stanford University, 1975.

Spence, M., "Job Market Signaling," this *Journal,* LXXXVII (Aug. 1973), 355–79.

——, *Market Signaling* (Cambridge: Harvard University Press, 1974).

Stiglitz, J. E., "Perfect and Imperfect Capital Markets," paper presented to Econometric Society Meeting, New Orleans, 1971.

——, "Education as a Screening Device and the Distribution of Income," mimeo, Yale University, 1972.

——, "Demand for Education in Public and Private School Systems," *Journal of Public Economics,* III (Nov. 1974a), 349–86.

——, "Pure Theory of Local Public Goods," in M. Feldstein ed. IEA Conference Volume (Turin, 1974b.).

——, "The Theory of Screening, Education, and Distribution of Income," *American Economic Review,* LXV (June 1975), 283–300.

Westhoff, Frank H., "The Theory of Local Public Goods," Ph.D. thesis, Yale University, 1974.

Wilson, Charles A., "Equilibrium in a Class of Self-Selection Models," Ph.D. thesis, University of Rochester, 1976.

[9]

Moral hazard in teams

Bengt Holmstrom*

This article studies moral hazard with many agents. The focus is on two features that are novel in a multiagent setting: free riding and competition. The free-rider problem implies a new role for the principal: administering incentive schemes that do not balance the budget. This new role is essential for controlling incentives and suggests that firms in which ownership and labor are partly separated will have an advantage over partnerships in which output is distributed among agents. A new characterization of informative (hence valuable) monitoring is derived and applied to analyze the value of relative performance evaluation. It is shown that competition among agents (due to relative evaluations) has merit solely as a device to extract information optimally. Competition per se is worthless. The role of aggregate measures in relative performance evaluation is also explored, and the implications for investment rules are discussed.

1. Introduction

■ Orthodox economic theory has little to offer in terms of understanding how nonmarket organizations, like firms, form and function. This is so because traditional theory pays little or no attention to the role of information, which evidently lies at the heart of organizations. The recent development of information economics, which explicitly recognizes that agents have limited and different information, is a welcome invention, which promises to be helpful in understanding the intricacies of organizational design. Particularly important in this context are questions concerning the control of agents' incentives, which to a large degree dictate the structure of organizations and set the limits of its performance potential (Arrow, 1974).

The members of an organization may be seen as providing two kinds of services: they supply inputs for production and process information for decisionmaking. Along with this dichotomy goes a taxonomy for incentive problems. Moral hazard refers to the problem of inducing agents to supply proper amounts of productive inputs when their actions cannot be observed and contracted for directly. Adverse selection refers to a situation where actions can be observed, but it cannot be verified whether the action was the correct one, given the agent's contingency, which he privately observes.

This article is concerned with moral hazard in teams.[1] By a team I mean rather

* Northwestern University.

This article grew out of my discussion of Stan Baiman and Joel Demski's paper, "Economically Optimal Performance Evaluation and Control Systems," presented at the Chicago Conference of Accounting, 1980. Their paper provided ample sources of inspiration for which I am grateful. I have also benefited from comments by Froystein Gjesdal, Milt Harris, Richard Kihlstrom, Ed Lazear, Paul Milgrom, Steve Ross, Karl Shell, an anonymous referee, and seminar participants at Yale, the Universities of Pennsylvania, California (San Diego), Chicago and Iowa. Financial support from the Center for Advanced Studies in Managerial Economics at Northwestern and from a J. L. Kellogg and NSF research grant is gratefully acknowledged.

[1] Earlier work on moral hazard in a single-agent setting includes Wilson (1969), Spence and Zeckhauser (1971), Ross (1973), Mirrlees (1976), Harris and Raviv (1979), Shavell (1979), Holmstrom (1979), and Grossman and Hart (1980). Models with many agents have been studied by Baiman and Demski (1980), Lazear and Rosen (1981), and Radner (1980). Papers contemporaneous and independent of this article are Atkinson and Feltham (1980), Green and Stokey (1982), and Nalebuff and Stiglitz (1982).

loosely a group of individuals who are organized so that their productive inputs are related.[2] The objective of the analysis is to derive some positive and normative implications regarding the organization of production with many agents whose inputs are imperfectly observed. The analysis will focus on two features that are specific to multiagent organizations: the problem of free riding when there is joint production and the role of competition in controlling incentives.

I start by considering the free-rider issue (Section 2). In contrast to the single-agent case, moral hazard problems may occur even when there is no uncertainty in output. The reason is that agents who cheat cannot be identified if joint output is the only observable indicator of inputs. Indeed, I show that noncooperative behavior will always yield an inefficient outcome if joint output is fully shared among the agents.

In a well-known paper, Alchian and Demsetz (1972) argue that efficiency can (and will) be restored by bringing in a principal who monitors the agents' inputs. My first point will be that the principal's role is not essentially one of monitoring. I show that under certainty group incentives alone can remove the free-rider problem. Such incentives require penalties that waste output or bonuses that exceed output. In both cases the principal is needed, either to enforce the penalties or to finance the bonuses. Thus, the principal's primary role is to break the budget-balancing constraint. The fact that capitalistic firms feature separation of ownership and labor implies that the free-rider problem is less pronounced in such firms than in closed organizations like partnerships.

Group incentives can also work quite well under uncertainty, but their effectiveness will be limited if there are many agents and if the agents are risk averse. This makes monitoring important. As a refinement of earlier results on monitoring in the single-agent context (Holmstrom, 1979; Shavell, 1979), I show in Section 3 that agents' sharing rules can, without loss in welfare, be written on a statistic of all observations if and only if this statistic is sufficient in the sense of statistical decision theory. This result parallels those in decision theory, but is not the same, since the context is a strategic game where agents rather than Nature choose the parameters of the distribution.

The most interesting implications of the sufficient statistic condition concern relative performance evaluation. These are explored in Section 4. One finds that relative performance evaluation will be valuable if one agent's output provides information about another agent's state uncertainty. Such will be the case if and only if agents face some common uncertainties. Thus, inducing competition among agents by tying their rewards to each other's performance has no intrinsic value. Rather, competition is the consequence of the efficient use of information.

An example of performance evaluation that can be rationalized in this fashion is the use of rank-order tournaments, which have recently been studied by Lazear and Rosen (1981). But since rank order is not a sufficient statistic for individual output except in special circumstances, rank-order tournaments will generally imply an inefficient use of available information. In contrast, I show that aggregate measures like peer averages may often provide sufficient information about common uncertainties and thus schemes that compare agents with such aggregate measures will be efficient. An example of relative performance evaluation of this kind is given by the new executive incentive packages, which base rewards on explicit comparisons with firms within the same industry.

For another application of the sufficient statistic condition, I show that the cost of common uncertainties can be essentially eliminated when the number of agents grows large. What remains to be coped with are the idiosyncratic risks of individual agents. This implies a particular concern for idiosyncratic risks in managerial decisions about invest-

---

[2] Although "team" is the most natural term to describe the setting I study, it should be noted that the term "team" has another precise technical meaning within team theory (Marschak and Radner, 1972), which is inconsistent with incentive problems. My model is also similar in structure to what Wilson (1968) called a syndicate.

ments, since only idiosyncratic risk will enter the process of evaluating managers. Thus, an agency-theoretic perspective implies changes in the normative implications of standard asset pricing models, which hold that systematic risk is the only risk that carries a premium.

The article concludes with some remarks on facets of the multiagent problem that are not addressed here but deserve consideration.

2. Group incentives and the role of the principal

■ **Certainty.** Consider the following simple model of team production. There are n agents. Each agent, indexed i, takes a nonobservable action $a_i \in A_i = [0, \infty)$, with a private (nonmonetary) cost $v_i: A_i \to \mathbb{R}$; v_i is strictly convex, differentiable, and increasing with $v_i(0) = 0$. Let $a = (a_1, \ldots, a_n) \in A = \overset{n}{\underset{i=1}{\mathsf{X}}} A_i$ and write

$$a_{-i} = (a_1, \ldots, a_{i-1}, a_{i+1}, \ldots, a_n), a = (a_i, a_{-i}).$$

The agents' actions determine a joint monetary outcome $x: A \to \mathbb{R}$, which must be allocated among the agents. The function x is assumed to be strictly increasing, concave, and differentiable with $x(0) = 0$. Let $s_i(x)$ stand for agent i's share of the outcome x. The preference function of agent i is assumed (for simplicity) to be additively separable in money and action, and linear in money. Hence, it is of the form $u_i(m_i, a_i) = m_i - v_i(a_i)$. Agents' initial endowments of money are finite and normalized to be zero.

The question is whether there is a way of fully allocating the joint outcome x so that the resulting noncooperative game among the agents has a Pareto optimal Nash equilibrium. That is, we ask whether there exist sharing rules $s_i(x) \geq 0$, $i = 1, \ldots, n$, such that we have budget-balancing

$$\sum_{i=1}^{n} s_i(x) = x, \qquad \text{for all } x, \tag{1}$$

and the noncooperative game with payoffs,

$$s_i(x(a)) - v_i(a_i), \qquad i = 1, \ldots, n, \tag{2}$$

has a Nash equilibrium a^*, which satisfies the condition for Pareto optimality,

$$a^* = \underset{a \in A}{\operatorname{argmax}} \, [x(a) - \sum_{i=1}^{n} v_i(a_i)]. \tag{3}$$

If the sharing rules are differentiable, we find, since a^* is a Nash equilibrium, that

$$s_i' x_i' - v_i' = 0, \qquad i = 1, \ldots, n, \tag{4}$$

where $x_i' \equiv \partial x / \partial a_i$. Pareto optimality implies that

$$x_i' - v_i' = 0, \qquad i = 1, \ldots, n. \tag{5}$$

Consistency of (4) and (5) requires $s_i' = 1$, $i = 1, \ldots, n$. But this is in conflict with (1), since differentiating (1) implies

$$\sum_{i=1}^{n} s_i' = 1. \tag{6}$$

Therefore, with differentiable sharing rules we cannot reach efficient Nash equilibria. The same is true more generally as stated in the following:

Theorem 1. There do not exist sharing rules $\{s_i(x)\}$ which satisfy (1) and which yield a^* as a Nash equilibrium in the noncooperative game with payoffs (2).

Proof: See Appendix.

Theorem 1 extends the intuition of the inconsistency of (4)–(6) to the case of arbitrary sharing rules. As long as we insist on budget-balancing—that is, (1)—and there are externalities present ($x'_i \neq 0$), we cannot achieve efficiency. Agents can cover improper actions behind the uncertainty concerning who was at fault. Since all agents cannot be penalized sufficiently for a deviation in the outcome, some agent always has an incentive to capitalize on this control deficiency.

The result indicates that in closed (budget-balanced) organizations like a labor-managed firm or a partnership, free-rider problems are likely to lead to an insufficient supply of productive inputs like effort. This observation is the starting point for Alchian and Demsetz' (1972) well-known theory of the firm. They argue that the inefficiency of a partnership will cause an organizational change. To secure a sufficient supply of effort, firms should hire a principal to monitor the behavior of agents. The monitor should be given title to the net earnings of the firm so that he has the proper incentives to work. Such an arrangement will restore efficiency. At the same time, it will change the partnership into a capitalistic firm with the monitor acting effectively as the owner.

There is a simpler solution, however, at least under certainty. The free-rider problem is not solely the consequence of the unobservability of actions, but equally the consequence of imposing budget-balancing. If we relax (1) to read:

$$\sum_i s_i(x) \leq x, \tag{7}$$

then there will exist efficient Nash equilibria.

Theorem 2. There exists a set of feasible sharing rules $s_i(x) \geq 0$, $i = 1, \ldots, n$, satisfying (7), such that a^* is a Nash equilibrium.

Proof: Let

$$s_i(x) = \begin{cases} b_i & \text{if} \quad x \geq x(a^*) \\ 0 & \text{if} \quad x < x(a^*). \end{cases} \tag{8}$$

Choose b_i's so that $\sum_i b_i = x(a^*)$ and $b_i > v_i(a_i^*) > 0$. This is possible because $x(a^*) - \sum_i v_i(a_i^*) > 0$ by Pareto optimality. It is clear that a^* is a Nash equilibrium when sharing rules are chosen in this fashion. *Q.E.D.*

The purpose of relaxing the budget-balancing constraint in (1) is to permit group penalties that are sufficient to police all agents' behavior. It is worth noting that the scheme in (8) does not violate individual endowment constraints and works independently of the team size. This feature is specific to the certainty case.

Schemes like (8) are observed in some types of contracting with labor teams. Usually it takes the form of a flat wage and a group bonus to be paid if a target is attained (whether one views the discontinuity in (8) as a bonus or a penalty appears immaterial). An extreme example of group punishment is the dismissal of the board of directors of a firm.

In a dynamic context the punishment in (8) can be interpreted as a threat to discontinue cooperation. There is a problem, however, with enforcing such group penalties if they are self-imposed by the worker team. Suppose something less than $x(a^*)$ is produced. *Ex post* it is not in the interest of any of the team members to waste some of the outcome. But if it is expected that penalties will not be enforced, we are back in the situation with budget-balancing, and the free-rider problem reappears. In the language of game theory, self-imposed penalties lead to an imperfect equilibrium in the sense of Selten (1975).

The enforcement problem can be overcome only by bringing in a principal (or a party) who will assume the residual of the nonbudget balancing sharing rules. The principal will not renegotiate the contract if for some reason the proper level of output is not attained. Note that it is important that the principal not provide any (unobservable) productive inputs or else a free-rider problem remains.

Of course, the scheme in (8) is only one of many possible solutions to the free-rider problem when (1) is not imposed. Bonding, where each agent pays up front $x(a^*)$ and receives a share $s_i(x) = x$, is another alternative, though it may be infeasible when there are endowment constraints. My point here is therefore not that group punishments are the only effective scheme, but rather that budget breaking is the essential instrument in neutralizing externalities from joint production. The primary role of the principal is to administer incentive schemes that police agents in a credible way rather than to monitor agents as in Alchian and Demsetz' story. The reason capitalistic firms enjoy an advantage over partnerships in controlling incentives is that they can (and will) independently of the level of internal monitoring employ schemes that are infeasible in closed (budget-balancing) organizations. There is little to suggest that either of the two forms of organization would stand at a comparative advantage when it comes to monitoring alone.

The theme that budget balancing and efficiency are inconsistent when externalities are present is certainly not novel. A celebrated solution to the resulting free-rider problem in the public goods context is Groves' scheme (Groves, 1973). I note that Groves' solution is possible only by breaking the budget constraint; it does not balance the budget (barring exceptional cases), because by analogy with Theorem 1 balancing the budget would necessarily result in inefficiencies.[3]

☐ **Uncertainty.** The reader may have noticed that when agents choose a^*, as they should in equilibrium, there will be no residual left with a scheme like (8). This fact may make the certainty solution appear extreme. That is not true, however. Penalties may work quite effectively under uncertainty as well. This was first observed by Mirrlees (1974) in a model with one agent. The argument is here extended to the multiagent case.

For the moment agents are assumed to be risk neutral.[4] Input costs are as above, output $x(a, \theta)$ is random through the state of nature θ, and agents have homogeneous beliefs concerning θ.

It is more convenient and illuminating to suppress θ and to consider the distribution function of x parameterized by a. (See Holmstrom (1979) for a more detailed argument.) Denote the conditional distribution of x, given the action vector a, by $F(x, a)$ and the conditional density function by $f(x, a)$. Assume that the partial derivatives $F_i(x, a)$ $= \partial F(x, a)/\partial a_i$ and $f_i(x, a) = \partial f(x, a)/\partial a_i$ exist for all i and (x, a). The following assumptions regarding distributions will be used in the theorems below.

Assumption 1. $F(x, a)$ is convex in a.

Assumption 2. $F_i(x, a)/F(x, a) \rightarrow -\infty$ as $x \rightarrow -\infty$ (or its lower bound).

Assumption 3. $F_i(x, a)/(1 - F(x, a)) \rightarrow -\infty$ as $x \rightarrow +\infty$ (or its upper bound).

Technically, the role of Assumption 1 will be to assure global optimality of the agents' actions. Unfortunately, it is not an assumption that is satisfied by natural specifications of $x(a, \theta)$, for example, $x(a, \theta) = (\Sigma a_i)\theta$ with θ normally distributed. It has an economic interpretation, though. Since $F(x, \lambda a_1 + (1 - \lambda)a_2) \leq \lambda F(x, a_1) + (1 - \lambda)F(x, a_2)$, the distribution on the left dominates the distribution on the right in the sense of first-order

---

[3] The idea of breaking the budget-balancing constraint to resolve externalities has figured more or less explicitly in many articles on property rights. This is particularly true of the bonding solution. Part of the analysis in Green (1976) is closely related to the one presented here, although its context and emphasis are different.

[4] Note that risk neutrality does not here mitigate the moral hazard problem as is the case with a single agent (Harris and Raviv, 1979).

stochastic dominance. Therefore, Assumption 1 corresponds to a particular form of stochastically diminishing returns to scale.

Assumptions 2 and 3 are implied by $f_i/f \to -\infty$ as $x \to -\infty$ and $f_i/f \to +\infty$ as $x \to +\infty$, respectively, which hold for many natural specifications of $x(a, \theta)$. These are likelihood ratio conditions and can be interpreted as stating that for very small or very large values of x, one can discern very precisely whether the right actions were taken (Milgrom, 1981).

Let output x be shared according to sharing rules $s_i(x)$, $i = 1, \ldots, n$, satisfying (7). For the time being I omit consideration of endowment constraints. The following theorem extends the insights about group incentives from the certainty case to the uncertainty case. The idea of the proof is taken from Mirrlees (1974).

Theorem 3: Under assumptions 1 and 2, a first-best solution can be approximated arbitrarily closely by using group penalties.

Proof: Consider the following sharing rules:

$$s_i(x) = \begin{cases} s_i x, & x \geq \bar{x}, \\ s_i x - k_i, & x < \bar{x}, \end{cases} \tag{9}$$

where $k_i > 0$, and $\Sigma\, s_i = 1$. Evidently (9) satisfies (7). The rules in (9) prescribe a penalty k_i to each agent i if a critical output level $\bar{x}$ is not achieved. Otherwise, the entire output is shared. For a^* to be a Nash equilibrium with (9), it is necessary and sufficient (by Assumption 1) that

$$s_i E_i(a^*) - k_i F_i(\bar{x}, a^*) - v_i'(a_i^*) = 0, \qquad i = 1, \ldots, n, \tag{10}$$

where $E(a) = Ex(a)$, the expected value of x, given a, and $E_i(a) = \partial Ex(a)/\partial a_i$. For fixed $\bar{x}$, choose k_i so that (10) holds. The expected residual is given by $W = \sum_i k_i F(\bar{x}, a^*)$. I need to show that W can be made arbitrarily small. From (10),

$$k_i = A_i/F_i(\bar{x}, a^*), \qquad \text{with} \qquad A_i = s_i E_i(a^*) - v_i'(a_i^*). \tag{11}$$

Let $\bar{x}$ decrease and adjust k_i so that (11) holds. Then the residual is given by

$$W = \sum_i A_i F(\bar{x}, a^*)/F_i(\bar{x}, a^*), \tag{12}$$

which, by Assumption 2, goes to zero with $\bar{x}$. Q.E.D.

From (10) and Assumption 2 it follows that the k_i's generally go to infinity as $\bar{x}$ is decreased. Finite endowments will make this arrangement infeasible. If the x-distribution is tight in the sense that there is an $\bar{x}$-value for which $|F_i|$ is large while $|F/F_i|$ is small, then we can get good approximations to first best even with endowment constraints. But if the distribution has much spread, so that $|F_i|$ is small for all $\bar{x}$ (as is the case for a lognormal distribution when the variance is big), then efficiency losses become substantial with wealth constraints. Assuming that the distribution of output becomes more diffuse when the number of agents grows large (more specifically that $|F_i| \to 0$ for all x), while $E_i(a)$ stays bounded, implies that a^* will converge to 0 because of (10) and that $s_i \to 0$ (because $\Sigma\, s_i = 1$). Thus, in contrast to the certainty case, endowment constraints will generally limit the size of a team that can effectively be policed by penalties.

A resolution of this dilemma can occasionally be found by paying bonuses as the following theorem indicates:

Theorem 4: Under Assumptions 1 and 3, the first best can be enforced at a negligible cost to a principal with unbounded wealth, even when agents' endowments are limited.

The proof is omitted because it is similar to that of Theorem 3. The scheme that the principal will use pays a bonus b_i if $x > \bar{x}$ and pays $s_i x(a^*)$, $(\Sigma\, s_i = 1)$, if $x \leq \bar{x}$. The

330 / THE BELL JOURNAL OF ECONOMICS

bonuses and $\bar{x}$ can be adjusted simultaneously so that a^* remains an equilibrium, while the principal's expected cost $(\Sigma\ b_i)(1 - F(\bar{x}, a^*))$ goes to zero because of Assumption 3.

The theorems above were developed under risk neutrality assumptions. If agents are risk averse with utility tending to $-\infty$ as wealth decreases, Theorem 3 remains valid (Mirrlees, 1974). Theorem 4, however, appears quite dependent on the risk neutrality assumption. An unverified conjecture is that asymptotic risk neutrality suffices.

3. Sufficient statistics

■ The preceding analysis suggests that under some circumstances efficient team production can be approached via simple penalty or bonus schemes. The role of the principal is important even if there are no risk-sharing advantages, which contrasts with the single-agent case. In the case of penalties the principal is needed to enforce them, and in the case of bonuses he is needed to pay them. The central feature is that the principal allows the budget-balancing constraint to be broken.

If there is uncertainty in production and if agents are risk averse or have limited endowments, monitoring becomes an important instrument in remedying moral hazard, since the first best is not attainable. I shall investigate below what type of monitoring provides valuable information in the sense that it helps improve welfare.

The model includes a risk-neutral principal and n risk-averse agents. The ith agent's utility function is additively separable in money and action, with $u_i(m_i)$ denoting the agent's utility of money function and $v_i(a_i)$ the agent's disutility of action. Since the principal is risk neutral, there are no gains to risk-sharing *per se*. To the extent output is used in determining agents' payoffs, its value is solely in providing incentives. Put differently, output will merely be used as a signal about the actions taken by the agents.

Let y be the vector of signals observed, so that y can be used as the basis for sharing.[5] This vector may or may not contain x. The distribution of y as a function of a is given by $G(y, a)$, with density $g(y, a)$. I assume that the derivative of g with respect to a_i, denoted g_{a_i}, exists for all i. The welfare problem can be stated as

$$\max_{a, s_i(y)} \int \{E(x|y, a) - \sum_i s_i(y)\} dG(y, a),\qquad(13)$$

subject to:

(i) $\quad \int u_i(s_i(y)) dG(y, a) - v_i(a_i) \geq \bar{u}_i, \qquad i = 1, \ldots, n.$

(ii) $\quad a_i \in \underset{a'_i}{\operatorname{argmax}} \int u_i(s_i(y)) dG(y, a'_i, a_{-i}) - v_i(a'_i), \qquad i = 1, \ldots, n.$

Here, $E(x|y, a)$ is the expected output of x, given y and a. Of course, it equals x if x is part of y. Condition (ii) implies that a is a Nash equilibrium. This behavioral assumption may be unreasonable at times, but the results to be presented do not depend on it in a critical way. (See p. 333.)

The following definition is an extension of that in Holmstrom (1979).

Definition:[6] A function $T_i(y)$ is said to be *sufficient for y with respect to a_i,* if there exist functions $h_i(\cdot) \geq 0$, $p_i(\cdot) \geq 0$ such that:

---

[5] It is not necessarily enough, as the literature frequently suggests, that y is observable to the principal and the agent for $s(y)$ to be enforceable. Legal enforceability requires that the enforcing authorities are also able to observe y when needed. On the other hand, implicit contracts may include signals that are not observed perfectly by the agents.

[6] Gjesdal (1982) provides a related extension of my earlier sufficient statistic condition.

$$g(y, a) = h_i(y, a_{-i})p_i(T_i(y), a), \qquad \text{for all } y \text{ and } a \text{ in the support of } g. \tag{14}$$

The vector $T(y) = (T_1(y), \ldots, T_n(y))$ is said to be sufficient for y with respect to a, if each $T_i(y)$ is sufficient for a_i.

Equation (14) is the well-known condition for a sufficient statistic in ordinary statistical decision theory (deGroot, 1970). Note, however, that the action a_i is a parameter chosen not by Nature but by a strategic agent. This notwithstanding, it will be shown below (Theorems 5 and 6) that agent i's sharing rule should be based solely on $T_i(y)$ if and only if T_i is sufficient, which parallels results in statistical decision theory.

Theorem 5. Assume $T(y) = (T_1(y), \ldots, T_n(y))$ is sufficient for y with respect to a. Then, given any collection of incentive schemes $\{s_i(y)\}$, there exists a set of schemes $\{\hat{s}_i(T_i)\}$ that weakly Pareto dominates $\{s_i(y)\}$.

Proof: I consider first the case of a single agent, dropping subscripts throughout. Define $\hat{s}(T)$ as follows:

$$u(\hat{s}(T)) = \int_{T(y)=T} u(s(y))g(y, a)dy/p(T, a) = \int_{T(y)=T} u(s(y))h(y)dy. \tag{15}$$

By Jensen's inequality (15) implies:

$$\int \hat{s}(T(y))g(y, a)dy \leqslant \int s(y)g(y, a)dy. \tag{16}$$

From (14) and (15) it follows that the agent will enjoy the same expected utility for all a, whether faced with $s(y)$ or $\hat{s}(T)$. Thus, he will take the same action under $\hat{s}(T)$ as he takes under $s(y)$. From this and (16), it follows that the principal is at least as well off with $\hat{s}(T)$ as with $s(y)$.

With n agents, the proof is identical once it is observed that the other agents' actions can be viewed as known constants because they can be inferred from the equilibrium. *Q.E.D.*

The converse to Theorem 5 requires brief preparation. I wish to state that if $T(y)$ is not sufficient, then we can strictly improve welfare by observing y. There is a problem, however, with the meaning of an insufficient statistic $T(y)$. Equation (14) may not hold for all a and yet a particular $T(y)$ will be sufficient in the sense that welfare improvements cannot be made. Such is obviously the case if we take $T(y)$ equal to the vector of optimal sharing rules.[7] Moreover, for a fixed a, equation (14) can always be satisfied by an appropriate choice of $h_i(\cdot)$ and $p_i(\cdot, \cdot)$.

To handle such cases, I shall define $T(y)$ as *sufficient at* a if it is the case that for all i and all T_i,

$$\frac{g_{a_i}(y_1, a)}{g(y_1, a)} = \frac{g_{a_i}(y_2, a)}{g(y_2, a)} \qquad \text{for almost all } y_1, y_2 \in \{y|T_i(y) = T_i\}. \tag{17}$$

Note that (17) follows from (14). Conversely, (17) implies (14) (by integrating) if it holds for all a. I shall say that $T(y)$ is *globally sufficient* if (17) is true *for all a and i* and *globally insufficient* if *for some i* (17) is false *for all a*.

Theorem 6. Assume $T(y)$ is globally insufficient for y. Let $\{s_i(y) = \hat{s}_i(T(y))\}$ be a collection of nonconstant sharing rules such that the agents' action choices are unique in equilibrium. Then there exist sharing rules $\{\hat{s}_i(y)\}$ that yield a strict Pareto improvement. Moreover,

---

[7] I am indebted to Steve Ross for this observation.

$\{\hat{s}_i(y)\}$ can be chosen so as to induce the same equilibrium actions as the rules $\{s_i(y)\}$ do.[8]

Proof: Again, for notational simplicity, I consider only the single-agent case. The fact that improvements can be achieved by keeping the agent's action unaltered implies that changes in one agent's sharing rule will not affect the other agents' behavior. Therefore, the steps shown here for a single agent can be repeated for all other agents in turn. The strategy of the proof is to show that if $T(y)$ is globally insufficient, there exists a different set of sharing rules that (i) leave the agent's action unchanged and (ii) leave the principal no worse off and the agent better off in terms of risk sharing.

Since $T(y)$ is globally insufficient, there exist a T_1 and sets of positive measure Y_{11}, Y_{12} which are disjoint and subsets of $Y_1 = \{y | T(y) = T_1\}$ such that

$$\frac{g_a(Y_{11}, a)}{g(Y_{11}, a)} \neq \frac{g_a(Y_{12}, a)}{g(Y_{12}, a)}, \tag{18}$$

where a is the agent's response to $s(y)$. Here $g(Y_{kl}, a) = \Pr\{y \in Y_{kl} | a\}$. Since $s(y)$ is not constant, there exists a $T_2 \neq T_1$ such that the set $Y_2 = \{y | T(y) = T_2\}$ is of positive measure and $\hat{s}(T_1) \neq \hat{s}(T_2)$. Define the following variation:

$$\hat{s}(y) = \hat{s}(T(y)) + I_{11}(y)ds_{11} + I_{12}(y)ds_{12} + I_2(y)ds_2,$$

where $I_{11}(y)$ is the indicator function for the event $\{y \in Y_{11}\}$ and similarly for $I_{12}(y)$, $I_2(y)$; and ds_{11}, ds_{12}, and ds_2 are numbers that we shall choose.

The effect on the principal's (P) and the agent's (A) welfare (*excluding any change in action*) from a change to $\hat{s}(y)$ is given by

$$\Delta P = -[ds_{11}g(Y_{11}, a) + ds_{12}g(Y_{12}, a) + ds_2g(Y_2, a)], \tag{19}$$

$$\Delta A = u_1'[ds_{11}g(Y_{11}, a) + ds_{12}g(Y_{12}, a)] + u_2'ds_2g(Y_2, a). \tag{20}$$

Here $u_1' = u'(\hat{s}(T_1))$ and $u_2' = u'(\hat{s}(T_2))$. Since $\hat{s}(T_1) \neq \hat{s}(T_2)$, $u_1' \neq u_2'$. Assume for concreteness that $u_2' > u_1'$.

The sign of the effect on the agent's action from the variation $\hat{s}(y)$ is given by

$$\operatorname{sgn}(\Delta a) = \operatorname{sgn}[u_1'(ds_{11}g_a(Y_{11}, a) + ds_{12}g_a(Y_{12}, a)) + u_2'ds_2g_a(Y_2, a)]. \tag{21}$$

Choose ds_{11}, ds_{12}, ds_2 as follows. Fix $ds_2 > 0$ and require that $\Delta P = 0$ and $\Delta a = 0$ so that

$$ds_{11}g(Y_{11}, a) + ds_{12}g(Y_{12}, a) = -ds_2g(Y_2, a), \text{ and} \tag{22}$$

$$ds_{11}g_a(Y_{11}, a) + ds_{12}g_a(Y_{12}, a) = -u_2'/u_1'ds_2g_a(Y_2, a). \tag{23}$$

From (20) and (22), it follows that $\Delta A > 0$, because $u_2' > u_1'$. The system (22) and (23) has a solution because (18) implies that the determinant is nonzero. This shows that ds_{11}, ds_{12}, ds_2 can be chosen so that $\Delta P = 0$, $\Delta A > 0$, and $\Delta a = 0$, in other words so that the principal is no worse off and the agent is better off in terms of risk sharing while the action remains unchanged. *Q.E.D.*

The main import of Theorem 5 is that randomization does not pay if the agent's utility function is separable.[9] Indeed, any pure noise should be filtered away from the

[8] The assumption that sharing rules are nonconstant is not an essential restriction; a constant sharing rule does not provide any incentives for effort and would obviously not be employed.

The assumption that actions are unique is restrictive. For conditions that guarantee uniqueness at the optimum, see Grossman and Hart (1980).

[9] Separability of the utility function is crucial for the result that pure randomization does not pay; see Gjesdal (1982). On the other hand, Karl Shell alerted me to the fact that even if the utility function is not separable, $T(y)$ is all we need to know about y, since randomization, when desired, can be generated in other ways than through the noninformative part of y.

agent's sharing rule. To the extent the sharing rule is random, it should be through signals that are informative about the agent's action.

Conversely, Theorem 6 states that if $T(y)$ is not a sufficient statistic for y (at the optimal a), we can do *strictly* better by using all of y instead of $T(y)$ as a basis for the sharing rule. The intuition, of course, is that y reveals more information about a than $T(y)$ does if and only if $T(y)$ is not sufficient for y.

Theorems 5 and 6 differ somewhat from my earlier result on informativeness, which dealt with a comparison of the two information systems $\eta_1 = x$ and $\eta_2 = (x, z)$. In η_1, the outcome x is observed, while in η_2 both the outcome x and an additional signal z are observed. In Holmstrom (1979), I called z an informative signal if $T(x, z) = x$ is not sufficient for (x, z) as defined in (14), and I proved that z is valuable if and only if z is informative.[10] Obviously, Theorems 5 and 6 generalize this result.

More importantly, though, for the application to the multiagent case, Theorem 6 shows that if $T(y)$ is not sufficient, welfare improvements can be made without changing the agents' actions, but merely by improving risk sharing. The proofs in Holmstrom (1979) and Shavell (1979) both do the reverse: maintain the same level of risk sharing, while providing incentives for the agent to change the action in a direction desirable for the principal. Such changes in action would complicate considerably the situation with many agents, since the whole equilibrium would then change.[11]

Working with risk sharing improvements, while keeping actions intact, has another advantage: the results do not hinge critically on the Nash equilibrium assumption made in the earlier formulation of the problem (see (13)). Theorem 5 is valid no matter what behavior is assumed; in particular, cooperation among agents would be acceptable. Theorem 6 is not so insensitive, because in the proof the agents' payoffs (as a function of actions) are changed globally, and this may induce collusive behavior. But as long as actions are chosen noncooperatively, the specific equilibrium concept is inessential, even in Theorem 6.

The sufficient-statistic results above are closely related to Blackwell's well-known theorem in decision theory. Blackwell's theorem states that all decisionmakers in all decision situations will prefer one information system (that is, experiment) to another if and only if the former is sufficient for the latter. (I shall explain shortly what this means.) But, Theorems 5 and 6 are not corollaries of Blackwell's results. Most importantly, the agency problem does not fit directly the framework of statistical decision theory. No inferences are being drawn from y concerning a, because actions are determined by the choice of the incentive scheme. In fact, the outcome y does not tell the principal anything at all about the actions of the agents! It is quite appealing, therefore, that the agency results conform with the intuition that information is being extracted from y, although logically that is not what is occurring.[12]

Secondly, Theorem 6 does not have a counterpart in Blackwell's analysis. Whether the necessary part of Blackwell's theorem, that information systems cannot be compared unless one is sufficient for the other, is true in the agency framework is still an open question.

Grossman and Hart (1980) and Gjesdal (1982) discuss the value of different infor-

---

[10] The sufficiency part was also proved by Shavell (1979) without explicitly using the notion of a sufficient statistic.

[11] Baiman and Demski (1980) prove a special case of Theorem 6 by using an extra assumption that appears unnecessary. This assumption is called for, since they do not exploit the possibility of improving risk-sharing benefits, but rather use the line of proof in Holmstrom (1979).

[12] Mathematically, the agency problem can be set up as a statistical decision problem with the restriction that the "decision rule," $s(y)$, has to satisfy the agents' incentive constraints. These are nonconvex in general, which explains why randomization may be valuable (see Gjesdal (1982) for an example). Randomization is never worthwhile in Blackwell's set-up.

mation systems from the point of view of Blackwell's notion of sufficiency. The following discussion will reveal its relationship to the sufficiency property used here.[13]

Let $\eta_1 = y_1$ and $\eta_2 = y_2$ be two information systems. Blackwell calls η_1 sufficient for η_2 if we have for all y_2, a:

$$g_2(y_2, a) = \int h(y_2, y_1)g_1(y_1, a)dy_1 , \qquad (24)$$

where g_2 and g_1 are the marginal densities of y_2 and y_1. Condition (24) looks much like (14), but is conceptually quite different, since (24) involves only marginal distributions, whereas (14) presumes a joint distribution for $y = (y_1, y_2)$. But the solutions to the Pareto problem (13) corresponding to η_1 or η_2 do not depend on the joint distribution of y_1 and y_2. Hence we may define a joint density by letting

$$g(y_1, y_2, a) = h(y_2, y_1)g_1(y_1, a). \qquad (25)$$

This will have as its marginals g_1 and g_2 (as in (24)). But (25) says that $T(y_1, y_2) = y_1$ is sufficient for (y_1, y_2). Hence, we get as good results by basing the sharing rule on y_1 as we do by basing it on (y_1, y_2). Therefore, $\eta_1 = y_1$ is as good an information system as $\eta = (y_1, y_2)$. But, of course, η can be no worse than $\eta_2 = y_2$. The conclusion is that η_1 is as good as η_2 if η_1 is sufficient for η_2 in the Blackwell sense. The Blackwell ordering can therefore be viewed as a corollary to the results of Theorems 5 and 6. The converse is true as well, since (24) is weaker than (14).

4. Relative performance evaluation and competition among agents

■   The result on sufficient statistics has many useful applications in agency theory. I shall illustrate its applicability by analyzing relative performance evaluation, which is of considerable relevance in the multiagent setting.

Theorem 6 lends support to the effort firms make in creating information systems that separate out individual contributions to total output. It is easy to show (by using (18)) that two independent measures of joint output are together more informative than a single measure of output. Thus, refined budgetary measures have positive value when costs are excluded.

Now consider the case where the information system is so rich that total output can be itemized according to the contribution of each individual; that is,

$$x(a, \theta) = \sum_i x_i(a_i, \theta_i), \qquad \theta = (\theta_1, \ldots, \theta_n),$$

where all x_i's are separately observed. If the θ_i's are not random, then efficiency can be achieved by holding each agent responsible for his own output.[14] This is in accordance with the general principles of responsibility accounting. What will be examined here is when under uncertainty it will be valuable to deviate from this general principle and actually have s_i, the sharing rule of i, depend on the vector of outcomes $x = (x_1, \ldots, x_n)$ rather than on x_i alone.

We frequently observe agents being evaluated on the basis of peer performance. In almost all organizations, agents compete with each other in one form or another. Sometimes there is an explicit prize for the best ones, as for instance, among sales personnel ("salesman of the month" awards, etc.). The special case of rank-order tournaments, in which relative performance is measured by rank alone, has been analyzed by Lazear and

---

[13] I am grateful to Paul Milgrom for discussing this relationship.

[14] In an earlier version of this article, I showed a partial converse: to achieve efficiency under certainty by using monitoring alone, n measures are needed that locally separate the contributions of individuals as in (26); this was shown under the restriction that sharing rules and measures are monotonic functions.

Rosen (1981). Related examples are provided by recent executive incentive packages in which performance is compared with that in competing firms.

The rationale for relative performance evaluation is easjly understood in light of the results on the value of information given in the previous section. The following theorem shows how those results apply.

Theorem 7:[15] Assume the x_i's are monotone in θ_i. Then the optimal sharing rule of agent i depends on individual i's output alone if and only if outputs are independent.

Proof: If the θ_i's are independent, then

$$f(x, a) = \prod_{i=1}^{n} f_i(x_i, a_i), \tag{26}$$

which obviously implies that $T_i(x) = x_i$ is sufficient for x with respect to a_i. By Theorem 5, it will be optimal to let s_i depend on x_i alone.

Suppose instead that θ_1 and θ_2 are dependent. Since, in equilibrium, the value of a_2 can be inferred, we can, without loss of generality, assume $x_2 = \theta_2$. Keeping a_2 at its equilibrium value (and suppressing, it notationally), the joint distribution of x_1 and $x_2 = \theta_2$ conditional on a_1 is given by

$$f(x_1, \theta_2, a_1) = \tilde{f}(x_1^{-1}(a_1, x_1), \theta_2), \tag{27}$$

where x_1^{-1} is the inverse of $x_1(a_1, \theta_1)$ and $\tilde{f}(\theta_1, \theta_2)$ is the joint distribution of (θ_1, θ_2). It follows that

$$\frac{f_{a_1}(x_1, \theta_2, a_1)}{f(x_1, \theta_2, a_1)} = \frac{\tilde{f}_1(x_1^{-1}(a_1, x_1), \theta_2)}{\tilde{f}(x_1^{-1}(a_1, x_1), \theta_2)} \frac{\partial x_1^{-1}(a_1, x_1)}{\partial a_1}. \tag{28}$$

Since θ_1 and θ_2 are dependent, $\tilde{f}_1/\tilde{f}$ depends on θ_2. Thus, (17) does not hold, and Theorem 6 applies. Consequently, the sharing rule for agent 1 should depend on both x_1 and x_2. *Q.E.D.*

An important implication of Theorem 7 is that forcing agents to compete with each other is valueless if there is no common underlying uncertainty. In this setting, the benefits from competition itself are nil. What is of value is the information that may be gained from peer performance.[16] Competition among agents is a consequence of attempts to exploit this information.

At this point it is appropriate to comment on the use of rank-order tournaments (Lazear and Rosen, 1981). A rank-order tournament awards agents merely on their performance rank, not on the value of the output itself. With n agents there are n prizes, $w_1 \geqslant \ldots \geqslant w_n$. The agent with the highest output gets w_1, second highest gets w_2, and so on.

From Theorem 7 it follows that if the agents' outcomes are unrelated, then rank-order tournaments will perform worse than rewarding agents on the basis of their individual outcomes alone. Pitting agents against each other will only result in more randomness in the reward scheme without any gains in the power of inference about actions.[17] On the other hand, as first noted by Lazear and Rosen, rank-order tournaments may be valuable if outcomes are related. The analysis above supports this contention. But it should be observed that rank-order tournaments may be informationally quite wasteful

---

[15] A related result is proved in Baiman and Demski (1980).

[16] In the extreme, if agents' outputs are completely dependent, in the sense that any x_j will reveal all θ_i, $i \neq j$, then the first-best outcome can be easily achieved by using relative performance evaluations.

[17] Lazear and Rosen (1981) find that rank-order tournaments may dominate piece rates even if agents' outputs are independent. Theorem 7 shows that this is the case not because of the value of competition, but because piece rates are sometimes far from optimal in the single-agent case.

if performance levels can be measured cardinally rather than ordinally. It is clear that the mapping from the agents' outcomes $x = (x_1, \ldots, x_n)$ into the statistic $T(x) = (k_1(x), \ldots, k_n(x))$, where $k_i(x)$ is the rank order of agent i, is not a sufficient statistic for a, except in trivial cases. Therefore, Theorem 6 tells us that there should be a better way of making use of x than what the rank-order tournament does. (Of course, if the output is very complex so that only ordinal measures are possible, then rank-order tournaments will be the best one can do.)

A general characterization of how information about the optimal use of peer performance with many agents can be developed formally as an extension of the characterization in Mirrlees (1976) or Holmstrom (1979). I shall not pursue that issue here. Instead I shall indicate how the sufficient statistic condition can be used to rationalize schemes that only use aggregate information about peer performance.

I shall restrict attention to the following two particular output structures:

I:
$$x_i(a_i, \theta_i) = a_i + \eta + \epsilon_i, \qquad i = 1, \ldots, n,$$

II:
$$x_i(a_i, \theta_i) = a_i(\eta + \epsilon_i), \qquad i = 1, \ldots, n.$$

Here $\theta_i = (\eta, \epsilon_i)$, where η is a common uncertainty parameter, while the ϵ_i's are independent, idiosyncratic risks.

Theorem 8: Let the technology be given by either I or II. Assume that $\eta, \epsilon_1, \ldots, \epsilon_n$ are independent and normally distributed. Let $\bar{x} = \Sigma \alpha_i x_i$ be a weighted average of the agents' outcomes. In the case of technology I, let $\alpha_i = \tau_i/\bar{\tau}$, where τ_i is the precision (the inverse of the variance) of ϵ_i and $\bar{\tau} = \Sigma \tau_i$. In the case of technology II, let $\alpha_i = \tau_i/\bar{\tau}a_i$, where a_i is the equilibrium response of agent i. In both cases, an optimal set of sharing rules $\{s_i(x)\}$ will have s_i depend on $\bar{x}$ and x_i alone.

Proof: Consider technology I. The joint density function for x, given a, is:

$$f(x, a) = K \int \exp\{-\frac{1}{2}[\sum_j \tau_j(x_j - a_j - \mu_j - \eta)^2 + \tau_0(\eta - \mu_0)^2]\}d\eta, \qquad (29)$$

where K is a constant, τ_0 is the precision of η, μ_0 is the mean of η, and τ_j, μ_j are the precision and mean of ϵ_j. In view of Theorem 5, we need to show that we can write (29) in the form of (14) for each $i = 1, \ldots, n$. Let

$$\bar{z}_{-i} = \sum_{k \neq i} (\tau_k/\bar{\tau}_{-i})(x_k - a_k - \mu_k), \qquad \bar{\tau}_{-i} = \sum_{k \neq i} \tau_k.$$

Then we can write:

$$\sum_j \tau_j(x_j - a_j - \mu_j - \eta)^2 = \sum_{j \neq i} \tau_j(x_j - a_j - \mu_j - \bar{z}_{-i} + \bar{z}_{-i} - \eta)^2 + \tau_i(x_i - a_i - \mu_i - \eta)^2$$

$$= \sum_{j \neq i} \tau_j(x_j - a_j - \mu_j - \bar{z}_{-i})^2 + (n - 1)(\bar{z}_{-i} - \eta)^2 + \tau_i(x_i - a_i - \mu_i - \eta)^2.$$

Substituting this expression into (29), we find upon integrating over η that we can write $f(x, a) = h_i(x, a_{-i})\hat{p}_i(\bar{z}_{-i}, x_i, a)$. But, since

$$\bar{z}_{-i} = (\bar{\tau}\bar{x} - \tau_i x_i)/\tau_{-i} - \sum_{k \neq i} (\tau_k/\bar{\tau}_{-i})(a_k + \mu_k),$$

we have $\hat{p}_i(\bar{z}_{-i}, x_i, a) = p_i(\bar{x}, x_i, a)$, which completes the proof of writing (29) in the form (14).

The proof for technology II is similar and is omitted. *Q.E.D.*

Theorem 8 suggests that sometimes an aggregate measure like the weighted average of peer performance will capture all the relevant information about the common uncertainty. This provides a rationale for the common practice of comparing performance against peer aggregates, although, of course, the sufficiency of a weighted average is a specific feature of the normal distribution.

Notice that Theorem 8 does *not* make the claim that s_i should depend on $x_i - \bar{x}$, only that it will have the form $s_i(x_i, \bar{x})$. The fact that the outputs of different agents are generally weighted differently in calculating $\bar{x}$ reflects possible differences in scale and in the value of these information sources. Differences in scale are corrected for by dividing x_j by a_j, which can be interpreted as a rate of return measure. Information values differ if ϵ_j's have different precision. If ϵ_j has high precision (low variance), then x_j tells rather sharply the value of η and should receive more weight in the average. This is another way of saying that x_j's which are correlated strongly with x_i should be more significant indicators in evaluating agent i's performance. Conversely, as $\tau_j \to 0$, x_j will essentially tell nothing about η because of the noise in ϵ_j, and hence should count very little.

The predictions of Theorem 8 conform well with the recent trend in executive incentive design. After stock options lost their tax advantage (and perhaps also because the market had been depressed in general), performance incentive packages became popular. These tie executive compensation to performance measured explicitly in relation to other firms in the industry (in particular, industry averages).

Let me turn finally to an analysis of large teams under the simplifying (but unnecessary) assumption that the technology is given by I or II. First, note that if we knew η *ex post*, this common uncertainty could and should (by Theorem 5) be filtered away to yield an improved solution to the agency problem. Also, if we knew η *ex post*, there would be no need to compare individual agents' outputs, since conditional on η they are independent (cf. Theorem 7). Thus, the solution to the incentive problem with n agents coincides with the solution of the n individual agency problems when η is known *ex post*. For these individual problems, the optimal schemes will depend on $a_i + \epsilon_i$ (for I) and $a_i\epsilon_i$ (for II), since the observation of η will allow us to observe these variables.

Now suppose η is not observed *ex post*. It is intuitively clear that as the number of agents grows large, we can essentially observe η by inferring it from the independent signals about η provided by the x_i's. Therefore, we would expect that with many agents we would be able to achieve approximately the same solution as if there were no common uncertainty at all. This intuition is correct.

Theorem 9: Consider technology I or II. Assume η, $\epsilon_1, \ldots, \epsilon_n$ are independent with uniformly bounded variance. Assume that in the solution to the single-agent problem without common uncertainty (i.e., $\eta = 0$) the agent's response is unique. Then this solution can be approximated arbitrarily closely as the number of agents grows large.

Proof: Consider technology I. Define $q_j = \eta + \epsilon_j$, $j = 1, \ldots, n$, and $\bar{q}_{-i} = 1/(n-1) \sum_{j \neq i} q_j$, $i = 1, \ldots, n$. Let $s_i^*(x_i)$ be the optimal solution to the single-agent problem when there is no common uncertainty, and let a_i^* be the agent's optimal response.

By the strong law of large numbers, $\bar{q}_{-i}$ goes almost surely to η. Therefore,

$$\int u_i(s_i^*(a_i + \eta + \epsilon_i - \bar{q}_{-i}))dP(\eta, \epsilon_1, \ldots, \epsilon_n)$$

converges uniformly to

$$\int u_i(s_i^*(a_i + \epsilon_i))dP(\epsilon_i).$$

Since a_i^* is a unique solution to

$$\max_{a_i} \int u_i(s_i^*(a_i + \epsilon_i))dP(\epsilon_i) - v_i(a_i),$$

we find that for large enough n, the agent will choose an action arbitrarily close to a_i^*

when solving

$$\max_{a_i} \int u_i(s_i^*(a_i^* + \eta + \epsilon_i - \bar{q}_{-i}))dP(\eta, \epsilon_1, \dots, \epsilon_n) - v_i(a_i).$$

Since $\bar{q}_{-i}$ can be inferred from the other agents' outcomes by calculating $x_j - a_j = \eta + \epsilon_j$, where a_j is the response of agent j, this proves the claim. The proof for technology II is similar. *Q.E.D.*

It is clear that constraining attention to technology I or II is not essential. The important thing is that all common uncertainty can be discerned in the limit and therefore removed from the agent's responsibility. The specifications above were just simple ways to illustrate the point.

The result that one may use relative performance measures to filter away common uncertainties has some interesting implications for financial theory. A standard model of financial markets is the capital asset pricing model (CAPM). One of its normative implications is that investments carried out by firms should be decided upon without reference to the investment's idiosyncratic risk as the market, through diversification, can neutralize such risk (see, e.g., Mossin (1969)). Investment decisions should be made solely with reference to systematic risk.

The analysis above shows that when incentives are a relevant concern, the normative implications of CAPM are altered. A new cost component related to moral hazard must be added. The interesting fact is that the costs due to moral hazard depend only on the idiosyncratic risk, which is precisely the converse of the costs due to risk bearing in the market. Therefore, the total costs of investment risk can be separated into two components: a price for the systematic risk given by the market according to CAPM (or more generally by arbitrage pricing) and a price for idiosyncratic risk determined by the project-specific returns to effort and the risk preferences of the manager.[18]

The agency perspective implies that between two projects with the same level of systematic risk, the one with lower idiosyncratic risk is strictly preferred. Consequently, diversification within the firm can be useful, since it helps to measure more accurately the manager's input. Furthermore, the concern for more accurate performance evaluation tends to make the firm choose projects which are more correlated with the market portfolio than efficient risk taking would prescribe. This implies that in their efforts to reduce idiosyncratic risk, firms provide society with a market portfolio which is not so diversified as (and hence riskier than) it would be were there no incentive problems present.[19]

This last point has a counterpart in the internal organization of a firm. Specialization is good from a purely technological point of view. In this respect agents' tasks should be well diversified. But problems with performance evaluation place a limit on the value of specialization. Thus, it may be optimal to have agents' tasks overlap (or duplicate) each other. One manifestation of this principle comes in the form of job rotation, which provides independent readings of the circumstances in which tasks are being carried out and thereby reduces moral hazard costs.

5. Concluding remarks

■ This article has made two general points. One is that the free-rider problem, which may arise in a multiagent setting, can largely be resolved if ownership and labor are partly

---

[18] Note, however, that including agency costs does not require a change in the positive theories of asset pricing. Prices of assets are based on expected returns in which agents' actions have already been factored. Whether expected returns are high because of the state variable in the outcome function $x(a, \theta)$ or because of the agent's action is immaterial for pricing the asset.

[19] One should not interpret insufficient diversification due to moral hazard as an inefficiency, since the framework is second best. There is a source of true inefficiency, though, when investment decisions are made independently. A firm which moves its project portfolio closer to the market's for improved performance evaluation does not account for the benefits that accrue to other firms from such a move.

separated. This gives capitalistic firms an advantage over partnerships. The other point is that relative performance evaluation can be helpful in reducing moral hazard costs, because it provides for better risk sharing. It is worth noting that many of the insights in the literature on rank-order tournaments and the value of competition (Lazear and Rosen, 1981; Green and Stokey, 1982; Nalebuff and Stiglitz, 1982) are fundamentally derivatives of the sufficient-statistic condition and therefore of much broader scope as shown here. In this respect generality proved both tractable and rich in implications.

There are other factors of the multiagent problem that have not been addressed in this article, but are worth studying. One concerns the possibility of collusion among agents when relative performance evaluations are used. Collusion may imply restrictions on reward structures. In this regard rank-order tournaments, which induce a zero-sum game between the agents, seem to have an advantage over schemes which are not zero-sum.

Another important issue relates to monitoring hierarchies. In this article monitoring technologies were exogenously given. In reality, they are not. The question is what determines the choice of monitors; and how should output be shared so as to provide all members of the organization (including monitors) with the best incentives to perform? Satisfactory answers to these questions would take us a big step toward understanding nonmarket organization.

Appendix

Proof of Theorem 1

■ Let $s_i(x)$, $i = 1, \ldots, n$, be arbitrary sharing rules satisfying (1). I shall show that the assumption that a^* is a Nash equilibrium will lead to a contradiction.

From the definition of a Nash equilibrium

$$s_i(x(a_i, a^*_{-i})) - v_i(a_i) \leq s_i(x(a^*)) - v_i(a^*_i), \ \forall \ a_i \in A_i. \tag{A1}$$

Let $\{\alpha^l\}$ be a strictly increasing sequence of real numbers converging to $x(a^*)$. Let $\{a_i^l\}$ be the corresponding n sequences satisfying

$$\alpha^l = x(a_i^l, a^*_{-i}). \tag{A2}$$

The sequences $\{a_i^l\}$ are well defined (starting from a large enough l if necessary), since $a^* \in$ int A, $x'_i(a^*) \neq 0$, and $x(a)$ is strictly concave. Pareto optimality implies $v'_i(a^*_i)$ $= x'_i(a^*)$, $\forall$ i. This in turn implies, using (A2), that $v_i(a^*_i) - v_i(a_i^l) = x(a^*) - x(a_i^l, a^*_{-i})$ $+ o(a_i^l - a^*_i)$, $\forall$ i, $\forall$ l, where $o(h)/h \rightarrow 0$ as $h \rightarrow 0$. Substituting into (A1), using (A2) gives

$$x(a^*) - \alpha^l + o(a_i^l - a^*_i) \leq s_i(x(a^*)) - s_i(\alpha^l), \ \forall \ i, \ \forall \ l. \tag{A3}$$

Sum (A3) over i, use (1), rearrange and multiply by $n/(n - 1)$. This gives:

$$\sum_{i=1}^{n} \{x(a^*) - \alpha^l + o(a_i^l - a^*_i)\} \leq 0, \ \forall \ l,$$

which can be written

$$\sum_{i=1}^{n} \{-x'_i(a^*)(a_i^l - a^*_i) + o(a_i^l - a^*_i)\} \leq 0, \ \forall \ l. \tag{A4}$$

Since $\alpha^l < x(a^*)$ by the choice of α^l, and $x'_i(a^*) \neq 0$, the first term in the bracket is strictly positive. For large enough l, this term dominates, which contradicts (A4). Hence, the assumption that a^* is a Nash equilibrium has led to a contradiction and must be false. *Q.E.D.*

340 / THE BELL JOURNAL OF ECONOMICS

References

ALCHIAN, A. AND DEMSETZ, H. "Production, Information Costs, and Economic Organization." *American Economic Review*, Vol. 62 (1972).

ARROW, K. *Limits to Organization.* New York: Norton & Co., 1974.

ATKINSON, A.A. AND FELTHAM, G.A. "Information in Capital Markets: An Agency Theory Perspective." Mimeographed, University of British Columbia, July 1980.

BAIMAN, S. AND DEMSKI, L. "Economically Optimal Performance Evaluation and Control Systems." *Journal of Accounting Research*, Supplement (1980).

DEGROOT, M. *Optimal Statistical Decisions.* New York: McGraw-Hill, 1970.

GJESDAL, F. "Information and Incentives: The Agency Incentive Problem." *Review of Economic Studies*, Vol. 49(3), No. 157 (July 1982).

GREEN, J. "On Optimal Structure of Liability Laws." *Bell Journal of Economics*, Vol. 7, No. 2 (Autumn 1976).
——— AND STOKEY, N. "A Comparison of Tournaments and Contracts." Working Paper No. 840, NBER, January 1982.

GROSSMAN, S. AND HART, O. "An Analysis of the Principal-Agent Problem." CARESS WP No. 80-17, University of Pennsylvania, April 1980 (forthcoming in *Econometrica*).

HARRIS, M. AND RAVIV, A. "Optimal Incentive Contracts with Imperfect Information." *Journal of Economic Theory*, Vol. 24 (1979).

HOLMSTROM, B. "Moral Hazard and Observability." *Bell Journal of Economics*, Vol. 10, No. 1 (Spring 1979).
———. "A Discussion of Economically Optimal Performance Evaluation and Control Systems." *Journal of Accounting Research*, Supplement (1980).

LAZEAR, E. AND ROSEN, S. "Rank-Order Tournaments as Optimum Labor Contracts." *Journal of Political Economy*, Vol. 89, No. 5 (1981).

MARSCHAK, J. AND RADNER, R. *Economic Theory of Teams.* New Haven: Yale University Press, 1972.

MILGROM, P. "Good News and Bad News: Representation Theorems and Applications." *Bell Journal of Economics*, Vol. 12, No. 2 (Autumn 1981).

MIRRLEES, J. "Notes on Welfare Economics, Information and Uncertainty" in Balch, McFadden, and Wu, eds., *Essays on Economic Behavior under Uncertainty*, Amsterdam: North Holland, 1974.
———. "The Optimal Structure of Incentives and Authority within an Organization." *Bell Journal of Economics*, Vol. 7, No. 1 (Spring 1976).

MOSSIN, J. "Security Pricing and Investment Criteria in Competitive Markets." *American Economic Review*, Vol. 59 (1969).

NALEBUFF, B. AND STIGLITZ, J. "Prizes and Incentives: Toward a General Theory of Compensation and Competition." Research Memorandum No. 293, Princeton University, January 1982.

RADNER, R. "Optimal Equilibria in Some Repeated Games with Imperfect Monitoring." Bell Laboratories Discussion Paper, May 1980.

ROSS, S. "The Economic Theory of Agency: The Principal's Problem." *American Economic Review*, Vol. 63 (May 1973).

SELTEN, R. "Reexamination of the Perfectness Concept for Equilibrium Points in Extensive Games." *International Journal of Game Theory*, Vol. 4 (1975).

SHAVELL, S. "Risk Sharing and Incentives in the Principal and Agent Relationship." *Bell Journal of Economics*, Vol. 10, No. 1 (Spring 1979).

SPENCE, A.M. AND ZECKHAUSER, R. "Insurance, Information and Individual Action." *American Economic Review*, Vol. 61 (May 1971).

WILSON, R. "The Theory of Syndicates." *Econometrica*, Vol. 36 (January 1968).
———. "The Structure of Incentives for Decentralization under Uncertainty." *La Decision*, No. 171 (1969).

[10]

Hierarchies and Bureaucracies: On the Role of Collusion in Organizations

JEAN TIROLE
Massachusetts Institute of Technology

1. INTRODUCTION

This research derives its motivation (and borrows unrestrainedly) from sociological studies of collusive behavior in organizations. Like the sociology literature, it emphasizes that behavior is often best predicted by the analysis of group as well as individual incentives; and it gropes toward a precise definition of concepts such as "power," "cliques," "corporate politics," and "bureaucracy" (Crozier, 1963; Cyert and March; Dalton; Scott). It differs from this literature in that it tries to incorporate the acquired knowledge of modern information economics into the analysis.

The research also borrows a considerable amount from the principal/agent paradigm of information economics. This paradigm, mainly developed for two-tier organizations, emphasizes the productive inefficiency associated with asymmetric information and insurance motives (or limited liability constraints).[1] Formally, organizations can be seen as networks of overlapping or nested principal/agent relationships. A theme of the paper, however, is that the analysis of hierarchical structures does not boil down to a compounding of the basic inefficiency, due to the fact that going from the simple two-tier principal/agent structure to more complex ones introduces the possibility of

1. See, e.g., Ross; Mirrlees, 1975; Shavell; Holmström, 1979; and Grossman and Hart.

The author is very grateful to Kenneth Arrow, Patrick Bolton, Eric Maskin, Oliver Williamson, various colleagues and students at MIT, and participants at the LEO workshop at Yale Law School for helpful comments and suggestions, and to two anonymous referees for carefully executed reports. The research was supported by the French Planning Board (Commissariat Général au Plan), the National Science Foundation, and the Sloan Foundation.

Journal of Law, Economics, and Organization vol. 2, no. 2 Fall 1986
© 1986 by Yale University. All rights reserved. ISSN 8756–6222

182 / JOURNAL OF LAW, ECONOMICS, AND ORGANIZATION II:2, 1986

collusion. This research departs from the existing information economics literature in that it views an organization as a network of contracts that interplay rather than as a single contract.

The consideration of coalitions in incentive theory certainly deserves some motivation. It raises the questions of how coalitions can form and whether they, in fact, do form. Part 2 reviews and classifies some evidence on the existence of coalitions and on their enforcement mechanism. The examples given there bring direct evidence that coalitions do matter. Since the emergence of coalitions ought to be anticipated at the organization design stage, the mere observation of real-world collusive behavior understates their significance.

Part 3 develops a simple three-tier principal/supervisor/agent model. The agent is the productive unit. He makes an unobservable decision, called "effort," which, together with an exogenous productivity shock, affects the principal's profit. Productivity can be low or high. Neither the level of productivity nor the level of effort is observed by the principal. The supervisor's role is to obtain more information about the agent's activity than is available to the principal. He is a mere conduit; his supervisory effort is assumed exogenous in order to focus on the transmission of information. He observes either the true level of productivity (and then has verifiable evidence about it) or nothing. His degree of freedom is whether to report to the principal when he observes the productivity (given that he can claim to have observed nothing).

The effect of coalitions on the optimal incentive scheme is then examined with reference to the supervisor/agent coalition. In addition to the usual incentive compatibility and individual rationality constraints, new constraints must be introduced. The supervisor here acts naturally as an advocate for the agent. More generally, however, all types of coalitions need to be considered. The relevant coalition occurs at a "nexus of informed parties," that is, within a group of parties that can manipulate the information received by the rest of the organization.

Part 4 suggests some implications of coalitions for organizational behavior. Concluding remarks are offered in part 5.

2. COALITIONS AND COVERT TRANSFERS

HIERARCHIES

Vertical structures in this paper are represented by three-layer hierarchies: principal/supervisor/agent. The roles of the three parties will be described in detail; for the moment, it suffices to think of the principal as the owner of the structure or as the buyer of the agent's product, of the agent as a party picking a productive action affecting the principal, and of the supervisor as a party collecting information to help the principal control the agent. Like the two-tier representation of the classic principal/agent model, this three-tier description is a convenient abstraction. Most organizations are more complex than the idealization considered here. First, one can easily think of higher-order vertical structures. Second, horizontal elements can be superimposed on the vertical frame. For example, the supervisor may monitor several agents (see part 4), or the agent may be monitored by several supervisors.

The evidence supplied in the next section focuses on collusion within a firm A prototypical example concerns the hierarchy manager/foreman/worker. It is clear, however, that these internal organization examples have much in common with collusive behaviors in other structures (even though these structures may differ in other respects: nature and flows of rewards, selection process for the agent, interplay with other horizontal and vertical elements, and so forth). Thus, I expect most conclusions will apply to hierarchies such as voter/government agency/defense contractor (or regulated firm),[2] brass/colonel/regiment, or economics profession/Ph.D. adviser/Ph.D. student.[3] These examples motivate the following axioms, which underly the model presented in part 3.

Axiom 1: The principal, who is the owner of the vertical structure or the buyer of the good produced by the agent, or, more generally, the person who is affected by the agent's activity, lacks either the time or the knowledge required to supervise the agent.

Axiom 2: It is not efficient to divide the supervisory job among several supervisors.

Axiom 3: The supervisor lacks either the time or the resources required to run the vertical structure.

Axiom 3 is posited only to motivate at the current stage the presence of a principal (so that the vertical structure does not boil down to a two-tier one). In the model I will actually dispense with Axiom 3 by allowing the principal to sell to the supervisor. Axiom 2 rules out the use of a team of supervisors. It can be justified either by a cost of duplication of the supervisory function or by a collusive behavior between supervisors. Some circumstances under which several supervisors can efficiently be used by the principal are described in part 4.3. Axiom 1 vindicates the supervisory function. It can be motivated by the possibilities that the principal overlooks and coordinates many agents or that he is technically unable to supervise the agent (in some of the examples

2. For example of collusion in procurement, see Scherer (1964: 100) and Williamson (1967a: 233); for the theory of regulatory capture, see Stigler and Posner; see also Rose-Ackerman and Caillaud et al.

3. To give a few other examples: shareholder/manager/worker; firm/auditor/manger; investor/broker/firm; restaurant owner/maître d'/waiter; Department of Defense/contractor/subcontractor; train company/ticket inspector/passenger.

184 / JOURNAL OF LAW, ECONOMICS, AND ORGANIZATION II:2, 1986

above, the introduction of a supervisor also helps solve the free rider problem associated with the supervision by several principals).

The model set up in part 3 will focus on the supervisory function by assuming that the supervisor has no management or production activity. This assumption is restrictive. In general, the supervisor creates a joint output: supervision of the agent and contribution to production. The productive part may involve the selection of the agent (for example, a contractor selects a subcontractor), the organization and coordination of production and the supply of tools, and the advisory function. Focusing on the supervisory function enables me to make my main points without undue complexity. I do, however, feel that the interplay between the supervisory and production functions is an important question, which I shall tackle in part 5.

2.2. COALITIONS AND COVERT TRANSFERS

The starting point and the tangible effect of the coalition is the manipulation of the information received by the principal. There are several ways in which information may be manipulated: the existing evidence may be concealed or distorted, or the evidence may not be created. Several examples below will illustrate these three possibilities.

Second, the object of the coalition is to benefit one or several members of the coalition. We can distinguish between one-sided favors—one member manipulates the information to the benefit of another member—and shared favors—the manipulation benefits both members. One-sided favors usually go with an explicit or implicit promise of a counterbalancing favor from the beneficiary of the original favor to the other member. The delivery of this promise can be simultaneous or delayed.

The evidence on coalitions and covert transfers I now present is based on sociological studies of the internal organization of firms. In particular, I rely heavily on the very insightful work of Crozier and Dalton,[4] to whom I refer for more details. The general observation is that it is usually hard to obtain information from the intermediate levels of a hierarchy. Both Crozier and Dalton insist that very often common sense directs the controller to falsify his information to allow the monitored group to obtain better results;[5] that is, the controller is not in a position that allows him to give trustworthy information. Both sociologists strongly emphasize the existence of coalitions (Crozier talks about "clans and groups of members of different categories" and Dalton about "cliques.")[6]

As mentioned earlier, one way of manipulating the information is to ignore

4. I am grateful to Woody Powell for the Dalton reference.
5. See, e.g., Crozier, 1963: 51, 52, 56, and 280.
6. See also Selznick's idea that expertise tends to create a caste spirit and temptations of collusion with groups that depend on that expertise.

As mentioned earlier, one way of manipulating the information is to ignore it. This is the case when minor "thefts" and perquisites are not reported. Such private benefits include the use of material and services for personal ends (tools, clerical supplies, long-distance phone calls, use of the firm's employees to redecorate a home, and so forth), days off, plush offices, expense accounting.[7] Sometimes information may be hard to dispose of; it may then be useful not to obtain it: "Inside [the firm] nominal surprise was also a preventive of conflict. For example, safety and health inspectors usually telephoned in advance of visits so that they would not see unsafe practices or conditions they would feel obliged to report" (Dalton, 1959: 48).

Another way to manipulate the information is to distort it. The effect of collusion on auditing is now well documented.[8] Examples of ingenious distortions of records abound, from the creation of fictitious personnel on payroll to changes of job titles, reports of nonexistent pieces, and so forth. Note also that accounting distortions are not the only type of auditing distortions; for example, quality tests can be manipulated.[9]

Manipulation of information is also very common when a shop or a group of employees decides not to implement changes it did not originate. For instance, the supervisor does not enforce the official procedures and the subordinates act cooperatively: the subordinates "keep key persons among interlocking departments informed of change in unofficial methods, and, at the proper time, they teach new members the distinctions between their practices and *official misleading instructions*" (Dalton p. 56; emphasis in text). It is also common not to apply safety rules. Accidents are then kept off the record.[10]

I would like to stress the importance of reciprocity in these examples. This aspect is emphasized in the contributions quoted above, and it is more generally developed in Gouldner (1961), who insists on the universality of the norm of reciprocity. Thus, one-sided favors call for reciprocated ones. For instance, a foreman manipulates the information relevant to the appraisal of his workers' performance. In return, workers can do a number of favors for their foreman. These can include refraining from activities such as unrest, going on strike, leapfrogging for complaints. Also, when facing difficulties, employees place the responsibility not on their supervisors, but on higher

---

7. See Dalton, chap. 7.

8. See, e.g., Dalton (1959: 32), Williamson (1975: 146), and Antle (1984). In other contexts, see also Williamson (1967a) and Schmalensee.

9. Dalton (1959: 85–86) has observed that chemists manipulate the sample experiments to "prove" that the standards of quality are met. In this example, line foremen in return "notify the chemists, rather than their superior, of anything 'going wrong' that would reflect on them, and cooperate to reduce the number of analyses the chemists have to make."

10. See Dalton (pp. 80–85) for a discussion of how and why workers may cooperate in such a deception.

186 / JOURNAL OF LAW, ECONOMICS, AND ORGANIZATION II:2, 1986

levels of the hierarchy (Crozier, 1963: 52). Other nonmonetary transfers include mutual affection and respect, as emphasized by the Human Relations School (for example, see Etzioni, 1964: 34). The foreman, by defending his workers, obtains a better climate within his shop and he is thus more likely to avoid trouble (Crozier, p. 56).

Covert transfers are diverse in nature. First, many of the transfers described earlier are linked to the manipulation by one party of the information possessed about another party (for example, the supervisor conceals information that is detrimental to the agent, and conversely). Some transfers come from direct actions that benefit the other party.[11] A widespread enforcement mechanism for the coalition under such transfers has to do with the repetition of the relationship between the colluding parties. I will emphasize this aspect in part 4.

Second, there is another type of transfer, one which is somewhat out of the (current) realm of economics but which is very important in practice. It has to do with face-to-face relationships, and includes mutual affection and respect. It applies even to relationships that are not repeated.[12] It is just very unpleasant to hurt someone one is facing.

The model developed in part 3 chooses to formalize yet another type of covert transfer: monetary ones. Although such transfers do exist—monetary bribes in contracting; private discounts in business (for example, frequent flyer bonuses received by executives rather than by their firms);[13] auditors obtaining management advisory service contracts from or (now illegally) holding shares of their clients—they are usually fairly limited. The reason why this is so is easily understood. A monetary transfer may be observed by parties that do not belong to the coalition and may be used as evidence of its existence. Nonmonetary transfers are not as conspicuous; or at least, they are harder to use as evidence of a coalition.[14]

Thus, most covert transfers are nonmonetary. The purpose of positing monetary transfers in the theoretical model of part 3 is expositional convenience. This will enable me to make a number of my points using standard economic analysis. I do believe, however, that considering only monetary transfers is restrictive. Although my results are strongly suggestive of what

11. Note that, at a formal level, the two types of transfers are very similar. The delegation of actions to parties mainly stems from informational problems. This lack of distinction is well illustrated by a promotion example: what is the difference between the supervisor's concealing information detrimental to the agent and his promoting the agent directly?

12. Think of the very strict rules that can be imposed on employees checking on people they will never see again (e.g., conductors on trains).

13. Note that firms could force their employees to return their bonuses. Thus, the outcome may well be interpreted as a coalition against the taxpayer.

14. Note that in some cases the covert transfers can actually be observed by the principal but the latter can hardly use this observation, as there is some probability that the transfer is justified. In other words, the principal is unable to show that the transfer is the outcome of a coalition against him. For example, the defense contractor can always argue that he hires the civil servant because of the latter's great talent.

occurs under nonmonetary transfers, the latter should originate new features. [15]

Observed collusive behaviors are only the tip of the iceberg. Anticipating that their members have incentives to collude, organizations can and do set up incentive schemes that restrict the formation and thus the effect of coalitions. In some cases, in equilibrium, no coalition forms that can be observed by outsiders (see the equivalence principle in part 3). However, coalitions are latent and do influence organizational behavior. Thus, the mere observation of collusive behavior understates the influence of coalitions on an organization.

Later I shall emphasize the restrictions on communication in organizations. Nonverifiable reports will hardly be requested. Even verifiable reports will have a somewhat limited effect on rewards (see part 3). This limited communication, which is consistent with both detailed and casual evidence, is a piece of the submerged part of the iceberg. [16] I will analyze other pieces in part 4.

3. THE THEORY

3.1. THE MODEL

Consider the following simple principal/supervisor/agent hierarchy.

The parties. The *agent* is the productive unit. The profit x created by the agent's activity depends on a productivity parameter θ and on the effort $e > 0$ he exerts:

$$x = \theta + e.$$

The agent's disutility of effort is equal, in monetary terms, to $g(e)$, where g is increasing, strictly convex, and $g(0) = g'(0) = 0$. The principal receives profit x, and gives wage W to the agent. The latter has an increasing, differentiable, and strictly concave Von Neumann–Morgenstern utility function U. We will assume that there exists w such that

$$\lim_{W \to w} U(W) = -\infty.$$

15. For instance, they may not add up to zero within a coalition; some may be inefficient, even from the point of view of the coalition (sexual harassment); others may be desirable, even from a social point of view (acts of cooperation).

16. As Katz and Kahn observe: "The typical upward communication loop is small and terminates with the immediate supervisor. He or she may transmit some of the information to the next higher level, but generally in a modified form."

188 / JOURNAL OF LAW, ECONOMICS, AND ORGANIZATION II:2, 1986

The agent's expected utility is $EU[W - g(e)]$ (the uncertainty will be described later).

There exists an *ex- ante* competitive supply of agents, with reservation wage W_0, and reservation utility $\bar{U} \equiv U(W_0)$. The agent's participation (individual rationality) constraint is

$$EU[W - g(e)] \geq \bar{U}.$$

The *supervisor's* role will be described along with the uncertainty and the informational assumptions. For the moment, let us just assume that the supervisor exerts no effort, receives a wage S from the principal, and has an increasing, differentiable, and strictly concave Von Neumann–Morgenstern utility function V. The supervisor's expected utility is $EV(S)$.

There exists *ex- ante* a competitive supply of supervisors, with reservation wage S_0, and reservation utility $\bar{V} \equiv V(S_0)$. The supervisor's participation (individual rationality) constraint is

$$EV(S) \geq \bar{V}.$$

In the discussion below, I will assume that $S_0 = 0$. This assumption corresponds to the case in which the principal must hire a supervisor for other purposes than supervision (organization, advising, coordination, and so forth). The opportunity cost of the supervisory function is then zero because of the supervisor's dual role. More generally, one can admit $S_0 \geq 0$. The decision of whether to hire a supervisor is then endogenous. The results obtained below remain valid on the condition that a supervisor is hired.

Finally, the *principal* is the owner of the technology used by the agent (or else is the buyer of the good produced by the agent). He designs the main contract and offers it to the supervisor and the agent. He is risk-neutral. His expected utility is $E(x - S - W)$. (I assume that the principal is risk-neutral so that the supervisor plays no role in insuring the principal.)

Uncertainty and Information.   The productivity parameter can take two values: $\underline{\theta}$ and $\bar{\theta}$, such that $0 < \underline{\theta} < \bar{\theta}$. $\underline{\theta}$ and $\bar{\theta}$ will later be called the bad (low) and good (high) states of *productivity*. Let $\Delta\theta \equiv \bar{\theta} - \underline{\theta}$.

There are four states of *nature*, indexed by i. State of nature i has probability p_i ($\sum_{i=1}^{4} p_i = 1$). The agent always observes θ before choosing his effort. The supervisor may or may not observe θ. In the following description of the four states of nature, S and A stand for supervisor and agent:

State 1: A and S observe $\underline{\theta}$.
State 2: A observes $\underline{\theta}$, S observes "nothing."
State 3: A observes $\bar{\theta}$, S observes "nothing."
State 4: A and B observe $\bar{\theta}$.

For a given θ, the supervisor's signal s can thus take two values: $|\theta, \emptyset|$, where $\emptyset$ denotes observation "nothing."

The agent's information structure is finer than the supervisor's, which is finer than the principal's. For simplicity, I assume the agent knows whether the supervisor learns the true state of productivity; that is, the agent knows the state of nature.

Lastly, I assume the agent's effort e is not observable by the other two parties.

Timing. The principal first offers a contract. For the moment I do not distinguish between the main contract and side contracts. The latter will be introduced shortly. The contract specifies the transfers S and W to the supervisor and the agent, as functions of the commonly observed variables. These observables are the profit x and the supervisor's report r to the principal.

I shall assume that the supervisor's information is "hard." By this I mean that his report is *verifiable* in the following sense: when he observes the state of productivity, he can convey this information to the principal in a credible way (the principal can look at the evidence and convince himself that the supervisor has announced the true state of productivity). However, the supervisor can lie and announce he has observed nothing, that is, conceal the evidence. (He can also announce the wrong state of nature, but this claim, which cannot be substantiated, is assumed to be interpreted as the absence of observation). Thus,

$$\text{if } s = \theta, \ r \ \varepsilon \ \{\theta, \emptyset\}$$

and

$$\text{if } s = \emptyset, \ r = \emptyset.$$

Let us briefly examine the notion of verifiability. The report can be thought of as the communication of the outcome of a quality test on the agent's product, or as a report on other shops, divisions, or firms facing a state of productivity correlated with that of the agent, or else as a credible statement by the supervisor on the agent's activity (the supervisor makes a "convincing case"). This leads us to three questions. First, are there circumstances in which the agent cannot supply a verifiable report himself? Second, if the agent can supply a verifiable report himself, is there still room for the supervisory function? Third, are nonverifiable reports of any interest? The first two questions will be analyzed in sections 4.1 and 3.2 respectively. I will not attempt to address the third question in detail. In section 4.5 I give an example in which nonverifiable reports can be useful. In general, however, nonverifiable reports create hazards. Indeed, in the accounting literature, Ijiri, Gjesdal, and Antle (1982, 1984) have warned us against the use of "soft" (that is, nonverifiable) information.[17] In my model, in the absence of collusion, it does not matter whether information is "hard" (verifiable), as is assumed here, or "soft." If the supervisor and the agent collude, however, soft information becomes useless, as is easily seen. Thus, I focus on hard information.

If the contract is accepted, the agent learns the state of nature; and the supervisor learns his signal, that is, he observes or does not observe the state of productivity. The agent then exerts effort. The profit is realized and the supervisor produces a report (the exact timing of the report can actually be a choice variable for the principal). The principal then rewards the supervisor and the agent.

The timing is summarized in the following diagram:

Contract	A learns θ	A chooses e	Profit $x = \theta + e$	Transfers
	S learns s		S reports r	$S(x,r)$
				$W(x,r)$

The Symmetric Information Allocation (First Best). For purposes of comparison, I consider the case in which the state of productivity is observed by the principal. The supervisor then has no supervisory function. He receives S_0 in all states of nature. The effort exerted by the agent is also observable by the principal. The optimal level of effort e^* maximizes the profit minus the disutility of effort:

$$\text{Max}_{e}\{\theta + e - g(e)\} \rightarrow g'(e^*) = 1 \text{ for all } \theta.$$

At the optimum, for any state of nature, the marginal disutility of effort is equal to the marginal profit. I will denote $g^* \equiv g(e^*)$ the corresponding disutility of effort. The agent also receives a wage that is independent of the state of nature: $W_i = W_0 + g^*$.

Asymmetric Information and Overt Contract. From now on, I consider the information structure described above as the four states of nature. I first derive the optimal contract, assuming that side contracts are infeasible (coalitions do not form).

Note that, when given a constant wage S_0, the supervisor is fully insured and obtains his reservation utility. Furthermore, he has no incentive to lie (conceal the evidence). Thus, the principal can obtain the supervisor's information at "minimal cost."

17. Antle (1984) studies soft information and shows that even in the absence of side transfers between the auditor (supervisor) and the manager (agent), the optimal auditor's contract may not depend on the auditor's report if one requires that the auditor has a dominant strategy (telling the truth in our context). Antle also allows for a supervisory effort.

The three-tier structure boils down to the two-tier principal/agent one, in which the principal pays a lump sum S_0 and inherits the supervisor's information structure.

Thus consider program (CF) (where CF stands for "coalition free"):

$$\text{Max}_{\{W_i, e_i\}} \sum_i p_i(\theta_i + e_i - W_i)$$

(CF) s.t.

$$(AIR) \sum_i p_i U[W_i - g(e_i)] \geq \bar{U}$$

$$(AIC)\ W_3 - g(e_3) \geq W_2 - g(e_2 - \Delta\theta).$$

The agent's individual rationality constraint (AIR) states that the agent must obtain at least his reservation utility. The agent's incentive compatibility constraint (AIC) comes from the fact that the principal has incomplete information about the state of nature in state 3. The agent can always exert effort $(e_2 - \Delta\theta)$ in state 3 to claim the state is actually 2 and obtain wage W_2. (A similar incentive compatibility constraint also exists in state 2 $[W_2 - g(e_2) \geq W_3 - g(e_3 + \Delta\theta)]$; but, as is usual, this constraint is not binding at the optimum. The issue is to induce the agent to reveal that the state of productivity is good, not that it is bad.)

Program (CF) leads to

Proposition 1: In the absence of coalitions, the optimal contract is equivalent to the optimal contract between the principal and the agent when the principal has the supervisor's information structure. The supervisor's wage is equal to S_0 in all states of nature. Furthermore:

$$W_3 > W_1 = W_4 > W_2$$

and

$$e_1 = e_3 = e_4 = e^* > e_2.$$

The proof of proposition 1, which is a straightforward extension of familiar proofs in contract theory, is supplied in the appendix. The supervisor's honesty implies that the principal has full information in states of nature 1 and 4 (when the supervisor observes the true state). The first best level of effort can then be required from the agent. Optimal insurance implies that the agent's wage is the same in these two states. In states of nature 2 and 3, the principal has incomplete information about the state of productivity. The agent's wage must be higher in state 3 than in state 2, in order to provide the

192 / JOURNAL OF LAW, ECONOMICS, AND ORGANIZATION II:2, 1986

agent with sufficient incentives not to shirk in state 3 (that is, not to claim that the productivity is low). Under asymmetric information, the principal must reward a high performance and punish a low one. The optimum also involves a suboptimal effort in the low state of productivity (this makes it less attractive to shirk in the good state of productivity, once the corresponding reduction in W_2 is taken into account).

3.2. SUPERVISOR/AGENT COALITION

Let us now introduce the possibility of a coalition between the supervisor and the agent. Suppose that after (or simultaneously with) having signed the main contract offered by the principal, and before the uncertainty is resolved, the supervisor and the agent sign a side (covert) contract. This side contract specifies transfer $t(x,r)$ from the agent to the supervisor as a function of the realized profit and the supervisor's report. (Making t depend also on the supervisor's signal would not affect the analysis, because as is easily seen, the signal can in equilibrium be recovered from the profit and the report.) The supervisor's and the agent's gross incomes become $\{S(x,r) + t\ (x,r)\}$ and $\{W(x,r) - t(x,r)\}$. Note that I formalize the side transfer t as being monetary.

I assume that either the side transfer t is not observable by the principal or the main contract does not contain a clause forbidding further bilateral contracts (the same outcome arises if the principal signs a main contract with the supervisor only, and lets the supervisor "subcontract" with an agent any way the supervisor wants).

Under a supervisor/agent coalition, the allocation given by proposition 1 is no longer sustainable. In state of nature 4, the supervisor is indifferent between reporting he has observed the good state of productivity and "remaining silent" (claiming he has observed nothing); but the agent prefers the supervisor to remain silent. Thus, the agent has an incentive to bribe the supervisor to prevent him from revealing that the technology is favorable to the agent.

More generally, the supervisor and the agent ought to sign a side contract that induces the supervisor to report r in the feasible set of reports so as to maximize the total wage bill $\{W(x,r) + S(x,r)\}$ for any state of nature and profit x.[18]

The issue of how the supervisor and the agent split the surplus generated by their side contract is a matter of bargaining power and is not germane to the points made here. Therefore, I will make only the following assumptions on the bargaining process.

18. Note that this point and the subsequent analysis would not be affected if the principal asked the agent to send a "message" as well. The agent and the supervisor can always coordinate on what message to send. Thus, the wage bill can only depend on hard information (verifiable report and profit).

A1. The supervisor and the agent choose a side contract that is Pareto optimal for these two parties.

A2. Each of the two parties can guarantee itself the no-side-contract outcome.

Given that the supervisor and the agent bargain under symmetric information, these two assumptions are indeed quite weak.

I use the following methodology: in a first step I derive a set of contraints that the *final* (post side contract) allocation must satisfy; to the usual individual rationality and individual incentive compatibility constraints, I add a set of "coalition incentive compatibility constraints." In the second step I maximize the principal's expected payoff subject to this enlarged set of constraints, assuming that no coalition is formed. The third (and trivial) step consists in showing that the optimal contract does not generate a side contract between the supervisor and the agent (that is, is coalition-proof).

Let us start by deriving a set of constraints that must be satisfied by the final allocation. This allocation will be represented by $\{S_i, W_i, e_i\}$ for all i (S_i and W_i now include the side transfer).

i) The participation—or individual rationality (*IR*)—constraints for the supervisor and the agent must be satisfied. Otherwise, under rational expectations, the main contract would not be signed. Thus, we can impose

$$(SIR) \qquad \sum_i p_i V(S_i) \geqslant \bar{V}$$

and

$$(AIR) \qquad \sum_i p_i U[W_i - g(e_i)] \geqslant \bar{U}.$$

ii) The agent in state of nature 3 should not claim that the state of nature is 2 (remember he is the only party who can distinguish between those two states). To claim so, he would have to exert effort $(e_2 - \Delta\theta)$. Thus, the incentive compatibility constraint for the agent is

$$(AIC) \qquad W_3 - g(e_3) \geqslant W_2 - g(e_2 - \Delta\theta).$$

Similarly, in state of nature 2, the agent should not behave as in state of nature 3. But, as usual, this second incentive constraint will not be binding and can be ignored for the moment. We will later check to see that it indeed is satisfied.

iii) Let us now derive the coalition incentive constraints (*CIC*). In states of nature 1 and 4, the supervisor can conceal his information. Hence, if the supervisor and the agent choose a Pareto-optimal side contract, the total wage bill net of the disutility of effort in states 1 and 4 cannot be lower than that in states 2 and 3 respectively. Thus, we get

$(CIC\ 1)$ $S_1 + W_1 - g(e_1) \geq S_2 + W_2 - g(e_2)$

$(CIC\ 2)$ $S_4 + W_4 - g(e_4) \geq S_3 + W_3 - g(e_3).$

It must also be the case that the supervisor cannot bribe the agent to behave in state 3 as in state 2. This constraint can be written:

$(CIC\ 3)$ $S_3 + W_3 - g(e_3) \geq S_2 + W_2 - g(e_2 - \Delta\theta).$[19]

Note that, if (AIC) is binding, $(CIC\ 3)$ reduces to $(CIC\ 3')\ S_3 \geq S_2.$

There are two constraints that we ignore for the moment: the agent IC constraint in state 2 $(W_2 - g(e_2) \geq W_3 - g(e_3 + \Delta\theta))$ and the coalition IC constraint in state 2 $(S_2 + W_2 - g(e_2) \geq S_3 + W_3 - g(e_3 + \Delta\theta))$. These constraints will indeed be automatically satisfied by the solution to our problem.

Next, let us compute the optimal contract for the principal when the latter anticipates that no coalition forms but must respect the previous constraints. That is, we look for the solution to program (C):

$$\underset{\{S_i, W_i, e_i\}}{\text{Max}}\ \ \sum_i p_i(\theta_i + e_i - S_i - W_i)$$

(C) s.t. (SIR), (AIR), (AIC), $(CIC\ 1)$, $(CIC\ 2)$, and $(CIC\ 3)$.

Note that the coalition necessarily hurts the principal, because (C) involves more constraints than (CF). The solution to (C) is derived in the appendix and is described in the following lemma.

---

19. Imagine that $(CIC\ 3)$ is not satisfied. Let us show that the supervisor and the agent can sign a side contract that leads to a Pareto-superior allocation for them. The supervisor is willing to accept a "certainty equivalent" wage S_e in states 2 and 3, such that

$$S_e \leq p_2' S_2 + p_3' S_3$$

where $p_i' \equiv p_i/(p_2 + p_3)$. Futhermore, from (AIC) and the fact that $(CIC\ 3)$ is not satisfied, $S_2 > S_3$ and $S_2 > S_e$.

The agent claims that the state is 2 in both states 2 and 3, and obtains expected utility, conditional on the state being one of these two states:

$$p_2'U[W_2 + S_2 - S_e - g(e_2)] + p_3'[W_2 + S_2 - S_e - g(e_2 - \Delta\theta)].$$

instead of

$$p_2'U[W_2 - g(e_2)] + p_3'U[W_3 - g(e_3)].$$

The latter expected utility is strictly lower than

$$p_2'U[W_2 - g(e_2)] + p_3'U[W_2 + S_2 - S_3 - g(e_2 - \Delta\theta)].$$

The agent's net income with the new contract dominates the income $[W_2 - g(e_2); W_2 + S_2 - S_3 - g(e_2 - \Delta\theta)]$. Thus, one can construct a Pareto-improving side contract that perturbs the assumed final allocation.

Lemma 1: The solution to (C) has the following features:
a) $S_4 > S_1 > S_2 = S_3$
b) $W_3 - g(e_3) > W_4 - g(e_4) > W_1 - g(e_1) > W_2 - g(e_2)$
c) $S_4 + W_4 = S_3 + W_3$
d) $e_1 = e_3 = e_4 = e^* > e_2$
e) All the constraints in (C), except (CIC 1), are binding (have strictly positive shadow prices).[20]

Note that the principal cannot hope to do better than the solution to (C), as the constraints in (C) must be satisfied by the final allocation. But if the principal offers the contract defined by the solution to (C), there is no state of nature in which the total wage bill net of the disutility of effort can be increased by changing the report or the effort level. Furthermore, by construction, (C) embodies the optimal insurance scheme (subject to the AIC constraint) between the supervisor and the agent. Thus, no side contract between the supervisor and the agent forms, and the principal can indeed guarantee himself the solution to (C). We call this fact the *equivalence principle*: the principal can restrict himself to contracts that do not induce the agent and the supervisor to collude, once the relevant coalition incentive constraints are introduced.[21]

We have thus obtained

Proposition 2: When the supervisor and the agent can collude, the final allocation satisfies conditions (a) through (e) of lemma 1.

Let us now comment on the outcome under collusion. Lemma 1 (d) says that a distortion in effort is imposed only when the state of productivity is low and is not observed by the supervisor; (c) stems from (CIC 2) and the fact that the effort is the same in states 3 and 4. Thus, the total wage bill is the same in states 3 and 4. However, the supervisor's and the agent's wages vary between these two states, in spite of risk aversion. The point is that in state 3, the agent

---

20. Let me check that the ignored constraints are also satisfied by the solution to (C). From (e), we know that

$$W_3 - g(e_3) = W_2 - g(e_2 - \Delta\theta).$$

Together with (d) and the convexity of g, this equality implies

$$W_3 - g(e_3 + \Delta\theta) < W_2 - g(e_2),$$

so that the agent's incentive compatibility constraint in state 2 is satisfied. Furthermore, from (a), we have

$$S_3 + W_3 - g(e_3 + \Delta\theta) < S_2 + W_2 - g(e_2),$$

so that the coalition incentive compatibility constraint in state 2 is also satisfied.

21. The coalition then does not form. Note that the allocation between the supervisor and the agent that results from (C) is optimal given the (conditional) wage bill and the agent's IC constraint; thus the solution to (C) could also be obtained by the principal by letting the supervisor and the agent collude. An extreme example occurs when the principal gives the supervisor the total (conditional) wage bill and lets the supervisor subcontract with an agent.

can claim that the state of productivity is low and the supervisor cannot provide evidence to the contrary. The agent must then be paid a high wage in order not to shirk. In state 4, optimal insurance calls for a lower wage for the agent than in state 3. But the supervisor must then obtain a higher wage in state 4 than in state 3, in order for the agent not to bribe the supervisor to conceal the state of productivity. This increase in the supervisor's wage represents a cost of obtaining the information.

The coalition incentive compatibility constraint in state 1—which induces the supervisor to reveal that the state of productivity is low—is not binding. This is very natural because in the low state of productivity, the agent prefers to have an excuse for generating a low profit. We interpret the result that (*CIC* 1) is not binding, while (*CIC* 2) is, as the idea that the supervisor naturally acts as an *advocate* for the agent.

To make it less costly to induce the supervisor to reveal that productivity is high (state of nature 4), the principal would want to give him a low salary (S_3) is he claims he has observed nothing and the profit is high. However, the supervisor's wage in state 3 cannot be lower than that in state 2 (from [CIC 3']). Thus $S_3 = S_2$. This constraint in turn leads to a lower S_2. This explains why the supervisor's wage in state 1 is higher than in state 2, despite the fact that the supervisor is quite willing to reveal the low state of productivity.

The two extreme cases of risk aversion for the supervisor lead to particularly simple results (see the appendix for a derivation). The supervisor is risk-neutral if V is linear; he is infinitely risk-averse if he cares only about his lowest possible wage.

Proposition 3: If the supervisor is risk-neutral, the principal realizes the same profit as in the collusion-free case. Up to a fixed cost S_0, everything is *as if* the principal monitored the agent directly and had the information structure $\{s_1 = \underline{\theta}, s_2 = s_3 = \emptyset, s_4 = \overline{\theta}\}$ (that is, the supervisor's information structure).

Proposition 4: If the supervisor is infinitely risk-averse, the principal pays a fixed wage S_0 to the supervisor; he then has the information structure $\{s_1 = \underline{\theta}, s_2 = s_3 = s_4 = \emptyset\}$ to monitor the agent.

The interpretation of propositions 3 and 4 is as follows.

A risk-neutral supervisor can own (be a residual claimant for) the vertical structure without any loss in terms of insurance. Thus, the principal can sell the vertical structure to the supervisor at a price equal to the expected profit minus the supervisor's reservation wage. The hierarchy then boils down to a two-tier structure between the supervisor and the agent. But we know that there is no room for collusion in a two-tier structure. Thus, the outcome is the collusion-free one.

In the examples mentioned in part 2, the supervisor is far from being made the residual claimant for the vertical structure. This suggests that proposition 3 is of limited interest in many cases.

The case of infinite risk aversion is clearly extreme. The motivation for studying it is that it very starkly illustrates the nature of the supervisor-agent coalition. The supervisor receives a constant wage like in the collusion-free case; however, he deliberately ignores the information he receives about the good state of productivity. He reveals only the information he receives about the bad state of productivity. Again, this behavior amounts to acting as an advocate for the agent.

As mentioned above, we may wonder what would happen if the agent were able to produce verifiable reports himself. Let us assume away the supervisory function, and let us endow the agent with full information in all states of nature (as earlier) and with verifiable information about the state of productivity in states 1 and 4 (thus, we transfer the supervisor's technology to the agent). Do we obtain the same outcome as with a supervisor (the outcome with a supervisor is the solution to [C], whether or not the agent can produce verifiable information in states 1 and 4)? The answer is provided in

Proposition 5: Assume the agent can produce verifiable information himself. Except in the case of supervisor's infinite risk aversion, there is still scope for a supervisory function.

The idea behind proposition 5 (the proof of which is straightforward and therefore not provided) is simple. In the absence of a supervisor, the agent will release only information that is favorable to him, that is, only evidence about the bad state of nature. In particular, we have $W_3 = W_4$ (and $e_3 = e_4$). Thus, the solution differs from (and is dominated by) the solution with a supervisor. This point is particularly clear in the case of the supervisor's risk neutrality. The supervisor, who is then the owner of the vertical structure, prefers to be informed about the good state of productivity, information he can obtain only if he collects verifiable information himself.

3.3. GENERAL COALITIONAL STRUCTURES

In the previous section, we assumed that only the supervisor and the agent can form a coalition. There is no a priori reason to impose such a restriction.

Consider first the outcome obtained in part 3.1, when no coalition is feasible, and introduce the possibility of a supervisor-principal coalition. This coalition could induce the supervisor not to release the evidence in state 1 or in state 4. Clearly, there is no point in doing so in state 4 ($W_3 > W_4$ and $e_3 = e_4$). It can also be shown that the main contract can be designed so that the supervisor reveals his signal in state 1.[22] Thus, the collusion-free

---

22. There is a subtle point to be addressed here: What happens if the outcome is not foreseen (i.e., not one of the four outcomes specified) by the main contract? For instance, in state 1 the agent could exert effort e^*, anticipating that the supervisor reports the evidence. But the supervisor might not do so. The profit would then differ from that expected in state 2, i.e. ($\underline{\theta} + e_2$).

The main contract can be designed so as to be immune to the supervisor/principal coalition.

198 / JOURNAL OF LAW, ECONOMICS, AND ORGANIZATION II:2, 1986

outcome is immune to a coalition between the supervisor and the principal. Similarly, it is easily seen that it is also immune to a coalition between the agent and the principal.

We now investigate what kind of allocation can be implemented by the principal when *all* types of bilateral coalitions are allowed. By allocation, we mean the *final* allocation that results from the parties' optimizing behavior given the main contract and the side contracts.

A final allocation is said to be coalition-proof if there exists no state of nature in which a coalition can increase its aggregate payoff by changing a variable (effort, report) that is controlled by a member of the coalition.

Proposition 6: The solution to (*C*) is coalition-proof.

Proposition 6 says that the main contract defined by program (*C*), in which a potential coalition between the supervisor and the agent is accounted for, is more generally coalition-proof. Thus, if the principal offers this contract, it is an equilibrium for the other parties to accept the contract and for all parties not to expect or suggest any side contract.[23]

The proof of proposition 6 (supplied in the appendix) starts by describing the mechanism more completely (in particular, it defines what happens if the observed {profit, report} pair is not one of the four equilibrium ones), and shows that the solution to (*C*) can indeed be implemented when all coalitions are allowed.

Proposition 6 shows that the principal need not worry about the effect that his potential coalitions with the agent and the supervisor have on the optimal contract for the supervisor-agent coalition. The corresponding coalition incentive compatibility constraints are not binding. In this sense, the relevant coalition is that between the supervisor and the agent. Thus, collusion naturally arises at the organization's *nexus of informed parties*, that is, within a group that can manipulate the information obtained by the rest of the organization (here, by the principal).[24]

I have not showed that the equivalence principle holds (while I did so when only the supervisor-agent coalition is feasible). Hence, we may wonder whether, given an extensive form for the formation of coalitions, the principal can do better when he can form coalitions than when he cannot (given, or course, that the other two parties correctly anticipate these coalitions if the main

---

Assume that the three parties are punished heavily in case of an "unforeseen outcome." Clearly, one equilibrium is the collusion-free one (the supervisor does not want to deviate unilaterally and conceal the evidence in state 1). To make sure that {$e = e_2$, $r = \emptyset$} is not another equilibrium in state 1 (in which the agent correctly anticipates that the other two parties form a coalition not to release evidence in state 1), it suffices that the main contract requires that the report be released *after* the profit is observed. This gives the agent a Stackelberg leadership. As he prefers state 1 to state 2, he can force the supervisor to announce the truth in state 1.

23. Here I am a bit loose on the extensive form for the formation of coalitions. See below.

24. In a sense, this property is an extension to group behavior of the classic principal/agent paradigm, in which the agent manipulates the information received by the principal.

contract gives scope for them). To answer this question, one must posit an extensive form for the game of coalition formation. For instance, suppose that in the coalition formation game, the supervisor and the agent form their coalition last. Then the constraints $(CIC\ 1)$ through $(CIC\ 3)$ must be satisfied by the final allocation. The final allocation must also satisfy (SIR), (AIR), and (AIC) (this last property holds for any game of coalition formation). Thus, the principal *cannot* do better than the solution to (C). Together with proposition 6, this implies that the outcome of the game with general coalitions is the same as the one with only the supervisor-agent coalition.

4. COALITIONS AND ORGANIZATIONAL BEHAVIOR

4.1. WHAT DO SUPERVISORS DO?

Before deriving some implications for hierarchical organizations, it is useful to discuss the role of supervisors in the light of the previous model. I again assume away productive activities by the supervisor to focus on the supervisory function. Also, I assume that the supervisor and the agent do collude (the factors of collusion are discussed in the next two sections).

We saw that the supervisor's information is more costly to obtain under collusion. For example, in the extreme case in which the supervisor is not willing to bear any income risk, everything is *as if* the principal hired a collusion-free (honest) supervisor who could observe that the agent's environment is unfavorable, but would never observe that this environment is favorable: the supervisor acts as an *advocate* (see proposition 4). But even in this extreme case, the supervisor is useful in producing verifiable evidence in the unfavorable state of productivity.

The behavior of the supervisor as an advocate for the agent may shed some light on the well-known and intriguing fact that *positive reinforcement is more reliable than negative reinforcement.*[25] Rewards work better than punishments. The usual, psychological explanation for this phenomenon is the trauma associated with punishments (issue of framing). It is harder to come up with an economic interpretation. Economists are not used to distinguishing rewards and punishments (punishments are just negative rewards). The theoretical model of part 3 shows that there may be an economic explanation as well, if one views organizations as a network of groups. For instance, a supervisor who is not willing to bear any income risk intervenes only to raise the agent's wage (in state 1), never to lower it. Thus, the supervisor's degree of freedom (object of intervention) is to reward the agent.[26] Except in the

25. See, e.g., Katz and Kahn (1978: 310).
26. If the supervisor is not infinitely risk-averse, the idea that rewards work better than punishments can still be formalized, albeit not in such a stark way. The supervisor needs no special incentive to reveal the environment is unfavorable (state 1), in the sense that the coalition

extreme case of an infinitely risk-averse supervisor, there is still scope for the supervisory function if the agent can produce the verifiable information himself. In the absence of a supervisor, there is no way to induce the agent to reveal that the environment is favorable (while he is always willing to demonstrate that the environment is unfavorable). A supervisor who is willing to bear some income risk can be given incentives to reveal that the environment is favorable, as long as the penalty imposed on the agent by this announcement is not so high that the agent bribes the supervisor not to reveal. (An alternative and more technical way to approach this result is to notice that the presence of a supervisor increases the set of contingencies over which an insurance-incentive contract can be signed with the agent.) In some cases, the agent may not be in a position to produce verifiable information himself. He may not be able to defend his case clearly ("lawyer's syndrome") or to provide quality tests. Alternatively, he may lack the time to do so.[27]

4.2. Who Colludes with Whom?

The reader might be misled by my emphasis on the supervisor-agent coalition and infer that (effective) coalitions naturally arise between the lower tiers of a vertical structure. The problem with this inference is that the conventional ordering in vertical structures is based on criteria that may not capture the issue studied here (for example, the ordering may stem from the initial distribution of authority or residual rights of control). Even though coalitions naturally form between a "supervisor" and an "agent," the notions of "supervisor" and "agent" may not fit conventional ordering.

For instance, the ordering of the hierarchies justice/police/convict and colonel/captain/conscript may not reflect their structures of information. One may think of instances in which the agent is the police or the captain, the principal the convict or conscript, and the supervisor the judicial system or the colonel. With this reordering, the agent may take an action that affects the principal, and the supervisor may check the agent's action. Thus, a coalition can form between the judicial system and the police against the convict, and between the colonel and the captain against the conscript. This means the

---

incentive constraint is not binding. By contrast, in state 4, the supervisor reveals that the environment is favorable only if his wage increase associated with the disclosure of information is at least equal to the corresponding reduction in the agent's wage (the coalition incentive constraint is binding).

27. The supervisor, from his dual function (planning, coordinating, advising, etc.) may devote more time to learning about outside units (shops, firms). If some other units are subject to productivity shocks that are statistically correlated with the agent's activity, the performance of these units can be used as a yardstick to infer the agent's behavior. Another possibility is that the supervisor supervises several agents. A common productivity shock affecting the agents may give rise to a free rider problem between the agents: each agent may be able to gather the evidence about the common shock and discuss it with upper tiers of the hierarchy, but he would prefer other agents to offer their time to do so.

theory is consistent with the existence of coalitions between members of what is traditionally called "upper tiers." The moral is that the identification of effective coalitions in an organization requires a careful consideration of the information structure. Similarly, a party may collude with different parties depending on the issue.[28]

4.3. THE LENGTH OF RELATIONSHIPS

Giving parties contract incentives or forcing them to have a long-run relationship has some desirable effects. First, as Williamson (1975) has forcefully argued, long-run relationships help foster the accumulation of specific assets. Second, as emphasized in the repeated moral hazard literature, repetition alleviates incentive problems (if the agent does not have access to perfect capital markets). On the other hand, it has been recognized that contracts should leave some flexibility for mutually advantageous "breaches."[29] In this section, I remark that the possibility of collusion suggests an alternative explanation of short-run relationships.

Collusions require side-transfers. As discussed in part 2, some types of transfers (monetary, personal interaction) may enforce coalitions in short-run relationships. The latter can also be enforced by a mutual threat (each member of the coalition threatens to release some piece of information that would be detrimental to the other member). Often, however, transfers and threats are not simultaneous: a party does a favor for the other party, who implicitly or explicitly promises to reciprocate later. The enforcement mechanism is then associated with repetition.

Keeping relationships short has the advantage of restricting side transfers and, thus, of limiting the influence of coalitions in organizations. As Kreps et al. have shown, cooperation between two parties at any given time increases with the time horizon of their relationship. It would be desirable to develop models of reputation that explain the common observation that the extent of collusion between two parties tends to increase over time. I expect such a formalization to follow one of the following two intuitive lines. First, trust may be slow to develop and the stakes of a cooperative behavior may accordingly rise over time. Higher stakes can be offered when one becomes reasonably sure that the other party is interested in cooperation.[30] Second,

28. In my model, the supervisor might share with the owner of the firm some information about demand for the product, say (like in the implicit contract literature). The supervisor then becomes a supervisor for the (so-called) principal and may collude with him not to release this information to the (so-called) agent. At the same time, he may collude with the agent regarding the release of the productivity information.

29. This aspect has been particularly emphasized by Aghion and Bolton in their reconsideration of the market foreclosure doctrine. In a somewhat different vein, see also Harris and Holmström's study of the sampling problem between two parties who, over time, lose information about the value of their relationship.

30. For a promising start on this, see Sobel's introduction of a stake into the Kreps—Milgrom—Roberts—Wilson model.

202 / JOURNAL OF LAW, ECONOMICS, AND ORGANIZATION II:2, 1986

and this argument is more specific to coalitions in organizations, past collusion may enforce current and future collusion. Once parties (for example, the supervisor and the agent) have started colluding, each possesses threats against the other in case of a breach. Disclosure by one party of information detrimental to the other party usually prompts immediate retaliation through release by the latter of information detrimental to the former.[31] This mutual blackmail, which makes the breakdown of collusion costly, forces the parties into a coalition to keep on colluding.[32]

There is some evidence that organizations give their members (especially at the managerial and supervisory levels) incentives to switch jobs within the organization.[33] Sometimes they even require it. In France one of the functions of the "Grands Corps" of civil servants is to provide decision makers and analysts who are mobile and fairly independent of pressures that come from inside the organizations with which they are working (because of their job and wage security as well as their mobility).

Another piece of evidence is the use of consulting firms to collect information. The latter are expensive and in many cases are limited in their access to information. However, their members have a short-run relationship with each firm for which they are working and therefore are almost (hidden) transfer-free.[34,35]

Similarly, outside recruiting may bring new blood to an organization, even when the new employee does not have superior ability or knowledge. (New employees are less subject to coalitional pressures because they do not yet know whom to trust).[36]

31. For instance, Dalton (1959: 77) mentions the case of a foreman colluding with operators not to "kill" a good rate. The foreman received an order to be completed at once. He decided to abide by the order, which led the engineers to investigate the operators' performance, which had unexplainably moved from a normal to a phenomenal level with no change in job or method. Enraged by the foreman's deception, the operators explained their remarkable rate by exposing the foreman's part in the deception.

32. A mitigating factor in this increase in collusion over time is the fact that at the beginning of the relationship each party can make the other party's life miserable for a longer period of time if the latter does not cooperate immediately (this effect is captured by Kreps et al.)

33. Monotony and the lack of further on-the-job learning may be motives to change jobs; but, to some extent, they are internalized by the member and do not require special incentives.

34. There is another use of consulting firms that is also related to coalitions: sometimes consultants are hired by the boss to tell him or her what he or she wants to hear (the threat in case of breakdown of collusion is the nonrenewal of the consulting contract).

35. In a similar spirit, Scherer suggested the use of an independent Program Evaluation Board to assess defense programs: "Serious problems of bias and lack of comparability are likely to arise when performance judgements are made by persons deeply involved in the programs" (1964: 329). Or the auctioning of defense contracts may break privileged relationships between contractors and Department of Defense officials. Let us also mention Niskanen's proposal to change committees after a limited time (1971: chap. 20); the frequent rotations of independent audit firms personnel among clients; and the high mobility in the diplomatic corps.

36. Greg Dow and Raaj Sah suggested to me that the desire to limit intertemporal side transfers may be a (very partial) explanation for Weber's observation that incumbents have no right to their office (in particular, cannot choose their successor). (For a model of reputation with overlapping parties, see Kreps's view of the firm as a reputation carrier.)

As a last example, let me point out that the advantage of a journal's anonymous reviewing process is that the referee-author relationship amounts to a one-shot relationship.

4.4. RULES VS. DISCRETION: THE EMERGENCE OF BUREAUCRACIES

The design of coalition-proof schemes has two facets. Should the principal rely on the supervisor's report to reward or punish the agent? Should the supervisor have discretion on the agent's reward or punishment? I take these two facets to be equivalent for the purpose of my single supervisor framework.

The main feature of a *rule* is that *it leaves no discretionary power to its enforcer*. In other words, a rule prevents the use of the enforcer's decentralized information. Rules are thus impersonal (suppress face-to-face relationships) and involve a loss of information. *Bureaucracies* are organizations mainly run by rules. The role of rules has been emphasized by, among others, Weber, Crozier, and Arrow.

The classical principal/agent paradigm in economics is already concerned, if not with rules, at least with limits on the discretionary power left to the informed party. In this model, the agent is simultaneously decision maker (because of his superior information)— and involved party. Therefore, he cannot be fully trusted and must be given an "incentive compatible" reward scheme (in some extreme cases, the principal may demand something like a profit or production target—in technical terms, may induce pooling or bunching—which is the theoretical analog of a rule). The idea that one may want to limit the discretion of a party who is simultaneously "judge and party" is well understood. By contrast, the observation that a party having relevant information to assess or affect *other* parties cannot fully be trusted to use this information to serve the goals of the organization may be more central to the reflections on rules and bureaucracies.

As we saw, collusion creates hazards to soft information, and even to a part of hard information (see, for example, proposition 4). The nonreliability of information transmitted by a supervisor naturally leads to the abandonment of this information or, equivalently, to the absence of supervisory discretion. For example, a foreman may not be entitled to allow a worker to be absent even if only he has the information relevant to this decision. More generally, foremen have almost no initiative as to personnel management and organization.[37]

---

37. Crozier (1963: 51–52, 56, 176, 238). Similarly, consider the familiar pronouncement by an employee of an administration: "I know that in your case the rule ought not to apply, but I have got to abide by it." The organization does not let the employee discriminate on the basis of his or her information for fear of letting face-to-face relationships (a type of collusive behavior) systematically bias the decision. It seems one might be able to use the law of large numbers: the employee would be entitled to some proportion of exceptions to the rule. But this arrangement requires that several conditions be met. The exceptions must be recorded, and the benefits of bookkeeping

If coalitions indeed foster bureaucratic tendencies, the previous reflections on the factors that influence the formation of coalitions ought to be relevant to explain why some organizations are more bureaucratic than others (that is, more run by rules). Let me offer some conjectures on this.

First, the theory of coalitions should predict that old organizations should be more bureaucratic than younger ones. This idea is based on the analysis of part 4.3. When organizations get started, their employees are not yet tied by a network of relationships (that is, cliques are not yet fully developed). When the organization matures, there is always at any point of time a substantial fraction of employees bound by their previous personal commitments. Thus, allowing employees to exercise discretion becomes more hazardous. (An alternative explanation for the development of rules over time is the idea that experience allows for a better description of tasks and, therefore, reduces discretion. This explanation, which does not involve coalitions, is certainly relevant. Let us, however, also note that it should not lead to the perception of rules as the lesser of two evils).

Second, the theory of coalitions may well predict that large firms should be more bureaucratic than smaller ones. The direct control of the veracity of one level of supervision's transmitted information—or, equivalently, its correct use of discretion—becomes harder and harder when the (vertical and horizontal) span of control rises.

4.5. MULTIAGENT SITUATIONS

Most of our conclusions apply to the case of "discriminatory hierarchical coalitions," in which a supervisor monitoring several agents favors some of them, not directly at the expense of the principal, but at that of other agents.[38]

Consider the principal/supervisor/multiagent situation, and suppose individual agent performance is observed only by the supervisor and is not

---

must exceed its costs (this leads to a standard argument in favor of rules). Futhermore, even if the basic technology of bookkeeping is reasonably cheap, it must be the case that it is not manipulated with the employee's supervisor's tacit agreement. More generally, an employee's discretion requires fine monitoring by the supervisor to make sure it is used appropriately. In the presence of a coalition, this in turn requires a fine control by the supervisor's supervisor, etc. This accumulation of monitoring costs (when they should have stopped at the first level of supervision in the absence of collusion) makes rules relatively appealing (checks by higher tiers are much cheaper, and can often be done randomly).

38. For instance, foremen or heads give better work conditions to their protégés. Or maintenance officers favor some operations heads. Such an example is given in Dalton (p. 34), in which some operation heads had hundreds of unfinished orders while others had none. The "dominant operation chiefs threatened to block their flow of informal favors to maintenance officers. These favors included (1) cooperation to 'cover up' errors made by maintenance machinists, or at least to share responsibility for them; (2) defense for the need of new maintenance personnel; (3) support in meetings against changes recommended by staff groups that maintenance forces opposed; (4) consideration, and justification to top management of material needed by Maintenance for its success and survival in meeting the demands of Operation."

Similarly, the Department of Defense may favor firms it has already dealt with (Scherer, 1964: 73); and, in business firms, managers may identify with a particular supplier (Pettigrew).

verifiable (by a court, say). In this case, all information is soft. Hence, if the supervisor colludes with the group of agents, he cannot be given any discretion over the agents' aggregate reward (like in part 3). However, he might be given authority to split a *fixed-size reward* among the agents as he likes. As long as he colludes only with the whole set of agents, he has no incentive to manipulate the announcements of individual performances.[39] If, however, he engages in discriminatory hierarchical coalitions, he destroys the link between individual performance and reward (that is, defeats the purpose of discretion) and, furthermore, promotes wasteful competition for the attainment of favors and privileged information among the agents.[40] Like the hierarchical coalition studied in this paper, the discriminatory hierarchical coalition fosters the abandonment of discretion (that is, the introduction of rules).

In a discriminatory hierarchical coalition, the supervisor must choose the agents with whom he wishes to collude. The previous thoughts on the availability of side transfers may shed some light on who is chosen. One factor is the length of the relationship. A transient agent may thus be at a disadvantage relative to agents with a similar but permanent position. A second factor lies in the preferences of parties. Thus, parties who are more prone to enforce collusion (or to use fear to coerce favors) will more likely be picked.

5. CONCLUSION

5.1. THEORIES OF ORGANIZATION

This section points out some of the features that identify the approach in terms of coalitions relative to complementary approaches. For ease of comparison, it focuses on features that distinguish if from other emanations of the basic principal/agent paradigm. For instance, it ignores the theory of bounded rationality,[41] which takes a very different route (in order to focus on the important phenomena of rules of thumb, limited attention, and imperfect communication, the latter approach abstracts from incentive problems and, in particular, from the malicious distortion of information).

Principal/Agent and Compounding Theories. There is not much point reviewing the now well-known principal/agent theory here. Several authors (Williamson, 1967b; Mirrlees, 1976; and Calvo and Wellisz) have extended this theory to multilayer contexts by assuming that intermediate layers have a

---

39. A similar argument is made by Bhattacharya and Malcomson to justify rank-order tournaments, an instance of a fixed-size reward.

40. Competition between agents can also be wasteful if mutual help between them is crucial for efficiency. It is then preferable to motivate them to form a productive team by suppressing discretion and offering only "low-powered" individual incentives (in the sense of Williamson, 1985).

41. See Simon; Nelson and Winter; Geanakoplos and Milgrom; Sah and Stiglitz.

choice of supervisory effort. For example, in the simple principal/ supervisor/ agent model, the principal monitors the supervisor who, in turn, supervises the agent (for instance, the probability of discovering that the agent shirks increases with the supervisor's effort). An interesting insight of this literature is to show how slack can trickle down a hierarchy: inappropriate incentives for the principal to monitor lead to a low supervisory effort in the middle tier, which leads to a low productive effort in the bottom tier (note that by making the supervisory effort exogenous, I emphasized the manipulation of information over supervisory slack). The literature also draws some conclusions about the optimal span of control and size of the vertical structure and about wage differentials.

In the compounding theory, any information held by a party about another party (the outcome of supervision broadly defined) is transmitted honestly. There are no side transfers and coalitions do not form. In terms of organizational design, the compounding theory (1) decomposes the search for the minimal cost of inducing a given organizational strategy (efforts, reports, and so on) into n subprograms; (2) puts no emphasis on the hazards associated with long-run relationships; (3) uses all information that does not reflect on parties that transmit it (that is, all supervisory information); and (4) favors, in multiagent contexts (in which individual performance is not verifiable), the use of (delegated) discretion to reward the agents. None of these properties holds in the presence of coalitions.[42]

Theory of Moral Hazard in Teams.   Moral hazard between members of a team arises when only the aggregate performance of the team is observable and verifiable. The associated free rider problem has been discussed much in the economics literature.[43]

Such a problem may arise in the simple principal/supervisor/agent structure. As I mentioned in part 2, the supervisor in general also has a productive function on top of the supervisory function: advising, selection, coordination, management, and so forth. Furthermore, the supervisor's productive performance is often observed only through the agent's. In other words, the supervisor and the agent form a productive team. This, of course, affects the supervisor's incentives when reporting on the agent's performance. For instance, a Ph.D. adviser may overstate the Ph.D. student's thesis quality, not because they are colluding, but because the adviser is eager to show that he or she obtains the good students and advises them well.

Thus, it would seem that the theories of moral hazard in teams and of coalitions lead to the same type of manipulation of information by the supervisor, in which the supervisor acts as an advocate for the agent. This is, however, false. To give an example, suppose, as in part 3, that the agent's performance

42. Property (1) does not hold because the cost of inducing a party to take some given action depends on the reward structure of other parties (through the coalition incentive constraints).
43. E.g., Alchian and Demsetz; Williamson, 1975; Holmström, 1982.

(x) depends on his effort (e) and on some productivity parameter (θ). Suppose further that the productivity parameter depends on the supervisor's productive effort. On the one hand, if the supervisor can manipulate the observation of performance, he has an incentive to overstate this performance, regardless of the existence of a coalition.[44] On the other hand, if the supervisor reports on the agent's effort or on the productivity parameter, his behavior is much influenced by the existence of a coalition with the agent. His best interest, in the absence of collusion, is to demonstrate that the agent exerts a low level of effort or faces a favorable productivity parameter. For example, for a given poor performance, the supervisor has every incentive to pass the responsibility for this poor performance on to the agent; and similarly, he tries to take credit for good performance. Thus, *everything that reflects poorly on the agent but not on the supervisor is reported by the latter*. For instance, in the absence of collusion the foreman ought to supply any evidence that the worker's task is an easy one. Or the Department of Defense ought to insist that the contracting firm could have avoided the cost overruns. This contrasts with the findings of part 3.

5.2. CONCLUDING REMARKS

By contrast with earlier work, this paper views an organization as a network of coalitions and contracts that interplay. The model developed in part 3 shows how the introduction of the relevant coalition incentive constraints modifies the optimal incentive scheme. It also shows that a natural coalition occurs between the agent and the supervisor. The words *agent* and *supervisor* must be taken in a broad sense; they do not necessarily reflect the traditional hierarchical ordering (as argued in part 6.2). At a more applied level, the ideas developed here are inspired by the direct evidence of the existence of coalitions and side transfers collected in the sociology literature. The indirect evidence was provided by the consistency of the suggestions of the model for organizational behavior with observed practice; among them: (1) the supervisor tends to act as an advocate for the agent; (2) short-run relationships may be desirable; and (3) the supervisor lacks the decision power that his central informational position should confer upon him. Hierarchies tend to be run by rules (that is, to be bureaucracies).

In our model, coalitions unambiguously decrease the efficiency of the vertical structure. Coalitions and their enforcement mechanism, side transfers, ought to be fought. This conclusion is extreme. In practice, some side transfers exist because organizations do not want to (rather than cannot) curb them. The medicine can do more harm than the illness; preventing long-run relationships between members of a hierarchy may result in efficiency losses.

---

44. The supervisor may manipulate the accounting procedure if x is a monetary performance (profit); or the quality evaluation if x a quality parameter.

208 / JOURNAL OF LAW, ECONOMICS, AND ORGANIZATION II:2, 1986

Employees then have lower incentives to develop knowledge specific to their positions or to their productive teamwork with other employees. Also, the moral hazard issue within teams of employees becomes more severe in the absence of a repeated relationship. Furthermore, an organization ought to encourage certain types of side transfers such as mutual help. Of course, such informal (covert) transfers can be used as vehicles for the formation of coalitions ("if you release this information about me, I will not help you adapt to your next task or problem"). But it is widely recognized by sociologists that without the countless acts of cooperation that take place everyday between members, most organizations would break down. They would also be poorly equipped to adapt to changes (which require an unusual amount of cooperation). In a similar vein, the benefits from authority are eliminated by the introduction of rules; as is now well recognized, many contingencies affecting an organization are hard to foresee or are costly to describe in advance. Allowing one of its members to make decisions when contingencies not contracted for (giving him or her "authority") gives flexibility to the organization (for instance, relative to rigid *ex ante* decisions). Of course, the member who is given authority acquires power because his or her decisions affect the other members, and this power can be used to generate favors. Again, the advantages and drawbacks of the authority relationship must be weighted against those of alternative arrangements (see also the discussion on discretion in multiagent situations).

The moral of this very incomplete discussion of the limits to the control of side transfers is that the very factors that give rise to coalitions may also give rise to desirable effects. This means that side transfers will be curbed (when possible) only if these other effects are small. A careful analysis of the trade-offs involved here would be quite worthwhile.

APPENDIX

A.1. PROOF OF PROPOSITION 1 (COLLUSION-FREE OUTCOME)

The Lagrangian for program (*CF*) is

$$L^{CF} = \sum_i p_i (\theta_i + e_i - W_i) + \mu \left(\sum_i p_i U(W_i - g(e_i)) - \bar{U} \right)$$
$$+ \gamma(W_3 - g(e_3) - W_2 + g(e_2 - \Delta\theta)).$$

This Lagrangian depends only on $(W_i - g(e_i))$ and $(e_i - W_i)$ for $i \neq 2$. This implies that $\{e_i - g(e_i)\}$ must be maximized for $i \neq 2$. That is:

$$i \neq 2 \rightarrow g'(e_i) = 1, \text{ or } e_i = e^*.$$

The first order conditions then boil down to

(1) $\mu\ U'\ (W_1 - g^*) = 1$

(2) $\mu\ U'\ (W_2 - g(e_2)) = 1 + \dfrac{\gamma}{p_2}$

(3) $\mu\ U'\ (W_3 - g^*) = 1 - \dfrac{\gamma}{p_3}$

(4) $\mu\ U'\ (W_4 - g^*) = 1$

(5) $(1 + \dfrac{\gamma}{p_2})g'(e_2) = 1 + \dfrac{\gamma}{p_2}g'(e_2 - \Delta\theta).$

If γ were equal to 0, the incentive constraint would be nonbinding and the first best solution would obtain. But we know that this first best solution is not incentive-compatible for the agent. Hence, γ is strictly positive, which, together with (5) and the strict convexity of g, implies that $e_2 < e^*$.

The ranking of the agent's utility levels in the various states of nature is given by equations (1) through (4).

The second order conditions are easily checked.

A.2. PROOF OF LEMMA 1 (SUPERVISOR/AGENT COALITION)

Let us know introduce the supervisor's *IR* constraint and the coalition incentive constraints. We ignore (*CIC* 1); we will later check that this constraint is satisfied. The new Lagrangian is

$$L^C = \sum_i p_i\ (\theta_i + e_i - S_i - W_i) + \upsilon\ (\sum_i p_iV(S_i) - \bar{V})$$

$$+ \mu(\sum_i p_iU(W_i - g(e_i)) - \bar{U}) + \gamma(W_3 - g(e_3) -$$

$$W_2 + g(e_2 - \Delta\theta))$$

$$+ \Pi(S_3 + W_3 - g(e_3) - S_2 - W_2 + g(e_2 - \Delta\theta))$$

$$+ \varepsilon\ (S_4 + W_4 - g(e_4) - S_3 - W_3 + g(e_3)).$$

First, notice that for $i \neq 2$, L^C depends on e_i and W_i only through $(e_i - W_i)$ and $(W_i - g(e_i))$. The optimum maximizes $(e_i - g(e_i))$, which leads to

$$i \neq 2 \rightarrow e_i = e^*.$$

210 / JOURNAL OF LAW, ECONOMICS, AND ORGANIZATION II:2, 1986

Taking the derivatives of L^C with respect to S_i, W_i, e_2 successively gives

(6) $\nu\, V'\,(S_1) = 1$

(7) $\nu\, V'\,(S_2) = 1 + \dfrac{\Pi}{p_2}$

(8) $\nu\, V'\,(S_3) = 1 + \dfrac{\varepsilon - \Pi}{p_3}$

(9) $\nu\, V'\,(S_4) = 1 + \dfrac{\varepsilon}{p_4}$

(10) $\mu\, U'\,(W_1 - g^*) = 1$

(11) $\mu\, U'\,(W_2 - g(e_2)) = 1 + \dfrac{\gamma + \Pi}{p_2}$

(12) $\mu\, U'\,(W_3 - g^*) = 1 - \dfrac{\gamma + \Pi - \varepsilon}{p_2}$

(13) $\mu\, U'\,(W_4 - g^*) = 1 - \dfrac{\varepsilon}{p_4}$

(14) $\left(1 + \dfrac{\gamma + \Pi}{p_2}\right) g'\,(e_2) = 1 + \dfrac{\gamma + \Pi}{p_2} g'\,(e_2 - \Delta\theta).$

Let us show that the agent *IC* constraint is binding, i.e., that $\gamma > 0$. Suppose that $\gamma = 0$. Equations (7), (8), (11), and (12) imply that Borch's rule hold between states 2 and 3:

(15) $\dfrac{V'\,(S_2)}{V'\,(S_3)} = \dfrac{U'\,(W_2 - g(e_2))}{U'\,(W_3 - g^*)}$.

But from (*AIC*),

(16) $W_3 - g^* \geq W_2 - g(e_2 - \Delta\theta) > W_2 - g(e_2).$

Equations (15) and (16) imply that

(17) $S_3 > S_2.$

From (16) and (17), (*CIC* 3) is not binding, which implies $\Pi = 0$. But then (11) and (12) imply

(18) $W_3 - g^* \leq W_2 - g(e_2)$,

which contradicts (16). Thus, $\gamma > 0$.

Let us now show that $(CIC\ 3)$ is binding, i.e., that $\Pi > 0$. Suppose that $\Pi = 0$. Equations (7) and (8) imply that $S_3 < S_2$, which is impossible from $(CIC\ 3)$ and the fact that (AIC) is binding. So, $\Pi > 0$, which implies that $S_2 = S_3$.

From (6) and (7), $S_1 > S_2$, and from (6) and (8) and the fact that $S_2 = S_3 < S_1$, $\varepsilon > \Pi$; (6) and (9) imply that $S_1 < S_4$.

Next, let us consider the agent's wage. Equations (10), (11), and (13) imply that $W_4 - g^* > W_1 - g^* > W_2 - g(e_2)$. Also, from $(CIC\ 2)$, $W_3 + S_3 = W_4 + S_4$, which implies that $W_3 > W_4$.

Last, observe that from (14), $g'\ (e_2) < 1$ or, $e_2 < e^*$.

Checking that $(CIC\ 1)$ is satisfied is trivial, as $S_1 > S_2$ and $W_1 - g^* > W_2 - g(e_2)$.

A.3. Proofs of Propositions 3 and 4 (Supervisor's Risk Neutrality and Extreme Risk Aversion)

Proposition 3. We know that for any specification of preferences, the principal cannot do better than in the collusion-free case, because he is facing more constraints. Conversely, let us show that he can do as well as in the collusion-free case if the supervisor is risk-neutral. Suppose he sells the vertical structure to the supervisor. In other words, the principal's profit is independent of the state of nature (which will imply that the final allocations is immune to a supervisor-agent coalition). The supervisor signs the optimal contract with the agent given the supervisor's information. Thus, the agent's allocation is the same as in the collusion-free outcome. The principal can then sell the vertical structure to the supervisor at a price such that the latter's expected profit net of the sale price is equal to his reservation wage (the supervisor bears risk, but cares only about his expected wage if he is risk-neutral).

A more formal way of proving proposition 3 is to compare (1) through (5) to (10) through (14). These equations give the same answer (for a given μ) if one takes $\Pi = \gamma = 0$ (i.e., if the coalition incentive constraints are not binding!); (6) through (9) are then satisfied by the appropriate choice of v.

Proposition 4. Let us now assume that the supervisor is infinitely risk-averse. Then the ratio of the supervisor's marginal utilities in two states of nature is infinite (or zero) unless the wages in these two states are equal. If the supervisor's wage is not a constant, then from (6) through (9) $\Pi = +\infty$ or $\varepsilon = +\infty$ (I am a bit informal here; the correct way to prove proposition 4 is to take the limit when V converges to the min function). Equations (10) through (13) then show that the agent's wage is $+\infty$ or $-\infty$ in some state of nature. We assumed that it cannot fall below w. But if the agent's wage is $+\infty$ in some state of nature, it must be $-\infty$ in another state, in order for the principal not to lose money. Again, this is impossible.

Hence, S_i is a constant (S_0). $(CIC\ 2)$ implies that $W_3 = W_4$; that is, the principal does not try to distinguish between states 3 and 4. It is then clear that

212 / JOURNAL OF LAW, ECONOMICS, AND ORGANIZATION II:2, 1986

the principal-agent contract is the optimal contract given that the principal has information structure $\{s_1 = \underline{\theta}, s_2 = s_3 = s_4 = \emptyset\}$.

A.4. PROOF OF PROPOSITION 6

The solution $\{S_i, W_i, e_i\}$ to (C) satisfies conditions (a) through (e) of lemma 1. If it is coalition-proof (which we want to show), it describes what happens on the equilibrium path for each state of nature. Of course, we are free to specify what happens off the equilibrium path, as long as we do not create scope for coalitions.

Thus, let us give a more complete description of the coalition-proof mechanism that implements the solution to (C). First, the supervisor produces his report after the profit is observed. Second, the supervisor gets wage S_1 and S_4 when he provides evidence that the state is 1 and 4, respectively (regardless of the profit level). Third, the three parties are heavily fined whenever the {report, profit} pair is not one of the four equilibrium pairs described by the solution to (C), with the exception of the supervisor when he produces evidence about states 1 and 4 (only the other two parties are then fined if the profit differs from $[\theta + e^*]$). These three points complete the description of the mechanism.

For simplicity, I assume that side contracts between two parties are not observed by the third party. By definition of (C), the mechanism is immune to a supervisor-agent coalition.

Let us show that it is immune to a principal-agent coalition. For this notice that in states 1 and 4, the supervisor has a dominant strategy: tell the truth. The supervisor's wage is lowest, and it is the same in states of nature 2 and 3. Hence, there is nothing that the principal and the agent can do to reduce the supervisor's wage.

Finally, let us show that the mechanism is immune to a principal-supervisor coalition. The object of this coalition can only be to induce the supervisor to hide the evidence in states 1 and 4. The agent's utility is higher in state 1 than in state 2. In state 1, the agent, by exerting effort e^*, forces the supervisor to reveal the evidence.[45] The agent's wage in state 4 is lower than in state 3 and his effort is the same in both states. Thus, a principal-supervisor coalition cannot gain by inducing the supervisor not to reveal the evidence in state 4. Hence, the principal-supervisor coalition cannot form either.

---

45. Unless the supervisor and the principal have signed a side contract that penalizes the supervisor when $\{x = \underline{\theta} + e^*, r = \underline{\theta}\}$ even more than the main contract does when $\{x = \underline{\theta} + e^*, r = \emptyset\}$. But the supervisor would not accept such a side contract, which would give him a very negative utility with probability p_1 (remember that side contracts are assumed not to be observable).

REFERENCES

Aghion, P., and P. Bolton. 1985. "Entry Prevention through Contracts with Customers." Mimeo, Massachusetts Institute of Technology.

Alchian, A., and H. Demsetz. 1972. "Production, Information Costs, and Economic Organization," *American Economic Review* 777.

Antle, R. 1982. "An Agency Model of Auditing," *Journal of Accounting Research* 503.

———. 1984. "Auditor Independence." *Journal of Accounting Research* 1.

Arrow, K. 1974. *The Limits of Organization.* New York: Norton.

Bhattacharya, S. 1983. "Tournaments, Termination Schemes and Forcing Contracts." Mimeo, University of California, Berkeley.

Caillaud, B., R. Guesnerie, P. Rey, and J. Tirole. 1985. "The Normative Economics of Government Intervention in Production." Stanford University, IMSSS TR #473.

Calvo, G., and S. Wellisz. 1978. "Supervision, Loss of Control, and the Optimal Size of the Firm," *Journal of Political Economy* 943.

Crozier, M. 1963. *Le Phenomene Bureaucratique.* Paris: Editions du Seuil. Translated by Crozier as *The Bureaucratic Phenomenon.* Chicago: University of Chicago Press, 1967.

Cyert, R., and J. March. 1963. *A Behavioral Theory of the Firm.* Englewood Cliffs: Prentice-Hall.

Dalton, M. 1959. *Men Who Manage.* New York: Wiley and Sons.

Downs, A. 1965. *Inside Bureaucracy.* Boston: Little, Brown, and Co.

Etzioni, A. 1964. *Modern Organizations.* Englewood Cliffs: Prentice-Hall.

Geanakoplos, J., and P. Milgrom. 1984. "A Theory of Hierarchies Based on Limited Managerial Attention." Mimeo, School of Management, Yale University.

Gjesdal, F. 1981. "Accounting for Stewardship," *Journal of Accounting Research* 208.

Gouldner, A. 1954. *Patterns of Industrial Bureaucracy.* New York: Free Press.

———. 1961. "The Norm of Reciprocity," *American Sociological Review* 161.

Green, J., and N. Stokey. 1983. "A Comparison of Tournaments and Contest," *Journal of Political Economy* 349.

Grossman, S., and O. Hart. 1983. "An Analysis of the Principal-Agent Problem," *Econometrica* 7.

Harris, M., and B. Holmstrom." 1983. "On the Duration of Agreements." Stanford University, IMSSS TR #424.

Hart, O. 1983. "The Market Mechanism as an Incentive Scheme" *Bell Journal of Economics* 366.

Holmström, B. 1979. "Moral Hazard and Observability," *Bell Journal of Economics* 74.

———. 1982. "Moral Hazard in Syndicates," *Bell Journal of Economics* 324.

Ijiri, Y. 1971. "A Defense of Historical Cost," R. B. Sterling, ed., in *Asset Valuation and Income Determination.* University of Kansas Press.

Katz, D., and R. Kahn. [1966] 1978. *The Social Psychology of Organizations,* 2d ed. New York: Wiley and Sons.

Kreps, D. 1984. "Corporate Culture and Economic Theory." Mimeo, Stanford University.

Kreps, D., P. Milgrom, J. Roberts, and R. Wilson. 1982. "Symposium on Finitely Repeated Models of Reputation," *Journal of Economic Theory* 245–52, 253–79, 280–312.

Lazear, E., and S. Rosen. 1981. "Rank Order Tournaments as Optimum Labor Contracts," *Journal of Political Economy* 841.

Malcomson, J. 1984. "Work Incentive, Hierarchy, and Internal Labor Markets," *Journal of Political Economy* 486.

214 / JOURNAL OF LAW, ECONOMICS, AND ORGANIZATION II:2, 1986

March, J., and H. Simon. 1958. *Organizations*. New York: Wiley and Sons.

Mirrlees, J. 1975. "The Theory of Moral Hazard and Unobservable Behavior, Part I." Mimeo, Nuffield College, Oxford.

————. 1976. "The Optimal Structure of Incentives and Authority within an Organizational," *Bell Journal of Economics* 105.

Mookherjee, D. 1984. "Optimal Incentive Schemes with Many Agents." *Review of Economic Studies* 433.

Nalebuff, B., and J. Stiglitz. 1983. "Prizes and Incentives: Towards a General Theory of Compensation and Competition," *Bell Journal of Economics* 21.

Nelson, R., and S. Winter. 1982. *An Evolutionary Theory of Economic Change*. Cambridge, Mass.: Harvard University Press.

Niskanen, W. 1971. *Bureaucracy and Representative Government*. Chicago: Athaton Aldine.

Olson, M. 1965. *The Logic of Collective Action: Public Goods and the Theory of Collective Action*. Cambridge, Mass.: Harvard University Press.

Peck, M., and F. Sherer. 1962. *The Weapons Acquisition Process: An Economic Analysis*. Harvard University, Graduate School of Business.

Pettigrew, A. 1972. "Information Control as a Power Resource," *Sociology* 187.

Posner, R. 1974. "Theories of Economic Regulation," *Bell Journal of Economics*.

Rose-Ackerman, S. 1978. *Corruption: A Study in Political Economy*. New York: Academic Press.

Ross, S. 1973. "The Economic Theory of Agency: The Principal's Problem," *American Economic Review* 134.

Sah, R., and J. Stiglitz. 1985. "Human Fallability and Economic Organzation," *American Economic Review* 292.

Scherer, F. 1964. *The Weapons Acquisition Process: Economic Incentives*. Harvard University, Graduate School of Business.

Schmalensee, R. 1980. *The Control of Natural Monopolies*. Lexington, Mass.: Lexington Books.

Scott, W. Richard. 1981. *Organization: Rational, Natural, and Open Systems*. Englewood Cliffs: Prentice-Hall.

Selznick, P. 1949. *TVA and the Grass Roots*. Berkeley and Los Angeles: University of California Press.

Shavell, S. 1979. "Risk-Sharing Incentives in the Principal and Agent Relationship," *Bell Journal of Economics* 55.

Simon H. 1976. *Administrative Behavior*, 3rd ed. New York: Macmillan.

Sobel, J. 1985. "A Theory of Credibility," *Review of Economic Studies* 557.

Stigler, G. 1971. "The Theory of Economic Regulation," *Bell Journal of Economics* 3.

Stiglitz, J. 1975. "Incentives, Risk, and Information: Notes towards a Theory of Hierarchy," *Bell Journal of Economics*.

Tullock, G. 1965. *The Politics of Bureaucracy*. Washington, D.C.: Public Affairs Press.

Weber, M. 1974. *The Theory of Social and Economic Organization*. New York: Oxford University Press.

Williamson, O. 1967a. "The Economics of Defense Contracting: Incentives and Performance," in R. McKean, ed., *Issues in Defense Economics*. New York: Columbia University Press.

————. 1967b. "Hierarchical Control and Optimal Firm Size," *Journal of Political Economy* 123.

————. 1975. *Markets and Hierarchies: Analysis and Antitrust Implications*. New York. Free Press.

————. 1985. *The Economics Institutions of Capitalism*. New York: Free Press.

[11]

Loyalty Filters

By GEORGE A. AKERLOF*

When people go through experiences, frequently their loyalties, or their values, change. I call these value-changing experiences "loyalty filters." This paper considers the case where these values are partially, but not totally, changeable. In addition, persons, by having a choice over their experiences, can exercise some choice over their values; or perhaps more typically, persons may choose for their children experiences that will lead them to have desired values. Insofar as this occurs, values are not fixed, as in standard economics, but are a matter of choice. Economic theory, which is largely a theory of choice, then becomes a useful tool in analyzing how these values are chosen. Most persons attempt to choose values for their children (and perhaps also for themselves) according to their economic opportunities that allow them to get along economically. According to Robert Coles' *Children of Crisis*, not only the wealthy (who will be discussed at some length in Section II), but also the poorest of the poor—immigrants, sharecroppers, and mountaineers—consciously teach their children values aimed at leading them best to survive economically.

The Wealth of Nations concerned itself with the issue of how the economy would behave if everyone were to behave selfishly. Adam Smith's famous answer to this question in terms of the invisible hand is the key result in economic theory. Since the time of Edgeworth (see Amartya Sen, 1977, p. 317), it has been fashionable for non-Marxist economic theorists to follow Smith's presumed worst-case assumption—that all persons are totally selfish. Yet as Sen points out, this assump-

tion is made for reasons of convenience, not because economists empirically assume that all persons act only out of selfishness.

This paper will explore the extent to which parents interested only in their children's economic welfare will teach them to be totally selfish. Section I gives an example in which children are taught to be honest, even to their own detriment. Such a teaching may cause children to act against their own short-run interest even while it serves their long-run economic interests. Similarly, Section II yields a model where children are taught to be loyal to their class interests; this teaching may not serve their individual short-run interest, but it does serve their individual long-run interest. Each of these models is motivated by an empirical observation. In the case of Section I, this observation concerns the economic well-being of the high-minded Quakers: if selfishness pays off, why should the Quakers do so well? Section II is motivated by Coles' studies of the way in which privileged children learn to view those less fortunate as "others," in contrast to "us."

The models of Sections I and II are meant to show economic man as not being undeviatingly selfish. In Section I, he is undeviatingly honest, even against his interest, and in Section II he is undeviatingly loyal to his class interest. Yet at the same time his long-run interests have been maximized by teaching him a code of conduct that leads him, insofar as possible, to act in his best long-run interest. Section III continues the process of making economic man less undeviatingly selfish. This section concerns economic and political elites who are the products of consciously styled elite academies. Examples of such elites come from military service academies, prestige universities, and other institutions that not only give technical training, but also teach loyalty to these institutions and the type of persons who are their faculty or alumni. Where these institutions are aligned with the government (or else

*University of California-Berkeley. I thank Donald Hayes, Hajime Miyazaki, and Janet Yellen for invaluable help and comments, and the Institute of Business and Economic Research, University of California-Berkeley, for logistical support. I also thank the National Science Foundation for financial support under research grant no. SES-8119150.

where their graduates have other monopoly powers), it is shown that the curriculum that best serves its alumni not only teaches technical skills, but also loyalty to the type of person who is a fellow graduate. In the model of this section, the elite graduate is unselfish in serving his country; nevertheless, due to the biases in his values, the interests of the elite end up being served, as well perhaps as the interest of the country. The picture emerges of well-trained, well-meaning civil servants who act selflessly according to their best conscience, yet nevertheless manage to earn more than the competitive wage due to the cultural biases that have been chosen.

Finally, before getting into the specific models, I would like to make a few remarks. Albert Hirschman's *Exit, Voice and Loyalty* (1970) is the only recent non-Marxist economics to emphasize the role of loyalty in economic theory.[1] Yet, for the most part, his book is unconcerned with how loyalties begin, which is the focus of this paper. I resisted the temptation to call this paper "Entrance, Voice, and Loyalty," which would have emphasized the contrast with Hirschman's work, because the title "Loyalty Filters" better conveys the generality of my subject matter. In this regard, I would like to remark on the particular and illustrative nature of the examples that follow. They fail in their particularity to reflect the many important possible types of loyalty filter. The agent who experiences the filter may consciously or unconsciously choose the experience. He may be conscious or unconscious of the effect of the experience on his loyalties. And the experience may not only be chosen by himself (or an agent such as his parents acting on his behalf), but instead by another

agent acting in his own selfish interest, such as an advertiser interested in fostering brand loyalty to the product he sells, or an employer interested in extracting unselfish performances from his employees.[2] Furthermore, according to George Homans (1950), loyalties change according to almost every role a person plays and almost every situation that involves him. The preceding rudimentary classification of loyalty filters according to choice/consciousness/agent choosing/role of agent should alert us to the great variety of loyalty filters. The examples given below are meant as an illustrative teaching device and as an invitation to the reader to roll his own examples of loyalty filters.

I. A Model of Honesty and Cooperative Behavior

A. *Motivation*

As mentioned above, the model in this section is motivated by the assumption of selfishness in economic models. It is also motivated by an experiment in social psychology (Fred Arnstein and Kenneth Feigenbaum, 1967). In this experiment, persons of different religious persuasions were asked to play a game of the prisoner's dilemma variety; in this game, noncooperative behavior improved considerably the lot of the noncooperative player provided the other player's behavior remained cooperative. Conversely, cooperative players fared quite poorly if the other players were noncooperative. It turned out that the Quakers, as might be expected, ranked quite high in terms of the trustfulness and cooperation of their responses, but low in terms of their economic rationality. This result is curious because in real life, Quakers are usually considered one of the wealthiest minority groups in the United States (Gordon Allport, 1958, p. 72). The model below is intended, accordingly, to show that honesty and cooperative behavior pay off; the honest person is not just a systematic "sucker."

---

[1] In Marxist terminology, this paper concerns how a class "in itself" becomes a class "for itself" (Anthony Giddens, 1975, p. 30). The prediction following Marx that most poverty stricken in society will be reactionary in attitude (Giddens, p. 37) accords exactly with that of the model of class loyalty in Section II. Only extra-economic attitudes will cause the poor to unite in their own class interests according to that model. That prediction is also consistent with the observation that most socialist revolutions have occurred in the wake of wars fought for reasons only incidental to the socialist takeover which later occurs.

[2] A very different type of loyalty filter from those in this paper is analyzed by myself and William Dickens (1982). I would like to record my debt to him for what I learned while jointly writing that paper.

The model is quite trivial; it corresponds exactly to a known observation: couriers who carry large sums of money are often "bonded." Apparently, it pays to bond such persons, which in effect is to guarantee their honesty. According to the model here, it pays persons to bond themselves by acquiring traits that cause them to appear honest. And the cheapest way to acquire such traits according to our model is, in fact, to be honest! This distinction between *appearance* and *actuality* of honesty has been discussed by Max Weber (1958).[3] Weber's essays on the Protestant ethic are the classic description of how different experiences result in different personality types, with important economic consequences.

B. *The Model*

The Nature of Jobs (from which labor demand is derived): Let there be only one type of job in the economy and let this job have a product y. Workers in this job, however, have an opportunity to embezzle an amount x with probability q unless there is surveillance. It would be straightforward to let there be surveillance costs, but complication is avoided by assuming these costs to be prohibitive.

The Nature of Workers (from which labor supply is derived): The utility of a worker depends on his income according to the util-

ity function $u(\cdot)$. Parents wish to maximize their children's welfare. They can train their children to be dishonest, which in this model means to embezzle whenever they can get away with it; or they can train their children to be honest.

Equilibrium Wages of Dishonest Workers: Employers are not fooled about the characters of their employees. A dishonest worker will be seen as such and his wage will be reduced by his expected embezzlement. Assuming risk-neutral competitive employers, a dishonest worker will receive a wage of $y - qx$, which is his product net of his expected embezzlement. Remember, however, that the worker has a chance to embezzle x with probability q. Thus with chance $(1-q)$, the dishonest worker has utility $u(y-qx)$, and with chance q, he has utility $u(y-qx+x)$. The net result is an expected utility given by

$$(1) \qquad E(u) = (1-q)u(y-qx)$$
$$+ qu(y+(1-q)x).$$

Equilibrium Wage of Honest Workers: Alternatively, according to the model, parents may train their children to be honest. Such training may require a cost to the parents, which we assume to be paid by the children. We call this cost c_h. Employers will pay honest persons their product y, so that their income net of training costs is $y - c_h$, and their utility is $u(y - c_h)$. Parents interested in maximizing their children's welfare will choose to make their children honest provided

$$(2) \quad u(y-c_h) > (1-q)u(y-qx)$$
$$+ qu(y+(1-q)x).$$

This last inequality always holds for given q, y, and x, provided c_h is sufficiently small and u has diminishing returns.

Very Dishonest Behavior: There is a final question. Children could presumably also be taught to act honest yet embezzle when they get a chance. I will assume that such training is quite costly. Suppose the cost of such training is c_{vd} (vd for very dishonest) and $c_{vd} - c_h > qx$. In this case, the costs of such

---

[3] The coincidence between Weber's view and that of this paper regarding honesty can be seen in the following discussion of Benjamin Franklin by Weber:

Now all Franklin's moral attitudes are coloured with utilitarianism. Honesty is useful, because it assures credit; so are punctuality, industry, frugality, and that is the reason they are virtues. A logical deduction from this would be that where, for instance, the appearance of honesty serves the same purpose that would suffice, and an unnecessary surplus of this virtue would evidently appear to Franklin's eyes as unproductive waste.... But in fact the matter is not by any means so simple. Benjamin Franklin's own character, as it appears in the unusual candidness of his autobiography belies that suspicion. The circumstance that he ascribes his recognition of the utility of virtue to a divine revelation which was intended to lead him in the path of righteousness shows that something more than mere garnishing for purely egocentric motives is involved. [pp. 52–53]

In the view of this paper, Franklin, no matter how utilitarian his beliefs, could not acquire the appearance of honesty without its actuality.

training exceed the gains from dishonesty qx, so that it never pays parents to train their children in this way. It may appear at first glance that it should not be difficult to teach people to dissemble their values. But persons often have a hard time hiding their true nature. The rareness of acting talent can be perceived any day of the week by a comparison of daytime and nighttime TV.

Furthermore, there is evidence that traits once acquired (in this case, honesty) are often difficult to lose even when they have become dysfunctional. Robert Merton describes how bureaucrats' "adherence to the rules, originally conceived as a means, becomes transformed into an end-in-itself" (1956, p. 253). In my model of childrearing, honesty may begin as a means for economic betterment, but then there is a displacement of goals so that the person so trained will refrain from embezzlement where there is no penalty. Psychological experiments with animals show similarly that animals may quite easily be trained to have dysfunctional behavior. See, for example, Henry Gleitman's example (1981, p. 148) of trained helplessness in dogs.

Remarks: The role of jointness of production in training in this model should be noted. It is assumed that at the cost c_h, parents can train their children to *appear* honest. But to make children appear honest, it is easiest to make them also *be* honest. There is a return to *appearing* honest, but not to *being* honest. It pays parents to teach their children to be honest because the individually functional trait of appearing honest is jointly produced with the individually dysfunctional trait of being honest.

It should also be noted that the word *embezzlement* need not be taken too literally. Any form of noncooperative behavior by workers, which the firm will find expensive and difficult to police, can play the exact same role as embezzlement. In many jobs, workers are given considerable scope for lack of cooperation before there will be retaliation by their supervisor. (See my 1982 article for an earlier discussion.) Such lack of cooperation has consequences similar to embezzlement in the model which has been presented. In the next section, a very similar model is proposed; embezzlement, however,

is replaced by the more general concept of noncooperation.

II. Class Loyalty

This section concerns a theory of class loyalty and formation. Although individualistic economic theory is based upon the assumption that individuals act selfishly out of their own interests, it is certainly empirically and theoretically possible that persons are loyal to other ideals. Coles' *Privileged Ones* describes how wealthy children think about poorer persons. The model in this section is motivated by his study.

A. *Studies of Social Identification (Coles, Allport)*

Coles' books, which are the result of fifteen years' intensive work by a trained child psychologist, may be the most complete and detailed study ever made of the formation of class loyalties. Nevertheless, the whole process whereby the socialization occurs is still a bit mysterious, even from Coles' detailed accounts. Why this mystery is of necessity the case is explained by Allport in his discussion of the learning of social values via identification of children with their parents:

> Learning through identification seems basically to involve a type of muscle strain or postural imitation. Supposing the child, hypersensitive to parental cues, senses a tightness or rigidity when his parents are talking about the Italian family that has moved in next door. In the very act of perceiving these parental cues, the child grows tight and rigid.... After this associated experience, he may tend, ever so slightly, to feel a tenseness (an incipient anxiety) whenever he hears (or thinks) of Italians. The process is infinitely subtle.   [1958, pp. 278–79]

Despite this subtlety, because of the intensity of his study, Coles is able to report, here and there, the emergence of social values among the wealthy as the younger children in his sample ask their mommy or daddy embarrassing questions such as why their family should not share their wealth with others. There are many answers to these questions, such as "Daddy works hard for what he earns"; "Mommy and Daddy give a great deal to charity"; "there are so many poor persons our contribution could only be very small." In some cases, the questions persist, particularly where the children identify with the maid and possibly also with her children. However, in these cases of persistence, these questions are usually abandoned when mommy (typically) makes it clear that it is not nice to annoy the loving daddy with such annoying and persistent questions. The children then re-immerse themselves in leading the "busy, busy lives" (Coles' phrase) which their parents have planned for them.

Although much of the process of socialization is difficult to see, it is clear that it is quite intentional on the part of these wealthy parents that their children are taught to view themselves as "different" from those who are less fortunate. This does not mean, typically, that "others" are to be despised; but almost all the wealthy children in Coles' book have a sense of identification with "us," children and families who are equally well to do, in contrast to "others" who are less fortunate.

The role of the difference in the lives of rich children and poor children in causing this sense of distinction and identification is made clear in the description of a young New Orleans girl at the time of the racial trouble in the early 1960's. I wish to stress, as does Coles, that the social meanings ascribed by this girl, although seen through the eyes of a child, are, nevertheless, exactly those intended by her parents. According to Coles, "'Our maid's children don't know about finger bowls,' a seven-year-old New Orleans girl says. She also says—the year is 1960— that 'the kids going into those [desegregated] schools don't know about finger bowls either; and they don't know how to smile and say thank-you to the people in the mobs'" (1977, p. 530).

The girl's plan of action for the black children going into the desegregated schools is to be unfailingly polite (i.e., to learn about finger bowls). This plan of action and the statement I have quoted are explained by Coles as correctly perceiving the role of manners in differentiating the wealthy from the poor. Displaying such politeness, in the view of the child, the black children will achieve her own status (and that of her family) and the mobs will cease to be hostile.

To summarize, wealthy parents tend to teach their children an identification with other persons of wealth and to view the less fortunate as others. Furthermore, this teaching is quite intentional, either learned through certain coded messages such as "manners" inherent in the way of life of the wealthy, in subtle demonstrations of annoyance or tension by parents, or, finally, occasionally, but except in rare cases only to younger children, by requests not to annoy mommy or daddy with needless questions. This section will construct a model wherein parents interested in maximizing their children's economic welfare will teach them such values. According to the technology, parents may teach their children to have such class values, but such values, as in the earlier model of honesty, cannot be dissembled. Thus persons cannot pretend to identify with other members of their class without actually being loyal.

B. A Model

The model will be quite similar to the one in the last section, only with some added generality. Let there be two types of persons, the wealthy, represented by W, and the poor, represented by P. Suppose that a W may be hired either by a P or a W, and that a W will have a marginal product, if cooperative, in a job provided by a W of y_{WW} and will have a chance of engaging in noncooperative behavior that will reduce this marginal product by x_{WW} with probability q_{WW}. The double subscript WW indicates that a W (the first subscript) is providing a job to a W (the second subscript). The probability that a W so hired will engage in noncooperative behavior will depend on his class loyalties. If loyal to the W, his probability of noncooperative behavior will be low; if loyal to the P, his probability of noncooperative behavior in such a job will be high. Again, as in the previous model, and again only for modeling convenience, assume that surveillance is not possible.

In the usual neoclassical model, contracts may be made between any two persons. Assume, therefore, similarly and symmetrically with the WW case, that a P may also hire a W. The marginal product of a W working for a P is y_{PW} with a chance of noncooperative behavior q_{PW} with cost to the employer of x_{PW}.

Consistent with the notation of the earlier model, the cost of instilling class loyalties is denoted by the letter c, with c_{WW} the cost of instilling loyalty of a W to the W and c_{PW} the cost of instilling loyalties of a W to the P.

The individual person maximizes his utility. This utility depends on his income and also on his behavior on the job, which may be cooperative or noncooperative. The individual benefits from noncooperative behavior, but it is not automatic that such behavior that costs the employer x_{WW} or x_{PW} will result in a benefit to the employee of equal amount. I will assume that the individual values the returns from noncooperative behavior at a fraction α, $0 \leq \alpha \leq 1$, of its cost. As before, let the individual have a utility function $u(\cdot)$, which in this case depends on the wage plus the value to him of being noncooperative, if he chooses that mode of behavior.

The individual has three choices: whether to work for a W or a P; whether to be loyal to the W or not; whether to be loyal to the P or not. In general, a person with a chance of noncooperation q at cost x in a job with cooperative product y, and with loyalties that are acquired at cost c, will receive a wage $y - qx$ and therefore have an expected utility

$$(3) \quad E(u) = (1-q)u(y - qx - c)$$
$$+ qu(y - qx + \alpha x - c).$$

Adoption of the following notation allows a single expression for the maximization problem of a W. Let e_{WW} be a dummy variable equal to unity if W is employed by a W, and equal to zero otherwise; let l_{WW} be a dummy variable equal to unity if W is loyal to the W, and equal to zero otherwise; and let l_{PW}

be a dummy variable, similarly, equal to unity if W is loyal to the P and equal to zero otherwise.

Accordingly, a W chooses for himself (or for his child) the variables e_{WW}, l_{WW}, l_{PW} to maximize $E(u)$, which is given by the expression:

$$(4) \quad E(u) = e_{WW}E_{WW}(u)$$
$$+ (1 - e_{WW})E_{PW}(u),$$

where $E_{WW}(u)$ and $E_{PW}(u)$ are the expected utilities of a W working for a W and a P, respectively. (An explicit expression for $E(u)$ can be derived as a function of e_{WW}, l_{WW}, and l_{PW} by use of (3). Let E_{WW} and E_{PW} be written as functions of l_{WW} and l_{PW} by insertion into (3) of the appropriate subscripts on $E(u), q, y, x$, and c, with q_{WW} and q_{PW} each an explicit function of its two arguments, l_{WW} and l_{PW}. Substitution of the expressions for E_{WW} and E_{PW} into (4) yields $E(u)$ as a function of the three optimizing variables, e_{WW}, l_{WW}, and l_{PW}.)

Assume that there are K_W units of capital owned by the W and K_P units of capital owned by the poor, and that both types of capital use both W and P labor with constant returns to scale. Then in equilibrium $E_{WW}(u) = E_{PW}(u)$, or, in words, the expected utility of a W working for a W and for a P are equal. The number of W working for W-capital and the number of W working for P-capital will be proportional to K_W and K_P respectively; thus the fraction of W working for W is $K_W/(K_P + K_W)$.[4]

---

[4] This intuitive result depends upon various assumptions in addition to constant returns to scale. The production functions with W and P owners of capital must be the same. In addition the following symmetry conditions are required: $q_{WW}(x, y) = q_{PW}(y, x)$, $q_{WP}(x, y) = q_{PP}(y, x)$, $x_{WW} = x_{PW}, x_{PP} = x_{WP}, c_{WW} = c_{PW}$, and $c_{PP} = c_{WP}$. These conditions guarantee that if the capital/W-labor and capital/P-labor ratios are the same with K_W and K_P, respectively, the expected marginal products and utilities of both W-labor (and also P-labor) will be equal on W-capital and on P-capital. The equilibrium condition that $E_{WW}(u) = E_{PW}(u)$ requires, of course, that some W are working for P, as well as W, capital. Despite the necessity of the stringent assumptions to show that the number of W working for W-capital is exactly proportional to K_W, the result that most workers will be working for W-capital if most capital is owned by W, will be quite robust.

In equilibrium, a W is indifferent to working for a W or a P, but if working for a W, the maximizer will choose loyalties to the W and not to the P; if working for the P, the opposite choices will be made, provided c_{WW} and c_{PW} are sufficiently small.

A W working for a W will receive expected utility which can be expressed (with appropriate use of subscripts in (3)) as

$$(5) \quad (1 - q_{WW}(l_{WW}, l_{PW}))$$
$$u(y_{WW} - q_{WW}(l_{WW}, l_{PW})x_{WW}$$
$$- l_{WW}c_{WW} - l_{PW}c_{PW}) + q_{WW}(l_{WW}, l_{PW})$$
$$u(y_{WW} - (q_{WW}(l_{WW}, l_{PW}) - \alpha)x_{WW}$$
$$- l_{WW}c_{WW} - l_{PW}c_{PW}).$$

Equation (5) is maximized (provided c_{WW} is sufficiently small, and given the assumptions that q_{WW} decreases with l_{WW} and increases with l_{PW}), by choosing loyalty to the W and no loyalty to the poor. In mathematical terms, this means choosing l_{WW} equal to unity, l_{PW} equal to zero.

Since most nonresidential capital is either owned or controlled by the wealthy, it may be assumed that K_W is large relative to K_P and hence it pays most W to train their children to be loyal to the W and not to the P.

C. Loyalties of the Poor

The previous model agrees with empirical findings regarding the loyalties of the wealthy as described by Coles. How does it fare with respect to its predictions regarding the loyalties of the poor?

Insofar as the assumptions of the stringent model hold, it predicts that the poor will also be loyal to the wealthy in proportion $K_W/(K_P + K_W)$. This is consistent with Coles' findings regarding the teaching of poor mothers to their children, although this loyalty may be instilled more out of passive acceptance of the system than out of genuine enthusiasm—as suggested by the words of one very poor migrant mother: "Do you

have a choice but to accept?... Once, when I was little I seem to recall asking my uncle if there wasn't something you could do, but he said no, there wasn't and hush up. Now, I have to tell my kids the same, that you don't go around complaining—you just don't" (Coles, 1967, p. 52).

Of course there are cases that run counter to the predictions of the model, where the poor have not been loyal to those who provide them with jobs. The model, in fact, gives predictions where such conditions are likely to occur because its assumptions are violated. Where willing cooperation is not necessary from workers, it is not necessary to secure their active loyalty. Such devices as the assembly line force workers to work at the pace of the line irrespective of their mental attitude. Also, such incentive schemes as piecework, where the worker who puts in less effort receives correspondingly less pay, reduce the cost to the employer of unwilling workers, and therefore causes there to be less reason why firms should demand positive loyalty. In contrast, servants' cooperative willingness is often of positive value; and, correspondingly, the term "loyal servant" is a standard figure of speech.

Furthermore, social institutions may change the loyalty incentive structure. As one example, unions that interpose themselves between workers and the firm regarding work conditions reduce the positive incentives for workers to be cooperative. Welfare is another agency that reduces the incentives for parents to teach their children traditions of cooperation with employers, either rich or poor.

While this model is all too simple to predict class loyalties in many complicated situations, particularly where feelings of justice and fairness play an important role, nevertheless, in capturing some of the economic incentives for being cooperative (vs. noncooperative), this model does allow some comparative static analysis of class loyalties. At the minimum it serves as a reminder that an important side effect of social policy (toward unions and welfare, for example) is the resultant change in loyalties due to the change in incentive structure.

VOL. 73 NO. 1   *AKERLOF: LOYALTY FILTERS*   *61*

III. Institutional Loyalties

The preceding sections have shown that parents eager to maximize their children's economic welfare may find it advantageous to teach honesty (Section I) and class loyalties (Section II) even though these traits may in some circumstances cause the individual to engage in nonmaximizing behavior. It pays parents to teach honesty and class loyalty because the *appearance* of honesty and class loyalty are beneficial; the easiest way to achieve these appearances is to *be* honest and loyal, even though honesty and loyalty themselves involve sacrifices.

This section presents a similar model of elite institutions. According to this model patriotism is jointly taught (i.e., jointly produced) with cultural values that are favorable to fellow graduates of the institution. This jointness of loyalties is reflected in the statement of President Eisenhower's defense secretary: "For years I have thought what was good for our country was good for General Motors and vice versa" (*New York Times*, 1954); likewise it is reflected in the college song which ends "for God, for country, and for Yale."

According to my model, loyalty to the institution has the effect that the services of graduates of the institution are highly valued—indeed, overvalued—by other graduates. Thus, while graduates of the institution may be patriotic even to the point of considerable self-sacrifice, the teaching of this patriotism may be of economic benefit to the graduates because it occurs jointly with the teaching of cultural biases in favor of the institution's graduates.

A. *Examples*

It may be helpful to give some concrete examples of institutions that, at least arguably, correspond to the model. In the United States, the military service academies teach loyalty to the academies themselves and also to the country. In Britain, Oxford and Cambridge—and, for some graduates, the public schools prior to university—teach loyalty to British values in general, and good govern-

ment in particular. In addition, there appears to be considerable loyalty to fellow graduates. As one indication of this loyalty, most MPs of both the Labour and Conservative parties are graduates of these two universities; more remarkable still, eighteen out of twenty-two of Mrs. Thatcher's current cabinet members are graduates of public schools, only two are nongraduates of Oxbridge or the Army-Navy service academies.

B. *The Model*

In this model, it is assumed that the public has a choice (as in fact may not actually occur) between government by elite-school graduates and nongraduates. It is assumed that the nongraduates are loyal to themselves (because they have not been taught the elite patriotism), while the elitists are patriotic but with elite biases. The public, interested in good government, chooses the elite-school graduates as ministers. These graduates are patriotic and self-sacrificing, but in such a way that the interests of graduates are served on the average.

Assume that there are two types of persons—graduates and nongraduates. The government needs ministers in number equal to a fraction α of all graduates. These ministers, like other graduates, have a marginal product w outside the government. Graduates, being patriotic, are willing to serve as ministers for remuneration which is a fraction β of w. Ministers award government contracts. Ministers who are graduates value the services of other graduates at $(1+\gamma)w$, whereas these services elsewhere only have value w. The fraction $(1-\alpha)$ of graduates who do not work as ministers are hired by the government as long as their wage paid there exceeds their marginal products elsewhere. β and γ are both functions of the curriculum, denoted c, of the elite institution.

Nongraduates have no cultural biases, but, by assumption, they do not have the patriotism of the elite. Consequently, they wish to award government contracts for their own benefit; by assumption, it is impossible to check on such misappropriation, and therefore the return to the public from nongraduates is zero. The expected return from government contracts awarded by graduates to a graduate is w at a cost $(1 + \gamma)w$. Since the benefit-cost ratio of a government of graduates, even if not optimal, is higher than of nongraduates, the public chooses the former type of government.

Now consider the expected return to graduates which, if the economic-maximizing curriculum c is chosen, will be

$$(6) \quad \max_c \{\alpha\beta(c)w + (1-\alpha)(1+\gamma(c))w\}.$$

In the case of an internal equilibrium where curriculum is a continuous variable, the curriculum which is the economic optimum for graduates will meet the condition that the marginal decrease in wages due to self-sacrifice just balances the marginal return to other graduates, due to the overvaluing of their services. Note that the economic optimum for graduates in this model is not the economic optimum for the public. For the public, the best curriculum is one that *maximizes* the benefits net of costs of contracts, including the costs of hiring fellow graduates.

C. Summary

The following phenomenon has been modeled. Graduates of elitist institutions are often excellent at their jobs and genuinely interested in the "common welfare" as they see it. While they give less than the best possible service because of that elitism per se, however, that is better yet than what would be given by persons who remain untrained in values of patriotism and loyalty to the organization. The graduates on the average, although they sometimes do genuinely sacrificial service, still have a positive economic return, because what is lost due to their sacrifice is more than offset by the overvalue by the government in the award of government contracts. The net result yields less than the optimum to the nongraduate public; control of the elite curriculum, or other government regulations such as "affirmative action" hiring of nongraduates, will improve government benefit-cost performance.

IV. Conclusion

This paper has presented examples of the concept of loyalty filters and their potential importance for economic theory. According to the key idea underlying this paper, as persons go through different experiences, their loyalties change. Loyalty filters have implications for how individuals and institutions will attempt to reach specified goals, as illustrated above, where, in each of the three examples, the goal was the maximization of economic welfare. Loyalty filters, as well, have implications concerning the goals that individuals attempt to attain. The modeling of each of these aspects of reality constitutes a departure of importance from standard economic models, capable of explaining such phenomena as cooperative behavior, class loyalties, and much institutional behavior.

REFERENCES

Akerlof, George A., "Labor Contracts as Partial Gift Exchange," *Quarterly Journal of Economics*, November 1982, 2.

_____ and Dickens, William T., "The Economic Consequences of Cognitive Dissonance," *American Economic Review*, June 1982, 72, 307–19.

Allport, Gordon W., *The Nature of Prejudice*, Anchor Books ed., Garden City: Doubleday and Company, Inc., 1958.

Arnstein, Fred and Feigenbaum, Kenneth D., "Relationship of Three Motives to Choice in Prisoner's Dilemma," *Psychological Reports*, June 1967, 20, 751–55.

Coles, Robert, *Migrants, Sharecroppers, Mountaineers*, Vol. II–*Children of Crisis*, Boston: Little, Brown and Company, 1967.

_____, *Privileged Ones: The Well-Off and the Rich in America*, Vol. V–*Children of Crisis*, Boston: Little, Brown and Company, 1977.

Giddens, Anthony, *The Class Structure of the Advanced Societies*, New York: Harper and Row, 1975.

Gleitman, Henry, *Psychology*, New York: W. W. Norton, 1981.

Hirschman, Albert O., *Exit, Voice, and Loyalty*, Cambridge: Harvard University Press, 1970.

Homans, George C., *The Human Group*, New York: Harcourt, Brace & World, 1950.

Merton, Robert K., *Social Theory and Social Structure*, New York: The Free Press, 1956.

Sen, Amartya K., "Rational Fools: A Critique of the Behavioral Foundations of Economic Theory," *Philosophy and Public Affairs*, Summer 1977, *6*, 317–44.

Weber, Max, *The Protestant Ethic and The Spirit of Capitalism*, New York: Scribner's, 1958.

New York Times, Section VI, 4:4, February 28, 1954.

[12]

TRANSACTION-COST ECONOMICS: THE GOVERNANCE OF CONTRACTUAL RELATIONS*

OLIVER E. WILLIAMSON
University of Pennsylvania

T HE new institutional economics is preoccupied with the origins, incidence, and ramifications of transaction costs. Indeed, if transaction costs are negligible, the organization of economic activity is irrelevant, since any advantages one mode of organization appears to hold over another will simply be eliminated by costless contracting. But despite the growing realization that transaction costs are central to the study of economics,[1] skeptics remain. Stanley Fischer's complaint is typical: "Transaction costs have a well-deserved bad name as a theoretical device . . . [partly] because there is a suspicion that almost anything can be rationalized by invoking suitably specified transaction costs."[2] Put differently, there are too many degrees of freedom; the concept wants for definition.

* This paper has benefited from support from the Center for Advanced Study in the Behavioral Sciences, the Guggenheim Foundation, and the National Science Foundation. Helpful comments by Yoram Ben-Porath, Richard Nelson, Douglass North, Thomas Palay, Joseph Sax, David Teece, and Peter Temin and from the participants at seminars at the Yale Law School and the Institute for Advanced Study at Princeton are gratefully acknowledged. The paper was rewritten to advantage after reading Ben-Porath's discussion paper, the F-Connection: Family, Friends, and Firms and the Organization of Exchange, and Temin's discussion paper, Modes of Economic Behavior: Variations on Themes of J. R. Hicks and Herbert Simon.

[1] Ronald Coase has forcefully argued the importance of transaction costs at twenty-year intervals. See R. H. Coase, The Nature of the Firm, 4 Economica 386 (n.s. 1937), reprinted in Readings in Price Theory 331 (George J. Stigler & Kenneth E. Boulding eds. 1952) and R. H. Coase, The Problem of Social Cost, 3 J. Law & Econ. 1 (1960). Much of my own work has been "preoccupied" with transaction costs during the past decade. See especially Oliver E. Williamson, Markets and Hierarchies: Analysis and Antitrust Implications (1975). Other works in which transaction costs are featured include: Guido Calabresi, Transaction Costs, Resource Allocation, and Liability Rules: A Comment, 11 J. Law & Econ. 67 (1968); Victor P. Goldberg, Regulation and Administered Contracts, 7 Bell J. Econ. 426 (1976); Benjamin Klein, Robert G. Crawford, and Armen A. Alchian, Vertical Integration, Appropriable Rents, and the Competitive Contracting Process, 21 J. Law & Econ. 297 (1978); and Carl J. Dahlman, The Problem of Externality, 22 J. Law & Econ. 141 (1979). For an examination of Pigou in which transaction costs are featured, see Victor P. Goldberg, Pigou on Complex Contracts and Welfare Economics (1979) (unpublished manuscript).

[2] S. Fischer, Long-Term Contracting, Sticky Prices, and Monetary Policy: Comment, 3 J. Monetary Econ. 317, 322 n. 5 (1977).

Among the factors on which there appears to be developing a general consensus are: (1) opportunism is a central concept in the study of transaction costs;[3] (2) opportunism is especially important for economic activity that involves transaction-specific investments in human and physical capital;[4] (3) the efficient processing of information is an important and related concept;[5] and (4) the assessment of transaction costs is a comparative institutional undertaking.[6] Beyond these general propositions, a consensus on transaction costs is lacking.

Further progress in the study of transaction costs awaits the identification of the critical dimensions with respect to which transaction costs differ and an examination of the economizing properties of alternative institutional modes for organizing transactions. Only then can the matching of transactions with modes be accomplished with confidence. This paper affirms the proposition that transaction costs are central to the study of economics, identifies the critical dimensions for characterizing transactions, describes the main governance structures of transactions, and indicates how and why transactions can be matched with institutions in a discriminating way.

I am mainly concerned with intermediate-product market transactions. Whereas previously I have emphasized the incentives to remove transactions from the market and organize them internally (vertical integration),[7] the analysis here is symmetrical and deals with market, hierarchical, and intermediate modes of organization alike. The question of why there is so much vertical integration remains interesting, but no more so than the question of why there are so many market- (and quasi-market) mediated transactions. A discriminating analysis will explain which transactions are located where and give the reasons why. The overall object of the exercise essentially comes down to this: for each abstract description of a transaction, identify

---

[3] Opportunism is a variety of self-interest seeking but extends simple self-interest seeking to include self-interest seeking with guile. It is not necessary that all agents be regarded as opportunistic in identical degree. It suffices that those who are less opportunistic than others are difficult to ascertain ex ante and that, even among the less opportunistic, most have their price. For a more complete discussion of opportunism, see Oliver E. Williamson, *supra* note 1, at 7-10, 26-30. For a recent application see Benjamin Klein, Robert G. Crawford, & Armen A. Alchian, *supra* note 1.

[4] The joining of opportunism with transaction-specific investments (or what Klein, Crawford, and Alchian refer to as "appropriable quasi rents") is a leading factor in explaining decisions to vertically integrate. See Oliver E. Williamson, The Vertical Integration of Production: Market Failure Considerations, 61 Am. Econ. Rev. 112 (Papers & Proceedings, May 1971); Oliver E. Williamson, *supra* note 1, at 16-19, 91-101; and Benjamin Klein, Robert G. Crawford, & Armen A. Alchian, *supra* note 1.

[5] But for the limited ability of human agents to receive, store, retrieve, and process data, interesting economic problems vanish.

[6] See Carl J. Dahlman, *supra* note 1.

[7] See note 4 *supra*.

the most economical governance structure—where by governance structure I refer to the institutional framework within which the integrity of a transaction is decided. Markets and hierarchies are two of the main alternatives.

Some legal background to the study of transactions is briefly reviewed in Section I. Of the three dimensions for describing transactions that I propose, investment attributes are the least well understood and probably the most important. The special relevance of investments is developed in the context of the economics of idiosyncrasy in Section II. A general contracting schema is developed and applied to commercial contracting in Section III. Applications to labor, regulation, family transactions, and capital markets are sketched in Section IV. Major implications are summarized in Section V. Concluding remarks follow.

I. Some Contracting Background

Although there is widespread agreement that the discrete-transaction paradigm—"sharp in by clear agreement; sharp out by clear performance"[8]—has served both law and economics well, there is increasing awareness that many contractual relations are not of this well-defined kind.[9] A deeper understanding of the nature of contract has emerged as the legal-rule emphasis associated with the study of discrete contracting has given way to a more general concern with the contractual purposes to be served.[10]

[8] I. R. Macneil, The Many Futures of Contract, 47 S. Cal. L. Rev. 691, 738 (1974) [hereinafter cited without cross-reference as Macneil, Many Futures of Contract].

[9] With respect to commercial contracts, see Karl N. Llewellyn, What Price Contract?—An Essay in Perspective, 40 Yale L. J. 704 (1931); Harold C. Havighurst, The Nature of Private Contract (1961); Lon L. Fuller, Collective Bargaining and the Arbitrator, 1963 Wis. L. Rev. 3; id., The Morality of Law (1964); Stewart Macaulay, Non-Contractual Relations in Business, 28 Am. Soc. Rev. 55 (1963); Lawrence M. Friedman, Contract Law in America (1965); Arthur Allen Leff, Contract as a Thing, 19 Am. U. L. Rev. 131 (1970); I. R. Macneil, Many Futures of Contracts; id., Contracts: Adjustment of Long-Term Economic Relations under Classical, Neoclassical, and Relational Contract Law, 72 Nw. U. L. Rev. 854 (1978) [hereinafter cited without cross-reference as Macneil, Contracts]; and Victor P. Goldberg, Toward an Expanded Economic Theory of Contract, 10 J. Econ. Issues 45 (1976). Labor lawyers have made similar observations regarding contracts governing the employment relationship. See Archibald Cox, The Legal Nature of Collective Bargaining Agreements, 57 Mich. L. Rev. 1 (1958); Clyde W. Summers, Collective Agreements and the Law of Contracts, 78 Yale L. J. 525 (1969); and David E. Feller, A General Theory of the Collective Bargaining Agreement, 61 Cal. L. Rev. 663 (1973).

[10] The technical versus purposive distinction is made by Clyde Summers, *supra* note 9. He distinguishes between "black letter law," on the one hand (539, 543, 548, 566) and a more circumstantial approach to law, on the other (549-51, 561, 566). "The epitome of abstraction is the *Restatement*, which illustrates its black letter rules by transactions suspended in mid-air, creating the illusion that contract rules can be stated without reference to surrounding circumstances and are therefore generally applicable to all contractual transactions" (566). He observes that such a conception does not and cannot provide a "framework for integrating rules and principles applicable to all contractual transactions" (566) but that this must be sought in a more

Ian Macneil, in a series of thoughtful and wide-ranging essays on contract, usefully distinguishes between discrete and relational transactions.[11] He further supplies twelve different "concepts" with respect to which these differ.[12] Serious problems of recognition and application are posed by such a rich classificatory apparatus. More useful for my purposes is the three-way classification of contracts that Macneil offers in his most recent article, where classical, neoclassical, and relational categories of contract law are recognized.

A. Classical Contract Law

As Macneil observes, any system of contract law has the purpose of facilitating exchange. What is distinctive about classical contract law is that it attempts to do this by enhancing discreteness and intensifying "presentiation,"[13] where presentiation has reference to efforts to "make or render present in place or time; to cause to be perceived or realized at present."[14] The economic counterpart to complete presentiation is contingent-claims contracting—which entails comprehensive contracting whereby all relevant future contingencies pertaining to the supply of a good or service are described and discounted with respect to both likelihood and futurity.[15]

Classical contract law endeavors to implement discreteness and presentiation in several ways. For one thing, the identity of the parties to a transaction is treated as irrelevant. In this respect it corresponds exactly with the "ideal" market transaction in economics.[16] Second, the nature of the agreement is carefully delimited, and the more formal features govern when formal (for example, written) and informal (for example, oral) terms are contested. Third, remedies are narrowly prescribed such that, "should the initial presentiation fail to materialize because of nonperformance, the consequences are relatively predictable from the beginning and are not open-

---

affirmative view of the law in which effective governance relations are emphasized. Contract interpretation and completing contracts are among these affirmative functions.

[11] See especially Macneil, Many Futures of Contract; Macneil, Contracts; and references to related work of his cited therein.

[12] Macneil, Many Futures of Contracts 738-40; Macneil, Contracts 902-05.

[13] Macneil, Contracts 862.

[14] *Id.* at 863 n. 25.

[15] For a discussion of complex contingent-claims contracting and its mechanics, see Kenneth J. Arrow, Essays in the Theory of Risk Bearing 121-34 (1971); J. E. Meade, The Controlled Economy 147-88 (1971); and Oliver E. Williamson, *supra* note 1, at 20-40.

[16] As Lester G. Telser & Harlow N. Higinbotham put it: "In an organized market the participants trade a standardized contract such that each unit of the contract is a perfect substitute for any other unit. The identities of the parties in any mutually agreeable transaction do not affect the terms of exchange. The organized market itself or some other institution deliberately creates a homogeneous good that can be traded anonymously by the participants or their agents." Organized Futures Markets: Costs and Benefits 85 J. Pol. Econ. 969, 997 (1977).

ended."[17] Additionally, third-party participation is discouraged.[18] The emphasis, thus, is on legal rules, formal documents, and self-liquidating transactions.

B. *Neoclassical Contract Law*

Not every transaction fits comfortably into the classical-contracting scheme. In particular, long-term contracts executed under conditions of uncertainty are ones for which complete presentation is apt to be prohibitively costly if not impossible. Problems of several kinds arise. First, not all future contingencies for which adaptations are required can be anticipated at the outset. Second, the appropriate adaptations will not be evident for many contingencies until the circumstances materialize. Third, except as changes in states of the world are unambiguous, hard contracting between autonomous parties may well give rise to veridical disputes when state-contingent claims are made. In a world where (at least some) parties are inclined to be opportunistic, whose representations are to be believed?

Faced with the prospective breakdown of classical contracting in these circumstances, three alternatives are available. One would be to forgo such transactions altogether. A second would be to remove these transactions from the market and organize them internally instead. Adaptive, sequential decision making would then be implemented under common ownership and with the assistance of hierarchical incentive and control systems. Third, a different contracting relation which preserves trading but provides for additional governance structure might be devised. This last brings us to what Macneil refers to as neoclassical contracting.

As Macneil observes, "Two common characteristics of long-term contracts are the existence of gaps in their planning and the presence of a range of processes and techniques used by contract planners to create flexibility in lieu of either leaving gaps or trying to plan rigidly."[19] Third-party assistance in resolving disputes and evaluating performance often has advantages over litigation in serving these functions of flexibility and gap filling. Lon Fuller's remarks on procedural differences between arbitration and litigation are instructive:

. . . there are open to the arbitrator . . . quick methods of education not open to the courts. An arbitrator will frequently interrupt the examination of witnesses with a request that the parties educate him to the point where he can understand the testimony being received. This education can proceed informally, with frequent interruptions by the arbitrator, and by informed persons on either side, when a point

[17] Macneil, Contracts 864.

[18] *Id.*

[19] *Id.* at 865.

needs clarification. Sometimes there will be arguments across the table, occasionally even within each of the separate camps. The end result will usually be a clarification that will enable everyone to proceed more intelligently with the case. There is in this informal procedure no infringement whatever of arbitrational due process.[20]

A recognition that the world is complex, that agreements are incomplete, and that some contracts will never be reached unless both parties have confidence in the settlement machinery thus characterizes neoclassical contract law. One important purposive difference in arbitration and litigation that contributes to the procedural differences described by Fuller is that, whereas continuity (at least completion of the contract) is presumed under the arbitration machinery, this presumption is much weaker when litigation is employed.[21]

C. *Relational Contracting*

The pressures to sustain ongoing relations "have led to the spin-off of many subject areas from the classical, and later the neoclassical, contract law system, e.g., much of corporate law and collective bargaining."[22] Thus, progressively increasing the "duration and complexity" of contract has resulted in the displacement of even neoclassical adjustment processes by adjustment processes of a more thoroughly transaction-specific, ongoing-administrative kind.[23] The fiction of discreteness is fully displaced as the relation takes on the properties of "a minisociety with a vast array of norms beyond those centered on the exchange and its immediate processes."[24] By contrast with the neoclassical system, where the reference point for effecting adaptations remains the original agreement, the reference point under a truly relational approach is the "entire relation as it has developed . . . [through] time. This may or may not include an 'original agreement'; and if it does, may or may not result in great deference being given it."[25]

II. THE ECONOMICS OF IDIOSYNCRASY

Macneil's three-way discussion of contracts discloses that contracts are a good deal more varied and complex than is commonly realized.[26] It further-

[20] Lon L. Fuller, *supra* note 9, at 11-12.

[21] As Lawrence Friedman observes, relationships are effectively fractured if a dispute reaches litigation. *Supra* note 9, at 205.

[22] Macneil, Contracts 885.

[23] *Id.* at 901.

[24] *Id.*

[25] *Id.* at 890.

[26] To be sure, some legal specialists insist that all of this was known all along. There is a difference, however, between awareness of a condition and an understanding. Macneil's treatment heightens awareness and deepens the understanding.

more suggests that governance structures—the institutional matrix within which transactions are negotiated and executed—vary with the nature of the transaction. But the critical dimensions of contract are not expressly identified, and the purposes of governance are not stated. Harmonizing interests that would otherwise give way to antagonistic subgoal pursuits appears to be an important governance function, but this is not explicit in his discussion.

That simple governance structures should be used in conjunction with simple contractual relations and complex governance structures reserved for complex relations seems generally sensible. Use of a complex structure to govern a simple relation is apt to incur unneeded costs, and use of a simple structure for a complex transaction invites strain. But what is simple and complex in contractual respects? Specific attention to the defining attributes of transactions is evidently needed.

As developed in Section III, the three critical dimensions for characterizing transactions are (1) uncertainty, (2) the frequency with which transactions recur, and (3) the degree to which durable transaction-specific investments are incurred. Of these three, uncertainty is widely conceded to be a critical attribute;[27] and that frequency matters is at least plausible.[28] The governance ramifications of neither, however, have been fully developed—nor can they be until joined with the third critical dimension: transaction-specific investments. Inasmuch as a considerable amount of the "action" in the study of governance is attributable to investment differences, some explication is needed.

A. *General*

The crucial investment distinction is this: to what degree are transaction-specific (nonmarketable) expenses incurred. Items that are unspecialized among users pose few hazards, since buyers in these circumstances can easily turn to alternative sources, and suppliers can sell output intended for one order to other buyers without difficulty.[29] Nonmarketability problems arise

---

[27] For a recent study of contractual relations in which uncertainty is featured, see Peter Temin, Modes of Economic Behavior: Variations on Themes of J. R. Hicks and Herbert Simon (March 1979) (Working Paper No. 235, MIT Dep't of Econ.).

[28] Gordon Whinston emphasizes frequency in his "A Note on Perspective Time: Goldberg's Relational Exchange, Repetitiveness, and Free Riders in Time and Space" (October 1978) (unpublished paper).

[29] See Lester A. Telser & Harold N. Higinbotham, *supra* note 16; also Yoram Ben-Porath, The F-Connection: Families, Friends, and Firms and the Organization of Exchange (December 1978) (Report No. 29/78, The Hebrew University of Jerusalem) and Yoram Barzel, Measurement Cost and the Organization of Markets (April 1979) (unpublished paper). Note that Barzel's concern with standardization is mainly in connection with final-product markets, whereas I am more interested in nonstandard investments. The two are not unrelated, but identical quality can often be realized with a variety of inputs. I am concerned with specialized (transaction-specific) inputs.

when the *specific identity* of the parties has important cost-bearing consequences. Transactions of this kind will be referred to as idiosyncratic.

Occasionally the identity of the parties is important from the outset, as when a buyer induces a supplier to invest in specialized physical capital of a transaction-specific kind. Inasmuch as the value of this capital in other uses is, by definition, much smaller than the specialized use for which it has been intended, the supplier is effectively "locked into" the transaction to a significant degree. This is symmetrical, moreover, in that the buyer cannot turn to alternative sources of supply and obtain the item on favorable terms, since the cost of supply from unspecialized capital is presumably great.[30] The buyer is thus committed to the transaction as well.

Ordinarily, however, there is more to idiosyncratic exchange than specialized physical capital. Human-capital investments that are transaction-specific commonly occur as well. Specialized training and learning-by-doing economies in production operations are illustrations. Except when these investments are transferable to alternative suppliers at low cost, which is rare, the benefits of the set-up costs can be realized only so long as the relationship between the buyer and seller of the intermediate product is maintained.

Additional transaction-specific savings can accrue at the interface between supplier and buyer as contracts are successively adapted to unfolding events, and as periodic contract-renewal agreements are reached. Familiarity here permits communication economies to be realized: specialized language develops as experience accumulates and nuances are signaled and received in a sensitive way. Both institutional and personal trust relations evolve. Thus the individuals who are responsible for adapting the interfaces have a personal as well as an organizational stake in what transpires. Where personal integrity is believed to be operative, individuals located at the interfaces may refuse to be a part of opportunistic efforts to take advantage of (rely on) the letter of the contract when the spirit of the exchange is emasculated. Such refusals can serve as a check upon organizational proclivities to behave opportunistically.[31] Other things being equal, idiosyncratic exchange rela-

---

[30] This assumes that it is costly for the incumbent supplier to transfer specialized physical assets to new suppliers. On this, see Oliver E. Williamson, Franchise Bidding for Natural Monopolies—in General and with Respect to CATV, 7 Bell J. Econ. 73 (1976). Klein, Crawford, & Alchian use the term "appropriable quasi rent" to refer to this condition. Use versus user distinctions are relevant in this connection: "The quasi-rent value of the asset is the excess of its value over its salvage value, that is, its value in its next best *use* to another renter. The potentially appropriable specialized portion of the quasi rent is the portion, if any, in excess of its value to the second highest-valuing *user*." Benjamin Klein, Robert G. Crawford, & Armen A. Alchian, *supra* note 1, at 298.

[31] Thorstein Veblen's remarks on the distant relation of the head of a large enterprise to transactions are apposite. He observes that under these impersonal circumstances "The mitigating effect which personal conduct may have in dealings between man and man is . . . in great

tions which feature personal trust will survive greater stress and display greater adaptability.

Idiosyncratic goods and services are thus ones where investments of transaction-specific human and physical capital are made and, contingent upon successful execution, benefits are realized. Such investments can and do occur in conjunction with occasional trades where delivery for a specialized design is stretched out over a long period (for example, certain construction contracts). The transactions that I wish to emphasize here, however, are exchanges of the recurring kind. Although large-numbers competition is frequently feasible at the initial award stage for recurring contracts of all kinds, idiosyncratic transactions are ones for which the relationship between buyer and supplier is quickly thereafter *transformed* into one of bilateral monopoly—on account of the transaction-specific costs referred to above. This transformation has profound contracting consequences.

Thus, whereas recurrent spot contracting is feasible for standardized transactions (because large-numbers competition is continuously self-policing in these circumstances), such contracting has seriously defective investment incentives where idiosyncratic activities are involved. By assumption, cost economies in production will be realized for idiosyncratic activities only if the supplier invests in a special-purpose plant and equipment or if his labor force develops transaction-specific skills in the course of contract execution (or both). The assurance of a continuing relation is needed to encourage investments of both kinds. Although the requisite incentives might be provided if long-term contracts were negotiated, such contracts are necessarily incomplete (by reason of bounded rationality). Appropriate state-contingent adaptations thus go unspecified. Intertemporal efficiency nevertheless requires that adaptations to changing market circumstances be made.

How to effect these adaptations poses a serious contracting dilemma, though it bears repeating that, absent the hazards of opportunism, the difficulties would vanish—since then the gaps in long-term, incomplete contracts could be faultlessly filled in an adaptive, sequential way. A general clause, to which both parties would agree, to the effect that "I will behave responsibly rather than seek individual advantage when an occasion to adapt arises," would, in the absence of opportunism, suffice. Given, however, the unenforceability of general clauses and the proclivity of human agents to make false and misleading (self-disbelieved) statements, the follow-

measured eliminated. . . . Business management [then] has a chance to proceed . . . untroubled by sentimental considerations of human kindness or irritation or of honesty." The Theory of Business Enterprise 53 (1927). Veblen evidently assigns slight weight to the possibility that those to whom negotiating responsibilities are assigned will themselves invest the transactions with integrity.

ing hazard must be confronted: joined as they are in an idiosyncratic condition of bilateral monopoly, both buyer and seller are strategically situated to bargain over the disposition of any incremental gain whenever a proposal to adapt is made by the other party. Although both have a long-term interest in effecting adaptations of a joint profit-maximizing kind, each also has an interest in appropriating as much of the gain as he can on each occasion to adapt. Efficient adaptations which would otherwise be made thus result in costly haggling or even go unmentioned, lest the gains be dissipated by costly subgoal pursuit. Governance structures which attenuate opportunism and otherwise infuse confidence are evidently needed.

B. *Examples*

Some illustrations may help to motivate what is involved in idiosyncratic transactions. Specialized physical capital is relatively straightforward. Examples are (1) the purchase of a specialized component from an outside supplier or (2) the location of a specialized plant in a unique, proximate relation to a downstream processing stage to which it supplies vital input.

Thus assume (*a*) that special-purpose equipment is needed to produce the component in question (which is to say that the value of the equipment in its next-best alternative use is much lower), (*b*) that scale economies require that a significant, discrete investment be made, and (*c*) that alternative buyers for such components are few (possibly because of the organization of the industry, possibly because of special-design features). The interests of buyer and seller in a continuing exchange relation are plainly strong under these circumstances.

Plant-proximity benefits are attributable to transportation and related flow-process (inventory, thermal economy, and so on) economies. A specialized plant need not be implied, but long life and a unique location are. Once made, the investment preempts the unique location and is not thereafter moveable (except at prohibitive cost). Buyer and supplier again need to satisfy themselves that they have a workable, adaptable exchange agreement.[32]

Idiosyncratic investments in human capital are in many ways more interesting and less obvious than are those in physical capital. Polanyi's discussion of "personal knowledge" is illuminating:

The attempt to analyze scientifically the established industrial arts has everywhere led to similar results. Indeed even in the modern industries the indefinable knowledge is still an essential part of technology. I have myself watched in Hungary a new, imported machine for blowing electric lamp bulbs, the exact counterpart of which

---

[32] The *Great Lakes Carbon* case is an example of the latter, 1970-1973 Trade Reg. Rep. Transfer Binder ¶ 19,848 (FTC Dkt No. 8805).

was operating successfully in Germany, failing for a whole year to produce a single flawless bulb.[33]

And he goes on to observe with respect to craftsmanship that:

. . . an art which has fallen into disuse for the period of a generation is altogether lost. . . . It is pathetic to watch the endless efforts—equipped with microscopy and chemistry, with mathematics and electronics—to reproduce a single violin of the kind the half-literate Stradivarius turned out as a matter of routine more than 200 years ago.[34]

Polanyi's discussion of language also has a bearing on the argument advanced above that specialized code words or expressions can and do arise in the context of recurring transactions and that these yield economies. As he puts it, "Different vocabularies for the interpretation of things divide men into groups which cannot understand each other's way of seeing things and acting upon them."[35] And subsequently he remarks that:

To know a language is an art, carried on by tacit judgments and the practice of unspecifiable skills. . . . Spoken communication is the successful application by two persons of the linguistic knowledge and skill acquired by such apprenticeship, one person wishing to transmit, the other to receive, information. Relying on what each has learnt, the speaker confidently utters words and the listener confidently interprets them, while they mutually rely on each other's correct use and understanding of these words. A true communication will take place if, and only if, these combined assumptions of authority and trust are in fact justified.[36]

Babbage reports a remarkable example of transaction-specific value in exchange that occurred in the early 1800s. Although he attributes the continuing exchange in the face of adversity to values of "established character" (trust), I believe there were other specialized human and physical investments involved as well. In any event, the circumstance which he describes is the following:

The influence of established character in producing confidence operated in a very remarkable manner at the time of the exclusion of British manufactures from the Continent during the last war. One of our largest establishments had been in the habit of doing extensive business with a house in the centre of Germany; but, on the closing of the continental ports against our manufacturers, heavy penalties were inflicted on all those who contravened the Berlin and Milan decrees. The English manufacturer continued, nevertheless, to receive orders, with directions how to con-

---

[33] Michael Polanyi, Personal Knowledge: Towards a Post-Critical Philosophy 52 (2d ed. 1962).

[34] *Id.* at 53.

[35] *Id.* at 112.

[36] *Id.* at 206.

sign them, and appointments for the time and mode of payment, in letters, the handwriting of which was known to him, but which were never signed, except by the Christian name of one of the firm, and even in some instances they were without any signature at all. These orders were executed; and in no instance was there the least irregularity in the payments.[37]

While most of these illustrations refer to technical and commercial transactions, other types of transactions also have an idiosyncratic quality. Justice Rhenquist refers to some of these when speaking of the general class of cases where "the litigation of an individual's claim of deprivation of a right would bring parties *who must remain in a continuing relationship* into the adversarial atmosphere of a courtroom"[38]—which atmosphere he plainly regards as detrimental to the quality of the relationship. Examples that he offers include reluctance to have the courts mediate collective bargaining disputes[39] and to allow children to bring suit against parents.[40]

But surely we must ask what is distinctive about these transactions. I submit that transaction-specific human capital is central to each. Why else would it take the Hungarians so long to operate the German light-bulb machine? And what else explains the loss of Stradivarius's craftsmanship? Likewise the understanding and trust which evolve between Babbage's transmitter and receiver are valued human assets which, once developed, will be sacrificed with reluctance. And the disruption of continuing relationships to which Justice Rhenquist refers occasions concern precisely because there are no adequate substitutes for these idiosyncratic relations.[41]

The general argument of this paper is that special governance structures supplant standard market-cum-classical contract exchange when transac-

---

[37] Charles Babbage, On the Economy of Machinery and Manufacturers 220-21 (1832). More recent examples of contracts wherein private parties can and evidently do "ignore" the law, even at some peril, when the law and the interests of the parties are at variance are offered by Stewart Macaulay, The Use and Nonuse of Contracts in the Manufacturing Industry, 9 Practical Lawyer 13, 16 (1963): "Requirements contracts probably are not legally enforceable in Wisconsin and a few other States. Yet, chemicals, containers, and a number of other things are still bought and sold there on the basis of requirements contracts.

"Decisions of the United States Court of Appeals for the Seventh Circuit indicate that a clause calling for a 'seller's price in effect at time and place of delivery' makes a contract unenforceable. The Wisconsin cases are not clear. Yet steel and steel products usually are sold in this way."

[38] Remarks of Mr. Justice Rhenquist, The Adversary Society, Baron di Hirsch Meyer Lecture, University of Miami School of Law, February 2, 1978, at 19 (emphasis added).

[39] *Id.* at 11-13.

[40] *Id.* at 16-19.

[41] As Ben-Porath puts it, "The most important characteristic of the family contract is that it is embedded in the identity of the partners without which it loses its meaning. It is thus specific and non-negotiable or nontransferable." Yoram Ben-Porath, *supra* note 29, at 6.

tion-specific values are great. Idiosyncratic commercial, labor, and family relationships are specific examples.

III. COMMERCIAL CONTRACTING

The discussion of commercial contracting begins with a brief statement on economizing. The proposed schema for characterizing transactions and their governance is then developed, including the relation of the schema with Macneil's three-way classification of contract.

A. *Economizing*

The criterion for organizing commercial transactions is assumed to be the strictly instrumental one of cost economizing. Essentially this takes two parts: economizing on production expense and economizing on transaction costs.[42] To the degree that transaction costs are negligible, buying rather than making will normally be the most cost-effective means of procurement.[43] Not only can static scale economies be more fully exhausted by buying rather than making, but the supplier who aggregates uncorrelated demands can realize collective pooling benefits as well. Since external procurement avoids many of the bureaucratic hazards of internal procurement (which hazards, however, are themselves of a transaction-cost kind),[44] external procurement is evidently warranted.[45]

As indicated, however, the object is to economize on the *sum* of production and transaction costs. To the degree production-cost economies of external procurement are small and/or the transaction costs associated with external procurement are great, alternative supply arrangements deserve serious consideration. Economizing on transaction costs essentially reduces

---

[42] More generally, the economizing problem includes choice between a special-purpose and a general-purpose good or service. A general-purpose item affords all of the advantages of market procurement, but possibly at the sacrifice of valued design or performance characteristics. A special-purpose item has the opposite features: valued differences are realized but market procurement here may pose hazards. For the purposes of this paper, intermediate-product characteristics are mainly taken as given and I focus principally on production and transaction-cost economies. A more general formulation would include product characteristics in the optimization.

[43] This ignores transient conditions, such as temporary excess˙ capacity. (In a zero-transaction-cost world, such excesses vanish as assets can be deployed as effectively by others as they can by the owner.)

[44] On these hazards and their transaction-cost origins, see Oliver E. Williamson, *supra* note 1, at 117-31.

[45] Dennis Carlton shows that economies of "vertical integration" can frequently be realized in a market where, absent integration, buyers and suppliers are randomly paired. As he defines vertical integration, however, this can be accomplished as effectively by long-term contract as it can by in-house production. Dennis W. Carlton, Vertical Integration in Competitive Markets under Uncertainty, 27 J. Indus. Econ. 189 (1979).

to economizing on bounded rationality while simultaneously safeguarding the transactions in question against the hazards of opportunism. Holding the governance structure constant, these two objectives are in tension, since a reduction in one commonly results in an increase in the other.[46]

Governance structures, however, are properly regarded as part of the optimization problem. For some transactions, a shift from one structure to another may permit a simultaneous reduction in both the expense of writing a complex contract (which economizes on bounded rationality) and the expense of executing it effectively in an adaptive, sequential way (by attenuating opportunism). Indeed, this is precisely the attraction of internal procurement for transactions of a recurrent, idiosyncratic kind. Not only are market-aggregation economies negligible for such transactions—since the requisite investments are transaction-specific—but market trading in these circumstances is shot through with appropriable quasi-rent hazards. The issues here have been developed elsewhere.[47] The object of this paper is to integrate them into a larger contractual framework.

Note in this connection that the prospect of recovering the set-up costs associated with specialized governance structures varies with the frequency with which transactions recur. Specialized governance structures are much easier to justify for recurrent transactions than for identical transactions that occur only occasionally.

B. *Characterizing Transactions*

I asserted earlier that the critical dimensions for describing contractual relations are uncertainty, the frequency with which transactions recur, and the degree to which investments are idiosyncratic. To simplify the exposition, I will assume uncertainty exists in some intermediate degree and focus initially on frequency and the degree to which the expenses incurred are transaction-specific. The separate importance of uncertainty will then be developed in Section III.D. Three frequency and three investment categories will be recognized. Frequency can be characterized as one-time, occasional, and recurrent; and investments are classed as nonspecific, mixed, and idiosyncratic. To further simplify the argument, the following assumptions are made: (1) Suppliers intend to be in business on a continuing basis; thus the special hazards posed by fly-by-night firms can be disregarded. (2) Potential suppliers for any given requirement are numerous—which is to say that *ex ante* monopoly in ownership of specialized resources is assumed away. (3)

---

[46] Thus a reduction in monitoring commonly gives rise to an increase in opportunism. Monitoring the employment relation, however, needs to be done with special care. Progressively increasing the intensity of surveillance can elicit resentment and have counterproductive (for example, work-to-rule) results. Such perversities are less likely for interfirm trading.

[47] See note 30 *supra*.

The frequency dimension refers strictly to buyer activity in the market.[48] (4) The investment dimension refers to the characteristics of investments made by suppliers.[49]

Although discrete transactions are intriguing—for example, purchasing local spirits from a shopkeeper in a remote area of a foreign country to which one never again expects to visit nor to refer his friends—few transactions have this totally isolated character. For those that do not, the difference between one-time and occasional transactions is not apparent. Accordingly, only occasional and recurrent frequency distinctions will be maintained. The two-by-three matrix shown in Figure I thus describes the six types of transactions to which governance structures need to be matched. Illustrative transactions appear in the cells.

		Investment Characteristics		
		Nonspecific	Mixed	Idiosyncratic
Frequency	Occasional	Purchasing Standard Equipment	Purchasing Customized Equipment	Constructing a Plant
	Recurrent	Purchasing Standard Material	Purchasing Customized Material	Site-Specific Transfer of Intermediate Product Across Successive Stages

FIGURE I
ILLUSTRATIVE COMMERCIAL TRANSACTIONS

C. *Governance Structures*

Three broad types of governance structures will be considered: non-transaction-specific, semi-specific, and highly specific. The market is the classic nonspecific governance structure within which "faceless buyers and sellers . . . meet . . . for an instant to exchange standardized goods at

---

[48] This seems reasonable for most intermediate-product market transactions.

[49] Production aspects are thus emphasized. Investments in governance structure are treated separately.

equilibrium prices."[50] By contrast, highly specific structures are tailored to
the special needs of the transaction. Identity here clearly matters. Semi-
specific structures, naturally, fall in between. Several propositions are suggested immediately. (1) Highly standardized transactions are not apt to require specialized governance structure. (2) Only recurrent transactions will
support a highly specialized governance structure.[51] (3) Although occasional
transactions of a nonstandardized kind will not support a transaction-
specific governance structure, they require special attention nonetheless. In
terms of Macneil's three-way classification of contract, classical contracting
presumably applies to all standardized transactions (whatever the frequency), relational contracting develops for transactions of a recurring and
nonstandardized kind, and neoclassical contracting is needed for occasional,
nonstandardized transactions.

1. *Market Governance: Classical Contracting.* Market governance is the
main governance structure for nonspecific transactions of both occasional
and recurrent contracting. Markets are especially efficacious when recurrent
transactions are contemplated, since both parties need only consult their
own experience in deciding to continue a trading relationship or, at little
transitional expense, turn elsewhere. Being standardized, alternative purchase and supply arrangements are presumably easy to work out.

Nonspecific but occasional transactions are ones for which buyers (and
sellers) are less able to rely on direct experience to safeguard transactions
against opportunism. Often, however, rating services or the experience of
other buyers of the same good can be consulted. Given that the good or
service is of a standardized kind, such experience rating, by formal and
informal means, will provide incentives for parties to behave responsibly.

To be sure, such transactions take place within and benefit from a legal
framework. But such dependence is not great. As S. Todd Lowry puts it,
"the traditional economic analysis of exchange in a market setting properly
corresponds to the legal concept of *sale* (rather than contract), since sale
presumes arrangements in a market context and requires legal support
primarily in enforcing transfers of title."[52] He would thus reserve the concept of contract for exchanges where, in the absence of standardized market

---

[50] Yoram Ben-Porath, *supra* note 29, at 7.

[51] Defense contracting may appear to be a counterexample, since an elaborate governance
structure is devised for many of these. This reflects in part, however, the special disabilities of
the government as a production instrument. But for this, many of these contracts would be
organized in-house. Also, contracts that are very large and of long duration, as many defense
contracts are, do have a recurring character.

[52] S. Todd Lowry, Bargain and Contract Theory in Law and Economics, 10 J. Econ. Issues
1, 12 (1976).

alternatives, the parties have designed "patterns of future relations on which they could rely."[53]

The assumptions of the discrete-contracting paradigm are rather well satisfied for transactions where markets serve as a main governance mode. Thus the specific identity of the parties is of negligible importance; substantive content is determined by reference to formal terms of the contract; and legal rules apply. Market alternatives are mainly what protect each party against opportunism by his opposite.[54] Litigation is strictly for settling claims; concentrated efforts to sustain the relation are not made because the relation is not independently valued.[55]

2. *Trilateral Governance: Neoclassical Contracting.* The two types of transactions for whic:a trilateral governance is needed are occasional transactions of the mixed and highly idiosyncratic kinds. Once the principals to such transactions have entered into a contract, there are strong incentives to see the contract through to completion. Not only have specialized investments been put in place, the opportunity cost of which is much lower in alternative uses, but the transfer of these assets to a successor supplier would pose inordinate difficulties in asset valuation.[56] The interests of the principals in sustaining the relation are especially great for highly idiosyncratic transactions.

Market relief is thus unsatisfactory. Often the setup costs of a transaction-specific governance structure cannot be recovered for occasional transactions. Given the limits of classical contract law for sustaining these transactions, on the one hand, and the prohibitive cost of transaction-specific (bilateral) governance, on the other, an intermediate institutional form is evidently needed.

Neoclassical contract law has many of the sought-after qualities. Thus rather than resorting immediately to strict reliance on litigation—with its

---

[53] *Id.* at 13.

[54] Although recurrent, standard transactions are ones for which an active spot market commonly exists, term contracting may also be employed—especially as planning economies are thereby realized by the parties. See Dennis W. Carlton, Price Rigidity, Forward Contracts, and Market Equilibrium, J. Pol. Econ. (forthcoming). The duration of these contracts will not be long, however, since the assets in question can be employed in other uses and/or in the service of other customers. The result is that changing market circumstances will be reflected relatively quickly in both price and quantity and relatively stringent contracting attitudes may be said to prevail.

[55] "Generally speaking, a serious conflict, even quite a minor one such as an objection to a harmlessly late tender of the delivery of goods, terminates the discrete contract as a live one and leaves nothing but a conflict over money damages to be settled by a lawsuit. Such a result fits neatly the norms of enhancing discreteness and intensifying . . . presentiation." Macneil, Contracts 877.

[56] See the articles cited in note 30 *supra*.

transaction-rupturing features—*third-party assistance* (arbitration) in resolving disputes and evaluating peformance is employed instead. (The use of the architect as a relatively independent expert to determine the content of form construction contracts is an example.)[57] Also, the expansion of the specific-performance remedy in past decades is consistent with continuity purposes—though Macneil declines to characterize specific performance as the "primary neoclassical contract remedy."[58] The section of the Uniform Commercial Code which permits the "seller aggrieved by a buyer's breach . . . unilaterally to maintain the relation"[59] is yet another example.

3. *Transaction-specific Governance: Relational Contracting.* The two types of transactions for which specialized governance structures are commonly devised are recurring transactions of the mixed and highly idiosyncratic kinds. The nonstandardized nature of these transactions makes primary reliance on market governance hazardous, while their recurrent nature permits the cost of the specialized governance structure to be recovered.

Two types of transaction-specific governance structures for intermediate-production market transactions can be distinguished: bilateral structures, where the autonomy of the parties is maintained, and unified structures, where the transaction is removed from the market and organized within the firm subject to an authority relation (vertical integration). Bilateral structures have only recently received the attention they deserve and their operation is least well understood.

(a) *Bilateral Governance: Obligational Contracting.* Highly idiosyncratic transactions are ones where the human and physical assets required for production are extensively specialized, so there are no obvious scale economies to be realized through interfirm trading that the buyer (or seller) is unable to realize himself (through vertical integration). In the case, however, of mixed transactions, the degree of asset specialization is less complete. Accordingly, outside procurement for these components may be favored by scale-economy considerations.

As compared with vertical integration, outside procurement also is good in eliciting cost control for steady-state supply. Problems, however, arise when adaptability and contractual expense are considered. Whereas internal adaptations can be effected by fiat, outside procurement involves effecting adaptations across a market interface. Unless the need for adaptations has been contemplated from the outset and expressly provided for by the contract,

---

[57] Macneil, Contracts 866.

[58] *Id.* at 879.

[59] *Id.* at 880. The rationale for this section of the Code is that "identification of the goods to the contract will, within limits, permit the seller to recover the price of the goods rather than merely damages for the breach. . . , ([where the] latter may be far less in amount and more difficult to prove)." *Id.*

which often is impossible or prohibitively expensive, adaptations across a market interface can be accomplished only by mutual, follow-on agreements. Inasmuch as the interests of the parties will commonly be at variance when adaptation proposals (originated by either party) are made, a dilemma is evidently posed.

On the one hand, both parties have an incentive to sustain the relationship rather than to permit it to unravel, the object being to avoid the sacrifice of valued transaction-specific economies. On the other hand, each party appropriates a separate profit stream and cannot be expected to accede readily to any proposal to adapt the contract. What is needed, evidently, is some way for declaring admissible dimensions for adjustment such that flexibility is provided under terms in which both parties have confidence. This can be accomplished partly by (1) recognizing that the hazards of opportunism vary with the type of adaptation proposed and (2) restricting adjustments to those where the hazards are least. But the spirit within which adaptations are effected is equally important.[60]

Quantity adjustments have much better incentive-compatibility properties than do price adjustments. For one thing, price adjustments have an unfortunate zero-sum quality, whereas proposals to increase, decrease, or delay delivery do not. Also, except as discussed below, price-adjustment proposals involve the risk that one's opposite is contriving to alter the terms within the bilateral monopoly trading gap to his advantage. By contrast, a presumption that exogenous events, rather than strategic purposes, are responsible for quantity adjustments is ordinarily warranted. Given the mixed nature of the exchange, a seller (or buyer) simply has little reason to doubt the representations of his opposite when a quantity change is proposed.

Thus buyers will neither seek supply from other sources nor divert products obtained (at favorable prices) to other uses (or users)—because other sources will incur high setup costs and an idiosyncratic product is nonfungible across uses and users. Likewise, sellers will not withhold supply because better opportunities have arisen, since the assets in question have a specialized character. The result is that quantity representations for idiosyncratic products can ordinarily be taken at face value. Since inability to adapt both quantity and price would render most idiosyncratic exchanges nonviable, quantity adjustments occur routinely.

---

[60] As Stewart Macaulay observes, "Disputes are frequently settled without reference to the contract or to potential or actual legal sanctions. There is a hesitancy to speak of legal right or to threaten to sue in . . . negotiations" where continuing business is valued. Stewart Macaulay, *supra* note 9, at 61.

The material which follows in this subsection was originally developed in connection with the study of inflation. See Michael L. Wachter & Oliver E. Williamson, Obligational Markets and the Mechanics of Inflation, 9 Bell J. Econ. 549 (1978).

Of course, not all price adjustments pose the same degree of hazard. Those which pose few hazards will predictably be implemented. Crude escalator clauses which reflect changes in general economic conditions are one possibility. But since such escalators are not transaction-specific, imperfect adjustments often result when these escalators are applied to local conditions. We should therefore consider whether price adjustments that are more closely related to local circumstances are feasible. The issue here is whether interim price adjustments can be devised for some subset of conditions such that the strategic hazards described above do not arise. What are the preconditions?

Crises facing either of the parties to an idiosyncratic exchange constitute one class of exceptions. Faced with a viability crisis which jeopardizes the relationship, ad hoc price relief may be permitted. More relevant and interesting, however, is whether there are circumstances whereby interim price adjustments are made routinely. The preconditions here are two: first, proposals to adjust prices must relate to exogenous, germane, and easily verifiable events; and second, quantifiable cost consequences must be confidently related thereto. An example may help to illustrate. Consider a component for which a significant share of the cost is accounted for by a basic material (copper, steel). Assume, moreover, that the fractional cost of the component in terms of this basic material is well specified. An exogenous change in prices of materials would under these circumstances pose few hazards if partial but interim price relief were permitted by allowing pass-through according to formula. A more refined adjustment than aggregate escalators would afford thereby obtains.

It bears emphasis, however, that not all costs so qualify. Changes in overhead or other expenses for which validation is difficult and which, even if verified, bear an uncertain relation to the cost of the component will not be passed through in a similar way. Recognizing the hazards, the parties will simply forgo relief of this kind.

(b) *Unified Governance: Internal Organization.* Incentives for trading weaken as transactions become progressively more idiosyncratic. The reason is that, as the specialized human and physical assets become more specialized to a single use, and hence less transferable to other uses, economies of scale can be as fully realized by the buyer as by an outside supplier.[61] The choice of organizing mode then turns on which mode has superior adaptive

---

[61] This assumes that factor prices paid by buyer and outside supplier are identical. Where this is not true, as in some unionized firms, buyers may choose to procure outside because of a differential wage rate. This is a common problem in the automobile industry, which has a very flat and relatively high wage scale.

properties. As discussed elsewhere, vertical integration will invariably appear in these circumstances.[62]

The advantage of vertical integration is that adaptations can be made in a sequential way without the need to consult, complete, or revise interfirm agreements. Where a single ownership entity spans both sides of the transactions, a presumption of joint profit maximization is warranted. Thus price adjustments in vertically integrated enterprises will be more complete than in interfirm trading. And quantity adjustments, of course, will be implemented at whatever frequency serves to maximize the joint gain to the transaction.

Unchanging identity at the interface coupled with extensive adaptability in both price and quantity is thus characteristic of highly idiosyncratic transactions which are vertically integrated. Obligational contracting is supplanted by the more comprehensive adaptive capability afforded by administration.

The match of governance structures with transactions that results from these economizing efforts is shown in Figure II.

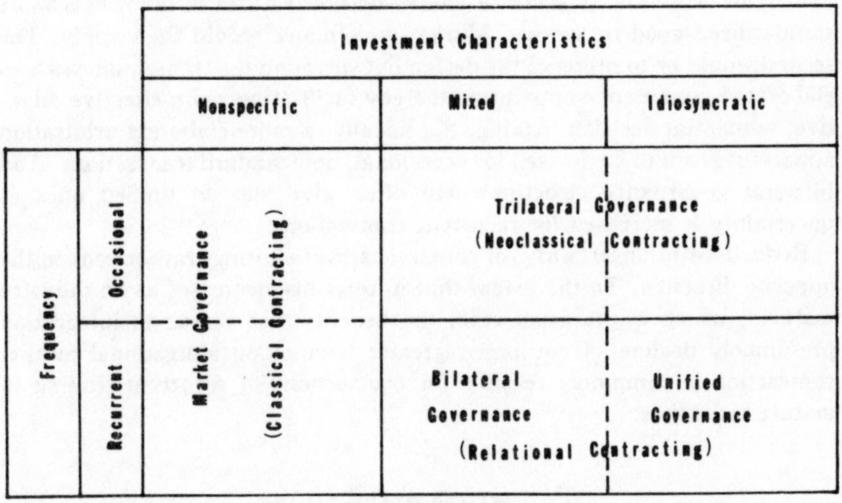

	Investment Characteristics		
	Nonspecific	Mixed	Idiosyncratic
Occasional	Market Governance (Classical Contracting)	Trilateral Governance (Neoclassical Contracting)	
Recurrent		Bilateral Governance (Relational Contracting)	Unified Governance

(Frequency — left axis label; Occasional / Recurrent — row labels)

FIGURE II
MATCHING GOVERNANCE STRUCTURES WITH COMMERCIAL TRANSACTIONS

D. *Uncertainty*

Transactions conducted under certainty are relatively uninteresting. Except as they differ in the time required to reach an equilibrium-exchange

[62] See the references cited in note 4 *supra*.

configuration, any governance structure will do. More relevant are transactions where uncertainty is present to an intermediate or high degree. The foregoing has dealt with the first of these. The question here is how the governance of transactions is affected by increasing the degree of uncertainty.

Recall that nonspecific transactions are ones for which continuity has little value, since new trading relations are easily arranged. Increasing the degree of uncertainty does not alter this. Accordingly, market exchange continues and the discrete-contracting paradigm (classical contract law) holds across standardized transactions of all kinds, whatever the degree of uncertainty.

Matters are different with transaction-specific investments. Whenever investments are idiosyncratic in nontrivial degree, increasing the degree of uncertainty makes it more imperative that the parties devise a machinery to "work things out"—since contractual gaps will be larger and the occasions for sequential adaptations will increase in number and importance as the degree of uncertainty increases. This has special relevance for the organization of transactions with mixed investment attributes. Two possibilities exist. One would be to sacrifice valued design features in favor of a more standardized good or service. Market governance would then apply. The second would be to preserve the design but surround the transaction with an elaborated governance apparatus, thereby facilitating more effective adaptive, sequential decision making. Specifically, a more elaborate arbitration apparatus is apt to be devised for occasional, nonstandard transactions. And bilateral governance structures will often give way to unified ones as uncertainty is increased for recurrent transactions.

Reductions in uncertainty, of course, warrant shifting transactions in the opposite direction. To the extent that uncertainty decreases as an industry matures, which is the usual case, the benefits that accrue to integration presumably decline. Accordingly, greater reliance on obligational market contracting is commonly feasible for transactions of recurrent trading in mature industries.

IV. Other Applications

The three dimensions for describing transactions—frequency, investment idiosyncrasy, and uncertainty—apply to transactions of all kinds. The same general considerations that apply to governance structures for commercial transactions carry over as well. The specific governance structures for organizing commercial transactions do not, however, apply without modification to the governance of other types of transactions. Applications of the framework to the study of labor markets, regulation, family law, and capital markets are briefly sketched here.

A. *Labor*

Occasional labor-market transactions typically take the form of repair or replacement services—the plumber, electrician, and so forth. Especially in older homes or structures, these transactions can take on an idiosyncratic quality. Although such transactions can be interesting, the transactions on which I want to focus are recurrent labor-market transactions of the nonspecific, mixed, and idiosyncratic kinds.

Clyde Summers's examination of collective agreements in relation to the law of contracts disclosed that, while the collective bargain differed greatly from the ordinary bargain of commerce, collective agreements are nonetheless a part of the "mainstream of contract."[63] He suggested that the study of contract proceed on two levels: the search for an underlying framework and, within that framework, an examination of the distinctive institutional attributes that distinguish each type of transaction. With respect to the first of these he conjectured that "the principles common to the whole range of contractual transactions are relatively few and of such generality and competing character that they should not be stated as legal rules at all."[64]

I am persuaded that Summers's two-part strategy for studying contract leads to a deeper understanding of the issues. And I believe that the framework set out in the preceding sections of this paper provides much of the underlying unity called for by Summers. What differs as one moves across various contracting activities is the institutional infrastructure.

(1) *Nonspecific Transactions.* Nonspecific labor-market transactions are ones where employer and employee are largely indifferent to the identity of each. Migrant farm labor is an example. Although an unchanging employment association between firm and worker may be observed to continue over long intervals for some of these employees, each party is essentially meeting bids in the spot market. A valuable ongoing relationship, in which specific training and on-the-job learning yield idiosyncratic benefits, is thus not implied. Both wages and employment are variable and market governance applies to transactions of this kind. Consider, therefore, mixed and idiosyncratic labor-market transactions.

(2) *Mixed Transactions.* Probably the most interesting labor-market transactions are those where large numbers of workers acquire an intermediate degree of firm-specific skill. Note that, inasmuch as the degree of idiosyncrasy is a design variable, firms would presumably redesign jobs to favor more standardized operations if it were impossible to devise governance structures which prevented antagonistic bargaining relations from developing between firms and idiosyncratically skilled employees. Although

---

[63] Clyde W. Summers, *supra* note 9, at 527.

[64] *Id.* at 568.

least-cost production technologies would be sacrificed in the process, net gains might nevertheless be realized since incumbent workers would realize little strategic advantage over otherwise qualified but inexperienced outsiders.

Justice Rhenquist has observed that "Adjudicatory review of the decisions of certain institutions, while perhaps insuring a 'better' decision in some objective sense, can only disrupt on-going relationships within the institution and thereby hamper the institution's ability to serve its designated societal function."[65] Examples of adjudicatory review with respect to which he counsels caution include collective bargaining agreements.

The reasons for this are that adjudicatory review is not easily apprised of the special needs of the transaction and the prospect of such review impairs the incentive of the parties to devise bilateral governance structure. The *Vaca v. Stipes* holding, which Justice Rhenquist cites, is fully consistent with this interpretation. There the Court held that an individual could not compel his union to take his grievance to arbitration, since if the law were otherwise "the settlement machinery provided by the contract would be substantially undermined, thus . . . [introducing] the vagaries of independent and unsystematic negotiations."[66] Archibald Cox elaborates as follows:[67]

. . . giving the union control over all claims arising under the collective agreement comports so much better with the functional nature of a collective bargaining agreement. . . . Allowing an individual to carry a claim to arbitration whenever he is dissatisfied with the adjustment worked out by the company and the union . . . discourages the kind of day-to-day cooperation between company and union which is normally the mark of sound industrial relations—a relationship in which grievances are treated as problems to be solved and contracts are only guideposts in a dynamic human relationship. When . . . the individual's claim endangers group interests, the union's function is to resolve the competition by reaching an accommodation or striking a balance.

The practice described by Cox of giving the union control over arbitration claims plainly permits group interests—whence the concern for system viability—to supersede individual interests, thereby curbing small-numbers opportunism.

General escalator or predetermined wage adjustments aside, wages are unchanging under collective bargaining agreements.[68] Interim adaptations are nonetheless essential. These take three forms: (1) quantity adjustments,

---

[65] Remarks of Mr. Justice Rhenquist, *supra* note 38, at 4.

[66] 386 U.S. 171, 191 (1967).

[67] Archibald Cox, *supra* note 9, at 24.

[68] The reason, of course, is that it is very costly and apt to be unproductive to reopen wage bargaining during the period covered by a contract. Since to reopen negotiations for one type of job is to invite it for all, and as objective differences among jobs may be difficult to demonstrate, wage bargaining is foreclosed except at contract-renewal intervals.

(2) assignment changes, and (3) refinement of working rules as a result of grievances.

Quantity adjustments are made in response to changing market opportunities. Either the level or the mix of employment is adjusted as economic events unfold. Given that valuable firm-specific training and learning reside in the workers, layoffs with a presumption of reemployment when conditions improve are common. Conformably, the degree to which the machinery governing access to jobs is elaborated ought to vary directly with the degree to which jobs in a firm are idiosyncratic. Thus promotion ladders in firms where a succession of interdependent jobs are highly idiosyncratic should be long and thin, with access mainly restricted to the bottom, whereas promotion ladders in nonidiosyncratic activities should be broadly structured.[69] Likewise, promotion on merit ought to be favored over promotion strictly by seniority in firms where jobs are more idiosyncratic.[70]

(3) *Highly Idiosyncratic Transactions.* Recall that idiosyncratic transactions involve not merely uniqueness but uniqueness of a transaction-specific kind. Also recall that our concern in this section is with recurring transactions. Thus, although there are many uniquely skilled individuals (artists, athletes, researchers, administrators), unique skills are rarely of a transaction-specific kind. On the contrary, most of these individuals could move to another organization without significant productivity losses.

The exceptions are those where the benefits which accrue to experience (inside knowledge) and/or team interaction effects are great. Whereas commercial transactions of a highly idiosyncratic nature are unified under a common ownership, limits on indenture foreclose this option for labor-market transactions. Instead of "merger," complex contracts designed to tie the interests of the individual to the organization on a long-term basis are negotiated. Severe penalties are provided should either party seek unilateral termination. Nonvested, long-term, contingent reward schemes are devised. More generally, transaction-specific infrastructure will be highly individuated for such transactions.

B. *Regulation of Natural Monopoly*

Again the argument is that specialized governance structure is needed to the degree efficient supply necessarily joins buyers and sellers in a bilateral

---

[69] Michael L. Wachter & Oliver E. Williamson, *supra* note 60, at 567.

[70] Thus although both nonidiosyncratic and idiosyncratic jobs may be organized collectively, the way in which the internal labor markets associated with each are organized should reflect objective differences between them. Additionally, the incentive to provide an orderly governance structure varies directly with the degree to which efficiencies are attributable thereto. *Ceteris paribus*, nonidiosyncratic jobs ought to be organized later and the governance structure less fully elaborated than for idiosyncratic jobs. Both propositions are borne out by the evidence.

trading relation of a continuing nature. And again, the object of governance is to (1) protect the interests of the respective parties and (2) adapt the relationship to changing circumstances.

Although differing in details, both Victor Goldberg[71] and I[72] have argued that specialized governance structure is needed for services for which natural monopoly features are great. Such structure presumably has the purpose of providing sellers (investors) and buyers with security of expectations, which is a protective function, while at the same time facilitating adaptive, sequential decision making. Rate-of-return regulation with periodic review has these features. To the extent, however, that such regulation is observed in conjunction with activities where transaction-specific investments are insubstantial (as, for example, in the trucking industry), the case for regulation is not at all apparent—or, if it is to be made, must appeal to arguments very different from those set out here.

C. *Family Law*

The issue here is whether the role of adjudication should be *expanded* to help govern family relationships. Granting that adjudication as ultimate relief can and often does serve a useful role for sustaining family relations, such relations are plainly idiosyncratic to an unusual degree and a specialized governance structure is surely the main mode of governance. As the role of adjudication is expanded, reliance upon internal structure is apt to be reduced. Therefore, except when individual rights are seriously threatened, withholding access to adjudication may be indicated.

Justice Rhenquist's remarks concerning the corrosive effects of adversary hearings on the family are apposite: "Any sort of adversary hearing which pits parent against child is bound to be disruptive, placing stresses and tensions on the intra-familial relationships which in turn weaken the family as an institution."[73] Whether, as this suggests, parent-child family relations are optimized where adjudication is zero or negligible is beyond the scope of this paper. It suffices for my purposes merely to note that valued family relations are recurrent and idiosyncratic and that a specialized, transaction-specific governance structure must be encouraged lest the parties withhold investing heavily in the institution.[74]

---

[71] Victor P. Goldberg, *supra* note 1.

[72] Oliver E. Williamson, *supra* note 30.

[73] Remarks of Mr. Justice Rhenquist, *supra* note 38, at 19.

[74] For a more extensive discussion of family transactions, see Yoram Ben-Porath, *supra* note 29, at 4-7.

D. *Capital Market Transactions*

The ease of verification is critical to the operation of capital markets.[75] Where verification is easy, markets work well and additional governance is unnecessary. Where verification is difficult or very difficult, however, additional governance may be indicated. Occasional transactions are apt to benefit from third-party assistance, while recurring transactions are ones for which bilateral or unified governance will presumably be observed. Assessing capital-market transactions within the proposed framework is thus accomplished by substituting "ease of verification" for "degree of transaction-specific investment." Once this is done, the governance structures appropriate to capital markets are broadly similar to those within which commercial transactions are organized.

V. IMPLICATIONS

Dimensionalizing transactions and examining the costs of executing different transactions in different ways generate a large number of institutional implications. Some of these are summarized here.

A. *General*

1. Nonspecific transactions, either occasional or recurrent, are efficiently organized by markets.

2. Occasional transactions that are nonstandardized stand most to benefit from adjudication.

3. A transaction-specific governance structure is more fully developed where transactions are (1) recurrent, (2) entail idiosyncratic investment, and (3) are executed under greater uncertainty.

B. *Commercial Transactions*

1. Optimization of commercial transactions requires simultaneous attention to (1) production economies, (2) transaction-cost economies, and (3) component design.

2. The reason why Macaulay observes so few litigated cases in business[76] is because markets work well for nonspecific transactions, while recurrent, nonstandard transactions are governed by bilateral or unified structures.

3. As uncertainty increases, the obligational market-contracting mode will not be used for recurrent transactions with mixed investment features. Such transactions will either be standardized, and shifted to the market, or organized internally.

---

[75] This feature was called to my attention by Sanford Grossman.

[76] Stewart Macaulay, *supra* note 9.

4. As generic demand grows and the number of supply sources increases, exchange that was once transaction-specific loses this characteristic and greater reliance on market-mediated governance is feasible. Thus vertical integration may give way to obligational market contracting, which in turn may give way to markets.

5. Where inventory and related flow-process economies are great, site-specific supply and transaction-specific governance (commonly vertical integration) will be observed. Generic demand here has little bearing.

6. The organization of the interface between manufacturing and distribution reflects similar investment considerations: goods and services that can be sold without incurring transaction-specific investment will be distributed through conventional marketing channels while those where such investments are great will be supported by specialized—mainly bilateral (for example, franchising) or unified (forward integration)—governance structures.

7. The governance of technical change poses special difficulties. The frequently noted limits of markets[77] often give way to more complex governance relations, again for the same general reasons and along the same general lines as are set out here.[78]

C. *Other Transactions*

1. The efficiency benefits of collective organization are negligible for nonspecific labor. Accordingly, such labor will be organized late, often only with the assistance of the political process.

2. Internal labor markets become more highly individuated as jobs become more varied and idiosyncratic.

3. Regulation can be interpreted in part as a response to the transactional dilemma posed by natural monopoly.

4. A transaction-cost justification for regulating activities for which transaction-specific investments are lacking (for example, trucking) is not apparent. The possibility that politics is the driving consideration in such industries warrants consideration.

5. Adjudication should proceed with caution in the area of family law lest valued transaction-specific investments be discouraged.

6. Ease of verification is the capital-market counterpart of transaction-specific investments. Upon making this substitution, the organization of capital markets and intermediate-product markets is broadly similar.

---

[77] Kenneth J. Arrow, Economic Welfare and the Allocation of Resources for Invention, in The Rate and Direction of Economic Activity 609 (1962).

[78] Aspects are discussed in Oliver E. Williamson, *supra* note 1, at 203-05.

VI. Concluding Remarks

Transaction-cost economics is an interdisciplinary undertaking that joins economics with aspects of organization theory and overlaps extensively with contract law. It is the modern counterpart of institutional economics and relies heavily on comparative analysis.[79] Frictionless ideals are useful mainly for reference purposes.

Although mathematical economics captures only a fraction of the transaction-cost phenomena of interest,[80] this has not been the only obstacle. Headway with the study of transaction-cost issues has been impeded by lack of verbal definitions. Identifying the critical dimensions with respect to which transactions differ has been a significant omission.

This paper attempts to rectify this deficiency and identifies uncertainty, frequency of exchange, and the degree to which investments are trans-action-specific as the principal dimensions for describing transactions. The efficient organization of economic activity entails matching governance structures with these transactional attributes in a discriminating way.

Although the main applications in this paper are to commercial contract-ing, the proposed approach generalizes easily to the study of labor contracts. It also has ramifications for understanding both public utility regulation and family relations. A unified approach to contract thus emerges.

The fact that the broad features of so many varied transactions fit within the framework is encouraging. The importance of transaction costs to the organization of economic activity is thus confirmed. But the world of con-tract is enormously complex,[81] and the simple economizing framework pro-posed here cannot be expected to capture more than main features. Elaborat-ing the framework to deal with microanalytic phenomena, however, should be feasible. And extending it to include additional or substitute dimensions (of which the ease of verification, in the case of capital-market transactions, is an example) may sometimes be necessary.

[79] Reliance on comparative analysis has been repeatedly emphasized by R. H. Coase, *supra* note 1.

[80] See Carl J. Dahlman, *supra* note 1, at 144-47.

[81] Benjamin Klein, Robert C. Crawford, & Armen A. Alchian, *supra* note 1, at 325.

[13]

The Costs and Benefits of Ownership:
A Theory of Vertical and Lateral Integration

Sanford J. Grossman

Princeton University

Oliver D. Hart

Massachusetts Institute of Technology

Our theory of costly contracts emphasizes that contractual rights can be of two types: specific rights and residual rights. When it is costly to list all specific rights over assets in the contract, it may be optimal to let one party purchase all residual rights. Ownership is the purchase of these residual rights. When residual rights are purchased by one party, they are lost by a second party, and this inevitably creates distortions. Firm 1 purchases firm 2 when firm 1's control increases the productivity of its management more than the loss of control decreases the productivity of firm 2's management.

I. Introduction

A. General Introduction

What is a firm? What are the determinants of how vertically or laterally integrated the activities of the firm are? This paper builds on the foundations laid by Coase (1937), Klein, Crawford, and Alchian (1978), and Williamson (1979), which emphasize the benefits of "con-

Research was supported by the National Science Foundation, the Alfred P. Sloan Foundation, and the International Centre for Economics and Related Disciplines at the London School of Economics. This is an extensively revised version of an earlier paper (Grossman and Hart 1984). We gratefully acknowledge helpful comments from Debra Aron, Peter Diamond, Richard Epstein, Naava Grossman, Paul Joskow, John Minahan, Jim Poterba, Andrew Postlewaite, Peter Thistle, Martin Weitzman, Oliver Williamson, Charles Wilson, Toni Zabalza, and two referees.

[*Journal of Political Economy*, 1986, vol. 94, no. 4]

trol" in response to situations in which there are difficulties in writing or enforcing complete contracts (see also Williamson 1971, 1983; Williamson, Wachter, and Harris 1975; Teece 1980). We define the firm as being composed of the assets (e.g., machines, inventories) that it owns. We present a theory of costly contracts that emphasizes that contractual rights can be of two types: specific rights and residual rights. When it is too costly for one party to specify a long list of the particular rights it desires over another party's assets, it may be optimal for that party to purchase all the rights except those specifically mentioned in the contract. Ownership is the purchase of these residual rights of control. We show that there can be harmful effects associated with the wrong allocation of residual rights. In particular, a firm that purchases its supplier, thereby removing residual rights of control from the manager of the supplying company, can distort the manager's incentives sufficiently to make common ownership harmful. We develop a theory of integration based on the attempt of parties in writing a contract to allocate efficiently the residual rights of control between themselves.

We begin by reviewing some transactions cost–based arguments for integration. Coase (1937) suggested that transactions will be organized in the firm when the cost of doing this is lower than the cost of using the market. He added some content to this idea by proposing that the costs of constant recontracting with an outside firm or manager can be high relative to those of signing a long-term contract with an employee in which the employee agrees to carry out the commands of the employer. Klein et al. (1978) and Williamson (1979) added further content by arguing that a contractual relationship between a separately owned buyer and seller will be plagued by opportunistic and inefficient behavior in situations in which there are large amounts of surplus to be divided ex post and in which, because of the impossibility of writing a complete, contingent contract, the ex ante contract does not specify a clear division of this surplus. Such situations in turn are likely to arise when either the buyer or seller must make investments that have a smaller value in a use outside their own relationship than within the relationship (i.e., there exist "asset specificities").

While these statements help us understand when the costs of contracting between separately owned firms may be high, they do not elucidate what the benefits are of "organizing the transaction within the firm." In particular, given that it is difficult to write a complete contract between a buyer and seller and this creates room for opportunistic behavior, the transactions cost–based arguments for integration do not explain how the scope for such behavior changes when one of the self-interested owners becomes an equally self-interested employee of the other owner. Furthermore, if vertical integration always reduces transaction costs, any buyer A and seller B that have a contractual relationship should be able to make themselves better off as follows: (i) A buys B and makes the previous owner of B the manager of a new subsidiary; (ii) A sets a transfer price between the subsidiary and itself equal to the contract price that existed when the firms were separate enterprises; and (iii) A gives the manager of B a compensation package equal to the profit of the subsidiary. Given this, however, how can integration ever be strictly worse than nonintegration; that is, what limits the size of the firm?[1]

A second question raised by the transactions cost–based arguments concerns the definition of integration itself. In particular, what does it mean for one firm to be more integrated than another? For example, is a firm that calls its retail force "employees" more integrated than one that calls its retail force "independent but exclusive sales agents"?

Existing theories cannot answer these questions because they do not give a sufficiently clear definition of integration for its costs and benefits to be assessed. It is not clear whether these theories are designed to explain the types of people called employees or instead the types of assets under the control of a single ownership unit. We define integration in terms of the ownership of assets and develop a model to explain when one firm will desire to acquire the assets of another firm. We will argue that, if one party gets rights of control, then this diminishes the rights of the other party to have control. To the extent that there are benefits of control, there will always be potential costs associated with removing control (i.e., ownership) from those who manage productive activities.

B. What Is Integration?

We define a firm to consist of those assets that it owns or over which it has control; we do not distinguish between ownership and control

---

[1] See Evans and Grossman (1983) for an elaboration of the critique of the transactions cost–based arguments for integration. Coase (1937) states that the size of the firm is limited by the managerial capacity of the single owner to manage many activities. As noted in the text, this is unconvincing since the owner could always hire another manager. The other authors do not give any clear statement as to what limits the size of the firm but appear to accept Coase's view that integration transforms a hostile supplier into a docile employee; thus the contracting problems associated with independent ownership are greatly diminished. However, there are some references to increased bureaucracy and its associated cost. See Williamson (1967), Rosen (1982), Keren and Levhari (1983), and Waldman (1984) for specific models of how the number of people involved in production affects the overall cost of production. None of these papers makes any distinction between the activities carried out via contract between separate owners and the activities carried out in a single ownership unit. That is, the theories are equally valid descriptions of how a firm can use hierarchies of outside contractors as they are theories of employment within the firm.

and virtually define ownership as the power to exercise control. In a corporation the shareholders as a group have control and delegate this control to the board of directors (i.e., management). Of course, control or ownership is never absolute. For example, a firm that owns a machine may not be able to sell it without the permission of the lenders for which the machine serves as collateral; more generally, a firm may give another firm specific authority over its machines. However, ownership gives the owner all rights to use the machine that he has not voluntarily given away or that the government or some other party has not taken by force. We believe that this terminology is roughly consistent with standard usage.[2]

In our attempt to explain asset ownership, we do not distinguish between employees and outside contractors in the case in which the firm provides all the tools and other assets used by the contractor. For example, in insurance retailing a firm may use its own employees as commissioned agents or use independent agents. The important difference between the two forms of retailing is that the employee-agent does not own the list of his clients, while the independent agent does own the list. If the firm owned the list and all the other important assets of the independent agents, then we would say that such a company had the same degree of integration as a company in which the retail sales force was composed of "employees." (A detailed discussion of the insurance industry may be found in Sec. IV.) As another example, consider vertical integration in shoe manufacturing. In the eighteenth century much of the manufacturing of shoes switched from the "putting out" system, in which the worker sewed the upper and lower halves of the shoe at home, to factory work, in which the factory owner's machines were used by the worker to put the shoes together (see Chandler 1977, p. 54). Even if workers are paid by the piece in both cases, the firm is more integrated in the latter case because it owns more of the machines used in production.

The examples above illustrate that the issue of ownership can be separated from the issue of contractual compensation. A firm may pay another firm or person by the piece or a fixed amount (salary), irrespective of the ownership of the machines. As Coase points out, the benefits of integration must surely be more than the ability to choose a new payment method. We assume that a payment method,

---

[2] Richard Posner, whose opinion on the legal definition of ownership we solicited, has referred us to the following statement by Oliver Wendell Holmes (1881/1946, p. 246): "But what are the rights of ownership? They are substantially the same as those incident to possession. Within the limits prescribed by policy, the owner is allowed to exercise his natural powers over the subject-matter uninterfered with, and is more or less protected in excluding other people from such interference. The owner is allowed to exclude all, and is accountable to no one but him."

whether it be salary compensation to an employee in the integrated company or a price for goods to be delivered between companies, is some function of the observable states of nature and the observable performance of the parties to the contract. We further assume that integration in itself does not make any new variable observable to both parties. Any audits that an employer can have done of his subsidiary are also feasible when the subsidiary is a separate company.[3]

It may be extremely costly to write a contract that specifies unambiguously the payments and actions of all parties in every observable state of nature. We assume that integration in itself does not change the cost of writing down a particular contractual provision.[4] What it does change is who has control over those provisions not included in the contract. Consider, for example, a contract between a publisher and a printer for a particular number of copies of a book. If the contract has no provision for an additional print run but the publisher receives some new information that makes it profitable for another run, then it is obvious that the right to decide whether or not to have the run belongs to the owner of the printing press. This is the simplest possible illustration of our assumption that the owner of an asset has the residual rights of control of that asset, that is, the right to control all aspects of the asset that have not been explicitly given away by contract.

C. Introduction to the Model

In order to be more specific about the costs and benefits of integration, it is necessary to set up a formal model of the relationship between two firms. This is done in Section II. For simplicity, the relationship, which may be either vertical or lateral, is assumed to last 2 periods.[5] In the first (i.e., the ex ante) period, the manager of each

---

[3] Arrow (1975) has analyzed the benefits of vertical integration based on the assumption that without integration it is more costly for one firm to communicate information to another than with integration. We do not see why any new method of communication becomes feasible under integration. The incentives of people to lie may change if their incentive structure changes, but Arrow does not explain how integration changes the set of feasible incentive structures. However, it might be the case that the right to audit is sometimes a residual right rather than a contractible right, in which case the theory developed below can explain the dependence of information on ownership patterns.

[4] Williamson (1983 pp. 523–24) gives an example of a contract written between nonintegrated firms in which there is no penalty for cancellation. He assumes that under vertical integration, or via the use of hostages, it is possible to extract a penalty from the buyer when he fails to take delivery of the seller's product. We shall ignore the possibility that there are artificial legal barriers to cancellation penalties and that integration is used by the parties as a way of getting around these.

[5] We model the relationship as a "once and for all" event. To the extent that the relationship is repeated, the incentives for vertical integration may be different from

firm makes relationship-specific investments, while in the second (i.e., the ex post) period, some further production decisions are taken and the benefits from the relationship are realized. A basic assumption of the model is that the production decisions, represented by q, are sufficiently complex that they cannot be specified completely in an initial contract between the firms. We have in mind a situation in which it is prohibitively difficult to think about and describe unambiguously in advance how all the potentially relevant aspects of the production allocation should be chosen as a function of the many states of the world. To simplify, we suppose that *no* aspect of q is ex ante contractible.[6] The noncontractibility of q creates the need to allocate residual rights of control since, if it is not specified how q will be chosen, there must be some implicit or explicit default that allows some party to choose the relevant components of q in the second period. We assume that the owner of each asset has the right to control that asset in the case of a missing provision.

Although q is ex ante noncontractible, we suppose that, once the state of the world is determined, the (small number of) relevant aspects of the production allocation become clear and the parties can negotiate or recontract over these (costlessly). That is, q is ex post contractible. Since the parties are assumed to have symmetric information, costless recontracting will always lead to an ex post efficient allocation, whatever is the initial allocation of ownership rights.[7] The *distribution* of ex post surplus, however, will be sensitive to ownership rights. For example, in the case of the printer and the publisher, while it may be efficient to have another print run, the printer will extract more surplus if he owns the printing plant and can therefore refuse to have the additional printing if negotiations fail.

Through their influence on the distribution of ex post surplus, ownership rights will affect ex ante investment decisions. That is, although ex post efficiency (relative to investment decisions) is guaranteed under any ownership structure, each ownership structure

those we give here. See Telser (1980) and Kreps (1984) for the role of reputation in long-term relationships as an enforcement device and Williamson (1979) for arguments on the role of repetitive idiosyncratic purchases in providing a cost to nonvertical integration. None of these papers deals with the influence of reputation on the ownership of assets. To the extent that reputation helps to enforce implicit agreements, repetition of the relationship is likely to increase the parties' surplus whether they are separate firms or part of the same firm. It is therefore unclear why reputation should have any particular implications concerning the ownership of assets.

[6] See Grossman and Hart (1984) for models in which some components of q are contractible while others are not.

[7] In a more complex model ex post inefficiencies will also appear in conjunction with costs of renegotiation. See Grossman and Hart (1984, sec. 2) for a model of ownership in which ex post inefficiencies rather than ex ante inefficiencies are analyzed.

will lead to a (different) distortion in ex ante investment. The ex ante investments that we are referring to are those that cannot be specified in the contract either because they are too complex to be described or because they stand for nonverifiable managerial effort decisions. We suppose that the parties allocate ownership rights in such a way that the ex ante investment distortions are minimized. The implications this has for the desirability of integration are the main focus of the paper and are analyzed in Section III.

It is worth asking why, in the context of our model, the usual argument that the feasible set can only become larger under integration fails. Given the existence of residual rights of control, if firm 1 buys firm 2, the owner of firm 1 will have the power to intervene in firm 2 in ways that may distort the incentives of firm 1's manager. Moreover, the owner cannot commit himself to intervene selectively in his subsidiary's operations since by their very definition residual rights refer to powers that cannot be specified in advance (at least in the detail required to make them part of an enforceable contract). It follows that integration can impose costs as well as benefits.

Since there are features of our theory that lack quantitative completeness, in Section IV we show how the theory can be applied to a particular industry, the insurance industry. Finally, Section V contains conclusions.

II. The Model

Consider two firms, 1 and 2, engaged in a relationship, which for simplicity we suppose lasts 2 periods. We assume that each firm is run by a manager who receives the full return from his firm's activities (the reason for this extreme assumption will become clear below). The firms sign a contract at date 0, and soon after managers 1 and 2 make relationship-specific investments, denoted by a_1 and a_2, respectively. At date 1, some further actions q_1 and q_2 are taken and the gains from trade are realized. We write the benefit of firm i's manager from the relationship at date 1, net of investment costs, as

$$B_i[a_i, \, \phi_i(q_1, q_2)]. \tag{1}$$

All costs and benefits are measured in date 1 dollars. We will often interpret the relationship as a vertical one in which upstream firm 2 supplies downstream firm 1 with an input. In this case $B_2 < 0$ may be a cost. However, another interpretation is that the relationship is a lateral one, for example, between two retail stores with adjacent locations. For technical reasons, we have assumed that B_i depends on some function ϕ_i of q_1 and q_2 and is increasing in ϕ_i. We shall be interested in cases in which there is a conflict of interest in the $\mathbf{q}$'s; for example, B_i might be increasing in $\mathbf{q}_i$ and decreasing in $\mathbf{q}_j$.[8]

The $\mathbf{q}_i$'s represent rights of control over firm i's assets, which are assumed to be ex ante noncontractible (as of date 0) but ex post contractible (as of date 1). As noted in the Introduction, we have in mind a situation in which it is extremely difficult to think about and describe in advance how the production allocation should depend on the "state of the world" but in which it is relatively easy to specify production decisions ex post once the state of the world is realized (a more detailed discussion of this may be found in n. 14). Since $\mathbf{q}_i$ is ex ante noncontractible, it qualifies as a residual right of control, and our assumption is that the owner of firm i has the right to choose it at date 1. Given that $\mathbf{q}_i$ is ex post contractible, however, firm i's owner may be prepared to give up this right in exchange for a side payment as part of renegotiation of the contract at date 1.

The ex ante investments $\mathbf{a}_i$ are also supposed to be noncontractible either because they are too complex to be described (they are multidimensional, not just dollar amounts) or because they stand for managerial effort decisions that are not verifiable (to third parties, such as the courts); for example, $\mathbf{a}_i$ might be manager i's effort in setting up a well-functioning firm. Investment decisions are assumed to be made independently and noncooperatively by the two managers just after the contract is signed at date 0. We shall suppose that each manager observes the other's investment decision after it has been made; in this model, there will be no asymmetries of information between the managers.

After investment decisions are made ex ante and ϕ_i is determined ex post through the choice of $\mathbf{q}_1$ and $\mathbf{q}_2$, manager i receives the benefit B_i. This benefit is again supposed to be nonverifiable and hence noncontractible. That is, B_i is a private benefit, accruing directly to firm i's manager, that does not show up in firm i's accounts. For example, B_i might stand for managerial perquisites or effort. A consequence of B_1 and B_2's not being verifiable is that it is impossible to write in the date 0 contract that firm 1, say, should transfer its benefit B_1 to firm 2.

We can summarize our assumptions so far as follows: (1) None of the variables $\mathbf{a}_i$, $\mathbf{q}_i$, and B_i is ex ante contractible, although the managers have symmetric information about these variables. Hence all the date 0 contract can do is to allocate ownership rights or residual rights of control to the two managers. (2) After the contract is signed, $\mathbf{a}_1$ and $\mathbf{a}_2$ are chosen simultaneously and noncooperatively by managers 1 and 2. (3) At date 1, the owner of firm i (i.e., the manager who has

---

[8] Here $\mathbf{a}_i$ and $\mathbf{q}_i$ are vectors in compact subsets of Euclidean spaces A_i and Q_i, respectively, and B_i and ϕ_i are continuous functions.

been given ownership rights in the date 0 contract) has the right and power to choose q_i.[9] If there is no further negotiation, the choices of different owners are made simultaneously and noncooperatively. Given that the q's become contractible at date 1, however, the contract may be *renegotiated* (costlessly). Then B_1 and B_2 are realized.

It should be stressed that we assume that separate managers are needed to choose a_i and a_j under any ownership structure (but see Sec. III, remark 1).[10]

Finally, we assume that there is a competitive market in identical potential trading partners at date 0, which determines the ex ante division of the surplus between the two managers. Given this ex ante division, an optimal contract simply maximizes one manager's benefit subject to the other manager's receiving his reservation utility (note that there is no uncertainty). We make the standard assumption that the functions B_1 and B_2, as well as the domains of the variables q_i and a_i, are common knowledge at date 0.

An example may be useful. Imagine that firm 1 is an electricity generating plant that is located next to a coal mine in order to use the mine's coal to make electricity (for a detailed analysis of long-term contracts between mine-mouth electricity generating plants and coal mines, see Joskow [1985]). Let $\phi_1(q_1, q_2)$ represent the quality of the coal delivered. Suppose that the boiler firm 1 installs to burn coal does not function well if the coal supplied is impure. Ex ante there may be many potential impurities, and it may be impossible to allow for each of these in the contract. Ex post, however, it may be clear what the relevant impurity is—high ash content, say. Our supposition is that, if firm 1 owns firm 2, it can, ex post, exercise its rights of control over firm 2's assets to direct that the coal should be taken from a deposit with low ash content (i.e., firm 1 chooses a subvector of q_2). In contrast, if firm 2 owns firm 1, it can exercise its right of control over firm 1's assets to direct that the boiler should be modified to accept coal with high ash content.

An alternative to ownership in this example is a contract that gives firm 1, say, the specific right to direct the areas of the mine in which coal is dug out. This would clearly be reasonable for any one particular right of control. However, we have in mind a situation in which there are many aspects of a firm's operations, each of which may be important in a different contingency, and thus the costs of assigning

---

[9] We suppose that no special skills are required to choose q_i. This means that the owner of firm i can contract with a subordinate to implement the choice of q_i; moreover, since there are many subordinates available, none is in a position to refuse to carry out the owner's wishes or to argue about terms.

[10] The contrary assumption that integration is useful because it substitutes one manager for two has been advanced by Aron (1984) and Mann and Wissink (1984).

specific rights of control ex ante are much higher than the costs of assigning generalized control.

It may be useful if we comment briefly on the motivation for our assumption that a_i, q_i, and B_i are all ex ante noncontractible. We shall see in the next section that, if either the a_i's or the q_i's are ex ante contractible, the first-best can be achieved under any ownership structure, and so the degree of integration of the firms is irrelevant. The same is true if the B_i's are contractible since in this case the parties can always write a contract that transfers firm i's benefit to firm j, thus removing all conflicts of interest. Hence, in order to develop an interesting theory of ownership, it is necessary to assume that the a_i's, q_i's, and B_i's are all at least partly noncontractible. It is nonetheless very strong to assume that *no* aspects of these variables are contractible. In any realistic situation, some parts of a firm's performance will be reflected in verifiable shareholders' profit, even if other parts, such as managerial well-being, are not. Similarly, in a vertical relationship, while the parties may have difficulty in specifying the quality of input to be exchanged in advance, they can surely at least contract on the *quantity* of input. While we are confident that some version of our results will continue to hold when a_i, q_i, and B_i are partly contractible, the formal extension of our analysis to this case is by no means straightforward. As a first step, it therefore seems reasonable to study the case in which no date 1 variables are contractible at date 0.[11]

III. Analysis of the Optimal Contract, Including the Allocation of Ownership Rights

An optimal contract maximizes one manager's benefit subject to the other manager's receiving his reservation utility. Given that there is no uncertainty and that monetary transfers are available, it follows that an optimal contract must maximize the total ex ante net benefits or surplus of the two managers,

$$B_1[a_1, \phi_1(q_1, q_2)] + B_2[a_2, \phi_2(q_1, q_2)]. \tag{2}$$

[11] Elsewhere we have considered the effect of date 0 contractibles for the special case in which no revisions of the date 0 contract are permitted at date 1 (see Grossman and Hart 1984). In the present model, however, in which revisions are allowed, the introduction of contractibles complicates matters greatly. With a contractible, not only can the parties agree on a schedule relating the payment from firm i to firm j to the contractible, but they can also agree on a way of revising this price schedule at date 1 according to messages manager i and manager j send reflecting the choice of the sunk investments a_1, a_2 (for an analysis of this in a special case, see Hart and Moore [1985]). With no contractibles, the payment from firm i to firm j at date 1 is just a constant, and any attempt to make it sensitive to the environment will fail since price revisions are a zero-sum game from the point of view of the buyer and seller.

It is useful to consider as a benchmark the first-best, where contrary to our assumptions above a_1 and a_2 are verifiable and q_1 and q_2 are ex ante contractible.

DEFINITION. Let a_1^*, a_2^*, q_1^*, and q_2^* be the (assumed unique) maximizers of $B_1 + B_2$ subject to $a_i \in A_i$, $q_i \in Q_i$ ($i = 1, 2$).

The first-best contract would state that manager i must choose a_i^* at date 0 and q_i^* at date 1 (if not he must pay manager j a large penalty) and would specify a monetary transfer between the two managers.

In fact it is possible to achieve the first-best as long as the q_i are ex ante contractible, even if the a_i are not. For if the date 0 contract specifies that $q_i = q_i^*$, party i has an incentive to choose a_i to maximize $B_i[a_i, \phi_i(q_1^*, q_2^*)]$, that is, to set $a_i = a_i^*$.[12] If neither the q_i nor the a_i are ex ante contractible, however, the first-best cannot generally be achieved, as we shall now see.

Under our simplifying assumption that no date 1 variables are contractible as of date 0, the contract will consist simply of an allocation of ownership rights and a transfer payment between the managers. There are three interesting cases to consider. In the first case, the firms remain separately owned or nonintegrated; that is, manager 1 owns and controls firm 1's assets and manager 2 owns and controls firm 2's assets. In the second case, firm 1 owns firm 2; that is, manager 1 owns and controls the assets of both firms (we call this firm 1 control). In the third case, firm 2 owns firm 1 (we call this firm 2 control). There is a fourth case in which manager 1 owns firm 2's assets and manager 2 owns firm 1's assets. This case appears less interesting than the others since it seems likely in practice to give a much lower level of surplus than case 1. We therefore ignore it in what follows.[13]

A. Case 1: Nonintegration

In this case manager 1 has the right to choose q_1 and manager 2 has the right to choose q_2 at date 1. It is useful to start at date 1 and work backward. At date 1, a_1 and a_2 are predetermined, and the only question concerns the choices of q_1 and q_2. If no further negotiation takes place, q_1 and q_2 will be chosen simultaneously and noncooperatively by managers 1 and 2 to maximize $\phi_1(q_1, q_2)$ and $\phi_2(q_1, q_2)$, respectively (since B_i is increasing in ϕ_i). We make the following assumption.

ASSUMPTION 1. There exists a unique pair $(\hat{q}_1, \hat{q}_2)$ satisfying: $q_1 =$

---

[12] This depends on our simplifying assumption that a_i does not affect B_j. The results presented below can be extended to the case of externalities in the a's without difficulty.

[13] There is also a class of more complicated contracts that make asset ownership at date 1 a function of messages the managers of firms i and j send after they have observed each other's investment decision. An example of this is an option to own contract. Our results are not affected by the existence of such contracts, and so for simplicity we ignore them.

$\hat{\mathbf{q}}_1$ maximizes $\phi_1(\mathbf{q}_1, \hat{\mathbf{q}}_2)$ subject to $\mathbf{q}_1 \in Q_1$, and $\mathbf{q}_2 = \hat{\mathbf{q}}_2$ maximizes $\phi_2(\hat{\mathbf{q}}_1, \mathbf{q}_2)$ subject to $\mathbf{q}_2 \in Q_2$.

In other words the game in which each manager i maximizes ϕ_i has a unique Nash equilibrium. Note the role of the separability assumption on B_i; it ensures that $\hat{\mathbf{q}}_1$ and $\hat{\mathbf{q}}_2$ are independent of $\mathbf{a}_1$ and $\mathbf{a}_2$.

Of course, given $\mathbf{a}_1$ and $\mathbf{a}_2$, the noncooperative equilibrium $(\hat{\mathbf{q}}_1, \hat{\mathbf{q}}_2)$ is unlikely to be ex post efficient in the sense of maximizing

$$B_1[\mathbf{a}_1, \phi_1(\mathbf{q}_1, \mathbf{q}_2)] + B_2[\mathbf{a}_2, \phi_2(\mathbf{q}_1, \mathbf{q}_2)]. \tag{3}$$

Therefore, the two parties can gain from writing a new contract at date 1 that specifies that $\mathbf{q}_1 = \mathbf{q}_1(\mathbf{a}_1, \mathbf{a}_2)$, $\mathbf{q}_2 = \mathbf{q}_2(\mathbf{a}_1, \mathbf{a}_2)$, where these are the maximizers of (3) (if there are several maximizers, choose any pair). We will use the notation $\hat{\mathbf{q}} \equiv (\hat{\mathbf{q}}_1, \hat{\mathbf{q}}_2)$ and $\mathbf{q}(\mathbf{a}) \equiv [\mathbf{q}_1(\mathbf{a}), \mathbf{q}_2(\mathbf{a})]$, where $\mathbf{a} = (\mathbf{a}_1, \mathbf{a}_2)$. The new contract is feasible since $\mathbf{q}_1$ and $\mathbf{q}_2$ are ex post contractible. It will specify a transfer price p that serves to allocate the gains from renegotiation. Because we do not want to get into the details of contract renegotiation, we shall simply assume that the parties split the increase in total surplus $50:50$; that is, the transfer price p satisfies

$$
\begin{aligned}
B_1\{\mathbf{a}_1, \phi_1[\mathbf{q}(\mathbf{a})]\} - p = {} & B_1[\mathbf{a}_1, \phi_1(\hat{\mathbf{q}})] + \tfrac{1}{2}(B_1\{\mathbf{a}_1, \phi_1[\mathbf{q}(\mathbf{a})]\} \\
& + B_2\{\mathbf{a}_2, \phi_2[\mathbf{q}(\mathbf{a})]\} - B_1[\mathbf{a}_1, \phi_1(\hat{\mathbf{q}})] \\
& - B_2[\mathbf{a}_2, \phi_2(\hat{\mathbf{q}})]) \equiv \xi_1(\mathbf{a}, \hat{\mathbf{q}}),
\end{aligned}
\tag{4}
$$

$$
\begin{aligned}
p + B_2\{\mathbf{a}_2, \phi_2[\mathbf{q}(\mathbf{a})]\} = {} & B_2[\mathbf{a}_2, \phi_2(\hat{\mathbf{q}})] + \tfrac{1}{2}(B_1\{\mathbf{a}_1, \phi_1[\mathbf{q}(\mathbf{a})]\} \\
& + B_2\{\mathbf{a}_2, \phi_2[\mathbf{q}(\mathbf{a})]\} - B_1[\mathbf{a}_1, \phi_1(\hat{\mathbf{q}})] \\
& - B_2[\mathbf{a}_2, \phi_2(\hat{\mathbf{q}})]) \equiv \xi_2(\mathbf{a}, \hat{\mathbf{q}}).
\end{aligned}
\tag{5}
$$

This is in fact the Nash bargaining solution. Note that most bargaining solutions will yield an ex post Pareto-optimal outcome given our assumptions that the parties have the same information and that bargaining (i.e., contract renegotiation) is costless (see, e.g., Rubinstein 1982). It should be clear from what follows that our results will generalize to many other divisions of the surplus.

We assume that $\mathbf{a}_1$ and $\mathbf{a}_2$ are chosen noncooperatively by the agents at date 0, taking into account the renegotiation at date 1, that is, with regard to the overall payoffs ξ_1 and ξ_2. A Nash equilibrium in date 0 investments is a pair $(\bar{\mathbf{a}}_1, \bar{\mathbf{a}}_2) \in A_1 \times A_2$ such that

$$\xi_1(\bar{\mathbf{a}}_1, \bar{\mathbf{a}}_2, \hat{\mathbf{q}}) \geq \xi_1(\mathbf{a}_1, \bar{\mathbf{a}}_2, \hat{\mathbf{q}}) \quad \text{for all } \mathbf{a}_1 \in A_1, \tag{6}$$

$$\xi_2(\bar{\mathbf{a}}_1, \bar{\mathbf{a}}_2, \hat{\mathbf{q}}) \geq \xi_2(\bar{\mathbf{a}}_1, \mathbf{a}_2, \hat{\mathbf{q}}) \quad \text{for all } \mathbf{a}_2 \in A_2. \tag{7}$$

The total ex ante surplus from the relationship in this equilibrium is then

$$B_1\{\bar{\mathbf{a}}_1, \phi_1[\mathbf{q}(\bar{\mathbf{a}})]\} + B_2\{\bar{\mathbf{a}}_2, \phi_2[\mathbf{q}(\bar{\mathbf{a}})]\}. \tag{8}$$

A sufficient condition for the existence of a Nash equilibrium in date 0 investments is that A_i is convex and ξ_i is concave in $\mathbf{a}_i$ ($i = 1, 2$).

We have seen how to compute total surplus in the case of nonintegration.[14] This will generally be less than the first-best level of surplus since the ex ante investments will be inefficient. To see this, note that the first-order conditions for a Nash equilibrium are

$$\frac{\partial \xi_i}{\partial \mathbf{a}_i} = \frac{1}{2} \frac{\partial B_i}{\partial \mathbf{a}_i} [\mathbf{a}_i, \phi_i(\hat{\mathbf{q}})] + \frac{1}{2} \frac{\partial B_i}{\partial \mathbf{a}_i} \{\mathbf{a}_i, \phi_i[\mathbf{q}(\mathbf{a})]\} = 0, \quad i = 1, 2, \quad (9)$$

where we are using the envelope theorem to eliminate remaining terms involving the ex post efficient $\mathbf{q}(\mathbf{a})$. This contrasts with the first-order conditions for the solution of (2),

$$\frac{\partial B_i}{\partial \mathbf{a}_i} \{\mathbf{a}_i, \phi_i[\mathbf{q}(\mathbf{a})]\} = 0, \quad i = 1, 2. \quad (10)$$

The inefficiency arises, then, because manager i puts 50 percent weight on the noncooperative outcome $\hat{\mathbf{q}}$, which is generally ex post inefficient, instead of all the weight on the cooperative outcome, which is ex post efficient; this is in spite of the fact that the noncooperative outcome never occurs! To the extent that the marginal and total benefits of $\mathbf{a}_i$ move in the same direction, the choice of the $\mathbf{a}_i$ can be substantially distorted. It is worth emphasizing that in this model all the inefficiency is due to the wrong choice of ex ante investment levels. The assumption of costless renegotiation ensures that there is no ex post inefficiency, and so if ex ante investments (more

---

[14] The reader may be concerned about our assumption that the manager can think clearly enough about $\mathbf{q}$ to solve (6) but that it is too costly to contract for $\mathbf{q}$ or design a mechanism to implement a particular $\mathbf{q}$. This assumption can be understood if we imagine that the noncontractible represents a special service that will be required of a firm at date 1 and that the type of service that is appropriate depends on the realization of a state of nature. Let there be N states of nature. The states are defined in such a way that state s requires the choice of activities from an M-dimensional space denoted by Q_s. The idea is that different activities are required for different states; i.e., while elements of Q_s, Q_t, $s \neq t$, are both M-dimensional Euclidean vectors, their coordinates refer to entirely distinct activities (different machines, e.g.). Further, in state s, the benefit function B is assumed to depend on the noncontractibles only through the chosen element $\mathbf{q}_s$ in Q_s, say $B = B(a, \mathbf{q}_s; s)$; if in state s some vector of activities in Q_t is chosen, $t \neq s$, no benefits are derived. Suppose in addition that we can normalize the spaces of activities so that $B(\mathbf{a}, \mathbf{q}_s, s) = B(\mathbf{a}, \mathbf{q})$, where $\mathbf{q}$ lies in a single space Q (where the coordinates of $\mathbf{q}$, of course, continue to refer to different activities in different states). Then, from an ex ante point of view, the manager, taking each s as equally likely, thinks of his objective as $B(\mathbf{a}, \mathbf{q})$, where $\mathbf{q}$ is a typical value assigned to the vector $\mathbf{q}_s$. Further, any element $\mathbf{q}$ in Q is contractible ex post (so that ownership has some value). However, to make $\mathbf{q}$ ex ante contractible, it would be necessary to specify different coordinates of $\mathbf{q}$ for each of the N states, and we assume that this is too costly.

precisely the noncontractible ones) are unimportant, the first-best can always be achieved.[15]

B. Case 2: Firm 1 Control

In this case firm 1 owns firm 2, and so manager 1 has the right to choose q_1 and q_2 at date 1. At date 1, manager 1 will now choose (q_1, q_2) to maximize ϕ_1 if no further negotiation takes place. We make the following assumption.

ASSUMPTION 2. There is a unique pair ($\bar{q}_1$, $\bar{q}_2$) such that ($\bar{q}_1$, $\bar{q}_2$) solves: maximize $\phi_1(q_1, q_2)$ subject to (q_1, q_2) $\in Q_1 \times Q_2$.

The pair ($\bar{q}_1$, $\bar{q}_2$) will generally not be ex post Pareto optimal, and so recontracting at date 1 will lead to the pair $q_1(a)$, $q_2(a)$, as in the case of nonintegration. *We will continue to assume that the parties split the gains from renegotiation 50:50.* That is, owning an additional firm increases a manager's bargaining power only by raising his status quo utility, that is, his utility in the event of no renegotiation (relative to given a_1 and a_2). Given the 50 percent sharing rule, manager i's final payoff is as in (4)–(5) with ($\bar{q}_1$, $\bar{q}_2$) replacing ($\hat{q}_1$, $\hat{q}_2$). The date 0 Nash equilibrium in investments and the final level of surplus are also defined as in the case of nonintegration, again with ($\bar{q}_1$, $\bar{q}_2$) replacing ($\hat{q}_1$, $\hat{q}_2$). Firm 1 control will generally lead to inefficient ex ante investments since ($\bar{q}_1$, $\bar{q}_2$) $\neq$ [$q_1(a)$, $q_2(a)$] (see [9]–[10]).

C. Case 3: Firm 2 Control

In this case, firm 2 owns firm 1, and so manager 2 has the right to choose q_1 and q_2 at date 1. Now, at date 1, manager 2 will choose (q_1, q_2) to maximize ϕ_2 if no further negotiation takes place. We make the following assumption.

ASSUMPTION 3. There is a unique pair ($\underset{\sim}{q}_1$, $\underset{\sim}{q}_2$) such that ($\underset{\sim}{q}_1$, $\underset{\sim}{q}_2$) solves: maximize $\phi_2(q_1, q_2)$ subject to (q_1, q_2) $\in Q_1 \times Q_2$.

This case is the same as the previous one with ($\underset{\sim}{q}_1$, $\underset{\sim}{q}_2$) replacing ($\bar{q}_1$, $\bar{q}_2$) everywhere. Again ex ante investments will generally be inefficient.

We consider now which of the three cases above represents the optimal ownership structure. We saw in (9) that the inefficiency in the a's is due to the fact that manager i puts 50 percent weight on the noncooperative solution ($\hat{q}_1$, $\hat{q}_2$)—which equals ($\hat{q}_1$, $\hat{q}_2$) under non-

[15] The result that the conflict over the division of surplus at date 1 can lead to a distortion in investment at date 0 is similar to the finding of Grout (1984). In Grout's model, however, investment expenditure is observable, there are no noncontractibles, and the inefficiency in ex ante investment results from the assumed impossibility of writing binding contracts.

integration, $(\bar{\mathbf{q}}_1, \bar{\mathbf{q}}_2)$ under firm 1 control, and $(\mathbf{q}_1, \mathbf{q}_2)$ under firm 2 control—instead of 100 percent on the cooperative solution $[\mathbf{q}_1(\mathbf{a}), \mathbf{q}_2(\mathbf{a})]$. It is clear, therefore, that if one of the pairs $(\hat{\mathbf{q}}_1, \hat{\mathbf{q}}_2)$, $(\bar{\mathbf{q}}_1, \bar{\mathbf{q}}_2)$, $(\mathbf{q}_1, \mathbf{q}_2)$ happens to be very close to $[\mathbf{q}_1(\mathbf{a}), \mathbf{q}_2(\mathbf{a})]$, there will be little inefficiency in the $\mathbf{a}$'s and the corresponding ownership structure will achieve approximately the first-best. Examples of this are provided in proposition 1.

PROPOSITION 1. (A) Suppose that ϕ_i depends primarily on $\mathbf{q}_i$ in the sense that $\phi_1(\mathbf{q}_1, \mathbf{q}_2) = \alpha_1(\mathbf{q}_1) + \epsilon_1\beta_1(\mathbf{q}_2)$, $\phi_2(\mathbf{q}_1, \mathbf{q}_2) = \alpha_2(\mathbf{q}_2) + \epsilon_2\beta_2(\mathbf{q}_1)$, where $\epsilon_1, \epsilon_2 > 0$ are small. Then nonintegration yields approximately the first-best, while firm 1 and firm 2 control generally do not. (B) Suppose that ϕ_2 hardly depends on $\mathbf{q}_1$ and $\mathbf{q}_2$ in the sense that $\phi_2(\mathbf{q}_1, \mathbf{q}_2) = \alpha_2 + \epsilon_2\delta_2(\mathbf{q}_1, \mathbf{q}_2)$, where $\epsilon_2 > 0$ is small. Then firm 1 control yields approximately the first-best, while nonintegration and firm 2 control generally do not. (C) Suppose that ϕ_1 hardly depends on $\mathbf{q}_1$ and $\mathbf{q}_2$ in the sense that $\phi_1(\mathbf{q}_1, \mathbf{q}_2) = \alpha_1 + \epsilon_1\delta_1(\mathbf{q}_1, \mathbf{q}_2)$, where $\epsilon_1 > 0$ is small. Then firm 2 control yields approximately the first-best, while nonintegration and firm 1 control generally do not.

To understand (and establish) part A, note that, under nonintegration, manager 1 chooses $\mathbf{q}_1 = \hat{\mathbf{q}}_1$ to maximize $\alpha_1(\mathbf{q}_1)$ and manager 2 chooses $\mathbf{q}_2 = \hat{\mathbf{q}}_2$ to maximize $\alpha_2(\mathbf{q}_2)$. If A holds, however, it is clear that in the limit $\epsilon_1 = \epsilon_2 = 0$ and $\hat{\mathbf{q}}_i$ is ex post efficient; that is, $[\mathbf{q}_1(\mathbf{a}), \mathbf{q}_2(\mathbf{a})]$ $= (\hat{\mathbf{q}}_1, \hat{\mathbf{q}}_2)$ for all $\mathbf{a}_1$ and $\mathbf{a}_2$. Hence (4)–(5) imply that in the limit $\mathbf{a}_i = \bar{\mathbf{a}}_i$ maximizes $B_i[\mathbf{a}_i, \alpha_i(\hat{\mathbf{q}}_i)]$, and so $\mathbf{a}_1 = \bar{\mathbf{a}}_1$ and $\mathbf{a}_2 = \bar{\mathbf{a}}_2$ are ex ante efficient. Therefore, by continuity, for ϵ_1 and ϵ_2 small, nonintegration achieves approximately the first-best.

Firm 1 or firm 2 control, in contrast, may lead to great inefficiencies in case A. Under firm 1 control, in the absence of renegotiation, manager 1 chooses $\mathbf{q}_1 = \hat{\mathbf{q}}_1$ to maximize $\alpha_1(\mathbf{q}_1)$ (which is ex post efficient) and $\mathbf{q}_2 = \bar{\mathbf{q}}_2$ to maximize $\beta_1(\mathbf{q}_2)$ (which is ex post inefficient). This means that in the limit $\epsilon_1 = \epsilon_2 = 0$, $\mathbf{a}_1$ is chosen efficiently, but $\mathbf{a}_2$ is chosen to maximize

$$\tfrac{1}{2}B_2[\mathbf{a}_2, \alpha_2(\bar{\mathbf{q}}_2)] + \tfrac{1}{2}B_2[\mathbf{a}_2, \alpha_2(\hat{\mathbf{q}}_2)], \tag{11}$$

which may be very inefficient if $\bar{\mathbf{q}}_2$ is far from $\hat{\mathbf{q}}_2$. Similarly under firm 2 control, $\mathbf{a}_2$ is chosen efficiently while $\mathbf{a}_1$ is not.

Parts B and C follow similarly. Under B, firm 2 cares little about $\mathbf{q}_1$ and $\mathbf{q}_2$, and so if firm 1 has control over these, it will make an approximately ex post efficient choice. This will in turn lead to approximately ex ante efficient choices of $\mathbf{a}_1$ and $\mathbf{a}_2$. Under C, firm 2 control over $\mathbf{q}_1$ and $\mathbf{q}_2$ leads to approximately efficient ex post and ex ante outcomes.

Proposition 1 says that if the noncontractibles $\mathbf{q}_l$ ($l = 1$ or 2) have a small effect on firm j's benefit B_j, it is efficient for firm i to control them. The reason is that, if firm j controls them, j will use these rights in such a way that i's ex ante expenditure is distorted, while if i owns them, there will be only a negligible distortion in j's investment (since j does not care about them). Note that j's ownership of $\mathbf{q}_l$ will lead to a serious distortion in i's expenditure only if $\partial^2 B_i[\mathbf{a}_i, \phi_i(\mathbf{q})]/\partial \mathbf{q}_l\partial \mathbf{a}_i$ is large, that is, if the marginal product of $\mathbf{a}_i$ is sensitive to $\mathbf{q}_l$. If $B_i[\mathbf{a}_i, \phi_i(\mathbf{q})] = f_i(\mathbf{a}_i) + \phi_i(\mathbf{q}_l)$, say, there is no distortion at all. To put it another way, proposition 1 tells us only that a particular ownership structure is optimal. It does not quantify the costs of being at a suboptimal structure. However, by choosing $(\partial/\partial \mathbf{q}_l)(\partial B_i/\partial \mathbf{a}_i)$ appropriately, we may easily construct examples in which this loss is extremely large.

REMARK 1. An interesting application of proposition 1 is to the special case in which one manager, manager 1, say, can run both firms by himself without any loss in efficiency (as in Aron [1984] and Mann and Wissink [1984]); that is, the firms may be engaged in complementary activities, and manager 1 may have some spare "capacity." This case can be captured by supposing that B_2 is approximately zero. We see from proposition 1 that under these conditions firm 1 control will dominate nonintegration or firm 2 control.

Proposition 1 deals with the special case in which the noncontractibles are important to one party but not to another. In general, both parties will care about the noncontractibles, and, as a result, each ownership structure will lead to a distortion in ex ante investments. The crucial question then is, Which ownership structure leads to the least significant distortion? Progress can be made in the analysis of this if we make some further assumptions. Recall that $B_i[\mathbf{a}_i, \phi_i(\mathbf{q}_1, \mathbf{q}_2)]$ is increasing in ϕ_i. We now make the following assumptions.

ASSUMPTION 4. Investment decisions are scalars and A_1, A_2 are intervals of the real line.

ASSUMPTION 5.

$$\frac{\partial^2 B_i}{\partial \phi_i \partial \mathbf{a}_i}[\mathbf{a}_i, \phi_i(\mathbf{q}_1, \mathbf{q}_2)] > 0.$$

That is, marginal benefit is high when average benefit is high.

ASSUMPTION 6.

$$\frac{\partial^2 B_i}{\partial \mathbf{a}_i^2}[\mathbf{a}_i, \phi_i(\mathbf{q}_1, \mathbf{q}_2)] < 0.$$

ASSUMPTION 7. The maximizers $\mathbf{q}_1(\mathbf{a})$ and $\mathbf{q}_2(\mathbf{a})$ of (3) are independent of $(\mathbf{a}_1, \mathbf{a}_2)$ in the relevant range; we write them as $\mathbf{q}_1^*$ and $\mathbf{q}_2^*$.

The fourth of these is a strong assumption. It says that the ex post efficient choice of the noncontractibles is independent of ex ante actions. The assumption is not reasonable if B_1 and B_2 are differentiable functions of the $\mathbf{q}$'s. However, it may hold if the $\mathbf{q}$'s take on only discrete values. In any case the argument that follows can be generalized to the case in which assumption 7 is violated, at the cost of additional complexity.

The first-order conditions for the choice of ex ante investment by the managers are given by (9), where we replace $\phi_i(\hat{q})$ by $\bar{\phi}_i = \phi_i(\bar{q}_1, \bar{q}_2)$, the prerenegotiation outcome. Given assumption 7, (9) therefore becomes

$$\frac{1}{2} \frac{\partial B_i}{\partial a_i} (\bar{a}_i, \bar{\phi}_i) + \frac{1}{2} \frac{\partial B_i}{\partial a_i} (\bar{a}_i, \phi_i^*) = 0, \tag{12}$$

where $\phi_i^* = \phi_i(q_1^*, q_2^*)$. On the other hand, the first-best investment decisions are characterized by

$$\frac{\partial B_i}{\partial a_i} (a_i^*, \phi_i^*) = 0. \tag{13}$$

Using assumption 5, we see that the left-hand side of (12) is positive (respectively negative) at $a_i = a_i^*$ if $\bar{\phi}_i > \phi_i^*$ ($< \phi_i^*$). Hence, by assumption 6,

$$\bar{a}_i \lessgtr a_i^* \quad \text{as} \quad \bar{\phi}_i \lessgtr \phi_i^*. \tag{14}$$

Proposition 1 dealt with the case in which one of the ownership structures gave rise to a $(\bar{q}_1, \bar{q}_2)$ very close to (q_1^*, q_2^*). Our concern now, however, is with cases in which $(\hat{q}_1, \hat{q}_2)$, $(\bar{q}_1, \bar{q}_2)$, and $(\underline{q}_1, \underline{q}_2)$ are all quite "far" from (q_1^*, q_2^*). We illustrate the situation in figure 1. The curve represents the efficient $\phi_2 - \phi_1$ combinations. We have drawn it to be continuous, but it could equally well be a set of discrete points. If firm 1 or firm 2 has control, the noncooperative outcome $(\bar{\phi}_1, \bar{\phi}_2)$ will lie on the efficiency frontier since one party controls q_1 and q_2. Under nonintegration, in contrast, the noncooperative outcome $(\hat{\phi}_1, \hat{\phi}_2)$ may well be highly inefficient because of the uncoordinated choice of (q_1, q_2).

We can use figure 1 to determine the nature of the investment distortions corresponding to the different ownership structures. Since $\bar{\phi}_1 > \phi_1^*$ and $\bar{\phi}_2 < \phi_2^*$, (14) implies that $\bar{a}_1 > a_1^*$ and $\bar{a}_2 < a_2^*$; that is, under firm 1 control, firm 1 overinvests relative to the first-best and firm 2 underinvests. On the other hand, since $\underline{\phi}_1 < \phi_1^*$ and $\underline{\phi}_2 > \phi_2^*$, (14) implies that, under firm 2 control, firm 2 overinvests relative to the first-best and firm 1 underinvests. Nonintegration is more complicated since the nature of the distortion depends on the relationship of $(\hat{\phi}_1, \hat{\phi}_2)$ to (ϕ_1^*, ϕ_2^*). However, if the outcome $(\hat{\phi}_1, \hat{\phi}_2)$ is highly inefficient—which seems plausible in a number of cases—it will quite likely lie to the southwest of (ϕ_1^*, ϕ_2^*), that is, $\hat{\phi}_1 < \phi_1^*$ and $\hat{\phi}_2 < \phi_2^*$. Hence in this case $\hat{a}_1 < a_1^*$ and $\hat{a}_2 < a_2^*$; that is, nonintegration leads to underinvestment by both firms.

It may be useful to put these results in words. Under firm i control,

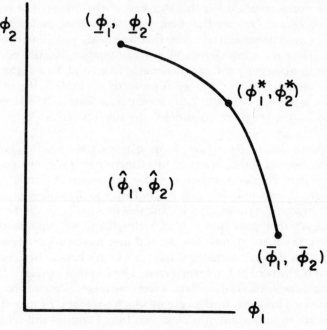

Fig. 1

firm i has a great deal of power ex post and hence will receive a high benefit in any date 1 renegotiation. Under assumption 5, however, high total benefits go together with high marginal benefits of investment, and so the consequence will be that firm i will overinvest. Firm j, on the other hand, with a low total and marginal benefit, will underinvest. Nonintegration, in contrast, gives both firms some power and will lead to moderate investment levels by each (note that, if $\hat{\phi}_2 > \bar{\phi}_2$ and $\hat{\phi}_1 > \underline{\phi}_1$, then $\hat{a}_2 > \bar{a}_2$ and $\hat{a}_1 > \underline{a}_1$; i.e., firm i's investment under nonintegration is greater than under firm j control).

The trade-offs should now be fairly clear. Firm 1 control will be desirable when firm 1's ex ante investment is much more important than firm 2's (so that firm 2's underinvestment under firm 1 control is relatively unimportant) and when overinvestment by firm 1 under firm 1 control is a less severe problem than underinvestment by firm 1 as in, for example, the nonintegrated solution. Firm 2 control will be desirable when firm 2's investment decision is much more important than firm 1's and when overinvestment by firm 2 is a less severe problem than underinvestment. Finally, nonintegration is desirable if a_1 and a_2 are both "important" in some sense, so that it is preferable to have both of them at a medium level than to have one very high and the other very low as under integration.

It is worth emphasizing that, because of the overinvestment problem, we cannot be sure that firm 1 control will be desirable even if firm 2's investment is irrelevant; that is, $\partial B_2/\partial \mathbf{a}_2 \equiv 0$. The overinvestment effect is a consequence of our assumption that the benefits B_j accrue to manager j and are inalienable from him. In a slight variant of our model, however, B_2, say, is perfectly alienable in the sense that there is a way for manager 1 to capture B_2 as long as he controls firm 2's assets. Under these conditions, the overinvestment effect disappears.

In particular, let $B_2 = f_2[\mathbf{a}_2, \phi_2(\mathbf{q}_1, \mathbf{q}_2)] - C_2(\mathbf{a}_2)$, where f_2 is a date 1 variable benefit and C_2 is a sunk investment cost. Imagine that, if firm 1 owns firm 2's assets, manager 1 has the option at date 1 of firing manager 2 and replacing him by another equally skilled manager at date 1 (training is unimportant), and this new manager can be offered a contract that pays him $-f_2$ (for simplicity, we suppose that the opportunity costs of both the old and new managers are zero). This means that if firm 1's manager has control, his benefit becomes $B_1 + f_2$; that is, the benefit f_2 is transferred. The fact that manager 2 will not receive f_2 will, of course, have a very adverse effect on his date 0 incentives. However, in the case in which manager 2's date 0 investments are unimportant, it is clear that firm 1 control will achieve the first-best since firm 1 will face the social objective function. We see then that the alienability of B_j and the irrelevance of $\mathbf{a}_j$ are jointly sufficient conditions for firm i control to be optimal.[16]

REMARK 2. One simplifying assumption we have made is that, when firm i owns firm j, it can control *all* the residual rights, $\mathbf{q}_j$. In reality, a subvector $\mathbf{q}_j^j$ of $\mathbf{q}_j$ may always remain under the control of manager j, say because manager j is the only person with the ability to control this particular aspect of the firm's operation. Our analysis can easily be generalized to this case. The main difference is that, even under integration, the prerenegotiation choice of $(\mathbf{q}_i, \mathbf{q}_j)$ will involve a lack of coordination by firms 1 and 2. Note that ownership rights are likely to be less important the more components of $\mathbf{q}_j$ remain under manager j's control. For example, suppose firm j is a law firm with a single lawyer and firm i is firm j's single client. Then if the client buys the law firm he may no more be able to get the lawyer to provide a special service than if the lawyer were in private practice. That is, the value of controlling firm j's assets may be very small in this case.

---

[16] In practice, the replacement of a manager may well be publicly observable and, hence, a contractible. So that we can stick with our framework in which there are no contractibles, we suppose that a replacement involves a move from one job to another in the company, which may not be verifiable (the manager may be "kicked upstairs" to a job with no perquisites, e.g.). That is, a replacement is part of the noncontractible $\mathbf{q}_2$.

IV. An Application

The main result of the last section can be stated as follows. If total and marginal benefits of investment move together, firm i ownership of firms i and j will lead to overinvestment by firm i and underinvestment by firm j. On the other hand, nonintegration will lead to moderate investment levels by each firm. The optimal ownership structure will be chosen to minimize the overall loss in surplus due to investment distortions. We now apply this result to the insurance industry.

Any real industry is, of course, far more complex than our model. One important difference is that in practice some variables will be contractible at date 0. We will therefore interpret our model with considerable latitude in what follows.

In the insurance industry some firms have a sales force that sells primarily its own company's products.[17] These companies are called direct writers, and their sales force may include employees (with virtually no ownership rights to office equipment) or agents who are independent contractors (who may own their office equipment and the building housing their agency office). Aside from the ownership of some office equipment, there are no major differences between employees and nonemployees; typically, both are on commissions, and the differences in commissions between the two types just reflect in an obvious way the differences in who bears office expenditures. However, in all cases direct writers are distinguished by the fact that the insurance company and not the agent owns the list of policyholders. Ownership of the list of policyholders entitles the insurance company to sell insurance to the policyholder if the agent terminates the relationship with the insurance company. Insurance company ownership of the list also means that the agent has no right to renew the insurance policy with a different company; he cannot leave the company and take his clients with him.

Insurance companies that are not direct writers sell insurance through independent agents and brokers (whom we will lump together as independent agents in distinction to the "captive" agents discussed above). The independent agents are distinguished by the fact that they, rather than the insurance company, own the list. An independent agent can sell any insurance company's product to his client. If the agent terminates his relationship with a particular insurance company, that company has no right to solicit the business from

[17] Our statements about the structure of the insurance industry are based on Strickler (1981), Webb et al. (1984), and conversations with professionals in the insurance industry. We are very grateful to Naava Grossman for her help in finding general information and data sources and for providing general information herself. We would also like to thank Peter Thistle.

the agent's list. Even without termination of the relationship, if the agent thinks that a client would be happier with the insurance of another company, the agent can encourage the client to change companies.

An insurance company has a number of expenditures that, given characteristics of the (contractible) commission structure to be explained below, can create ex post surplus between the insurance company and its agents or brokers. These expenditures include training of agents, client list-building expenditures (such as advertising), product development, and policyholder services. An insurance agent can have similar expenditures. To the extent that the efforts of the parties in generating these expenditures are not verifiable, they cannot be reimbursed directly without the creation of moral hazards. Instead the contract between the parties will specify payments as a function of observables, for example, commissions to the agent for policies produced for the insurance company.

We will use our framework to analyze the determinants of who owns the list of policyholders. (We assume that the agent does not want to own the whole insurance company.) Note that, since there is only one asset here (namely the client list), the choice is, in the language of our model, between firm 1 control and firm 2 control. Nonintegration has no meaning. To proceed, we must provide a model of the insurance industry. Space limitations permit only the simplest model. We assume that the agent devotes effort that is not verifiable to acquiring and keeping clients. The greater this effort, the more likely it is that a typical client will renew his insurance in the future, that is, that he will be persistent. Examples of such effort are the care with which the agent tailors the initial policy to the client's needs and the efficiency with which he deals with a claim once the policy is in force. Note that it is important for what follows that this effort yield dividends in the future, not just at the time when it is incurred; for example, a claim dealt with speedily today is likely to encourage the client to renew next year and the year after. To simplify the exposition, we assume that the agent can either "work" and produce only persistent clients or "not work" and produce only temporary clients, and that, if effort were verifiable, the insurance company would be prepared to compensate the agent for the extra effort of delivering persistent clients. An immediate implication of these assumptions is that, if the agent is paid a commission for the initial acquisition of the client and no later commission as a function of the persistence of the client, then the agent will deliver only temporary clients, and this is inefficient relative to the first-best. (Note that similar incentive problems will arise if some clients are naturally more persistent than others and the agent must devote extra effort to *finding* the more persistent clients; the analysis below applies also to this case.)

In order to induce the agent to produce persistent clients, the commission structure must be back-loaded to reward the agent's initial effort costs. Specifically, the agent must get an initial commission somewhat lower than the acquisition cost of a client but get renewal commissions that are in excess of the agent's servicing costs associated with obtaining the renewal; that is, the renewal premium must have some component of a reward for the effort of delivering persistent clients.

The back-loading of commissions, in and of itself, has no particular implication for who owns the list, unless there are noncontractibles. We will be concerned with two kinds of noncontractibles that could interfere with the commission structure above: (1) noncontractibles that can hurt the agent if the company owns the list and (2) noncontractibles that can hurt the company if the agent owns the list.

Important examples of type 1 have to do with the fact that the insurance company can make the product it is selling less competitive (e.g., by raising its price or lowering the quality of its services relative to other insurance companies) and hence make the client more likely to want to switch insurance companies. For example, an insurance company can decide that it does not want to insure automobiles in a particular region, so it raises its prices or lowers the quality of its services in that region. Or the insurance company can change the type and quality of its advertising, which affects the likelihood that a client will renew his policy. It is very difficult for an insurance company to write a contract with agents that specifies all the relevant ways in which, and contingencies under which, the company will support the competitive position of its particular products; that is, these actions really are noncontractible. Such noncontractibles can seriously distort the agent's effort decision if the firm owns the list and the commission structure is back-loaded. In particular, once the commission structure is back-loaded, the agent will lose the renewal premium and thus be unable to recover his cost of delivering persistent clients when the company takes actions that lead the client to want to switch insurance companies. On the other hand, if the agent owns the list, then the back-loading of the commission structure does not distort the agent's action because the agent can switch the client to another company when the first company is a bad match for the client. In the notation of our model, this is a case in which the q of the insurance company is very important for the agent's ex ante effort.

There are also type 2 noncontractibles, that is, noncontractibles that can hurt the company if the agent owns the list. First, if the company develops an unanticipated new insurance product, then the agent's clients cannot be solicited without the agent's permission when the agent owns the list. Second, when the agent owns the list, he can encourage his clients to switch to other companies if this seems advantageous (to him or to them). In some states of the world, such a switch may be efficient, but in other states it will merely increase the agent's profits at the expense of those of the company. The ability of the agent to switch customers in this way will distort the company's ex ante investments.[18]

So the trade-off between the different ownership structures is as in Section III. As in that section, we suppose that marginal benefits are small when average benefits are small. It follows that, if the company owns the list, the agent will have an insufficient incentive to deliver persistent clients; that is, he will underinvest in this activity. The company, on the other hand, will have at least the socially correct incentive to invest in list building and similar activities; that is, it will if anything overinvest in these activities. In contrast, if the agent owns the list, the company will underinvest in list building, but the agent will work hard to deliver persistent clients.

Further understanding about list ownership can be gained by considering what would happen if the reason for the back-loading of commissions disappeared. Recall that the back-loading was necessary because (*a*) the agent devoted nonverifiable effort to the servicing of clients and (*b*) the persistence of the client was sensitive to this effort. Much can be explained by noting that some kinds of insurance policies are more likely to be renewed than others, and this can make reason *b* much less of a factor. An example is "whole life" insurance. A life insurance policy will involve a longer-term contract than automobile insurance or fire and casualty insurance because a short-term policy gives very little protection to a person against the event that he will be sick but not die during the term of the life insurance policy and then be uninsurable thereafter. As a result, a life insurance customer has less of a tendency to switch insurance companies than does an automobile insurance customer. Moreover, to the extent that life insurance renewals do not occur, it is not because the agent has given the customer bad service on his claims! When renewals are relatively

---

[18] In each of the examples of noncontractibles we have indicated actions each party could take that would put the other party at a disadvantage. In some of these cases, e.g., the insurance company changing the support it provides to a given product, the noncontractible action does not involve direct manipulation of the item of which we are trying to explain the ownership, namely the client list. We have taken as given that the insurance agent does not want to own the whole insurance company. Hence the relevant variable that will allow the agent to increase his control over the renewal premiums to be generated by a particular client is the ownership of the list rather than direct control over the insurance company's marketing and product support program.

insensitive to the agent's actions, the commission structure need not be as back-loaded, and hence the argument for the agent to own the list is weakened. Further, even with some back-loading, to the extent that one company's q's do not affect the desire of a client to switch given that his insurance is a long-term contract, the agent has less need to own the list (see proposition 1).

Our analysis therefore predicts that, in products in which the renewal is not guaranteed and is sensitive to the agent's actions, the agent will be more likely to own the list, whereas in products in which the renewal is more certain and is less sensitive to the agent's actions, the company will be more likely to own the list. We now argue that these predictions are consistent with facts characterizing the insurance industry.

One important fact is that about 65 percent of the premiums in property-casualty insurance are generated by agents who own the client list, while in life insurance about 12 percent of the premiums are generated by agents who own the list.[19] Most property-casualty insurance is sold for a shorter term than most life insurance. Table 1 gives a more detailed breakdown for life insurance. It can be seen that term insurance is sold far more often by agents who retain list ownership than is whole life insurance. Note that term life insurance is for a period of a few years and then must be renewed. Hence the renewal is more important for term than for whole life insurance.

Another important fact is that there is great variation regarding list ownership among products in the property-casualty product area. For example, independent agents have a 47 percent share of the market for private passenger automobile liability insurance, while they have a 96 percent share of surety insurance (see Webb et al. 1984, 1:85–88). Marvel (1982) has shown that there is a positive correlation across property-casualty products between the importance of independent agents (as measured by their market share) and the size of an agent's client acquisition costs (as measured by advertising and other acquisition expenses). We think that this is some support in favor of our conclusion that the agent will own the list when the agent's marginal incentives are relatively important in generating the renewal.[20] Table 1 is suggestive of a similar point for life insurance.

---

[19] The property-casualty number comes from Webb et al. (1984, 1:85); the life insurance number is from Life Insurance Marketing and Research Association (LIMRA) (1977, p. 9) and is the fraction of premiums written by insurance brokers (as opposed to captive agents) in 1977 for the United States. The LIMRA study also estimates that brokers tend to specialize somewhat in term policies rather than whole life policies.

[20] Marvel (1982) offers an alternative explanation for the correlation. He argues that there are situations in which it is more efficient for the company to advertise than for the agent. In these situations, the insurance company helps bring the client to the agent. According to Marvel, an agent who did not have an exclusive dealings contract

TABLE 1

LIFE INSURANCE

Product	Importance of Agent List Ownership*
Substandard insurance	55.9
Term insurance	46.2
Group/pension	43.1
Whole life insurance	19.4

SOURCE.—Czepiec (1984), table 1.

NOTE.—An agent who uses a brokerage insurance company as the insurance provider for his client is an agent who is the owner of his client list. The percentage figure refers to agents who claim to "frequently" place their clients with a brokerage insurance company. A brokerage insurance company is an insurance company that uses independent "agents" who are called brokers because they do not have a legal agency relationship with the company but instead represent the client.

* Measured as percentage of agents who use brokerage companies to sell the indicated product.

The selling of substandard insurance and group/pension insurance involves substantial effort on the part of the agent to find an insurer that is a good match for the client. The willingness of the client to

---

with the insurance company could then switch the customer to another insurance company that does not advertise and thus can pay higher commissions. This argument faces the following difficulty. First, if the company advertises the *specific* benefits of *its* product, why should the customer allow the agent to switch him to another insurance company? Marvel seems to be assuming that the agent uses a "bait and switch" sort of tactic against his customers. Second, if the insurance company convinces the customer about the *general* benefits of insurance, then how does an exclusive dealings contract protect the insurance company? The customer will just go to a cheaper company that advertises somewhat less (which he can find in the Yellow Pages rather than through television). Another piece of evidence that Marvel presents in favor of his argument is that exclusive dealings companies tend to spend more on advertising than do companies without exclusive dealings contracts. This correlation is consistent with our explanation as well. If, for any reason, a company is assured of more policies per customer it acquires, then it may spend more on acquisition costs. Further, Marvel does not explain the fact that life insurance tends to be sold through captive agents far more frequently than property-casualty insurance. He also does not distinguish ownership of the renewal from exclusive dealings. A company can own the renewal without having an exclusive dealings contract. Industry sources are emphatic in pointing out that "the most important characteristic of the independent agency system in comparison with the exclusive agency system is the independent agent's 'ownership of renewals or expirations' " (Strickler 1981, p. 294). *The renewal plays no role in Marvel's argument.* Nevertheless, Marvel's argument can be modified to supplement ours as follows. First, an exclusive dealings contract is one method of enforcing list ownership rights. Second, if, unlike Marvel, we assume that the company is advertising the specific high quality of its agent force (e.g., "your State Farm agent is always available"), then an exclusive dealings contract would be a method of recovering the expenditures from its agents. Note that an insurance company that is involved in selling for a longer time than any one agent or customer has reputational incentives to choose agents of high quality so that its advertising is to some extent truthful. We would then argue that companies will have exclusive dealings contracts when they are better able to convince customers of the agent's quality than is the agent or they are able to select agents of high quality.

maintain his insurance coverage with the agent depends on the quality of the match. Hence the ownership of the list by the agent provides him with more protection from the noncontractible acts of the insurance company than he would receive with company list ownership and the back-loading of the commissions.

V. Conclusions

When two parties enter into a relationship in which assets will be used to generate income, the parties can, in principle, contractually specify exactly who will have control over each dimension of each asset in each particular future contingency. We have argued that there is often a low-cost alternative to contracts that allocate all specific rights of control. In particular, when it is too costly for one party to specify a long list of the particular rights it desires over another party's assets, then it may be optimal for the first party to purchase all rights except those specifically mentioned in the contract. Ownership is the purchase of these residual rights of control. Vertical integration is the purchase of the assets of a supplier (or of a purchaser) for the purpose of acquiring the residual rights of control.

The literature on transactions costs has emphasized that incomplete contracts can cause a nonintegrated relationship to yield outcomes that are inferior to those that would be achieved with complete contracts. It is implicitly assumed that integration yields the outcome that would arise under complete contracts. We argue that the relevant comparison is not between the nonintegrated outcome and the complete contract outcome but instead between a contract that allocates residual rights to one party and a contract that allocates them to another. We have emphasized the symmetry of control—namely, that when residual rights are purchased by one party they are lost by a second party—and this inevitably creates distortions. That is, integration shifts the incentives for opportunistic and distortionary behavior, but it does not remove these incentives.

Our model emphasizes the distortions, due to contractual incompleteness, that can prevent a party from getting the ex post return required to compensate for his ex ante investment. To the extent that the marginal and average values of investment move together, the allocation of ownership rights, by changing the average investment return, will affect the level of investment. We have seen that, if firm i owns firm j, firm i will use its residual rights of control to obtain a large share of the ex post surplus, and this will cause firm i to overinvest and firm j to underinvest. Under nonintegration, on the other hand, the ex post surplus will be divided more evenly, and so each firm will invest to a moderate extent. Integration is therefore optimal when one firm's investment decision is particularly important relative to the other firm's, whereas nonintegration is desirable when both investment decisions are "somewhat" important.

It should be noted, however, that contractual incompleteness can lead to other distortions. For instance, even if all ex ante investments can be verified and hence are reimbursable, residual rights may matter if the ex post distribution of the surplus is important for other reasons, for example, because of the risk aversion of the parties. An example is where manager 1 has an investment project but does not wish to finance it entirely himself since he would then bear all the risk. One possibility is to raise the funds externally from the market, which is risk neutral, say. The outside investors, who we suppose are led by manager 2, should then receive as their return a sizable fraction of the project's benefits. If manager 1 retains control of the project, however, he may be able to divert these benefits ex post from the investors to himself through his choice of noncontractibles, and knowing this, the investors may withhold some of their funds. In order to encourage outside investment, therefore, manager 1 may have to hand over some control to manager 2, for example, by giving him ownership rights over some of the assets.[21]

It should also be noted that if there is some barrier to ex post renegotiation, caused, for example, by the presence of transaction costs or asymmetric information, control of residual rights will be important in affecting the *size* of the ex post surplus as well as its *distribution* (even in the absence of ex ante investments). An analysis of the costs and benefits of ownership in this case may be found in Grossman and Hart (1984). A related idea is discussed by Farrell (1985).

Though we have emphasized residual rights of control over assets in order to explain who owns which assets, we can also use our theory to explain residual rights over actions. In particular, an employer-employee relationship differs from a contractor-contractee relationship in the allocation of residual rights of control over actions. An employer-employee relationship is typically characterized by the fact that many details of the job to be carried out are left to the employer's discretion; that is, the employer has many of the residual rights of control. In a contractor-contractee relationship, the job is specified in much greater detail, and the contractee typically has many of the residual rights of control over nonspecified actions. It may be useful in future work to apply our model to an analysis of the relative advantages of contractor-contractee and employer-employee relationships.

[21] We would like to thank John Minahan for a helpful discussion about this example.

It is worthwhile to consider which of the assumptions of the "Coase theorem" we drop in order to reach the conclusion that the distribution of ownership rights has efficiency consequences. The model of Sections II and III permits ex post bargaining of the type suggested in Coase (1960), but the ex ante efficiency of the relationship between the two parties will depend on how residual rights of control are allocated. The impossibility of ex ante bargaining over all aspects of the product to be delivered, that is, the incompleteness of the contract, is the source of our conclusion that the distribution of property rights has efficiency consequences.

References

Aɪon, Debra J. "Ability, Moral Hazard, and Firm Diversification, Part I." Mimeographed. Chicago: Univ. Chicago, Dept. Econ., May 1984.

Arrow, Kenneth J. "Vertical Integration and Communication." *Bell J. Econ.* 6 (Spring 1975): 173–83.

Chandler, Alfred D., Jr. *The Visible Hand.* Cambridge, Mass.: Harvard Univ. Press, 1977.

Coase, Ronald H. "The Nature of the Firm." *Economica* n.s. 4 (November 1937): 386–405. Reprinted in *Readings in Price Theory,* edited by George J. Stigler and Kenneth E. Boulding. Homewood, Ill.: Irwin (for American Econ. Assoc.), 1952.

———. "The Problem of Social Cost." *J. Law and Econ.* 3 (October 1960): 1–44.

Czepiec, Helena. "Measuring the Extent of Life Insurance Brokerage and Its Impact on Marketing Strategies." *Chartered Life Underwriters J.* (January 1984): 52–55.

Evans, David S., and Grossman, Sanford J. "Integration." In *Breaking Up Bell: Essays on Industrial Organization and Regulation,* edited by David S. Evans. New York: North-Holland, 1983.

Farrell, Joseph. "Allocating and Abrogating Rights: How Should Conflicts Be Resolved under Incomplete Information?" Mimeographed. Waltham, Mass.: GTE Labs, 1985.

Goldberg, Victor P., and Erickson, John E. "Long-Term Contracts for Petroleum Coke." Working Paper no. 206. Davis: Univ. California, Dept. Econ., September 1982.

Grossman, Sanford J., and Hart, Oliver D. "Vertical Integration and the Distribution of Property Rights." Mimeographed. Chicago: Univ. Chicago, Dept. Econ., 1984.

Grout, Paul A. "Investment and Wages in the Absence of Binding Contracts: A Nash Bargaining Approach." *Econometrica* 52 (March 1984): 449–60.

Hart, Oliver D., and Moore, J. "Incomplete Contracts and Renegotiation." Working Paper no. 367. Cambridge: Massachusetts Inst. Tech., 1985.

Holmes, Oliver Wendell. *The Common Law.* 1881. Reprint. Boston: Little, Brown, 1946.

Joskow, Paul. "Vertical Integration and Long-Term Contracts: The Case of Coal Burning Electric Generating Plants." *J. Law, Econ. and Organization* 1 (Fall 1985): 33–80.

Keren, Michael, and Levhari, David. "The Internal Organization of the Firm and the Shape of Average Costs." *Bell J. Econ.* 14 (Autumn 1983): 474–86.

Klein, Benjamin. "Transaction Cost Determinants of 'Unfair' Contractual Arrangements." *A.E.R. Papers and Proc.* 70 (May 1980): 356–62.

Klein, Benjamin; Crawford, Robert G.; and Alchian, Armen A. "Vertical Integration, Appropriable Rents, and the Competitive Contracting Process." *J. Law and Econ.* 21 (October 1978): 297–326.

Kreps, David M. "Corporate Culture and Economic Theory." Mimeographed. Stanford, Calif.: Stanford Univ., 1984.

Life Insurance Marketing and Research Association. "Brokerage Ordinary Life Insurance Production by Ordinary Agencies and Branch Offices, United States and Canada in 1977." Research Report 1979-3. Farmington, Conn.: Life Insurance Marketing and Res. Assoc., 1977.

Mann, Duncan P., and Wissink, Jennifer P. "Inside vs. Outside Production: A Contracting Approach to Vertical Integration." Manuscript. Philadelphia: Univ. Pennsylvania, Center Study Organizational Innovation, 1984.

Marvel, Howard P. "Exclusive Dealing." *J. Law and Econ.* 25 (April 1982): 1–25.

Rosen, Sherwin. "Authority, Control, and the Distribution of Earnings." *Bell J. Econ.* 13 (Autumn 1982): 311–23.

Rubinstein, Ariel. "Perfect Equilibrium in a Bargaining Model." *Econometrica* 50 (January 1982): 97–109.

Strickler, Nancy E., ed. *Marketing Life and Health Insurance.* Atlanta: Life Office Management Assoc., 1981.

Teece, David J. "Economies of Scope and the Scope of the Enterprise." *J. Econ. Behavior and Organization* 1 (September 1980): 223–47.

Telser, Lester G. "A Theory of Self-enforcing Agreements." *J. Bus.* 53 (January 1980): 27–44.

Waldman, Michael. "Worker Allocation, Hierarchies and the Wage Distribution." *Rev. Econ. Studies* 51 (January 1984): 95–109.

Webb, Bernard L.; Laumie, J. J.; Rokes, W. P.; and Baglimi, N. A. *Insurance Company Operations.* 3d ed. Malvern, Pa.: American Inst. Property and Liability Underwriters, 1984.

Williamson, Oliver E. "Hierarchical Control and Optimum Firm Size." *J.P.E.* 75 (April 1967): 123–38.

———. "The Vertical Integration of Production: Market Failure Considerations." *A.E.R. Papers and Proc.* 61 (May 1971): 112–23.

———. "Transaction-Cost Economics: The Governance of Contractual Relations." *J. Law and Econ.* 22 (October 1979): 233–61.

———. "Credible Commitments: Using Hostages to Support Exchange." *A.E.R.* 73 (September 1983): 519–40.

Williamson, Oliver E.; Wachter, Michael L.; and Harris, Jeffrey E. "Understanding the Employment Relation: The Analysis of Idiosyncratic Exchange." *Bell J. Econ.* 6 (Spring 1975): 250–78.

[14]

Vertical Integration and Long-term Contracts: The Case of Coal-burning Electric Generating Plants

PAUL L. JOSKOW
Massachusetts Institute of Technology

1. INTRODUCTION

What factors determine the institutional arrangements that govern supply relationships between input suppliers and their customers? Why are some transactions internalized through vertical integration? Why are many market transactions governed by complex long-term contracts? What determines the structure of such contracts and why are they used instead of simple spot market transactions? Over the past several years, a substantial amount of theoretical work has attempted to answer these questions. A much smaller quantity of empirical work devoted to testing alternative theories and expanding our understanding of vertical integration and contracting has appeared. Most of the empirical work has focused on examining the choice between vertical integration and "the market."[1] Empirical analysis of contracts has been minimal. Aside from Macaulay's classic paper and a recent paper by Goldberg and Erickson, most of the empirical analysis of contracts has been limited to examples based on interpretations of facts obtained from court decisions or secondary sources.[2] In this paper I provide a theoretical

I am grateful to Fred Dunbar, Victor Goldberg, Edmund Kitch, Oliver Williamson, Dick Schmalensee, Oliver Hart, and Steve Shavell for help and comments. I also want to thank National Economic Research Associates, Inc. for giving me access to its coal contract library.

1. Monteverde and Teece is an excellent example of this type of empirical work.
2. This is not to say that the examples have not been useful. The example presented by

Journal of Law, Economics, and Organization vol. 1, no. 1, Fall 1985
© 1985 by Yale University. All rights reserved. ISSN 8756–6222

34 / JOURNAL OF LAW, ECONOMICS, AND ORGANIZATION I:1, 1985

and empirical analysis of the structure of vertical arrangements governing coal supply transactions between electric utilities and coal suppliers.[3] I examine coal supply arrangements between electric utilities and coal suppliers in general but focus on the structure of these vertical relationships for mine-mouth coal plants.

Theoretical work devoted to the analysis of vertical arrangements has taken a number of different approaches.[4] I am particularly interested in what has been called the "transactions cost approach," which I attribute to Coase, Williamson, Klein, Goldberg, and others working in their tradition.[5] My plan in this paper is to use the transactions cost framework developed by these authors as the theoretical basis for analyzing coal supply arrangements and to make use of the empirical results to "test" the validity of the theory as a framework for understanding the structure of vertical relationships.

1.1. POTENTIAL BIASES

Before proceeding further it is useful to answer a question likely to be in the reader's mind. Why study coal supply arrangements involving electric utilities? Since the buyers in this case are subject to economic regulation by state and federal regulatory agencies, we are confronted with a potentially complicating set of incentives that would not arise in studying the supply arrangements of unregulated firms. My reasons are quite simple. Detailed knowledge of a variety of characteristics of buyers and sellers seems essential for applying and testing transactions cost theory empirically. I already possess considerable information about electric utilities, power plants, and coal markets as a result of earlier research. Furthermore, in part because they are regulated, there is a lot of information available about particular utilities, their power plants, and their coal supply arrangements. It is even possible to obtain a large set of actual coal supply contracts and related documents. The opportunity to analyze data at this level of microeconomic detail is extremely rare.

Nevertheless, it is necessary to be sensitive to potential biases in supply arrangements that may be caused by economic regulation. It is my belief that economic regulation of electric utilities (including both the incentive created by price regulation and the direct restrictions on mergers and acqui-

---

Klein, Crawford, and Alchian of the evolution of the supply relationship between General Motors and Fisher Body was instrumental in getting me interested in pursuing this project. Empirical studies of contract by Palay and by Masten have been published while this paper was in progress.

3. This is part of a larger project examining vertical relationships between electric utilities and input suppliers.

4. Some of the alternative approaches are discussed in Williamson (1983; 520–21) and Williamson (1984).

5. These papers include Coase (1937, 1972); Williamson (1971, 1975, 1979, 1983, and 1984); Klein, Crawford, and Alchian; Klein; Monteverde and Teece; and Goldberg.

sitions imposed by state and federal law) tends to discourage vertical integration. State regulators tend to be hostile to vertical integration and both state and federal regulators have, especially in recent years, treated the recovery of costs from captive (integrated) mines quite harshly.[6] There may be a similar bias against long-term contracts. The prospect of "automatic" pass-through of fuel costs through fuel adjustment clauses may also make electric utilities less responsive to the kinds of costs that motivate unregulated firms to adopt vertical arrangements that minimize costs.

I argue below that, particularly for mine-mouth plants, transaction cost theory implies that vertical integration or complex long-term contracts will be used to support exchange. Thus, data involving electric utilities are more likely to lead to rejection of the transactions cost theory than might otherwise be the case if one side of the transaction were not regulated. In an effort to at least partially control for any regulatory biases, I try to make comparisons between different types of electric generating plants. By making comparisons between supply arrangements for different types of plants with different transaction characteristics but subject to the same types of regulatory restrictions, I should be able to get a feeling for whether regulation is driving the results (in which case there should be no differences) or whether the transaction cost considerations hypothesized are important.

2. VERTICAL SUPPLY ARRANGEMENTS: AN OVERVIEW OF THE TRANSACTIONS COST APPROACH

In this section I provide a synthesis of what I take to be the primary theoretical foundations and implications of the transaction cost literature that I attribute to Coase, Williamson, Klein, Goldberg, and others. I have integrated ideas developed over time and across commentators and added my own interpretations.[7]

2.1. THE BASIC THEORY

Economic institutions (or governance structures) emerge to minimize the costs of making transactions. These costs include both ordinary production costs (land, labor, capital, materials, and supplies) that make up the components of a neoclassical cost function and certain transactions costs associated with establishing and administering an ongoing business relationship. These transactions costs (which are identified more completely below) are real economic costs that must be taken into account along with ordinary production costs in structuring cost-minimizing economic institutions.

6. See McGraw-Hilll (1981: 371–73), *Electrical Week*, August 23, 1982, and *Electrical Week*, April 5, 1982. Some state commissions and FERC have been paying increasing attention to purchases made from subsidiaries and purchases made under long-term contracts.

7. The primary references are contained in n. 5.

36 / JOURNAL OF LAW, ECONOMICS, AND ORGANIZATION   I:1, 1985

There exists a continuum of *potential* governance structures for vertical relationships. At one extreme we have vertical integration. At the other extreme we have Walrasian auction markets. In between we have a wide array of potential contracting institutions that mediate transactions through the market but involve the use of a variety of specialized contractual provisions that arise as a consequence of efforts by firms to minimize the total cost of transactions over time. The nature, magnitude, and institutional response to transactions costs depends upon particular identifiable characteristics of the transactions involved. Thus, specific combinations of transactional characteristics, as they interact with more conventional production opportunities, lead to predictable cost-minimizing organizational and contractual responses.

2.2. TRANSACTIONS COSTS AND TRANSACTION CHARACTERISTICS

Transactions costs include the following: costs of negotiating and writing contingent contracts; costs of monitoring contractual performance; costs of enforcing contractual promises; and costs associated with breaches of contractual promises. In each case these costs may include the costs of acquiring and processing information, legal costs, organizational costs, and costs associated with inefficient (in the neoclassical sense) pricing and production behavior.

There appear to be four important characteristics of transactions that have been identified as affecting the nature and magnitude of these transactions costs in important ways.[8] These include:

    a. the extent to which the contemplated transactions are characterized by uncertainty and complexity;

    b. the extent to which cost-minimizing transactions (in the neoclassical cost function sense) require one or both parties to a transaction to make durable transaction-specific (idiosyncratic) sunk investments;

    c. the extent to which there are diseconomies associated with vertical integration that must be traded off against transactions costs that arise when market transactions are relied upon (these may include economics of scale, scope, or learning associated with supplying similar inputs in multiple vertical supply relationships; they also include incentive and command and control costs associated with bringing additional activities

---

8. I believe that information asymmetries can and should be further integrated into this literature and added to the list. The transactions cost literature I focus on here has either ignored or placed in the background both information asymmetries and differences between agents in the costs of bearing risks. The principle-agent literature, which is concerned with related problems, relies on assumptions about information asymmetries and risk aversion, but ignores transaction-specific investments. See Holmstrom, Shavell, and Hart. It would be productive to integrate the two approaches, but this is well beyond the scope of this paper.

inside a firm that would not arise when "market" transactions are relied upon);[9]

d. the "frequency" of transactions or more generally reputational constraints.

As uncertainty and complexity become more important in a vertical relationship the expected costs of writing, administering, and enforcing full contingent contracts increases. When uncertainty and complexity are important it becomes uneconomical to write full contingent contracts, and "market contracts" will tend to be incomplete. A contract is incomplete in the sense that it does not specify unambiguously the obligations of each party in every possible state of nature.

Contractual incompleteness sets the stage for ex post performance problems. When contingencies arise that are not fully and unambiguously covered by formal contractual provisions, one or both parties to the transaction may have incentives to "behave badly" by taking actions that increase the costs or reduce the revenues that will be obtained by the other party. The anticipation at the contract formation stage that "bad behavior" will occur when certain contingencies arise affects the cost-minimizing structure of the initial vertical relationship.

The "bad behavior" that may occur has been termed "opportunism" by Williamson. As I understand it, opportunism refers both to behavior that does not maximize joint profits (and is inefficient) when a particular contingency arises and also behavior that involves the appropriation of wealth of one party by the other in some states of nature without necessarily inducing distortions in supply or demand. In either case, upon realization that opportunistic behavior may occur, the governance structure and the terms and conditions of any arrangement chosen are adjusted ex ante. Contracts that pose more serious hazards are provided with greater safeguards.

The theory generally assumes that markets are competitive ex ante (many buyers and sellers). Opportunism can emerge ex post because certain characteristics of the supply relationship give one or both parties to the transaction some monopoly power when certain contingencies arise. In most of the recent work in this tradition, the primary source of monopoly power is the presence of durable transaction-specific sunk investments (see below). However, there appears to be a natural relationship between opportunism in this sense and more conventional notions of moral hazard that arise because of information asymmetries.[10] In the latter case, incentive problems arise because one party to the transaction both can affect (uncertain) outcomes by his own behavior and has better (less costly) access to information about the

9. Thus there are both costs and benefits associated with internal production. Grossman and Hart provide an interesting analysis of this issue.

10. Holmstrom, Shavell, and Hart are excellent examples of the approach taken in this growing literature.

38 / JOURNAL OF LAW, ECONOMICS, AND ORGANIZATION I:1, 1985

causes of observed outcomes. The agent can exploit an information monopoly to its advantage.

Following the theoretical and empirical work in this tradition, I focus on durable transaction-specific sunk investments and largely ignore problems associated with information asymmetries and differences in the costs of bearing risk. Williamson (1983: 526) identifies four different types of transaction-specific sunk investments:

a. *Site specificity*: buyer and seller are in a "cheek-by-jowl" relation with one another, reflecting ex ante decisions to minimize inventory and transportation expense.

b. *Physical asset specificity*: when one or both parties to the transaction make investments in equipment and machinery that involves design characteristics specific to the transaction and which have lower values in alternative uses.

c. *Human-capital specificity*: arising as a consequence of learning-by-doing, investment, and transfer of skills (specific human capital) specific to a particular relationship.

d. *Dedicated assets*: general investments that would not take place but for the prospect of selling a significant amount of product to a particular customer. If the contract is terminated prematurely, it would leave the supplier with significant excess capacity.

Given contractual incompleteness due to uncertainty and complexity, as durable transaction-specific investments become more important, the transactions costs associated with mediating vertical relationships using conventional "spot markets" increase. Very simply, the argument is that transaction-specific sunk investments generate a stream of potentially appropriable quasi-rents equal to the difference between the anticipated value in the use to which the investments were committed and the next best use. The presence of transaction-specific investments creates incentives for one party to "hold up" the other ex post and can lead to costly haggling. When transaction-specific investments are important, governance structures will emerge ex ante to reduce the incentives either party has to exploit them ex post. Considerable emphasis has been placed on the proposition that vertical integraion is more likely to emerge when cost-minimizing (in the neoclassical sense) transactions involve durable transaction-specific sunk investments. Williamson's recent work and a great deal of Klein's work, however, consider contractual alternatives to vertical integration where transactions costs are important. If vertical integration is not economical because of diseconomies associated with internal production, contractual arrangements to govern exchange between independent agents will emerge to economize on these transactions costs. The structure of these market contracts will reflect efforts to create incentives and restrictions that reflect anticipted performance problems so that agents will perform as initially promised when different contingencies arise.

The theory also assumes that there is a strong incentive to structure contracts to minimize reliance on the legal system (which is costly and confronts grave difficulties in distinguishing promised behavior from "bad behavior") and therefore to structure vertical arrangements to achieve a "private ordering" that does not rely on legal enforcement. Nevertheless, people do sue one another for breach of contract, and various rules for defining breach and calculating damages exist (Muris). Thus, contractual arrangements should at least evolve in the shadow of the law, with recognition that court enforcement remains an option. Opportunities to specify contractual agreements in a clear and unambiguous way so as to strengthen the credibility and reduce the costs and uncertainty of legal sanctions should be taken advantage of.

The reliance of vertical integration is constrained by any diseconomies that may be associated with it. A supplier of some input that involves transaction-specific investments, for example, may achieve economies as a consequence of engaging in similar types of transactions with other buyers. There may be economies of scale associated with shared inputs across transactions or learning economies associated with repetitive production in many separate relationships. Internal incentive and command and control problems may limit the economic desirability of vertical integration.

Finally, the market may provide a natural deterrent to agents behaving badly and eliminate the need to rely on either vertical integration or complex "non-standard" contracts. There is a potential cost to breaches of written or implied contractual promises: the loss of future business from either this buyer or other buyers. In markets where buyers and sellers frequently engage in similar types of transactions, and where it is possible at low cost to distinguish "bad behavior" from "promised behavior" (perhaps combined with bad luck), reputational constraints will mitigate hold-up incentives and allow agents to more comfortably use simple auction markets, recognizing that the market provides penalties for inefficient behavior. These considerations may help to explain Macaulay's findings regarding the informality of contracts in business.

3. OVERVIEW OF U.S. COAL MARKETS

The primary market for coal today is the electric power industry, which accounts for more than 80 percent of domestic coal consumption. The second most important source of coal demand is coke plants (about 10 percent), which produce coke for the iron and steel industry. All other industrial consumers in the aggregate account for most of the remainder, with a small amount of coal continuing to be used in the residential/commercial sectors (see table 1). Coal is used to generate more than 50 percent of the electricity produced in the U.S. and accounts for more than 70 percent of fossil fuel utilization.

Coal reserves are not distributed uniformly across the country in terms of either quantity or quality. The Bureau of Land Management divides the

Table 1. U.S. Coal Consumption by Sector, 1980 and 1982

	1980		1982	
Sector	Tons (millions)	%	Tons (millions)	%
Electric utilities	569	81	594	84
Coke plants	67	10	41	6
Other industrial	60	9	64	9
Residential/commercial	6	1	8	1
	702		707	

SOURCE: *Quarterly Coal Report*, U.S. Department of Energy (DOE/EIA-0121), September 1983.

country into more than twenty coal-producing districts, but the bulk of the coal supplies are conveniently grouped into a handful of areas: the Appalachian region, the Interior (Midwestern) region, the Western region (often divided into the North Plains and Mountain regions), and Texas. Historically, most of the coal produced came from the Appalachian and Midwestern regions. Coal production in the Western region has increased dramatically in the past decade, reflecting the attractive economics of large strip-mining operations, declining productivity and labor problems in the East that increased costs, and an increasing demand for low-sulfur coal to meet air pollution restrictions.

There are substantial differences between the regions in terms of coal quality and optimal mining techniques and scale. Coal in the Appalachian region generally has a high BTU content, a sulfur content that varies from 1 to 3 percent, and ash content that varies from 10 to 15 percent (see table 2). The coal in the Interior region generally has a lower BTU content and a higher sulfur content. There is relatively little low-sulfur (1 percent or less) coal in the Midwest. Coal in the Western region varies widely in BTU content and ash content, with average BTU content significantly lower than the other regions. But Western coal generally has a very low sulfur content and relatively low mining costs (see below), making it especially attractive in midwestern states subject to sulfur emissions restrictions despite high transport costs. The coal being produced in Texas is almost all lignite, with low BTU content, low sulfur, and high ash content.

Topography and the nature of coal deposits affect the optimal type and scale of mining, and these characteristics also vary significantly among the regions. In Appalachia, underground mining accounts for about 60 per-

VERTICAL INTEGRATION AND LONG-TERM CONTRACTS / 41

cent of production and underground mines are relatively small (see table 3). Underground mines in the East appear to have relatively small minimum efficient scales (MES) (Zimmerman: 17–36), although the observed size distribution is somewhat misleading since it contains a large number of old and marginal mines which are very small. The topography of the Appalachian region makes necessary the use of relatively small mobile machinery for surface mining (Zimmerman: 26) and the MES of a strip-mining operation here is also relatively small.

In the Midwest, surface mining accounts for about 70 percent of coal production and both underground and surface mines are much larger than in the Appalachian area. The topography of the Interior region makes it eco-

Table 2. Regional Coal Characteristics, 1982 Production

Region/state/BLM district	BTU/lb	% sulfur	% ash
Appalachian			
Alabama	12,154	1.3	11.8
Georgia	12,338	1.5	11.7
Ohio	11,565	3.3	12.5
Pennsylvania			
1	12,228	1.9	14.5
2	12,233	2.0	12.1
Tennessee			
8	12,349	1.5	10.9
13	12,293	0.9	12.3
Virginia			
8	12,592	1.0	10.9
West Virginia			
3	12,708	2.3	10.7
6	12,109	3.9	11.4
8	12,213	0.9	11.8
Kentucky/East	12,184	1.1	10.6
Interior			
Illinois	10,959	2.7	10.2
Indiana	10,942	2.6	10.2
Kentucky/West	11,446	3.2	11.2
Missouri	10,276	4.8	17.1
Kansas	10,463	4.7	20.7
Texas	6,445	0.8	15.5
Western			
Wyoming	8,686	0.4	6.2
Montana	8,958	0.6	6.8
New Mexico	9,342	0.7	19.0
North Dakota	6,590	0.6	8.2
Utah	11,643	0.5	10.3
Washington	8,100	0.8	15.7

SOURCE: *Cost and Quality of Fuels for Electric Utility Plants*, U.S. Department of Energy (DOE/EIA-0191(82). August 1983, table 53.

42 / JOURNAL OF LAW, ECONOMICS, AND ORGANIZATION I:1, 1985

Table 3. Underground and Surface Mining by Region, 1982

Region	% Underground	Annual output per mine	
		Underground	Surface
Appalachian	60	138,900	100,003
Interior	30	760,590	411,650
Western	11	441,810	2,646,040
U.S. total	40	170,040	242,540

SOURCE: Calculated from *Coal Data (1981/82)*, National Coal Association, II–11 and II–12.

nomical to use larger equipment and to better exploit economies of scale in strip mining than in the East. The MES of surface mines is larger in the Midwest as a result. In the Western region almost all of the coal comes from large strip mines (most of the underground mining takes place in Utah and Colorado). The topography and the nature of the deposits permits the use of large draglines and shovels, allowing fuller exploitation of surface-mining scale economies and larger MES (Zimmerman: 24–35). Surface mines are generally substantially more capital intensive than underground mines, and surface-mining technology seems to be characterized by substantial scale economies.

The bulk of the coal produced (about 75 percent) is carried by railroad (sometimes in conjunction with barge transport) (National Coal Association, 1984: 28). Transportation costs account for a large part of the delivered costs of coal on average. About half of the coal transported by rail is shipped by unit trains consisting of 100 or more specialized cars (often owned or leased by the utility buying the coal). Unit train shipments are generally acknowledged to be the most economical way of moving large volumes of coal by train. About 20 percent of the coal transported is carried by inland barges for at least part of the trip. Trucks account for a small part of the "mine-to-market" transportation but are used at both the loading end and the receiving end of the trip to collect and distribute coal (National Coal Association, 1984: 29). Coal slurry pipelines are a fourth transport option, but only one is currently operating.

Transportation opportunities vary from region to region. There appears to be more inter- and intra-mode competition in the East than in the West. For coal produced in the Interior and Western regions, rail transportation is essentially the only alternative to mine-mouth operations. Many of these producing areas must rely on one or perhaps two railroads to move coal out of these areas, and direct rail linkages between coal fields and potential load centers often do not exist.

Overall, most analysts have concluded that the coal supply market is quite competitive in the ex ante bidding sense used by Williamson (Gordon: 67–69). Concentration in mining and reserve ownership is low and entry ap-

VERTICAL INTEGRATION AND LONG-TERM CONTRACTS / 43

pears to be relatively easy. Any monopoly problems are generally attributed to the railroads.

4. COAL SUPPLY ARRANGEMENTS FOR ELECTRIC GENERATING PLANTS AND TRANSACTION-SPECIFIC INVESTMENTS

When a utility considers building a new base-load generating plant it must make a number of interrelated decisions.[11] The most important decisions that must be made concern the following:

1. How large should the generating unit(s) be?
2. What type of fuel should they burn?
3. Where should the plant be located?
4. How should the generating unit's boiler be designed to minimize expected fuel costs over the life of the unit?
5. If a coal burning plant is built, what types of coal will the plant utilize, what is it likely to cost, and where is this type of coal likely to come from?
6. How will the coal be transported from the mine to the plant and what are the expected costs of transportation?

For purposes of discussion here we will assume that the optimal size of the generating units has been determined and that a decision has been made to utilize coal as the primary fuel for generating electricity in the plants that are built. In the spirit of transaction cost theory we first consider the cost minimizing options that utilities have in each of the remaining dimensions given the "ordinary" or neoclassical cost opportunities they face. We then discuss the importance of transaction-specific investments associated with four "stylized" cost minimizing investment/coal procurement strategies and the associated implications for the choice of governance structure to support cost minimizing exchange in each case.

A utility considering building a new coal plant can choose between two primary locational strategies. It can build a plant (independently or jointly with other utilities) in or near its own service territory, reflecting the electrical requirements of its system, land and cooling water availability, transportation facilities, etc., and arrange for transportation of the coal from one or more mines to the plant. This has been the approach taken for most operating coal plants. Alternatively, the utility can build (itself or jointly with other utilities) a plant adjacent to coal reserves from which coal will be mined for that plant, with effectively zero coal transportation costs, and then use a high

---

11. A base-load unit is a unit that is designed to operate at full capacity throughout the year, regardless of variations in total system demand. Demand variations are accommodated with "cycling" or "peaking" units. Almost all coal-burning units are designed to operate as base-load units for a substantial fraction of their useful lives, on the order of twenty years.

44 / JOURNAL OF LAW, ECONOMICS, AND ORGANIZATION I:1, 1985

voltage transmission system to transport the power from the supply point to load centers. Such plants are referred to as mine-mouth plants. For utilities whose service territories are far from coal-mining areas, the choice between these two alternatives is quite discrete. Obviously, however, a utility whose electric loads are also close to coal-producing areas can take advantage of the best of both alternatives.

The decision to choose one locational strategy rather than another (ignoring transactions costs) depends on the prices of coal at the mine in different locations, the availability and costs of coal transport alternatives, the costs and institutional constraints associated with the transmission of electricity, and any institutional constraints affecting the ownership and operation of coal units in states other than those in which the utility is chartered to provide service.

A generating unit is typically designed optimally to burn coal with particular characteristics (BTU content, sulfur content, ash content, chemical composition, grindability, etc.). The use of coal that differs from the design specifications of a plant can lead to a loss in thermal efficiency or to increases in plant outages and maintenance costs. Exactly how tightly a plant is designed is, within some range, a variable of choice for the utility. The design decision depends on a utility's anticipated fuel procurement strategy, the variation in coal quality in the areas from which the utility is likely to purchase coal, the quantities of different types of coal available in these areas and the number of suppliers producing it, and the costs of building more fuel flexibility into the plant. For a mine-mouth plant, the design is necessarily governed by the characteristics of the coal in the areas adjacent to the plant.

In general, cost-minimizing coal procurement strategies and plant design are intimately related. A utility could plan to buy coal for a plant through spot market purchases or short-term contracts from a wide variety of different suppliers. If this strategy is chosen, boiler design flexibility is likely to be an important consideration, unless coal in the areas where the utility anticipates buying in this way is of fairly uniform quality. At the other extreme a utility could plan to purchase all of its coal requirements from one specific mine over the life of the plant. In this case, the plant could be designed optimally to burn coal with the characteristics expected to be available from this mine. Intermediate strategies involving more or less burning flexibility and more or less flexibility in procurement can also be pursued. A utility can choose to purchase from existing mines that are already supplying coal for other utilities and plants or contract in advance from a mine that has not yet been developed.

The cost-minimizing coal procurement strategy will depend on a number of factors. The expected f.o.b. price of coal in various areas is a primary consideration, along with the expected costs of transporting coal from the mines to the plant. Air pollution restrictions are likely to sharply constrain the kinds of coal that some utilities can burn economically. The economics of mining is likely to affect coal procurement strategies as well. If there are substantial economies of scale in mining, a utility may be able to reduce its coal costs by committing itself to purchase all of its coal from one large mine.[12] If economies of scale in mining are not important, there is little advantage to doing so. The availability of alternative transportation opportunities may also affect the strategy.

If the decision is made to build a mine-mouth plant, the location, design, and coal procurement strategy generally go hand in hand with one another. The plant is consciously located near specific coal reserves, is designed to optimally burn coal of the quality that will be mined there, and the utility expects to acquire coal for the plant from one or more adjacent mines over a large portion of the expected life of the plant.

There are numerous possible combinations of plant design strategies, coal procurement strategies, and transportation strategies that are possible. Let me identify four stylized cases for further discussion.

Case 1: The utility expects to purchase coal from a large number of existing suppliers located at different points in a fairly large geographical area through spot market purchases and simple short-term contracts. The elasticity of supply of coal of like quality from this general area is fairly high and numerous utilities are active in purchasing coal there. The identity of the particular mines from which coal is purchased is not of any importance to the utility. It anticipates making transportation arrangement with a variety of railroads and barge companies, contracting for delivery as it contracts for coal. It designs its plant with enough flexibility to accept coal of the variable quality that would be available from any of the mines in the general area.

Case 2: The utility expects to purchase coal from a relatively small number of existing mines located close to one another and producing similar types of coal. The mines currently supply coal to other utilities. To economically meet the anticipated demand the mines must make modest investments to increase their capacity. The utility expects to rely on these mines for several years but anticipates the possibility of switching suppliers, sub-

---

12. My reasoning here is related to Williamson's notion of dedicated assets. The development of a mine requires durable investments. The mine operator chooses both an optimal level of capacity and an optimal mining technique to meet expected demand. Mining techniques vary in capital intensity. More capital-intensive techniques are optimal at larger scales, other things equal. Without a long-term commitment by buyers to take specific quantities, the mine operator will treat nominal contract demand as being uncertain with an expected value that is less than the nominal contract demand. Mine capacity and mining technique will be chosen to reflect this expected demand and the unit cost of coal and prices determined based on this expected demand. If a buyer can commit itself to a firm demand equal to the nominal demand, it can induce the mine operator to expand capacity, reducing unit costs. Some of the savings can be passed along as a lower price than would otherwise prevail if the contract demand were treated as being uncertain. The more significant the scale economies, the greater the associated price reduction.

46 / JOURNAL OF LAW, ECONOMICS, AND ORGANIZATION I:1, 1985

ject to contractual restrictions, if economic opportunities arise to do so. It anticipates relying on two different railroads to transport the coal, but alternative transportation arrangements can be made at a small cost penalty. Other suppliers of coal of this quality in proximate areas exist, but the elasticity of supply in the short run is very low. The longer-run supply elasticity is fairly large, however. The utility designs its boiler to burn coal of the type available from these two mines, applying tighter design specifications than in the case above. It recognizes that switching suppliers may make it difficult to obtain coal with the same characteristics as its initial suppliers but coal quality is sufficiently uniform in the areas where alternative suppliers are likely to be located that coal quality deviations can be accommodated with only small increases in costs.

Case 3: The utility anticipates obtaining supplies from one or two specific mines for the life of the plant. The mines are currently in operation but will make substantial investments to increase capacity in anticipation of these purchases. The quantities of coal that the utility expects to purchase do not exhaust the economic capacity of these mines, and the mine owners eventually anticipate making sales to other utilities at similar prices. There are very limited supplies available in the short run from other mines in this area, and coal quality varies widely from mine to mine in the same general geographical area. The utility anticipates relying on a single railroad to transport the coal and plans to invest in unit trains to carry the coal on this railroad's tracks. The plant is designed with tight specifications to optimally burn the coal from these mines including specific investments in pollution control equipment.

Case 4: The utility builds a mine-mouth plant and anticipates obtaining all supplies from one or two adjacent mines. The plant is designed specifically to optimally burn coal from these mines. The mine would not be built but for the existence of the plant, and opportunities to sell coal at the same price to other buyers is uncertain. The utility makes extensive investments in transmission capacity to move the power from mine to load centers.

These four cases involve very different degrees of transaction-specific investments. In the first case, the buyer makes specific investments to design its plant to burn coal of the quality produced in a fairly large geographical area, but the value of the investments would not be reduced by shifting suppliers on short notice since there is an elastic supply of coal of similar quality available from this area. Multiple transport options combined with ease of shifting suppliers does not make the value of the plant economically dependent on the behavior of a particular railroad. Suppliers have not made investments specific to the purchases of this particular plant or utility. None of the four potential types of transaction-specific sunk investments seem to be important.

In the second case, transaction-specific investments are likely to be somewhat more important. The plant has tighter design specifications. Sudden switching of suppliers could be costly because the elasticity of supply is small, although if appropriate notice is given additional mining capacity can be brought into production to satisfy additional demand at approximately the same price. Only two railroads are utilized, but alternative transport options are available at a small increase in cost. The suppliers have made some investments in direct response to the anticipated demand of this utility, but the associated mines are already operating, and alternative purchasers of the coal would probably emerge with some lag. Thus, the power plant investment is characterized by some physical asset specificity and some of the mining investments may fall into the dedicated assets category.

In the third case, transaction specific investments are much more important. The utility has designed its plant to burn coal from a particular mine. It has invested in unit trains to transport that coal. The mine owners will make investments to increase the capacity of the mine almost completely as a response to the expected demand by this utility. The utility effectively ties itself to a single transport option, although by owning the rail cars that will carry the coal it has some control over the availability of transportation and simplifies the problem of writing a contract for transport services with the railroad. In this case the investment in the plant is characterized by a greater degree of physical asset specificity. The mining investment has the character of a dedicated asset. Although the vertical relationship is not of the "cheek-by-jowl" nature implied by the concept of site specificity, the existence of a single railroad and utility investments in rolling stock to be used on that railroad seem to lead to a similar result.

The fourth case is a mine-mouth plant and is characterized by at least three of the four types of asset specificity identified by Williamson: (a) site specificity—the plant and mine are deliberately located next to one another to minimize costs; (b) physical asset specificity—the plant is designed to burn the particular types of coal located in the adjacent reserves; and (c) dedicated assets—the mine would not be built but for the promise of purchases from the adjacent plant, and the plant would not be built but for the availability of coal from the adjacent mine.[13] Human (or organizational) asset specificity "that arise in a learning-by-doing fashion" as identified by

---

13. The importance of dedicated assets is made clearly by one of the contracts for a mine-mouth plant that is analyzed below.

Buyers will construct, own and operate a coal fired steam-electric generating plant . . . adjoining coal lands of Seller, based upon the assurance of a dependable supply of coal of specified quality and characteristics for the useful life of the plant.

The Buyers would not design and construct a plant of this type [at this site] . . . but for the availability of a dependable supply of coal from seller through December 31, 2019. . . .

It is essential to the Seller, because of the substantial capital investment it must make in order to have the capability to supply Buyers' requirements, that buyers purchase all of their coal requirements for said plant from Seller. (From the coal supply agreement between the five joint owners of units 3 and 4 of the Colstrip generating plant in Montana and Western Energy Company, dated July 2, 1980.)

48 / JOURNAL OF LAW, ECONOMICS, AND ORGANIZATION I:1, 1985

Williamson may also be important especially with regard to coordination between the plant operator and the mine operator, but I will not treat this fourth form of asset specificity in this discussion.

Let us consider the implications of asset specificity for the optimal choice of governance structure in each case, assuming for now that contracts will be incomplete and reputational constraints are not important (we look at these issues in more detail below as part of the detailed analysis of mine-mouth plants). According to transaction cost theory, other things being equal, the potential for opportunism should vary directly with the importance of transaction specific investments. These problems of opportunism should in turn affect the nature of the contractual relationships between buyers and sellers. In case 1 opportunism should be minimal and reliance on spot market purchases and simple contracts should be adequate. In case 2, there is a potential for opportunistic behavior by the buyer and the seller, but this is sharply constrained since transaction-specific investments are modest. Alternatives to spot market transactions and simple short-term contracts are likely to be desirable to provide some protection for buyers and sellers from ex-post hold-up problems. Vertical integration is not a viable option, however, given the procurement strategy of the utility. In case 3, both the buyer and the seller make transaction-specific investments and opportunism is potentially quite serious. The potential for the railroad to act opportunistically is another real complication. Long-term contracts with extensive protection for both the buyer and the seller from opportunistic behavior is suggested. Vertical integration is a possibility, although if the utility also sinks investments in the mine the railroad's incentives to hold it up may be even greater. Long-term coal supply contracts with utility performance contingent on performance of the railroad may be desirable.

Asset specificity appears to be most important for mine-mouth plants and opportunism potentially the most severe. Such plants appear to be prime candidates for the use of complex long-term contracts or vertical integration to support exchange.

In the case of mine-mouth plants we can assume that neoclassical cost considerations led to this locational choice, and we can examine the choice of governance structures that have been made in response to the associated transaction cost considerations. For other plants, we have no easy way of identifying directly the underlying neoclassical cost conditions that might make one of the other strategies economical for particular plants. However, in light of the general characteristics of coal supply and transportation discussed above, we can make at least some qualitative statements about the likely incidence of each of the three cases.

For the strategy covered by case 1 to be economical (transaction cost considerations aside), several characteristics of supply and transportation must prevail. The supply areas where the utility can most economically obtain coal should have coal of fairly uniform quality, should have numerous producing mines, and should be supplying quantities of coal that are very large relative to the demands of any particular plant. Economies of scale in coal mining should not be important, so that it is not advantageous for a plant to commit itself to long-term supplies with a single supplier. In addition, transport cost savings associated with the use of several competing transport alternatives should be greater than the savings associated with the use of unit trains to transport large quantities of coal from a single point to the plant. Alternatively, the mines must be close enough together to economically move the coal to a local point for onward transport by unit trains.

These characteristics of coal supply and transportation do not appear to be satisfied in most areas of the country. To the extent that this extreme case would be an economical coal procurement strategy anywhere, it is likely to be so for some plants located in the East which utilize coal from certain areas in Appalachia and for one reason or another cannot make efficient use of unit trains.[14]

The second case is likely to be more consistent with the supply and transportation opportunities faced by many plants located in the East and especially in the eastern half of the Midwest which secure supplies from Appalachia and the eastern Interior region. This reflects potential benefits associated with making at least limited commitments to particular mines, the costs of efficiently operating plants with variable coal quality, and economies associated with concentrating coal transportation and investments in unit trains. Longer-term contracts with some protection from opportunism would be more likely in this case, although there seems to be little reason for vertical integration.

As we move further west, the advantages of reliance on a small number of mines because of scale economies, transport economies, and variations in coal quality become more important. Potential opportunism becomes more severe and reliance on spot markets or simple contracts more problematical. Long-term contracts with appropriate protective provisions become more likely. Utilities in the Midwest and West that rely on supplies of coal from the West to satisfy air pollution requirements or which take advantage of cheap lignite and subbituminous coal—and must make very specific plant investments to burn it effectively—are likely to have arrangements similar to those suggested in case 3. Procurement strategies that lie between cases 2 and 3 are likely to reflect opportunities faced by other plants in the Midwest.

Overall, this suggests that (excluding mine-mouth plants) as we move

14. The age of the plant is also likely to be relevant. Over time, technological change has made it possible to build more efficient plants that produce steam at higher temperatures and pressures. The newer high-pressure units, especially supercritical units, tend to be more sensitive to variations in coal quality. See Joskow and Rose for a discussion of changes in generating-unit technology over time.

from East to West, we should see less reliance on spot market purchases and more reliance on long-term contracts. There should be relatively little reliance on spot market purchases generally since the supply, transportation, and generating technology conditions conducive to cost-minimizing supply strategies that do not involve at least some asset specificity by either the buyer or the seller are likely to exist for a relatively small fraction of all coal-burning power plants. Mine-mouth plants are the prime candidates for complex long-term contracts or vertical integration.

5. VERTICAL INTEGRATION, SPOT MARKETS, AND CONTRACT SALES

The previous discussion suggests that we should observe considerable variation in coal supply arrangements. Spot market transactions and simple short-term contracts will be economical choices for some plants, tending to be older plants located in the East. Vertical integration is most likely for mine-mouth plants, but such plants account for a relatively small fraction of total coal utilization (on the order of 15 percent—see below). If vertical integration is not chosen to govern supply for mine-mouth plants, contracts will have to be structured to mitigate opportunism in the context of a supply relationship governed by complex long-term contracts. Most coal-burning plants are likely to face economic opportunities that fall somewhere between these two extremes and will not rely extensively on either spot markets or vertical integration or the very long and tight contracts that simulate the opportunism-mitigating features of vertical integration.

We now turn to an examination of the extent to which vertical integration, spot markets, and other contractual arrangements are utilized to support exchange between coal-generating plants and their suppliers for the industry as a whole.

Table 4 lists the utilities that are integrated into coal production in one way or another and their coal subsidiaries (where the latter information is available).[15] The table also provides information on the extent of vertical integration (percent of coal requirements provided by coal subsidiaries) for each of these companies. Less than 15 percent of coal consumed by utilities is supplied to plants by a coal company owned by the owner of the plant (or one of the owners in the case of jointly owned plants). Another 3 percent or

15. Exactly what constitutes vertical integration is far from obvious. Some utilities own a plant themselves and have a mining division or subsidiary that operates the mines. Other utilities own plants themselves, own both coal reserves and the mines, but contract with independent operators to produce the coal. Still other utilities own the reserves, but contract with independent contractors to both develop and operate the mines. In other cases, the plant is jointly owned by several utilities, only one of which has an ownership interest in the mines serving the plant. I classify any of these cases as vertical integration and make finer distinctions in the discussion of mine-mouth plants below.

VERTICAL INTEGRATION AND LONG-TERM CONTRACTS / 51

so of U.S. coal consumption is produced by coal companies owned by utilities but supplied to plants not owned by the integrated utility in question. The extent of vertical integration into coal production in the electric utility industry is substantally less than in the coking (iron and steel) industry, where about 65 percent of requirements come from integrated coal suppliers.

About half of the utilities owning coal-producing subsidiaries are fully integrated, supplying all of their coal requirements (and often supplying coal to other utilities as well). The others generally supply only a small fraction of their coal needs. Those utilities that are integrated tend to be relatively large consumers of coal, but more than half of the twenty largest utility consumers of coal are not integrated. A few utilities are currently attempting to divest

Table 4. Vertical Integration into Coal Mining by Electric Utilities

Utility/subsidiaries	1980 production		Extent
	(tons)	(state)	
Texas Utilities	27,590,768	(TX)	100% requirements
Pacific P&L/NERCO			
Bridger Coal (joint owner)	6,453,302	(WY)	100% requirements by
Decker Coal (joint owner)	5,534,429	(MT)	company-owned mines or
Glenrock Coal	3,800,000	(WY)	mines owned by joint-
Sond Mountains Minerals	500,000	(AL)	owners of plants + substan-
Spring Creek Coal	100,000	(MT)	tial third-party sales.
Bankhead Coal	390,000	(AL)	
Total	16,777,331		
American Electric Power			~30% of requirements
Windsor Power House			
Southern Ohio Coal			
Central Ohio Coal			
Southern Appalachian Coal			
Cedar Coal			
Central Appalachian			
Simco/Peabody (joint owner)			
Price River Coal		(UT)	
Total	16,057,181		
Montana Power			
Western Energy	10,448,000	(MT)	100% of requirements + third-party sales.
Washington Water Power	5,140,000	(WA)	Requirements of Centralia, system's only coal plant.
Utah P&L	4,600,000	(UT)	~65% of requirements; mines operated by contractor.
Montana/Dakota Utilities			100% of requirements +
Knife River Coal	4,788,967	(MT, ND)	third-party sales.

52 / JOURNAL OF LAW, ECONOMICS, AND ORGANIZATION I:1, 1985

Table 4. Vertical Integration into Coal Mining by Electric Utilities, *continued*

Utility/subsidiaries	1980 production		Extent
	(tons)	(state)	
Pennsylvania P&L			
Pennsylvania Mines	2,928,211	(PA)	~50% of requirements
Greenwich Collieries	1,528,807	(PA)	
Lady Jane Collieries	200,963	(PA)	
Total	4,657,981		
Black Hills P&L			100% of requirements incl.
Wyodak Resources	2,500,000	(WY)	all of Wyodak plant.
Duke Power			
Eastover Mining Co.	2,084,000	(PA)	~15% of requirements. Subsid. up for sale in 1983.
Duquesne L&P	900,000	(PA)	~20% of requirements
Iowa PS Co.			
Energy Dev. Co.	877,631	(WY)	NA
VEPCO			~15% requirements
Laurel Run Mining	619,981	(WV)	(Mt. Storm plant)
Tampa Electric			
Cal-Glo Coal	388,000	(KY)	~10% of requirements
Ohio Edison	188,439	(OH)	~5% of requirements
Carolina P&L			
Leslie Coal (80%)	545,800	(KY)	~5% of requirements
McInnes Coal (80%)	—		
Total production by utility-controlled mines			83,000,000 tons
Sales to third parties (excl. joint plant owners)			13,000,000
Net integrated production			70,000,000
% of total utility coal use (tons):	14		
% of total utility coal use (BTUs):	12		

SOURCE: Compiled from data in 1982 *Keystone Coal Manual, Moody's Public Utility Manual* (various years), annual reports, and 10-K filings.

themselves of coal subsidiaries, largely as a consequence of unfavorable regulatory treatment of coal obtained from captive mines.[16]

Thus, about 85 percent of the coal used to generate electricity is supplied through some type of market transaction mechanism. Readily available data on coal supply arrangements breaks utility coal transactions down into spot transactions and contract transactions (see table 5). Generally, spot transactions involve coal supply agreements for relatively small fixed quantities of coal with delivery schedules extending for less than a year. Transactions that involve deliveries extending over a period of more than a year generally fall in the contract category. The proportion of spot transactions varies consider-

16. Duke Power has been actively seeking a buyer for its coal subsidiary. Carolina Power and Light and Pennsylvania Power and Light are also considering selling their coal subsidiares. See, for example, *Electrical Week*, August 23, 1982.

Table 5. Spot and Contract Transactions

Year	% spot	% contract
1974	23.8	76.2
1975	18.2	81.8
1976	14.0	86.0
1977	19.4	80.6
1978	21.2	78.8
1979	12.8	87.2
1980	11.5	88.5
1981	13.1	86.9
1982	9.6	90.4

Regional Breakdown: 1982	
Region	% spot
Appalachian	17.4
Interior	7.4
Texas	8.1
Western	1.6
Total	9.6

SOURCE: Calculated from *Cost and Quality of Fuels for Electric Utility Plants*, U.S. Department of Energy (DOE/EIA-0191(82)). August 1983, table 53.

ably from year to year. The relatively high values from 1974–75 and 1977–78 appear to reflect coal strikes that took place during portions of these periods. There is also substantial regional variation in the volume of coal made available through spot market transactions. The spot market accounts for a much larger fraction of transactions in the East than elsewhere, and there is essentially no spot market for coal in the West.

The contract category includes everything from one-year contracts to fifty-year contracts, and individual contracts vary widely in the annual tonnage provided for. There is probably relatively little difference from a transactional perspective between spot sales and contract sales with deliveries spread over one or two years, so it would be useful to break down the contract category further by duration and volume. Additional information on contract deliveries by duration and annual quantities is not as easily obtained from standard government sources as the initial breakdown between spot and contract. However, I have analyzed a sample of more than 200 coal contracts that accounted for more than 30 percent of contract coal deliveries in 1979 (see table 6).[17] Over 80 percent of the coal sold under these contracts involved delivery commitments for more than five years and more than 70 percent involved commitments extending over a period of more than ten

17. The contract information was obtained from Pasha Publications, *1980 Guide to Coal Contracts*, for another project. Data on 270 contracts was collected but only 205 contained both information on duration and delivered quantities for 1979.

54 / JOURNAL OF LAW, ECONOMICS, AND ORGANIZATION   I:1, 1985

years. This breakdown is roughly equivalent to the survey information Gordon (55–58) obtained for 1969. Longer contract periods are generally associated with larger annual volumes of coal as well.

These results are broadly consistent with the previous discussion. About 60 percent of the coal supplied to electric utilities involves relatively long-term contracts (more than five years). The spot market is not a significant governance mechanism for coal supply arrangements between utilities and coal producers. It is most important in the East and essentially nonexistent in the West. Vertical integration is not particularly important either, accounting for a somewhat smaller fraction of coal supplied.

Table 6. Distribution of 205 Contracts by Duration and Annual Tonnage

Duration	% of coal deliveries	Tons/year/contract
less than or 5 years	17	267,000
6-10 years	12	556,000
11-20 years	37	885,000
21–30 years	17	1,309,000
more than 30 years	17	2,411,000

SOURCE: See text and n. 17.

6. COAL SUPPLY ARRANGEMENTS FOR MINE-MOUTH PLANTS IMPLIED BY TRANSACTION COST CONSIDERATIONS

I argued above that coal supply transactions for mine-mouth plants are characterized by at least three of the four types of asset specificity identified by Williamson (1983: 26). From a transactional perspective, these plants are distinguished from the "typical" coal plant primarily by the unusual importance of durable transaction-specific investments. Transaction cost theory suggests that mine-mouth plants should be much more likely to be integrated or make use of complex long-term contracts than the typical generating plant. Before proceeding further it is worth considering briefly the other characteristics of transactions that are likely to affect the governance structure for coal plants generally and mine-mouth coal plants in particular:

Uncertainty/complexity: There is no easy way to measure the extent to which a particular type of transaction is subject to uncertainty or complexity. Indeed, it is not at all obvious from the literature how one even would conceptualize either a cardinal or ordinal measurement procedure. Precise measurement is not critical, however. Uncertainty and complexity are important to the extent that buyers and sellers cannot write unambiguous and easily enforceable full contingent claims contracts. When full contingent claims contracts cannot be written, contracts are necessarily incomplete. Contractual incompleteness is not the source of transactional difficulties, but rather sets the stage for contractual difficulties in the presence of transaction-specific investments or information asymmetries.

From the perspective of a utility considering investment in a coal plant with an expected life of thirty-five years or more, it is certainly reasonable to assume that there is enough uncertainty about coal demand in the short run and over the life of the plant to make it difficult to write a full contingent claims contract. Coal demand will vary with the utilization rate of the plant and the thermal efficiency of the plant. Both of these vary over time in a nondeterministic way. As a plant ages and moves higher in the dispatch profile, plant utilization will also vary with total electrical load and with the prices of fuels burned by other plants on a utility's system. Air pollution restrictions and cooling water availability may limit plant utilization and affect both the quantity and the types of coal required. Furthermore, because coal quality is very important and numerous coal characteristics are relevant for plant design and plant performance, the "simple" product *coal* is a much more complex product than first appears.

From the perspective of a mine owner considering investing in a new mine or expanding an existing mine, there is also likely to be considerable uncertainty about mining costs and coal quality over the life of the mine. Ex ante, there is at least some uncertainty about mining costs, cleaning requirements, and reserves given prevailing input prices. Over time, the nominal and real costs of mining are inherently uncertain, depending not only on the physical characteristics of the reserves, but also on changes in input prices, contract work rules, government regulations affecting mining costs, and technologies.

For the purposes of examining governance structures for coal supplied to electric utilities, I think that it is fair to assume that contracts will necessarily be incomplete. This is especially true for mine-mouth plants, where both parties make long-term reliance investments contingent on the performance of the other over many years.

Reputational constraints: Is it likely that the threat of losing future purchases (in the case of the mining company) or the prospect that buyers will have to pay higher transactions prices in future contracts (reflecting a price for anticipated breaches on the part of the buyer) will deter the kinds of "bad behavior" that the transactions cost literature is concerned with? Reputational constraints depend primarily on the importance of repeat purchase activity and the ability to distinguish bad (good) outcomes (such as high mining costs or failures to deliver promised quantities) that arise because of inefficient (efficient) behavior from bad (good) outcomes that arise simply because of bad (good) luck. Reputational constraints are likely to be most important when utilities find it economical (in the neoclassical sense) to adopt procurement strategies such as those outlined in case 1 and case 2 above. There is extensive repeat purchase activity, sales are made to many sellers

56 / JOURNAL OF LAW, ECONOMICS, AND ORGANIZATION   I:1, 1985

from the same mines, and the utility buys from several different sellers. These constraints are not likely to be significant in the case of mine-mouth operations, however.

Individual mine-mouth operations have many idiosyncrasies that make it difficult for third parties to distinguish poor performance due to actions by either party from poor performance resulting from exogenous factors that are not subject to control by either party. Especially in the last ten or fifteen years, regulatory changes and labor problems have had profound effects on mining costs and production. Many generating units built over the past twenty years have experienced much poorer heat rates and availabilities than had been anticipated. It is likely to be difficult to determine how much of this change was due to exogenous factors and how much can be associated with suboptimal levels of effort by either party. Overall, it seems unlikely that reputational constraints can provide protection from opportunistic behavior in the case of mine-mouth plants.

Diseconomies of internal production: I have no way of evaluating objectively whether there are important economies that a large coal producer with production activity and experience from other supply arrangements would bring to a transaction that a utility embarking on coal production itself would not be able to take advantage of. I suspect that there are some economies of scale or experience in this sense that utilities would not be able to take advantage of, but I have seen no evidence that would allow me to make a definitive statement.[18] Nor is there any way to estimate empirically internal incentive and command and control problems that might increase costs from integrated production compared to the costs of market procurement and necessarily limit the economic extent of vertical integration. There is little reason to believe, however, that these considerations are more important for mine-mouth plants than they are for other types of plants.

In summary, these observations suggest the following. The assumption of incomplete contracts is probably a good one for all types of generating plants. This sets the stage for opportunism if transaction-specific investments are necessary for structuring a minimum cost supply relationship. Transaction-specific sunk investments are considerably more important for mine-mouth plants than for other types of plants. Reputational constraints are not likely to be particularly effective in the case of mine-mouth plants. Diseconomies of internal production are likely to affect the economics of vertical integration equally, regardless of the particular type of plant involved.

18. The utility owners of Western Coal (formed to supply the San Juan plant) did apparently consider taking over mining responsibilities from Utah-International, the developer and operator of the adjacent mine. Among other things they concluded that Utah could take advantage of some economies associated with its mining operations at Four Corners. See letter from Western Coal Co. to Tucson Gas and Electric and Public Service of New Mexico regarding negotiations between Western (jointly owned by the two utilities) and Utah-International (dated February 21, 1978, on file).

This all implies that coal supply transactions for a mine-mouth operation are prime candidates for the choice of vertical integration as a transaction cost-minimizing governance structure. Regulatory considerations, coal supplier economies, and other diseconomies of vertical integration may make vertical integration less attractive than alternative contractual governance structure, or even impossible. If vertical integration is not chosen, some type of long-term contractual arrangement containing provisions that anticipate performance difficulties and designed to effectuate a smooth and efficient relationship between the buyer and the seller should be forthcoming. Reliance on a spot market or even relatively short-term contracts are not likely to prove to be a cost-minimizing alternative.

Let's assume that for one reason or another a mine-mouth plant operator chooses to secure supplies through contract rather than vertical integration. What are the characteristics of an efficient contractual relationship? What contractual provisions will emerge as the parties negotiate a mutually acceptable supply agreement in response to anticipated transactions costs and contract execution difficulties? Are the resulting arrangements efficient?

From a normative (efficiency) perspective we would expect a coal supply arrangement to emerge with these desirable features:

a. The contemplated mine-mouth operation will go forward if it is the cost-minimizing way for the utility to generate electricity; the parties will be able to strike a deal.

b. Once a plant and mine are built, the plant operator will continue to take supplies from the adjacent mine as long as this is the least cost source of supply, without the buyer switching to a (socially) uneconomical supplier.

c. The seller will produce coal efficiently.

d. The seller will continue to supply the quantities and quality of coal promised as long as it represents the least cost source of supply for the plant. The seller will not uneconomically shift supplies to other buyers.

e. The agreement will be flexible enough to allow supply and demand by the supplier/purchaser to adjust to changes in economic conditions. If the current supplier is not the minimum cost producer, the agreement should provide a mechanism to shift suppliers, reduce production, etc.

f. Minimization of haggling over price and production levels that may disrupt efficient supply arrangements but may be a natural outcome of the bilateral monopoly situation that emerges once each party sinks costs in reliance on the agreement.

g. Avoidance of litigation and litigation costs.

The actual provisions that emerge will reflect efforts by each party to maximize profits with due recognition of the costs of writing, monitoring, and enforcing contractual promises. A variety of price and nonprice provisions are potentially available to support exchange and mitigate opportunism. The optimal price and nonprice provisions are likely to be related to

58 / JOURNAL OF LAW, ECONOMICS, AND ORGANIZATION   I:1, 1985

one another and it is difficult to discuss them independently. It is even more difficult to discuss them together.

Let me assume, to begin, that the costs of producing coal do not change over time due to changes in input prices, technological change, government regulation, contractual changes in work rules, and so on, and that a price (level and structure) is negotiated at the start of the contract and is *anticipated* to be fixed over the term of the contract, although either party is free to try to exploit any ex post monopoly power to force the other to agree to a higher or lower price after production begins. I assume that other changes in market conditions may take place over time which affect the value of the coal to the buyer and the opportunity cost to the seller of supplying to the adjacent plant. Given these assumptions, I can suggest the kinds of nonprice terms that we should expect to find in these contracts to mitigate opportunism and then relax the assumptions about the costs of producing coal to examine alternative patterns for determining prices over the life of the contract.

6.1. NONPRICE PROVISIONS

Given the three types of investment specificity that characterizes this type of production, neither the utility nor the coal supplier will want to be the first mover. The utility is not going to start building a power plant on this site without some supply agreement because it would be subject to hold-up by the owner(s) of adjacent reserves. The same is true of the coal supplier vis-à-vis the utility. Furthermore, effective design of the mine-mouth operation requires cooperation between both the utility and the coal supplier. Thus, a firm governance structure is likely to be in place before any substantial plant investments are made by either party.

I expect to see very long-term contracts negotiated which specify purchasing (take) and supply obligations for the plant and the mine over a substantial fraction of the life of the plant—at least twenty years. Neither the power plant owner nor the supplier is likely to want to enter into a relationship which involves frequent renegotiation of terms after each incurs transaction-specific sunk investments.

I would expect to see extensive use of requirements contracts. The quantity of coal to be delivered under the contract must be specified somehow. Coal requirements will vary from month to month and year to year. Some of this variation can be dealt with through a coal inventory accumulation, although one of the desirable features of a mine-mouth plant is the ability to minimize inventories that might otherwise be necessary to insure against transportation problems. Ideally, the power plant owner would simply like the mine to deliver enough coal to satisfy the requirements of the plant. Since requirements vary, the easiest way to specify quantities from the viewpoint of the plant operator is simply to write the contract as a requirements contract.

There are strategic reasons for the utility to write the contract as a requirements contract as well and to include provisions to restrict sales to third parties. Reducing promised deliveries during the anticipated term of the contract may be perceived as a supplier-credible threat as part of an effort to hold up the utility, because the utility's initial investment is larger, longer-lived, and less easily redeployed than those of the mining company. The mine operator could credibly reduce supplies over time by ceasing to make replacement and expansion investments and use this threat to extract better terms from the utility. Furthermore, depending on the pricing provisions in the contract, changing market conditions could make it profitable for the mining company to breach the contract to supply even if it is not efficient to do so. Clear language that the contract is for plant requirements over a specified period of time makes court enforcement easier if disputes arise between the plant owner and the mine owner that cannot be resolved otherwise. It also suggests that provisions for dealing with sales to third parties and the dedication of specific reserves to the agreement along with the requirements provisions will protect the utility from the threat and potential costs of diverting supplies to other buyers.[19]

A requirements contract serves to protect the seller in similar ways. Threats by the buyer to switch to alternative suppliers are made less credible both because comparable suppliers will not be waiting in the wings to take up the slack and because breach is easier to detect and penalize through legal sanctions.

Coal quality is of particular importance to the utility, and the mining company is in a position to affect coal quality by its mining practices. The mining company may be able to reduce its costs by mining low-quality deposits, shirking on cleaning, and increase effective prices (especially in per ton priced contracts) by increasing the quantity of "junk" in the coal. The utility may have difficulty distinguishing coal quality problems that arise because of poor mining practices and coal quality problems that arise because the reserves are of generally lower quality than had been anticipated when the contract was negotiated. The supplier may also have an interest in the precise definition of the expectations about coal quality ex ante since claims of poor coal quality may be used by a utility as an excuse to breach the contract. One would expect substantial ex ante investigation of reserve characteristics to verify that the promised quality specifications can be achieved. I would also expect the contract itself not only to specify minimum acceptable coal quality but also to define clearly the specific reserves on which ex ante

19. This is especially true if the pricing provisions of the contract have a significant cost plus component.

60 / JOURNAL OF LAW, ECONOMICS, AND ORGANIZATION I:1, 1985

quantity/quality evaluations were made and to provide for the dedication of these reserves to production for this plant. To the extent that variations in coal quality can be easily "priced," I would expect pricing provisions expanded to do so.

Williamson (1983) discusses the desirability of "protective governance structures" to deal with potential hold-up problems when "hostage arrangements" cannot be structured to eliminate expropriation incentives possessed by one or both parties. Contractual incompleteness and the potential for haggling are a serious potential problem in unintegrated mine-mouth operations. While court enforcement remains an option and coal contract disputes do occasionally lead to litigation, arbitration clearly represents an opportunity to provide a dispute resolution system that does not entail the costs (broadly defined) of litigation. Thus, I expect to see arbitration provision contained in these contracts as well as other cooperative arrangements that allow for the smooth functioning of a complex agreement and the settlement of disputes without resorting to litigation.

6.2. PRICING PROVISIONS

Establishing a pricing formula to govern compensation arrangements for contracts lasting many years that provide incentives to both the buyer and the seller to perform as promised without leading to serious inefficiencies itself is not an easy task. Dealing with the kinds of ex post performance problems addressed in the transactions cost literature and providing mechanisms for smooth adjustments in obligations as various contingencies arise is complicated by the uncertainty governing future costs and market conditions that are inherent in this relationship. Input prices are likely to change over time, technological developments may reduce the current and expected future costs of mining from similar reserves, labor agreements may change work rules and increase or decrease productivity, new government regulations may increase mining costs, unanticipated mining problems may emerge, new property and severance taxes may be applied, and so on. General changes in supply and demand are likely to lead to changes in the value of the coal at the mine-mouth operation both from the buyer's perspective and the seller's perspective.

The compensation arrangements should reflect two interrelated objectives. First, they should be structured to eliminate the incentives either party has to behave opportunistically. Second, the pricing provisions should be structured in such a way that efficient demand and supply decisions are made by both the buyer and the seller. It would, for example, be undesirable if a pricing formula gave one or both parties the incentive to reach their purchase and supply promises if this would increase the social costs of supplying coal or producing electricity. Let us examine four different methods for establishing prices over time.

1. *Market price contracts.* If the product under consideration were a homogeneous product sold in a competitive auction market and carrying a clear market price, the simplest way of determining prices might be just to stipulate that payments would be made at some fraction of an appropriate market price indicator. This is not likely to be a particularly attractive alternative as the sole determinant of prices for coal supplied for a mine-mouth operation, however.

Coal is not a homogeneous commodity with regard to the characteristics of the coal or the location of the coal. The mine-mouth supply price includes both the cost of coal and (implicitly) the cost of transportation. There simply will not be any meaningful market price for coal of this particular type delivered to the plant. This is especially problematical in the West, where there is essentially no spot market to tie anything to. Market price contracts may make a lot of sense for a homogeneous commodity like uranium, or even for coal in some areas of the country and when other types of plants are involved, but not for mine-mouth plants.

2. *Fixed price contracts:* An alternative to a market price contract is a simple fixed price contract (as I assumed above). Risk allocation problems aside, this contract has poor incentive properties with regard to continuing performance. The primary problem is that if the supplier's actual costs rise significantly above the fixed price when certain contingencies arise, the supplier will have strong incentives to breach (reduce quantities provided in the short run, cease making investments to expand its capacity to continue to supply, run down the value of the equipment, etc.) even if such behavior is inefficient. Similarly, if the expected price of coal available from alternative suppliers falls below the fixed price (due to cost reductions generally, changing market conditions, etc.) the plant operator may find it profitable to breach even if it is inefficient to do so.

Expectations of secular increases in input prices, reserve depletion, and changes in work rules and government regulations that are likely to reduce productivity make these problems worse. A long-term fixed price contract must assure that the present discounted value (PDV) of expected revenues is greater than or equal to the PDV of expected costs or the supplier will not agree to enter into the supply arrangement. Given expectations of nominal cost increases over time, this implies a fixed price that will "front load" the cash flow so that in early years the supplier is getting revenues substantially above current costs, while in later years he may receive revenues substantially below the then current cost. At some point the fixed contract price may fall below current incremental costs, and the supplier will have an incentive to abandon the mine, substantially reduce production, cease making investments, and so on.[20] Fixed prices in long-term contracts do not appear to me

20. This depends on the length of the contract, the capital output ratio, the durability of the investments, the expected rate of inflation, and the discount rate used. I have performed some simulations of the relationship between the fixed price and the incremental costs for a variety of

62 / JOURNAL OF LAW, ECONOMICS, AND ORGANIZATION   I:1, 1985

to be credible because the specification of a fixed price is so likely to provide incentives to one or both parties to threaten to breach and to trigger renegotiation.

3. *Cost plus profit contracts:* A third alternative is to negotiate a cost plus profit contract in which the supplier is compensated for all of the costs incurred in production, including the cost of capital. Risk allocation considerations aside, if it could be assured that the supplier would produce efficiently, such a contract has some desirable properties. It is unlikely that the buyer would have a strong incentive to breach, because it is unlikely that he could get the coal more cheaply elsewhere over the duration of the contract, unless the market value of the coal increases or decreases faster than production costs, since the mine-mouth supplier is presumably facing the same changes in input prices, regulations, technological change, etc., as are other comparable suppliers.

A cost-based price also ensures that prices are high enough so that the supplier does not have an incentive to walk away from the supply arrangement when costs increase due to input price changes, productivity changes due to changes in health and safety regulation, land reclamation costs, and so on, as might occur with a fixed price contract. A cost-based price of course does not eliminate the incentives a supplier might have to ship supplies to buyers if there is a large unanticipated increase in the value of the coal, for example, as a result of an increase in the demand for low-sulfur coal, making it more valuable in the market than it is under the contract (i.e., the long-run supply function for low-sulfur coal is upward sloping and the economic rent associated with an assumed inframarginal reserve rises). And it is unlikely that it would be efficient for the supplier to shift to another buyer if such a contingency arose. Similar inefficient responses by buyers can be expected if the value of coal falls and the "costs" used in the pricing formula reflect generated rents based on ex ante expectations.

An important problem with a cost plus contract is that it has poor incentive properties with regard to the supplier's incentives to minimize costs. Without more, the supplier has little incentive to produce efficiently. If costs rose high enough the buyer would have incentives to switch to other suppliers, but there is likely to be a potentially large wedge for inefficiency, since the next best alternative would on average be more costly to the buyer than an efficiently operated mine-mouth facility.

4. *Indexed contracts:* The fourth and final type of contract that I consider is an indexed contract. This is a natural alternative to a fixed price contract. Rather than try to set a fixed price that rolls in revenues for anticipated fu-

---

reasonable assumptions. Reasonable assumptions about expected input price inflation suggests that the abandonment problem becomes serious for contracts that are longer than fifteen or twenty years. The mines at mine-mouth plants are often organized as separate subsidiaries of larger coal companies and it is possible that a utility would have difficulty making a claim against the parent company.

VERTICAL INTEGRATION AND LONG-TERM CONTRACTS / 63

ture changes in input prices, costs of government regulations, changes in union work rules, and so on, we can set a base price that is adjusted over time as input prices rise. For example, the base price can be broken down into components (labor, materials and supplies, depreciation, profit, property taxes) and then each component escalated according to an appropriate input price and productivity index. This type of contract seems to deal with some of the undesirable properties of both the fixed price and cost plus contracts. Prices now rise over time as input prices rise and productivity opportunities change, and we do not have to front-load cash flow. Prices rise as the supplier's input prices rise and production opportunities change but are independent of the actual production decisions made by the supplier. If the supplier can increase productivity more than provided for by the index, his actual costs will rise by less than the indexed price. If his costs rise—because of bad mining practices, for example—his net revenues are reduced as a result. This type of contract provides incentives for the supplier to minimize costs (given coal quantity and quality). Furthermore, the increases in input prices, technological change, and so forth will have similar effects on the costs of proximate alternative suppliers as well. Although this type of pricing provision cannot guarantee that contract prices will move in lockstep with the prices that might be charged by competing suppliers over time, it does account for several important causes of changing supply prices. An indexed contract therefore appears to dominate either a fixed price or cost plus contract.

An indexed contract is not without problems, however. It may be difficult to index some components of mining cost that will affect the costs of producing from this mine and "comparable" mines (actual and potential). New labor contracts may change work rules, increasing labor costs. New mining regulations may increase costs substantially. Technological change may reduce costs and substantially alter the cost-minimizing weights used to index the price. This kind of adjustment mechanism can also get very complicated if we try to break down the base price into numerous components. The indexed price could move far away from the economic costs of production, giving either the buyer or the seller increased incentives to breach the agreement. Complexity would encourage haggling and litigation.

In addition to general provisions for adjusting the *level* of prices, the price *structure* could be adapted to provide additional financial protection against expropriation and uneconomic buyer/supplier switching. For example, Williamson (1983) and Goldberg and Erickson suggest that nonlinear prices may be used as a device to help to insure that the buyer performs. A seller concerned that a buyer will shift to other suppliers might find a fixed annual payment (to cover sunk costs) plus a commodity charge attractive or include minimum take or pay provisions in the contract. We should recognize, however, that optimally adjusting nonlinear price schedules over time may be even more complicated than adjusting simple (linear) unit prices.

64 / JOURNAL OF LAW, ECONOMICS, AND ORGANIZATION I:1, 1985

None of the price adjustment mechanisms is ideal, in the sense that the method of setting the level and structure of prices alone can deal effectively with all of the performance problems that can arise in a long-term coal supply arrangement. Thus, whatever method is used to determine prices, I also expect to see substantial reliance for protection on the kinds of nonprice provisions discussed above.

Finally, there is the problem of "surprises" that affect either the price or nonprice terms of a contract, events that were not anticipated with positive probability by either party to the contract when the contract was negotiated. The expected effects of surprises are not reflected in the terms of the contract. As I have argued elsewhere (1977: 157), "bounded rationality" suggests that there are some contingencies that are simply not contemplated by the parties when they negotiate a supply arrangement. These contingencies may involve the effects of unexpected changes in government regulation, dramatic changes in supply or demand in the market, or other changes that would impose a large financial burden on one of the parties if it performed as required by literal interpretation of the contract—a burden that was not reflected, for example, in the base price or adjustment provisions. Both parties to the contract should recognize ex ante that surprises will occur and I would expect to find general provisions in contracts, such as force majeur or gross inequity clauses, that specify a process for dealing with such unspecified contingencies if they arise.

7. COAL SUPPLY ARRANGEMENTS FOR MINE-MOUTH COAL PLANTS: GENERAL CHARACTERISTICS

Table 7 lists all of the mine-mouth coal plants with first units that began operating no earlier than 1960 (with one exception) that I was able to identify.[21] The method used to identify these plants is discussed in the appendix. There are twenty-one plants, which accounted for about 15 percent of electric utility coal deliveries. Most of the plants are multiunit facilities and more than half are jointly owned by at least two utilities. Only two of the plants used any coal purchased on the spot market and in both cases spot sales accounted for only a small fraction of total consumption.

Table 8 provides general information on the coal supply arrangements that have been made for each plant. In 1982, ten of the plants obtained all of their coal supplies from either a coal-mining division or a subsidiary of one of the utilities owning the plant (i.e., coal supply arrangements involved some form of vertical integration). One plant (Mt. Storm) obtained part of its supplies from a coal-mining subsidiary of the utility (but this accounted for 100

---

21. The initial source I used to date the units at different plant sites gave the wrong date for the first unit of the Montrose plant (1960 rather than 1958). I decided to leave it on the list. There are two or three other utilities with mine-mouth plants which predate the sample period.

Table 7. Mine-Mouth Coal Plants

Unit names	Utility/state	Joint owners	Units (yrs)	Capacity (MWE) 1982	Coal deliveries (tons)
Big Brown	Texas Util. (TX)	No	71, 72	1186	5,963,000
Martin Lake	Texas Util. (TX)	No	77, 78, 79	2379	11,413,000
Monticello	Texas Util. (TX)	No	74, 75	1980	9,797,000
Hunter	Utah P&L (UT)	No	78, 80 (83, 85)	892	2,525,000
Huntington	Utah P&L (UT)	No	74, 77	892	2,492,000
Naughton	Utah P&L (WY)	No	63, 68, 71	707	2,040,000
Wyodak	Pacific P&L (WY)	Yes	78	331	1,812,000
Centralia	Pacific P&L (WA)	Yes	72, 72	1329	4,400,000
Bridger	Pacific P&L (WY)	Yes	74, 75, 76, 77	2034	6,025,000
San Juan	Pub. Serv. NM (NM)	Yes	73, 76, 79, 82	1708	5,071,000
Colstrip	Montana Power (MT)	Yes	75, 76 (84, 85)	716	2,103,000
Four Corners[a]	Arizona PS (NM)	Yes	63, 63, 64, 69, 70	2269	7,291,000
Young	Minkotta Coop (ND)	Yes	70, 77	673	2,983,850
Coyote	Mont./Dakota (ND)	Yes	81	450	1,669,000
Montrose	Kan. City P&L (MO)	No	58, 60, 64	536	1,326,700
Craig	Col.-Ute Coop (CO)	Yes	79, 80 (83)	894	2,303,000
Asbury	Emp. Dist. (MO)	No	70	212	707,000
Keystone[b]	Penn. Elec (PA)	Yes	67, 68	1872	3,543,000
Homer City	Penn. Elec (PA)	Yes	69, 71, 77	2012	3,811,000
Conemaugh[b]	Penn. Elec (PA)	Yes	70, 71	1872	2,668,000
Mt. Storm	VEPCO (WV)	No	65, 66, 73	1662	3,100,000

a. Units 4 and 5 jointly owned.
b. Pennsylvania Electric operates plant for joint owners but has no direct ownershhip interest. Other GPU subsidiaries own part of the plants along with other utilities.
SOURCE: See appendix.

percent of mine's capacity). In the case of jointly owned plants with coal supplied by a coal subsidiary of one of the plant owners, there is typically a formal contract written between the owners of the plant and the coal subsidiary. I have noted these in table 8 by using the term *integrated/contract* to reflect this state of affairs.

Together, mine-mouth power plants account for about 50 million tons of "integrated" coal supplies per year. This is about 60 percent of all coal supplied to utilities by coal companies owned by one of the owners of a plant. In other words, mine-mouth plants account for about 15 percent of total coal utilization but 60 percent of all coal supply arrangements governed by some form of vertical integration. A mine-mouth plant is thus about six times more likely to rely on vertical integration to support exchange than is any other type of coal-burning power plant.

The remaining ten plants all rely primarily on long-term contracts for the supply of coal.[22] The contracts vary in duration from twenty years to fifty years, with thirty-five years being typical. The "integrated/contract" supply

22. Note that the Huntington and Hunter plants were initially supplied under long-term contracts, but the utility eventually acquired the mines. Coal supply arrangements for the San Juan plant moved in the opposite direction.

66 / JOURNAL OF LAW, ECONOMICS, AND ORGANIZATION I:1, 1985

arrangements generally involve long-term contracts with thirty-five-year durations as well. Referring back to table 6 it is clear that very long contracts are far more likely to emerge to govern coal supply arrangemenuts for mine-mouth plants than they are to govern supply arrangements generally in the electric utility industry. On average less than 20 percent of the coal supplied under the 200 sample contracts had durations of greater than thirty years (and most of this is accounted for by mine-mouth plants). Both the extensive reliance on vertical integration and very long-term contracts are quite consistent with the predictions of transaction cost theory.

8. NONPRICE PROVISIONS OF LONG-TERM CONTRACTS FOR MINE-MOUTH PLANTS

I was able to obtain the actual contracts governing transactions between the coal supplier and the power plant owners for sixteen of the twenty-one mine-mouth plants on the list.[23] Since some plants have more than one contract, either because separate contracts were written for different units or (in one case) contracts were written with two adjacent mining companies, I have twenty-one contracts in all, plus amendments and revisions, covering sixteen plants. These contracts may be "incomplete," but many of them are very complicated. These were not just documents dashed off because the companys' lawyers said they should have a legal document to "confirm their orders."

Table 9 summarizes the incidence of various nonprice provisions of the coal supply contracts reflecting the discussion above.

Duration: As indicated above, most of the contracts have durations of thirty years or more, with thirty-five years being most typical. And these are real long-term contracts. Sixteen of the contracts have no scheduled renegotiation provisions. Three contracts provide for price renegotiation (subject to certain constraints) after twenty years. One provides for renegotiation of the escalation weights only. One contract allows the buyer to terminate after six years but obligates him to reimburse the mining company for all fixed costs. Short-term renegotiation provisions and options to terminate on short notice are generally not provided for, as they sometimes are in other coal contracts (McGraw-Hill, 1981: 352–53). It is also clear from reading the contracts that are available that these supply agreements are generally negotiated several years before the initial units for which the coal is to be supplied are placed in service. Neither party moves first; they move together.

Requirements contracts/dedication of reserves: Almost all of the contracts are full requirements contracts. Of those that are not, one contract simply

23. This includes the initial contracts and amendments for Hunter and Huntington.

VERTICAL INTEGRATION AND LONG-TERM CONTRACTS / 67

Table 8. Coal Supply Arrangements for Mine-Mouth Plants

Unit	Supply Arrangements	Initial contract	Duration
Big Brown	Integrated	None	NA
Martin Lake	Integrated	None	NA
Monticello	Integrated	None	NA
Huntington	Initially long-term contract; util. acquired mines in 1977	1971	35 yrs
Hunter	Initially long-term contract; util. acquired mines in 1977	1974	35 yrs
Naughton	Long-term contract	1957	40 yrs
Wyodak	Integrated/contract	1977	35 yrs
Centralia	Integrated/contract	1970	35 yrs
Bridger	Integrated/contract	1974	35 yrs
San Juan	Initially coal subsidiary contracted with mining co. to build and operate mine on util. sub. reserves. Reserves later sold to mining co. and supplies now provided under long-term contract.	1972, 1980	37 yrs
Colstrip	Integrated/contract (units 1, 2)	1971	35 yrs
	(unit 3)	1980	36 yrs
Four Corners	Long-term contracts (units 1, 2, 3)	1960, 1963	35 yrs
	(units 4, 5)	1966	35 yrs
Young	Long-term contract	1966	50 yrs
Coyote	Integrated contract	1978	35 yrs
Montrose	Long-term contracts (units 1, 2)	1956	~30 yrs
	(unit 3, different mine)	1959	~35 yrs
Craig	Long-term contract	1973	35 yrs
Asbury	Long-term contract + some spot	1966	20 yrs
Keystone	Long-term contract	1964	~30 yrs
Homer City	Long-term contracts (2)	1966	~30 yrs
Conemaugh	Long-term contracts	196?	~30 yrs
Mt. Storm	Initial supply arrangements unknown; currently coal comes from adjacent company-owned mine (100% of output plus contract purchases from other suppliers with different durations, plus some spot purchases.	NA	NA

SOURCE: See appendix.

specifies annual supplies for each of twenty years, one contract specifies annual quantities (plus or minus 10 percent) for each of thirty-five years, one 90 percent requirements contract, and one plant that has two contracts each for 50 percent of requirements (with flexibility to go down to 40 percent). In all but one case specific reserves are dedicated to fulfilling the contract as well. Most of the contracts also have explicit restrictions on sales to third parties which require the approval of the plant operator, or most favored nations clauses.

Coal quality: Coal quality is handled in one or both of two ways. Most of the contracts include "contract" coal quality characteristics and "minimum" coal quality characteristics, often along with various bonus/penalty provisions if certain coal quality specs (usually BTU content) fall above or below

68 / JOURNAL OF LAW, ECONOMICS, AND ORGANIZATION I:1, 1985

those specified in the contract. BTU content of coal, sulfur content, size, moisture, and ash content are the most frequently specified characteristics. If coal quality specifications are not included, the contract provides for "run-of-mine" deliveries free of certain impurities from specified reserves. Some contracts have as many as sixteen coal quality characteristics specified.

Maximum delivery commitments: In addition to providing requirements obligations for the buyer and seller, the contracts typically specify maximum monthly and annual quantities that the suppliers are committed to deliver. These are often adjustable within some range if the purchasers give adequate notice to the supplier. These provisions sometimes get very complicated, especially when a sequence of generating units is planned. Even if a utility claims its requirements are greater than the maximum, the supplier has no contractual obligation to supply more than the maximum.

Arbitration: All but three of the contracts have specific arbitration provisions to deal with disputes arising under the contracts. Two of the

Table 9. Summary of Selected Nonprice Provisions of Contracts (21 contracts)

Duration
    Mean: 35 yrs
    Median: 35 yrs
    Mode: 35 yrs
    Min: 20 yrs
    Max: 50 yrs

Requirements contracts
    Full requirements: 16
    Partial (%) req.:   3
    Annual quantities: 2

Min take/min payment
    Yes: 16
    Not mentioned: 5 (2, cost plus or two-part tariff; 1, added by amendment)

Arbitration
    Yes: 18
    Not mentioned: 3

Scheduled renegotiation
    Yes: 5 (3, after 20 years; 1, escal. weights only; 1, buyer pays fixed costs on termination)
    No: 16

Coal quality specs
    Yes: 14
    No: 7 (run of mine for specified reserves)

Specification/dedication of reserves
    Yes: 20
    Not mentioned: 1

Specific restrictions on third-party sales
    Yes: 13
    Not mentioned: 8

Gross inequity
    Yes: 12
    Not mentioned: 9 (3, cost plus; 3, integrated/contract; 1, "fair profit" provision)

SOURCE: See appendix.

three contracts without these provisions were eventually terminated after utility acquisition of the mines. A few of the contracts also provide for a joint utility/supplier committee to facilitate the smooth operation of the coal supply arrangements and to avoid disputes.

9. PRICING PROVISIONS IN LONG-TERM CONTRACTS

There are two general types of formulas used to determine prices in the actual coal contracts that I have reviewed. The predominant form (fourteen of twenty-one contracts) of pricing involves the specification of a base price (either per ton or per million BTUs) which is broken down into several different components (labor, materials, depreciation, profit, taxes, etc.) with an escalation provision specified for each. Usually some of the components are indexed in some way, while other components are adjusted for changes in actual cases. There is some variation among contracts in this regard. These contracts thus represent a mixture of the indexed and cost plus contracts discussed above. They recognize explicitly that prices will have to be adjusted over time (up or down) to reflect changes in input prices and several categories of real cost changes that are not subject to the control of the mining company. Prices are not, however, formally tied to market prices, nor do changes in the relationship between contract prices and market prices automatically trigger renegotiation. The older contracts tend to have a fraction of the price which is not escalated, and it is quite clear that uncertainty due to inflation and unanticipated exogenous events affecting real mining costs have been of increasing importance in structuring long-term contracts between utilities and independent suppliers over time.

The second primary type of compensation arrangement (seven contracts plus one indexed contract with a cost plus option) is a cost plus profit contract. These contracts normally specify that the buyer will pay all operating costs, depreciation, amortization, property and severence taxes, plus an allowance for profit (normally per ton or per BTU with a couple of exceptions). These contracts generally recognize explicitly that pure cost plus arrangements raise incentive problems and include specific incentive provisions.

Table 10 summarizes a number of the key provisions governing price adjustments over time.

9.1. BASE PRICE ESCALATION CONTRACTS (14 contracts)

Wages and benefits: Labor costs are normally broken down into several categories to reflect wages, benefits, employment taxes, etc. A base hourly wage rate is typically indexed to changes in wage rates (including benefits, taxes, etc.) as specified in collective bargaining agreements applicable to the area in which the mine is located (if it is unionized and sometimes if it is not) or

Table 10. Summary of Pricing Provisions in Contracts

General pricing provisions: Base price plus escalation: 14
                             Cost plus profit: 7 and 1 with option

ESCALATION PROVISIONS IN BASE PRICE PLUS ESCALATION CONTRACTS

Components of base price
Wages/benefits
  Indexed: 11
  Actual costs: 3
Materials and supplies
  Indexed: 13
  Actual costs: 1
Depreciation/amortization
  Indexed: 4 (2 partial, 1 full)
  Actual costs: 3
  Fixed: 2
  Aggregated with other components: 4
  Other: 1
Profit
  Indexed: 5
  ROI: 1
  Fixed: 3
  Aggregated with other components: 4
  Other: 1
Residual aggregate
  Indexed: 4
  Fixed: 2
  None: 8
Taxes/royalties
  Actual costs: 14
Costs due to changes in gov't regulations
  Actual costs: 12
  Not mentioned: 2 (subsequently added by amendement)
Changes in contract/union work rules
  Actual costs: 13
  Fixed: 1 (contract has cost plus option)

COST PLUS PROFIT CONTRACTS

Treatment of base profit per unit
  Indexed: 6
  ROI: 2 (includes contract with cost plus option)
Incentive Provisions
  Bonus/penalty based on "standard cost" comparisons: 3
  Bonus/penalty based on market price comparions: 3
  Option to rebid mining agreement: 1
  Contractual promise to develop incentive provision: 1

NONLINEAR RATE STRUCTURE (in addition to/along with minimum take): 5 of 21

to the average wage rate actually paid to workers at the mine, including changes in government-mandated tax and benefit payments. I have identified the treatment of wages and benefits as indexed if the wage component had a fixed weight in the base price, excluding adjustments for contractual or legal changes in work rules, and was adjusted only for changes in prevailing wage rates. Several contracts have manning tables attached to indicate how the average wage rate is to be determined. In three of the contracts all increases in labor costs per unit output were passed through, so that changes in labor costs due to both input price changes and changes in realized productivity were reflected in transactions prices. These are denoted as adjustments based on "actual cost."

Materials and supplies (M&S): The M&S component of the base price is almost always indexed using a weighted average of several components of the wholesale price index (WPI). As many as nine separate components of the WPI are sometimes used. One contract contains a pass-through for changes in actual M&S costs. Two contracts adjust M&S costs using the same index used to adjust wages (one contract was written in 1957 and the other has an unusual cost plus option). Explosives and electricity are often indexed separately.

The fraction of the base price attributable to labor costs and materials and supplies varies considerably but generally falls within the range of 50 to 70 percent of the base price.

Depreciation/amortization: This capital cost component is treated in a variety of ways. In about half the cases it is indexed directly (one case partially indexed and one case fully indexed), using either the WPI or the consumer price index (CPI), or aggregated with a profit component and residual costs and then indexed. In three cases actual costs were passed through and in two cases this component was fixed. One contract had a more complicated treatment of depreciation and profits, which used a fixed component unless profits fell below some lower boundary, in which case prices would be adjusted upward.

Profit: In five cases a specific profit component was indexed either by the WPI or the CPI. In one case prices were adjusted upward or downward if the rate of return on sales fell above or below some range specified in the contract. In three cases the profit component was fixed. In four cases it was aggregated with depreciation and other residual costs and then indexed in three cases and was fixed in the other.

Costs due to changes in government regulations: Costs associated with complying with new government regulaions are generally treated as a cost to be passed on to the buyer. The provisions for calculating these costs are sometimes quite vague and are often subject to arbitration. The two contracts which did not contain such a provision were subsequently amended to include it. Both of these contracts were written in the 1960s.

Changes in taxes (excluding income) and royalties: These cost changes are generally simply passed through. Since they are usually changes in tax rates it is as if they were indexed.

Changes in contract/union work rules: In all but one of the contracts, provisions were made to adjust the labor component for changes in contract working hours, overtime pay, vacation time, etc. Several contracts contain detailed examples of the computations that should be made to implement this provision.

9.2. COST PLUS CONTRACTS (8 contracts)

Seven of the twenty-one contracts were primarily cost plus contracts and an additional contract gave the seller the option to switch from an indexed contract to a cost plus arrangement on six months' notice (it is counted twice in the totals). In six of these contracts the profit component is indexed to the CPI or the WPI. In two contracts the profit is based on a fair rate of return on investment.

Seven of the eight contracts (including the contract with the cost plus option) have formal incentive provisions. The eighth has vague language in the contract indicating that an incentive plan would be developed through negotiation after three years (the mine involved was subsequently acquired by the utility, before the date which would have triggered this provision). In three of the contracts there is a bonus/penalty provided for, in the form of an adjustment to the profit component based on a comparison with market prices. In one of these contracts the incentive payment is tied to a comparison between the unit cost increase under the contract and the increase in a weighted average of local, regional, and national coal prices. The other two contracts provide for a reward if the coal produced is the lowest cost of any comparable mine in the state.

Three of the contracts provide for a bonus/penalty based on the relationship between the actual costs and an indexed "standard cost." The indexed standard cost is constructed in a way similar to the construction of the base price plus escalation prices in the first set of contracts. Components are specified and then either indexed (mostly) or adjusted for some actual cost changes. The indexed standard cost is then compared to the actual cost per ton. There is a sliding scale that adjusts the profit component upward if the actual cost is below the standard cost and vice versa. The sliding scale bonus/penalty adjustment has a minimum and maximum. In each of these contracts explicit provisions are made as well for the utility to acquire the assets of the mines at net book value. In at least two of the three contracts, the utilities financed the initial development of the mines and hold mortgages on the property.[24]

The contract which gives the mining company the option to change from an indexed contract to a cost plus contract also gives the buyers the option to put the mining contract up for competitive bids if the cost plus option is exercised. The contract provides that a new mining company can acquire the assets at depreciated book cost or fair market value, whichever is lower.

---

24. This is probably true of Keystone as well, although I was unable to find documents indicating that utility financing had been provided.

In these cost plus contracts, the utility frequently has the contractual right not only to audit the books and submit the reasonableness of costs incurred to arbitration, but also to approve mining plans, capital expenditures, and budgets. Indeed, the distinction between vertical integration and "contract" in several of these cost plus contracts becomes almost a matter of semantics rather than a sharp distinction given the joint control, the presence of utility financing, and the cost plus nature of the pricing provisions.

9.3. OTHER PROVISIONS

Nonlinear pricing/minimum take or pay: five of the contracts had nonlinear price schedules (although one had ten components with prices *increasing* as aggregate production increased). Most of the contracts have minimum take or pay provisions. Of the five contracts without minimum take or pay provisions, one was a cost plus contract, one had a two-part tariff, and one had a minimum take or pay provision added by amendment.

Gross inequity/force majeur: Many of the contracts recognize explicitly that the pricing provisions specified can track the "prudent" costs incurred by the mining company only imperfectly. While the contracts intend both parties to bear some price/cost risk, it is not the intent of the contract to impose inequitable losses on the mining company or (in fewer cases) allow it to earn inequitable profits as a result of "surprises." These contracts contain a fairly vague provision that allows one or both parties to reopen the contract by asserting that its continuance constitutes a gross inequity. Thirteen of the contracts have gross inequity provisions and in at least a few cases these provisions were used to reopen the contracts. All of the contracts recognize that certain contingencies may arise that make it impossible for the plant to continue to operate or that make it impossible for it to continue to burn coal from this mine. Fairly standard force majeur provisions are included in all of the contracts. In a few cases considerable detail regarding what does and what does not constitute force majeur and how compensation will be made during force majeur periods is contained in the contracts.

10. EXPERIENCE WITH CONTRACT EXECUTION OVER TIME

A complete analysis of coal supply arrangements for mine-mouth plants would ideally include a detailed discussion of how these supply arrangements worked out over time. Did one party to the contract try to hold up the other? Were there haggling problems? Was there uneconomical supplier switching? Did the contractual provisions allow for smooth adjustments in obligatons? Did the parties continue to perform as economic conditions changed? Did the parties resort to litigation to get contractual promises enforced?

Most of the information that one would need to do such an in-depth analy-

74 / JOURNAL OF LAW, ECONOMICS, AND ORGANIZATION   I:1, 1985

sis is not publicly available. I will discuss the fragments of evidence that I have been able to put together, however.

Most of the initial supply arrangements that were made at the time the construction of a mine-mouth plant was planned have continued to govern supply arrangements up until the present time, despite fairly dramatic changes in coal prices, mining costs, and air pollution restrictions. However, many of the contracts have been amended, in several cases numerous times, for a variety of reasons. The contracts negotiated in the 1960s and early 1970s often had pricing provisions that did not provide adequate protection to the mining company for the kinds of cost increases that occurred in the 1970s. Amendments revising the base price and escalation provisions appear to be quite common. Sometimes these amendments are made in the course of negotiating a new supply agreement to accommodate additional generating units on the site. The gross inequity provisions have also been used to adjust prices. In several cases initial provisions for annual price adjustments were amended to provide for semi-annual, quarterly, or monthly base price adjustments as the inflation rate increased in the 1970s. In a few cases there were amendments clarifying the operation of the pricing provisions contained in the contracts, no doubt following a dispute between the parties. I was surprised at how enduring these relationships have been and how few modifications there have been made to the initial supply arrangements, given the many changes that have occurred in coal markets over the last twenty years.

Two of the twenty-one plants identified experienced significant changes in their initial supply arrangements. The owners of the San Juan plant initially created a jointly owned coal subsidiary (Western Coal Company), which owned the reserves and coal cleaning facilities.[25] They contracted with a subsidiary of Utah-International to build and operate a mine to produce coal from these reserves in 1972. The mining contract gave either party the option to terminate the agreement after six years, in which case the plant owners would have to acquire the mining assets. The contract price (apparently) contained a large fixed component. Utah notified the owners that it would exercise its option to terminate after six years since it was losing money. It offered to renegotiate the supply arrangement and preferred a cost plus contract. After determining that they could not produce the coal any cheaper and that an alternative fixed price contract offered by Utah was too expensive, the joint owners of the plant signed a new mining agreement with a cost plus profit pricing formula. Subsequently, Western Coal sold the

25. See letter from Western Coal Co. to Tucson Gas and Electric and Public Service of New Mexico regarding negotiations with Utah-International (dated February 21, 1978, on file).

reserves to the mine operator as well, and the utilities signed a revised thirty-seven year cost plus contract with Utah-International.

Utah Power & Light initially secured coal supplies for the Hunter and Huntington units under two long-term contracts with Peabody Coal. The first contract signed in 1971 provided for the requirements of the first two units of the Huntington plant. The second contract signed in 1974 (involving a second mine) provided for supplying the requirements of the first two units of the Hunter plant. Both contracts were for thirty-five years. The first used a base price plus escalation formula. The second used a cost plus formula with no explicit incentive provision. They both also contain unusually wide ranges in acceptable coal quality and no bonus/penalty payments tied to coal quality. Both mines were acquired by Utah Power & Light in 1977 and are operated by an independent operator under a thirty-year agreement.[26] The mining agreement does not contain coal quality specs or a bonus/penalty system. The plants encountered serious operating problems due to poor coal quality and wide variations in coal quality both before *and* after the acquisition of the mines. The utility never rejected any coal under the agreements.

I could find only one supply arrangement in the group where a dispute led to litigation. In 1973 Colorado-Ute Electric Cooperative signed a long-term requirements contract with Utah-International to supply coal for the first two units of the Craig generating station. The contract specified that the units would each have a capacity of 350 MWE. The requirements contract specified both a minimum take (and associated minimum payments) by the utility and a maximum monthly and yearly delivery obligation by the supplier. Deliveries above the maximum were at the discretion of the seller. Without telling the supplier, Colorado-Ute subsequently increased the actual size of each generating unit by about 20 percent. The year before deliveries were to commence the supplier sued for breach of contract, requesting that it be obligated only to deliver the minimum takes specified in the contract. Colorado-Ute argued that it was entitled to deliveries up to the maximum specified in the contract. The federal district court (425 F.Supp. 1093 [D. Colo. 1976]) found for the supplier, allowing him to rescind part of the agreement. Deliveries are being made under the contract, but only at the minimum take levels. A commentary on the case suggests that market conditions had changed after the contract was negotiated, that the seller could get higher prices by selling the additional coal to others, and perhaps that it could extract a higher price from Colorado-Ute.[27]

26. McGraw-Hill (1981: 392). This publication does not identify the utility and plants by name, but it is clear from the information provided that the utility is Utah Power and Light and the plants are Hunter and Huntington.

27. McGraw-Hill (1981: 486). Additional coal was eventually purchased from another supplier.

76 / JOURNAL OF LAW, ECONOMICS, AND ORGANIZATION I:1, 1985

11. DISCUSSION

The empirical results are quite consistent with the predictions of the transactions cost theory. Spot markets and short-term contracts account for a relatively small fraction of coal supply transactions for electric utilities. For the utility industry as a whole, long-term contracts rather than vertical integration is the preferred governance structure. Vertical integration is much more prevalent for mine-mouth plants than it is for other coal-fired generating stations, however. Although mine-mouth plants account for only 15 percent of total coal consumption by electric utilities, they account for more than half of the supplies governed by some form of vertical integration. When contracts are chosen in lieu of vertical integration (or, in a sense, in addition to it for jointly owned generating plants) for mine-mouth plants, the parties rely on very long-term contracts to support exchange. These contracts, while certainly "incomplete," are often quite complex, containing numerous price and nonprice provisions to protect both parties from breach and to help ensure the smooth operation of the supply relationship over time.

Although my research examining coal supply arrangements for non-mine-mouth generating plants is not yet complete, preliminary results suggest that there are important differences, on average, between contracts governing exchange for mine-mouth plants compared to other types of generating plants. The contractual duration of coal supply agreements for mine-mouth plants is substantially longer than for other types of plants and involves substantially larger annual delivery commitments (compare table 6 and table 8). Preliminary analysis of about sixty contracts for other coal plants suggests that these figures may understate the differences in length of commitment. Several of the non–mine-mouth contracts contain renegotiation and termination provisions that specifically allow one or both parties to terminate the agreement without paying damages long before the stated term of the contract is reached. This is not generally the case for mine-mouth plants. Contracts for mine-mouth plants are generally written as requirements contracts. This is rarely the case for the other contracts that I have examined.[28]

Although long-term contracts establish pricing provisions ex ante, this does not mean that prices are rigid. The pricing formulas used allow for frequent price adjustments based on input price changes and other cost changes that are attributable to exogenous events. While prices will not gen-

---

28. I have performed a preliminary analysis of 60 contracts that do not involve mine-mouth plants. The average duration of the contracts is about thirteen years. Only four are requirements contracts. Only three involved mines that had not been developed at the time the contract was signed. Eighteen of these contracts provide for scheduled price renegotiation during the term of the contract.

erally track short-term movements in market prices, they do respond in the long run to changes in the costs of producing coal. Recent contracts often provide for quarterly or monthly adjustments, and some older contracts have been amended to do so.

The pricing provisions, along with certain nonprice provisions, also reflect an interest by buyers that their suppliers produce efficiently. Two-thirds of the contracts make extensive use of indexing provisions to adjust prices so that the price the seller receives is partially independent of his production decisions. If the seller can beat the index he can increase his profits, and if the seller does not mine efficiently his profits will fall. All of the cost plus profit contracts recognize explicitly that pure cost plus pricing has bad incentive properties with regard to efficient production. All but one of these contracts contains additional provisions to give suppliers incentives to produce efficiently.

Overall, I have found the transactions cost framework to be an extremely powerful vehicle for gaining a better understanding of the nature of vertical supply relationships between power plant owners and their coal suppliers.

APPENDIX

This appendix summarizes the methods used for collecting the information on vertical integration and contracts that is discussed in the text.

VERTICAL INTEGRATION

I started with lists of captive coal mines contained in the McGraw-Hill *Keystone Coal Manual* and Gordon. Individual utility entries in *Moody's Public Utilities Manual* were reviewed to verify the information provided there and to resolve differences between the two lists. Next, Pasha Publications' *Guide to Coal Contracts* was searched for additional information on utility ownership of mines. Then, the entries for the 25 largest utility consumers of coal in *Moody's* were reviewed in an effort to identify additional utility-owned mines. Finally, the ownership of all suppliers identified in the contracts with mine-mouth plants was determined from another listing in the *Keystone Coal Manual*.

Annual production figures by mines and consumption figures for utilities were obtained from the *Keystone Coal Manual*, the Department of Energy's *Cost and Quality of Fuels for Electric Utilities, Moody's* and annual reports.

MINE-MOUTH PLANTS

The definition of a mine-mouth plant is at least partially subjective and no general list of such plants appears to exist. I searched for plants that were deliberately located adjacent to specific coal reserves in order to exploit these reserves to generate electricity and where the adjacent mining facilities were built in reliance on these plants. The *Guide to Coal Contracts* has extensive information on coal transportation modes

78 / JOURNAL OF LAW, ECONOMICS, AND ORGANIZATION I:1, 1985

used to serve many plants. Mine-mouth plants are frequently noted explicitly. In a few cases, mine-mouth plants were identified when conveyor belts or short-haul rail spurs were designated as the coal transportation mode. Gordon contains a discussion of mine-mouth plants and identifies a few. The *Keystone Coal Manual* also provides information to identify mine-mouth plants. These sources were supplemented by searches of annual reports and various government publications. I identified more plants than appear on the list but eliminated plants which had first units which began operating before 1960, since I thought that it would be difficult to obtain information on initial supply arrangements for plants that began operating so long ago. One plant (Montrose) that began supplying electricity before 1960 is on the list because the start-date that I initially identified turned out to be incorrect. I left it on the list since I had already collected the information on coal supply arrangements. Almost all of the older plants that were dropped from the list obtain at least some of their coal from utility-owned coal subsidiaries. In several cases these plants were greatly expanded with large units built in the 1960s or 1970s and rely on contracts for a large fraction of their supplies. It is possible that this selection process did not capture all mine-mouth plants in existence.

CONTRACTS

General information on the contract characteristics for each plant was obtained from the *Guide to Coal Contracts*. Individual contracts, amendments, etc., were obtained from the *Washington Service Bureau*. These contracts in turn were obtained primarily from SEC files. National Economic Research Associates gave me access to their coal contract library, where these contracts are filed. In a few cases I was able to obtain additional information by making telephone calls to individual utilities and reviewing 10-K filings.

The contracts are sometimes long and complicated. Just reading them is not very productive. I used a coding sheet which contained entries for a variety of contract characteristics based on the discussion of the implications of transactions cost theory contained in the text. Each contract was read to fill in the relevant characteristics that had been identified. In several cases it is necessary to make interpretations of provisions which are unclear or ambiguous, so the coding of the contracts involves some subjective evaluations as well. I read every contract, amendment, and any associated correspondence myself.

REFERENCES

Coase, Ronald H. 1937. "The Nature of the Firm," 4 *Economica* 386–405.
———. 1972. "Industrial Organization: A Proposal for Research," in Victor R. Fuchs, ed., *Policy Issues and Research Opportunities in Industrial Organization*, vol. 3. New York: National Bureau of Economic Research.
Goldberg, Victor P. 1976. "Regulation and Administered Conracts," 7 *Bell Journal of Economics* 426–48.
——— and John E. Erickson. Undated. "The Law and Economics of Long-Term Contracts: A Case Study of Petroleum Coke," mimeo.
Gordon, Richard L. 1975. *U.S. Coal and the Electric Power Industry*. Washington, D.C.: Resources for the Future, Johns Hopkins University Press.

Grossman, Sanford J., and Oliver Hart. 1984. "The Cost and Benefits of Ownership: A Theory of Vertical Integration," London: London School of Economics, mimeo.

Hart, Oliver D. 1983. "Optimal Labour Contracts under Asymmetric Information: An Introduction," 50 *Review of Economic Studies* 3–36.

Holmstrom, Bengt. 1979. "Moral Hazard and Observability," 10 *Bell Journal of Economics* 74–91.

Joskow, Paul L. 1977. "Commercial Impossibility, The Uranium Market and the Westinghouse Case," 6 *Journal of Legal Studies* 119–76.

———and Nancy Rose. 1984. "The Effects of Technological Change, Experience and Environmental Regulation on the Construction Costs of Coal-Burning Generating Units," MIT Department of Economics Discussion, paper.

Klein, Benjamin. 1980. "Transaction Cost Determinants of 'Unfair' Contractual Relations," 70 *American Economic Review* 356–62.

———, R. A. Crawford and A. A. Alchian. 1979. "Vertical Integration, Appropriable Rents, and the Competitive Contracting Process," 21 *Journal of Law and Economics* 297–326.

Macaulay, Stewart. 1963. "Non-Contractual Relations in Business," 28 *American Sociological Review* 55–70.

Masten, Scott E., 1984. "The Organization of Production: Evidence from the Aerospace Industry," 23 *Journal of Law and Economics* 403–19.

McGraw-Hill, Inc. 1981. *How to Negotiate and Administer a Coal Supply Agreement*. New York.

———. 1982. *Keystone Coal Industry Manual*. New York.

Monteverde, Kirk, and David J. Teece 1982. "Supplier Switching Costs and Vertical Integration in the Automobile Industry," 13 *Bell Journal of Economics* 206–13.

Moody's Investors Services. (Various Years.) *Moody's Public Utility Manual*, New York.

Muris, Timothy J. 1981. "Opportunistic Behavior and the Law of Contracts," 65 *Minnesota Law Review* 521–90.

National Coal Association. 1983. *Coal Data (1981/82)*. Washington, D.C.

———. 1984. *Facts about Coal (1984/85)*. Washington, D.C.

———. (Various years.) *Steam Electric Plant Factors*. Washington, D.C.

Palay, Thomas M. 1984. "Comparative Institutional Economics: The Governance of Freight Rail Contracting," 13 *Journal of Legal Studies* 265–88.

Pasha Publications. (1981, 1983). *Guide to Coal Contracts*. Arlington, VA.

Shavell, Steven. 1979. "Risk Sharing and Incentives in the Principal and Agent Relationship," 10 *Bell Journal of Economics* 55–73.

U.S. Department of Energy. (Various years.) *Inventory of Power Plants in the United States*, DOE/EIA-0095. Washington, D.C.: Government Printing Office.

———. (Various years.) *Cost and Quality of Fuels for Electric Utility Plants*, DOE/EIA-0191. Washington, D.C.: Government Printing Office.

———. (Various issues.) *Quarterly Coal Report*, DOE/EIA-0121. Washington, D.C.: Government Printing Office.

———. 1983. *Coal Production–1982*, DOE/EIA-0118(82). Washington, D.C.: Government Printing Office.

Williamson, Oliver E. 1971. "The Vertical Integration of Production: Market Failure Considerations," 61 *American Economic Review* 112–23.

———. 1975. *Markets and Hierarchies: Analysis and Antitrust Implications*, New York: Free Press.

———. 1979. "Transaction Cost Economics: The Governance of Contractual Relations," 22 *Journal of Law and Economics* 233–61.

———. 1983. "Credible Commitments: Using Hostages to Support Exchange," 73 *American Economic Review* 519–40.

———. 1984. *The Economic Institutions of Capitalism*. Draft manuscript.

Zimmerman, Martin. 1981. *The U.S. Coal Industry: The Economics of Policy Choice*. Cambridge: MIT Press.

[15]

The Role of Market Forces in Assuring Contractual Performance

Benjamin Klein

University of California, Los Angeles

Keith B. Leffler

University of Washington

The conditions under which transactors can use the market (repeat-purchase) mechanism of contract enforcement are examined. Increased price is shown to be a means of assuring contractual performance. A necessary and sufficient condition for performance is the existence of price sufficiently above salvageable production costs so that the nonperforming firm loses a discounted stream of rents on future sales which is greater than the wealth increase from nonperformance. This will generally imply a market price greater than the perfectly competitive price and rationalize investments in firm-specific assets. Advertising investments thereby become a positive indicator of likely performance.

I. Introduction

An implicit assumption of the economic paradigm of market exchange is the presence of a government to define property rights and

We thank Armen Alchian, Thomas Borcherding, Harold Demsetz, James Ferguson, Jack Hirshleifer, Matt Lindsay, Roy Kenney, John Long, Ian Macneil, Kevin Murphy, Phillip Nelson, Joseph Ostroy, Peter Pashigian, Sam Peltzman, George Priest, John Riley, Jonathan Skinner, George Stigler, Earl Thompson, and participants at seminars at UCLA and the University of Chicago during 1977–78 for helpful suggestions and comments. Jonathan Skinner also provided valuable research assistance. The Foundation for Research in Economics and Education and the University of Chicago Law School Law and Economics Program provided Klein with research support, and the Center for Research in Government Policy and Business, University of Rochester, provided Leffler with research support.

[*Journal of Political Economy*, 1981, vol. 89, no. 4]

enforce contracts. An important element of the legal-philosophical tradition upon which the economic model is built is that without some third-party enforcer to sanction stealing and reneging, market exchange would be impossible.[1] But economists also have long considered "reputations" and brand names to be private devices which provide incentives that assure contract performance in the absence of any third-party enforcer (Hayek 1948, p. 97; Marshall 1949, vol. 4, p. xi). This private-contract enforcement mechanism relies upon the value to the firm of repeat sales to satisfied customers as a means of preventing nonperformance. However, it is possible that economic agents with well-known brand names and reputations for honoring contracts may find it wealth maximizing to break such potentially long-term exchange relationships and obtain a temporary increase in profit. In particular, the determinants of the efficacy of this market method of contract performance and therefore the conditions under which we are likely to observe its use remain unspecified.

This paper examines the nongovernmental repeat-purchase contract-enforcement mechanism. To isolate this force, we assume throughout our analysis that contracts are not enforceable by the government or any other third party. Transactors are assumed to rely solely on the threat of termination of the business relationship for enforcement of contractual promises.[2] This assumption is most realistic for contractual terms concerning difficult-to-measure product characteristics such as the "taste" of a hamburger. However, even when the aspects of a contract are less complicated and subjective and therefore performance more easily measurable by a third party such as a judge, specification, litigation, and other contract-enforcement costs may be substantial. Therefore, explicit guarantees to replace or repair defective goods (warranties) are not costless ways to assure contract performance. Market arrangements such as the value of lost repeat purchases which motivate transactors to honor their promises may be the cheapest method of guaranteeing the guarantee.

While our approach is general in the sense that the value of future exchanges can motivate fulfillment of all types of contractual prom-

---

[1] Hobbes ([1651] 1955, pp. 89–90) maintains that ". . . he that performeth first, has no assurance the other will perform after; because the bonds of words are too weak to bridle men's ambition, avarice, anger, and other Passions, without the fear of some coercive Power; which in the condition of here Nature, where all men are equal, and judges of the justness of their own fears cannot possibly be supposed."

[2] This assumption is consistent with the pioneering work of Macaulay (1963), where reliance on formal contracts and the threat of explicit legal sanctions was found to be an extremely rare element of interfirm relationships. Macaulay provides some sketchy evidence that business firms prevent nonfulfillment of contracts by the use of effective nonlegal sanctions consisting primarily of the loss of future business. This "relational" nature of contracts has been recently emphasized by Macneil (1974), and also by Goldberg (1976) and Williamson (1979).

ises, we focus in this paper on contracts between producers and consumers regarding product quality. In order for a repeat-sale enforcement mechanism to operate, we assume that the identity of firms is known by consumers[3] and that the government enforces property rights to the extent that consumers voluntarily choose whom to deal with and must pay for the goods they receive.[4] In addition, managers of firms are assumed to be wealth maximizing and to place no value on honesty per se.

In Section II, the conditions are outlined under which firms will either honor their commitments to supply a high level of quality or choose to supply a quality lower than promised. In order to emphasize the ability of markets to guarantee quality in the absence of any government enforcement mechanism, a simple model is presented which assumes that consumers costlessly communicate among one another. Therefore, if a firm cheats and supplies to any individual a quality of product less than contracted for, all consumers in the market learn this and all future sales are lost. A major result of our analysis is that even such perfect interconsumer communication conditions are not sufficient to assure high quality supply. Cheating will be prevented and high quality products will be supplied only if firms are earning a continual stream of rental income that will be lost if low quality output is deceptively produced. The present discounted value of this rental stream must be greater than the one-time wealth increase obtained from low quality production.

This condition for the "notorious firm" repeat-purchase mechanism to assure high quality supply is not generally fulfilled by the usual free-entry, perfectly competitive equilibrium conditions of price equal to marginal and average cost. It becomes necessary to distinguish between production costs that are "sunk" firm-specific assets and those production costs that are salvageable (i.e., recoverable) in uses outside the firm. Our analysis implies that firms will not cheat on

---

[3] Nonidentification of firm output leads to quality depreciation via a standard externality argument; i.e., supply by a particular firm of lower than anticipated quality imposes a cost through the loss of future sales not solely on that firm but on all firms in the industry (see Akerlof 1970; Klein 1974).

[4] For simplicity, we assume that "theft," as opposed to nonfulfillment of contract, is not possible. While "fraud," in the sense of one party to the transaction intentionally supplying less than contracted for, is analytically similar to "theft," we draw a distinction along this continuum by assuming that the government only permits "voluntary" transactions in the sense that transactors choose whom to trade with. Therefore, while consumers cannot "steal" goods, they can, in principle, pay for the goods they receive with checks that bounce; and while firms cannot rob consumers, they can, in principle, supply goods of lower than promised quality. Although we recognize the great difficulty in practice of separating the underlying government enforcement mechanisms, e.g., property law, from the private promise-enforcing mechanisms we are attempting to analyze, this distinction between theft and fraud is analytically unambiguous.

promises to sell high quality output only if price is sufficiently above salvageable production costs. While the perfectly competitive price may imply such a margin above salvageable costs, this will not necessarily be the case. The fundamental theoretical result of this paper is that market prices above the competitive price and the presence of nonsalvageable capital are means of enforcing quality promises.[5]

In Section III our theoretical model of quality-guaranteeing price premiums above salvageable costs is extended to examine how the capital value of these price-premium payments can be dissipated in a free-entry equilibrium. The quality-guaranteeing nature of nonsalvageable, firm-specific capital investments is developed. Alternative techniques of minimizing the cost to consumers of obtaining an assured high quality are investigated. We also explore market responses to consumer uncertainty about quality-assuring premium levels. Advertising and other production and distribution investments in "conspicuous" assets are examined as competitive responses to simultaneous quality and production-cost uncertainties. Finally, a summary of the analysis and some concluding remarks are presented in Section IV.

II. Price Premiums and Quality Assurance

Assume initially that consumers costlessly know all market prices and production technologies but not the qualities of goods offered for sale. For simplicity, the good being considered is assumed to be characterized by a single objective quality measure, q, where quality refers to the level of some desirable characteristic contained in the good. Examples are the quietness of appliance motors, the wrinkle-free or colorfast properties of clothing, or the gasoline mileage of an automobile. We also assume that the economy consists of consumers who consider buying a product x each period, where the length of a period is defined by the life (repurchase period) of product x, and who are assumed to costlessly communicate quality information among one another. Therefore, if a particular firm supplies less-

---

[5] The notion that an increased price can serve as a means of assuring high quality supply by giving the firm a rental stream that will be lost if future sales are not made is not new. Adam Smith ([1776] 1937, p. 105) suggested this force more than 200 years ago when he noted that "the wages of labour vary according to the small or great trust which must be reposed in the workman. The wages of goldsmiths and jewellers are everywhere superior to those of many other workmen, not only of equal, but of much superior ingenuity; on account of the precious metals with which they are intrusted. We trust our health to the physician; our fortune and sometimes our life and reputation to the lawyer and attorney. Such confidence could not safely be reposed in people of a very mean or low condition." Similar competitive mechanisms recently have been analyzed by Becker and Stigler (1974) and Klein (1974).

ASSURING CONTRACTUAL PERFORMANCE 619

than-contracted-for quality to one consumer, the next period all consumers are assumed to know. In addition, this information is assumed not to depreciate over time.[6]⌐j

Identical technology is assumed to be available to all entrepreneurs. Hence, there are many potential firms with identical total cost functions, $C = c(x,q) + F(q)$, where F is fixed (invariant to rate) costs. Higher quality and larger quantities require higher production costs, $F_q > 0$, $c_q > 0$, $c_x > 0$, and marginal cost is assumed to increase with quality, $c_{xq} > 0$. Fixed costs are assumed initially to be expenditures made explicitly each period rather than capital costs allocated to the current period. For example, they may include a payment on a short-term (one-period) rental agreement for a machine but not the current forgone interest on a purchased machine or the current period's payment on a long-term rental agreement—both of which imply long-term and hence capital commitments.

We therefore are explicitly distinguishing between "fixed" costs in the sense employed here of constant (invariant to output) current costs and "sunk" (nonsalvageable) capital costs. The usual textbook proposition that a firm will not shut down production as long as price is greater than average variable cost blurs this distinction and implicitly assumes that all fixed costs are also sunk capital costs. Our assumption of the complete absence of any long-term commitments is analytically equivalent to perfect salvageability of all capital assets. If all long-term production-factor commitments were costlessly reversible, that is, all real and financial assets such as the machine or the long-term machine rental contract could be costlessly resold and hence perfectly salvageable, there also would not be any capital costs. Only the nonsalvageable part of any long-term commitment should be considered a current sunk capital cost.

If buyers are costlessly informed about quality, the competitive price schedule, P_c, for alternative quality levels is given by the minimum average production costs for each level of quality and is designated by $P_c = P_c(q)$. This is represented in figure 1 for two alternative quality levels, q_h and q_{min}, by the prices P_1 and P_0. Suppose, however, that the quality of product x cannot be determined costlessly before purchase. For simplicity, assume prepurchase inspection reveals only whether quality is below some minimum level, q_{min}, and that

[6] If we modify the assumptions of our model to make interconsumer communication less than perfect and allow inflows of new ignorant consumers over time and permit individuals to forget, the potential short-run cheating gain by firms would be increased. Therefore, the quality-assuring price premium would be higher than we derive below. In this case increased firm size, by making it more likely that the individuals one is sharing product-quality information with (e.g., family and friends) have purchased from the same firm, lowers the potential short-run cheating gain by essentially reducing the repurchase period.

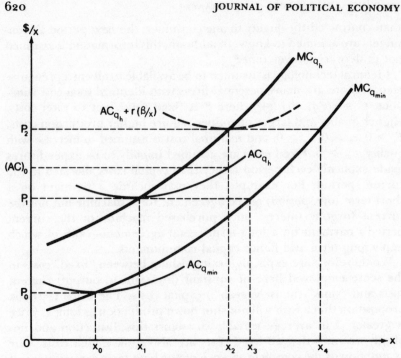

FIG 1.—Pricing and production of alternative quality levels

the costs are prohibitive of determining whether quality is above q_{min} prior to purchase.[7] Obviously, whenever the market price that consumers will pay for asserted high quality exceeds the cost of producing minimum quality output, the firm can increase its initial period profits by producing the minimum quality output and deceptively selling it as a higher quality product.

If producers are to have an incentive to produce high quality products (in the absence of governmentally enforceable contracts), consumers must somehow reward high quality production and punish low quality production. We assume in this competitive framework that consumers will purchase from particular sellers randomly chosen from the group of homogeneous sellers over which consumer information is transmitted. If a consumer receives a product of a quality at least as high as implicitly contracted for, he will continue to purchase randomly from this group of sellers. On the other hand, if quality is less than contracted for, all consumers cease to purchase from the particular sampled "cheating" firm.

[7] The quality of the good beyond the minimum level is therefore what Nelson (1970) has labeled as an "experience" characteristic. Making the minimum quality level endogenous does not substantially change the following analysis.

ASSURING CONTRACTUAL PERFORMANCE   621

Consider now an initial "competitive" equilibrium in which a single firm contemplates selling a quality below that expected by customers. Given the competitive market price for some high quality, $P_c(q_h) \equiv P_1$ in figure 1, this particular firm could increase its initial period quasi rents by producing minimum quality and selling it at the high quality price. However, since buyers are assumed to communicate fully with one another, all future customers of high quality output, that is, sales at prices greater than $P_c(q_{min}) \equiv P_0$ in figure 1, are lost. That is, a firm that cheats will become known as a "notorious" cheater, and consumers will not purchase from the firm any product the quality of which cannot be determined prepurchase.[8]

Whether sales of high or minimum quality will maximize the firm's wealth depends on whether the capital value of future quasi rents from continued high quality production exceeds the differential initial period quasi rents from quality depreciation. In terms of figure 1, at the perfectly competitive price for high quality output, P_1, price is equal to the average costs of high quality production. Therefore, the quasi rents from continued high quality production are zero. If, alternatively, the firm were to deceptively produce minimum quality output, as a price taker it would expand its production to x_3 (where $P_1 = MC_{q_{min}}$) and receive a one-period quasi rent, the present value of which is equal to:

$$W_1 = \frac{1}{1+r}\left\{(P_1 - P_0)x_3 - \int_{x_0}^{x_3}[MC_{q_{min}}(x) - P_0]dx\right\}. \quad (1)$$

Therefore, at the perfectly competitive price for any quality above q_{min} firms will always cheat consumers and supply q_{min}.

Faced with this possibility, consumers would recognize that regardless of producers' promises they will not obtain the higher quality product. Therefore, consumers would be willing to pay only the costless information price of the minimum quality product whose quality they can verify prepurchase, P_0. Because of such rational consumer anticipations, firms will not be able to cheat, but desired high quality output will not be supplied.

There may, however, be a price higher than the perfectly competitive price of high quality output, P_1, that if it were the equilibrium market price would (a) motivate honest production of the high quality good and (b) not completely dissipate the consumers' surplus from purchase of higher quality. Consider a price such as P_2 in figure 1. A

---

[8] A terminated firm cannot begin business in this industry under a new name. However, the highest valued alternative use of the entrepreneurial skills is included in salvageable fixed production costs. The firm considered here is assumed to face the same opportunities elsewhere as the firms that are honest in production of x. Therefore, the cheating firm can elect to enter a new industry.

firm supplying high quality output will now expand its production to x_2. The price premium $\tilde{P}$, defined as the increase in the price above minimum average cost of high quality, provides firms supplying high quality with a perpetual stream of quasi rents the present value of which (assuming unchanging cost and demand conditions over time) is equal to:

$$W_2 = \frac{1}{r}\left\{\tilde{P}x_2 - \int_{x_1}^{x_2}[MC_h(x) - P_1]dx\right\}. \tag{2}$$

The price premium also increases the gains to a firm from supplying minimum quality at the high price. A firm that chooses to cheat will now expand its output (in terms of fig. 1 to x_4) and earn the extra premium on all units sold.[9] Therefore, the capital value of the quasi rents from supplying quality less than promised is:

$$W_3 = \frac{1}{1+r}\left\{[\tilde{P} + (P_1 - P_0)]x_4 - \int_{x_0}^{x_4}[MC_{q_{min}}(x) - P_0]dx\right\}. \tag{3}$$

A firm will honor its implicit quality contract as long as the difference between the capital values of the noncheating and cheating strategies, $W_2 - W_3$, is positive. Consider the quasi-rent flow of the cheating and noncheating alternatives, that is, the terms in braces in our expressions (2) and (3). Define QR_2 equal to rW_2 and QR_3 equal to $(1 + r)W_3$. A firm will then elect not to cheat if and only if:

$$\frac{QR_3}{QR_2} \leq \frac{(1+r)}{r}. \tag{4}$$

Therefore, there will be a price premium that motivates firms to honestly produce high quality as long as:

$$\lim_{\tilde{P}\to\infty}\left(\frac{QR_3}{QR_2}\right) \leq \frac{(1+r)}{r}. \tag{5}$$

Using L'Hospital's rule, equation (5) will be satisfied as long as

$$\frac{1}{r} > \frac{(x_4 - x_2)}{x_2} \tag{6}$$

for all $P > P_3$, where P_3 is some finite price. Intuitively, as the price increases it is only the increase in quasi rents on the additional units of minimum quality output that favors the deceptive strategy. Equation (6) insures that price increases beyond some level increase W_2 more than W_3 such that eventually W_2 is greater than W_3.

---

[9] Note that although x_2 may be greater or less than x_3, depending on the price premium chosen, given upward-sloping supply functions and the condition that $MC_{q_h}(q) > MC_{q_{min}}(q)$ for all q, it must be the case that $x_4 > x_2 > x_1$.

The condition specified in equation (6) is quite reasonable. It will be satisfied as long as a cheating firm does not accompany cheating with very large output increases. If, for example, the real interest rate were .05 we require only that the output increase by a cheating firm not be more than 20 times the total output that would be produced if the firm were not cheating. Hence, under very general cost conditions a price premium will exist that motivates competitive firms to honor high quality promises because the value of satisfied customers exceeds the cost savings of cheating them.[10]

While we cannot state broad necessary conditions for the form the cost function must take to imply the existence of a quality-assuring price, "reasonable" sufficient conditions can be stated. In particular, all cases of vertically parallel marginal cost curves, as illustrated in figure 1, where quality is produced by a fixed input not subject to decreasing returns to scale (such as the use of a better motor) and where the second derivative of marginal cost is greater than or equal to zero imply the existence of a quality-assuring price. The Appendix contains simulation results under the more unrealistic assumption of isoelastic marginal cost functions. These simulations indicate the exceptional nature of the conditions when equation (6) is not satisfied. When a quality-assuring price does not exist, the cost functions are generally such that at reasonable premiums cheating output would be expanded by very large factors (often factors of many thousands). Since marginal cost functions for most products can be expected to become quite steep if not vertical at output expansions of much less than these factors, a quality-assuring price premium can generally be expected to exist.

Throughout the remainder of the paper we assume the existence of a quality-assuring price. For given cost and demand conditions, the minimum quality-assuring price will depend upon the level of quality

[10] The potential function of price premiums as quality guarantors is also applicable to markets in which firms face downward-sloping demands. In this case, the inability of firms to increase sales without reductions in price limits the gains available from deceptive minimum quality production as price increases. The existence of a price sufficient to guarantee quality now depends on the elasticity of demand in addition to the cost savings from quality reductions at various quantities. In addition, when price-searching firms do not have stable future demands, consumer knowledge of cost and current demand conditions is not sufficient to estimate the quality-assuring price. The anticipated future demand vis-à-vis current demand is also relevant. For example, where consumers expect a growing demand for the output of a firm that continues to produce high quality output, the rate of quasi-rent flow from high quality (or future deceptive minimum quality) production increases over time. As compared to a firm with the same initial but constant demand, the growing firm will receive a larger capital value return at any price from high quality production in the initial period. Firms facing expected demand growth will therefore require smaller quality-assuring price premiums. See Klein, McLaughlin, and Murphy (1980) for an analysis of the less than perfectly elastic firm demand case.

considered and is denoted by $P^* = P^*(q, q_{min}, r)$. Our analysis implies that the quality-assuring price will increase as quality increases, as minimum quality decreases (for all q greater than q_{min}), and as the interest rate increases. These conditions are consistent with the familiar recognition that, given a particular quality level, quality-cheating problems are less severe the higher the level of quality that can be detected prepurchase and the shorter the period of repurchase.[11]

Intuitively, the quality-assuring price treats the potential value of not producing minimum quality as an explicit opportunity cost to the firm of higher quality production. Hence the quality-assuring price must not only compensate the firm for the increased average production costs incurred when quality above that detectable prior to purchase is produced, but must also yield a normal rate of return on the forgone gains from exploiting consumer ignorance. This price "premium" stream can be thought of as "protection money" paid by consumers to induce contract performance. Although the present discounted value of this stream equals the value of the short-run gain the firm can obtain by cheating, consumers are not indifferent between paying the "premium" over time or permitting the firm to cheat. The price "premium" is a payment for high quality in the face of prepurchase quality-determination costs. The relevant consumer choice is between demanding minimum quality output at a perfectly competitive (costless information) price or paying a competitive price

[11] We can complicate our model by dropping the assumption that nondeceiving firms are anticipated to produce forever. If firms have a finite life, and the last period of production is known by both firms and consumers, there will be no premium sufficient to guarantee quality. No matter how high the premium paid by consumers for a high quality good in the last period, firms will supply "deceptive" minimum quality because there are no future sales to lose. Consumers aware of the last period will therefore demand only the minimum quality in that period. But then the next to the last period becomes the last period in the sense that, independent of the price premium, firm wealth is maximized by supplying minimum quality and going out of business. Consumers will then only pay for minimum quality output in the next to last period, and so on. High quality will never be produced. However, the necessary unraveling of the premium solution to assure high quality requires prior consumer knowledge of a date beyond which the firm will not produce. If consumers merely know that firms have finite lives but cannot with certainty specify a date beyond which a particular firm will not exist, price premiums may assure quality. While consumers are aware that some transactions will be with firms in their last period and hence cheating will occur, the expected gain from purchasing high promised quality can be positive. Our price premium–repeat business quality enforcement mechanism is analytically equivalent in form to the "super-game" solutions to the prisoner's dilemma problem developed in the game-theory literature. A general result of that analysis is that a cooperative solution can exist if one assumes either an infinitely long super game (as we have assumed in our model), or a super game of finite length but with transactors who have sufficient uncertainty regarding the period when the super game will end (see, e.g., Luce and Raiffa [1957], pp. 97–102, or, for a more recent solution to the problem that is similar in emphasis to our approach, Telser [1980]).

"premium," which is both necessary and sufficient, for higher quality output.[12]

There is a possibility that the required quality-guaranteeing price premium may exceed the increased consumer surplus of purchasing higher quality rather than the minimum quality product. If consumers can easily substitute increased quantity of the low quality product for increased quality, then the value of guaranteed high quality will be relatively low. Therefore, although a quality-guaranteeing price exists, a higher than minimum quality product may not be produced. For those goods where the substitution possibilities between quality and quantity are lower (e.g., drugs), consumer demand for confidence will be relatively high and the high quality guarantee worth the price premium. We assume throughout that we are dealing with products where some demand exists for the high quality good in the range of prices considered.

III. Competitive Market Equilibrium: Firm-specific Capital Investments

Our analysis has focused on the case where costless information (perfectly competitive) prices do not imply sufficient firm-specific rents to motivate high quality production. A price premium was therefore necessary to induce high quality supply. Thus, if price assures quality, the firms producing quality greater than q_{min} appear to earn positive economic profits. However, this cannot describe a full market equilibrium. When the price is high enough to assure a particular high level of quality, additional firms have an incentive to enter the industry. But if additional firms enter, the summation of the individual firms' outputs will exceed the quantity demanded at the quality-assuring price. Yet this output surplus cannot result in price reductions since the quality-assuring price is, in effect, a minimum price constraint "enforced" by rational consumers. All price-taking firms supplying a particular promised quality q above the minimum face a horizontal demand curve at $P^* = P^*(q)$, which is of an unusual nature in that prices above or below P^* result in zero sales. Consumers know that any price below P^* for its associated quality results in the

---

[12] As opposed to the Darby and Karni (1973) analysis, this particular model implies an equilibrium quantity of "fraud" equal to zero, where fraud is the difference between anticipated and actual quality. Given the symmetrical information assumptions regarding cost functions, parties to a contract know when and by how much a contract will be broken. An unanticipated broken quality contract is therefore not possible. The implicit economic (as opposed to common usage) concept of "contract" refers to anticipated outcomes and not to verbal promises or written agreements; thus there will be no broken quality "contracts."

supply of q_{min}. They therefore will not purchase from a firm promising that quality at a price lower than P^*.

A. Brand Name Capital Investments

Competition to dissipate the economic profits being earned by existing firms must therefore occur in nonprice dimensions. However, the zero-profit equilibrium is consistent with only a very particular form of profit-absorbing nonprice competition. The competition involves *firm-specific capital* expenditures. This firm-specific capital competition motivates firms to purchase assets with (nonsalvageable) costs equal to the capital value of the premium rental stream earned when high quality is supplied at the quality-assuring price. That is, if $P^*(q)$ is not to increase, the investment leading to zero profits must be highly firm specific and depreciate to zero if the firm cheats and supplies q_{min} rather than the anticipated quality. Such firm-specific capital costs could, for example, take the form of sunk investments in the design of a firm logo or an expensive sign promoting the firm's name. Expenditures on these highly firm-specific assets are then said to represent brand name (or selling) capital investments.

The competitive process also forces the firm-specific capital investments to take the form of assets which provide the greatest direct service value to consumers. The consumers' "effective" price of purchasing a quality-assured good, where the effective price is defined as the purchase price of a product, P^*, less the value of the services yielded by the jointly supplied brand name assets, is thereby minimized. Competition among firms in seeking and making the most highly valued firm-specific brand name capital investments will occur until the expected wealth increase and, therefore, the incentive to enter the industry are eliminated.

If the firm decides to cheat it will experience a capital loss equal to its anticipated future profit stream. Since $P^*(q)$ is derived so that the threat of loss of this future profit stream motivates guaranteed quality, the zero-profit equilibrium "brand-name capital," β, which serves as an explicit hostage to prevent cheating, equals, in terms of figure 1, where $P^*(q_h) = P_2$,

$$\beta = \frac{[P_2 - (AC)_0]x_2}{r}. \tag{7}$$

That is, the market value of the competitive firm's brand name capital is equal to the value of total specific or "sunk" selling costs made by the firm which, in turn, equals the present value of the anticipated premium stream from high quality output. If we continue to assume that there are no capital (and therefore "sunk") costs of production, the zero-profit equilibrium is shown in figure 1 where average "total" cost (which includes average production costs, AC_{q_h}, plus average brand-name capital [i.e., nonsalvageable "selling"] costs, $r[\beta/x]$) just equals price, P_2.

What assures high quality supply is the capital loss due to the loss of future business if low quality is produced. Since the imputed value of the firm's brand name capital is determined by the firm's expected quasi rents on future sales, this capital loss from supplying quality lower than promised is represented by the depreciation of this firm-specific asset. The expenditures on brand name capital assets are therefore similar to collateral that the firm loses if it supplies output of less than anticipated quality and in equilibrium the premium stream provides only a normal rate of return on this collateral asset.

Note that the "effective" price paid by consumers, which equals the quality-assuring price less the value of the consumer services yielded by the brand name capital, may be minimized by the investment in specific selling assets with some positive salvage value. Even though this results in an increased quality-guaranteeing price, assets with positive salvage values may yield differentially large direct consumer service flows. All brand name capital assets must, however, satisfy a necessary condition that the salvage value per unit of output be less than the consumer service value. Firms competing to minimize the effective price will choose specific assets by trading off increased consumer service value with decreased salvage value. This may explain why stores which supply high quality products often have amenities (such as a luxurious carpet cut to fit the particular store) even though only small direct consumer services may be yielded relative to cost.[13]

B. Nonsalvageable Productive Assets

The market equilibrium we have developed implies an effective price for high quality output that is higher than what would exist in a zero information cost world. While the costless-information solution is meaningless as an achievable standard of "efficiency," alternative marketing arrangements may be usefully compared to this benchmark. Viable, competitive firms will adopt the arrangements which, considering all transacting and contracting costs, minimize the devia-

[13] If the "sunk" asset yields absolutely no consumer services, then the firm will not use it. Even though profits would be eliminated by purchase of such an asset, consumers would be indifferent between a firm that invested in the asset and a firm that did not. In a world where consumers do not possess full knowledge of cost conditions, however, use of obviously specific assets may be employed even if yielding no direct consumer service flow because they may efficiently inform consumers regarding the sunk capital cost to the firm. This is discussed in greater detail in Sec. IIIC.

tions between the costless-information price and the effective price. One potentially efficient alternative or supplement to the pure price-premium method of guaranteeing quality may be the use of nonsalvageable productive assets rather than brand name (selling) assets.

In order to simplify the analysis of price premiums in guaranteeing quality, we have assumed that all production costs, including fixed costs, were noncapital costs and therefore, by definition, salvageable. More realistically, firms can control both the capital intensity of production and the salvage value of any fixed assets employed in the production process. In particular, if the firm uses a production process that has a nonsalvageable capital element, the normal rate of return (quasi-rent stream) on this element of production capital effectively serves as a quality-assuring premium. In terms of our model, the capital value of the quasi-rent stream when a firm cheats (eq. [3]) is now modified so that the net gain from cheating equals W_3 minus this nonsalvageable capital cost. Alternatively, in the zero-profit equilibrium the total level of collateral must still equal the potential gross gains from cheating, but part of the collateral is now provided by the nonsalvageable production assets rather than the brand name capital assets.

For example, if a machine is somewhat illiquid, buying it rather than renting it short term provides some of this collateral and lowers the quality-guaranteeing price. In fact, because of positive selling costs, capital assets generally have a salvage value less than cost. Thus capital inputs, especially those that have a high turnover cost, will have a value in terms of providing quality assurance in addition to their productive value. Even if the asset is not firm specific, if there is any time delay after the firm cheats and is terminated by consumers in selling the asset to another firm, the firm loses the real rate of interest for that time period on the capital. In addition to physical capital, human capital costs, especially entrepreneurial skills, are also often highly nonsalvageable in the face of consumer termination and therefore also provide significant quality assurance.

The general theoretical point is that the presence of positive quality-information costs favors an increase in the capital intensity of production, including the extent of long-term, illiquid contractual arrangements with suppliers of productive inputs. In particular, the minimum-cost production technique is no longer necessarily that which minimizes solely the average cost of production. "Sunk" production capital now accomplishes two functions—the supply of production services and the supply of quality-assuring services. Therefore, increases in average production costs accompanied by larger increases in sunk production assets may minimize the effective consumer product price. Profit maximization requires firms to trade off "inefficient" production technologies and the quality-assurance cost savings implied by the presence of firm-specific (sunk) capital assets in the productive process and hence the reduced necessity for the firm to make sunk selling cost (brand name capital) investments. Although the more capital intensive production technology may increase the perfectly competitive price of high quality output, P_0, it reduces the price premium, $P_2 - P_1$, necessary to assure the supply of that high quality. In fact, even a very slight modification of the minimum production cost technology, such as an alteration in some contractual terms, may imply the existence of large enough nonsalvageable assets so that the need for a quality-guaranteeing price premium is eliminated entirely.[14]

C. Consumer Cost Uncertainty: A Role for Advertising

The discussion to this point has assumed complete consumer knowledge of firms' costs of producing alternative quality outputs and knowledge of the extent to which any capital production costs or brand name capital selling costs are salvageable. This knowledge is necessary and sufficient to accurately calculate both the quality-guaranteeing premium and price. However, consumers are generally uncertain about cost conditions and therefore do not know the minimum quality-guaranteeing price with perfect accuracy. In fact, consumers cannot even make perfect anticipated quality rankings across firms on the basis of price. That one firm has a higher price than another may indicate a larger price premium or, alternatively, more inefficient production. In this section, we examine how the more realistic assumption of consumer cost uncertainty influences market responses to prepurchase quality uncertainty.

We have shown that increases in the price premium over average recoverable cost generally increase the relative returns from production of promised (high) quality rather than deceptive minimum (low) quality. The existence of a high price premium also makes expenditures on brand name capital investments economically feasible. The magnitude of brand name capital investments in turn indicates

---

[14] For example, franchisers can assure quality by requiring franchisee investment in specific production capital. A general arrangement by which this is accomplished is by not permitting the franchisee to own the land upon which its investments (e.g., capital fixtures) are made. Rather, the franchiser owns or leases the land and leases or subleases it to the franchisee, thereby creating for the franchisee a large nonsalvageable asset if he is terminated by the franchiser. This highly franchiser-specific asset can therefore serve as a form of collateral and potentially eliminate any need for a price premium. See Klein (1980) for a more complete discussion of this franchising solution, including the potential reverse cheating problem that is created by such contractual arrangements.

the magnitude of the price premium. When a consumer is uncertain about the cost of producing a particular high quality level of output and therefore the required quality-assuring premium, information about the actual level of the price premium will provide information about the probability of receiving high quality. If consumers are risk averse, this uncertainty about receiving anticipated high or deceptively low quality output will increase the premium that will be paid. The premium will include both a (presumably unbiased) estimate of the quality-assuring premium and an extra payment to reduce the risk of being deceived.

Thus, when consumers do not know the minimum quality-guaranteeing price, the larger is a firm's brand name capital investment relative to sales, the more likely its price premium is sufficient to motivate high quality production. Competitive investment in brand name capital is now no longer constrained to assets which yield direct consumer service flows with a present discounted value greater than the salvage value of the assets. Implicit information about the sufficiency of price as a guarantee can be supplied by "conspicuous" specific asset expenditures. Luxurious storefronts and ornate displays or signs may be supplied by a firm even if yielding no direct consumer service flows. Such firm-specific assets inform consumers of the magnitude of sunk capital costs and thereby supply information about the quasi-rent price-premium stream being earned by the firm and hence the opportunity cost to the firm if it cheats. Both the informational services and the direct utility producing services of assets are now relevant considerations for a firm in deciding upon the most valuable form the brand name capital investment should take.

The value of information about the magnitude of a firm's specific or "sunk" capital cost, and therefore the magnitude of the price premium, is one return from advertising. Indeed, the role of premiums as quality guarantors provides foundation for Nelson's (1974) argument that advertising, by definition, supplies valuable information to consumers—namely, information that the firm is advertising. A sufficient investment in advertising implies that a firm will not engage in short-run quality deception since the advertising indicates a nonsalvageable cost gap between price and production costs, that is, the existence of a price premium. This argument essentially reverses Nelson's logic. It is not that it pays a firm with a "best buy" to advertise more, but rather that advertising implies the supply of "best buys," or more correctly, the supply of promised high quality products. Advertising does not directly "signal" the presence of a "best buy," but "signals" the presence of firm-specific selling costs and therefore the magnitude of the price premium. We would therefore expect, ceteris paribus, a positive correlation not between advertising intensity and "best buys," as Nelson claims, but between advertising intensity and the extent of quality that is costly to determine prepurchase.[15]

Conspicuous sunk costs such as advertising are, like all sunk costs, irrelevant in determining future firm behavior regarding output quality. However, consumers know that such sunk costs can be profitable only if the future quasi rents are large. In particular, if the consumer estimate of the initial sunk expenditure made by the firm is greater than the consumer estimate of the firm's possible short-run cheating gain, then a price premium on future sales sufficient to prevent cheating is estimated to exist. Our analysis therefore implies that independent of excludability or collection costs, advertising that guarantees quality will be sold at a zero price and "tied in" with the marked-up product being advertised.[16]

Our theory also suggests why endorsements by celebrities and other seemingly "noninformative" advertising such as elaborate (obviously costly to produce) commercials, sponsorships of telethons, athletic events, and charities are valuable to consumers. In addition to drawing attention to the product, such advertising indicates the presence of a large sunk "selling" cost and the existence of a price premium. And because the crucial variable is the consumers' estimate of the stock of advertising capital (and not the flow), it also explains why firms advertise that they have advertised in the past (e.g., "as seen on 'The Tonight Show'"). Rather than serving a direct certifying function (e.g., as recommended by *Good Housekeeping* magazine), information about past advertising informs consumers about the magnitude of the total brand name capital investment.[17]

Firms may also provide valuable information by publicizing the

[15] Nelson's argument is based on an assumption similar to the Spence (1973)-type screening assumption regarding the lower cost to more productive individuals of obtaining education. Nelson's argument, however, is circular since consumers react to advertising only because the best buys advertise more and the best buys advertise more only because consumers buy advertised products. Schmalensee (1978) has shown that the Nelson scenario may imply "fly-by-night" producers who advertise the most and also deceptively produce minimum quality. Like Spence's signaling model, the government could, in principle, tax this investment and thereby save real resources without reducing the effectiveness of this information if consumers were aware of the tax rate. However, advertising serves many purposes. In particular, advertising also can supply valuable consumer information about the particular characteristics and availability of products. For optimality the government would therefore have to determine the appropriate tax rate for each advertising message and consumers would have to be aware of each of these particular tax rates.

[16] Mishan (1970) has argued for legislation which would require advertising to be sold separately at a price which covers advertising costs. This would completely destroy the informational value of advertising we are emphasizing here.

[17] Note, however, that just as firms may deceive consumers about quality to be supplied, they may also attempt to deceive them about the magnitude of the advertising investments made, e.g., purchasing a local spot on "The Tonight Show" and advertising the advertising as if an expenditure on a national spot was made.

large fees paid to celebrities for commercials. Information about large endorsement fees would be closely guarded if the purpose were to simulate an "unsolicited endorsement" of the product's particular quality characteristics rather than to indicate the existence of a price premium. Viewed in this context, it is obviously unnecessary for the celebrity to actually use the particular brand advertised. This is contrary to a recent FTC ruling (see Federal Trade Commission 1980).

This analysis of advertising implies that consumers necessarily receive something when they pay a higher price for an advertised brand. An expensive name brand aspirin, for example, is likely to be better than unadvertised aspirin because it is expensive. The advertising of the name brand product indicates the presence of a current and future price premium. This premium on future sales is the firm's brand name capital which will be lost if the firm supplies lower than anticipated quality. Therefore, firms selling more highly advertised, higher priced products will necessarily take more precautions in production.[18]

We have emphasized the informational value of advertising as a sunk cost. Other marketing activities can serve a similar informational role in indicating the presence of a price premium. For example, free samples, in addition to letting consumers try the product, provide information regarding future premiums and therefore anticipated quality. Such free or low-price samples thus provide information not solely to those consumers that receive the samples but also to anyone aware of the existence and magnitude of the free or low-price sample program. More generally, the supply by a firm of quality greater than anticipated and paid for by consumers is a similar type of brand name capital investment by the firm. By forgoing revenue, the firm provides information to consumers that it has made a nonsalvageable investment of a particular magnitude and that a particular future premium stream is anticipated to cover the initial sunk alternative cost.[19]

---

[18] The greater is the cost to consumers of obtaining deceptively low quality, the greater will be the demand for quality assurance. The very low market share of "generic" children's aspirin (1 percent) vis-à-vis generic's share of the regular aspirin market (7 percent) is consistent with this implication (see IMS America, Ltd. 1978). Many individuals who claim "all aspirin is alike" apparently pay the extra price for their children where the costs of lower quality are greater and therefore quality assurance is considered more important.

[19] Our analysis of advertising also illuminates the monopolistic competition debate. Chamberlin's (1965) distinction between production costs, defined as what is included in the "package" that passes from seller to buyer, and selling costs (e.g., advertising), which are not part of the package transferred, suggests that selling costs usefully may be considered as a privately supplied collective factor. For example, a firm which holds selling costs, such as expenditures on a store sign, constant as his sales increase does not appear to be decreasing the average "quality" of his product. Demsetz (1959, 1968) made the contrary assumption that average quality does fall as sales increase, holding

Finally, even when consumers systematically underestimate the quality-assuring price because of downward-biased estimates of production or marketing costs or upward-biased estimates of anticipated demand growth, firms in a monopolistically competitive environment may not cheat. Such price-setting firms may possess specific nonsalvageable assets (such as trademarks) upon which they are earning a sufficient quasi-rent premium to induce high quality supply. However, the existence of independent competitive retailers that do not have any ownership stake in this firm-specific asset and yet can significantly influence the quality of the final product supplied to consumers creates a severe quality-cheating problem for the manufacturer. In this context, rational but imperfectly informed consumers will not demand a sufficient premium to prevent retailer cheating. Manufacturers may protect their trademarks by imposing constraints on the retailer competitive process including entry restrictions, exclusive territorial grants, minimum resale price maintenance, and advertising restrictions that will assure quality by creating a sufficiently valuable premium stream for the retailers. If this manufacturer-created premium stream is greater than the potential short-run retailer return from deceptive low quality supply, the magnitude of which is determined in part by the manufacturer by its level of direct policing expenditures, the retailer will not cheat and the consumer will receive anticipated high quality supply.[20]

IV. Conclusion

We have shown that even the existence of perfect communication among buyers so that all future sales are lost to a cheating firm is not sufficient to assure noncheating behavior. We have analyzed the

selling costs constant, by merely ignoring Chamberlin's distinction and its possible theoretical significance and identifying quality costs with selling costs (aggregating both into the concept "demand increasing costs"). However, since in a monopolistically competitive environment the price premium that will assure quality depends upon the demand expected in the future, the quality incentive implied by an advertising investment also depends upon consumers' expectations about future demand. In particular, the relevant variable indicating an incentive to produce high quality is the level of advertising capital compared to anticipated future sales. Hence advertising is not a pure public good in a firm's production function as Chamberlin implicitly assumed, and the arbitrary contrary assumption made by Demsetz is possibly justifiable.

[20] See Klein et al. (1980) for a complete analysis of this case applied to the FTC Coors litigation. Coors appears to have employed exclusive territories on the wholesale level and resale price maintenance on the retail level to create a sufficient premium to encourage the necessary refrigeration of their nonpasteurized beer. Implications of this analysis in terms of providing a possible rationale for similar constraints on the competitive process enforced by trade associations and government regulatory agencies are also examined.

generally unrecognized importance of increased market prices and nonsalvageable capital as possible methods of making quality promises credible. We obviously do not want to claim that consumers "know" this theory in the sense that they can verbalize it but only that they behave in such a way as if they recognize the forces at work. They may, for example, know from past experience that when a particular type of investment is present such as advertising they are much less likely to be deceived. Therefore, survivorship of crude decision rules over time may produce consumer behavior very similar to what would be predicted by this model without the existence of explicit "knowledge" of the forces we have examined.

Our analysis implies that consumers can successfully use price as an indicator of quality. We are not referring to the phenomenon of an ignorant consumer free riding on the information contained in the market price paid by other more informed buyers but rather to the fact that consumer knowledge of a gap between firm price and salvageable costs, that is, the knowledge of the existence of a price premium, supplies quality assurance. The former argument, that a naive buyer in a market dominated by knowledgeable buyers can use price as a quality signal because the relative market price of different products reflects differences in production costs and therefore differences in quality, crucially depends upon a "majority" of the buyers in the market being knowledgeable.

As Scitovsky (1945, p. 101) correctly notes, ". . . the situation becomes paradoxical when price is the index by which the average buyer judges quality. In a market where this happens price ceases to be governed by competition and becomes instead an instrument wherewith the seller can influence his customer's opinions of the quality of his wares." However, even when the "average" buyer uses price as an index of quality, we need not fear, as Scitovsky does, the havoc this supposedly wreaks on the economic theory of choice. All consumers in a market may consistently use price, given their estimates of salvageable production costs, as an indicator of the firm's price-premium stream and therefore as an indicator of the anticipated quality of the output to be supplied by the firm. Scitovsky did not consider that price not only influences buyers' expectations but also influences producers' incentives.

We do not wish to suggest that use of implicit (price premium–specific investment) contracts is always the cheapest way to assure quality supply. When quality characteristics can be specified cheaply and measured by a third party, and hence contract enforcement costs are anticipated to be low, explicit contractual solutions with governmentally enforced penalties (including warranties) may be a less

ASSURING CONTRACTUAL PERFORMANCE 635

costly solution. When explicit contract costs are high and the extent of short-run profit from deceptively low quality supply and hence the quality-assuring price premium is also high, governmental specification and enforcement of minimum quality standards may be an alternative method of reducing the costs of assuring the supply of high quality products.[21] And, finally, vertical integration, which in this consumer-product context may consist of home production or consumer cooperatives, may be a possible alternative arrangement (see Klein, Crawford, and Alchian 1978).

The three major methods in which to organize transactions can be usefully considered within this framework as (*a*) explicit contractual or regulatory specification with third-party enforcement, (*b*) direct (two-party) enforcement of implicit contracts, and (*c*) one-party organization or vertical integration. This paper has analyzed the brand name repeat-purchase mechanism represented by the second alternative. More generally, however, all market transactions, including those "within" the firm such as employer-employee agreements, consist of a combination of the two basic forms of contractual arrangements. Some elements of performance will be specified and enforced by third-party sanctions and other elements enforced without invoking the power of some outside party to the transaction but merely by the threat of termination of the transactional relationship.

Our analysis implies that, given a particular level of explicit contract costs, we are more likely to observe an increased reliance on the brand name contract-enforcement mechanism the lower the rate of interest and the lower the level of prepurchase quality-determination costs. The lower the interest rate the greater the capital cost to a firm from the loss of future sales and therefore the lower the equilibrium price premium. Hence we can expect the termination of future exchange method of enforcing contracts to be more effective. More generally, since the interest rate in our model refers to the period of product repurchase, the quality assurance will be less costly for less durable goods that have greater repurchase frequency. Franchising chains, for example, take advantage of this effect by making it possible for

[21] Such governmental regulations, however, do not avoid the contractual problems of ex ante explicitly defining in an enforceable manner all major elements of performance. Nor do they necessarily avoid the implicit contractual conditions of a price-premium stream (created by entry restrictions, an initial forfeitable bond, and/or minimum price restraints) to effectively enforce the governmental regulations (see Klein et al. 1980). In addition, by making it illegal to supply less than the regulated quality, individuals that would voluntarily demand lower quality than the regulated standard incur a loss of consumer surplus. Distribution effects are created, since while the regulation may decrease the cost of supplying high quality output it increases the cost of supplying lower quality output.

consumers to pool information from sales of seemingly disparate sellers, thereby decreasing the period of repurchase and the quality-assuring price.

Similarly, purchase from a diversified firm increases the frequency of repeat purchase and lowers the necessary price premium. As long as consumers react to receiving unexpectedly low quality from a diversified firm by reducing purchases of the firm's entire product line, all the firm's nonsalvageable capital serves to assure the quality of each product it produces. This economy of scale in communicating quality-assurance information to consumers may be one motivation for conglomerate mergers. If a firm sells a set of products, each of which is produced by capital with salvage value less than costs, the quality-guaranteeing price premium on each product will be lower than if production were done by separate firms.

Finally, we can expect greater reliance on the non-third-party method of contract enforcement the lower the direct costs to the consumer of determining quality of the product prepurchase. The higher the costs of producing the minimum quality output that cannot be distinguished prepurchase from a given promised high quality output and the faster these minimum quality production costs rise with increased output, the lower the potential short-run cheating gain and therefore the lower the price premium. When the low quality cost function is such that a cheating firm can expand output a substantial amount with little increase in cost, use of the brand name enforcement mechanism is unlikely.

When the low quality cost function becomes so flat that the premium solution does not exist, the implicit contract-enforcement mechanism we have analyzed will not be used. When this condition is combined with an extremely high cost of quality assurance via explicit contractual guarantees, governmental supply may be the cheapest alternative. An obvious example is the good "money," where the marginal cost of production is essentially zero, the short-run cheating potential extremely large, and where the cost of a commodity money or the necessary bullion reserves to assure performance via convertibility is also extremely high. Governmental supply is the generally adopted but far from costless solution (see Klein 1974). Other products where the "hold-up" potential is very large and where explicit contract costs are high (such as police or fire protection services) are also generally supplied by non-profit-maximizing government agencies rather than by unregulated profit-maximizing firms earning large quasi rents on unsalvageable (firm-specific) capital assets. In general, minimization of the cost of assuring performance will imply an optimal combination of governmental regulation and/or supply, explicit contractual enforcement, vertical integration, and the implicit (brand name) contractual enforcement mechanism we have analyzed.

Appendix

Simulation of the Quality-assuring Price

If we assume that output of high and low (minimum) quality is produced by constant-elasticity cost functions of the form:

$$C_h = F_h + \beta_h x_h^\alpha, \tag{A1}$$

$$C_l = F_l + \beta_l x_l^\alpha, \tag{A2}$$

the quality-assuring price premium, $\tilde{P}$, will be given by:[22]

$$\tilde{P} = \left\{ \frac{\left[1 - \frac{(F_l/F_h)r}{1+r} \right]}{1 - \frac{r}{1+r}\left(\frac{\beta_l}{\beta_h} \right)^{1/(\alpha-1)}} \right\}^{(\alpha-1)/\alpha} \tag{A3}$$

This expression indicates that as the ratio of low to high quality fixed costs, (F_l/F_h), decreases the quality-guaranteeing price-premium increases (because the short-run profit from cheating increases). But, as long as F_l can be assumed to be less than or equal to F_h, fixed costs cannot affect the existence of the quality-guaranteeing price premium. Similarly, as the interest rate, r, increases, the quality-guaranteeing price premium increases but will always exist. It is the marginal cost elasticity, $[1/(\alpha - 1)]$, and the ratio of the marginal cost slopes, (β_l/β_h), that determine the existence of a quality-assuring price premium. An increase in the elasticity of marginal cost or a decrease in the ratio of the low to high quality marginal cost slopes, by increasing the possible expansion of the low quality output at the high quality-guaranteeing price, increases the quality-guaranteeing price premium and the likelihood that it may not exist. Simulation results as a function of these parameters are presented in table A1 below. The ratio of the quality-assuring price to the minimum average cost of high quality production, P_2/P_1 in terms of figure 1, along with the ratio of low quality output at the quality-assuring price relative to the minimum high quality average cost output, x_4/x_1 in terms of figure 1, is presented. When the quality-assuring price does not exist, the ratio of low quality output at a P_2/P_1 ratio of 2 to the output at the minimum average cost of low quality output, x_0, is presented in brackets to indicate the shape of the low quality cost function. The results indicate that these cases of nonexistence generally occur where the low quality cost curve is so flat relative to the high quality cost curve that cheating output can be expanded dramatically relative to the noncheating output. For example, when the marginal cost elasticity is assumed to be 10.0 and the ratio of marginal cost slopes is assumed to be 0.25, it implies that low quality output can be profitably expanded by more than a billion times beyond its minimum average cost rate when the market price is double the perfectly competitive high quality price.

[22] The derivation is available to readers upon request.

TABLE A1

SIMULATION OF QUALITY-ASSURING PRICES

Interest Rate r	Ratio of Fixed Costs (F_I/F_N)	Marginal Cost Elasticity $[1/(\alpha - 1)]$	Ratio of Marginal Cost Slopes (β_I/β_N)	Price-Premium Ratio (P_2/P_1)	Output Ratio (x_N/x_1)
.03	.5	.5	.25	1.031	2.03
.03	.5	.5	.50	1.018	1.43
.03	.5	.5	.75	1.013	1.16
.03	.5	2.0	.25	1.227	24.07
.03	.5	2.0	.50	1.037	4.30
.03	.5	2.0	.75	1.013	1.82
.03	.5	4.0	.25	Does not exist	$[4.10 \times 10^3]$
.03	.5	4.0	.50	1.130	26.12
.03	.5	4.0	.75	1.017	3.37
.03	.5	10.0	.25	Does not exist	$[1.07 \times 10^9]$
.03	.5	10.0	.50	Does not exist	$[1.05 \times 10^6]$
.03	.5	10.0	.75	1.067	33.97
.03	1.0	.5	.25	1.021	2.02
.03	1.0	.5	.50	1.008	1.42
.03	1.0	.5	.75	1.003	1.16
.03	1.0	2.0	.25	1.221	23.84
.03	1.0	2.0	.50	1.032	4.26
.03	1.0	2.0	.75	1.008	1.81
.03	1.0	4.0	.25	Does not exist	$[4.10 \times 10^3]$
.03	1.0	4.0	.50	1.127	25.81
.03	1.0	4.0	.75	1.013	3.34
.03	1.0	10.0	.25	Does not exist	$[1.07 \times 10^9]$
.03	1.0	10.0	.50	Does not exist	$[1.05 \times 10^6]$
.03	1.0	10.0	.75	1.066	$[1.82 \times 10^4]$
.09	.5	.5	.25	1.097	2.09
.09	.5	.5	.50	1.056	1.45
.09	.5	.5	.75	1.039	1.18

.09	.5	2.0	.25	Does not exist	[64.0]
.09	.5	2.0	.50	1.127	5.08
.09	.5	2.0	.75	1.040	1.92
.09	.5	4.0	.25	Does not exist	$[4.10 \times 10^3]$
.09	.5	4.0	.50	Does not exist	$[2.56 \times 10^7]$
.09	.5	4.0	.75	1.053	3.89
.09	.5	10.0	.25	Does not exist	$[1.07 \times 10^9]$
.09	.5	10.0	.50	Does not exist	$[1.05 \times 10^9]$
.09	.5	10.0	.75	Does not exist	$[1.82 \times 10^9]$
.09	1.0	.5	.25	1.065	2.06
.09	1.0	.5	.50	1.026	1.43
.09	1.0	.5	.75	1.009	1.16
.09	1.0	2.0	.25	Does not exist	[64.0]
.09	1.0	2.0	.50	1.111	4.93
.09	1.0	2.0	.75	1.024	1.87
.09	1.0	4.0	.25	Does not exist	$[4.10 \times 10^3]$
.09	1.0	4.0	.50	Does not exist	$[2.56 \times 10^7]$
.09	1.0	4.0	.75	1.044	3.76
.09	1.0	10.0	.25	Does not exist	$[1.07 \times 10^9]$
.09	1.0	10.0	.50	Does not exist	$[1.05 \times 10^9]$
.09	1.0	10.0	.75	Does not exist	$[1.82 \times 10^9]$

640   JOURNAL OF POLITICAL ECONOMY

References

Akerlof, George A. "The Market for 'Lemons': Quality Uncertainty and the Market Mechanism." *Q.J.E.* 84 (August 1970): 488–500.

Becker, Gary S., and Stigler, George J. "Law Enforcement, Malfeasance, and Compensation of Enforcers." *J. Legal Studies* 3 (January 1974): 1–18.

Chamberlin, Edward H. *The Theory of Monopolistic Competition: A Re-Orientation of the Theory of Value.* 8th ed. Cambridge, Mass.: Harvard Univ. Press, 1965.

Darby, Michael R., and Karni, Edi. "Free Competition and the Optimal Amount of Fraud." *J. Law and Econ.* 16 (April 1973): 67–88.

Demsetz, Harold. "The Nature of Equilibrium in Monopolistic Competition." *J.P.E.* 67, no. 1 (February 1959): 21–30.

———. "Do Competition and Monopolistic Competition Differ?" *J.P.E.* 76, no. 1 (January/February 1968): 146–48.

Federal Trade Commission, Office of the Federal Registrar. *Guides concerning Use of Endorsements and Testimonials in Advertising.* 16 CFR, pt. 255. Washington: Government Printing Office, 1980.

Goldberg, Victor P. "Toward an Expanded Theory of Contract." *J. Econ. Issues* 10 (March 1976): 45–61.

Hayek, Friedrich A. "The Meaning of Competition." In *Individualism and Economic Order.* Chicago: Univ. Chicago Press, 1948.

Hobbes, Thomas. *Leviathan.* Oxford: Blackwell, 1955, first published 1651.

IMS America, Ltd. *U.S. Pharmaceutical Market, Drug Stores and Hospitals, Audit of Purchases.* Bergen, N.J.: IMS America, 1978.

Klein, Benjamin. "The Competitive Supply of Money." *J. Money, Credit and Banking* 6 (November 1974): 423–53.

———. "Borderlines of Law and Economic Theory: Transaction Cost Determinants of 'Unfair' Contractual Arrangements." *A.E.R. Papers and Proc.* 70 (May 1980): 356–62.

Klein, Benjamin; Crawford, Robert G.; and Alchian, Armen A. "Vertical Integration, Appropriable Rents, and the Competitive Contracting Process." *J. Law and Econ.* 21 (October 1978): 297–326.

Klein, Benjamin; McLaughlin, Andrew; and Murphy, Kevin M. "Resale Price Maintenance, Exclusive Territories, and Franchise Termination: The Coors Case." Working Paper, UCLA, 1980.

Leffler, Keith B. "The Role of Price in Guaranteeing Quality." Working Paper no. CPB77-5, Univ. Rochester, June 1977.

Luce, R. Duncan, and Raiffa, Howard. *Games and Decisions: Introduction and Critical Survey.* New York: Wiley, 1957.

Macaulay, Stewart, "Non-contractual Relations in Business: A Preliminary Study." *American Soc. Rev.* 28 (February 1963): 55–67.

Macneil, Ian. "The Many Futures of Contracts." *Southern California Law Rev.* 47 (May 1974): 691–816.

Marshall, Alfred. *Principles of Economics: An Introductory Volume.* 8th ed. New York: Macmillan, 1949.

Mishan, Edward J. *21 Popular Economic Fallacies.* New York: Praeger, 1970.

Nelson, Phillip. "Information and Consumer Behavior." *J.P.E.* 78, no. 2 (March/April 1970): 311–29.

———. "Advertising as Information." *J.P.E.* 82, no. 4 (July/August 1974): 729–54.

Schmalensee, Richard. "A Model of Advertising and Product Quality." *J.P.E.* 86, no. 3 (June 1978): 485–503.

ASSURING CONTRACTUAL PERFORMANCE 641

Scitovsky, Tibor. "Some Consequences of the Habit of Judging Quality by Price." *Rev. Econ. Studies* 12, no. 2 (1945): 100–105.

Smith, Adam. *An Inquiry into the Nature and Causes of the Wealth of Nations.* New York: Modern Library, 1937, first published 1776.

Spence, A. Michael. "Job Market Signaling." *Q.J.E.* 87 (August 1973): 355–74.

Telser, Lester G. "A Theory of Self-enforcing Agreements." *J. Bus.* 22, no. 1 (January 1980): 27–44.

Williamson, Oliver E. "Transaction-Cost Economics: The Governance of Contractual Relations." *J. Law and Econ.* 22 (October 1979): 233–61.

Part III
Strategic Behaviour and Competition

[16]

Two Systems of Belief About Monopoly

Harold Demsetz*

I

The old adage "seeing is believing" contains a double measure of truth, for there also is much merit in the notion that "believing is seeing." Facts must be placed into a system of belief before they yield to interpretation. The same astronomical observations in the Copernican theory convey an entirely different image of the universe in the Ptolemaic theory, and phenomena assume new meaning when we shift from the Newtonian system to the Einsteinian system. Economic facts also require a system of belief before they can be interpreted. There is an impression that economists share a common system of belief about monopoly and competition into which the facts about concentration and profits, whatever they may be, can be fitted neatly. But this is not so, and the illusion of unanimity is now being shattered.

This disillusionment stems partly from the fact that students of monopoly and competition now are being asked to respond to policy alternatives of greater significance than those posed since the decade of the thirties. The renewed attempt to link monopoly to inflation via some type of "cost-push" inflation theory has thrust the monopoly problem into policy areas usually reserved to Keynesians and Monetarists. But more important has been the continuing attempt to incorporate the monopoly model, as that term often is understood or misunderstood, into legislation that would bring about a radical restructuring of industry. Such legislation was recommended by President Johnson's antitrust task force, and, in much stronger form, currently is sought by Senator Hart. These legislative programs already have brought the debate among economists before the public and have forced closer questioning of our beliefs and evidence about the operation of the economic system.

In addition, there recently have been factual findings that are difficult to explain with the accepted doctrine about the relationship between competition and industry structure. These new findings must, at the least, stimulate a reexamination of doctrine and, possibly, a revolution in doctrine. All of this should make the workday of the economist more interesting and that of the policymaker more hesitant.

Two competing theories about monopoly are heading for a showdown. Our understanding of the operation of the economic system depends largely on which of these two systems of belief is adopted. The currently most familiar belief conceives of monopoly power as producible by a firm or an industry without any substantial aid from the government. I shall call this the "self-

* Professor of Economics, The University of California at Los Angeles, and Senior Research Fellow, The Hoover Institution. For further biographical information, see Appendix D.

sufficiency" theory. A second belief, which may be named the "intervention-ism" theory, sees monopoly power as a derivative of governmental interventions. These two views refer to a difference in belief about the source of *most* monopoly power, not to every instance of monopoly power.

It is true that the government's agreement to provide protection from would-be competitors is secured at least partly through the activities of firms, and therefore, that the interventionism theory of monopoly is a variant of the self-sufficiency theory. Nonetheless it is useful to preserve the substantive distinction of these competing views when we deal with the problem of how we can best cope with monopoly power. Should we try to reduce the degree of government intervention, or should we seek to restructure industries and to modify the competitive tactics used by firms? Those who hold to the belief of self-sufficient monopoly will answer this question by seeking more intervention, while those who see the source of monopoly in government intervention will seek to reduce the role of government in our economy.

This brief description suggests a clearer distinction of these competing beliefs than actually exists. Proponents of either view might see one source of monopoly in explicit agreements to collude, and both groups might consider it desirable to make such agreements illegal. The existence of such agreements might be interpreted as a self-sufficient source of monopoly; or alternatively, the legality of such agreements might be seen as government intervention to help enforce the agreements. Setting aside such problems about specific practices, a correct difference in emphasis is nonetheless captured by this description. The belief in a self-sufficient source of monopoly generates a view of the unregulated economy as one that is monopoly prone, while the belief that government intervention is the prime source of monopoly sees the unregulated economy as essentially competitive. The self-sufficiency theory suggests that political intervention is required; market concentration is seen as an important inhibitor of competition from within the industry, and large capital requirements, intensive advertising, and "predatory" pricing are viewed as important obstacles to competition from outside the industry. The belief that monopoly arises because of government intervention considers these to be relatively unimportant sources of monopoly so long as the government does not use its coercive powers to create and police legal barriers to competition; this viewpoint suggests that the regulation of transport, the imposition of tariffs, the various agricultural programs, the enforcement of licensure, the control of prices, and the legal restrictions imposed on entry and on the use of competitive tactics are the origins of more serious monopoly problems.

II

The intellectual origin of the interventionist theory of monopoly can be traced at least to Adam Smith's attack on mercantilism. In several chapters of *The Wealth of Nations*, Smith explored inefficiencies caused by governmental measures to protect and subsidize industries. This view of the nature of the monopoly problem dominated the thinking of economists until the first quarter of the twentieth century — after which it became quiescent, only to be res-

urrected recently in work dealing with the economic theory of political behavior. The quiescent period began after an important restructuring of industry
had taken place, brought about partly because transport cost had fallen
rapidly (thereby making it feasible for larger firms to sell across obsolete geo-
graphic market boundaries), and partly because the laws of incorporation had
been revised in ways that facilitated the massing of large amounts of capital
at low cost through public stock subscription.

Coincidentally with this restructuring, the economic theory of monopoly became increasingly explicit as to its assumptions and narrow as to its applications. The theory contrasted two industry structures and the prices that could
be deduced from each: an atomistic structure comprised of an extremely large
number of firms, and a monopoly structure containing but one firm. The atomistic structure denied any firm the power to control price. The one-firm structure
conveyed complete control over price to the single firm. Increasingly these two
structures were interpreted as descriptions of counterparts in real markets. I
believe this interpretation errs seriously, but, in any case, the search for the
source of monopoly power began to shift from government protection to industry structure.

Although markets had become more concentrated at the turn of the century
(but, in general, not since then), only a very few were so dominated by one
firm that they could be thought to resemble closely the one-firm industry assumed in the monopoly model. Nonetheless, the system of belief had so shifted
that many economists came to view many actual industrial structures as near-
enough approximations to the single-firm structure of monopoly theory. There
was a growing expectation that monopoly was significantly correlated with
market concentration, and this expectation soon hardened into a market concentration doctrine.

No serious theoretical basis yet exists for this doctrine, notwithstanding
Weiss's efforts to demonstrate the existence of such a basis. Weiss does
marshal enough "theories" of oligopoly to make a very convincing case. But
the case he makes is mine.

The essence of monopoly power is the ability to prevent an expansion of
capacity when price exceeds unit cost; yet not one of the oligopoly theories he
described deals with the problem posed for colluding oligopolists by potential
and actual entry; not one tells us how price can be maintained above a competitive level even *if* oligopolists should succeed in eliminating competition
among existing firms. These models thus share a seldom recognized characteristic of the basic monopoly model from which they derive; the monopoly model
assumes that monopoly power exists, it does not explain *how* monopoly power
is acquired and maintained; the theory then proceeds to show how such power
will be exercised.

The structure of an industry is determined largely by the degree to which
scale economies prevail, or by the comparative efficiencies of firms; but no
good theoretical link has been forged between the structure of the industry
and the degree to which competitive pricing prevails, because no good explanation has been provided for how present and potential rivals are kept

from competing without some governmentally provided restrictions on competitive activities.

What these descriptions of oligopoly behavior attempt to explain is: how oligopolists will act *if* there is no concern about entry. Even at this much more restricted game, these descriptions, with the exception of Stigler's, can hardly be dignified as theories. One theory assumes that each oligopolist believes that his rivals will not change their outputs no matter what he does; another assumes that rivals will keep their prices unchanged no matter what; others reach no definite equilibrium price or fail to explain how the equilibrium price is established. Stigler's theory of oligopoly is the only one that assumes sensible behavior on the part of oligopolists; but even his theory, which is worked out much better than the others, neglects the problems posed by open entry and by the need to discipline firms that compete.

Note that I have been discussing the absence of a well-worked-out theory supporting the link between industry structure and *monopoly* power. The testing of the market concentration doctrine has relied extensively on a search for a correlation between industry structure and *profit rates*. This implies that there is good reason to expect collusion among oligopolists to record higher profit rates as these are measured by accountants. There are, of course, many problems in the use of accounting data as approximations for economic concepts; but even if these measurement problems are set aside, there remain serious theoretical problems which I will discuss later.

Confirmation of the market concentration doctrine was offered first in the work of Professor Joe Bain[1] who, in 1951, published his famous study of the relationship between market concentration and profit rates in 42 selected industries. He found that profit rates were higher for industries in which the largest eight firms accounted for at least 70 percent of industry value added. Table 7 summarizes his results.

Continuing through the decades of the fifties and sixties with the work of Bain and others, there was growing acceptance of the market concentration doctrine. Soon it became the dominant view of economists working in this area. It was taught in economics departments throughout the land at the time that most persons at this conference were attending college. Its influence spread beyond the narrow confines of professional economics and filtered into the world of politics and antitrust law. It has become part of the conventional wisdom of intellectuals and policymakers. "Oligopoly," "shared monopoly," "conscious parallelism in pricing," and "barriers to entry," not yet household words, have become establishment clichés.

When a profession accepts a new system of belief, research is guided by that belief to rationalize observed phenomena in ways that confirm it. The belief in a self-sufficient theory of monopoly power offers no exception. Several studies followed quickly on Bain's and, although a few produced contrary results, most found confirmation of the new paradigm. A weak but gen-

---

1. Joe S. Bain, "Relation of Profit-Rate to Industry Concentration: American Manufacturing, 1936-1940," *Quarterly Journal of Economics*, 65 (August 1951), p. 293.

TABLE 7

Average of Industry Average-Profit Rates Within Concentration
Deciles, 42 Selected Industries, 1936-1940

Value Added, Supplied by 8 Largest Firms	Average of Industry Average-Profit Rates	Number of Industries
90-100.0%	12.7%	8
80- 89.9	9.8	11
70- 79.9	16.3	3
60- 69.9	5.8	5
50- 59.9	5.8	4
40- 49.9	8.6	2
30- 39.9	6.3	5
20- 29.9	10.4	2
10- 19.9	17.0	1
0- 9.9	9.1	1

Source: Joe S. Bain, "Relation of Profit-Rate to Industry Concentration: American Manufacturing, 1936-1940," *Quarterly
Journal of Economics*, 65 (August 1951), p. 293.

erally persistent correlation between market concentration and profit rates is
a fairly accurate description of these findings. Alternative explanations for
these data generally were ignored because the market concentration doctrine
had won the imagination of investigators and had given direction to their
thoughts, much as Ptolemaic astronomy provided the signposts for the study
of heavenly bodies during the four hundred years surrounding the life of
Christ.

How did concentrated markets remain concentrated if they yielded above-
average profits and were not protected by the government? Why did Bain
observe lower profit rates for the smaller firms relative to the larger ones that
occupied the same concentrated industries? What distortion is implied when
industry profits are measured primarily by the profits of the larger firms in the
industry? Why did nine industries with concentration ratios between 50 and
70 percent have lower profit rates than the eleven less concentrated industries
contained in Bain's sample? (See Table 7). These matters generally were set
aside during the period when most of the confirmatory studies were produced,
although some attention was given by Bain (and his student H. Michael Mann)
to the problem of why a positive relationship between concentration and profit
rates should be resilient in the face of entry threats. It was decided — largely
by intuition, not analysis — that the use of advertising and capital, as well as
the existence of economies of scale, created what Bain called barriers to the
entry of resources from outside the industry. No clear rationale was given as
to why the use of particular kinds of inputs should create such barriers when
these same inputs are available to firms both inside and outside the industry.

But Bain and Mann did find a stronger correlation between concentration and profits for those industries that used these inputs very intensely.

By 1960, then, collected evidence indicated a weak but generally positive correlation between concentration and profit rates. One large study covering a different time span, by George J. Stigler,[2] did not support these findings nor did a few smaller studies. Nonetheless, the balance of evidence, when measured by a number of studies, clearly favored the market concentration doctrine. In addition, there was the smaller amount of work indicating a potential explanation for this relationship in the intensive use of advertising and capital. Those who believed in the self-sufficient source of monopoly power had found confirmation.

During the middle sixties, development less clearly favored the belief in self-sufficient monopoly. It is true that Stigler[3] did construct a formal rationale for the market concentration doctrine in 1964, and Comanor and Wilson[4] in 1967 presented statistical evidence that higher profit rates were associated with more intensive use of advertising. But both studies really gave less support to the market concentration doctrine than might be supposed. Comanor and Wilson found that after account was taken of advertising expenditures and capital requirements, there no longer existed any correlation between market concentration and profit rates; and Stigler's theoretical analysis indicated that it takes relatively few firms to reduce significantly the gains from a collusive arrangement. Moreover, Stigler's study took no account of the role that entry would play in making such arrangements even less profitable.

Largely unnoticed, there appeared several studies during the late fifties and the decade of the sixties that provided cumulating evidence in favor of the belief that government intervention is a major source of monopoly power. It had always been recognized that tariffs, oil import quotas, the agricultural program, and the legal support of unions constructed impediments to the free flow of resources and created higher returns for small segments of the economy at greater cost to the more dispersed masses. But it generally was believed that government regulation of industry as provided for in the Act to Regulate Commerce, the Maritime Act, the Federal Communications Act, the Air Transport Act, etc., worked to the advantage of consumers. These studies provided arguments and evidence that this was not the case, and that, in general, this type of regulation protected the regulated industries from competition at the expense of consumers. Even at the local level, regulations such as those limiting entry into the taxi business and into housing through zoning requirements were shown to be protective devices creating serious impediments to the efficient use of resources.

2. George J. Stigler, *Capital and Rates of Return in Manufacturing* (Princeton Univ. Press 1963).

3. George J. Stigler, "A Theory of Oligopoly," *Journal of Political Economy*, 72 (February 1964), p. 44.

4. W. S. Comanor and T. A. Wilson, "Advertising, Market Structure, and Performance," *Review of Economics and Statistics*, 49 (November 1967), p. 423.

170   *Harold Demsetz*

These studies offered support for the belief that government intervention plays a substantial role in the creation of monopoly power, but they did not undermine the evidence that had been accumulating in favor of the belief in self-sufficient monopoly power, nor did they lead many economists to doubt the market concentration doctrine. The way of looking at economic phenomena remained fairly fixed by the belief in self-sufficient monopoly power. But, beginning with the present decade, new evidence raised doubts about the main statistical supports and theoretical conjectures of the market concentration doctrine.

Yale Brozen[5] attempted to find evidence that would substantiate the rationalization used by President Johnson's Task Force on Antitrust Policy in its call for a Concentrated Industries Act for the purpose of reducing market concentration. The task force based its recommendation on its belief that there existed a large body of evidence showing a *persistent* relationship between concentration and high rates of return. The task force report stated that:

> It is the persistence of high profits over extended time periods and over whole industries . . . that suggest[s] artificial restraints on output and the absence of fully effective competition. The correlation of evidence of this kind with very high levels of concentration appears to be significant.[6]

Brozen found that none of the studies supporting the market concentration doctrine had looked at the question of the persistence over time of the correlation between profit and concentration; their results were based essentially on observations of a cross-section of industries during a given time interval. He examined the question of persistence directly by carrying forward in time three studies that supported the market concentration doctrine. (These were the basic study by Bain, a follow-up study by Mann, and a second, smaller study by Stigler that had found a correlation between profit and concentration for a group of 17 highly concentrated industries.) Brozen found no confirmation of the persistence in these correlations. The correlations degenerated within a few years, and high and low profit rates tended to converge toward a common level.

Why should the period used by Bain, 1936-1940, support the market concentration doctrine when subsequent time periods did not? Brozen[7] answered this puzzle by enlarging the sample used by Bain from 42 to 80 industries, and, in some industries, Brozen also increased the number of firms used to measure profit rates. Bain had used only 42 out of the 340 industries for which census data were available. The information in which Bain was interested was available for only 149 of these, because he relied on profit data

---

5. Yale Brozen, "The Antitrust Task Force Deconcentration Recommendation," *Journal of Law and Economics*, 13 (October 1970), p. 279.

6. White House Task Force on Antitrust Policy, "Report 1," in *Role of the Giant Corporations* (1968), p. 883.

7. Yale Brozen, "Bain's Concentration and Rates of Return Revisited," *Journal of Law and Economics*, 14 (October 1971), p. 351.

reported by the Securities and Exchange Commission. Another group of industries was omitted because Bain felt that the market definitions used by the census were inaccurate. Brozen was able to enlarge this sample by using information not earlier available to Bain. The enlarged sample, examined for the same time period studied by Bain, failed to reveal any significant correlation between concentration and profits. Apparently Bain's findings were not representative of the population from which he selected his industries.

The undermining of the evidence favoring the market concentration doctrine continued with a recent article by Stanley Ornstein.[8] Ornstein found profit rates to be related significantly to industry and firm growth rates, and to the minimum efficient scale of production, but not to market concentration. Meanwhile, other studies have revealed a high degree of temporal instability in correlations between profit rates and market concentration, and some of these correlations are negative.

These new studies constitute a fundamental challenge to the empirical work underlying the market concentration doctrine. Doubts have been raised as to whether there exists a positive correlation between profit rates and concentration, and the proposition that any such relationship holds persistently through time seems to be discredited.

Weiss has provided us with a tabulation of most of the empirical studies bearing on the market concentration doctrine [Table 11]. His detailed critical review of these, however, is limited to those studies whose results are inconsistent with the market concentration doctrine. These he dismisses in some cases because their methodology was poor, because the time period covered was inflationary, or because regional industries were treated as if they had national markets. But almost all of the studies in support of the market concentration doctrine either have methodological problems, or are very heavily influenced by deflationary periods, or treat regional industries as national. If the criteria that Weiss adopts to criticize nonconfirmatory studies are applied to all studies, we are left with very little acceptable evidence about the relationship between profit rates and concentration.

Apparently, we now confront the proposition that successful collusion is practiced only during noninflationary periods by firms that advertise or use capital intensely — unless, of course, market concentration should be less than 70 percent! The theories to which Weiss has appealed tell us very little about oligopoly behavior, and they certainly do not tell us that collusion fails to work when the Consumer Price Index turns upward or when the 8-firm concentration ratio dips below 70 percent.

Brozen's study is selected for special criticism by Weiss. He contends that it was improper for Brozen to classify a few industries as concentrated or unconcentrated. For example, Weiss charges that Brozen was incorrect to include beet and cane sugar among his concentrated industries, because they compete on the same market and "their combined 8-firm concentration ratio was probably less than 70." The reader might suppose from Weiss's discussion that

    8. Stanley Ornstein, "Concentration and Profits," Journal of Business, 45 (October 1972), p. 519.

these problems were not discussed by Brozen, but the appendix to Brozen's paper [see n. 7 *supra*] discusses the very industries referred to by Weiss, and I recommend a reading of that appendix for those who are curious about why Brozen constructed the sample as he did. For example, Brozen writes:

> Bain excluded the sugar industries (beet and cane) on the ground that the separation of close substitutes "would tend seriously to overstate the true concentration for the theoretical industry within which the outputs in question fell." If we assume that no cane suger refiner produced beet sugar and take the proportion of the output of the leading eight cane sugar refiners of total refined sugar (beet and cane) sales, thus obtaining the lower limit of the possible sugar refining concentration ratio, it exceeds 70 percent and puts the sugar industry in Bain's more concentrated groups.

Brozen did not specially select his sample as seems to be implied by Weiss, but chose to use the complete Federal Trade Commission sample that had been used by the commission to conduct one of the studies quoted by Weiss as support for the market concentration doctrine. Brozen merely shifted the time period to that examined by Bain.

We have already seen that Weiss is simply wrong in saying that the combined 8-firm concentration ratio for the sugar industry was less than 70 percent. Weiss also removed several industries because of their regional character, but it is not proper to exclude an industry from the unconcentrated category merely because it is regional. An accepted procedure is to require regional industries to exhibit very low national concentration measures before they are allowed to enter the unconcentrated category. A national 4-firm concentration ratio less than 20 percent has been found acceptable to other investigators. If we use this criterion, Weiss should not have removed the bread and bakery products industry from the unconcentrated category, nor should he have removed nonalcoholic beverages or malt liquors. The cement industry profits in 1939 and 1940 were below the average for the unconcentrated group, where the industry was placed in Brozen's sample. If it were removed from this category, as Weiss suggests, and placed instead in the concentrated industries category, as was done in Mann's study, the results would have turned out even more favorable to a rejection of Bain's findings. For alcoholic beverages, a strong case can be made that the market was national in scope; for example, most of the beer sold by the top brewers was sold nationwide from single plants. Finally, I am not sure how blast furnace products should be handled, since it is difficult to discover the extent of competition between pig iron producers and integrated steel mills.

Weiss's techniques, of course, can be applied to studies favoring the market concentration doctrine. For example, Bain was not so careful as Weiss implies. Bain did not eliminate all industries with regional characteristics. He used cement and also cast iron pipe. He didn't use the locomotive industry, although it clearly is highly concentrated and manufactures a single product. It earned only 1.7 percent, and its inclusion in Bain's sample would have lowered the concentrated industries' rate of return.

But even after Weiss recasts the FTC sample, he gets a 2.2 percent difference in return between concentrated and nonconcentrated industries for one year — no small reduction from the 4.4 percent difference found by Bain. And in the other year there is no significant difference. The guts of Brozen's study hold their shape very well even when operated on by Weiss.

We have seen that the theoretical basis for the market concentration doctrine is weak at best, and that the empirical work is not clear cut as to results. The situation is much worse when we turn to the notion of self-created barriers to entry. The lack of a theoretical justification for identifying certain types of expenditures as "barriers to entry" is even more glaring than is the lack of a theoretical basis for the market concentration doctrine. The costliness of producing commodities does, of course, limit the amounts that will be made available at particular prices; in this sense cost does create a "barrier" to production, but no pejorative interpretation can be given to such a "barrier to entry." Indeed, it would be wasteful to produce additional units when the cost of doing so exceeds the value of these units to prospective purchasers. Cost, whether incurred to acquire labor or capital or to inform prospective buyers, sets proper limits on the production and marketing of commodities.

What does it mean to say that advertising expenditures and capital outlays constitute barriers to entry? One meaning is that firms must make such expenditures if they are to produce and communicate about the commodities they hope to sell. Such expenditures are no more barriers than are expenditures on labor and material. A second meaning is that existing firms are more efficient in the employment of such inputs than are firms not yet in the industry. If this is so, the existing firms deserve applause, not divestiture. A third meaning is that existing firms have an *undesirable* advantage in the use of these inputs. Since all firms can borrow in the capital markets and can purchase advertising campaigns, it is difficult to see wherein the unfair advantage lies. If large firms are better risks to lenders and, therefore, if they can borrow at lower rates (internally or externally) than can small or new firms, then this element of superiority for the large-scale, older firm is properly recognized by capital markets. Similarly, if buyers have more confidence in, and are more knowledgeable about, well-established products, then this also is a real efficiency not to be denied to firms that have invested in building substantial reputations. Nor should buyers who do not desire to bear the risk of consuming and the cost of searching for *possibly* equally good but less well-known alternatives be denied the advantage of trading with older, larger firms.

Objections based on problems of accounting methods have been raised about the notion that advertising creates a barrier to entry. There is a suspicion that the empirical correlation between advertising intensity and profit rate is an accounting artifact brought about by the fact that accountants treat advertising as a current expense even though the returns from advertising may be earned over several years. Critics have argued that it is this accounting artifact and not barriers to entry that produces this correlation. Two studies have attempted to take into consideration the investment-like quality of advertising. Weiss[9] adjusted Comanor and Wilson's study by introducing a depreciation rate for advertising, but he found that this did not significantly reduce the correlation between profit rates and advertising that had been uncovered by Comanor and Wilson. A doctoral dissertation by H. Bloch[10] using different methods and data, however, concluded that the correlation between these variables disappears when the accounting data are corrected to allow for the investmentlike quality of advertising.

When Weiss modified the Comanor and Wilson study, he applied a uniform advertising depreciation rate to all industries. This is likely to result in a bias if advertising depreciation rates actually differ among industries. R. Ayanian, in a dissertation now being completed at UCLA, has estimated depreciation rates for various industries and found that they do differ. When he uses the different depreciation rates applicable to different industries, he finds no correlation between profit rates and advertising intensity.

The current popularity of "barriers to entry" is puzzling. It is said that existing firms have created a preference for their products through the use of advertising and, therefore, that new competitors need to advertise even more intensely if they are to attract customers. But the firms now in the industry once needed to attract customers away from the established products of other industries, to an unknown new product, so it is not at all clear that new entrants suffer a disadvantage as compared with those who showed the way. Furthermore, the inputs most likely to create a differential advantage for existing firms are those that might make it more difficult for new firms to learn the source of strength enjoyed by old firms. Old firms may have developed particular trade secrets or ways of organizing that are relatively difficult for new firms to learn about. But the use of advertising and large amounts of capital are there for everyone to see and duplicate. Even the particular type of sales pitch used by successful firms can be imitated with relative ease. The use of advertising and capital would seem to me to be the least likely candidates for the role of barriers to entry. One grandfather's clause is worth a very, very large advertising budget.

In summary then, we can conclude that the theoretical support of the market concentration doctrine, including its barriers-to-entry variant, is weak or nonexistent. On the empirical side, it is clear that more studies reveal a positive correlation between profits and concentration than do not. There are enough of those that fail to show such a correlation, however, that the policymaker ought not suppose that conclusive evidence of this statistical relationship exists. What is needed is a thoroughgoing fresh look at the data and methodology. But even if this should reveal a positive correlation, there would still remain a serious problem for policy, for what can be inferred from a positive correlation?

9. L. Weiss, "Advertising, Profits, and Corporate Taxes," *Review of Economics and Statistics,* 51 (November 1969), p. 421.

10. H. Bloch, "Advertising, Competition, and Market Performance" (unpublished Ph.D. thesis, Univ. of Chicago 1971).

III

That any meaning can be given to persistent correlations between profit and concentration is attributable to the fact that accounting measures are necessarily poor approximations to the theoretical concepts they represent. The most important imperfection is their weakness in attaching appropriate values to those assets that are likely to be associated with the preservation of monopoly or the attainment of superior efficiency. If proper economic values were given on these assets, then all firms, whether monopolies or competitive, could be expected to yield the same rate of return. Thus, the trucking industry obtains a grandfather's clause to block entry. This increases the value of the licenses to operate, but accountants are unlikely to value these licenses at anything like their market value; if they were so valued, the rate of return recorded by trucking firms would be no different than that recorded by free-entry industries. A correct evaluation of assets would capitalize monopoly profits into the value of the assets which shield the firms from competition. Similarly, an explicit or implicit agreement to collude, if successful, is an undervalued asset to companies. Hence it is possible to look at accounting returns and form some guess as to the degree of monopoly that is present.

Unfortunately, it is not only sources of monopoly that are undervalued by accountants but also sources of efficiency. For example, General Motors has made a decision to push ahead with a rotary-engine car. No element of monopoly is present in that decision, since Ford and Chrysler also could have adopted the same course of action. But they did not. Let us suppose that GM's decision turns out to be correct, and that it gains both profit and market share, which it holds for many years because of the difficulty of quickly imitating that decision, the uncertainty among all firms as to whether the rotary engine will continue to be successful, and the tendency of consumers in this industry to rate experience highly. Accounting procedures are essentially backward-looking, but the uncertain value of such a decision rests in the future. Hence, for many years GM may record high profits and high market share even though monopoly is absent.

It might be supposed that management wages would reflect the value of a correct decision, but they will do so only imperfectly and with long lags. Indeed, if the full value of such decisions accrued to management, there would be no reason for GM stock to appreciate. Part of the reason that salaries will not capture the full value of such decisions is because some of the reward accrues to shareholders who had a role in selecting a productive (or lucky) team. Another reason is that it is difficult to forecast how long the decision will remain the correct decision. The better the decision turns out in retrospect, the more undervalued (relatively) will have been the management. Finally, the goodness of the decision may not reflect the ability of one man but the ability of an entire management team. No one member of such a team can hope to obtain a salary elsewhere that reflects his value as a member of this team; hence there is no reason for the market to push such salaries to the point where all the gain from the correct decision is exhausted in wages; nor should the market do so, since it is the firm itself, as a team, that has created this value. Similar problems arise in the case of monopoly profits. Since management is "responsible" for the decisions that create monopoly, it might be expected that the monopoly gains will be fully absorbed in managerial salary.

Higher accounting profit rates can arise either for reasons of monopoly or for superior efficiency, because accountants simply cannot appropriately value the assets or the decisions that may give rise to the profits. (Similarly, incorrect or unwise decisions will produce lower accounting profit rates.) Sometimes there will be an element of both efficiency and monopoly. Patent and copyright privileges may deliver to innovative firms some protection from competition and also may lead to higher concentration. To the extent that accounting procedures undervalue such legal protection, there will exist a positive correlation between profit and concentration. But this is cause for alarm only if we believe that the proper workings of the incentive system do not require such protection against easy imitation.

One difference in the implications of the source of high returns should be noted. If firms succeed in colluding to raise price, this may give rise to an increase in accounting profits because this agreement is undervalued by accountants. But these profits and the undervaluing of the agreement will be short-lived if firms cannot control competition in other directions. There will be great incentives to improve product quality and services in order to sell more at the collusive price. Such competition will raise cost towards price and dissipate the profitability of the agreement. This will not be the case if the cause of the higher profits is superior efficiency; there is no reason for a superior firm to dissipate its gains in such a fashion.

We do not yet understand the permanence that can be attached to either source of high accounting rates of return. Collusive agreements, even when enforced by government, do not last forever. The competition for government protection that sometimes creates new monopoly also may do away with old monopoly. Similarly, basic decisions having nothing to do with monopoly sometimes turn out well but other times turn out poorly. The Ford Motor Company acquired a dominant profitable position in the automobile industry by virtue of Henry Ford's decision to produce a standard model with mass-production techniques; but after several years of this, the same decision-maker lost share and profits to GM. In some cases, the effects of monopoly or of superior decisions may be felt for many years, and, in part, this could explain any persistence in high accounting rates of return.

A phenomenon that is likely to generate fairly persistent differences in accounting rates of returns is the fact that some products are more efficiently produced by firms possessing a large share of the market, while in other industries large market shares are not necessary for efficiency. Those firms that first act on the belief that large scale is an advantage, and that invest in the marketing and production techniques prerequisite to executing the move to large scale, will possess a competitively secured advantage in timing and in obtaining early consumer acceptance that will be difficult to overcome in a short time period. The market may not have grown large enough to accommodate more than a handful of such firms. These firms can produce at lower unit cost than smaller firms. They are superior in this respect, and they command an economic rent for achieving primacy. This rent will be measured as profit by accountants. Even though such firms can achieve generally low unit cost, at the margin their capacity may be strained and price will be high enough to allow smaller, higher unit cost firms to accommodate that part of the market not easily serviced by the larger firms. If and when the market grows enough to accommodate additional large firms, such firms will form, perhaps by merger of the smaller firms.

If industries are *persistently* concentrated, the fundamental reason will be the prevalence of large scale advantages. Such firms will record higher profits because the market has not yet grown sufficiently; in order to bring smaller, less efficient firms into production, price will need to be high enough to cover their unit cost, and this means that price will need to be high enough for *accounting* profits to be recorded by the large firms in these industries. Of course, these industries will be the highly concentrated ones.

Since most of the earlier studies of the relationship between profit and concentration relied heavily on the rate of return of only larger firms, it is difficult to know whether monopoly or superior efficiency accounts for the positive correlations frequently found. Does the market concentration doctrine, *unaided by this "efficient structure"* explanation, adequately explain the pattern of profit rates and market concentration? Do higher profits in concentrated industries reflect only monopoly? Or are they in whole or part brought about by the efficiency of large firms in these industries? [11] Some light can be shed on these questions by examining profit–concentration correlations after taking account of firm size. Firms of each size class should have profit rates that increase with concentration if collusion is more successful in concentrated markets. The absence of such correlations for most size classes of firms would be difficult to reconcile with the market concentration doctrine.

Table 8 tabulates the correlation between profit rates and concentration for firms in five different size categories and for each of five years. [12] Each entry shows the size of the correlation (which can vary from -1, for a perfect inverse relationship, to $+1$ for a perfect direct relationship) and indicates the level of significance that can be attached to the measured correlation. The most important information in Table 8 is that after the size of the firm is taken into account, *no* significant correlation between profit rate and market con-

11. Earlier empirical work exploring this problem can be found in H. Demsetz, "The Market Concentration Doctrine" (AEI-Hoover Policy Studies, August 1973), and H. Demsetz, "Industry Structure, Market Rivalry, and Public Policy," *Journal of Law and Economics,* 16 (April 1973), p. 1.

12. Four size classes were used when this paper was originally presented. At that time the largest class size was $50 million and up, but L. Weiss objected that the three smaller classes did not contain large enough firms. In response to this point, a fifth class size has been added. No cell in Tables 2 and 3 has less than 63 industries represented, and most have over 90.

TABLE 8

Correlations Between Rate of Return and Concentration by Asset Size of Firms

Asset Size ($000)	No. of industries:	94	116	116	116	76
	Year:	1958 [a]	1963	1966	1967	1970
$0-500		.29 [b]	−.19 [c]	−.09	−.01	−.38 [b]
500-5,000		.11	−.00	−.06	−.07	−.01
5,000-50,000		.14	.11	.04	−.05	−.00
50,000-100,000		−.01	.01	.09	.10	−.03
100,000 and up		.03	.16	.16	.16	.28 [c]
All asset sizes		.28 [b]	.35 [b]	.28 [b]	.19 [c]	.27 [c]

Note: Concentration is based on 4-digit census industries weighted by employment to match IRS profit data. The 1958 data were not yet complete, with 14 industries still to be tabulated.

a. Sample coverage for 1958 is small, and the data for 1958 must be interpreted with caution.

b. Significant at 1 percent confidence level.

c. Significant at 5 percent confidence level.

centration is apparent even though the correlations which ignore firm size are positive. It would appear that most, if not all, of the positive correlations between profit rates and concentration uncovered by some earlier studies can be attributed to variations in the size of firms, not the degree to which markets are concentrated. This general pattern of profit rate/concentration correlations cannot be explained by recognized oligopoly or monopoly theory. Indeed, it could be argued, with no more casualness than other arguments surrounding the market concentration doctrine, that the positive correlations should be strongest for moderate- and small-sized firms, since the large firms need to adhere more to the collusive agreement than do moderate-sized firms.

The strongest positive correlations tend to be found in the largest class size; and even though these fail to meet the standard tests of statistical significance, there no doubt will be attempts to link this fact to market power. One such explanation deserves attention. In effect, it is a compromise explanation. Larger firms in concentrated industries have lower cost because there are scale economies in these industries or because of some inherent superiority of the larger firms in these industries. Nonetheless they succeed in colluding so that *their* profit rates are relatively high. The prices they set in this collusion are not so high as to yield high profits for less efficient, more moderately sized smaller firms. Hence we observe a stronger positive correlation between profit rates and market concentration for the largest firms than for other firms.

In this rationalization of the data, the cost of production to moderate-sized firms in concentrated markets apparently sets the upper limit to the prices that are (can be?) set through the collusion of large firms; otherwise, firms of moderate size would exhibit higher profits in concentrated industries than in unconcentrated. Presumably, this limit to profits is effective because higher profits would lead new firms, possibly large new firms, and existing smaller firms to merge or expand capacity in the industry. All of this, of course, implies that existing large firms possess superior characteristics that are difficult to imitate. Their methods of organizing production, of providing service, and of establishing buyer confidence must yield lower cost than can be obtained by newer or smaller firms.

This compromise explanation hardly can justify a call for deconcentration, because considerable economies of large-scale production or other advantages of existing large firms would then be lost with no compensation in the form of lower prices. If the sizes of all firms are limited by deconcentration policies to be no larger than moderate-sized firms in their industries, then it will be the costs of the moderate-sized firms that determine prices. But that is how price is constrained without deconcentration if we accept this rationalization of these data. Since persistent market concentration seems to be associated with economies of scale or other forms of superior performance by existing larger firms in concentrated industries, a move to deconcentrate such industries is very *likely* to increase, not decrease, cost even *if* it were true that collusion is more successful in these industries. Embracing the market concentration doctrine through legislation is thus very likely to penalize the success and superior performance upon which depends the progress and wealth of this nation.

Table 8 reveals that most of the correlation between accounting profit rates and concentration can be attributed to firm size, not market concentration. The remaining correlation might only reflect accounting artifacts or special sources of efficiency other than size. There is a suspicion that the accounting treatment accorded advertising expenditures tends to exaggerate the rates of return recorded by those firms that advertise intensely, because accountants fail to treat advertising as a long-lived asset.

It might well be the case that some of the correlations in Table 8 reflect variations in advertising intensity and not variations in market concentration. It is possible to examine what happens to the correlations shown in Table 8 when variations in advertising intensity are taken into account. Table 9 recasts Table 8 after the effect of variations in advertising intensity are removed from the data. The entries in Table 9 thus isolate to a finer degree than Table 8 the relationship between accounting profit rates and concentration for given size classes of firms. The effect of taking account of advertising intensity is to weaken substantially the correlations between profit rates and concentration.

A closer look at Table 9 is rewarding. For firms with asset sizes larger than $1 million, the correlations prevalent in Table 8 all but disappear. Moreover, the correlations which ignore asset sizes turn out to be insignificant in 1967 and 1970 where before they were significant, and the correlations for 1963 and 1966 are weakened. Only the correlation for 1958 is strengthened, but oddly enough only the smallest firms reveal a significant positive relationship between profit rates and concentration for that year; this hardly can constitute strong evidence of collusion among large firms. The years 1958, 1967, and

180   *Harold Demsetz*

TABLE 9
Correlations Between Rate of Return and Concentration by Asset Size of Firms

Asset Size ($000)	1958 [a]	1963	1966	1967	1970
$0-500	.29 [b]	—.18 [c]	—.11	.00	—.41 [b]
500-5000	.12	—.03	—.05	—.11	—.08
5000-50,000	.17	.02	—.03	—.14	—.12
50,000-100,000	—.01	—.07	.04	.04	—.11
100,000 and up	.04	.06	.06	.06	.11
All asset sizes	.36 [b]	.29 [b]	.21 [c]	.09	.08

Note: All data identical to data underlying Table 8, but correlations between profit and concentration are partial correlations derived by taking account of the partial correlation between profit rates and advertising sales ratios.

a. Sample coverage for 1958 is small, and the data for 1958 must be interpreted cautiously.

b. Significant at 1 percent confidence level.

c. Significant at 5 percent confidence level.

1970 no longer yield evidence confirming the market concentration doctrine. The year 1966 yields weak evidence on an overall basis, but not for firms smaller than $50 million in asset size. Only 1963 retains a very significant overall correlation, but even here the smaller firms do not provide confirming data. It happens that 1963 is the year chosen by Weiss to correlate "profit margins" with concentration and advertising intensity. But 1963 appears to be a very atypical year with respect to this correlation, a fact to which I called attention in earlier work.[13] Table 9 does not offer convincing evidence for the market concentration doctrine. This is especially true since the correlations presented in that table are based on "one-tailed" tests of significance. Such tests seek to ascertain the probability that a positive correlation between profits and concentration exists. In view of the severe problems of securing dependable accounting data and the very weak theory underlying the market concentration doctrine, it might be wiser to ascertain whether the correlations differ significantly from zero in either a positive or a negative direction. Such a two-tailed test would cut (approximately in half) the remaining significance of the correlations shown in Table 9.

The role played by advertising in producing the results of Table 9 is still difficult to interpret. In some yet-to-be-described way, advertising might be associated with "barriers to entry." However, much of the correlation between profit rates and concentration found in earlier studies may be due to the inappropriate accounting treatment accorded to advertising; evidence for this exists in other studies referred to above. On the other hand, a true source

13. See Demsetz, "The Market Concentration Doctrine," *supra* n. 11, at 16.

of superior efficiency may exist in the use of advertising by large firms in concentrated industries.

IV

Let us now complete the circle, returning to discuss the relative merits of the "self-sufficiency" and "interventionist" views of the monopoly problem. The evidence that has been cumulating in recent years must raise doubts about the importance of self-sufficient sources of monopoly and must increase our estimate of the importance of government intervention to protect industries from competition. It is possible, I think, to give good reasons for believing that this new evidence is indicative of the underlying truth.

The key to sustained monopoly power is the ability of an industry to restrict or retard the expansion and utilization of productive capacity. Government can offer to industry much greater powers of coercion to accomplish this end than can be supplied by the industry itself. Most of the resources supplied by the Department of Agriculture at taxpayer expense have been used to subsidize the policing of output restrictions that never could have been obtained without such aid. Moreover, an industry attempting to restrict capacity by its own efforts would need to rely on much less effective techniques than are available when the laws of the land can be marshaled toward this end. For example, if existing firms attempt to block entry by "predatory" pricing, they must all suffer reductions in their profits. The techniques available to firms without the aid of government are not very specific to penalizing only entrants. But the use of CAB or FCC to restrict competitive entry through the use of licensure or certificates of convenience and necessity specifically penalizes prospective entrants. An investment by an industry to obtain government aid to monopolize is likely to yield much more control than the investment of the same sum without the aid of governmental techniques. Some would argue that without government aid such an investment would generally be unprofitable.

More important than this, however, is the greater ease of securing the funds for such an investment if the restrictions are to be achieved through the government. In the absence of government cooperation there are important incentives for not contributing to an effort to restrict output. First, such an effort might very well run afoul of the antitrust laws. Secondly, to the extent that the agreement to restrict output is likely to succeed, a firm would find it profitable to remain outside the agreement; the firm could then expand its output to take full advantage of any higher prices brought about through the private efforts of other firms. These factors, which undermine the success of efforts to collude, are not as important if restrictions are to be achieved through the good offices of the government.

The government and the courts have been careful to protect the constitutional right of petition. If the firms in an industry cooperate in an in-house attempt to restrict output, they are in violation of the antitrust laws; but if they cooperate to obtain the aid of the White House and the Congress in building tariff barriers or in increasing agricultural support prices, they are not in violation of the antitrust laws. The basic conflict between the fundamental right of collective petition and the illegality of attempting to collude has been decided in favor of the right to petition.

The *Noerr* case in 1961[14] dealt explicitly with this conflict. In that case the Court of Appeals for the Third Circuit had held that no violation of the Sherman Act can be predicated upon mere attempts to influence the passage or enforcement of laws even if two or more persons associate in an attempt to persuade the legislature or the executive to take particular action that would produce a restraint or a monopoly. (There was some backing away from this decision in a later case, but this tended to emphasize the illegality of restricting one's competitors from easy access to the judicial or legislative machinery.) The antitrust laws are not violated by agreements to petition the government to restrict competition — but are violated when such agreements do not involve the government, even if those agreements fail to achieve their ends. The legal route of monopoly runs through Washington and the state capitals.

More important than the legality of a collusive agreement, perhaps, is the greater difficulty that would confront a firm which seeks to take advantage of an agreement secured and acted upon by other firms when this agreement works through the law. If such an agreement were to operate outside the law, a firm not joining in the agreement could hope to expand its output in response to the higher price brought about by the output restrictions which other firms imposed on themselves. The propensity to stay out of such an agreement or to secretly break its terms constitutes a serious impediment to collusion outside the law. But if the government is brought into the collusive agreement, then higher powers of coercion can be brought into play to make sure that firms in the industry do not undermine the agreement. How else can individual farmers be prevented from increasing output when prices rise? How else can individual owners of oil-rich land be prevented from increasing crude oil output when oil prices rise or when imports are restricted? In one case the discipline is obtained through the federal government's agricultural program, and in the other through the prorationing programs of state governments.

For these reasons and others, including the statistical evidence that has come to light recently, it is quite plausible to believe that government intervention constitutes the main threat to a competitive economy. It is important that this threat be recognized, because our belief on this score governs how we deploy resources to ensure that competition will flourish. What is called for is a redirection of our efforts. Government intervention that has created and sustained monopoly should be our primary target.

How such a redirection can be brought about is hardly the province of the economist. I doubt that monstrosities such as the agricultural program can be modified significantly until basic changes in the political makeup of this nation continue for several more years. But I see no basic political beliefs of the

14. Eastern R.R. Presidents Conference v. Noerr Motor Freight, Inc., 365 U.S. 127 (1961).

voters of this nation that predispose them to rejoice when the FCC protects established networks and movie theaters from the competition of pay TV. Nor are there obvious cheers from the electorate when the ICC exercises its control over minimum freight rates, or when it prevents truckers and railroads from competing with each other. John Q. Public does not rise to salute when the SEC cooperates with the attempts of the NYSE to protect itself from competition within and without, nor does he exude great pleasure at the efforts of the CAB to keep airlines from setting lower fares. These regulatory actions have benefited special interests in situations where the typical citizen suffers no great illusion as to where his interest lies.

If we can not do away with such regulation, let us at least make it easier for the Justice Department (or some other agency not beholden to any particular industry) to ask whether the decisions of our regulatory tribunals are in the public interest, and, when it feels that they are not, to bring the issue before the courts of this land. I commend the Justice Department for recent moves that it has made on the question of fixed commissions on our organized exchanges. This is a welcome indirect challenge of the authority of the SEC as the sole arbiter of the public interest in the operation of capital markets. But it should be made easier for some agency to question the merits of regulatory decisions and to represent consumer interests in affairs of these industries.

I do not suggest that we abandon the search for private conspiracy, but I do think that it is time to pay much less attention to the structure of industry and virtually no attention to the notion of nongovernmental barriers to entry. A commitment to the machinery of competitive organization requires that we generally accept the consequences of effective competition. For antitrust, this means that market share and profits can be expected to shift in favor of successful rivals.

Unfortunately, our antitrust laws are being used to protect competitors and penalize efficiency. Competitive pricing policies, effective advertising campaigns, and the efficient management of resources are as likely to run afoul of antitrust as are attempts to collude. To an increasing extent, the *United States Steel* [15] and *Alcoa* [16] cases typify the reasoning in contemporary antitrust cases.

The United States Steel Corporation escaped dissolution by refraining from competitive pricing, thus escaping any charge that it used its power to make life difficult for smaller rivals, but Alcoa was found to violate antitrust laws because it behaved competitively. Alcoa had claimed that it never excluded competitors, but Judge Learned Hand clearly described the source of illegality in his reply: "[W]e can think of no more effective exclusion than progressively to embrace each new opportunity as it opened, and to face every newcomer with new capacity already geared into a great organization having the advantage of experience, trade connections, and the elite of personnel." [17]

15. United States v. United States Steel Corp., 251 U.S. 417 (1920).
16. United States v. Aluminum Company of America, 148 F.2d 416 (2nd Cir. 1945).
17. *Id.* at 431.

184   *Leonard W. Weiss*

Those who seek freedom, productivity, and protection through market competition must believe that there is a steady stream of competition that disciplines even those who best their rivals on a given day or during a given decade. The history of market economies provides overwhelming evidence that this belief is based on experience. A public policy based on this belief should cease to be alarmed when effective competition *actually* shifts market share and profits, and certainly should not interfere with competitive processes in *anticipation* of such consequences. Such a cool and unconcerned posture must contemplate the possibility of a modicum of monopoly power for short periods of time in some instances, but this is a small cost to bear in order to avoid the attempt to tune finely the operation of competitive forces. The inadequacies of attempted fine-tuning are readily revealed in contemporary antitrust and in the substitution of regulatory restrictionism and favoritism for market rivalry.

Present trends in antitrust make it difficult to refrain from asking whether present practices encourage more competition than they inhibit. The answer cannot be given yet with any certainty, but there are numerous instances where judicial "cartelization" seems to have taken place. Given these uncertainties, it would seem wise to redirect our efforts to the task of reducing governmentally protected monopolies.

[17]

The Economic Journal, 90 (*March* 1980), 95–106
Printed in Great Britain

THE ROLE OF INVESTMENT IN
ENTRY-DETERRENCE*

The theory of large-scale entry into an industry is made complicated by its game-theoretic aspects. Even in the simplest case of one established firm facing one prospective entrant, there are some subtle strategic interactions. The established firm's pre-entry decisions can influence the prospective entrant's view of what will happen if he enters, and the established firm will try to exploit this possibility to its own advantage.

The earliest treatments met these problems by adopting the Bain–Sylos postulate, where the prospective entrant was assumed to believe that the established firm would maintain the same output after entry as its actual pre-entry output. Then the established firm naturally acquired a Stackelberg leadership role. However, the assumption is dubious on two opposing counts. First, faced with an irrevocable fact of entry, the established firm will usually find it best to make an accommodating output reduction. On the other hand, it would like to threaten to respond to entry with a predatory increase in output. Its problem is to make the latter threat credible given the prospective entrant's knowledge of the former fact. (A detailed exposition of the Bain–Sylos model and its critique can be found in Scherer (1970, ch. 8).)

In a seminal treatment of games involving such conflicts, Schelling (1960, ch. 2) suggested that a threat which is costly to carry out can be made credible by entering into an advance commitment which makes its fulfilment optimal or even necessary. This was applied to the question of entry by Spence (1977), who recognised that the established firm's prior and irrevocable investment decisions could be a commitment of this kind. He assumed that the prospective entrant would believe that the established firm's post-entry output would equal its pre-entry capacity. In the interests of entry-deterrence, the established firm may set capacity at such a high level that in the pre-entry phase it would not want to utilise it all, i.e. excess capacity would be observed.

The Bain–Sylos and Spence analyses were extended in Dixit (1979) by considering whether the established firm will find it best to prevent entry or to allow it to occur. However, the basic assumptions concerning the post-entry developments were maintained.

Since it is at best unclear whether such assumptions will be valid, it seems useful to study the consequences of some alternatives. In reality, there may be no agreement about the rules of the post-entry game, and there may be periods of disequilibrium before any order is established. Financial positions of the firms may then acquire an important role. However, even when the two have a common understanding of the rules of the post-entry duopoly, there are several possibilities. An obvious case is where a Nash equilibrium will be established

* I am grateful to Gunnar Bramness and Michael Waterson for useful comments on an earlier version.

after entry, either in quantities as in Cournot (see also Wenders (1971)) or in prices as in Bertrand. Yet another case is where the entrant is destined to take over Stackelberg leadership in setting quantities (see Salop (1978)).

In this paper I examine some of these possibilities. The basic point is that although the *rules* of the post-entry game are taken to be exogenous, the established firm can alter the *outcome* to its advantage by changing the initial conditions. In particular, an irrevocable choice of investment allows it to alter its post-entry marginal cost curve, and thereby the post-entry equilibrium under any specified rule. It will be seen that it can use this privilege to exercise limited leadership.

I. THE MODEL

The basic point is most easily seen in a simplified model. I shall reduce the dynamic aspects to the barest essentials by ignoring all lags. Either entry does not occur at all, in which case the established firm continues in a stationary state, or else it occurs at once, and the post-entry equilibrium is also established at once, so that the resulting duopoly continues in its stationary state. It is as if the two players see through the whole problem and implement the solution immediately.[1] The result is that we can confine attention to the constant streams of profits, avoiding the complication of reducing a varying pair of profit flows to discounted present values. However, once the underlying principle is understood, an added complication in this respect is not difficult to admit in principle.

The second simplification made in the main body of the analysis is with regard to the costs of production. Let the subscript 1 denote the established firm and 2 the prospective entrant. Each firm will be supposed to have a constant average variable cost of output, and a constant unit cost of capacity expansion, and a set-up cost. If firm i has capacity k_i and is producing output x_i (with $x_i \leqslant k_i$), its cost per period will be

$$C_i = f_i + w_i x_i + r_i k_i, \tag{1}$$

where f_i is the fixed set-up cost, r_i the constant cost per unit of capacity (both expressed in per period or flow terms), and w_i the constant average variable cost for output. The possibility that the two firms have the same cost functions ($f_1 = f_2$, etc.) is not excluded. The special form (1) has some analytical and empirical merit; I examine a more general cost function in Section III.

The revenues per period for the two firms will be functions $R^i(x_1, x_2)$. Each will be increasing and concave in that firm's output. Also, each firm's total and marginal revenue will be decreasing in the other's output.

The rules of the game are as follows. The established firm chooses a pre-entry capacity level k_1. This may subsequently be increased, but cannot be reduced. If the other firm decides to enter, the two will achieve a duopoly Cournot-Nash equilibrium with quantity-setting. Otherwise the established firm will prevail as a monopoly.

[1] Compare the exchange between Moriarty and Holmes in *The Final Problem*: 'All that I have to say has already crossed your mind', said he. 'Then possibly my answer has crossed yours', I replied.

First suppose that firm 1 has installed capacity k_1. If it is producing output within this limit, i.e. if $x_1 \leqslant k_1$, its total costs are

$$C_1 = f_1 + r_1 k_1 + w_1 x_1.$$

However, if it wishes to produce greater output, it must acquire additional capacity. If $x_1 > k_1$, therefore,

$$C_1 = f_1 + (w_1 + r_1) x_1.$$

Correspondingly, firm 1's marginal cost is w_1 so long as its output does not exceed k_1, and $(w_1 + r_1)$ thereafter. Firm 2 has no prior commitment in capacity. For all positive levels of output x_2, it acquires capacity k_2 to match, yielding

$$C_2 = f_2 + (w_2 + r_2) x_2$$

and a marginal cost of $(w_2 + r_2)$. The choice of k_1 thus affects the shape of the marginal cost curve of firm 1, which in turn affects its reaction curve. When the two firms interact, the resulting duopoly equilibrium depends on k_1, and therefore so do the profits of the two firms in it. If the profits for the second firm are positive, it will enter; otherwise it will not. Bearing this in mind, firm 1 will choose that k_1 which maximises its profit. Whether this is done by preventing entry or by allowing it to occur remains to be seen. However, I shall assume for simplicity of exposition that the established firm's maximum profit is positive, i.e. exit is not its best policy.

The analysis follows the scheme just outlined. For a given k_1, Fig. 1 shows the marginal cost curve for the established firm, MC_1, as the heavy kinked line.

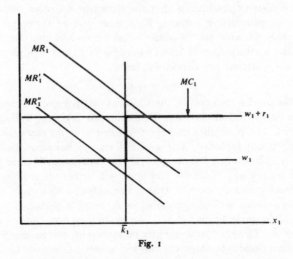

Fig. 1

It equals w_1, the marginal cost when there is spare capacity, up to the output level k_1 and $(w_1 + r_1)$, the marginal cost including capacity expansion cost, thereafter. On this we superimpose the marginal revenue curve, the position of which depends on the assumed output level x_2 of the other firm. For a sufficiently low value of x_2, the curve is in a position like the one labelled MR_1, and the first firm's profit-maximising choice of x_1 lies to the right of its previously fixed capacity level. For successively higher levels of x_2, the marginal revenue curve shifts downwards to occupy positions like MR_1' and MR_1'', yielding choices of x_1 at, or below, the capacity level. This response of x_1 to x_2 is just the established firm's reaction function to the entrant's output.

This function can be shown in a more familiar direct manner in the space of two quantities, and this is done in Fig. 2. I have shown two 'reference' curves MM' and NN'. The first becomes the reaction function if capacity expansion costs matter, and the second if there is spare capacity. Therefore the first is relevant for outputs above k_1 and the second for outputs below this level. For fixed k_1, then, the reaction function is the kinked curve shown in heavy lines.

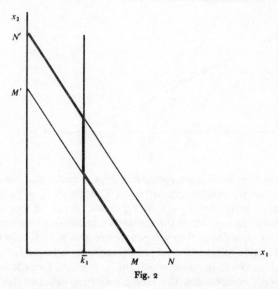

Fig. 2

Let the points M and N have respective coordinates $(M_1, 0)$ and $(N_1, 0)$. The quantities M_1 and N_1 can be interpreted as follows. Both are profit-maximising quantity choices of firm 1 when the output level of firm 2 is held fixed at zero, i.e. when the possibility of entry is ignored. However, M_1 is the choice when capacity expansion costs matter, and N_1 is relevant when there is sufficient capacity already installed and only variable costs matter.

Since firm 2 has no prior commitment in capacity, its reaction function RR' is straightforward. I assume that it intersects both MM' and NN' in a way that corresponds to the usual 'stable' Cournot solution, in order to minimise complications other than those of immediate interest (see Fig. 3).

For given k_1, we have a duopoly Nash equilibrium at the intersection of the two reaction functions. However, the established firm has the privilege of choosing k_1 in advance, and thus determining which reaction function it will present in the post-entry duopoly. Suppose firm 2's reaction function meets MM' at $T = (T_1, T_2)$ and NN' at $V = (V_1, V_2)$ as shown in Fig. 3. Clearly T and V can be interpreted as Nash equilibria under alternative extreme circumstances, T when capacity expansion costs matter for firm 1, and V when

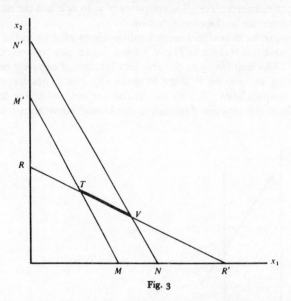

Fig. 3

they do not. It is then evident on comparing Figs. 2 and 3 that for a choice of $k_1 \leqslant T_1$, the post-entry equilibrium will be at T, while for $k_1 \geqslant V_1$, it will occur at V. Most importantly, for $T_1 \leqslant k_1 \leqslant V_1$, it will occur at the appropriate point on the heavy line segment of the entrant's reaction function lying between T and V. Here the established firm will produce output $x_1 = k_1$, and the entrant will produce the same output as would a Stackelberg follower faced with this x_1. It is in this sense that, even when the post-entry game is accepted as leading to a Nash equilibrium, the established firm can exercise leadership over a limited range by using its capacity choice to manipulate the initial conditions of that game.

However, the qualification of the limited range is important. In particular, it means that capacity levels above V_1 are not credible threats of entry-deterrence. When a prospective entrant is confident of its ability to sustain a Nash equilibrium in the post-entry game, it does not fear such levels. And when the established firm knows this, it does not try out the costly and empty threats.

Since $N_1 > V_1$, we see a fortiori the futility of maintaining capacity levels above N_1 as threats to deter entry. Nor are such capacity levels justified by considerations of pre-entry production; in fact a monopolist saddled with capacity above N_1 will choose to leave the excess idle. Under the rules of the game assumed here, therefore, we will not observe the established firm installing capacity above N_1. The Spence excess capacity strategy will not be employed.

Nor will we ever see the established firm installing pre-entry capacity of less than T_1: if entry is to occur it will want more capacity, and if entry is not to occur it will want capacity of at least $M_1 > T_1$.

In the model used by Spence, it is simply assumed that a prospective entrant expects the established firm will respond to entry by producing an output level equal to its pre-entry capacity, no matter how high that may be. It is then possible that constrained monopoly profits made by keeping capacity at the entry-deterring level and producing at N exceed what is possible with a lower capacity leading to a Stackelberg duopoly equilibrium. This is the excess-capacity strategy of entry prevention. When the credibility of the threat is questioned, matters can be different, and the above argument shows that they are indeed different under the particular modification of the rules of the game.

II. CLASSIFICATION OF OUTCOMES

The discussion so far was confined to the post-entry duopoly, i.e. both firms were assumed to have incurred the set-up costs. When we come to the ex ante decision about whether to enter, set-up costs matter, and the choice is governed by the sign of the profits net of them. (Dixit (1979) uses an alternative geometric approach involving discontinuous reaction functions.)

We have seen above that at all points that are ever going to be observed without or with entry, the established firm will be producing an output equal to its chosen pre-entry capacity. Therefore we may write the profits of the two firms as functions of their outputs alone, i.e.

$$\pi_i(x_1, x_2) = R^i(x_1, x_2) - f_i - (w_i + r_i) x_i.$$

It will often be convenient to indicate the point of evaluation (x_1, x_2) by a letter label such as that used in the corresponding figure. I have assumed that the maximum value of π_1 is always positive. Depending on the sign of π_2, various cases arise. Note that along firm 2's reaction function, its profit decreases monotonically from T to V. Therefore we can classify the possibilities as follows.

Case 1. $\pi_2(T) < 0$. Now the prospective entrant cannot make a profit in any post-entry equilibrium. So it will not try to enter the industry at all. Entry being irrelevant, the established firm will enjoy a pure monopoly by setting its capacity and output at M_1.

Case 2. $\pi_2(V) > 0$. Here the prospective entrant will make a positive profit in any post-entry equilibrium, so the established firm cannot hope to prevent entry. It can only seek the best available duopoly position. To this end, it will compute its profit along the segment TV. Since all these choices involve output equal to capacity, we can simply use the conventional iso-π_1 contours in (x_1, x_2) space and find the highest contour along the segment TV. If there is a Stackelberg tangency to the left of V, that is firm 1's best choice. However, if the conventional tangency occurs to the right of V, we now have a corner solution at V, which can then be thought of as a sort of generalised Stackelberg leadership point.

Case 3. $\pi_2(T) > 0 > \pi_2(V)$. This presents the richest set of possibilities. Now there is a point $B = (B_1, B_2)$ along such TV that $\pi_2(B) = 0$. If the established firm sets its capacity above B_1, the prospective entrant will reckon on making a negative profit in the post-entry Nash equilibrium, and therefore will not enter. Thus the capacity level B_1 is the entry-barring level. Knowing this, firm 1 wants to know whether it is worth its while to prevent entry.

Sub-case i. If $B_1 < M_1$, then the established firm's monopoly choice is automatically sufficient to deter entry. In Bain's terminology, entry can be said to be blockaded.

If $B_1 > M_1$, the established firm can only bar entry by maintaining capacity (and output) at a level greater than it would want to as a monopolist; thus it is faced with a calculation of the costs and benefits of entry-prevention. To prevent entry, it needs a capacity of just greater than B_1. Since $B_1 < V_1 < N_1$, we know that it will want to use all this capacity in its monopoly choice of output, so its profit will be $\pi_1(B_1, 0)$. The alternative is to allow entry and settle for the best duopoly point, which may be a tangency in the segment TV, or a corner solution at V. Whichever it is, call it the generalised Stackelberg point S, with coordinates (S_1, S_2). Then we have:

Sub-case ii. $\pi_1(S) < \pi_1(B_1, 0)$, when it is better to prevent entry by choosing a limit-capacity or limit-output at B_1. There is a corresponding limit-price. In Bain's usage, entry is effectively impeded. Incidentally, for this sub-case to arise, it is sufficient to have $S_1 \geqslant B_1$. For, with $B_1 > M_1$, we have $\pi_1(S_1, S_2) < \pi_1(S_1, 0) \leqslant \pi_1(B_1, 0)$.

Sub-case iii. $\pi_1(S) > \pi_1(B_1, 0)$, when it is better to allow entry, i.e. entry is ineffectively impeded, and a duopoly solution is observed at S. Remember that S is the post-entry Nash equilibrium.

An alternative way of distinguishing between the sub-cases *ii* and *iii* is to draw the iso-π_1 contour through S and see if it intersects the x_1-axis to the right or the left of B_1. This would follow Dixit (1979), except for one new feature: the Stackelberg point S can be at the corner solution V.

For particular demand functions, we can evaluate all these profit expressions explicitly, and thereby express the classification of outcomes in terms of the underlying parameters.

III. EXTENSIONS AND MODIFICATIONS

Of the numerous extensions conceivable, I consider three. The first involves an alternative and rather extreme post-entry equilibrium, where the rules of the game are that the entrant acquires the role of quantity leadership (see Salop (1978)). Thus firm 2 chooses a point on firm 1's post-entry reaction function to maximise its own profit. However, firm 1, by its initial commitment to capacity, can decide which reaction function to present to the entrant, and can manipulate this choice to its own advantage.

Fig. 4 shows the possibilities. The notation is the same as in Fig. 3, with some additions. Let $F = (F_1, F_2)$ be the ordinary Stackelberg point where firm 2 is the leader and firm 1 the follower, taking into account capacity expansion costs, i.e. using the reference curve MM'. If firm 1 sets its capacity k_1 at a level less than F_1, then its reaction function as drawn in Fig. 2 will drop from NN' to MM' at k_1 to the left of F. Firm 2's profit will then be maximised on this reaction function at the tangency point F. For k_1 between F_1 and T_1, there will be a maximum at the kink in firm 1's reaction function where it meets MM', yielding an equilibrium at the appropriate point along the segment FT.

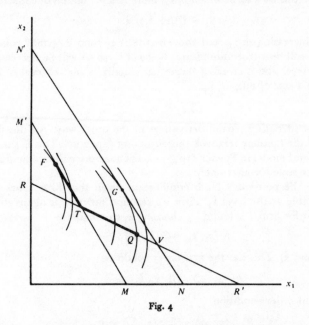

Fig. 4

For a while to the right of T, we will have a tangency solution along TV, an iso-π_2 contour being tangential to the vertical portion of firm 1's reaction function. Let G be the point where an iso-π_2 contour is tangential to NN', and let this contour meet RR' at $Q = (Q_1, Q_2)$. Then the vertical tangency will be the best choice for firm 2 so long as $k_1 \leqslant Q_1$. For $k_1 > Q_1$, however, it will prefer the tangency at G.

By its choice of k_1, the established firm can therefore secure as the post-entry equilibrium any point along the kinked line segment FTQ, shown in heavy ink in the figure, and the isolated point G. In other words, even though the rules of the game require it to surrender post-entry quantity leadership, the established firm can use its commitment to capacity to seize a limited initiative back from the entrant. It remains to choose the best available point. Now G is clearly inferior from the point of view of firm 1 to the point directly below it on the segment TQ. Similarly, all points along FT are worse than T. However, there is a genuine choice to be made, i.e. leadership exercised, along the segment TQ. This is smaller than the segment TV which was available when the post-entry rules led to a Nash equilibrium. But the qualitative features are unchanged, and all of my earlier analysis applies on replacing V by Q throughout.

The second extension I consider allows a more general cost function. The form (1), up to the given capacity level, has marginal cost constant at the level w_1, and since capacity cannot be exceeded, the marginal cost of output can be said to jump to infinity where output hits capacity. An increase in capacity then lowers marginal cost from infinity to w_1 over the added range. Now I replace this by a form which has a more flexible notion of capacity. Let

$$C_1 = C^1(x_1, k_1). \tag{2}$$

This will be increasing in x_1, and convex at least beyond a certain point. For each x_1 there will be a cost-minimising choice of k_1, so C^1 will be decreasing in k_1 up to this level and increasing thereafter. Finally, a higher level of k_1 will lower marginal cost of output, i.e.

$$C^1_{x_1 k_1} < 0, \tag{3}$$

with subscripts denoting partial derivatives in the usual way. All this follows the theory of the familiar textbook short-run cost functions. This is similar to the more general model in Spence (1977) except that price discipline does not break down completely after entry.

Begin with the post-entry Nash equilibrium given that firm 1 has set its capacity variable at the level k_1. Firm 2's reaction function is again straight-forward. That for firm 1 is found by choosing x_1 to maximise

$$R^1(x_1, x_2) - C^1(x_1, k_1)$$

for given x_2 and k_1. This has the first-order condition

$$R^1_{x_1}(x_1, x_2) - C^1_{x_1}(x_1, k_1) = 0 \tag{4}$$

and the second-order condition

$$R^1_{x_1 x_1}(x_1, x_2) - C^1_{x_1 x_1}(x_1, k_1) < 0. \tag{5}$$

Equation (4) defines firm 1's post-entry reaction function, and also tells us how it shifts as k_1 changes. Total differentiation gives

$$dx_1 = [-R^1_{x_1 x_2}/(R^1_{x_1 x_1} - C^1_{x_1 x_1})] dx_2 + [C^1_{x_1 k_1}/(R^1_{x_1 x_1} - C^1_{x_1 x_1})] dk_1.$$

Given our assumption that the commodities are substitutes in the sense that an increased quantity of the second lowers the marginal revenue for the first, and using (5), we see that the reaction function slopes downward. Also, using (3) and (5), we see that it shifts to the right as k_1 increases.

Fig. 5 shows a collection of firm 1's reaction functions for different choices of k_1, as a set of dashed lines. Where each meets firm 2's reaction function RR', there is a post-entry Nash equilibrium for the appropriate choice of k_1. Thus, once again, firm 1 by its choice of capacity can achieve any one of a range of points along firm 2's reaction function. This is almost as if it acquired the privilege of quantity leadership. There are two limitations. First, the possible reaction functions found by varying k_1 may trace out only a limited part of firm 2's reaction function, as happened in the case of Section I. Secondly, in any post-entry Nash equilibrium, the k_1 which achieves it is not the ideal choice for producing the x_1 that prevails there; so the policy involves a cost that does not appear in straightforward quantity leadership. To see this, we must examine the equilibrium in more detail. Firm 2 maximises $R^2(x_1, x_2) - C^2(x_2)$ in obvious notation, so its reaction function is given by

$$R^2_{x_2}(x_1, x_2) - C^2_{x_2}(x_2) = 0. \tag{6}$$

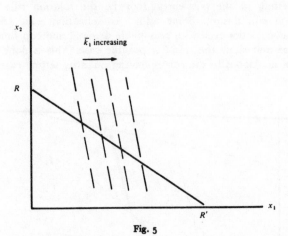

Fig. 5

Then (4) and (6) define the duopoly equilibrium as a function of k_1. Differentiating the equations totally, we have

$$\begin{bmatrix} R^1_{x_1 x_1} - C^1_{x_1 x_1} & R^1_{x_1 x_2} \\ R^2_{x_1 x_2} & R^2_{x_2 x_2} - C^2_{x_2 x_2} \end{bmatrix} \begin{bmatrix} dx_1 \\ dx_2 \end{bmatrix} = \begin{bmatrix} C^1_{x_1 k_1} dk_1 \\ 0 \end{bmatrix}. \tag{7}$$

Write Δ for the determinant of the coefficient matrix; it is positive by the stability condition for the equilibrium. Then we have the solution

$$\begin{bmatrix} dx_1 \\ dx_2 \end{bmatrix} = \frac{1}{\Delta} \begin{bmatrix} R^2_{x_2 x_2} - C^2_{x_2 x_2} \\ -R^1_{x_1 x_2} \end{bmatrix} C^1_{x_1 k_1} dk_1. \tag{8}$$

Firm 1 uses this in its choice to k_1 to maximise its profit, therefore

$$d\pi_1 = (R^1_{x_1} - C^1_{x_1}) dx_1 + R^1_{x_2} dx_2 - C^1_{k_1} dk_1$$

$$= -(R^1_{x_2} R^2_{x_1 x_2} C^1_{x_1 k_1} / \Delta + C^1_{k_1}) dk_1. \tag{9}$$

At the best duopoly point, the coefficient of dk_1 in (9) is zero. Since all three factors in the numerator of the first term are negative while Δ is positive, we see that at this point,

$$C^1_{k_1} > 0,$$

i.e. firm 1 carries its capacity to a point beyond what is optimum for producing its output.

Once again the analysis can be completed by examining the sign of firm 2's profits, and the desirability of entry-prevention for firm 1. This more flexible notion of capacity can be interpreted in terms of other types of investment such as dealer networks and advertising, and this provides a basis for arguments that such expenditures can be used by an established firm in its efforts to deter entry. This counters recent expressions of pessimism (e.g. Needham (1978) pp. 177–9) concerning the effectiveness of such tactics.

For the last modification, I revert to a rigid concept of capacity, but consider price-setting in the post-entry duopoly, the solution rule being the Bertrand–Nash equilibrium. Some added complications can arise due to possible non-convexities even with reasonable demand and cost functions, but I ignore these and show the simplest possible case. This is done in Fig. 6, with notation analogous to the corresponding quantity-setting case of Fig. 3.

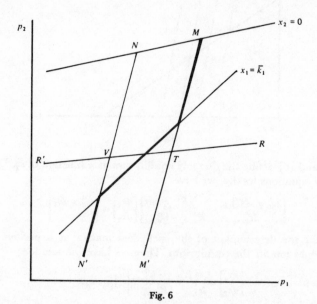

Fig. 6

The prospective entrant's reaction function is RR'. For the established firm, we have two reference curves MM' and NN', the former when capacity expansion costs matter and the latter when they do not. Their relative positions are naturally reversed as compared to the quantity-setting case. The former is relevant for $x_1 \geqslant k_1$ and the latter for $x_1 \leqslant k_1$, where x_1 is found from the demand function $D^1(p_1, p_2)$. The boundary curve $x_1 = k_1$ is shown for a particular k_1, and the corresponding reaction function for the established firm is shown by the heavy lines. It is then clear that by varying k_1, the established firm can secure any point along the segment TV of the prospective entrant's reaction function as the post-entry Nash equilibrium. Once again, we observe a limited leadership possibility arise by virtue of the established firm's advantage in being the first to make a commitment to capacity.

IV. CONCLUDING COMMENTS

The theme of the paper is that the role of an irrevocable commitment of investment in entry-deterrence is to alter the initial conditions of the post-entry game to the advantage of the established firm, for any fixed rule under which that game is to be played. This was illustrated in several simple models. Prominent among the conclusions was the observation that if the post-entry game is agreed to be played according to Nash rules, the established firm will not wish to install capacity that would be left idle in the pre-entry phase. This contrasts with the results of Spence (1977), where the post-entry game involves leadership by the established firm, and its threat of producing at a level equal to its pre-entry capacity is assumed to be believed by the prospective entrant. It is not possible to claim universal validity for either of these models. However, in the absence of any asymmetrical advantage possessed by the established firm in the post-entry phase, the Nash solution has considerable appeal.

Salop (1979) provides some examples of similar prior commitments that create an advantage for the established firm. Spence (1979) can be thought of as developing the same theme. In this model, capacity can only be acquired slowly, and the two firms differ in their abilities in this regard. This difference governs how the industry evolves, including issues of whether the second firm will enter, and what kind of equilibrium will result if it does. Much of the interesting dynamics is lost in my formulation, but the compensating advantage is that the basic idea becomes much more transparent. It is hoped that the distinction between the *rules* of the post-entry game and its *initial conditions* will prove useful in future work. I have assumed the rules to be understood and accepted by both firms. Investment then helps deter entry by changing the initial conditions. Within this framework, there is scope for several extensions: several periods and firms could be introduced, and constraints arising from capital markets could be imposed. The question of whether one firm can change the rules in its own favour is more interesting, but much more difficult.

University of Warwick AVINASH DIXIT

Date of receipt of final typescript: July, 1979

REFERENCES

Dixit, A. (1979). 'A model of duopoly suggesting a theory of entry barriers.' *Bell Journal of Economics*, vol. 10, no. 1 (Spring) pp. 20–32.
Needham, D. (1978). *The Economics of Industrial Structure, Conduct and Performance.* London: Holt, Rinehart and Winston.
Salop, S. (1978). 'A note on self-enforcing threats and entry deterrence'. University of Pennsylvania, Discussion Paper No. 14.
——(1979). 'Strategic entry deterrence.' *American Economic Review*, Papers and Proceedings.
Schelling, T. C. (1960). *The Strategy of Conflict.* Cambridge, Mass.: Harvard University Press.
Scherer, F. M. (1970). *Industrial Market Structure and Economic Performance.* Chicago: Rand-McNally.
Spence, M. (1977). 'Entry, investment and oligopolistic pricing.' *Bell Journal of Economics*, vol. 8, no. 2 (Autumn), pp. 534–44.
—— (1979). 'Investment, strategy and growth in a new market.' *Bell Journal of Economics*, vol. 10, no. 1 (Spring), pp. 1–19.
Wenders, T. (1971). 'Collusion and entry.' *Journal of Political Economy*, vol. 79, no. 6 (November–December), pp. 1258–77.

[18]

Contracts as a Barrier to Entry

By PHILIPPE AGHION AND PATRICK BOLTON*

It is shown that an incumbent seller who faces a threat of entry into his or her market will sign long-term contracts that prevent the entry of some lower-cost producers even though they do not preclude entry completely. Moreover, when a seller possesses superior information about the likelihood of entry, it is shown that the length of the contract may act as a signal of the true probability of entry.

Most of the literature on entry prevention deals with the case of two duopolists (the established firm and the potential entrant) who compete with each other to share a market, where one of the duopolists (the incumbent) has a first-move advantage.[1] This basic paradigm has been studied under various assumptions: about the strategy space of the players; the information structure of the game; and the time horizon. Recently, the model has been enlarged to allow for several entrants, several incumbents, several markets, and third parties.[2]

We propose here to extend the entry-prevention model in one other direction, which to our knowledge has not yet been formalized; namely, we consider whether optimal contracts between buyers and sellers deter entry and whether they are suboptimal from a welfare point of view. It has been pointed out by many economists that contracts between buyers and sellers in intermediate-good industries may have significant entry-prevention effects and that such contracts may be bad from a welfare point of view.[3]

On the other hand, it is a widespread opinion among antitrust practitioners that contracts between buyers and sellers are socially efficient.[4] There have been a number of antitrust cases involving exclusive dealing contracts and often the decision reached by the judge has lead to considerable controversy. One famous case, *United States v. United Shoe Machinery Corporation* (1922), illustrates quite clearly the nature of the debate: the United Shoe Machinery Corporation controlled 85 percent of the shoe-machinery market and had developed a complex leasing system of its machines to shoe manufacturers, a leasing system against which, it was thought, other machinery manufacturers would have difficulty competing. The judge ruled that these leasing contracts were in violation of the Sherman Act; his decision has been repeatedly criticized by leading antitrust experts (see Richard Posner, 1976, and Robert Bork, 1978). The main argument against the decision has been expressed by Posner: "The point I particularly want to emphasize is that the customers of United would be unlikely to participate in a campaign to strengthen United's monopoly position without insisting on being compensated for the loss of alternative and less costly

*Department of Economics, Harvard University, Cambridge, MA 02138, and University of California, Berkeley, CA 94720, respectively. We are greatly indebted to Jean Tirole for helping us formulate the model. We also thank Jerry Green and Oliver Hart for their useful suggestions and kind encouragement. We have been most fortunate to benefit from many helpful discussions with Dilip Abreu, Richard Caves, Nancy Gallini, Andreu Mas-Colell, and Eric Maskin.

[1] See, for example, the seminal contributions by Michael Spence (1977) and Avinash Dixit (1979, 1980).

[2] For a recent survey, see Drew Fudenberg and Jean Tirole (1986).

[3] Spence (p. 544), for example, briefly mentioned contracts as a method for impeding entry; see also

Oliver Williamson (1979). Furthermore, there is a literature on barriers to entry and vertical integration that is relevant to our discussion, since most of the time what vertical integration achieves in this literature can also be done through an appropriate contract. (See Roger Blair and David Kaserman, 1983.)

[4] This position has been forcefully defended by Robert Bork (1978), for example.

(because competitive) sources of supply" (p. 203). Exactly the same point is made by Bork (p. 140), who concludes that when we find exclusive dealing contracts in practice, then these contracts could not have been signed for entry-deterrence reasons.

Both Posner and Bork are right in pointing out that the buyer is better off when there is entry and that he (she) will tend to reject exclusive dealing contracts that reduce the likelihood of entry unless the seller compensates him (her) by offering an advantageous deal. Nevertheless, we show that contracts between buyers and sellers will be signed for entry-prevention purposes.

When the buyer and the seller sign a contract, they have a monopoly power over the entrant. They can jointly determine what fee the entrant must pay in order to be able to trade with the buyer; that is to say, if the buyer signs an exclusive contract with the seller and then trades with the entrant, he must pay damages to the seller. Thus he will only trade with the entrant if the latter charges a price which is lower than the seller's price minus the damages he pays to the seller. These damages, which are determined in the original contract (liquidated damages), act as an entry fee the entrant must pay to the seller. We show that the buyer and the seller set this entry fee in the same way that a monopoly would set its price, when it cannot observe the willingness to pay of its customers. Thus, the main reason for signing exclusive contracts, in our model, is to extract some of the surplus an entrant would get if he entered the seller's market.

These contracts introduce a social cost, for they sometimes block the entry of firms that may be more efficient than the incumbent seller. Entry is blocked because the contract imposes an entry cost on potential competitors. This cost takes two different forms: an entrant must either wait until contracts expire, or induce the customers to break their contract with the incumbent by paying their liquidated damages.

The waiting cost is larger, other things being equal, the longer the contract. We are thus led to study the question of the optimal length of the contract. It is a well-known principle in economics that if agents engage in mutually advantageous trade, it is in their best interest to sign the longest possible contract. A long-term contract can always replicate what a sequence of short-term contracts achieves.

This principle, however, sharply contrasts empirical evidence: In practice most contracts are of an explicit finite duration. Many economists have been puzzled by this obvious discrepancy between the theory and empirical evidence, and several authors have attempted to provide an explanation for why contracts are of a finite duration; most notably Oliver Williamson (1975, 1979) and Milton Harris and Bengt Holmström (1983).

We argue here that looking only at the length of a contract is misleading. What is important is to what extent a contract of a given length locks the parties into a relationship. Thus we are led to make the distinction between the *nominal length* of the contract (the length that is specified in the contract) and the *effective length* of the contract (the actual length that the parties expect the relationship to last at the time of signing). Liquidated damages constitute an implicit measure of the effective length of the contract.

The paper is organized as follows: Section I looks at optimal contracts between a single buyer and the incumbent seller, when both parties have the same information about the likelihood of entry. Section II analyzes optimal contracts when there is asymmetric information about the probability of entry. Section III deals with optimal contracts when there are several buyers. Finally, Section IV offers some concluding comments.

I. Optimal Contracts Between One Buyer and the Incumbent Seller

We consider a two-period model, where a single producer supplies one unit to a buyer. The latter has a reservation price, $P = 1$, and buys at most one unit. The seller faces a threat of entry, which is modeled as follows: At the time of contracting the seller's unit cost is $c = \frac{1}{2}$, while the entrant's cost of producing the same homogenous good is not known. For simplicity we assume that the entrant's cost, c_e, is uniformly distributed in

390   *THE AMERICAN ECONOMIC REVIEW*   *JUNE 1987*

$[0,1]$.[5] Furthermore, if entry occurs and no contract has been signed between the incumbent and the buyer, both suppliers compete in prices, so that the Bertrand equilibrium price is given by $P = \max\{\frac{1}{2}, c_e\}$. When there is no entry, the potential entrant makes zero profits. Thus entry will only occur if $c_e \leq \frac{1}{2}$ and the probability of entry is given by

$$(1) \qquad \phi = Pr\left(c_e \leq \tfrac{1}{2}\right) = \tfrac{1}{2}.$$

We attempt here to model in the simplest way the view of the world where there are many investors at each period of time who try to invest their funds in the markets where they hope to get the highest returns. The distribution of profits across markets, however, changes stochastically over time. Therefore entry into a given market may also be stochastic. In this story it is implicitly assumed that investors do not have an unlimited access to funds and/or that there are diminishing returns to managing more investment projects. If neither of these assumptions hold, then investment will take place until the marginal return on the last investment project is equal to the interest rate. Many good reasons have been given for why investors only have a limited access to funds (see for example, Joseph Stiglitz and Andrew Weiss, 1981, or Williamson, 1971).

The timing of the game is as follows: At date 1 the incumbent seller and the buyer negotiate a contract, then entry either takes place or does not. Finally at date 2, there is production and trade.[6] We assume that the

entrant's cost, c_e, is *not observable* but the parties to the contract know the distribution function of c_e. Therefore, contracts contingent on c_e cannot be written.[7]

If no contract is signed at date 1, the buyer's expected payoff is given by

$$(2) \qquad (1-\phi)\cdot 0 + \phi \cdot \tfrac{1}{2} = \tfrac{1}{2}\cdot\tfrac{1}{2} = \tfrac{1}{4}.$$

That is, with probability $(1-\phi)$ there is no entry and the seller sets the price equal to one. Hence, the buyer gets no surplus. With probability ϕ, entry occurs and Bertrand competition drives the price down to the incumbent's unit cost $c = \frac{1}{2}$. Now, Posner's point simply was that any contract that is acceptable to the buyer must give him an expected surplus of at least $\frac{1}{4}$ (assuming that the buyer is risk neutral). We shall show that even though the seller faces this constraint, there are gains to signing long-term contracts and in preventing entry.

The buyer and the incumbent seller could conceivably sign very complicated contracts even in this simple setting. For example, the price specified in the contract may be contingent on the event of entry or even contingent on the entrant's offer.[8] We shall, however, restrict ourselves to simple contracts of the form $c = \{P, P_0\}$ and show that there is no loss of generality in considering only this type of contract. Here P is the price of the good when the buyer trades with the incumbent and P_0 is the price the buyer must

---

[5] The choice of a uniform distribution is entirely for the sake of computational simplicity. In our 1985 paper, we show that the qualitative results obtained here are valid for any continuous density $f(x)$ with a support such that the lower bound is finite and that contains the interval $[0\ \frac{1}{2}]$.

[6] When production takes place before entry, the analysis is slightly modified. When the buyer switches to the entrant, the incumbent must now incur a loss of $c = \frac{1}{2}$. Thus the Bertrand equilibrium in the post-entry game now is $P = c_e$, so that entry will be precluded (since the entrant always makes nonpositive profits). To avoid an outcome where *ex post* competition (after entry) drives out *ex ante* competition (see Partha Dasgupta and Stiglitz, 1984), we then need to assume that the entrant

sometimes makes losses when he does not enter into the incumbent's market. In other words, the entrant sometimes has a negative opportunity cost (see our earlier paper).

[7] In general, what matters is not the actual unit cost of the entrant but his opportunity cost of not entering. If one takes this interpretation, then nonobservability of the entrant's opportunity cost is a mild assumption.

[8] One often observes contracts where a retailer provides a minimum price warranty of the form: "If the buyer is offered a lower price by another retailer for the same good, within t periods, he can then claim back the difference between the high and the low price." These are examples of contracts which are contingent on the entrant's offer. Of course, if such contracts are written then entry is precluded (since the entrant makes zero profits). See our discussion of these contracts in Section IV.

pay if he does not trade with the incumbent. In other words, P_0 represents *liquidated damages*.

When a contract $c = \{P, P_0\}$ is signed, the buyer gets a surplus of $1 - P$ if there is no entry. Furthermore, if there is entry, he will only switch to the entrant if the latter offers a surplus of at least $1 - P$. We shall assume that when the buyer is indifferent between switching and not switching, he trades with the entrant. Thus in the post-entry equilibrium, the buyer also gets a surplus of $1 - P$. Then a contract $c = \{P, P_0\}$ is acceptable to the buyer only if

$$(3) \qquad 1 - P \geq \tfrac{1}{4}.$$

Next, an entrant can only attract the buyer if he sets a price $\tilde{P}$, such that

$$(4) \qquad \tilde{P} \leq P - P_0$$

(in equilibrium the entrant sets, $\tilde{P} = P - P_0$). And entry only occurs if the entrant makes positive profits:

$$(5) \qquad \tilde{P} - c_e \geq 0.$$

Thus, when a contract $c = \{P, P_0\}$ is signed the probability of entry becomes

$$(6) \qquad \phi' = \max\{0; P - P_0\}.$$

The incumbent now faces the following program:

$$(7) \qquad \max_{P, P_0} \phi' \cdot P_0 + (1 - \phi')(P - c),$$

subject to $\qquad 1 - P \geq \tfrac{1}{4}.$

It is straightforward to verify that the optimal contract is then given by $c = \{\tfrac{3}{4}; \tfrac{1}{2}\}$.

There are several conclusions to be drawn. First, the incumbent's expected payoff of signing the contract $c = \{\tfrac{3}{4}, \tfrac{1}{2}\}$ is given by $\pi = \tfrac{1}{16} + \tfrac{1}{4}$. If he had not signed a contract, or if he had signed a contract that completely blocks entry, his expected payoff would be $\tfrac{1}{4}$. Hence he is strictly better off signing this contract and the buyer is not worse off.

Second, when $c = \{\tfrac{3}{4}, \tfrac{1}{2}\}$ is signed, the probability of entry is $\phi' = \tfrac{3}{4} - \tfrac{1}{2} = \tfrac{1}{4}$. Thus the optimal contract prevents entry to some extent but does not preclude entry completely. The contract $c = \{P, P_0\}$ changes the entry game in a subtle way. On the one hand, it sets a large entry fee, P_0, to the entrant. This reduces the likelihood of entry. But $P_0 = \tfrac{1}{2}$, does not completely eliminate entry, since the contract commits the incumbent to set a price $P = \tfrac{3}{4}$. Thus all entrants with costs $c_e \leq \tfrac{1}{4}$ will find it profitable to enter. Furthermore, even if the incumbent had the opportunity of lowering the price P below $\tfrac{3}{4}$ in the post-entry game, he would not want to do this. *The incumbent is strictly better off when the buyer switches to the entrant* in the post-entry game, for then he gets a surplus of $\tfrac{1}{2}$ compared with a maximum surplus of $P - c = \tfrac{1}{4}$, if he retained the buyer.

By signing a contract, the incumbent and the buyer form a coalition which acts like a nondiscriminating monopolist with respect to the entrant. The coalition sets P_0 like a monopolist sets its price when it cannot discriminate between buyers with different willingnesses to pay.[9] If c_e were observable, the contract could specify P_0 as a function of c_e and the coalition would be able to extract all of the entrant's surplus ($P_0 = \tfrac{1}{2} - c_e$).

The idea that the incumbent and the buyer can get together and extract some of the entrant's rent is very general. It does not depend, for instance, on the assumption that the seller sets the contract. Peter Diamond and Eric Maskin (1979) have obtained a similar result in the context of a model of search with breach of contract, where neither the buyer nor the seller has the power of making take-it-or-leave-it offers. Rather, Diamond and Maskin assume that the outcome of the bargaining game between a buyer and a seller is given by the Nash-bargaining solution.

---

[9] An interesting feature of the optimal contract is that if the probability of entry ϕ increases, then the optimal price P_0 may decrease. For example if the incumbent's unit cost is k then $\phi = k$ and $P_0^* = 1 - k(1 - k) - k/2$. Thus $dP_0^*/dk < 0$ for $k < \tfrac{3}{4}$.

Given that the incumbent and the buyer can only act as nondiscriminating monopolists, with respect to potential entrants, the optimal contract introduces a *social cost*, for it sometimes blocks the entry of a firm with a lower cost of production than the incumbent. When an optimal contract is signed, entrants with costs $c_e \in [\frac{1}{4}; \frac{1}{2}]$ do not enter.

To close this section we explain why the buyer and the seller can restrict themselves to simple contracts, $c = \{P, P_0\}$. The buyer and the seller can form a coalition whose value is $\frac{1}{2}$ when they do not allow entry into the market (the buyer's reservation price is one and the incumbent's cost is $c = \frac{1}{2}$). They can raise their payoff by allowing entry and making the entrant pay a fee, which in general will be a function of the entrant's cost, c_e. But the entrant's cost is private information so that the coalition faces a revelation of information problem. Now, a direct mechanism would specify a transfer from the entrant to the coalition, which is a function of the entrant's cost report: $t(c_e)$. This function $t(c_e)$ must satisfy the incentive-compatibility (*IC*) constraints: for all $c_e \in [0,1]$,

$$(IC) \quad \pi(c_e) - t(c_e) \geq \pi(c_e) - t(\hat{c}_e)$$

$$\text{for all } \hat{c}_e \in [0,1].$$

(Where $\pi(c_e)$ is the entrant's rent when his cost is c_e.) The *IC* constraints imply that $t(c_e) = t$ for all $c_e \in [0,1]$. In other words, the entry fee is independent of the entrant's cost.

Next, the entrant's rent is given by the difference between the incumbent's cost and his cost, c_e (i.e., $\pi(c_e) = \frac{1}{2} - c_e$). The coalition chooses t to maximize:

$$t \cdot Pr(\pi(c_e) \geq t) = t \cdot Pr(\tfrac{1}{2} - c_e \geq t)$$

$$= t(\tfrac{1}{2} - t).$$

Then the optimal transfer is $t^* = \frac{1}{4}$ and the expected surplus raised is $\frac{1}{16}$. Notice that the optimal contract $c = \{P = \frac{3}{4}; P_0 = \frac{1}{2}\}$ also raises a surplus of $\frac{1}{16}$ from the entrant. We can now appeal to the revelation principle (Dasgupta, Peter Hammond, and Maskin,

1979), which says that no indirect mechanism does better than the best direct mechanism. That is, no other contract exists that raises a higher surplus than $\frac{1}{16}$. Therefore there is no loss in restricting the contracts to be of the form $c = \{P, P_0\}$.[10]

II. Asymmetric Information About the Probability of Entry

In Section I it was assumed that both the incumbent and the buyer know the true probability of entry. This is not always realistic and one would expect that often the incumbent is better informed about the possibility of entry than the buyer. For example, if the incumbent is a high-tech firm and is the only one to have the know-how to produce a given intermediate good, then it is likely to be much better informed than its customers about the ability of a potential competitor in acquiring this know-how and thus produce the intermediate good. Hence, in this section we assume that the incumbent has some private information about the likelihood of entry.[11]

Asymmetric information has important consequences for the determination of the optimal nominal length of the contract. Under symmetric information, there is no incentive for writing a contract of finite nominal length. On the contrary, the incumbent always gains by locking the buyer into a contract in every period, for then an entrant cannot avoid paying the entry fee by entering at a time when the buyer is not bound by a contract to the incumbent. Under asymmetric information, on the other hand, the seller may wish to sign a contract of finite nominal length in order to signal to the buyer that entry is unlikely. Of course, the seller could also signal his information by

---

[10] In the above discussion we have restricted ourselves to deterministic mechanisms. Since all agents are assumed to be risk neutral, there is no loss of generality in considering only deterministic mechanisms (see Maskin, 1981).

[11] One can think of situations where the buyer is better informed about the probability of entry. Then we have a classic self-selection problem and all the results obtained in this section would also apply to this case.

offering a contract with lower liquidated damages, P_0. Such a contract would reduce the buyer's switching cost and could only profitably be offered by a seller facing a low probability of entry. We show however, that under certain conditions, signaling through the length of the contract is strictly better than signaling through liquidated damages.

To keep the analysis simple, we shall assume that the probability of entry is either "high" or "low." The incumbent knows the true probability but the buyer does not. Furthermore, as in Section I, the incumbent makes the contract offer. The situation described here is akin to an "informed Principal" problem (see Roger Myerson, 1983, and Maskin and Jean Tirole, 1985).

As in Section I, we shall assume that the entrant's costs are uniformly distributed on $[0,1]$. The incumbent's cost, on the other hand, is either $c = \frac{1}{2}$ or $c = k$, where $0 < k < \frac{1}{2}$. Then the probability of entry is low when $c = k$ and it is high when $c = \frac{1}{2}$, since when $c = k$, we have

$$(8) \qquad \underline{\phi} \equiv Pr(c_e \le k) = k < \frac{1}{2},$$

and when $c = \frac{1}{2}$, we have

$$(9) \qquad \bar{\phi} \equiv Pr(c_e \le \frac{1}{2}) = \frac{1}{2}.$$

The buyer's prior beliefs about the incumbent's costs are given by $m = Pr(c = k)$.

Under asymmetric information, it is no longer true that the seller can restrict himself with no loss to simple contracts, $c = \{P, P_0\}$. In fact, we show in our earlier paper that the incumbent seller can achieve the symmetric information optimal outcome by offering contracts of the form $c = \{P, P^e, P_0\}$ where P_0 is defined as in the previous section, P is the price the buyer pays if he trades with the incumbent and entry did not occur and P^e is the price the buyer pays if he trades with the incumbent and entry took place. Alternatively, when the incumbent only offers contracts of the form $c = \{P, P_0\}$, he can never attain the symmetric information optimal outcome. Thus simple contracts $c = \{P, P_0\}$ are suboptimal under asymmetric

information. Thus, if the more general contracts $c = \{P, P^e, P_0\}$ are feasible asymmetric information puts no restrictions on the nominal length of the contract.

We give the following argument for why such contracts may not be feasible: First, "entry" may be a very complicated event to describe, when a firm can enter with a non-homogeneous good. The incumbent must then decide what commodities qualify as "entrants" and, even if a list of such commodities can be defined, an entrant would have an incentive to produce a good which is not on that list whenever $P > P^e$. Alternatively, if $P^e > P$, there would be an incentive for the incumbent to claim that entry has occurred whenever there is an ambiguity about the event of entry. In short, the event of entry may be difficult to observe, let alone to verify.

Second, when $P > P^e$, the buyer could bribe someone to "enter" only to force the incumbent to lower his price. Vice versa, when $P < P^e$, the incumbent may want to bribe someone to enter.

When only simple contracts $c = \{P, P_0\}$ are feasible, asymmetric information can put restrictions on both the liquidated damages P_0, and the length of the contract. In the present model, contract length is somewhat artificially defined since production and trade take place only once. It should however be clear from what follows that the conclusions reached here carry over to a model with N periods of production and trade $(N \ge 2)$ where entry can take place in any of these N periods.

Here we compare the asymmetric information-contracting solution with the no-contracting solution and show that when the difference between high and low costs is sufficiently large, the low-cost incumbent is better off not signing a contract and leaving options open until the entry decision is taken by the potential competitor. In a model with N periods, this result would be modified and the low-cost incumbent would be better off signing a *shorter* contract than the high-cost incumbent.

When the seller makes a contract offer $c = \{P, P_0\}$, he conveys information about his type, so that the buyer's beliefs change.

Let the buyer's posterior beliefs be

(10) $\beta(c) = Pr(\phi = \bar{\phi}/c)$.

The buyer will only accept the contract if

(11) $1 - P \geq \beta(c)\bar{\phi}/2$

$$+ (1 - \beta(c))\underline{\phi}(1 - k)$$

From (8) and (9) we can rewrite (11) as

(12) $1 - P \geq (\beta(c)/4)$

$$+ (1 - \beta(c))k(1 - k)$$

When the incumbent signs a contract $c = \{P, P_0\}$, the probability of entry is given by

(13) $Pr(c_e \leq P - P_0) = P - P_0$.

Thus, the incumbent's payoff when he is respectively of type $\bar{\phi}$ or $\underline{\phi}$ is given by

(14)

$$V(c, \bar{\phi}) = (P - P_0)(P_0 - P + \tfrac{1}{2}) + P - \tfrac{1}{2}$$

$$V(c, \underline{\phi}) = (P - P_0)(P_0 - P + k) + P - k$$

for $P > P_0$, (otherwise $V(c, \bar{\phi}) = P - \tfrac{1}{2}$ and $V(c, \underline{\phi}) = P - k$). It is straightforward to verify that the Spence-Mirrlees condition is satisfied:

(15) $d/dk[-\partial V/\partial P/\partial V/\partial P_0] < 0$.

In other words, it is more costly for an incumbent facing a higher probability of entry to lower P_0 than it is for an incumbent facing a lower probability of entry. Given condition (12) we can draw Figure 1 where $\bar{c}^* = \{P = \tfrac{3}{4}; P_0 = \tfrac{1}{2}\}$ is the optimal symmetric information contract when $\phi = \bar{\phi}$. Notice that this contract will always be accepted by the buyer since the right-hand side in (12) is increasing in β and when $\beta = 1$ (12) becomes

(16) $1 - P \geq \tfrac{1}{4}$.

In addition, the contract $\bar{c}^*$ is the best con-

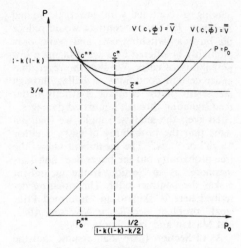

FIGURE 1

tract for the high-cost incumbent, among the class of contracts which generate beliefs $\beta(c) = 1$. It is common in signaling models to obtain a plethora of equilibria and our model is no exception to this rule. Any pair of contracts $(c, \bar{c}^*)$ where c is such that $P = 1 - k(1 - k)$ and $0 \leq P_0 \leq P_0^*$ (see Figure 1) constitutes a separating equilibrium. Furthermore, any point in the shaded area in the diagram may be a pooling or semiseparating equilibrium of the signaling game. Following David Kreps (1984), however, we can refine the Bayesian equilibrium concept by using dominance and stability arguments and thus single out the best separating equilibrium $(c^{**}, \bar{c}^*)$ where c^{**} is defined as $c^{**} = \{P = 1 - k(1 - k); P_0 = P_0^*\}$. How is P_0^* determined? It is the solution to the equation

$$V(c^{**}, \bar{\phi}) = V(\bar{c}^*, \bar{\phi}),$$

which can be rewritten as

(17) $(P - P_0)(P_0 - P + \tfrac{1}{2}) + P - \tfrac{1}{2} = \tfrac{1}{16} + \tfrac{1}{4}$,

where $P = 1 - k(1 - k)$.

Now P_0^* is the smaller root of this quadratic equation (see Figure 1) and is given by

(18) $P_0^* = \left((2P - \frac{1}{2}) - \sqrt{4P - 3}\right)/2.$

How does the optimal contract for the low-cost incumbent under asymmetric information compare with the optimal symmetric information contract given by $\underline{c}^* = \{P = 1 - k(1-k); P_0 = (2P - k)/2\}$?

The optimal contract under asymmetric information, c^{**} specifies the same price P as c^*, but it specifies lower liquidated damages: $P_0^* < P_0$. It is straightforward to compute that $P_0^* < P_0$ reduces to

(19) $1 + 4k^2 > 5k - \frac{1}{2}.$

And for all $0 < k < \frac{1}{2}$ this inequality is verified.

Intuitively, the incumbent with low costs signals his type by offering to reduce liquidated damages below the first-best level. His information is credibly transmitted since it is too costly for the high-cost incumbent to reduce P_0 to that level and thereby induce too much entry.

We now show that for small k, the low-cost incumbent is better off not signing a contract than signing c^{**}. If the low-cost seller does not sign a contract, his expected profits are given by

(20) $(1 - \phi)(1 - k) = (1 - k)^2.$

If he signs c^{**} he gets

(21) $V(c^{**}, \phi)$

$= (P - P_0^*)(k - (P - P_0^*)) + P - k,$

where $P = 1 - k(1 - k)$

and $P - P_0^* = \frac{1}{4} + \frac{1}{2}\sqrt{4(1 - k(1-k)) - 3}.$

It remains to show that for small k, we have

(22) $\left[\frac{1}{4} + \frac{1}{2}\sqrt{4(1 - k(1-k)) - 3}\right]k$

$- \left[\frac{1}{4} + \frac{1}{2}\sqrt{4(1 - k(1-k)) - 3}\right]^2$

$+ 1 - k(1 - k) - k \leq (1 - k)^2$

And (22) reduces to

(23) $k \leq \frac{1}{4} + \frac{1}{2}\sqrt{4(1 - k(1-k)) - 3}$

which is clearly verified for small k. Also, for k close to $\frac{1}{2}$, (23) is not satisfied. We summarize the above discussion in the following proposition:

PROPOSITION 1: *Under asymmetric information about the probability of entry (or equivalently about the incumbent's costs), the optimal contracting solution is such that*

(a) *the high-cost incumbent signs the optimal symmetric information contract* $\bar{c}^* = \{P = \frac{3}{4}; P_0 = \frac{1}{2}\}.$

(b) *the low-cost incumbent either signs the second-best contract*

$c^{**} = \{P = 1 - k(1 - k);$

$P_0^* = P - \frac{1}{4} - \frac{1}{2}\sqrt{4P - 3}\}$

(when k is close to $\frac{1}{2}$) or does not sign a long-term contract at all (when k is close to zero).

(c) c^{**} *is characterized by the property that liquidated damages (P_0^*) are lower than in the optimal symmetric information contract,*

$\underline{c}^* = \{P = 1 - k(1 - k); P_0 = P - (k/2)\}.$

One can explain Proposition 1(b) as follows. As k becomes smaller the price $P = 1 - k(1 - k)$ rises, which makes it more attractive for the high-cost firm to mimic the low-cost firm's behavior. In order to discourage the high-cost firm from cheating, the low-cost firm must therefore increase the gap $P - P_0 = [\frac{1}{4} + \frac{1}{2}(4(1 - k(1-k)) - 3)^{1/2}]$. But this is equivalent to raising the probability of entry after a contract has been signed (see equation (13)). There comes a point where $\phi' = P - P_0 \geq \phi = k$; that is, by raising $P - P_0$, the low-cost firm raises the *ex post* probability of entry (ϕ') above the *ex ante* probability of entry (ϕ) (see (23)). This essentially involves subsidizing some inefficient entrants to enter the market. The incumbent then gets a negative transfer from the entrant. He can do strictly better by not offering any transfer (i.e., by not signing a contract at all).

We have thus established that the *nominal* length of the contract may serve as a signal of the probability of entry. This result confirms the following basic intuition:

The buyer reasons as follows when he is offered a contract: "If the incumbent wants to sign a contract of a long duration he must be worried about entry, so that I infer from this that the probability of entry is high and I will only accept to sign this contract if he charges a low price. If, on the other hand, the incumbent offers a short-term contract, he reveals that he is not much preoccupied about entry, so that I will be willing to accept a higher price."

The result obtained in Proposition 1(c) implies that the social cost is smaller in the asymmetric information case than in the symmetric information case. That is, liquidated damages (P_0^*) are smaller in c^{**} than in $\underline{c}^*$; therefore fewer efficient firms will be kept out of the market. It is worth emphasizing this point, since one usually thinks of asymmetric information as a constraint that prevents agents from reaching a socially efficient outcome (a first-best optimum). This is a general theme in Agency theory (see Oliver Hart and Holmström, 1985). Here, on the contrary, asymmetric information about the incumbent's costs may actually force agents to choose the socially efficient outcome (whenever the condition in (23) is verified). *The informational asymmetry constrains the monopoly power of the incumbent and the buyer with respect to the entrant.* There is another interpretation of this result. Remember that the incumbent and the buyer are constrained in the first place by the informational asymmetry about the entrant's costs. Then, the conclusion reached here is that if there exists another informational asymmetry between the buyer and the incumbent (about the latter's cost) *the two informational constraints may cancel each other out.*

This is an important observation for agency theory. Informational constraints do not necessarily add up; they may cancel out.

III. Optimal Contracts with Several Buyers

One may wonder to what extent the results obtained in Sections I and II depend on the assumption that there is only one incumbent seller and one buyer? This section attempts to give a partial answer to this question. We compare in turn the situation where there is one buyer but several incumbent sellers, and the situation where there is one incumbent seller but several buyers. All the results established in Section I are valid in each case. Moreover, new interesting features are introduced in the latter situation, where a single incumbent negotiates with several buyers.

Consider first the situation where there are two or more identical sellers but only one buyer. Then, Bertrand competition essentially gives all the bargaining power to the buyer; he gets all of the surplus but the form of the optimal contract does not change. The buyer sets P_0 in the same way as the seller does, when the seller makes the contract offer.

The interesting situation is when there are several buyers and one seller. In this case, the entrant's profits depend on how many customers he can serve in the post-entry game. What is crucial, however, is how the size of the entrant's potential market affects the probability of entry. If the probability of entry is independent of the size of the market, then the case of several buyers reduces to the case of one buyer. In general, however, the size of the market will affect the probability of entry. For example, if the entrant must pay a fixed cost of entry, then his average cost is decreasing in the number of customers served and the probability of entry is increasing in the number of customers.

In this latter case, when one buyer signs a long-term contract with the incumbent, he imposes a negative externality on all other buyers. By locking himself into a long-run relation with the seller, he reduces the size of the entrant's potential market so that, *ceteris paribus*, the probability of entry will be smaller. As a result, the other buyers will have to accept higher prices. We show that the incumbent can exploit this negative externality to extract more (possibly all) surplus out of each buyer. In some cases, the seller can impose the monopoly price ($P = 1$) on each buyer, even though the *ex ante* probability of entry is arbitrarily close to one (*ex ante* refers to the no-contract situation). In addition, the seller can extract part of the entrant's surplus by choosing damages (P_0) appropriately, so that we get the paradoxical result that a seller facing a threat of entry may be better off than a natural monopoly. To reach this conclusion, we must push the logic of the game to its limits. This result is thus interesting mainly for illustrative purposes.

We will only consider the case of two buyers and one seller.[12] Both buyers are identical and have a reservation price $P = 1$. The incumbent is as described in Section I. The entrant has the same unit costs as in Section I; in addition, he may face a fixed cost of entry, $F \geq 0$. We shall first consider the problem where F is strictly positive. Then, in the absence of any contract, the entrant's profit is given by

$$(24) \qquad \pi_e = 2\left(\tfrac{1}{2} - c_e\right) - F.$$

Thus, the *ex ante* probability of entry is given by

$$(25) \qquad \phi = Pr(\pi_e \geq 0) = (1 - F)/2.$$

Suppose now that one of the buyers signs a contract with the incumbent where $P_0 = +\infty$. Then in the post-entry game, this buyer will never switch to the entrant. The latter can now hope to get at most:

$$(26) \qquad \hat{\pi}_e = \tfrac{1}{2} - c_e - F.$$

The other buyer therefore faces a lower likelihood of entry given by

$$(27) \qquad \hat{\phi} = Pr(\hat{\pi}_e \geq 0) = (1 - 2F)/2.$$

More generally, whenever one buyer signs a contract with the incumbent of the form

[12]We deal with the generalization to n buyers ($n \geq 2$) in our earlier paper.

$c = \{P, P_0\}$, the other buyer faces a new probability of entry given by

$$(28) \qquad \hat{\phi} = \max\left\{\frac{P - P_0 + \tfrac{1}{2} - F}{2}; \frac{1 - 2F}{2}\right\}.$$

We will analyze the negotiation game where the incumbent makes simultaneous contract offers to both buyers. The case where the incumbent makes sequential offers is considered in our earlier paper. There we establish that the timing of offers does not matter. The same outcome is obtained in the simultaneous offers case as in the sequential offers case.

The incumbent can without loss restrict the set of contracts to be of the form $c = \{P, P_0, P^r, P_0^r\}$, where

P = the price a buyer must pay if he trades with the incumbent and the other buyer has signed a long-term contract;

P_0 = the damages a buyer must pay if he switches to the entrant and the other buyer has signed a contract with the incumbent;

P^r = the price a buyer must pay if he trades with the incumbent and the other buyer did not sign a contract;

P_0^r = the damages a buyer must pay if he trades with the entrant and the other buyer did not sign a contract with the incumbent.

It is implicitly assumed here that all contracts are publicly observable. This is a strong assumption. In practice, all contracts are not observable. As a result, one can never be certain when a contract is observed, whether there does not exist a hidden contract which cancels the effects of the observed contract. In our model, however, the incumbent has an incentive to publicize all of his contracts, as will become clear below. Thus, hidden contracts are not a problem.

When the seller makes a contract offer $c = \{P, P_0, P^r, P_0^r\}$ to each buyer, B_1 and B_2, the latter play a noncooperative game where they have two pure strategies: "accept" and "reject." The payoff matrix of this game is represented in Table 1. By choosing P^r and P_0^r appropriately, the incumbent can ensure that $\hat{\phi} = (1 - 2F)/2$.

398   *THE AMERICAN ECONOMIC REVIEW*   *JUNE 1987*

TABLE 1 — B_1

	Accept		Reject	
Accept	$1-P$	$1-P$	$1-p^r$	$\hat{\phi}/2$
Reject	$\hat{\phi}/2$	$1-p^r$	$\phi/2$	$\phi/2$

Essentially, this involves choosing P_0^r large enough so that the buyer who accepted a contract will not switch to the entrant. Now, accept is a (weakly) dominant strategy when

$$(29) \qquad 1-P \geq \hat{\phi}/2 = (1-2F)/4;$$

$$(30) \qquad\qquad 1-P^r > \phi/2.$$

When the incumbent offers a contract to both buyers such that (29) and (30) are satisfied (and such that $\hat{\phi} = (1-2F)/2$), the unique Nash equilibrium is for both buyers to accept the contract offer. As a result, both buyers receive a strictly lower payoff in equilibrium than if they both rejected the contract, since $\hat{\phi} < \phi$.

Thus when there are several buyers contracting with the incumbent, there is another reason why rational buyers are willing to perpetuate the monopoly position of the seller. As Steven Salop puts it, contracts "...are valued by each buyer individually even while they create an external cost to all other buyers" (1986, p. 273). He calls this situation a "*free-rider effect in reverse*" (emphasis added).

In addition to this effect, the seller can set P_0 appropriately so as to extract the maximum expected surplus from the entrant. To summarize, in this simple model with simultaneous offers, the set of optimal contracts is given by

$$(31) \quad c^* = \left\{ P = 1 - \frac{(1-2F)}{4}; \right.$$

$$P_0 = P - \frac{F+1}{4};$$

$$\left. P^r < 1 - \frac{\phi}{2}; P_0^r > P^r + \tfrac{1}{2} + F \right\}.$$

And at the optimum the incumbent's expected payoff is given by

$$(32) \quad \pi = \left(2(P-P_0)-F\right)\left(2\left(P_0-P+\tfrac{1}{2}\right)\right)$$

$$+ 2\left(P - \tfrac{1}{2}\right)$$

$$= \frac{(1-F)^2}{2} + 1 - \frac{(1-2F)}{2}.$$

Suppose now that $F \geq \tfrac{1}{2}$, then $\hat{\phi} = 0$ and the incumbent is able to impose the monopoly price ($P = 1$) on the buyer. His expected payoff at the optimum is then given by

$$(33) \quad \pi = \left((1-F)^2/2\right) + 1.$$

Thus the incumbent does strictly better than a natural monopoly, since he can also extract some of the potential entrant's surplus. On the other hand, when $F = 0$, we have $\hat{\phi} = \phi = \tfrac{1}{2}$, and the "free-rider effect in reverse" disappears, so that the two buyers case reduces to a one-buyer case, where the customer purchases two units rather than one. In other words, when the probability of entry is independent of the size of the market, competition among buyers does not matter.

Thus the principles established in the one buyer-one seller case remain valid when we allow for either more than one buyer or more than one seller. The analysis is somewhat incomplete since we did not deal with the several buyers-several sellers case. The results obtained in Section I carry through to this more general model (see Diamond-Maskin). As far as the results in this section are concerned, it is likely that sellers will not be able to exploit to the same extent the free-rider effect in reverse.

IV. Conclusion

The principles formalized in this paper are very general. What is basically required for contracts to constitute a barrier to entry is that post-entry profits for the incumbent in the absence of any contract be lower than pre-entry profits (and vice versa for consumers). In addition, it is necessary that the incumbent cannot discriminate between entrants of various levels of efficiency. This is a rather mild assumption if one interprets the entrant's cost as an opportunity cost of entry as in our earlier paper. Throughout the paper we interpreted P_0 to be "liquidated damages," but P_0 may also represent down payments, deposits, collateral, future discounts, and benefits, etc. Thus, the analysis developed here has potentially a wide range of applicability.

Casual empiricism suggests that "endogenous switching costs" for customers are a widespread phenomenon. In the housing market, for example, advance deposits in rental contracts can be interpreted as serving this function (there are, of course, also moral hazard reasons for requiring deposits). Paul Klemperer (1986) provides a number of examples of endogenous switching costs, like frequent flyer programs, trading stamps, deferred rebates by shipping firms, etc. Also, fixed fees in franchise contracts may be used to extract some rent from a potential competitor. The contract between Automatic Radio Manufacturing Co. and Hazeltine Research (see *Automatic Radio Manufacturing Co. v. Hazeltine Research Inc.*, 1950) is a good example. Automatic Radio had to pay a fixed fee irrespective of whether it exploited the patents licensed by Hazeltine. Any new licensor therefore faced an entry barrier equal to the amount of this fee. Another striking example is the case of Bell Laboratories when it invented the transistor. There were other research institutes competing with Bell Laboratories. In order to preempt them, Bell Labs offered to publicize the technology to any potential licensee, in exchange for a fixed fee of $25,000. This fee served the same function as P_0, in the contract above. Moreover Bell Lab's strategy was to become the industry standard. Thus any individual licensee would have to take into account the additional switching cost of not being standardized (see E. Braun and S. Macdonald, 1978). Our analysis provides a rationale for the practices described here and explains why rational customers cooperate with firms in these anticompetitive practices. Unfortunately, the variety and potential complexity of these contractual clauses makes the task for antitrust authorities very difficult.

A rapidly growing literature on exogenous switching costs is related to our present study (see Klemperer for a recent thorough exposition). The welfare conclusions obtained in this research are radically different from ours. For example, in Klemperer, entry may be socially inefficient because consumers dissipate the gains from entry (in terms of lower prices and higher output) by incurring the socially wasteful switching costs. In our model, the social cost comes from insufficient entry; when entry occurs it is always welfare improving. Salop also studies the effect of various clauses, such as the "meeting the competition clause" or the "clause of the most favored nation" on competition. His emphasis is more on cartel coordination than entry prevention. In our model a "meeting the competition clause" would preclude entry since the entrant could never undercut the incumbent. *We have shown, however, that it is optimal not to eliminate entry completely.* Therefore, such clauses will never be adopted for entry-deterrence purposes; they may however be useful to facilitate cartel coordination, as Salop shows, since they increase the cost of price cutting.

Our theory of contract length is a substantial departure from existing theories. Most explanations have emphasized the idea that contract length is determined as a tradeoff between recontracting costs and the costs associated with the incompleteness of the contract (see Williamson, 1975, 1985; Ronald Dye, 1985a; Jo Anna Gray, 1976). A notable exception is Harris and Holmström. In practice, uncertainty about the future and the cost of writing complete contracts are without doubt important elements in the determination of contract length. The difficulty from a theoretical perspective is however that uncertainty about the future and "transaction costs" are notoriously vague categories. If contracts are to be incomplete what contingencies should the parties leave out of the contract? This is a very difficult question which has only received partial answers (see Dye, 1985b, and Hart-Holmström). Explanations of contract length based on contractual incompleteness crucially depend on how one answers this question (see Dye, 1985b). In this paper we have sidestepped the difficulty to provide a story based on asymmetric information. We believe that signaling aspects are important in the determination of contract length and view our explanation as complementary to the existing theories.

Recently, Benjamin Hermalin (1986) has developed another theory of contract length based on asymmetric information. He considers a competitive labor market where initially workers have private information about productivity but where in a later stage this information becomes public (for example, through output observations). He shows that by varying contract length, it is impossible for firms to *profitably* screen out low-productivity workers from high-productivity workers. Ideally, a firm wants to retain only high-productivity workers, but long-term contracts are most attractive to low-productivity workers. Thus, by screening out workers, the firm achieves the opposite of what it wants: it offers long contracts to low-productivity workers and short contracts to high-productivity workers. In equilibrium, either firms offer only short-term contracts, or they offer "trivial" long-term contracts that replicate the outcome achieved with short-term contracts. In our model, on the contrary, signaling (or screening) works. Moreover, when it is optimal for the low-cost incumbent to sign a short-term contract, there does not exist an alternative trivial long-term contract. One can view our explanation and Hermalin's as dual: in his model the high-productivity sellers do not want to be locked in a long-term contract; here it is the buyer who does not want to forego future opportunities.

REFERENCES

Aghion, Philippe and Bolton, Patrick, "Entry-Prevention through Contracts with Customers," unpublished, 1985.

Blair, Roger D. and Kaserman, David L., *Law and Economics of Vertical Integration and Control*, New York: Academic Press, 1983.

Bork, Robert H., *The Antitrust Paradox*, New York: Basic Books, 1978.

Braun, E. and Macdonald, S., *Revolution in Miniature: The History and Impact of Semiconductor Electronics*, New York: Cambridge University Press, 1978.

Caves, Richard, E., "Vertical Restraints in Manufacturer-Distributor Relations: Incidence and Economic Effects," mimeo., Harvard University, 1984.

Dasgupta, Partha and Stiglitz, Joseph, "Sunk Costs and Competition," mimeo., Princeton University, 1984.

_____, Hammond, Peter and Maskin, Eric, "The Implementation of Social Choice Rules: Some General Results on Incentive Compatability," *Review of Economic Studies*, April 1979, *46*, 185–206.

Diamond, Peter A. and Maskin, Eric, "An Equilibrium Analysis of Search and Breach of Contract, I: Steady States," *Bell Journal of Economics*, Spring 1979, *10*, 282–316.

Dixit, Avinash, "A Model of Duopoly Suggesting a Theory of Entry-Barriers," *Bell Journal of Economics*, Spring 1979, *10*, 20–32.

_____, "The Role of Investment in Entry Deterrence," *Economic Journal*, March 1980, *90*, 95–106.

Dye, Ronald, (1985a)"Costly Contract Contingencies," *International Economic Review*, February 1985, *26*, 233–50.

_____, (1985b)"Optimal Length of Labor Contracts," *International Economic Review*, February 1985, *26*, 251–70.

Fudenberg, Drew and Tirole, Jean, "Dynamic Models of Oligopoly," in J. Lesourne and H. Sonnenschein, eds., *Fundamentals of Pure and Applied Economics*, New York: Harwood Academic Press, 1986.

Gray, Jo Anna, "Wage Indexation: A Macroeconomic Approach," *Journal of Monetary Economics*, April 1976, *2*, 221–35.

Harris, Milton and Holmström, Bengt, "On the Duration of Agreements," mimeo., IMSSS, Stanford University, 1983.

Hart, Oliver and Holmström, Bengt, "The Theory of Contracts," in T. Bewley, ed., *Advances in Economic Theory*, New York: Cambridge University Press, 1985.

_____ and Moore, John, "Incomplete Contracts and Renegotiation," mimeo., MIT 1985.

Hermalin, Benjamin, "Adverse Selection and Contract Length," mimeo., MIT, 1986.

Klemperer, Paul, "Markets with Consumer Switching Costs," unpublished doctoral dissertation, Graduate School of Business, Stanford University, 1986.

Kreps, David M., "Signaling Games and Stable Equilibrium," mimeo., Stanford University, 1984.

Maskin, Eric, "Randomization in Incentive Problems," mimeo., 1981.

_____ **and Tirole, Jean,** "Principals with Private Information, II: Dependent Values," lecture notes, 1985.

Myerson, Roger B., "Mechanism Design by an Informed Principal," *Econometrica*, November, 1983, *51*, 1767–97.

Posner, Richard A., *Antitrust Law: An Economic Perspective*, Chicago: University of Chicago Press, 1976.

Salop, Steven, "Practices that (credibly) Facilitate Oligopoly Coordination," in J. Stiglitz and F. Mathewson, eds., *New Developments in the Analysis of Market Structure*, Cambridge: MIT Press, 1986.

Spence, A. Michael, "Entry, Capacity, Investment and Oligopolistic Pricing," *Bell Journal of Economics*, Autumn 1977, *8*, 534–44.

Stiglitz, Joseph and Weiss, Andrew, "Credit Rationing in Markets with Imperfect Information," *American Economic Review*, June 1981, *71*, 393–409.

Williamson, Oliver E., "The Vertical Integration of Production: Market Failure Considerations," *American Economic Review*, March 1971, *61*, 112–23.

_____, *Markets and Hierarchies: Analysis and Antitrust Implications*, New York: Free Press, 1975.

_____, "Assessing Vertical Market Restrictions: Antitrust Ramifications of the Transaction-Cost Approach," *University of Pennsylvania Law Review*, April 1979, *127*, 953–93.

_____, *The Economic Institutions of Capitalism*, New York: Free Press, 1985.

Automatic Radio Manufacturing Co. v. Hazeltine Research Inc., 339 U.S. 827, 834, 1950.

United States v. United Shoe Machinery Corporation, 258 U.S. 451, 1922.

[19]

Econometrica, Vol. 50, No. 2 (March, 1982)

LIMIT PRICING AND ENTRY UNDER INCOMPLETE INFORMATION: AN EQUILIBRIUM ANALYSIS[1]

By Paul Milgrom and John Roberts

Limit pricing involves charging prices below the monopoly price to make new entry appear unattractive. If the entrant is a rational decision maker with complete information, pre-entry prices will not influence its entry decision, so the established firm has no incentive to practice limit pricing. However, if the established firm has private, payoff relevant information (e.g., about costs), then prices can signal that information, so limit pricing can arise in equilibrium. The probability that entry actually occurs in such an equilibrium, however, can be lower, the same, or even higher than in a regime of complete information (where no limit pricing would occur).

1. INTRODUCTION

THE BASIC IDEA OF LIMIT PRICING is that an established firm may be able to influence, through its current pricing policy alone,[2] other firms' perceptions of the profitability of entering the firm's markets, and that the firm may thus set its prices below their short run maximizing levels in order to deter entry. As such, limit pricing has constituted a major theme in the industrial organization literature for at least the last thirty years, and during the past decade in particular it has been the subject of a number of papers employing formal models of maximizing behavior.[3] For the most part, these latter analyses have concentrated on the decision problem of the established firm, taking as given the limit-pricing assumption that a lower pre-entry price will deter or restrict entry. In this context, the typical conclusion is that an optimal price-output policy in the face of threatened entry will involve prices which are below the short-run monopoly level, but still above the level that would prevail after entry. This conclusion had led to some debate as to the appropriate public policy regarding such limit pricing, since there appears to be a trade-off between the benefits to society of lower pre-entry prices and the costs arising from entry being limited or deterred.

[1] Much of the work reported here first appeared in [11]. This work has been presented at a large number of conferences, meetings, and seminars, and we would like to thank our audiences at each of these events for their comments. We are particularly indebted to Eric Maskin, Roger Myerson, Steve Salop, Robert Wilson, and two referees for their helpful suggestions, to David Besanko for his excellent research assistance, and to Armando Ortega-Reichert, whose work on repeated competitive bidding [15] has influenced our thinking on the present subject. Finally, we gratefully acknowledge the financial support of the Graduate School of Business at Stanford, the J. L. Kellogg Graduate School of Management at Northwestern, and the National Science Foundation (Grants SOC 77-06000 to the IMSSS at Stanford and SOC 79-07542 and SES 80-01932 to Northwestern).

[2] Although some recent treatments of entry deterrence incorporate other strategic variables, the standard, traditional approach is to treat the choice of the pre-entry price as the firm's only decision and to assume no dependence of post-entry profits on this choice.

[3] The idea behind limit pricing can be traced back through the work of J. Bain [1] and J. M. Clark [2] at least to a paper by N. Kaldor [7]. The recent formal investigations begin with D. Gaskins [5], M. I. Kamien and N. L. Schwartz [8], and G. Pyatt [16]. See F. M. Scherer [18] and S. Salop [17] for further references.

443

P. MILGROM AND J. ROBERTS

In this paper we present a re-examination of the limit pricing problem. Our model differs from most of the existing literature in that we treat both the established firm and potential entrant as rational, maximizing economic agents. This naturally leads to a game-theoretic, equilibrium formulation. However, once one adopts this approach, it is not immediately obvious why limit pricing should emerge at all.

This point has been made explicitly by J. Friedman [3] in one of the few existing game-theoretic treatments of pricing in the face of potential entry of which we are aware. Friedman notes that, under the usual sort of assumptions on demand, the profits which would accrue should entry occur are completely independent of the pre-entry price. Since in Friedman's model both the established firm and the entrant are completely informed as to demand and cost conditions, these post-entry profits are fully known when the entry decision is made. Then the inescapable logic of (perfect) equilibrium (Selten [19]) requires that the entry decision be independent of the pre-entry price. This means that any attempt at limit pricing would serve only to squander pre-entry profits and so there would be no limit pricing.

Friedman's argument will be generally valid in any complete-information, game-theoretic model in which the established firm's pre-entry actions do not influence post-entry costs and demand. In such a model, then, the intuitive idea underlying the traditional concept of limit pricing—that potential entrants would read the pre-entry price as a signal concerning the price and market shares they can expect to prevail after entry—finds no formal justification. In contrast, a formalization of this intuition is the very heart of our model.

Specifically, we consider situations in which neither the established firm nor the potential entrant is perfectly informed as to some characteristic of the other which is relevant to the post-entry profits of both. The central example of such a characteristic, and the one on which we initially concentrate, is the other firm's unit costs. In such a situation, the pre-entry price may become a signal regarding the established firm's costs, which in turn are a determinant of the post-entry price and profits for the entrant. Thus the relationship assumed in the earlier literature emerges endogenously in equilibrium in our model: a lower price (by signalling lower costs) tends to discourage entry. Thus, too, limit-pricing behavior arises in equilibrium, with the established firm attempting to influence the entry decision by charging a pre-entry price which is below the simple monopoly level.

The entrant, meanwhile, will seek to infer the established firm's costs (and thus the profitability of entry) from observation of the pre-entry price. In making this inference, of course, it will have to employ some conjecture regarding the established firm's pricing policy, i.e., the relationship between the established firm's cost and the price it charges. In Nash equilibrium, this conjecture must be correct. Indeed the very definition of equilibrium in this context involves rational expectations by each firm about the other's behavior. Thus, the entrant will allow for limit pricing in making its inferences and its entry decision.

Thus, in equilibrium, the established firm practices limit pricing, but the entrant is not fooled by this strategy. Consequently, the probability that entry actually occurs in equilibrium need not be any lower than it would be in a world of full information, where limit pricing would not arise. Indeed, the probability of entry in the limit pricing equilibrium may even be higher than with complete information, even though the pre-entry price is lower. In particular, this means that the alleged trade-off for society between lower prices and delayed or deterred entry may never arise.

In the next section, we illustrate these claims in the context of a simple model with linear demand and constant unit costs. In this model we compute equilibria for two specific examples. One of these involves only two possible levels of costs for the entrants and for the established firm; the other involves a continuum of possibilities on each side. In Section 3 we consider a more general model. The final section contains our conclusions.

2. TWO EXAMPLES

Consider the market for a homogeneous good in which there is an established firm, denoted firm 1, and a potential entrant, firm 2. Initially, each firm knows its own unit cost, c_i, $i = 1, 2$, but it does not know the other firm's cost level. Firm 1 is a monopolist, and it must pick a quantity Q to produce (or a price to charge) as a monopolist, given its knowledge of c_1 and its beliefs about c_2. Firm 2 will observe this choice and then (knowing c_2 but not c_1) must either enter the market or decide to stay out. If it enters, it incurs an entry cost of K, each firm learns the other's cost, and then the two firms operate as Cournot duopolists. If it does not enter, firm 1 will henceforth enjoy its monopoly profits without further fear of entry.

We summarize the notation and profit formulae with linear demand and constant unit costs in Table I. To simplify the payoff formulae, we normalize the

TABLE I

Present value to i of $1 accruing after entry	δ_i
Unit production cost of firm i	c_i
Fixed cost of entry for firm 2	K
Inverse demand	$P = a - bQ$
Simple monopoly output	$m(c_1) = (a - c_1)/2b$
First period profit for firm 1	$\Pi_1^0(Q, c_1) = (a - bQ - c_1)Q$
Monopoly profit for firm 1	$\Pi_1^M(c_1) = (a - c_1)^2/4b$
Cournot profit for firm i	$\Pi_i^C(c_1, c_2) = (a - 2c_i + c_j)^2/9b$
Reward to firm 1 from deterring entry	$R(c_1, c_2) = \Pi_1^M(c_1) - \Pi_1^C(c_1, c_2)$
Payoff to 1 if entry occurs	$\Pi_1^0(Q, c_1)$
Payoff to 1 if no entry	$\Pi_1^0(Q, c_1) + \delta_1 R(c_1, c_2)$
Payoff to 2 if entry	$\delta_2 \Pi_2^C(c_1, c_2) - K$
Payoff to 2 if no entry	0
Range of possible c_i values	$[\underline{c}_i, \bar{c}_i]$
Probability distribution function for c_i (j's beliefs about c_i)	H_i

P. MILGROM AND J. ROBERTS

post-entry profits of the established firm to be zero if entry occurs, so it receives only its first period profit as its payoff in this event. If entry does not occur, its payoff is its first period profit plus the discounted value of a reward to deterring entry. This reward is equal to the excess of its monopoly profit over its profit as a Cournot duopolist.

The extensive form game corresponding to this set-up is one of incomplete information, since the players do not know the numerical values of the payoffs corresponding to any pair of decisions they make. Attempting to analyze such a game directly would easily lead one into a morass of infinite regress. The approach we adopt instead is that proposed by Harsanyi [6], which involves replacing this *incomplete* information game by a game of *complete* but *imperfect* information.[4] One then treats the Nash equilibria of this second game as the equilibria of the original game.

The imperfect information game involves another player, "Nature," which is indifferent over all possible outcomes. Nature moves first and selects c_1 and c_2 according to the probability distributions, H_i, giving the players' beliefs. Then player i is informed about c_i but not about c_j, and for each realization of c_1 and c_2 the game tree unfolds as above.

In any extensive form game, a player's strategy is a specification of the action it will take in any information set, i.e., the player's actions at any point can depend only on what it knows at that point. Here, the information sets for firm 1 are defined by the realized values of c_1 (given by "Nature's move") and those for firm 2 by a realization of c_2 and a choice of Q by firm 1. Thus, a (pure) strategy for 1 is a map s from its possible cost levels into the possible choices of Q and a (pure) strategy for 2 is a map t from $\mathbb{R}^2$ into $\{0,1\}$ giving its decision for each possible pair (c_2, Q), where we interpret 1 as "enter" and 0 as "stay out."

A pair of strategies constitutes an equilibrium if each maximizes the expected payoff of the player using it, given that the other is using its specified strategy. This is the standard Nash equilibrium notion. However, to accentuate the rational expectations character of Nash equilibrium, it is helpful to use the following, equivalent definition. An equilibrium consists of a pair of strategies (s^*, t^*) and a pair of conjectures $(\bar{s}, \bar{t})$ such that (i) firm 1's pricing policy s^* is a best response to its conjecture $\bar{t}$ about firm 2's entry rule, (ii) the strategy t^* is a best response for firm 2 to its conjecture $\bar{s}$, and (iii) the actual and conjectured strategies coincide. We formalize these conditions as follows: (i) for any $c_1 \in [\underline{c}_1, \bar{c}_1]$ and any $s : [\underline{c}_1, \bar{c}_1] \to \mathbb{R}_+$,

$$\Pi^0(s^*(c_1), c_1) + \delta_1 \int_{\underline{c}_2}^{\bar{c}_2} R(c_1, c_2)\left[1 - \bar{t}(c_2, s^*(c_1))\right] dH_2(c_2)$$

$$\geq \Pi^0(s(c_1), c_1) + \delta_1 \int_{\underline{c}_2}^{\bar{c}_2} R(c_1, c_2)\left[1 - \bar{t}(c_2, s(c_1))\right] dH_2(c_2),$$

---

[4] An extensive form game has imperfect information if some player at some point must make a move without having been fully informed about all the previous moves made by the other players.

(ii) for any $c_2 \in [\underline{c}_2, \bar{c}_2]$ and any $t : [\underline{c}_2, \bar{c}_2] \times \mathbb{R}_+ \to \{0, 1\}$,

$$\int_{\underline{c}_1}^{z_1} \left[\delta_2 \Pi_2^C(c_1, c_2) - K \right] t^*(c_2, \bar{s}(c_1)) \, dH_1(c_1)$$

$$\geq \int_{\underline{c}_1}^{z_1} \left[\delta_2 \Pi_2^C(c_1, c_2) - K \right] t(c_2, \bar{s}(c_1)) \, dH_1(c_1), \qquad \text{and}$$

(iii) $(s^*, t^*) = (\bar{s}, \bar{t})$.

Given this framework, we first study a parameterized family of examples where the H_i are two-point distributions and, for specific values of the parameters, compute equilibria. Later in this section we will allow for a continuum of possible cost levels ("types") for the two firms.

Thus, suppose that the demand curve is $P = 10 - Q$, that $K = 7$, that $\underline{c}_1 = 0.5$, $\underline{c}_2 = 1.5$, $\bar{c}_1 = \bar{c}_2 = 2.0$, that $\delta_1 = \delta_2 = 1$, and that the costs are independently distributed with $H_2(c_2 = \bar{c}_2) = p = 1 - H_2(c_2 = \underline{c}_2)$ and $H_1(c_1 = \bar{c}_1) = q = 1 - H_1(c_1 = \underline{c}_1)$.

With these specifications, the payoffs are as follows:

$$R(\underline{c}_1, \underline{c}_2) = 10.31, \qquad \Pi_2^C(\underline{c}_1, \underline{c}_2) - K = -0.75,$$

$$R(\underline{c}_1, \bar{c}_2) = 9.12, \qquad \Pi_2^C(\underline{c}_1, \bar{c}^2) - K = -2.31,$$

$$R(\bar{c}_1, \underline{c}_2) = 9.75, \qquad \Pi_2^C(\bar{c}_1, \underline{c}_2) - K = 2.00,$$

$$R(\bar{c}_1, \bar{c}_2) = 8.89, \qquad \Pi_2^C(\bar{c}_1, \bar{c}_2) - K = 0.11,$$

$$m(\underline{c}_1) = 4.75, \qquad \Pi_1^M(\underline{c}_1) = 22.56,$$

$$m(\bar{c}_1) = 4.00, \qquad \Pi_1^M(\bar{c}_1) = 16.00.$$

Note that if 1's costs were known to be $\underline{c}_1$, neither type of potential entrant would want to enter, while if c_1 were known to be $\bar{c}_1$, both would want to enter. Thus, the probability of entry, if the entrant were to be directly informed of the realized value of c_1, is simply q, the probability that $c_1 = \bar{c}_1$. Of course, if firm 2 were so informed, there would be no point to limit pricing and Q would simply be set at the short-run profit-maximizing level of $m(c_1)$.

Note, too, that if firm 2 were unable to observe Q and were uninformed about c_1, then it would want to enter if its expected profits were positive, i.e., if $q\Pi_2^C(\bar{c}_1, c_2) + (1 - q)\Pi_2^C(\underline{c}_1, c_2) - K \geq 0$. If $0.954 > q > 0.273$, then this inequality holds for $\underline{c}_2$ and not for $\bar{c}_2$, so the low cost entrant would come in and the high cost entrant would not. (For $q < 0.273$, neither would want to enter, and for $q > 0.954$, both would want to enter.)

In fact, if 2 is not directly informed about c_1 but can observe Q, it will attempt to make inferences about the actual value of c_1 from its observation of Q, using its conjectures about 1's behavior. Note that in equilibrium, the only values of Q which could be observed are $s^*(\underline{c}_1)$ and $s^*(\bar{c}_1)$. Now in this set-up there are only two possibilities: either $s^*(\underline{c}_1) = s^*(\bar{c}_1)$, or else the two values differ. An equilibrium with the first of these properties is called *pooling*, while in the other situation the equilibrium is *separating*. Thus, in pooling equilibrium, observing Q gives no information, while the observation of Q in a separating equilibrium allows the value of c_1 to be inferred exactly.

Thus, in a separating equilibrium (s^*, t^*), entry will occur if $s^*(\bar{c}_1)$ is observed and will not if $s^*(\underline{c}_1)$ is observed: *entry takes place in exactly the same circumstances as if the entrant had been informed about the value of* c_1, i.e., with prior probability q. Moreover, this will be true in any separating equilibrium of any model of this type: in any separating equilibrium, observing the equilibrium choice of the established firm allows a precise and accurate inference to be made about the firm's characteristic. Thus, in such an equilibrium, *limit pricing will not limit entry* relative to the complete information case (in which there would be no limit pricing because the possibility of influencing the entrant's decision does not arise).

In a pooling equilibrium, the entrant can infer nothing from observing Q and so enters if its expected profit is positive. Thus, as noted above, if $q \in (0.273, 0.954)$, only the low cost entrant will come in. Thus, in a pooling equilibrium, the probability of entry is $(1 - p)$, while in a separating equilibrium the probability of entry is q.

We now will show that, in this example, so long as p is not too small, there are both pooling and separating equilibria, that all equilibria involve limit pricing, and that the probability of entry in a pooling equilibrium may equal, exceed or fall short of that in a separating equilibrium (or, equivalently, under complete information).

First, we show that the following strategies constitute a separating equilibrium:

$$s^*(\underline{c}_1) = 7.2, \qquad s^*(\bar{c}_1) = m(\bar{c}_1) = 4.0,$$

$$t^*(c_2, Q) = \begin{cases} 1 & \text{if } Q < 7.2, \\ 0 & \text{otherwise.} \end{cases}$$

Note that since $s^*(\underline{c}_1) > m(\underline{c}_1)$, s^* is a limit pricing strategy. Notice too that from our earlier discussion, t^* is clearly a best response to s^*. Thus, we need to check that s^* is optimal, given t^*. First, note that unless the high cost established firm produces at least 7.2, it cannot deter any entry. But, this level is high enough that it is not worthwhile for $\bar{c}_1$ to produce it, even though in so doing it would eliminate all entry. To see this, note that producing $Q = s^*(\underline{c}_1)$ yields the payoff

$$\Pi_1^0(\bar{c}_1, s^*(\underline{c}_1)) + pR(\bar{c}_1, \bar{c}_2) + (1 - p)R(\bar{c}_1, \underline{c}_2) = 15.51 - 0.86p$$

while producing $m(\bar{c}_1)$ yields $\Pi_1^0(\bar{c}_1, m(\bar{c}_1)) = 16$, which exceeds $15.51 - 0.86p$ for all $p \geqq 0$. Finally, note that the low cost firm has no reason to produce more than $s^*(\underline{c}_1)$. If it produces less, it is sure to face entry, and thus its best choice in this range would be $m(\underline{c}_1)$. But $s^*(\underline{c}_1)$ yields an expected payoff of $26.87 - 1.19p$, which for all $p \leqq 1$ strictly exceeds the payoff $\Pi_1^M(\underline{c}_1) = 22.56$ from producing $m(\underline{c}_1)$. Thus, $s^*(\underline{c}_1)$ is also optimal.

We now demonstrate the existence of a pooling equilibrium given by

$$s^*(\underline{c}_1) = s^*(\bar{c}_1) = m(\underline{c}_1) = 4.75,$$

$$t^*(\underline{c}_2, Q) = 1,$$

$$t^*(\bar{c}_2, Q) = \begin{cases} 0 & \text{if } Q \geqq 4.75, \\ 1 & \text{otherwise.} \end{cases}$$

Note again that our earlier discussion indicates that t^* is a best response to s^*, given $q \in (0.273, 0.954)$. Further, it is evident that s^* is optimal if $c_1 = \underline{c}_1$, since any increase in Q would not deter entry, and any decrease in output would both increase entry and reduce first period profits. Finally, if the established firm has $c_1 = \bar{c}_1$, it similarly has no incentive to increase output, while cutting output could at best yield the monopoly first period return, but would induce certain entry. This gives a payoff of 16.00, which is, for $p > 0.063$, less than its current return of $\Pi_1^0(\bar{c}_1, 4.75) + pR(\bar{c}_1, \bar{c}_2) = 15.44 + 8.89p$. Thus, if $p > 0.063$, this is also an equilibrium, and since $s^*(\bar{c}_1) > m(\bar{c}_1)$, it, too, involves limit pricing.

To summarize, our pooling equilibrium required that the probability p of the entrant having high costs exceed 0.063 and that q lie in $(0.273, 0.954)$, while our separating equilibrium existed for all p and q. In a separating equilibrium, the probability of entry is q, which is just the probability that the established firm is of the high cost type, while in our pooling equilibrium, the probability of entry is $1 - p$, the probability of the entrant having low costs.[5] Clearly, we may have $1 - p$ greater than, less than, or equal to q and still meet the requirements for existence of both equilibria. *Limit pricing equilibria may involve less, the same, or more entry than occurs in the full information (no limit pricing) case.*

It is, of course, true in either type of equilibrium that if the limit-pricing firm were to charge a higher price than is called for by the equilibrium strategy, then it would face a greater threat of entry. This is because the entrant would interpret this high price as meaning that the firm's costs were higher than they in fact are, and thus entry would appear more attractive/ (Note that the entrant's inferences will be correct only if firm 1 adheres to its equilibrium strategy.)/ Indeed, it is this balancing of foregone first period profits against the reward to deterring entry which characterizes the equilibrium and it is this threat of increased entry which leads the established firm to maintain its expanded output. Thus, in this sense, limit pricing does limit entry.

A useful way to think about these results is to consider limit pricing as the outcome of competition between the types of the established firm, with high cost types attempting to mimic low cost ones and low cost firms attempting to distinguish themselves from the high cost ones. Then whether a pooling or a

---

[5] If $q < 0.273$, then there is a pooling equilibrium against which the probability of entry is zero. If $q > 0.954$, then entry would be certain if a pooling equilibrium were established. But then each type of established firm would find that its monopoly output represents a profitable deviation. Thus, there could be no such equilibrium.

separating equilibrium is established is a matter of whether it is the high or low cost type which is successful. This competition could, of course, be purely a conjectural one in the mind of the entrant, but it might also be more concrete. Specifically, one can imagine that there are a number of currently monopolized markets, all of which are identical except that a percentage p have high cost incumbents and the rest have low cost incumbents. There is also a limited supply of venture capital, which is available to an entrant whose costs are unknown a priori. Then the competition between types of established firms becomes real, with each established firm attempting to make entry into its market appear unattractive.[6]

The active role assigned to the entrant in this model and the corresponding significance of the beliefs and conjectures embodied in the entrant's strategy lead to the existence of a multiplicity of equilibria, both in this example and more generally. Our example actually has a continuum of both separating and pooling equilibria, where each class of equilibria is parameterized by the critical level of Q such that observation of a lower output than this level induces increased entry. In general, there is a large class of entrant's strategies t such that t and the best response to it constitute an equilibrium: many possible conjectures by the entrant as to the outcome of the competition among established firms are consistent with rational expectations. Thus, there is no unique limit price in these models.[7]

One way to attempt to narrow the set of equilibria is to place restrictions on the possible strategies for the entrant. For example, one could require that, conditional on observing *any* Q, the entrant assign probabilities to Q having been the choice of each type of established firm. Then one would require that, for each Q, $t^*(c_2, Q)$ be a best response, given these conjectures. This is the essence of the concept of sequential equilibrium due to David Kreps and Robert Wilson [10], and it is clearly in the spirit of the perfectness criterion for equilibria (Selten [19]).[8] However, as is easily verified, our equilibria already satisfy this condition, and still we have the unwanted multiplicity. Thus one might consider further restrictions on the entrant's conjectures. In particular, one might hypothesize that the entrant will not conjecture that the competition between types of established firm will be unnecessarily wasteful. This results in considering only those equilibria (s^*, t^*) for which there is no other equilibrium where the payoffs to the various types of established firms weakly dominate those under (s^*, t^*). The two particular equilibria we have identified here meet this condition. Other separating

---

[6]See E. Gal-or [4] for a more explicit model along these lines. Also see D. Kreps and R. Wilson [9] and P. Milgrom and J. Roberts [12] for multi-market models of entry deterrence through predation.

[7]There is a second source of non-uniqueness which involves the specification of $t^*(c_2, Q)$ for values of Q outside the range of s^*. Since such values of Q are observed with probability zero, the maximization of expected return places no constraint on t^* at these points. Then, even within the constraint that s^* be a best response to the entrant's strategy, there are typically many strategies t^* which constitute equilibria with s^*. However, all such t^* for a given s^* give the same evolution of the play of the game (the same Q values being chosen and the same entry decisions being made). Thus, this non-uniqueness is less crucial.

[8]This correspondence is not coincidence, as Kreps and Wilson [10] have shown: every perfect equilibrium is sequential.

equilibria all involve $s^*(\bar{c}_1) = m(\bar{c}_1)$ and $s^*(\underline{c}_1) > 7.2,$[9] other pooling equilibria must involve lower payoffs for the low cost established firm,[10] and neither equilibrium dominates the other.

Although there are no equilibria in this example where $s^* \equiv m$, the monopoly output, this strategy could arise in equilibrium with other specifications of the parameters. This would happen if the profit to a high cost firm in producing its monopoly output and then facing certain entry exceeded its profits from producing the monopoly output of the low cost firm and then avoiding all entry. However, if there are a continuum of types (cost levels) possible for the established firm and the H_i are atomless, this cannot happen: at most only a set of firms of measure zero could produce their monopoly outputs in equilibrium.

Both to establish this claim and to explore more completely the nature of the limit pricing problem in a framework with less discontinuity, we now examine a specification of the model with a continuum of possible cost levels. Thus, suppose that the distribution of c_j is given by a continuous density function $h_j(c_j)$ which is positive on $[\underline{c}_j, \bar{c}_j]$. We will initially concentrate on separating equilibria.

Assume that 2 conjectures that 1 will play some strategy $\bar{s}$. Then, for any Q in the range of $\bar{s}$, the entrant's best response is to act as if $c_1 \in \bar{s}^{-1}(Q)$, and to enter if and only if the expected value of $\delta_2 \Pi_2^C(c_1, c_2) - K$, conditional on $c_1 \in \bar{s}^{-1}(Q)$, is positive. If $\bar{s}$ is monotone decreasing, then $\bar{s}^{-1}(Q)$ is a singleton and so 2 should enter if and only if $c_2 \leqq \gamma(\bar{s}^{-1}(Q))$, where $\gamma(c_1) \equiv (a + c_1 - 3\sqrt{bK})/2$ is the highest level of c_2 permitting successful entry against a firm with costs c_1. Thus, for $Q \in$ range $\bar{s}$, 2's best response satisfies

$$t(c_2, Q) = \begin{cases} 1 & \text{if } c_2 \leqq \bar{g}(Q), \\ 0 & \text{otherwise}, \end{cases}$$

where $\bar{g} = \gamma \circ \bar{s}^{-1}$.

Now, suppose that 1's conjecture is that t is of this general form, so that 2 will be deterred from entering if c_2 exceeds some value $g(Q)$. Then 1's expected payoff is

$$G(c_1, Q) = \Pi_1^0(c_1, Q) + \delta_1 \int_{g(Q)}^{\bar{z}_2} R(c_1, c_2) h_2(c_2)\, dc_2.$$

Maximizing with respect to Q yields

$$0 = \frac{\partial \Pi_1^0}{\partial Q} - \delta_1 R(c_1, g(Q)) h_2(g(Q)) g'(Q).$$

---

[9]Note, in particular, that $s^* = m$ is not an equilibrium strategy, since the $\bar{c}_1$ firm would be willing to produce $m(\underline{c}_1)$ to eliminate all entry.

[10]While it might seem that any other pooling equilibrium would have $s^*(c_1) > m(\underline{c}_1)$, this need not be the case. However, if the entrant's conjectures regarding the value of c_1, given Q, are continuous in Q, pooling equilibria with higher than monopoly prices disappear. If, in addition, the probability assigned to $c_1 = \underline{c}_1$ rises sufficiently rapidly in Q, then only separating equilibria can exist. These continuity and monotonicity conditions are similar in spirit to Myerson's properness criterion [14].

But, in equilibrium, the conjectures must be correct (i.e., $\bar{s} = s^*$, $g = \gamma \circ s^{*-1}$), so we have that $s^*(c_1)$ must satisfy

$$(1) \qquad 0 = \frac{\partial \Pi_1^0(c_1, s^*(c_1))}{\partial Q} - \frac{\delta_1 R(c_1, \gamma(c_1)) h_2(\gamma(c_1)) \gamma'(c_1)}{ds^*(c_1)/dc_1}$$

Note that, so long as $R(c_1, \gamma(c_1))$, $h_2(\gamma(c_1))$, and $\gamma'(c_1)$ are positive and $ds^*/dc_1 < \infty$ (i.e., s^* is differentiable at c_1), then this first order condition implies that $\partial \Pi_1^0/\partial Q < 0$. Thus, the simple monopoly solution $m(c_1)$, which is defined by $\partial \Pi_1^0/\partial Q = 0$, cannot arise in equilibrium. If the entrant were to conjecture $\bar{s} = m$ and respond optimally, then by increasing output slightly from $m(c_1)$ to, say, $m(c_1) + \epsilon = \bar{s}(c_1')$, the established firm can eliminate the threat of entry from firms in the interval $(\gamma(c_1'), \gamma(c_1)]$. This increase in output has a first-order effect on Π_1^0 of zero, since $\partial \Pi_1^0/\partial Q = 0$ at $m(c_1)$, but a non-negligible first-order effect on the expected value of the reward to deterring entry. Thus, in any model of this type, so long as: (i) it is more profitable to be a monopolist than to share the market, (ii) beliefs are given by a positive density, and (iii) higher costs for the established firm encourage entry, essentially all established firms must be limit pricing in a separating equilibrium.

Of course, in such an equilibrium, s^* is invertible and so there is the same entry as if c_1 were known directly.

Now, to obtain an explicit solution for a particular specification, suppose that $\underline{c}_i = 0$ and that h_2 has, for $c_2 \geq \gamma(0)$, the particular form

$$h_2(c_2) = 8bp / \left[4(a - c_2)\sqrt{bK} - 7bK \right],$$

where the parameter ρ reflects the probability of there being a viable potential competitor. Also, assume that $\bar{c}_i < a/2$, which insures that the usual first-order conditions define a Cournot equilibrium after entry. As well, assume that $a \geq 7\sqrt{bK}/2$, which both insures that h_2 is a density for any choice of $\bar{c}_2 < a/2$ and also implies that $\gamma(0) > 0$, so that even low cost established firms are threatened by entry. Finally, assume that $\gamma(\bar{c}_1) < \bar{c}_2$, so that $h_2(\gamma(\bar{c}_1)) \neq 0$.

Then, substituting for $R(c_1, \gamma(c_1)) = [2(a - c_1)\sqrt{bK} - bK]/4b$ and h_1 and rearranging terms yields

$$\frac{ds^*}{dc} = \frac{\delta_1 \rho}{\left[a - c_1 - 2bs^*(c_1) \right]}.$$

This differential equation was derived on the assumption that s^* was monotone decreasing on $[\underline{c}_1, \bar{c}_1]$. The solutions meeting this condition and satisfying the non-negativity condition for expected profits form a non-intersecting family parameterized by a boundary condition, which we may take to be the value of $s^*(\bar{c}_1)$. Since each member of this family with the appropriate specification of t^*

can constitute an equilibrium,[11] the multiplicity of equilibria in the earlier example carries over.

As suggested earlier, it seems reasonable to concentrate on solutions which are Pareto efficient. There is a unique such solution among the separating equilibria. In it, the highest cost firm, which will stand revealed as a weakling in any case, does not limit price. Alternatively, we can also eliminate the multiplicity by imposing the condition that an entrant whose costs exceed $\gamma(\bar{c}_1)$ will never enter, no matter what value of Q is observed, since such an entrant could never expect to recoup the entry cost K. Under either of these specifications, the boundary condition becomes $s^*(\bar{c}_1) = m(\bar{c}_1) = (a - \bar{c}_1)/2b$. The corresponding solution of the differential equation is then given implicitly by

$$0 = m(c_1) - s^*(c_1) + \delta_1\rho - \delta_1\rho \exp\left[\frac{m(\bar{c}_1) - s^*(c_1)}{\delta_1\rho}\right].$$

Now, let t^* be specified by $t(c_2, Q) = 1$ iff $c_2 \leqq \gamma(s^{*-1}(Q))$ for Q in the range of s^* and, say, by $t(c_2, Q) = t(c_2, s^*(\underline{c}_1))$ for $Q > s^*(\underline{c}_1)$ and $t(c_2, Q) = t(c_2, s^*(\bar{c}_1))$ for $Q < m(\bar{c}_1)$. For s^* and t^* to be an equilibrium it is clearly sufficient that $G(c_1, Q)$ be pseudo-concave in Q for each c_1, so that the first order condition (1) guarantees an optimum. For this, it is in turn sufficient (see [11]) that

$$\frac{ds^*(z)}{dz} \leqq \inf_{c \in [0, \bar{c}_1]} \frac{\delta_1\gamma'(z)\big[R(c_1, \gamma(z)) - R(z, \gamma(z))\big]h_1(\gamma(z))}{(z - c)}$$

$$= \inf_{c_1} \frac{\delta_1(1/2)\big[(z - c_1)(24\sqrt{bK} - 6a - z + 7c_1)/36b\big]}{(z - c_1)}$$

$$\times \left(\frac{8b\rho}{2(a - z)\sqrt{bK} - bK}\right) = \frac{\delta_1\rho\big[24\sqrt{bK} - 6a - z\big]}{9\big[2(a - z)\sqrt{bK} - bK\big]}.$$

Since $ds^*/dz = -1/[2b(1 - \exp[(m(\bar{c}_1) - s(z))/\delta_1\rho])]$ is strictly decreasing and bounded above by $-1/(2b)$, if the right hand side of the inequality were always positive, i.e., $6a + \sup z < 24\sqrt{bK}$, we would then be assured that (s^*, t^*) is an equilibrium. Thus, since $\bar{c}_1 = \sup z < a/2$, $a < 48\sqrt{bK}/13$ provides a sufficient condition.

It is straightforward to obtain comparative statics results for this example. Let $A \equiv [m(\bar{c}_1) - s(c_1)]/(\delta_1\rho) \leqq 0$. Then

$$\partial s^*/\partial\rho = \delta_1 \frac{\big[1 + (A - 1)\exp A\big]}{1 - \exp A} > 0,$$

$$\partial s^*/\partial\delta_1 = \rho \frac{\big[1 + (A - 1)\exp A\big]}{1 - \exp A} > 0,$$

[11] So long as the first-order condition (1) actually gives a maximum.

454 P. MILGROM AND J. ROBERTS

and

$$\partial s^* / \partial \bar{c}_1 = \frac{\exp A}{2b(1 - \exp A)} > 0.$$

The intuition behind the first two results is clear. Regarding the third, the idea is that the possibility of there being higher cost firms leads the current $\bar{c}_1$ firm to limit price in order to distinguish itself, and then all lower cost firms must further increase their outputs.

Since the particular h function that we chose to permit computation resulted in $R(c_1, \gamma(c_1))h(\gamma(c_1))$ being constant, comparative statics with respect to a and b reveal the effects of changes in first period demand only. Note too that changes in these parameters affect both m and s^*, so interest centers on the effects on $s^* - m$. These are obtained by $\partial s^* / \partial a = 1/2b = \partial m / \partial a$, and $\partial s^* / \partial b < - (a - c_1)/2b^2 = \partial m / \partial b$: increases in a do not affect the amount of limit pricing, while increases in b reduce the amount of limit pricing by increasing the marginal cost of this activity (as measured by c_1 less the marginal revenue at $s^*(c_1)$) while leaving the marginal return (in the second period) unaffected.

Since the density function we used depends on K, comparative statics with respect to K cannot legitimately be interpreted in the natural way as indicating the effect of changing entry barriers.[12] To allow such an analysis, suppose instead that the established firm's beliefs are given by a density function which is independent of K. In this case, if $K = 0$, then $R(c_1, \gamma(c_1))h(\gamma(c_1)) \equiv 0$, and no limit pricing will occur. It is only the fact of positive K that causes the marginal entrant to enter with a strictly positive level of output. With no cost of entry, a marginal entrant comes in with an output which is essentially zero, and there is no return to deterring such entry. Similarly, if K is very large (Bain's blockaded entry case), no possible level of $\underline{c}_2$ will permit positive profits, the threat of entry disappears, and again no limit pricing will occur. In the particular example we calculated, K was such that $\gamma(\underline{c}_1) > \underline{c}_2$, so even low cost established firms were threatened and practiced limit pricing. A fourth possibility comes when K is high enough that $\gamma(\underline{c}_1) < \underline{c}_2$, so that there is a set $[\underline{c}_1, c_1^*)$ of firms against which no potential entrant would want to enter. An interesting aspect of our model is that even firms in this range may practice limit pricing. The essential cause of this is that, if $m(c_1') \leqq s(c_1'')$ for some $c_1' < c_1^* < c_1''$, then by producing $m(c_1')$, the low cost firm becomes identified with higher cost firms which are subject to entry. These latter firms may be expected to be limit pricing, so $s^*(c_1'') > m(c_1'')$, and thus $m(c_1') = s^*(c_1'')$ is possible. By increasing output to (slightly more than) $s^*(c_1^*)$, which, to a first approximation, does not reduce the value of Π^0, the low cost firm can eliminate the threat of entry and thus increase second period expected returns.

Finally, we should mention that although we have concentrated on separating equilibria, other equilibria are possible in the continuum of types framework. A

---

[12] The possibility of normalizing 2's payoff means that lowering δ_2 corresponds to raising K.

result of Milgrom and Weber [13] indicates that we need not concern ourselves with mixed strategy equilibria in games of this type. However, pure pooling equilibria are conceptually possible, as are equilibria where s^* is a decreasing step function.[13] In any pooling equilibrium, all types of the established firm are better off producing the equilibrium output Q^* than they are changing their output and facing the different probability of entry this different value of Q implies. For example, if entry is relatively unlikely when $Q = Q^*$ (perhaps because low values of c_1 are very likely a priori), and any deviation from Q^* brings certain entry, then if the $\bar{c}_1$ type is willing to produce Q^*, a pooling equilibrium will be maintained. In general, the form of the entrant's conjectures (as embodied in its strategy) which is necessary to support a pooling equilibria is typically discontinuous in Q, and the same sort of discontinuities underlie step-function equilibria.

It is clear that the extended example we have been discussing involves a number of special features, such as the linearity of demand and cost, and the assumption that post-entry competition yields the full information Cournot outcome. However, these assumptions serve mainly to simplify arguments and facilitate computation; they do not drive the results. Indeed, so long as the entrant's post-entry profits decrease in c_2 and increase in c_1 while the established firm strictly prefers to be a monopolist than to share the market ($R(c_1, c_2) > 0$), our principal conclusions remain: if pre-entry price can be a signal for post-entry profits, even if it does not directly influence profitability, then limit pricing will emerge in equilibrium, but entry need not be deterred relative to the complete information case. Moreover, as we shall argue in the next section, even if we allow for much more general uncertainty and for post-entry profits being dependent on pre-entry actions, a similar conclusion is valid.

3. ENTRY DETERRENCE AND RATIONAL EXPECTATIONS

In this section we consider a fairly general two-period model of entry deterrence and entry under incomplete information. While we do not provide a complete analysis of this model, we do indicate some of the implications of equilibrium for the firms' behavior.

Rather than setting up a general formal model from scratch, let us re-interpret the model in Section 2 with some modifications. In particular, we now view c_1 and c_2 as belonging to some arbitrary measurable spaces, and we will view Q as an action belonging to some other arbitrary space. Suppose further that 2 observes only some variable q which is correlated with Q, and suppose, too, that the payoffs depend not only on c_1, c_2 and the action y taken by the entrant (which may also now belong to some arbitrary space), but also on Q and possibly on a random variable θ, the realization of which is not revealed until the firms make their choices. Finally, let all the random variables have some arbitrary joint distribution.

---

[13] The possible equilibria are characterized in [11].

This framework is obviously very general. In particular, it allows for capital investment which affects marginal costs, advertising and other means of achieving brand loyalty, general forms of demand and cost functions, varying scales and forms of entry, imperfect observability of actions, uncertainty as to how the post-entry game will be played, and arbitrary dependencies among all the random elements of the model.

As before, it is useful to analyze equilibrium via strategies, s^* and t^*, and conjectures, $\bar{s}$ and $\bar{t}$. (These may be taken to be either pure or mixed strategies.) Thus, firm 1 conjectures that 2's strategy is $\bar{t}$, for each value of c_1 it will select an action $Q = s(c_1)$ to maximize the expected value of its perceived payoff, conditional on c_1. Unless expected second-period payoffs are insensitive to Q, both through any direct effect on second period profits and also through the effect on 2's conjectured action, the solution for the established firm's maximization problem will not be the same as the solution to the problem of maximizing the expected value of first period profits. Thus, we would generally expect that the threat of entry will alter behavior: some generalized form of limit pricing will be a characteristic of equilibrium.

In making its decision, the entrant will seek to maximize its expected payoff conditional on its private information c_2 and its (imperfect) observation of Q, given its conjecture $\bar{s}$. Should it happen that the observation of the signal q in equilibrium permits a precise inference via $\bar{s}$ about c_1, then entry will of course occur in precisely the same circumstances as if c_1 had been directly announced. In this case, the only effect of the generalized limit pricing on entry will be through the direct effect of Q on 2's post-entry profits (as, for example, when the choice of Q affects demand or cost). If this effect is zero, then, as in the example in Section 2, limit pricing will still occur, but it need not deter entry relative to the complete information case.

However, the unrestricted dimensionalities allowed for c_1 and Q suggest that an invertible strategy s^* is unlikely. Moreover, so long as the random noise term relating q and Q is neither perfectly correlated with c_1 nor degenerate, then even if s^* is an invertible function of Q one would not expect a noisy observation of Q via q to permit a precise inference of the value of c_1. Thus one must expect that such exact inferences will be impossible in equilibrium, and that residual uncertainty will remain concerning c_1 when the entry decision is made. In this case, the entrant must base its entry decision y on the expected value of its profits, as a function of Q, y and the exogenous uncertainty θ, conditional on the values of c_2 and q, and given its conjecture $\bar{s}$ about 1's behavior. With some abuse of notation, let us write this as

$$(2) \qquad E\big(\Pi_2(c_1, c_2, \bar{s}(c_1), y, \theta) \,|\, q(\bar{s}(c_1), \theta), c_2\big).$$

Then the question is that of whether the established firm can, through its choice of Q, cause the entrant in equilibrium to lower its estimate of the profitability of entry.

Consider what 2's estimate of its prospects are a priori, knowing c_2 but before observing q. This is just the expectation of expression (2), conditional on c_2. Then, in equilibrium, where $\bar{s} = s^*$, so that 2's conjecture is correct, this a priori estimate is

$$(3) \qquad E\big(E\big[\,\Pi_2(\mathbf{c}_1, c_2, s^*(c_1), y, \theta)\,\big|\,q(s^*(c_1), \theta), c_2\big]\,\big|\,c_2\big).$$

But, by a standard result in probability theory, expression (3) is equal to $E(\Pi_2(c_1, c_2, s^*(c_1), y, \theta)\,|\,c_2)$. But this, in turn, is simply what firm 2 would estimate its profits to be if it were to receive no information.

In this sense, then, the observation of the established firm's actions cannot, in equilibrium, systematically bias the entrant's expectations. If without any information it would have estimated its expected profits at $\overline{\Pi}$ then the fact that it will receive the signal cannot lead it to expect to receive less than $\overline{\Pi}$. Put a different way, if there are some values of c_1 and c_2 such that observing $s^*(c_1)$ (directly or indirectly) causes an entrant with characteristics c_2 to underestimate the profitability of entry, then there is an offsetting set of values for c_1 and c_2 where observing $s^*(c_1)$ causes the entrant to overestimate its prospects.

4. SUMMARY AND CONCLUSIONS

In his original analysis of limit pricing, Bain [1, p. 453] argued that although "current price . . . need play no direct role [in the entry decision], since the anticipated industry price *after entry* and the entrant's anticipated market share are the strategic considerations," the potential entrant may "regard this price as an indicator" of post-entry profitability. Given this, Bain developed his theory of limit pricing, from which a large literature has emerged. A weakness of this literature has been the failure to model both the established firm and the entrant as strategic agents. However, if one models the situation described by Bain as a game of complete information, no limit pricing can emerge in equilibrium [3].

In this paper we model the problem considered by Bain of entry deterrence and entry as a game of incomplete information. In this game, Bain's arguments are valid: although pre-entry actions by the established firm may not influence post-entry profitability, they may become signals for some unobservable determinants of profits. Limit pricing, or, more generally, deviations from short run maximizing behavior, then emerge in equilibrium, just as earlier analyses had found. However, an unsuspected feature also emerges. Since the entrant will, in equilibrium, recognize the incentives for limit-pricing, its expectations of the profitability of entry will not be consistently biased by the established firm's behavior. Then, depending on the particular equilibrium that is established and the parameters of the model, the probability of entry may fall short of, equal, or even exceed what it would be if there were complete information and thus no limit pricing.

One conclusion of this analysis is for the appropriate public policy towards limit-pricing. If pre-entry price does not influence post-entry demand and if the two-period modelling used here is appropriate, then limit pricing should not be discouraged, since it means lower prices and cannot, overall, limit entry. More generally, the admittedly incomplete analysis in Section 3 might suggest a stronger statement regarding strategic moves taken by established firms to deter entry. To the extent that these actions are not objectionable per se, but rather are of potential concern only because of signalling effects which it is feared may deter entry, then they are in fact benign. The question is whether either of these suggestions would stand up under a full examination of a richer model. In particular, it would seem that embedding the opportunity for limit pricing in a multi-period model where predation is possible and where reputations are a factor would be an important extension of the present analysis. This is a problem we hope to address in future work.

Northwestern University
and
Stanford University

Manuscript received March, 1980; revision received December, 1980.

REFERENCES

[1] BAIN, J.: "A Note on Pricing in Monopoly and Oligopoly," *American Economic Review*, 39(1949), 448–464.
[2] CLARK, J. M.: "Toward a Concept of Workable Competition," *American Economic Review*, 30(1940), 241–256.
[3] FRIEDMAN, J.: "On Entry Preventing Behavior," in *Applied Game Theory*, ed. by S. J. Brams, A. Schotter, and G. Schwodiauer. Wurzburg, Vienna: Physica-Verlag, 1979, pp. 236–253.
[4] GAL-OR, E.: "Limit Price Entry Prevention and its Impact on Potential Investors—A Game-Theoretic Approach," Ph.D. Dissertation, Northwestern University, 1980.
[5] GASKINS, D.: "Dynamic Limit Pricing: Optimal Pricing Under Threat of Entry," *Journal of Economic Theory*, 2(1971), 306–322.
[6] HARSANYI, J. C.: "Games with Incomplete Information Played by 'Bayesian' Players," Parts I, II and III, *Management Science*, 14 (November, 1967; January, 1968; and March, 1968), 159–182, 320–324, and 486–502.
[7] KALDOR, N.: "Market Imperfection and Excess Capacity," *Economica*, 2(1935), 33–50.
[8] KAMIEN, M. I., AND N. SCHWARTZ: "Limit Pricing and Uncertain Entry," *Econometrica*, 39(1971), 441–454.
[9] KREPS, D., AND R. WILSON: "On the Chain-Store Paradox and Predation: Reputation for Toughness," Discussion Paper 551, Graduate School of Business, Stanford University, 1980.
[10] ———: "Sequential Equilibria," Discussion Paper 584, Graduate School of Business, Stanford University, 1980.
[11] MILGROM, P., AND J. ROBERTS: "Equilibrium Limit Pricing Doesn't Limit Entry," Discussion Paper 399R, Center for Mathematical Studies in Economics and Management Science, Northwestern University, 1980.
[12] ———: "Predation, Reputation, and Entry Deterrence," Discussion Paper 427, Center for Mathematical Studies in Economics and Management Science, Northwestern University, 1980.
[13] MILGROM, P., AND R. WEBER: "Distributional Strategies for Games with Incomplete Information," Discussion Paper 428, Center for Mathematical Studies in Economics and Management Science, Northwestern University, 1980.
[14] MYERSON, R.: "Refinements of the Nash Equilibrium Concept," *International Journal of Game Theory*, 7(1978), 73–80.

[15] ORTEGA-REICHERT, A.: "Models for Competitive Bidding Under Uncertainty," Ph.D. dissertation, Stanford University, 1968.

[16] PYATT, G.: "Profit Maximization and the Threat of New Entry," *Economic Journal*, 81(1971), 242–255.

[17] SALOP, S. C.: "Strategic Entry Deterrence," *American Economic Review*, 69(1979), 335–338.

[18] SCHERER, F. M.: *Industrial Market Structure and Economic Performance*, Second Edition. Chicago: Rand McNally and Company, 1979.

[19] SELTEN, R.: "Reexamination of the Perfectness Concept for Equilibrium Points in Extensive Games," *International Journal of Game Theory*, 4(1975), 25–55.

[20]

JOURNAL OF ECONOMIC THEORY 27, 253–279 (1982)

Reputation and Imperfect Information

DAVID M. KREPS AND ROBERT WILSON

*Graduate School of Business, Stanford University,
Stanford, California 94305*

Received June 18, 1980; revised June 22, 1981

A common observation in the informal literature of economics (and elsewhere) is that in multistage "games," players may seek early in the game to acquire a reputation for being "tough" or "benevolent" or something else. But this phenomenon is not observed in some formal game-theoretic analyses of finite games, such as Selten's finitely repeated chain-store game or in the finitely repeated prisoners' dilemma. We reexamine Selten's model, adding to it a "small" amount of imperfect (or incomplete) information about players' payoffs, and we find that this addition is sufficient to give rise to the "reputation effect" that one intuitively expects. *Journal of Economic Literature*, Classification Numbers: 026, 213, 611.

1. INTRODUCTION

The purpose of this paper is to present some game-theoretic models that illustrate the role of a firm's reputation. Allusions to reputational effects recur in the industrial organization literature on imperfect competition, but formal models and analyses have been lacking. Scherer [21], for example, points to

the demonstration effect that sharp price cutting in one market can have on the behavior of actual or would-be rivals in other markets. If rivals come to fear from a multimarket seller's actions in Market A that entry or expansion in Markets B and C will be met by sharp price cuts or other rapacious responses, they may be deterred from taking agressive actions there. Then the conglomerate's expected benefit from predation in Market A will be supplemented by the discounted present value of the competition-inhibiting effects its example has in Markets B and C. (page 338)

The intuitive appeal of this line of reasoning has, however, been called the "chain-store paradox" by Selten [24], who demonstrates that it is not supported in a straightforward game-theoretic model. We shall elaborate Selten's argument later, but the crux is that, in a very simple environment, there is no means by which thoroughly rational strategies in one market could be influenced by behavior in a second, essentially independent market.

253

0022-0531/82/040253-27$02.00/0

What is lacking, apparently, is a plausible mechanism that connects behavior in otherwise independent markets.

We show that imperfect information is one such mechanism. Moreover, the effects of imperfect information can be quite dramatic. If rivals perceive the *slightest* chance that an incumbent firm might enjoy "rapacious responses," then the incumbent's optimal strategy is to employ such behavior against its rivals in all, except possibly the last few, in a long string of encounters. For the incumbent, the immediate cost of predation is a worthwhile investment to sustain or enhance its reputation, thereby deterring subsequent challenges.

The two models we present here are variants of the game studied by Selten [24]; several other variations are discussed in Kreps and Wilson [8]. The first model can be interpreted in the context envisioned by Scherer: A multimarket monopolist faces a succession of potential entrants (though in our model the analysis is unchanged if there is a single rival with repeated opportunities to enter). We treat this as a finitely repeated game with the added feature that the entrants are unsure about the monopolist's payoffs, and we show that there is a unique "sensible" equilibrium where, no matter how small the chance that the monopolist actually benefits from predation, the entrants nearly always avoid challenging the monopolist for fear of the predatory response. The second model enriches this formulation by allowing, in the case of a single entrant with multiple entry opportunities, that also the incumbent is uncertain about the entrant's payoffs. The equilibrium in this model is analogous to a price war: Since the entrant also has a reputation to protect, both firms may engage in battle. Each employs its aggressive tactic in a classic game of "chicken," persisting in its attempt to force the other to acquiesce before it would itself give up the fight, even if it is virtually certain (at the outset) that each side will thereby incur short-run losses.

After reviewing Selten's model in Section 2, we analyze these two models in Sections 3 and 4, respectively. In Section 5 we discuss our results and relate them to some of the relevant literature. In particular, this issue of the *Journal* includes a companion article by Milgrom and Roberts [13] that explores many of the issues studied here in models that are richer in institutional detail. Their paper is highly recommended to the reader.

2. THE CHAIN-STORE PARADOX

The models we analyze are variations on the chain-store game studied by Selten [24]. Consider a sequential game with two players called the *entrant* (or potential entrant) and the *monopolist*. The entrant moves first, electing either to *enter* or to *stay out*. Following entry, the monopolist chooses either to *acquiesce* or to *fight*. If the entrant stays out, the incumbent is not called

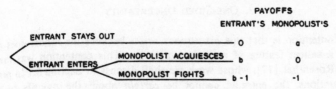

FIG. 1. Selten's chain-store game.

upon to move. Payoffs to the players, depending on the moves selected, are given in Fig. 1. We consider the case that $a > 1$ and $0 < b < 1$.

How will this game be played? If the entrant enters, the monopolist chooses between the payoffs 0 if it acquiesces and -1 if it fights, so surely it will acquiesce. Anticipating this response, the entrant chooses between 0 if it stays out and b if it enters, and so it will enter. This is one Nash equilibrium of the game, but there is another: If the entrant were to anticipate that the monopolist would fight entry, then the entrant would want to stay out. Note that it costs the monopolist nothing to adopt the strategy "fight if entry" if no entry occurs. So this is a second Nash equilibrium. But this second equilibrium is not so plausible as the first. It depends on an expectation by the entrant of the monopolist's behavior that, faced with the *fait accompli* of entry, would be irrational behavior for the monopolist. In the parlance of game theory, the second equilibrium is *imperfect*. We suppose that the entrant adopts the "rational expectation" that the monopolist will acquiesce to entry, and we expect the first equilibrium to ensue.

Consider next the case that the game in Fig. 1 is played a finite number of times. A single monopolist plays a succession of N different entrants, where the monopolist's total payoff is the sum of its payoffs in the N stage games. Allow the later entrants to observe the moves in all earlier stages of the game. Scherer's reasoning predicts that in this case the "reputation" effect might come to life: The monopolist, by fighting any early entry, might convince later opponents that it will fight, thus deterring later entries. Indeed, if this were the case, then also the early round opponents would not enter, not wishing to be abused for demonstration purposes. However, as Selten argues, this does not withstand scrutiny. In the last stage the monopolist will not fight because there are no later entrants to demonstrate for. So in the last stage, entry will surely occur. But then in the penultimate stage, the monopolist again has no reason to fight—it is costly in the short run and has no effect on the last stage. The next-to-last entrant, realizing this, will surely enter. This logic can be repeated, unraveling from the back: In each stage entry and acquiescence will occur. To be precise, this is the unique perfect Nash equilibrium of the game; cf. Selten [22, 23, 24]. Apparently, this model is inadequate to justify Scherer's prediction that reputational effects will play a role.

3. One-Sided Uncertainty

Our contention is that this inadequacy arises because the model does not capture a salient feature of realistic situations. (This contention was made first by Rosenthal [17], whose work we shall discuss in Section 5.) In practical situations, the entrants cannot be *certain* about the payoffs to the monopolist. They may be unsure about the monopolist's costs, or they may be uncertain about nonpecuniary benefits that the monopolist reaps—this may be a monopolist who enjoys being tough. The latter might be more colorfully stated by saying that the monopolist plays tough "irrationally"; according to Scherer [21, p. 247], "... fear of irrational or avowedly rapacious action, then, rather than the expectation of rational pricing responses, may be what deters the potential new entrant from entering on a large scale." For whatever reason, the entrants may initially assess some positive probability p that the monopolist's payoffs are not as in Fig. 1 but rather (in the simplest case) as in Fig. 2, reflecting a short-term benefit from a fighting response. In this case, later entrants, observing earlier moves, will revise their assessment p on the basis of what they see. Perhaps in this case the reputation effect will come alive.

We model this formally as follows. There are $N + 1$ players, for N a positive integer. One of the players is the *monopolist*; the others are called *entrant N, entrant N − 1,..., entrant* 1. The monopolist plays the game in Fig. 1 against each entrant in turn: First it plays against entrant N, then $N − 1$, etc. (We always index time backwards, and we refer to stage n as that part of the game that involves entrant n.) The payoffs for each entrant are given in Fig. 1.

The monopolist's payoffs are more complex: Its total payoff is the sum (undiscounted for now) of its payoffs in each stage, where the stage payoffs are either *all* as in Fig. 1 or *all* as in Fig. 2. The monopolist knows which payoff structure obtains. The entrants, on the other hand, initially assess probability δ that the monopolist's payoff structure is the second one. As the game progresses, each entrant (and the monopolist) observes all prior moves. Consequently, the history of moves prior to stage n may enable entrant n to revise this assessment if the history reveals some information about the relative likelihoods of the monopolist's two possible payoff structures.

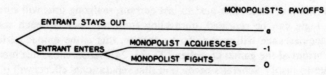

FIG. 2.   Payoffs for a tough monopolist.

This model conforms to Harsanyi's [7] formulation of a game with incomplete information. Alternatively, it is a game with imperfect information (among the entrants) and perfect recall, in which "nature" initially determines the monopolist's payoff structure, and nature's move is observed by the monopolist but not the entrants. In line with the first interpretation, we refer to the *weak monopolist* or the *strong monopolist*, meaning the monopolist if its payoffs are as in Fig. 1 or Fig. 2, respectively.

Since the players have perfect recall, there is no loss of generality in restricting attention to behavior strategies (Kuhn [10]). We wish to identify a Nash equilibrium of this game and, moreover, we wish the equilibrium identified to be *perfect*. That is, we wish to exclude equilibria that are based on expectations by one player of another's behavior that would not be rational for the latter to carry out if called upon to do so. Because our games have incomplete information, Selten's [22] concept of subgame perfection is inadequate. His concept of "trembling-hand" perfection (Selten [23]), on the other hand, is difficult to employ in games with strategy spaces as complex as those present here. So we use an analogous equilibrium concept called a *sequential equilibrium*. This is a refinement for extensive games of the usual Nash equilibrium that captures the spirit of Selten's perfectness criterion but that is much easier to apply. General definitions and properties of sequential equilibria are given in Kreps and Wilson [9], which we summarize here.

There are three basic parts to the definition of a sequential equilibrium: (a) Whenever a player must choose an action, that player has some probability assessment over the nodes in its information set, reflecting what that player believes has happened so far. (b) These assessments are consistent with the hypothesized equilibrium strategy. For example, they satisfy Bayes' rule whenever it applies. (c) Starting from *every* information set, the player whose turn it is to move is using a strategy that is optimal for the remainder of the game against the hypothesized future moves of its opponent (given by the strategies) and the assessment of past moves by other players and by "nature" (given by the assessment over nodes in the information set). The difference between this and the standard concept of a Nash equilibrium is that (c) is required for *every* information set, including those that will not be reached if the equilibrium strategies are followed. So each player will be willing to carry out its strategy at *every* point in the game, if ever it is called upon to do so. The properties are: Sequential equilibria exist for all finite extensive games. They are subgame perfect Nash equilibria. For a fixed extensive form and probabilities of nature's moves, as we vary the payoffs it is generic that all strict sequential equilibria are trembling-hand perfect, and the equilibrium path of each sequential equilibrium is an equilibrium path for some trembling-hand perfect equilibrium. Every trembling-hand perfect equilibrium is sequential.

In the context of the game analyzed here, the definition of sequential equilibrium specializes as follows. An equilibrium comprises a (behavior) strategy for each player *and*, for each stage $n = N,..., 1$, a function p_n taking histories of moves up to stage n into numbers in $[0, 1]$ such that: (a) Starting from any point in the game where it is the monopolist's move, the monopolist's strategy is a best response to the entrants' strategies. (b) For each n, entrant n's strategy (contingent on a history h_n of prior play) is a best response to the monopolist's strategy *given that* the monopolist is strong with probability $p_n(h_n)$. (c) The game begins with $p_N = \delta$. (d) Each p_n is computed from p_{n+1} and the monopolist's strategy using Bayes' rule whenever possible. (We will not write (d) precisely—it will be transparent when we give the equilibrium below. That (d) implies "consistency of beliefs" in the sense of Kreps and Wilson [9] may not be apparent, but it does follow from the simple structure of the game being considered here.) The interpretation is that p_n gives the probability assessed by entrant n that the monopolist is strong as a function of how the game has been played up to stage n. Note that in (a) the monopolist's assessment over nodes in its information set is omitted, because all of its information sets are singletons.

We now give a sequential equilibrium for this game. This particular sequential equilibrium has the fortuitous property that, in terms of play from stage n on, p_n is a sufficient statistic for the history of play up to date n. That is, the choices of the players at stage n depend only on p_n and (for the monopolist) the move of entrant n; and p_n is a function of p_{n+1} and the moves at stage $n + 1$. We are lucky to be able to find a sequential equilibrium with this simple structure; it is not generally the case that one can find sequential equilibria for which the players' assessments are sufficient statistics for past play. (See remark (A) below.)

We begin by giving the functions p_n. Set $p_N = \delta$. For $n < N$, if the history of play up to stage n includes *any* instance that entry was met by acquiescence, set $p_n = 0$. If every entry so far has been met by fighting, and if k is the smallest index ($> n$) such that there was entry at stage k, then set $p_n = \max(b^{k-1}, \delta)$. If there has been no entry, set $p_n = \delta$.

This corresponds to the following recursive definition:

(a) If there is no entry at stage $n + 1$, then $p_n = p_{n+1}$.

(b) If there is entry at stage $n + 1$, this entry is fought, and $p_{n+1} > 0$, then $p_n = \max(b^n, p_{n+1})$.

(c) If there is entry at stage $n + 1$ and either this entry is met by acquiescence or $p_{n+1} = 0$, then $p_n = 0$.

Now that we have described how p_n is computed at every node in the game tree, we can give the strategies of the players in terms of p_n.

Strategy of the Monopolist

(a) If the monopolist is strong, it always fights entry.

(b) If the monopolist is weak and entry occurs at stage n, the monopolist's response depends on n and p_n: If $n = 1$, the monopolist acquiesces. If $n > 1$ and $p_n \geqslant b^{n-1}$, the monopolist fights. If $n > 1$ and $p_n < b^{n-1}$, the monopolist fights with probability $((1 - b^{n-1}) p_n)/((1 - p_n) b^{n-1})$ and acquiesces with the complementary probability. (Note that when $p_n = 0$, the probability of fighting is zero, and when $p_n = b^{n-1}$, the probability of fighting is one.)

Strategies of the Entrants

If $p_n > b^n$, entrant n stays out. If $p_n < b^n$, entrant n enters. If $p_n = b^n$, entrant n randomizes, staying out with probability $1/a$.

PROPOSITION 1. *The strategies and beliefs given above constitute a sequential equilibrium.*

Proof. We only sketch the proof, leaving details to the reader. In the context of this game, there are two things to verify: First, the beliefs of the entrants must be consistent with the strategy of the monopolist, in the sense that Bayes' rule holds whenever it applies. Second, starting from any information set in the game, no player has the incentive (in terms of the payoff for the remainder of the game) to change its selection of move at that information set. For entrants, this verification is made using the beliefs given above. (Once this is verified, the Bellman optimality principle together with the fact that beliefs are Bayesian consistent ensures that no player can unilaterally change its strategy and benefit starting from any point in the game tree.)

The verification of Bayesian consistency is easy. If no entry takes place at stage n, nothing is learned about the monopolist, and we have $p_{n-1} = p_n$ in such instances. If $p_n \geqslant b^{n-1}$, then the monopolist is supposed to fight entry. If $p_n = 0$, then the monopolist is supposed to acquiesce. So in these cases, Bayes' rule implies that $p_{n-1} = p_n$ (as long as the monopolist follows its strategy). In each case, this is what we have. Finally, for $p_n \in (0, b^{n-1})$, there are positive probabilities that the monopolist will acquiesce and that it will fight entry. It only acquiesces if it is weak, and, indeed, in this case we have $p_{n-1} = 0$. If it fights, Bayes' rule requires that

$p_{n-1} = \text{Prob}(\text{monopolist strong} \mid \text{monopolist fights})$

$= \text{Prob}(\text{monopolist strong and fights})/\text{Prob}(\text{fights})$

$$= \frac{\text{Prob}(\text{fights} \mid \text{strong}) \cdot \text{Prob}(\text{strong})}{\text{Prob}(\text{fights} \mid \text{strong}) \cdot \text{Prob}(\text{strong}) + \text{Prob}(\text{fights} \mid \text{weak}) \cdot P(\text{weak})}$$

$$= \frac{1 \cdot p_n}{1 \cdot p_n + [((1 - b^{n-1}) p_n)/((1 - p_n) b^{n-1})][1 - p_n]} = b^{n-1},$$

260   **KREPS AND WILSON**

which is what we have posited. Thus beliefs and strategies are Bayesian consistent.

Note that there are two instances in which Bayes' rule does not apply: $p_n \geqslant b^{n-1}$ and the monopolist acquiesces to entry; $p_n = 0$ and the monopolist fights. In each case we set $p_{n-1} = 0$. In words, we assume that any acquiescence is viewed by the entrants as "proof" that the monopolist is weak, and the entrants are unshakeable in this conviction once it is formed. This assignment of beliefs off the equilibrium path is *somewhat* arbitrary—there are other assessments that work as well. But this assignment is not wholly capricious—there are assessments that would not give an equilibrium. (This will be discussed more fully below.)

(Repeating an earlier contention, this set of assessments is consistent in the sense of Kreps and Wilson [9]. A direct proof is not difficult.)

Verification that the entrants are playing optimally is straightforward. If $p_n \geqslant b^{n-1}$, entrant n expects entry to be fought, and so it stays out. If $p_n \in (b^n, b^{n-1})$, acquiescence will occur with positive probability, but with probability less than $1 - b$. Again it is better to stay out. If $p_n = b^n$, acquiescence follows entry with probability $1 - b$, and the entrant is indifferent. If $p_n < b^n$, the probability of acquiescence exceeds $1 - b$, and the entrant enters.

To see that the strong monopolist is playing optimally, note that if the entrants follow the strategy above, acquiescence at any point results in more future entries than does fighting. In the short run fighting is better for the strong monopolist, and in the long run fewer entries are better, so the strong monopolist will always fight.

Finally, for the weak monopolist, one can verify inductively that given that these strategies are followed from stage n to stage 1, the expected payoff to the weak monopolist from stages n to 1 is given by the following function of p_n:

$$
\begin{aligned}
v_n(p_n) &= a(t - k(p_n) + 1) + 1 && \text{if } \ b^n < p_n = b^{k(p_n)-1}, \\
&= a(t - k(p_n) + 1) && \text{if } \ b^n < p_n < b^{k(p_n)-1}, \\
&= 1 && \text{if } \ p_n = b^n, \text{ and} \\
&= 0 && \text{if } \ p_n < b^n,
\end{aligned}
$$

where $k(p) = \inf\{n : b^n < p\}$ for $p > 0$, and $k(0) = \infty$. Now suppose that entry occurs at stage n. By acquiescing, the monopolist receives zero both in this stage and in the rest of the game (since p_{n-1} will be set equal to zero). By fighting, the monopolist receives -1 in this stage and future expected payoffs of 0 if $p_n = 0$, 1 if $p_n \in (0, b^{n-1}]$, and more than 1 if $p_n > b^{n-1}$. Thus the weak monopolist is happy to follow the strategy given above. ∎

It is easiest to understand the nature of this equilibrium by tracing through the play of the game for "typical" values of δ and b, say $\delta = 1/10$ and $b = 1/2$. Note that in this case, $k(\delta) = 4$. Refer to Fig. 3. At stage N (presumed to be greater than 4) the game begins with $p_N = \delta$. At this stage, the monopolist would fight entry regardless of its payoffs, so entry is forestalled. The game evolves along arrow (a) to the point $p_{N-1} = p_N = \delta$. Note that *if* there is entry, the monopolist is willing *ex post* to fight—to acquiesce moves the game along arrow (b) to $p_{N-1} = 0$, from which point the monopolist nets zero. Fighting costs 1 immediately, but acquiescing costs much more in the future. (Note that all that is necessary is that acquiescence cost at least one—as long as acquiescence resulted in $p_{N-1} \leqslant 1/16$ this would

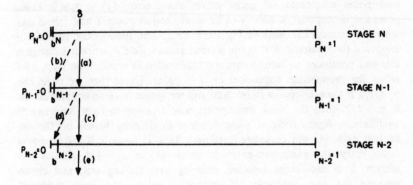

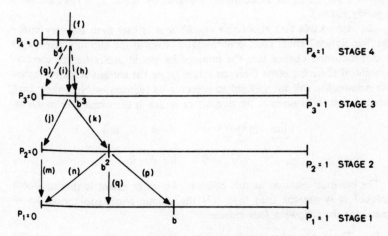

FIG. 3. Temporal evolution of the game.

be so in this case. So here is one place where the non-Bayesian reassessments need not be *precisely* as specified above to have an equilibrium. But note that $p_{N-1} \leqslant 1/16$ is necessary—otherwise the weak monopolist would rather acquiesce than fight at this stage.) The game continues in this fashion (arrows (c), (e), and (f)) until date 4 $(=k(\delta))$. At this date the monopolist might acquiesce if it is weak and if it is challenged—the strategy of the weak monopolist is chosen so that following entry, acquiescence leads to $p_3 = 0$ (arrow (g)) and fighting leads to $p_3 = b^3$ (arrow (h)). But this does *not* give entrant 4 enough incentive to enter—the game actually evolves along arrow (i) to $p_3 = \delta$. At date 3 the weak monopolist again will randomize if challenged (so that arrows (j) and (k) give the posteriors), and now there is high enough probability of acquiescence for entrant 3 to enter. If the monopolist acquiesces, the game moves along arrow (j) to $p_2 = 0$. At this point the monopolist is known to be weak, and entrants 2 and 1 both enter with the monopolist acquiescing each time. The monopolist thereafter is supposed to acquiesce; if it fights instead at, say, date 2, entrant 1 disregards this and continues to believe that the monopolist is weak. That is, $p_1 = 0$ if either the monopolist acquiesces *or* if it fights. (Note that we could have $p_1 \leqslant 1/2$ if the monopolist fights, and still we would have an equilibrium. But if $p_1 > 1/2$, then the weak monopolist would prefer to fight, upsetting the equilibrium. Again there is some freedom in defining beliefs off the equilibrium path, but not complete freedom.) Back at stage 3, if the monopolist fights entry, the game moves along arrow (k) to $p_2 = 1/4$. At this point entrant 2 is indifferent between entering and staying out, and chooses between the two randomly. If entrant 2 enters, the weak monopolist randomizes between acquiescence (arrow (n)) and fighting (arrow (p)). If entrant 2 stays out, the game moves along arrow (q) to $p_1 = 1/4$ (and entrant 1 surely enters).

The remarkable fact about this equilibrium is that even for very small δ, the "reputation" effect soon predominates. Even if the entrants assess a one-in-one-thousand chance that the monopolist would prefer (in the short run) to fight, if there are more than ten stages to go the entrant stays out because the monopolist will *surely* fight to preserve its reputation. Note the "discontinuity" that this causes as the number of stages in the game goes to infinity:

$$\lim_{N \to \infty} v_N(\delta)/N = a \qquad \text{if} \quad \delta > 0, \text{ and}$$

$$= 0 \qquad \text{if} \quad \delta = 0.$$

The obvious question at this point is: To what extent is this equilibrium unique? It is not the case that it is the unique Nash equilibrium for this game, for the following four reasons.

(a)   There are other Nash equilibria that are not sequential equilibria.

(That is, that are not, roughly speaking, perfect.) For example, it is a Nash equilibrium for the monopolist to fight any entry (regardless of its payoffs), and for the entrants never to enter. But this behavior is not "ex post rational" for the weak monopolist in stage one. In general, we wish to allow only sequential equilibria, and we confine attention to those for the remainder of this discussion.

(b) There are sequential equilibria where the strong monopolist acquiesces to entry. For example, if $N = 2$, $b = 1/2$, and $\delta = 2/3$ (very high probability that the monopolist is strong), it is a sequential equilibrium for entrant 2 to enter, the monopolist to acquiesce to this entry regardless of its payoffs, and for entrant 1 to adopt the strategy: Stay out if the monopolist acquiesces in stage 2; enter if the monopolist fights in stage 2. (In stage one, the monopolist responds with its ex post dominant action.) This is sequential because it is supported by the following beliefs of entrant 1:

$$\text{Prob(monopolist strong} \mid \text{acquiescence in stage 2)} = p_2 = 2/3,$$

$$\text{Prob(monopolist strong} \mid \text{fight in stage 2)} = 1/4.$$

For the given strategies, the first of these reassessments follows from Bayes' rule, and the second is "legitimate" because Bayes' rule does not apply: There is zero prior probability that the monopolist will fight in stage 2.

Although this is a sequential equilibrium, we contend that it is not very sensible. The flaw is in the beliefs of entrant one—if there is fighting in stage 2, entrant 1 revises *downward* the probability that the monopolist is strong. Intuitively it seems at least as likely that the strong monopolist would defect and fight as that the weak monopolist would do so. Thus it seems intuitive that entrant one will assess

$$\text{Prob(strong} \mid \text{fight)} \geqslant \text{Prob(strong} \mid \text{acquiesce)}.$$

But if we insist on this condition holding, then the equilibrium given immediately above is excluded.

Putting this formally, we will call the beliefs $\{p_n\}$ of the entrants *plausible* if given two histories h_n and h'_n of play up to stage n, if h_n and h'_n are the same except that some plays of "fight" in h_n are "acquiesce" in h'_n, then $p_n(h_n) \geqslant p_n(h'_n)$. We wish to allow only sequential equilibria that are supported by plausible beliefs. Note that this is not true of the equilibrium immediately above, but it is true of the equilibrium Proposition 1.

(c) In the sequential equilibrium given in this section, there is some freedom in describing what happens off the equilibrium path. For example, we have said that if $p_n = 0$ and the monopolist fights entry, then the entrants set $p_{n-1} = 0$. Thus once $p_n = 0$ in our equilibrium, every subsequent entrant enters. But we would also have an equilibrium if we set $p_{n-1} = b^{n-1}$ after such a defection from the equilibrium, and then entrant $n - 1$ would randomize between entering and staying out. Note well, this concerns the behavior of entrant $n - 1$ only off the equilibrium path, but in terms of strategies it is a different equilibrium. We cannot hope to have uniqueness off the equilibrium path.

(d) Finally, there is a bit of freedom in defining equilibria along the equilibrium path when $\delta = b^n$ for some $n \leqslant N$: The behavior of entrant n in this case need not conform to the strategy above—any randomization will work.

Except for these four problems, we do get uniqueness:

PROPOSITION 2. *If $\delta \neq b^n$ for $n \leqslant N$, then every sequential equilibrium with plausible beliefs has on-the-equilibrium-path strategies as described previously. Thus every sequential equilibrium with plausible beliefs has the value functions given above.*

The proof is by induction and is left to the reader. We simply note that in carrying out the induction one establishes the following:

(a) The value function of the strong monopolist (in equilibrium) will be a nondecreasing function of p_n, and the strong monopolist will therefore fight any entry.

(b) The value function of the weak monopolist will be a nondecreasing function of p_n and will be given by the formula in the proof of Proposition 1 for $\delta \neq b^n$, $m \leqslant n$.

(c) If there is entry at stage n and if the monopolist fights this entry, then entrant $n - 1$ must stay out with probability exactly $1/a$.

By going through this proof, the reader will see the intuition behind this equilibrium, which we will try to summarize here. As long as beliefs are plausible, the strong monopolist will always fight entry. Thus any acquiescence is conclusive proof that the monopolist is weak. Moreover, such evidence once given must result in zero payoff for the monopolist—the argument of Selten that we have given in Section 1 applies (with minor modifications). If entrant n is to enter, then it must be that there is probability $1 - b$ (at least) that the monopolist will acquiesce, which requires that the weak monopolist is randomizing or simply acquiescing. This also requires that $p_n \leqslant b$, and, from Bayes' rule, that *if* this entry is met by fighting, then $p_{n-1} \geqslant p_n/b$. Thus if we begin with $\delta > b^m$, there can be at most m entrants who have a positive probability of entering. As N gets large, then, the value to either monopolist must asymptote to aN, and, for $N > 2m$, the weak monopolist would always wish to fight entry. (In fact, in the equilibrium in turns out that this is true for $N \geqslant m$.)

We close this section by listing several extensions and embellishments of the basic model.

(A) We have dealt above with the case $a > 1$. If $0 < a \leqslant 1$, then the same basic structure for the equilibrium emerges, in that for sufficiently large n, entrants do not enter because the monopolist will fight with probability one. The play near the end of the game is more complicated however. In particular, one cannot obtain an equilibrium where entrant n's strategy depends only on p_n—it depends instead on p_n and the history of play in the last j rounds, where j is the smallest integer such that $ja > 1$.

(B) If the monopolist discounts its payoffs by a factor ρ per period, the following results. If $\rho > 1/a$, then the equilibrium is *precisely* as above except that the randomizing probabilities of the entrants must change. If $\rho \leqslant 1/(a + 1)$, then the equilibrium is quite different—the weak monopolist acquiesces at the first entry, so entrants enter if $p_n < b$ and stay out if $p_n > b$. For ρ such that $1/(a + 1) < \rho \leqslant 1/a$, the basic character of the equilibrium is just as in the case of $\rho > 1/a$—for large enough n entrants stay out because the monopolist will fight any entry. But the equilibrium is complicated for small n, resembling the equilibrium in the undiscounted case where $a < 1$.

(C) Suppose that instead of the sequential game depicted in Fig. 1, each stage consists of a two-by-two simultaneous move game, Table I, where the payoffs with probability $1 - \delta$ are shown in (a) and the payoffs with probability δ are shown in (b). (We assume $0 < b < 1$ and $a > 1$.) Otherwise the structure of the game is the same: One of these two bimatrices is chosen at the outset, according to the probabilities given. One monopolist plays against N entrants in sequence. The monopolist knows which bimatrix was chosen; the entrants do not.

For $\delta = 0$, the argument of Selten is easy adapted to show that the *unique* equilibrium (perfect or not) has row 2, column 1 played in each stage. This is because row 2 is strongly dominant in the stage game. But for $\delta > 0$ we get an equilibrium almost identical to the one discussed above: For stages n such that $b^n < \delta$, the monopolist plays row 1 regardless of which bimatrix was selected, and the entrant responds with column 2. (The play of the game is a bit different near the end of the game.) So we see that a little incomplete

TABLE I

		entrant				entrant	
		column 1	column 2			column 1	column 2
monopolist	row 1	-1, b-1	a-1, 0	monopolist	row 1	0, b-1	a, 0
	row 2	0, b	a, 0		row 2	-1, b	a-1, 0

(a)   (b)

information can not only make an imperfect equilibrium perfect (more accurately, sequential)—it can also make as part of a sequential equilibrium the play of an action that with very high probability is *strongly dominated* in the stage game.

(D) Paul Milgrom has pointed out to us that similar equilibria can be found even when every player in the game knows the payoffs of the monopolist, as long as this knowledge is not *common knowledge*. That is suppose all the entrants know the monopolist's payoffs, but they are not certain whether their fellow entrants have this information. Then (with the proper precise specification) they fear that the weak monopolist will fight (for large *n*), in order to maintain its reputation among the other entrants. This being so, the entrant will not enter. And the monopolist, even if it knows that all the entrants know that it is weak, may be willing to fight entry early on, in order to help "convince" subsequent entrants that it (the monopolist) is not sure that the entrants know this. (Precise arguments of this form are found in Milgrom and Roberts [13].) Selten's argument requires that it is common knowledge that the monopolist is weak. In real-life contexts this is a very strong assumption, and weakening it ever so slightly (more slightly than we have done above) can give life to the "reputation" effect.

(E) We have dealt exclusively with the case of a single monopolist playing against *N* different entrants. Another interesting case is where a single monopolist plays *N* times against a single entrant. For the game we have analyzed in this section, this turns out to have no effect on the equilibrium. (We leave this to the reader to verify.) But as we shall see in the next section, this is due (at least in part) to the fact that there is no uncertainty about the payoffs of the entrants.

4. Two-Sided Uncertainty

In this section we consider what happens when the monopolist is unsure about the payoffs of the entrants. The most interesting formulation of this problem is where a single monopolist plays the stage game of Fig. 1 a total of *N* times against a single opponent. The payoff to each player is the sum of the player's payoffs in each stage. The monopolist's payoffs are as in Fig. 1 or Fig. 2, with probabilities $1 - \delta$ and δ, respectively. The entrant's payoffs are as in Fig. 1, for some *b* such that $0 < b < 1$ with probability $1 - \gamma$ and for some other $b > 1$ with probability γ. Each player knows its own payoffs at the start of the game, and each is unsure of the payoffs of its opponent. The payoffs are statistically independent.

Continuing the terminology of Section 3, we shall refer to the weak entrant as the entrant if its payoffs satisfy $0 < b < 1$, and the strong entrant if its payoffs satisfy $b > 1$.

Note that the strong entrant does better to enter than to stay out in any stage, even if the monopolist is sure to fight. Because it seems plausible that entry will not decrease the probability that the monopolist will acquiesce subsequently, we look for equilibria where the strong entrant always enters. Thus any failure to enter brands the entrant as weak, at which point we are back to the situation of Section 3. (Recall that it did not matter there whether there was a single entrant or N entrants.) Similarly, we look for an equilibrium where the strong monopolist always fights. Thus any failure to fight brands the monopolist as weak, following which the entrant always enters and the monopolist always acquiesces. We search, then, for an equilibrium of the following sort: The strong entrant always enters. The strong monopolist always fights. The weak entrant chooses a strategy that is a mixture of "stopping rules": A stopping rule gives the date at which the entrant will "give in" and not enter if the monopolist has not acquiesced yet. (The entrant may later re-enter, as we will then follow the equilibrium of Section 3.) The weak monopolist will also mix among stopping rules: A stopping rule for the monopolist gives the date at which the monopolist will first acquiesce if the entrant has not retreated first. If one side or the other gives in, we move to either the situation of Section 3 or to where entry-acquiescence follows until the game ends.

Giving a complete specification of the equilibrium that is obtained is extraordinarily tedious, because it is based on some very involved recursions. Still, we can give a rough description of what happens. At any stage n the previous play of the game is summarized into two statistics: p_n, the probability assessed by the entrant that the monopolist is strong; q_n, the probability assessed by the monopolist that the entrant is strong. (The game begins with $p_N = \delta$ and $q_N = \gamma$.) Thus the "state space" of the game at stage n is the unit square, as depicted in Fig. 4. The edge $q_n = 0$ is the subject of

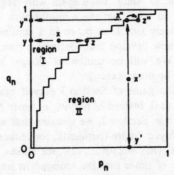

FIG. 4. State space of the game at stage n.

Section 3. The edge $p_n = 0$ can be analyzed using the argument of Selten with the conclusion: The entrant always enters, and the weak monopolist always acquiesces.

The square is divided into two regions by a curve, as shown. If (p_n, q_n) lies in region I, say at the point x, then the entrant enters regardless of its payoffs, and the weak monopolist randomizes. If the weak monopolist acquiesces, the game evolves to the point y (actually, to this point in the *next* square—the square for stage $n - 1$). If it fights, or if it is strong and hence fights, the entrant uses Bayes' rule to compute p_{n-1}, landing at the point z on the curve, and just *beyond* the curve in region II of the next square. If (p_n, q_n) lies in region II, say at x', then the weak entrant randomizes. If it stays out, the equilibrium of Section 3 ensues—and the next stage begins a the point y'. If it enters (or if it is strong and therefore enters), the monopolist recomputes the probability that it is strong, landing at the point x'' along the curve. Then the monopolist randomizes (if weak), and the game evolves to y'' or to z''. Both z and z'' are in region II of the next square, so the next round begins with randomization by the weak entrant, and so on.

Except for the very start of the game, when $p_N = \delta$ and $q_n = \gamma$, most of the play takes place along the curve. (Actually, the curve shifts slightly as n changes.) So we see an initial jump to the curve (or to one of the two edges), followed by a slow climb up the curve with ever present the chance that a jump to one of the edges will occur. With probability one, a weak player will eventually give in, so we either jump to an edge eventually or, if both players are strong, we reach the point $p_0 = q_0 = 1$. This is a game of "chicken," where once begun, each side (if weak) randomizes between a small probability of giving in and a large probability of daring the other side for one more round. The relative size of these probabilities is required by the conditions of an equilibrium: Daring once more costs something this round, but giving in is costly for the rest of the game. So it must be that daring once more does not give either player a substantial chance of *immediate* gain; the opponent must be about to "dare" once again with large probability.

While it is tedious to give the exact equilibrium in the discrete time formulation, it is relatively simple to do so in a continuous time version of the game. So we shall now develop that continuous-time version. (We should forewarn the reader: We will be somewhat sloppy in what follows. But everything we say can be made exact.)

To begin, consider the game of Section 3 played against a single entrant over the time period N to 0. Instead of playing at times $N, N - 1, ..., 1$, for the stakes (per stage) given in Section 3, we imagine that an integer K is given, and that the game is played "more frequently, for reduced stakes," with play at times $N, (KN - 1)/K, (KN - 2)/K, ..., 1/K$, for stakes $1/K$ times the stakes given. It is the *number* of times that the monopolist has left to demonstrate its "toughness" that is decisive in Section 3, so we find that if $k(\delta) = n$, the entrant stays out (and the monopolist would surely fight) at all times $t > n/K$. As K goes to infinity, we see that the entrant stays out until "the very last instant" of time.

With this limiting result as motivation, we now consider the "continuous-time" version of the above game, played over a time interval T to 0. At each time $t \in [T, 0]$, the entrant chooses whether to enter or to stay out, and the monopolist chooses whether to fight entry or to acquiesce. A realization of the entrant's strategy is formalized as a (measurable) function $e: [T, 0] \to \{0, 1\}$, where $e(t) = 1$ means that the entrant is entering at date t. A realization of the monopolist's strategy is formalized as a function $f: [T, 0] \to \{0, 1\}$, where $f(t) = 1$ means that the monopolist is fighting at date t. (We have a "closed-loop" game, so pure strategies would be a pair of functions e and f where $e(t)$ is $F((e(s), f(s)), s < t)$-measurable, and $f(t)$ is $F(f(s), s < t; e(s), s \leqslant t)$-measurable. We shall not try to be more precise about this here; instead we trust the reader's ability to see how to formalize what follows.) Given realizations e and f, payoffs to each side are determined by measuring the lengths of times during which there is not entry ($e(t) = 0$), during which entry is fought ($e(t) = 1$, $f(t) = 1$), and during which there is acquiescence to entry ($e(t) = 1$, $f(t) = 0$), and assigning payoffs accordingly. For example, if λ denotes Lebesgue measure, then the weak monopolist's payoff is

$$\lambda\{e(t) = 0\} \cdot a - \lambda\{e(t) = 1, f(t) = 1\}.$$

In this game, an equilibrium calls for the entrant to stay out as long as the monopolist does not acquiesce and to always enter after any acquiescence is observed; for the strong monopolist to fight any entry; and for the weak monopolist to fight as long as it has not acquiesced yet and to acquiesce forever after an acquiescence. The reader can easily verify that this is an equilibrium. Moreover, if by some "mistake" the entrant entered before time 0, the weak monopolist would want to fight: By acquiescing it saves an "instantaneous" one unit, but then it invites entry for the remainder of the game—a substantial loss that outweighs the instantaneous savings.

(The reader is entitled to be somewhat skeptical about this. By moving to a continuous-time formulation, we have obtained some of the features of the supergame (infinitely repeated) formulation. For example, the equilibrium above is "perfect" even if $\delta = 0$, just as in the supergame with $\delta = 0$. But in the case $\delta = 0$, this equilibrium is not the limit of discrete-but-more-rapid equilibrium play. What justifies this particular equilibrium in the case $\delta > 0$ is that it is the limit of discrete equilibria. We shall return to this point after we discuss the case of two-sided uncertainty.)

Now consider the continuous-time game where there is uncertainty on both sides. The formulation is as above, but now there is uncertainty (at the outset) about the entrant's payoffs as a function of the realizations of e and f.

We are looking for an equilibrium with the following characteristics: (1) The strong monopolist always fights. (2) The strong entrant always enters. (3) By virtue of (1), if the monopolist ever declines to fight an entry, it is revealed as weak. Thereafter, the entrant always enters and the weak monopolist always acquiesces. (4) By virtue of (2), if the entrant ever fails to enter it is revealed as weak. Assuming that the monopolist has not previously been revealed as weak, the game proceeds as above, with the weak entrant staying out until the end and the monopolist always ready to fight.

Just as in the discrete time formulation, an equilibrium with these features can be recast as an equilibrium in "stopping rules" for the weak entrant and monopolist—each choosing the date at which it will "give in" if its opponent has not given in yet. If the entrant gives in first (at date t), then regime (4) above takes effect, with the weak monopolist obtaining at for the rest of the game, and the weak entrant receiving 0. If the monopolist gives in first at t, regime (3) ensues, with the weak entrant receiving bt and the weak monopolist receiving 0. Until one side or the other gives in, the weak monopolist receives -1 per unit of time, and the weak entrant receives $b-1$ per unit of time. The equilibrium condition is that each player's stopping time should be optimal given the probability distribution of the other's, and given the assumption that the other player, if strong, will never give in. This game is very similar to the "war of attrition" game; cf. Riley [16] and Milgrom and Weber [14]. It is formally equivalent to a two-person competitive auction, where the stopping times are reinterpreted as bids. This observation will be especially useful later when we discuss the connection between this continuous-time formulation and the discrete-time formulation of the game. (We are indebted to Paul Milgrom for acquainting us with the "war of attrition" and for pointing out the relevance of his work with Weber.)

It is easiest and most illustrative to present the equilibrium using a diagram similar to Fig. 4. In Fig. 5 we have the "state space" of this game—the unit square, interpreted exactly as in Fig. 4. The bottom boundary is where the entrant is known to be weak. Along this boundary (excluding the left hand endpoint) the weak monopolist's payoff function (at date t) is $v_t(p, 0) = at$ and the weak entrant's is $u_t(p, 0) = 0$. The left hand boundary is where the monopolist is known to be weak—here (including the bottom endpoint) $v_t(0, q) = 0$ and $u_t(0, q) = bt$.

The nature of the equilibrium is just as in the discrete case: The state space is divided into two regions by a curve $f(p, q) = 0$ that passes through the points $(0, 0)$ and $(1, 1)$. If the initial data of the game place us in region I, then the game begins with the entrant entering for sure and the monopolist (if weak) randomizing between fighting and immediate capitulation. This randomization is such that if the monopolist does fight at time T, the entrant revises its assessment that the monopolist is strong so as

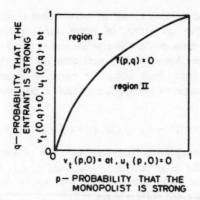

FIG. 5.   State space of the continuous-time game.

to go to the curve $f(p, q) = 0$. From region II it is the (weak) entrant that randomizes between immediate capitulation and entry—if it does enter, the monopolist revises its assessment that the entrant is strong up to a point where the curve $f(p, q)$ is reached. Thereafter, the weak monopolist and weak entrant randomize "continuously" between keeping up the fight and capitulating—this is done in a fashion so that as long as they continue to fight, the Bayesian reassessments of each side that the other is strong causes (p_t, q_t) to slide up along the curve toward $(1, 1)$. (Of course, if one side or the other capitulates, transition is made to the appropriate boundary.) There is a time $T^0 > 0$ such that by this time, one side or the other (if weak) has given in with probability one—if both sides are strong, at this time the point $(1, 1)$ has been reached, and we remain there until time $t = 0$.

The difference between this equilibrium and the one for the discrete time game (and the reason that this one is so much easier to compute) is that the curve $f(p, q) = 0$ does not change with t in the continuous-time case. This is so because in the continuous-time version of the game, a game of duration $T/2$ is strategically equivalent to a game of duration T, so long as the priors (δ, γ) are the same. All that changes is that everything takes place twice as rapidly—we could as well think of the game taking place at the same speed but for half the stakes. The values are half as large, but nothing else changes.

We now present a heuristic derivation of the equilibrium, assuming that it has the form outlined above. Note first that along the curve the value functions for each side must be identically zero. This is so because (by hypothesis) both sides are randomizing continuously, and one outcome of these randomizations transfers them to points (the lower boundary for the entrant and the left-hand boundary for the monopolist) where the value function is zero. Let $\pi_t(p_t, q_t)$ and $\rho_t(p_t, q_t)$ be the hazard rate functions associated with the weak monopolist's and entrant's randomizations at time t

with posteriors p_t and q_t lying along the curve. That is, in the time interval $(t, t - h)$ there is (up to terms of order $o(h)$) probability $(1 - p_t) \cdot \pi_t(p_t, q_t) \cdot h$ that the monopolist will give in, and $(1 - q_t) \cdot \rho_t(p_t, q_t) \cdot h$ that the entrant will give in. Assuming sufficient continuity, if the value functions are to be constant (and zero) along the curve, it is necessary that the expected change in value to the weak monopolist be zero. Up to terms of order $o(h)$, this is

$$-h + [(1 - q_t) \cdot \rho_t(p_t, q_t) \cdot h][at] = o(h).$$

That is, the weak monopolist's immediate cost $-h$ of keeping up the bluff should be offset by the small chance $(1 - q_t) \cdot \rho_t(p_t, q_t) \cdot h$ that the entrant will give in times the large gain at that will accrue in this event. The analogous argument for the entrant gives

$$(b - 1)h + (1 - p_t) \cdot \pi_t(p_t, q_t) \cdot hbt = o(h).$$

Dividing by h and passing to the limit, we get

$$\rho_t(p_t, q_t) = 1/(at(1 - q_t)) \quad \text{and} \quad \pi_t(p_t, q_t) = (1 - b)/(bt(1 - p_t)).$$

Consider next the evolution of the posteriors p_t and q_t. The probability table that the monopolist would construct at date t for the joint probability distribution that the entrant is weak or not and will give in or not in the interval $(t, t - h)$ is given in Table II (up to terms of order $o(h)$). Thus the conditional probability that the entrant is strong, conditional on not giving in over the interval $(t, t - h)$, is

$$q_{t-h} = q_t/[1 - (1 - q_t)\rho_t(p_t, q_t)h].$$

Thus, ignoring terms of order $O(h)$,

$$(q_t - q_{t-h})/h = q_t(1 - q_t)\rho_t(p_t, q_t).$$

Passing to the limit, this gives $\dot{q}_t = (q_t - q_t^2)\rho_t(p_t, q_t) = q_t/(at)$. Similarly $\dot{p}_t = p_t(1 - b)/(bt)$. Thus along the curve we must have

$$dq_t/dp_t = (q_t b)/((1 - b)\, ap_t).$$

TABLE II

	weak	strong	
give in	$(1 - q_t)\rho_t(p_t, q_t)h$	0	$(1 - q_t)\rho_t(p_t, q_t)h$
not	$(1 - q_t)(1 - \rho_t(p_t, q_t)h)$	q_t	$1 - (1 - q_t)\rho_t(p_t, q_t)h$
	$(1 - q_t)$	q_t	

This is independent of t, and it is easily integrated to give $q_t = k(p_t)^c$ where k is a constant of integration and $c = b/((1-b)a)$. To ensure that $(1, 1)$ is on the curve, we must have $k = 1$. Therefore the curve is given by

$$f(p, q) \equiv q^{(1-b)/b} - p^{1/a} = 0.$$

(Note well the normalization of k so that $(1, 1)$ is on the curve. This will be important later on.)

We can solve similarly for q_t and p_t. Integrating $\dot{q}_t = q_t/(at)$ yields $q_t = k't^{-1/a}$. Analogously, $p_t = k''t^{-(1-b)/b}$. The constants k' and k'' are determined by the initial conditions. Suppose, for example, that we initially have a prior (δ, γ) that lies in region II. Then the initial randomization is by the weak entrant and yields posterior $q_T = \delta^c$ if the entrant does enter. Solving for k' yields $k' = \delta^c T^{1/a}$. Solving for k'' yields $k'' = \delta T^{(1-b)/b}$. Thus

$$p_t = \delta(T/t)^{(1-b)/b} \quad \text{and} \quad q_t = \delta^c(T/t)^{1/a}.$$

Note that these yield $p_t = 1$ and $q_t = 1$ for $t = T\delta^{ac} = T\delta^{b/(1-b)}$. (Of course, both p_t and q_t hit one simultaneously as the curve has been normalized to pass through $(1, 1)$.) The point to note here is that in this equilibrium, the posterior $(1, 1)$ will be reached at a time T° strictly between T and 0 (unless $\delta = 0$ or 1) so long as neither player gives in previously. But of course, the posterior $(1, 1)$ can only be reached if with probability one both of the weak players would have given in. So, according to this equilibrium, if the two players are both strong, they will learn this before the game terminates. Put another way, the date T° previously referred to is $\delta^{b/(1-b)}T$ (for (δ, γ) in region II). The formulae change somewhat for (δ, γ) in region I, but the qualitative conclusions are the same.

Does this heuristic derivation hold up? That is, do we really have an equilibrium? There are two things to worry about. First, in several places the heuristic arguments that we give depend somewhat on sufficient regularity of the functions π_t and ρ_t. The reader can make these arguments rigorous for the functions that we derived. Second (and more substantially), the necessary conditions that were developed for π_t and ρ_t were necessary for the value functions to be *constant* along the curve. To have an equilibrium we require somewhat more: The value functions must be identically *zero* along this curve. This is where the normalization of the curve comes in: At the point $(1, 1)$, the value functions are clearly zero for each weak player, as each is certain that the other is strong. Put another way, suppose (once the curve is reached) that one side or the other is weak and decides *not* to randomize but simply to wait out its opponent. The conditions that gave us π_t and ρ_t ensure that the change in expected value is zero as this goes on. (For the technically minded, apply Dynkin's formula to the appropriate generalized Poisson process.) And at date T°, if nothing has happened the player that is waiting *knows* that its opponent is strong—it should immediately give in for a value of zero. Thus the value all along the curve is zero. This, with a little careful argument, suffices to show that we really do have an equilibrium.

Two final comments about this equilibrium seem in order. First, the value functions to each (weak) player are easily computed. In region II, they are $u_T(\delta, \gamma) = 0$ and $v_T(\delta, \gamma) = [(\delta^c - \gamma)/\delta^c] aT$; in region I, they are $u_T(\delta, \gamma) = [(\gamma^{1/c} - \delta)/\gamma^{1/c}] bT$ and $v_T(\delta, \gamma) = 0$. That is, they are simple linear interpolates of the value of zero along the curve and the values along the bottom boundary in region II and the left-hand boundary in region I.

Second, we noted earlier that the continuous-time formulation can introduce equilibria that are not limits of the equilibria for discrete-time models. We should like to know that the continuous-time equilibrium just presented is indeed the limit of the discrete-time equilibrium with which we began this section. We have not checked all the details, but we are quite sure that this is so. To see this, recall that the discrete time game can be posed as an optimal stopping problem where the entrant is limited to stopping at, say, discrete times $T, (TK - 1)/K,..., 1/K$ and the monopolist is limited to stopping at times (say) $T - 1/(2K), (TK - 3/2)/K,..., 1/(2K)$. The continuous-time problem is one where stopping at any time $t \in [T, 0]$ is possible. It is easy to move from the discrete-to-continuous-time versions of the problem when there is one-sided uncertainty, so we know that we have convergence of the value of "stopping" at particular times. As K goes to infinity, the sets of available strategies also converge, and the methods of Milgrom and Weber [14] apply to show convergence of the equilibria of the discrete games to the continuous-time version. (Indeed, Paul Milgrom has shown us how, by viewing the continuous-time game as a game in distributional strategies, it is simple to derive the equilibrium given above.)

Before concluding this section, we also note that this gives just one sort of formulation of the problem with two-sided uncertainty. We might consider what happens when a single monopolist plays against a succession of different entrants (each of whom plays the game once), where the monopolist is uncertain of the entrants' payoffs. In such a game we would have to specify the way in which the entrants' payoffs are related—they might all be identical (perfectly correlated, from the point of view of the monopolist), or they might be independently and identically distributed, or something between these two extremes. Both of these extreme cases are analyzed in detail in Kreps and Wilson [8]. The case of identical entrants gives the most interesting comparison with the model analyzed above: With identical entrants who only play the game once, the first entrant nearly always "tells the truth" by refusing to enter if weak, and the weak monopolist will with substantial probability fight the first few entries, just to keep the weak entrants "honest." What this illustrates is that the game of "chicken" that we see above requires *both* two-sided uncertainty *and* that each side has a stake in maintaining its reputation. When it is only one side that will participate in many stages, the other has little motivation to dissemble and will not fight too hard to attain/maintain its reputation. (Another interesting formulation of the problem is where there is a population of entrants and a population of monopolists, and in each round there is a random assignment of one monopolist to one entrant, in the manner of Rosenthal [18] and Rosenthal and Landau [19]. We have done no analysis of this formulation.)

5. DISCUSSION

We have presented these simple examples to illustrate formally the power of "reputation" in finitely repeated games. That reputation is powerful in reality is very well appreciated: In the context of Industrial Organization, recall the quotation from Scherer in Section 1. Consider the importance of reputation in contract and labor negotiations; in a firm's employment practices; in a firm's "good name" for its product; in the maintenance of a cartel (or in the prisoners' dilemma game); in international diplomacy. To each of these contexts, our analytical structure can be applied to yield the conclusions: If the situation is repeated, so that it is worthwhile to maintain or acquire a reputation, and if there is some uncertainty about the motivations of one or more of the players, then that uncertainty can substantially affect the play of the game. There need not be much uncertainty for this to happen. The power of the reputation effect depends on the nature of one's opponents; notably on whether they also seek to acquire a reputation.

Phenomena that bear the interpretation of "reputation" are not entirely new to the literature of formal game theory. They are implicit in much of the literature on super-games, where the stage game is repeated infinitely often, or where there is always high enough probability of at least one more repetition (Rubinstein [20] is a representative citation). Indeed, Dybvig and Spatt [6] make explicit use of the reputation interpretation in a super-game context. What is new in this paper (and in Milgrom and Roberts [13]) is the observation that with a very little imperfect information, these effects come alive in finitely repeated games. Comparing the two approaches is difficult, but it is worth noting that in the models reported here, the problem of multiplicity of equilibria that plagues the super-game literature is substantially alleviated. Also, we believe that we have interesting models of the sorts of "wars" that might go on between players to see which equilibrium will ensue. But we are far from ready to make a very informed comparison of the two approaches—at this point, we can only claim that this seems to be an interesting alternative way to produce reputation effects.

A point made briefly in Section 3 is worth repeating here. To keep matters simple, we posited the simplest type of uncertainty: Players are uncertain about the payoffs of their fellows. But it does nearly as well if there is no uncertainty about players' payoffs, but there is uncertainty about whether this is so. In the parlance of game theory, for these effects to disappear, payoffs must be common knowledge. (Milgrom and Roberts [13] present formal models to back up this contention.) This is a very strong assumption for any real-life application.

The reader may object that in order to obtain the reputation effect, we have loaded the deck. That is, we have a model where reputation is easily shattered, making it all the more valuable; there are at most two types of each player; and each player has only two possible actions. To the first of these criticisms we plead guilty: The power of reputation seems to be positively related to its fragility. As for the second, the models of Milgrom and Roberts [13] have continua of types of monopolists, so this does not seem crucial to our conclusions. And to the third, we do admit that this has made it easy for us to get a "pooling equilibrium" (to borrow a term from the insurance literature), where one type successfully mimics another. The analysis of Milgrom and Roberts [12] shows that with a continuum of actions, one can also get screening equilibria in these sorts of models. But this is not necessary: Crawford and Sobel [3] investigate a class of models with a continua of actions where some pooling is necessary in any equilibrium. The assumption of only two actions makes things easier for us, but we doubt that it is crucial.

What is evident from our simple examples is that a very little uncertainty "destabilizes" game-theoretic analysis in games with a fairly large number of stages. The reader may suspect that something more is true: By cleverly choosing the nature of that small uncertainty (precisely—its support), one can get out of a game-theoretic analysis whatever one wishes. We have no formal proposition of this sort to present at this time, but we certainly share these suspicions. If this is so, then the game-theoretic analysis of this type of game comes down eventually to how one picks the initial incomplete information. And nothing in the *theory* of games will help one to do this.

This reinforces a point made by Rosenthal [17]. Rosenthal investigates the original chain-store game and makes the point with which we began: The paradoxical result in Selten's analysis is due to the complete and perfect information formulation that Selten uses. In a more realistic formulation of the game, the intuitive outcome will be predicted by the game-theoretic analysis. Rosenthal does not provide this analysis, despairing of the analyst's ability to solve an adequate formulation. Instead, he suggests an analysis using the paradigm of Decision Analysis, where one tries to assess *directly* how the entrants will respond to early round fighting by the monopolist. Such an analysis can certainly lead to the intuitive outcome, as shown by Macgregor [11]. But, as Rosenthal notes, the weakness in this approach is the *ad hoc* assessment of entrants' behavior. We have carried out a game-theoretic analysis of *one* very simple incomplete information formulation. We therefore have avoided *ad hoc* assumptions about the entrants' behavior. But we have made *ad hoc* assumptions about their information, and we have found that small changes in those assumptions greatly influence the play of the game. So at some level, analysis of this sort of situation may require *ad hoc* assumptions.

We have presented models in this paper that demonstrate the reputation effect as simply and as powerfully as possible. In order to do this, we have not tried to model realistic settings from Industrial Organization or some other economic context. (Milgrom and Roberts [13] rectify this deficiency: They concentrate somewhat more on the application of these ideas.) To illustrate how these ideas might be applied, we close with two examples.

The first concerns the problem of entry deterrence, especially the papers of Spence [26] and Dixit [4, 5]. These papers take the basic framework of Bain [1] and Sylos [27] and ask: What can the monopolist do prior to the entrant's decision point to make predation optimal in the short run? (The answers they give include such things as expanded capacity, sales networks, etc.) The relevance of this question is that the *threat* of predation is only credible if predation is *ex post* the optimal response, so the monopolist must make it so in order to forestall entry. What our model suggests (and what can be demonstrated formally) is that in repeated play situations, the actions taken by the monopolist need not make predation actually ex post optimal—what they must do is to make predation *possible* and, perhaps, increase the probability assessed by the entrants that it is *ex post* optimal. If deterrence is the objective, the appearance and not the reality of *ex post* optimal predation may be what is important.

The second context is that of a monopolist producer of a durable capital good where, for whatever reason, the monopolist is unable to maintain a rental market but must sell outright his product. In a multiperiod setting, where the monopolist is assumed to be sequentially optimizing, this can severely diminish the monopolist's market power. (See Bulow [2] and Stokey [25].) Supposing the monopolist produces subject to a capacity constraint, the monopolist is often *better off* with a tighter constraint. This is because the constraint prevents the monopolist from "over-producing." Then, if that constraint is the matter of private information for the monopolist, a monopolist with a loose constraint can successfully (in an equilibrium) masquerade as having a more stringent constraint, thereby recouping some of his lost market power. In essence, as the number of periods goes to infinity (as one comes closer to a continuous-time formulation), the monopolist can successfully attain the reputation of a "low capacity" producer even if his capacity is (with probability approaching one) high. Moorthy [15] presents an example along these lines.

278   KREPS AND WILSON

ACKNOWLEDGMENTS

The authors express their gratitude to John Harsanyi, Mary Macgregor, Paul Milgrom, John Roberts, Robert Rosenthal, Reinhart Selten, Sylvain Sorin and many other colleagues for their helpful comments and criticisms. This research has been supported in part by National Science Foundation Grants SOC77-07741-A01, SOC75-21820-A01, SOC77-0600-A01 and SES80-06407 to the Institute for Mathematical Studies in the Social Sciences and the Graduate School of Business, Stanford University.

REFERENCES

1. J. S. BAIN, "Barriers to New Competition," Harvard Univ. Press, Cambridge, Mass., 1956.
2. J. BULOW, Durable goods monopolists, Stanford Graduate School of Business, mimeo, 1979; *J. Pol. Econ.*, in press.
3. V. CRAWFORD AND J. SOBEL, Stategic information transmission, University of California at San Diego, mimeo, 1981.
4. A. DIXIT, A model of duopoly suggesting a theory of entry barriers, *Bell J. Econ.* 10 (1979), 20–32.
5. A. DIXIT, The role of investment in entry-deterence, *Econ. J.* 90 (1980), 95–106.
6. P. DYBVIG AND C. SPATT, Does it pay to maintain a reputation, Financial Center Memorandum No. 32, Princeton University, 1980.
7. J. HARSANYI, Games with incomplete information played by Bayesian players, Parts I, II. and III, *Manag. Sci.* 14 (1967–1968), 159–182, 320–334, 486–502.
8. D. KREPS AND R. WILSON, "On the Chain-Store Paradox and Predation: Reputation for Toughness," Stanford University Graduate School of Business Research Paper No. 551, 1981.
9. D. KREPS AND R. WILSON, Sequential equilibria, *Econometrica* 50 (1982).
10. H. KUHN, Extensive games and the problem of information, *in* "Contributions to the Theory of Games, Vol. 2" (H. Kuhn and A. Tucker, Eds.), pp. 193–216, Princeton Univ. Press, Princeton, N.J., 1953.
11. M. MACGREGOR, A resolution of the chain-store paradox, University of California at Berkeley, mimeo, 1979.
12. P. MILGROM AND J. ROBERTS, "Limit Pricing and Entry under Incomplete Information: An Equilibrium Analysis," *Econometrica* 50 (1982), 443–460.
13. P. MILGROM AND J. ROBERTS, Predation, reputation, and entry deterrence, *J. Econ. Theory* 27 (1982), 280–312.
14. P. MILGROM AND R. WEBER, Distributional strategies for games with incomplete information, Northwestern University Graduate School of Management, mimeo, 1980.
15. S. MOORTHY, The Pablo Picasso problem, Stanford University Graduate School of Business, mimeo, 1980.
16. J. RILEY, Strong evolutionary equilibria and the war of attrition, *J. Theoret. Biol.* 82 (1980).
17. R. W. ROSENTHAL, Games of perfect information, predatory pricing and the chain-store paradox, *J. Econ. Theory* 25 (1981), 92–100.
18. R. W. ROSENTHAL, Sequences of games with varying opponents, *Econometrica* 47 (1979), 1353–1366.
19. R. W. ROSENTHAL AND H. J. LANDAU, A game-theoretic analysis of bargaining with reputations, Bell Telephone Laboratories, mimeo, 1979.

20. A. RUBINSTEIN, Strong perfect equilibrium in supergames, *Internat. J. Game Theory* 9 (1979), 1–12.

21. F. SCHERER, "Industrial Market Structure and Economic Performance," 2nd ed., Rand McNally College Publishing Company, Chicago, 1980.

22. R. SELTEN, Spieltheoretische behandlung eines oligopolmodells mit nachfragetragheit, *Z. Staatswissenschaft* 121 (1965).

23. R. SELTEN, Reexamination of the perfectness concept for equilibrium points in extensive games, *Internat. J. Game Theory* 4 (1975), 25–55.

24. R. SELTEN, The chain-store paradox, *Theory and Decision* 9 (1978), 127–159.

25. N. STOKEY, Self-fulfilling expectations, rational expectations, and durable goods pricing, Northwestern University, mimeo, 1979.

26. A. M. SPENCE, Entry, capacity, investment and oligopolistic pricing, *Bell J. Econ.* 8 (1977), 534–544.

27. P. SYLOS-LABINI, "Oligopoly and Technical Progress," trans. E. Henderson, Harvard Univ. Press, Cambridge, Mass., 1962.

[21]

The Fat-Cat Effect, The Puppy-Dog Ploy, and the Lean and Hungry Look

By DREW FUDENBERG AND JEAN TIROLE*

Let me have about me men that are
fat.... *Julius Caesar*, Act 1, Sc. 2

The idea that strategic considerations may
provide firms an incentive to "overinvest" in
"capital" to deter the entry or expansion of
rivals is by now well understood. However,
in some circumstances, increased investment
may be a strategic handicap, because it may
reduce the incentive to respond aggressively
to competitors. In such cases, firms may instead choose to maintain a "lean and hungry
look," thus avoiding the "fat-cat effect." We
illustrate these effects with models of investment in advertising and in *R&D*. We also
provide a taxonomy of the factors which
tend to favor over- and underinvestment,
both to deter entry and to accommodate it.
Such a classification, of course, requires a
notion of what it means to overinvest; that
is, we must provide a benchmark for comparison. If entry is deterred, we use a
monopolist's investment as the basis for
comparison. For the case of entry accommodation, we compare the incumbent's investment to that in a "precommitment" or
"open-loop" equilibrium, in which the incumbent takes the entrant's actions as given
and does not try to influence them through
its choice of preentry investment. We flesh
out the taxonomy with several additional
examples.

Our advertising model was inspired by
Richard Schmalensee's (1982) paper, whose
results foreshadow ours. We provide an
example in which an established firm will

underinvest in advertising if it chooses to
deter entry, because by lowering its stock of
"goodwill" it establishes a credible threat to
cut prices in the event of entry. Conversely,
if the established firm chooses to allow entry,
it will advertise heavily and become a fat cat
in order to soften the entrant's pricing
behavior. Thus the strategic incentives for
investment depend on whether or not the
incumbent chooses to deter entry. This
contrasts with the previous work on strategic investment in cost-reducing machinery
(Michael Spence, 1977, 1979; Avinash Dixit,
1979; our 1983a article) and in "learning by
doing" (Spence, 1981; our 1983c article) in
which the strategic incentives always encourage the incumbent to overaccumulate. Our
R&D model builds on Jennifer Reinganum's
(1983) observation that the "Arrow effect"
(Kenneth Arrow, 1962) of an incumbent monopolist's reduced incentive to do *R&D* is
robust to the threat of entry so long as the
R&D technology is stochastic.

Our examples show that the key factors in
strategic investment are whether investment
makes the incumbent more or less "tough"
in the post-entry game, and how the entrant
reacts to tougher play by the incumbent.
These two factors are the basis of our taxonomy. Jeremy Bulow et al. (1983) have independently noted the importance of the entrant's reaction. Their paper overlaps a good
deal with ours.

I. Advertising and Goodwill

In our goodwill model, a customer can buy
from a firm only if he is aware of its existence. To inform consumers, firms place
ads in newspapers. An ad that is read informs the customer of the existence of the
firm and also gives the firm's price. In the
first period, only the incumbent is in the
market; in the second period the entrant may

*University of California, Berkeley, CA 94707, and
CERAS, Ecole Nationale des Ponts et Chaussées, 75007
Paris, France. Much of this paper is drawn from
our survey (1983b). We would like to thank John
Geanakoplos, Jennifer Reinganum, and Richard
Schmalensee for helpful conversations. Research sup-
port from the National Science Foundation is gratefully
acknowledged.

enter. The crucial assumption is that some of the customers who received an ad in the first period do not bother to read the ads in the second period, and therefore buy only from the incumbent. This captive market for the incumbent represents the incumbent's accumulation of goodwill. One could derive such captivity from a model in which rational consumers possess imperfect information about product quality, as in Schmalensee (1982), or from a model in which customers must sink firm-specific costs in learning how to consume the product.

There are two firms, an incumbent and an entrant, and a unit population of *ex ante* identical consumers. If a consumer is aware of both firms, and the incumbent charges x_1, and the entrant charges x_2, the consumer's demands for the two goods are $D^1(x_1, x_2)$ and $D^2(x_1, x_2)$, respectively. If a consumer is only aware of the incumbent (entrant), his demand is $D^1(x_1, \infty)$ and $(D^2(\infty, x_2))$. The (net of variable costs) revenue an informed consumer brings the incumbent is $R^1(x_1, x_2)$ or $R^1(x_1, \infty)$ depending on whether the consumer also knows about the entrant or not, and similarly for the entrant. We'll assume that the revenues are differentiable, quasi concave in own-prices, and they, as well as the marginal revenue, increase with the competitor's price (these are standard assumptions for price competition with differentiated goods).

To inform consumers, the firms put ads in the newspapers. An ad that is read makes the customer aware of the product and gives the price. The cost of reaching a fraction K of the population in the first period is $A(K)$, where $A(K)$ is convex for strictly positive levels of advertising, and $A(1) = \infty$.[1] There are two periods, $t = 1, 2$. In the first period, only the incumbent is in the market. It advertises K_1, charges the monopoly price, and makes profits $K^1 \cdot R^m$. In the second period the entrant may enter.

To further simplify, we assume that all active firms will choose to cover the remaining market in the second period at cost A_2.

[1] See Gerard Butters (1977), and Gene Grossman and Carl Shapiro (1984) for examples of advertising technologies.

Then assuming entry, the profits of the two firms, Π^1 and Π^2, can be written

$$(1) \quad \Pi^1 = \left[-A(K_1) + K_1 R^m \right]$$
$$+ \delta \left[K_1 R^1(x_1, \infty) \right.$$
$$+ (1 - K_1) R^1(x_1, x_2) - A_2 \right]$$
$$\Pi^2 = \delta \left[(1 - K_1) R^2(x_1, x_2) - A_2 \right],$$

where δ is the common discount factor.

In the second period, the firms simultaneously choose prices. Assuming that a Nash equilibrium for this second-stage game exists and is characterized by the first-order conditions, we have

$$(2) \quad K_1 R_1^1(x_1^*, \infty)$$
$$+ (1 - K_1) R_1^1(x_1^*, x_2^*) = 0;$$

$$(3) \quad R_2^2(x_1^*, x_2^*) = 0,$$

where $R_j^i \equiv \partial R^i(x_1, x_2) / \partial x_j$, and x_i^* is the equilibrium value of x_i as a function of K_1.

From equation (2), and the assumption that $R_{ij}^i > 0$, we see that

$$R_1^1(x_1^*, \infty) > 0 > R_1^1(x_1^*, x_2^*).$$

The incumbent would like to increase its price for its captive customers, and reduce it where there is competition; but price discrimination has been assumed impossible.

Differentiating the first-order conditions, and using $R_{ij}^i > 0$, we have

$$(4) \quad \partial x_1^* / \partial K_1 > 0, \quad \partial x_1^* / \partial x_2^* > 0,$$
$$\partial x_2^* / \partial K_1 = 0, \quad \partial x_2^* / \partial x_1^* > 0.$$

The heart of the fat-cat effect is that $\partial x_1^* / \partial K_1 > 0$. As the incumbent's goodwill increases, it becomes more reluctant to match the entrant's price. The large captive market makes the incumbent a pacifistic "fat cat." This suggests that if entry is going to occur, the incumbent has an incentive to increase K_1 to "soften" the second-period equilibrium.

To formalize this intuition we first must sign the *total* derivative dx_1^*/dK_1. While one would expect increasing K_1 to increase the incumbent's equilibrium price, this is only true if firm 1's second-period reaction curve is steeper than firm 2's. This will be true if $R_{11}^1 \cdot R_{22}^2 > R_{12}^1 \cdot R_{21}^2$. If dx_1^*/dK_1 were negative the model would not exhibit the fat-cat effect.

Now we compare the incumbent's choice of K_1 in the open-loop and perfect equilibria. In the former, the incumbent takes x_2^* as given, and thus ignores the possibility of strategic investment. Setting $\partial \pi^1/\partial K_1 = 0$ in (1), we have

(5) $R^m + \delta \big(R^1(x_1^*, \infty)$

$\quad\quad - R^1(x_1^*, x_2^*) \big) = A'(K_1).$

In a perfect equilibrium, the incumbent realizes that x_2^* depends on K_1, giving first-order conditions

(6) $R^m + \delta \big(R^1(x_1^*, \infty) - R^1(x_1^*, x_2^*)$

$\quad\quad + (1 - K_1) R_2^1 (dx_2^*/dK_1) \big) = A'(K_1).$

As R_2^1 and dx_2^*/dK_1 are positive, for a fixed K_1 the left-hand side of (6) exceeds that of (5), so if the second-order condition corresponding to (6) is satisfied, its solution exceeds that of (5).

The fat-cat effect suggests a corollary, that the incumbent should underinvest and maintain a "lean and hungry look" to deter entry. However, while the "price effect" of increasing K_1 encourages entry, the "direct effect" of reducing the entrant's market goes the other way. To see this, note that

(7) $\Pi_K^2 = \delta \big[(1 - K_1) R_1^2 (dx_1^*/dK_1) - R^2 \big].$

The first term in the right-hand side of (7) is the strategic effect of K_1 on the second-period price, the second is the direct effect. One can find plausible examples of demand and advertising functions such that the indirect effect dominates. This is the case, for example, for goods which are differentiated by their location on the unit interval with linear

"transportation" costs, if first-period advertising is sufficiently expensive that the incumbent's equilibrium share of the informed consumers is positive. In this case, entry deterrence requires underinvestment.

II. Technological Competition

We now develop a simple model of investment in $R\&D$ to illustrate the lean and hungry look, building on the work of Arrow and Reinganum. In the first period, the incumbent, firm 1, spends K_1 on capital, and then has constant average cost $\bar{c}(K_1)$. The incumbent receives the monopoly profit $V^m(\bar{c}(K_1))$ in period 1. In the second period, both the incumbent and firm 2 may do $R\&D$ on a new technology which allows constant average cost c. If one firm develops the innovation, it receives the monopoly value $V^m(c)$. Thus the innovation is "large" or "drastic" in Arrow's sense. If both firms develop the innovation, their profit is zero. If neither firm succeeds, then the incumbent again receives $V^m(\bar{c})$. The second-period $R\&D$ technology is stochastic. If firm i spends x_i on $R\&D$, it obtains the new technology with probability $\mu_i(x_i)$. We assume $\mu_i'(0) = \infty$, $\mu_i' > 0$, $\mu_i'' < 0$. The total payoffs from period 2 on are

(9) $\Pi^1 = \mu_1(1 - \mu_2)V^m(c)$

$\quad\quad + (1 - \mu_1)(1 - \mu_2)V^m(\bar{c}) - x_1,$

$\Pi^2 = \mu_2(1 - \mu_1)V^m(c) - x_2.$

The first-order conditions for a Nash equilibrium are

(10) $\mu_1' \big[V^m(c) - V^m(\bar{c}) \big] (1 - \mu_2) = 1,$

$\quad\quad \mu_2' V^m(c)(1 - \mu_1) = 1.$

We see that since the incumbent's gain is only the difference in the monopoly profits, it has less incentive to innovate than the entrant. This is the Arrow effect.[2] We have

[2] For large innovations, the monopoly price with the new technology is less than the average cost of the old one. Richard Gilbert and David Newbery (1982) showed

derived it here in a model with each firm's chance of succeeding independent of the other's, so that we have had to allow a nonzero probability of a tie. Reinganum's model avoids ties, because the possibilities of "success" (obtaining the patent) are not independent.

Because $\mu_i' > 0$ and $\mu_i'' < 0$, the reaction curves in (10) slope downward—the more one firm spends, the less the other wishes to. Since increasing K_1 decreases the incumbent's gain from the innovator's we expect that the strategic incentive is to reduce K_1 to play more aggressively in period 2. As in our last example, this is only true if the reaction curves are "stable," which in this case requires $\mu_1'' \mu_2''(1 - \mu_1)(1 - \mu_2) > (\mu_1' \mu_2')^2$. This is true for example for $\mu_i(x) = \max(1, bx^{1/2})$, with b small. We conclude that to accommodate entry the incumbent has a strategic incentive to underinvest. Because K_1 has no direct effect on Π^2, we can also say that to deter entry the incumbent has an incentive to underinvest.[3]

III. Taxonomy and Conclusion

In the goodwill model the incumbent could underinvest to deter entry, while in the $R\&D$ model the strategic incentives always favored underinvestment. To relate these results to previous work, we next present an informal taxonomy of pre-entry strategic investment by an incumbent. In many cases, one might expect both "investment" and "production" decisions to be made post-entry. We have restricted attention to a single post-entry variable for simplicity. We should point out

that for "small" innovations, because the sum of the duopoly profits is (typically) less than $\Pi^m(c)$, the incumbent loses more than the entrant gains if the entrant obtains the patent. With a deterministic $R\&D$ technology, the incumbent's incentive to innovate thus exceeds the entrant's, because the incumbent's current patent is certain to be superceded and thus the current profits are not "sacrificed" by the incumbent's $R\&D$. Reinganum showed that with stochastic $R\&D$ and a small innovation, either effect can dominate. In her $R\&D$ model the reaction curves slope up.

[3] For small innovations the direct effect goes the other way.

that this involves some loss of generality. Strategic underinvestment requires that the incumbent not be able to invest after entry, or more generally that pre- and post-entry investments are imperfectly substitutable. This was the case in both of our examples. However, if investment is in productive machinery and capital costs are linear and constant over time, then underinvestment would be ineffective, as the incumbent's post-entry investment would make up any previous restraint.

Before presenting the taxonomy, it should be acknowledged that since Schmalensee's (1983) article, several authors have independently noticed the possibility of underinvestment. J. Baldani (1983) studies the conditions leading to underinvestment in advertising. Bulow et al. present a careful treatment of two-stage games in which either production or investment takes place in the first period, with production in the second, and costs need not be separable across periods. They focus on cost minimization as the benchmark for over- and underinvestment. The starting point for the Bulow et al. paper was the observation that a firm might choose not to enter an apparently profitable market due to strategic spillovers on other product lines. This point is developed in more detail in K. Judd (1983).

Our taxonomy classifies market according to the signs of the incentives for strategic investments. Because only the incumbent has a strategic incentive, given concavity, we can unambiguously say whether the incumbent will over- or underinvest to accommodate entry (compared to the open-loop equilibrium).[4] We continue to denote the incumbent's first-period choice K_1, the post-entry decisions x_1 and x_2, and the payoffs Π^1 and Π^2. For entry deterrence there are

[4] This does not generalize to the case in which both firms make strategic decisions. In our paper on learning by doing (1983c), we give an example in which one firm's first-period output declined in moving from the precommitment to the perfect equilibrium. The problem is that if, as expected, firm 1's output increases when it plays strategically, firm 2's strategic incentive to increase output can be outweighed by its response to firm 1's change.

two effects, as we noted before: the "direct effect" $\partial \Pi^2/\partial K_1$, and the "strategic effect" $\partial \Pi^2/\partial x_1^* \cdot \partial x_1^*/\partial K_1$. We saw in the goodwill case that these two effects had opposite signs, and so the overall incentives were ambiguous. In all the rest of our examples, these two effects have the same sign.

In Table 1, first the entry-accommodating strategy and then the entry-deterring one is given. The fat-cat strategy is overinvestment that accommodates entry by committing the incumbent to play less aggressively postentry. The lean and hungry strategy is underinvestment to be tougher. The top dog strategy is overinvestment to be tough; this is the familiar result of Spence and Dixit.

Last, the puppy-dog strategy is *underinvestment* that accommodates entry by turning the incumbent into a small, friendly, nonaggressive puppy dog. This strategy is desirable if investment makes the incumbent tougher, and the second-period reaction curves slope up.

One final caveat: the classification in Table 1 depends as previously on the second-period Nash equilibria being "stable," so that changing K_1 has the intuitive effect on x_2^*.

Our goodwill model is an example of Case I: goodwill makes the incumbent soft, and the second-period reaction curves slope up. The $R\&D$ model illustrates Case II. Case III is the "classic" case for investing in productive machinery and "learning by doing" (Spence, 1981; our paper, 1983c) with quantity competition. Case IV results from either of these models with price competition (Bulow et al.; our paper, 1983b; Judith Gelman and Steven Salop, 1983). A more novel example of the puppy-dog ploy arises in the P. Milgrom and J. Roberts (1982) model of limit pricing under incomplete information, if we remove their assumption that the established firm's cost is revealed once the entrant decides to enter, and replace quantity with price as the strategic variable. To accommodate entry, the incumbent then prefers the entrant to believe that the incumbent's costs are relatively high.

We conclude with two warnings. First, one key ingredient of our taxonomy is the slope of the second-period reaction curves. In many

TABLE 1

Slope of Reaction Curves	Investment Makes Incumbent:	
	Tough	Soft
Upward	Case IV	Case I
	A: Puppy Dog	A: Fat Cat
	D: Top Dog	D: Lean and Hungry
Downward	Case III	Case II
	A: Top Dog	A: Lean and Hungry
	A: Top Dog	A: Lean and Hungry

Note: A = Accommodate entry; D = Deter entry.

of our examples, downward slopes correspond to quantity competition and upward slopes to competition in prices.[5] These examples are potentially misleading. We do not intend to revive the Cournot vs. Bertrand argument. As David Kreps and José Scheinkman (1983) have shown, "Quantity Precommitment and Bertrand Competition Yield Cournot Outcomes." Thus, "price competition" and "quantity competition" should not be interpreted as referring to the variable chosen by firms in the second stage, but rather as two different reduced forms for the determination of both prices and outputs. Second, our restriction to a single post-entry stage eliminates many important strategic interactions. As our 1983a paper shows, such interactions may reverse the over- or underinvestment results of two-stage models.

[5] Bulow et al. point out that while these are the "normal" cases, it is possible, for example, for reaction curves to slope up in quantity competition.

REFERENCES

Arrow, Kenneth, "Economic Welfare and the Allocation of Resources to Innovation," in R. Nelson, ed., *The Rate and Direction of Economic Activity*, New York: National Bureau of Economic Research, 1962.

Baldani, J., "Strategic Advertising and Credible Entry Deterrence Policies," mimeo.,

Colgate University, 1983.

Bulow, J., Geanakoplos, J. and Klemperer, P., "Multimarket Oligopoly," Stanford Business School R. P. 696, 1983.

Butters, Gerard, "Equilibrium Distributions of Sales and Advertising Prices," *Review of Economic Studies*, October 1977, *44*, 465–96.

Dixit, A., "A Model of Duopoly Suggesting a Theory of Entry Barriers," *Bell Journal of Economics*, Spring 1979, *10*, 20–32.

Fudenberg, D. and Tirole, J., (1983a) "Capital as a Commitment: Strategic Investment to Deter Mobility," *Journal of Economic Theory*, December 1983, *31*, 227–50.

_____ and _____, (1983b) "Dynamic Models of Oligopoly," IMSSS T. R. 428, Stanford University, 1983.

_____ and _____, (1983c) "Learning by Doing and Market Performance," *Bell Journal of Economics*, Autumn 1983, *14*, 522–30.

Gelman, J. and Salop, S., "Judo Economics," mimeo., George Washington University, 1982.

Gilbert, R. and Newbery, D., "Preemptive Patenting and the Persistence of Monopoly," *American Economic Review*, June 1982, *72*, 514–26.

Grossman, G. and Shapiro, C., "Informative Advertising with Differentiated Goods," *Review of Economic Studies*, January 1984, *51*, 63–82.

Judd, K., "Credible Spatial Preemption," MEDS D. P. 577, Northwestern University, 1983.

Kreps, D. and Scheinkman, J., "Quantity Precommitment and Bertrand Competition Yield Cournot Outcomes," mimeo., University of Chicago, 1983.

Milgrom, P. and Roberts, J., "Limit Pricing and Entry under Incomplete Information," *Econometrica*, 1982, *50*, 443–60.

Reinganum, Jennifer, "Uncertain Innovation and the Persistence of Monopoly," *American Economic Review*, September 1983, *73*, 741–48.

Schmalensee, Richard, "Product Differentiation Advantages of Pioneering Brands," *American Economic Review*, June 1982, *72*, 349–65.

_____, "Advertising and Entry Deterrence: An Exploratory Model," *Journal of Political Economy*, August 1983, *90*, 636–53.

Spence, A. Michael, "Entry, Capacity, Investment, and Oligopolistic Pricing," *Bell Journal of Economics*, Autumn 1977, *8*, 534–44.

_____, "Investment Strategy and Growth in a New Market," *Bell Journal of Economics*, Spring 1979, *10*, 1–19.

_____, "The Learning Curve and Competition," *Bell Journal of Economics*, Spring 1981, *12*, 49–70.

12 On the Theory of Perfectly-Contestable Markets

W. J. Baumol

NEW YORK UNIVERSITY AND PRINCETON
UNIVERSITY, USA

J. C. Panzar

NORTHWESTERN UNIVERSITY, USA

and

R. D. Willig[1]

PRINCETON UNIVERSITY, USA

I INTRODUCTION

The purpose of this chapter is to provide an overview of the theory of perfectly-contestable markets.[2] The treatment here is deliberately schematic in order to focus on the logical structure of the theory.

Perfectly-contestable markets can be viewed as a benchmark for the study of industry structure – a benchmark based on an idealised limiting case. In this limiting case, potential entry imposes the strongest possible symmetric constraint upon incumbents: entry is without disadvantage and is perfectly reversible. As a result, no role is played by the sunk costs, precommitments, asymmetric information and strategic behaviour that characterise many real markets and that are the subject of much penetrating current research in industrial organisation. With irreversibilities and the inducements for strategic behaviour assumed away, industry structure in perfectly-contestable markets is determined by the fundamental forces of demand and of production technology.

Of course, this is also true of perfectly-competitive markets. However, this most-familiar idealised limiting case is not a satisfactory benchmark for the study of industry structure in general, because it is intrinsically inapplicable to a variety of significant cases. In particular, where increasing returns to scale are present, perfectly-competitive behaviour (with its marginal-cost pricing) is logically inconsistent with the long-run financial viability of unsubsidised firms.

Thus, in place of perfect competition, we propose perfect contestability as a general standard of comparison for more-complex and (usually) more-realistic models of industrial organisation. However, this alteration in general standard does not always produce a change in implications because, as is shown below, perfectly-competitive behaviour is necessary in perfectly-contestable markets in certain specifiable circumstances. In other words, perfect contestability is a generalisation of perfect competition – a generalisation that can be used where returns to scale are increasing, as well as where returns are decreasing or constant.

Section II defines perfectly-contestable markets, compares them with perfectly-competitive markets, derives some of the basic properties of sustainable prices and industry structures, and examines the implications of perfect contestability for industries that produce a single, homogeneous output. In that case, only outcomes that are Ramsey optimal (i.e., welfare maximising subject to the financial viability of unsubsidised firms), can be sustained in a perfectly-contestable market. Section III sketches a model in which profit-maximising potential entrants may or may not exhibit the aggressive behaviour required for perfect contestability, depending on the relative values of structural parameters which characterise the degree to which costs are sunk. The analysis reveals that a market is contestable if entrants can reverse their investments without loss and suffer no other disadvantages relative to incumbents. Section IV outlines some of the implications of perfect contestability for the structure of multi-product industries that are not perfectly competitive. The analysis identifies some qualitative properties of multi-output production costs that are significant determinants of industry structure in these circumstances and examines some normative properties of the equilibria. Section V concludes the chapter by indicating the relevance of the analysis for positive economics and empirical work.

II PERFECTLY CONTESTABLE MARKETS: DEFINITIONS AND BASIC PROPERTIES

The theory presented here lies in the realm of partial equilibrium. It deals with the provision of the set of products $N = \{1, \ldots, n\}$, some of which may not actually be produced, and which is a proper subset of all the goods in the economy. The prices of these products are represented by vectors $p \in R^n_{++}$, and other prices are assumed to be exogenous and are suppressed in the notation. $Q(p) \in R^n_+$ is the vector-valued market demand function for the products in N and it suppresses consumers' incomes, which are assumed to be exogenous. For any output vector $y \in R^n_+$, $C(y)$ is the cost at exogenously-fixed factor prices when production is efficient. The underlying technology is assumed to be freely available to all incumbent firms and to all potential entrants. Where necessary, $C(y)$ and $Q(p)$ will be assumed to be differentiable.

Definition 1 A *feasible industry configuration* is composed of m firms producing output vectors $y^1, \ldots, y^m \in R^n_+$, at prices $p \in R^n_{++}$, such that the markets clear, $\Sigma^m_{i=1} y^i = Q(p)$, and that each firm at least breaks even, $p \cdot y^i - C(y^i) \geq 0$, $i = 1, \ldots, m$.

Thus, the industry configuration is taken as comprised of m firms, where m can be any positive integer, so that the industry structure is monopolistic if $m = 1$; competitive if m is sufficiently large, or oligopolistic for intermediate values of m. The term 'feasibility' refers to the requirements (a) that each of the firms involved selects a non-negative output vector that permits its production costs, $C(\cdot)$, to be covered at the market prices, p, and (b) that the sum of the outputs of the m firms satisfies market demands at those prices.

Definition 2 A feasible industry configuration over N, with prices p and firms' outputs $y^1, \ldots, y^m$, is *sustainable* if $p^e \cdot y^e \leq C(y^e)$ for all $p^e \in R^n_{++}$, $y^e \in R^n_+$, $p^e \leq p$, and $y^e \leq Q(p^e)$.

The interpretation of this definition is that a sustainable configuration affords no profitable opportunities for entry by potential entrants who regard incumbents' prices as fixed (for a period sufficiently long to make $C(\cdot)$ the relevant flow-cost function for an entrant). Here, a feasible marketing plan for a potential entrant is comprised of prices, p^e, that do not exceed the incumbents' quoted prices, p, and a

342   *The Perfectly Contestable Market*

quantity vector, y^e, that does not exceed market demand at the entrant's prices, $Q(p^e)$. The configuration is sustainable if no such marketing plan for an entrant offers a flow of profit $(p^e \cdot y^e - C(y^e))$ that is positive.

Definition 3 A *perfectly-contestable market* (PCM) is one in which a necessary condition for an industry configuration to be in equilibrium is that it be sustainable.

A PCM so defined may be interpreted, heuristically, as a market subject to potential entry by firms that have no disadvantage relative to incumbents, and that assess the profitability of entry on the supposition that incumbents' prices are fixed for a sufficiently-long period of time. Then, since one requirement for equilibrium is the absence of new entry, an equilibrium configuration in a PCM must offer no inducement for entry; i.e., it must be sustainable.

In Section III, we explore in more detail the basic economic elements that make an industry perfectly-contestable by analysing the sort of entrant-behaviour that gives substance to the definition of sustainability. We shall argue that the key to the contestability of non-competitive markets is reversible entry and the absence of sunk costs. However, before focusing on that subject, we proceed to describe some of the properties of PCMs and the implications of sustainability.

Definition 4 A feasible industry configuration over N, p; $y^1, \ldots, y^m$, is a *long-run competitive equilibrium* if $p \cdot y \leq C(y)$ $\forall y \in R_+^n$.

So defined, a long-run competitive equilibrium has precisely the characteristics usually ascribed to it. Together, $p \cdot y^i \geq C(y^i)$ and $p \cdot y \leq C(y)$, $\forall y \in R_+^n$, imply that $p \cdot y^i = C(y^i)$ and that the $y^i \in$ arg $\max_y(p \cdot y - C(y))$. Thus, each firm in the configuration takes prices as parametric; chooses output to maximise profits; earns zero profit; and equates marginal costs to prices of produced outputs. It is now easy to show

Proposition 1[3] *A long-run competitive equilibrium is a sustainable configuration, so that a perfectly competitive market is a PCM.*

Proposition 2 *Sustainable configurations need not be long-run competitive equilibria, and a PCM need not be perfectly competitive.*

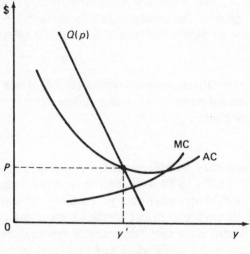

FIG. 12.1

The simplest example sufficient to prove this second proposition is
described in Figure 12.1. Here, the feasible configuration, comprised
of one firm producing and selling y^1 at the price p, is sustainable. This
follows because, at a price equal to or less than p, sale of any quantity
on or inside the demand curve yields revenue no greater than production cost; in this range, price does not exceed average cost (AC).
Yet, this configuration is not a long-run competitive equilibrium, as
defined above. This is because $py - C(y) > 0$, for $y > y^1$ and, at
y^1, p exceeds marginal cost (MC). In fact, because the only intersection of the demand and average cost curves occurs in the range of
increasing returns to scale, there is no possible long-run competitive
equilibrium. However, this intersection point does correspond to a
sustainable configuration.

   Hence, Propositions 1 and 2 show that the sustainable industry-
configuration is a substantive generalisation of the long-run competitive equilibrium, and that the PCM is a substantive generalisation of
the perfectly-competitive market. The following propositions sum-
marise some characteristics of equilibria in PCMs.

Proposition 3[4]   *Let p; y^1, . . ., y^m be a sustainable industry configuration. Then each firm must (i) earn zero profit by operating
efficiently, $p \cdot y^i - C(y^i) = 0$;   (ii)   avoid   cross-subsidisation,
$p_s \cdot y^i_s \geq C(y^i) - C(y^i_{N-s})$, $\forall S \subset N$ (where the vector x_T agrees with the*

344 *The Perfectly Contestable Market*

vector x in components j ϵ T and has zeros for its other components);
(iii) price at or above marginal cost, $p_j \geq \partial C(y^i)/\partial y_j$.

The interpretation of condition (ii) is that the revenues earned from the sales of any subset of the goods must not fall short of the incremental costs of producing that subset. Otherwise, in view of the equality of total revenues and costs, the revenues collected from the sales of the other goods must exceed their total stand-alone production cost. In PCMs, such pricing invites entry into the markets for the goods providing the subsidy.

Proposition 4[5] Let p; y^1, . . ., y^m be a sustainable configuration with $y_j^k < \sum_{h=1}^m y_j^h$. Then $p_j = \partial C(y^k)/\partial y_j$. That is, if two or more firms produce a given good in a PCM, they must select input–output vectors at which their marginal costs of producing it are equal to the good's market price.

The implications of this result are surprisingly strong. The discipline of sustainability in perfectly-contestable markets forces firms to adopt prices just equal to marginal costs, provided only that they are not monopolists of the products in question. Conventional wisdom implies that, generally, only perfect competition involving a multitude of firms, each small in its output markets, can be relied upon to provide marginal-cost prices. Here we see that potential competition by prospective entrants, rather than rivalry among incumbent firms, suffices to make marginal-cost pricing a requirement of equilibrium in PCMs, even in those containing as few as two active producers of each product. The conventional view holds that the enforcement mechanism of full competitive-equilibrium requires the smallness of each active firm in its product market, in addition to freedom of entry. We see that the smallness requirement can be dispensed with almost entirely, and exclusive reliance put on the freedom of entry that characterises PCMs.

Proposition 5[6] Let p; y^1, . . ., y^m be a sustainable configuration. Then, for any $\hat{y}^1$, . . ., $\hat{y}^k$ with $\sum_{j=1}^k \hat{y}^j = \sum_{j=1}^m y^j$, $\sum_{j=1}^k C(\hat{y}^j) \geq \sum_{j=1}^m C(y^j)$. That is, a sustainable configuration minimises the total cost to the industry of producing the total industry output.

This proposition is a generalisation to PCMs of a well known result for perfect competition. It can be interpreted as a manifestation of the power of unimpeded potential entry to impose efficiency upon the industry. For example, the proposition implies that if a monopoly occupies a PCM it must be a *natural* monopoly: production by a single firm must minimise industry-cost for the given output vector. Thus, Propositions 3, 4 and 5 are powerful tools for the analysis of industry structure in PCMs. Proposition 5 permits information on the properties of production costs to be used to assess the scale and scope of firms' activities in PCMs. Then, Propositions 3 and 4 permit inferences to be drawn about the corresponding equilibrium prices.

In particular, this analytic approach leads to very strong results in the single-product case. Propositions 3 to 5 show that there are only two possible types of sustainable configuration in single-product industries. The first type, represented in Figure 12.1, involves a single firm which charges the lowest price that is consistent with non-negative profit. The firm must be a natural monopoly when it produces the quantity that is demanded at this price. And, in this circumstance, the result maximises welfare, subject to the constraint that all firms in question be viable financially without subsidies. Such a second-best maximum is referred to as a 'Ramsey optimum'.

The second type of sustainable configuration involves production, by one or more firms, of outputs at which both marginal cost and average cost are equal to price. Here, in the long run, all active firms exhibit the behaviour that characterises perfectly competitive equilibrium. And, of course, the result involves both (first-best) welfare optimality and financial viability. Hence, in this case, Ramsey optimality and the first-best coincide. This establishes the result that, in a single-product industry, any sustainable configuration is Ramsey optimal.

However, in general, because of the 'integer problem', sustainable configurations may generally not exist. This problem arises, for example, where there is only one output at which a firm's marginal and average costs coincide, and where the quantity of output demanded by the market at the competitive price is greater than this, but is not an integer multiple of that amount. Then, no sustainable configurations exist.

There is, however, a plausible assumption, supported by empirical evidence, at least to some degree, that eliminates the integer problem. Suppose that a firm's average cost curve has a flat-bottom (as in Figure 12.2), rather than being 'U'-shaped. In particular, suppose that the minimum level of average cost is attained not only at one output, but (at least) at all outputs between the minimum efficient scale, y_m, and twice the minimum efficient scale. Then any industry

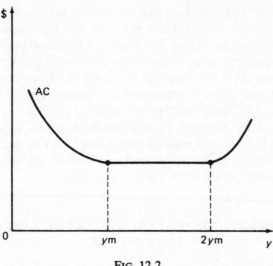

FIG. 12.2

output, y^1, that is at least equal to y_m can be apportioned among an integer number of firms each of which achieves minimum average cost. Specifically, y^1 can be divided evenly among $\lfloor y^1/y_m \rfloor$ firms (where $\lfloor x \rfloor$ is the largest integer not greater than x), and each firm's output, $y^1/\lfloor y^1/y_m \rfloor$, must lie in the (half-open) interval between y_m and $2y_m$. Hence, in this case, the Ramsey optimum can either be a sustainable configuration of two or more firms performing competitively, or a sustainable natural monopoly. Such a monopoly may either produce an output at which there are increasing returns to scale, when it will price at average cost. Or it may produce an output between y_m and $2y_m$ with locally constant returns to scale, when it will adopt a price equal both to average and marginal cost. This, together with the preceding argument, establishes the following result.

Proposition 6[7] In a single-product industry in which the firm's average cost curve has a flat-bottom between minimum efficient scale and twice minimum efficient scale, a configuration is sustainable if and only if it is Ramsey optimal.

This result shows that, under the conditions described, there is equivalence between welfare optimality and equilibrium in PCMs. This extends the corresponding result for perfectly-competitive equilibria to cases of increasing returns to scale. Moreover, since the behavioural assumptions required for a PCM are weaker than those underlying perfectly-competitive markets, the equivalence result is more sweeping. In particular, Proposition 6 implies that PCMs can be expected to perform well, whatever the number of firms participating in equilibrium. It is the potential competition of potential entrants, rather than the active competition of existing rivals, that drives equilibrium in PCMs to welfare optimality.

Because of the strength of this result, it seems appropriate to examine its behavioural underpinnings more closely before moving on, in Section IV to the richer multi-product situation in which the normative implications of PCMs are less clear.

III   PERFECT-CONTESTABILITY AS THE ABSENCE OF SUNK COSTS[8]

In this Section, we construct and analyse an explicit model of entry behaviour. We show that, in the limiting case without sunk costs, only sustainable industry configurations can withstand the threat of entry: i.e., the market is perfectly-contestable.

Since entry takes place over time, we must construct a model with a modicum of dynamic structure. At time zero, there is assumed to be an incumbent monopolist operating in the market with an initial capital stock, K_i^0, providing an instantaneous flow of output (y_i) via a technology whose flow of variable costs is given by the function $V(y, K)$. The (representative) potential entrant has access to the same technology and can purchase capital equipment at the price β per unit.

The key to the dynamic structure of the model is a *contract period* of length τ. The potential entrant can compete *for* the market by quoting a price p_e and, *if it is not matched* (or beaten) by the incumbent, make a *firm* contract with consumers for delivery of the flow of output $y_e \leq Q(p_e)$, at that price, for the period $[0, \tau]$. If the incumbent matches the potential entrant's price, the latter simply stays out of the market and incurs no costs. Should the entrant actually contract for delivery, it would be saddled with a capital outlay of βK_e^0. However, this investment may be only partially *sunk*, since we assume that at time τ, the end of contract period, the entrant may, if it chooses, 'scrap' its capital for a salvage price of α per unit, with $0 \leq \alpha \leq \beta$. If $\alpha = 0$ all capital costs are sunk, while if $\alpha = \beta$ no costs are sunk since all investments can be reversed fully at time τ.

(*Physical* depreciation of capital can be subsumed into $V(\cdot)$.) The amount of capital chosen by the entrant will depend upon both the properties of the variable cost function and on the prices α and β.

We shall not attempt, here, to provide a detailed model of the nature of the rivalry between the incumbent and a successful entrant once the initial contract period is over. However, it may plausibly be assumed that the present values, at τ, of future profits are functions of the *state variables* of the system at τ. Thus, the discounted future profits of the entrant and the incumbent can be expressed as $\pi^f_e(K^0_e, K^0_i)$ and $\pi^f_i(K^0_e, K^0_i)$. While the forms of these functions depend upon the behavioural model of future market rivalry, generally applicable lower bounds are yielded by the fact that either firm always has the option of selling its plant for salvage at time τ. Therefore,

$$\pi^f_e(K^0_e, K^0_i) \geqslant \alpha K^0_e \tag{1}$$

$$\pi^f_i(K^0_e, K^0_i) \geqslant \alpha K^0_i. \tag{2}$$

We are now in a position to examine the entry decision at time zero. The first issue is whether or not there exists any set of contracts (entry plan) which the entrant can offer and which, if *not* matched by the incumbent, would justify the expectation of positive *total* profits. In the simplest case, such 'contracts' consist of an offer price p_e less than the incumbent's posted price p^0_i and a flow rate of output y_e no larger than the (instantaneous) quantity demanded $Q(p_e)$. Anticipated total profits are thus given by:

$$\pi^T_e = \gamma_\tau[p_e y_e - V(y_e, K^0_e)] - \beta K^0_e + \pi^f_e e^{-r\tau}, \tag{3}$$

where r is the discount rate and $\gamma_\tau = (1 - e^{-r\tau})/r$. Formally, an *entry offering* will be made if and only if:

$$\pi^*_e \equiv \max_{\substack{K^0_e \geqslant 0, \\ p_e \leqslant p^0_i, y_e \leqslant Q(p_e)}} \pi^T_e > 0. \tag{4}$$

In order to shed some light on the conditions under which (4) will hold, we use the lower bound (1) to obtain,

$$\pi^T_e \geqslant \gamma_\tau[p_e y_e - V(y_e, K^0_e) - \rho_e K^0_e]. \tag{5}$$

Here ρ_e, the effective rental cost of capital to the potential entrant, is given by:

$$\rho_e = (\beta - \alpha e^{-r\tau})/\gamma_\tau = r\beta + (\beta - \alpha)r e^{-r\tau}/(1 - e^{-r\tau}). \tag{6}$$

This enables us to rewrite (5) in terms of an instantaneous cost function that is fully minimised for the given output vector:

$$\pi_e^\tau \geq \gamma_\tau [p_e y_e - C^e(y_e, \rho_e)] \tag{7}$$

where $C^e(y, \rho) \equiv \min_K (V(y, K) + \rho K)$. Equation (7) tells us that the total profit is bounded from *below* by what the entrant can earn during the initial contract period, when the effective instantaneous rental rate of capital ρ_e takes into account asset liquidation at the end of that period. If that value is positive for *any* allowable p_e and y_e, an entry offering will be made. Therefore, a *necessary* condition for *no* entry offering to be made at time zero is that

$$p_e y_e - C(y_e, \rho_e) \leq 0 \ \forall p_e \leq p_i^0, y_e \leq Q(p_e). \tag{8}$$

The only difference between (8) and Definition 2 (of sustainability) is that the effective rental rate of capital faced by the entrant may exceed that of the incumbent, namely $r\beta$, the interest on a unit of invested capital. The difference is attributable to the possibility that the entrant may find itself forced to write off its capital fully over the contract period. This possibility arises because nothing in our model precludes the incumbent from driving any entrant out of business at time τ. Yet, from (6), we see that if $\alpha = \beta$ so that there are no sunk costs, then $\rho_e = r\beta$. Also, note that $\lim_{\tau \to \infty} \rho_e = r\beta$. Thus, in view of (8), we have proven

Proposition 7   If there are no sunk costs (or if the contract period is sufficiently long), then the incumbent firm(s) will be immune from entry offerings only *if the industry configuration is sustainable.*

While we have built our model so that the incumbent always has the option of matching an entry offering, thereby preventing actual entry from occurring, to do so it must lower its price to a sustainable level for the *entire* period $[0, \tau]$. If the basic technology is freely available and potential entrants are sufficiently numerous, the incumbent faces a similar entry threat at *every instant*. Therefore, we have an immediate Corollary to Proposition 7:

Proposition 8   In the absence of sunk costs, entry deterrence requires the industry to operate in a sustainable configuration at all times.

Our model also permits an analytic derivation of an upper bound upon the rate of excess profits attainable by the incumbent. For example, in the single product case, the highest price (p_i^0) that the incumbent can charge without provoking an entry offering is given (in

350 *The Perfectly Contestable Market*

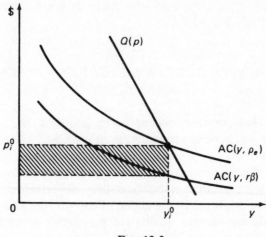

FIG. 12.3

Figure 12.3) by the intersection of the demand curve and the *entrant's* average cost curve $AC(y, \rho_e)$. The shaded area depicts the instantaneous rate of excess profit which the incumbent can earn by virtue of the fact that its effective rental rate of capital is less than the entrant's. (This assumes, of course, that p_i^0 is less than the simple monopoly price.)

To consider a simple example, suppose that $C(y, \rho) = \rho \bar{K} + cy$ for $y > 0$. Then p_i^0 is determined by the condition.

$$(p_i^0 - c) \, Q \, (p_i^0) \; = \; \rho \bar{K}_e \; = \; r\bar{K}(\beta + (\beta - \alpha)/(e^{rr} - 1)) \qquad (9)$$

This bound may be particularly useful because it is based on the actual capital stock employed by the incumbent.

To sum up briefly, this section provides a rather general model of the entry process. This makes it possible to derive a substantive upper bound on the economic value of any 'first-mover' advantages that accrue to an incumbent as a result of the need to sink costs *and* yields, as a readily-interpretable limiting case, precisely the same equilibrium conditions that characterise PCMs. In this model, the approach towards perfect-contestability is also 'continuous'. That is, as long as $\tau > 0$, if the degree to which costs are sunk, as measured by $\beta - \alpha$, declines smoothly towards zero, so does the upper bound on monopoly profits. Thus, in addition to providing a plausible model of the entry process resulting in perfect contestability as a limiting case, the analysis of this section also sheds some light on the 'robustness' of the theory. A small departure from the world of no sunk costs leads, via (9) or (13), only to a similarly small increase in the associated equilibrium price.[9]

IV   MULTI-PRODUCT PERFECTLY CONTESTABLE MARKETS

In industries that produce two or more goods, a rich variety of industry structures becomes possible, even in PCMs. Here, while the constraints imposed upon incumbents by perfect contestability are not nearly as effective in limiting the range of possible outcomes as they are in single product industries, they nevertheless provide a helpful basis for analysis. In particular, Propositions 3 to 5 indicate connections among various qualitative properties of multi-product cost functions and various elements of industry structure in PCMs. These connections constitute one theme of this section. The other theme is the normative evaluation of the industry structures that arise in multi-product PCMs.

Before proceeding, it may be useful to provide definitions of some of the multi-product cost properties that are used in the analysis.

Definition 5   Let $P = \{T_1, \ldots, T_k\}$ be a non-trivial partition of $S \subseteq N$. There are (weak) *economies of scope* at y_s with respect to the partition P if $\Sigma_{i=1}^{k} C(y_{T_i}) > (\geqslant) C(y_s)$. If no partition is mentioned explicitly, then it is presumed that $T_i = \{i\}$.

Definition 6   The *degree of scale economies* defined over the entire product set, $N = \{1, \ldots, n\}$, at y, is given by $S_N(y) = C(y)/y \cdot \nabla C(y)$. Returns to scale are said to be increasing, constant, or decreasing as S_N is greater than, equal to, or less than unity. This occurs as the elasticity of ray average cost with respect to t is negative, zero, or positive; where *ray average cost* is $\mathrm{RAC}(ty^\circ) \equiv C(y^\circ)/t$.

Definition 7   The *incremental cost* of the product set $T \subseteq N$ at y is given by $IC_T(y) \equiv C(y) - C(y_{N-T})$ The *average incremental cost* of T is $AIC_T(y) \equiv IC_T(y)/\Sigma_{j \epsilon T} y_j$. The average incremental cost of T is decreasing, increasing, or constant at y if $AIC_T(ty_T + y_{N-T})$ is a decreasing, increasing, or locally constant function of t at $t = 1$. These cases are labelled respectively, increasing, decreasing, or constant *returns to the scale of the product line T*. The degree of scale economies specific to T is $IC_T(y)/\Sigma_{i \epsilon T} y_i (\alpha C(y))/xy_i$.

Definition 8 A cost function $C(y)$ is *trans-ray convex* through some point $y^* = (y_1^*, \ldots, y_n^*)$ if there exists at least one vector of positive constants $w_1, \ldots, w_n$ such that for every two output vectors $y^a = (y_1^a, \ldots, y_n^a)$ and $y^b = (y_1^b, \ldots, y_n^b)$ that lie on the hyperplane $\Sigma w_i y_i = w_0$ through point y^*, $C[ky^a + (1 - k)y^b] \leq kC(y^a) + (1 - k)C(y^b)$ for $k \epsilon (0, 1)$.

In view of the general result that sustainable configurations minimise industry-wide costs (Proposition 5), these cost properties permit inferences to be drawn about industry structure in multi-product PCMs. The first issue that arises is when multi-commodity production is characteristic of equilibrium in a PCM.

Proposition 9[10] *A multi-product firm in a PCM must enjoy (at least weak) economies of scope over the set of goods it produces. When strict economies of scope are present, there must be at least one multi-product firm in any PCM that supplies more than one good.*

The second basic question that arises is whether there can be two or more firms actively producing a particular good in a PCM. If there are, then, by Proposition 4, marginal-cost pricing must result. The answer depends upon the availability of product-specific scale economies.

Proposition 10[11] *Any product with average incremental costs that decline throughout the relevant range (i.e., that offers product-specific increasing returns to scale) must be produced by only a single firm (if it is produced at all) in a PCM. Further, such a product must be priced above marginal cost, unless the degree of product-specific scale economies is exactly one.*

Thus, regardless of the presence or absence of economies of scope, globally-declining average incremental costs imply that a product must be monopolised in a PCM. It is an immediate corollary that if all goods in the set N exhibit product-specific scale economies, and if there are economies of scope among them all, then the industry is a natural monopoly that must be monopolised in a PCM.

Another route to this result is provided by the 'weak invisible-hand theorem of natural monopoly'.

Proposition 11[12] *Trans-ray convexity of costs together with global economies of scale imply natural monopoly. If, in addition, certain other technical conditions are met, a monopoly charging Ramsey-optimal prices is a sustainable configuration.*

In general, there may exist natural monopoly situations in which no sustainable prices are possible for the Ramsey optimal product set. Further, even where sustainable prices exist, the Ramsey optimal prices may not be among them. However, under the conditions of the weak invisible hand theorem, the Ramsey optimal prices for the Ramsey optimal product set are guaranteed to be sustainable, so that PCMs are consistent with (second-best) welfare optimal performance by a natural monopoly.

PCMs will yield first-best welfare optimality if there exist sustainable configurations with at least two firms actively producing each good. For, in this case, Propositions 4 and 5 guarantee industry-wide cost efficiency and marginal-cost pricing of all products. Here, two issues must be resolved: Does industry-wide cost minimisation require at least two producers of each good? And if so, do sustainable configurations exist?

The existence problem can be solved in a manner analogous to its solution in the case of single-product industries: by assuming that ray average costs remain at their minimum levels for output vectors that lie (on each ray) between minimum efficient-scale and twice minimum efficient-scale. And the presence of at least two producers (or one operating in the region where constant returns prevail) of each good is assured if the quantities demanded by the market at the relevant marginal-cost prices are no smaller than minimum efficient-scale (along the relevant ray) and if the cost function exhibits trans-ray convexity. Under conditions that represent these ideas formally, we have demonstrated the existence of a first-best sustainable configuration; i.e., one with competitive properties.[13]

(A) FIRMS ACTIVE IN BOTH MONOPOLY AND COMPETITIVE MARKETS

We have briefly discussed the equilibrium requirements and welfare implications which perfect contestability holds for markets in which industry cost minimisation requires either that one firm market all products (natural monopoly) or that each product be produced by two or more firms. In this sub-section we consider the 'mixed case' in which product 1 is characterised by globally-decreasing incremental costs and is linked by economies of scope to product 2, which, in stand-alone production, is 'naturally competitive'. What

The Perfectly Contestable Market

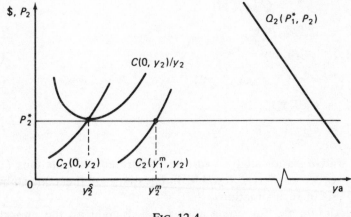

FIG. 12.4

does the theory of perfectly-contestable markets tell us about equilibrium in such cases?

We know from Propositions 5 and 10 that good 1 must be monopolised and that good 2 must be priced at marginal cost, if the market demand is large enough to require two or more active firms. But what role, if any, will the product 1 monopolist have in the market for product 2?

Figure 12.4 depicts the situation there. The equilibrium price in market 2 (p_2^*) is determined by the level of average costs at y_2^s, the minimum efficient scale in stand-alone production. Now the assumption of economies of scope guarantees that the average *incremental* cost curve of the (product 1) monopolist, $(C(y_1^m, y_2) - C(y_1^m, 0))/y_2$, lies everywhere below the average cost curve of specialty firms, $C(0, y_2)/y_2$. So, for example, at an output of y_2^s the revenues from participation in market 2, $p_2^* y_2^s = C(0, y_2^s)$, exceed the associated incremental costs. Thus, industry cost-minimisation requires participation in market 2 by the product 1 monopolist. Its level of output (y_2^m) will be that which equates its marginal cost to price. If, as may well be the case, economies of scope arise, in part, from *cost complementarities*, $C_{12} < 0$, then, as depicted in Figure 12.4, the monopolist's marginal cost curve for product 2 must lie to the right of that of the specialty firms, and its rate of output must be greater. The analysis is completed by the (simultaneous) determination of y_1^m, via the overall zero-profit condition for the product 1 monopolist. More specifically, the six endogenous variables y_1^m, y_2^m, y_2^s, p_1^*, p_2^* and (ignoring the integer problem), the number of specialty firms n_s, are determined by the following system of equations:

$$n_s y_2^s + y_2^m = Q_2(p_1^*, p_2^*) \tag{11}$$

$$y_1^m = Q_1(p_1^*, p_2^*) \tag{12}$$

$$p_2^* y_2^s = C(0, y_2^s) \tag{13}$$

$$p_1^* y_1^m + p_2^* y_2^m = C(y_1^m, y_2^m) \tag{14}$$

$$p_2^* = C_2(0, y_2^s) \tag{15}$$

$$p_2^* = C_2(y_1^m, y_2^m). \tag{16}$$

Comparative-statics analysis can be performed on equations (11)–(16) in order to derive testable implications of the contestability hypothesis in such situations.

In addition, the foregoing analysis sheds light on the important current issue of the proper policy approach to be taken towards regulated or public natural monopolies, whose products or services are technologically-related to those of structurally-competitive industries. It is clear that, under the conditions postulated, the monopoly firm should have a larger share of the market for product 2 than should the representative specialty firm. A policy of precluding it from such markets (or restricting it to producing y_2^s) would leave p_2^* unchanged, but would result in a higher price for product 1. Thus, participation in competitive markets by such firms *benefits* rather than burdens consumers of the monopoly product. Note, however, that such participation does have the effect of forcing *some* specialty providers out of market 2, and this may well be the source of political opposition to such participation by regulated or public enterprises.[14]

(B) MONOPOLISTIC COMPETITION[15]

The standard scenario of Chamberlinian monopolistic competition can be summarised in our terms. It is the case in which a multitude of products (actual or prospective) that are substitutes in demand are included in the product set, each such product having a U-shaped average cost curve, and in which there are no economies of scope among them.

The equilibrium concept which Chamberlin called the 'large group case' entails the adoption by each of the single-product firms of the price that maximises its profits, given the prices of its rivals – which offer differentiated, substitute products. Free entry of firms marketing additional product varieties then continues, until the maximal profit of each active firm is driven to zero, as shown in Figure 12.5.

356   *The Perfectly Contestable Market*

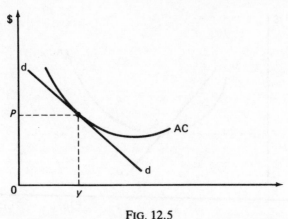

FIG. 12.5

Simultaneously, potential entrants are offered no profitable opportunity for entry, given the prices and product designs already supplied in the market. In this equilibrium, each active firm, of necessity,
equates its price to its average cost in the region of increasing returns
to scale, because of the requisite tangency between its downward-
sloping demand curve, dd, and the average cost curve.

Plainly, then, by its very definition, this Chamberlinian equilibrium
is a sustainable configuration over the set of potential products.
However, other sustainable configurations are also compatible with
the very same scenario. One such type, depicted in Figure 12.6,
involves average-cost pricing (point A) by each single-product firm,
but not the selection of those prices that maximise its profit on the
(not always plausible) assumption that the prices of other active firms
are given. Rather, each firm may choose to maximise its profit given
the behaviour of potential entrants, who would undercut it if it were
to raise its price above average cost. Of course, such a configuration
would not be sustainable if an entrant could earn a profit by supplying
a new product variant, given the prices and designs of those already
offered for sale. However, a large number of sustainable configurations of the form illustrated will generally exist in monopolistically-
competitive markets, with an industry-wide trade-off being made
between the number of available varieties and the price of each.
Notice that a sustainable solution (such as A) does not exhibit excess
capacity. That is, excess capacity in a monopolistically-competitive
market is not necessary for sustainability.

Another type of sustainable configuration in such a market would
arise if the quantity of a particular product-variety that was de-

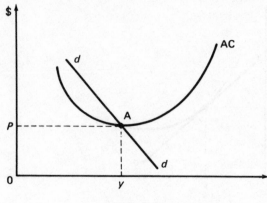

FIG. 12.6

manded in equilibrium were sufficiently large, relative to the minimum efficient scale, to require production by two or more firms for
industry efficiency. Then, it is required that any such product variant
should coexist with any less-popular variants (characterised by Figure
12.5 or 12.6) in equilibrium. Of course, the price of the popular
variant must simultaneously equal marginal and average cost, while
the others may conceivably be priced at average cost and above
marginal cost. This type of sustainable configuration can be consistent with Chamberlin's assumption that firms choose prices to maximise their profits, given the decisions of the other active firms. As
such, these configurations can perhaps provide the foundation for a
substantive and relevant generalisation of Chamberlinian monopolistic-
competition theory.

Chamberlin and his successors apparently never dealt with the incentive of a firm, in the standard framework, to produce *several* product
varieties in order to co-ordinate their prices. In general, the profit-
maximising prices for a pair of substitute products are both higher than
the prices that comprise a Nash-equilibrium between two non-co-
operating price-setting vendors. However, in contestable markets, such
co-ordinated prices are not sustainable in the absence of economies of
scope, so that in the absence of such economies Chamberlin's disregard
of the incentives for co-ordinated pricing can be justified.

Chamberlin suggested that outside the 'large group case', firms can
usefully be assumed to set their own prices on the basis of the
anticipated price reactions of their rivals, rather than on the basis of
the dd demand curve that takes rivals' prices to be fixed. The former
yields what he called the high-tangency equilibrium, pictured in

358   *The Perfectly Contestable Market*

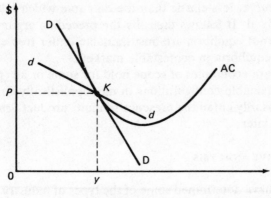

FIG. 12.7

Figure 12.7. Here, the demand curve DD is based on the assumption that rivals are expected to react to any one firm's price moves by changing their own prices in exactly the same way. Hence DD must be less elastic than the dd curve. The situation depicted in Figure 12.7 is purportedly a free-entry equilibrium of this kind, because the DD curve is tangent to the average-cost curve, yielding zero profits that are maximal given the assumed price reactions of rivals.

However, such a position cannot be an equilibrium in a contestable market. An entrant can duplicate closely or exactly the product design of the firm depicted, and enter at a lower price. Since dd is more elastic than the DD curve that is tangent to the AC curve, the dd curve necessarily cuts into and above the AC curve, as illustrated. Consequently, there exist (temporarily) profitable entry opportunities, and so 'high-tangency equilibria' cannot be equilibria in contestable markets. It should be noted that Chamberlin's discussion implies strongly that the markets of which he was thinking satisfied the free-entry requirements of contestability. Thus, it is of some significance for his analysis that his high-tangency solution turns out to be unsustainable.

It should be noted that, recently, important work on monopolistic competition by Spence and by Dixit and Stiglitz has assumed Cournot quantity-behaviour among rivals supplying differentiated products. The resulting 'free-entry equilibria' are analogous to those depicted in Figure 12.7. The assumption that rivals are expected to leave their outputs unchanged is equivalent, in a case of substitute products, to a conjecture that price decreases will induce rivals to respond by decreasing their prices, and to behave analogously when price increases occur. Thus, the corresponding demand curve is, like Chamberlin's DD curve, less-elastic than the dd curve which takes rivals' prices to be fixed. It follows then, by the preceding argument, that quantity Cournot equilibria are unsustainable under free entry, and are not truly equilibria in contestable markets.

Finally, where economies of scope hold for some or all (potential) products, sustainable configurations in monopolistically-competitive markets necessarily entail the presence of multi-product firms. These are discussed later.

(C) NORMATIVE ANALYSIS

Now that we have determined some of the types of industry structure for which sustainability is possible, so that they are consistent with equilibrium in contestable markets, it is appropriate to subject them to a normative analysis which studies their consequences for economic welfare. Should we find any sustainable oligopolistic or monopolistically-competitive structures that necessarily produce optimal results, given the relevant economic circumstances and feasibility constraints, we could infer that in those cases the invisible hand holds, far outside its normal domain. On the other hand, where sustainable solutions are not necessarily optimal, or are even inconsistent with optimality, some degree of market failure must be expected. Such cases of market failure are not those attributable to entry barriers or to friction, because in our analysis they occur in the world of frictionless and reversible free entry that characterises contestable markets. Rather, such market failures must be ascribed to the very nature of production technology, consumer preferences (as described by market demands) and, perhaps, to the system of non-discriminatory simple prices which are taken throughout the analysis to constitute the only form of prices available.

One of the principal lessons of PCMs is that monopoly does not necessarily entail such welfare losses. Rather, the weak invisible hand theorem shows that under certain conditions sustainability and Ramsey optimality are consistent. Hence, the total of consumers' and producers' surpluses may well be maximised (subject to the constraint that firms be self-supporting) in the equilibrium of a monopoly which operates in contestable markets.

Even stronger results follow from the discussion in earlier portions of this section and in Section II. We showed that, under certain conditions, sustainability and a first-best solution are consistent in an oligopoly with a small number of firms. When minimisation of industry cost requires that each good be produced by at least two firms, sustainability requires that any equilibrium should satisfy the necessary conditions for a first-best allocation of resources. Thus, in these cases, the invisible hand has the same power over oligopoly in contestable markets that it exercises over a perfectly-competitive industry.

However, in the other cases discussed in this section, there are systematic reasons indicating that unsustainability may plague the industry configurations that are Ramsey optimal. Industry configurations involving firms that are partial monopolies, as well as those that constitute generalised Chamberlinian structures, may be such. They may lie outside the set of market forms in which decentralised decision making, guided by the price system, can attain results as desirable as those achievable, in theory, by a perfectly-informed and beneficent planner, even if he is constrained to permit firms to break even.

Examination of the requirements of contestability in the 'mixed case' discussed above readily brings out the difficulties, though it is well known that (sustainable) Chamberlinian equilibria may not be even 'second-best'. Suppose the planner were given the task of maximising aggregate consumers' surplus in markets 1 and 2, subject to the constraint that, in aggregate, the *industry* (i.e., the product 1 monopolist and all the specialised firms) at least break-even: this is the case we have referred to as the *viable-industry Ramsey optimum*. Even without characterising this programme formally, it is easy to discern the qualitative properties of the solution. As long as the products are substitutes with finite own-price elasticities of demand, the usual Ramsey inverse-elasticity rule will require that there be a positive mark-up over the relevant *social* marginal cost for *each* product. For product 2, this social marginal cost is given by $C_2(0, y_2^s) = C_2(y_1^m, y_2^m) = p_2^*$. Thus, the viable-industry Ramsey optimum would require $p_2 > p_2^*$, which is clearly unsustainable because of the profit inducement thereby offered to entering specialty firms.

It is also easy to see that unsustainability remains a problem in this example. This is so even if we lower our sights a bit and instruct our planner to seek what we have called a *viable-firm Ramsey optimum* involving the maximisation of consumer's plus producers' surplus and subject to the constraints that *each* active firm earn a non-negative profit. For the solution to this programme, too, would require a $p_2 > p_2^*$, rendering it unsustainable.

It is far from clear that the failure of either type of Ramsey optimum to meet the requirements of sustainability should be viewed as a form of market failure. For it can be shown that contestability can still claim an achievement in such cases, ensuring what we have called 'autarkic Ramsey optimality'. Under this, each firm acts so as to maximise the welfare of its customers, subject to its own financial viability *given the behaviour of other firms*. It is not difficult to show that the achievement of a result superior to this would require intervention that, in effect, directed some firms to undertake actions harmful to their own interests and to those of their customers, in order to benefit other firms in the industry. This may be interpreted to mean that here contestable markets perform as well as one could hope with any decentralised markets employing the pursuit of self-interest and a price system in order to guide the allocation of resources.

V CONCLUDING COMMENT

Our book, *Contestable Markets and the Theory of Industry Structure*, began as an attempt at systematic exploration of the properties of multi-product cost functions that are crucial for the determination of market structure. However, we feel that, in addition, it makes two contributions to value theory. It provides a static (partial) equilibrium theory of industry structure, conduct and performance more generally applicable than what was available before. This static theory is, itself, replete with the kind of testable implications and refutable hypotheses required to satisfy the methodological tastes of Milton Friedman or the Samuelson of the *Foundations of Economic Analysis*. We hope others will continue to join us in drawing them out. The model in Section IV(A) provides one starting point. Second, we have gone further and offered another meta-hypothesis: i.e., that the theory of perfectly-contestable markets will yield good predictions for cases in which sunk costs are unimportant. This, too, is subject to empirical testing and refutation. Thus, in addition to the provision of normative benchmarks, we hope to have offered grist for the mill of positive economics.

NOTES

1. We are grateful for their generous support to the Economics Program of the Division of Social Sciences of the National Science Foundation, the Division of Information Science and Technology of the National Science Foundation, the Sloan Foundation, and to the organisers of the IEA Conference on New Developments in Market Structure. The views

362   *The Perfectly Contestable Market*

expressed are those of the authors and do not necessarily reflect those of the institutions with which they are affiliated.

2. Much of the material presented here is a summary of the analysis in Baumol, Panzar and Willig (1982). This work builds upon published writings by authors too numerous to list here. The book includes an extensive list of references that is, inevitably, incomplete.

3. *Proof* $p \cdot y \leq C(y)$, $\forall y \in R^n_+$, implies that $p^e \cdot y \leq C(y)$, $\forall y \in R^n_+$, for $p^e \leq p$. Then $p^e \cdot y \leq C(y)$ for $p^e \leq p$ and $y \leq Q(p^e)$.

4. *Proof* (i) Otherwise, $p^e = p$ and $y^e = y^i$ would be a profitable entry plan. (ii) Otherwise, if $p_S \cdot y^i_S < C(y^i) - C(y^i_{N-S})$, $p \cdot y^i = C(y^i)$ would imply that $p_{N-S} y^i_{N-S} > C(y^i_{N-S})$. Then $p^e = p$ and $y^e = y^i_{N-S}$ would be a profitable entry plan. (iii) Otherwise, $p^e = p$ and $y^e = y^i - \epsilon u^j$ would be a profitable entry plan, for some $\epsilon > 0$, where u^j is the jth unit co-ordinate vector.

5. *Proof* Suppose $y^k_j < \sum^m_{h=1} y^h_j = Q_j(p)$ and $p_j > C_j(y^k)$. Consider this function of the scalar t: $\psi(t) = p \cdot (y^k + tu^j) - C(y^k + tu^j)$, where u^j is the vector with zeros for each component except for the jth, which is unity. $\psi(t)$ is the profit earned by an entry plan replicating all of the activities of firm k with the exception of an increase by amount t in the output of good j. Evaluating it at $t = 0$, $\psi(0) = p \cdot y^k - C(y^k) = 0$, since a firm in a sustainable configuration must earn exactly zero profit. Differentiation yields $\psi'(t) = p_j - C_j(y^k + tu^j)$, and, at $t = 0$, $\psi'(0) = p_j - C_j(y^k) > 0$ which is positive by hypothesis. Thus, the profit earned by the entry plan increases from zero as t is increased from 0. Hence, there exists some $\bar{t} > 0$ such that $\psi(t) > 0$ for $0 < t < \bar{t}$. Moreover, the entry plan is feasible for $0 < t \leq Q_j(p) - y^k_j$ so that the entrant's output of good j, $y^k_j + t$, remains no greater than the amount demanded by consumers, $Q_j(p)$. Consequently, for $0 < t \leq \min(\bar{t}, Q_j(p) - y^k_j)$, the entry plan is both feasible and profitable, which contradicts the hypothesis that the industry configuration is sustainable. Our result follows: p_j must be equal to $C_j(y^k)$ for firm k's output vector to be part of a sustainable configuration in which firm k is not the sole producer of good j.

6. *Proof* The proof is by contradiction. Suppose there were another group of firms with output levels, $\hat{y}^1, \ldots, \hat{y}^k$, that could produce the same total output ($\sum^m_{i=1} y^i$) as that offered by a given sustainable configuration at lower cost. Thus, $\sum^k_{j=1} \hat{y}^j = \sum^m_{i=1} y^i$ and $\sum^k_{j=1} C(\hat{y}^j) < \sum^m_{i=1} C(y^i)$. Then at the original prices, p, the profits of the new group would, in total, be positive; i.e., $\sum^k_{j=1} (\hat{y}^j \cdot p - C(\hat{y}^j)) = \sum_j(\hat{y}^j \cdot p) - \sum_j C(\hat{y}^j) = p \cdot \sum_j \hat{y}^j - \sum_j C(\hat{y}^j) = p \cdot \sum_i y^i - \sum_i C(\hat{y}^j) > p \cdot \sum_i y^i - \sum_i C(y^i) = \sum_i(p \cdot y^i - C(y^i)) \geq 0$. Consequently, to some firm j in the new group, the old prices would have yielded a positive profit, $\hat{y}^j p - C(\hat{y}^j) > 0$. Hence, $p^e = p$ and $y^e = \hat{y}^j \leq \sum_i y^i = Q(p)$ would have constituted a profitable entry plan that rendered the given configuration unsustainable.

7. This result is extended in our book, in Proposition 2D3, to cases in which the minimum level of average cost extends over a smaller range of outputs.

8. While the *analytics* of this section are based upon those of Section 10H of our book, we are indebted to Sanford Grossman for pointing the way to the richer interpretation presented here.

9. The present analysis yields contestable behaviour as a consequence of less-stringent sufficient conditions than the assumptions of costless and instantaneous entry and exit and an incumbent's price adjustment lag implicit in the informal discussion of Baumol (1982). Thus, it provides us with an opportunity to clarify two issues raised by Martin Weitzman (1983) and by Marius Schwartz and Robert Reynolds (1983) in their critiques of the theory. (For a more complete discussion, see our 'Comment on the Comments'.) Both arguments are based on the mistaken belief that those strong sufficient conditions are also *necessary* for the theory of perfect contestability to be applicable.

Weitzman argued that our theory is incompatible with anything but constant returns to scale and thus is not a generalisation of perfect competition at all. For if entry and exit are perfectly costless and instantaneous, there can never be any economies of scale because a firm can produce as small a quantity of output as it desires by entering a market, producing at minimum efficient scale, however large it may be, but doing so for only a very brief period. If minimum efficient scale yields an output of 10 000 units per hour, the firm can produce 2500 units at the same unit cost by effecting production for only 15 minutes and then disbanding the production facilities, without incurring any exit cost. The firm can then sell the 2500 units over the course of the hour by storing it until customers materialise. Thus, a steady flow of demand at a rate of 2500 units per hour can be met at the same unit cost as the 10 000 unit flow of demand sufficient to keep a firm's production facilities continuously occupied at the cost-minimising output level.

Many outputs and production processes may fit this parable as a limiting case, but many do not. First, some items, notably services, cannot be stored at all. They perish the instant they are produced, and one cannot get around this problem by taking the time they are held in inventory to be very brief, approaching zero in the limit. Second, fixed investment does not always take the form of capacity capable of turning out a continuous steady flow of output. Rather, some types of processes require an irreducible amount of production *time* to be effective and in that time they yield some fixed minimum batch of output. More generally, the minimal average cost per unit produced may be achievable only if the production process is run at a particular intensity over a particular span of time. In these cases the technique of 'substituting' the perfect divisibility of time to compensate for other indivisibilities is inapplicable.

The Weitzman argument against the applicability of perfect contestability to non-constant returns to scale suffers from another more fundamental problem – a mischaracterisation of contestability resulting from a confusion between *economic* and technological notions of sunk costs. As we have just seen, to produce its results, even the limiting case of perfect contestability does *not* require entry and exit to be instantaneous. Rather, it is sufficient that the process be rapid enough so that the entrant does not find his investment vulnerable to a retaliatory response by the incumbent. The length of this time period is not exclusively a technological datum, but is also the result of business practice and opportunities in the market in question. This period can be as long as the longest period for which it is credible for buyers to commit their patronage to the entrant. Thus, perfect contestability can survive the technological imposition of a minimum production-time requirement $t^* \leq \tau$, while the Weitzman parable cannot.

The issue raised by Schwartz and Reynolds is very different and more significant. They point out, correctly, that the conditions required for *perfect* contestability are certain to be violated in reality, at least to some degree. It then becomes important to ask whether small deviations from such conditions are likely to alter substantially the conclusions of the analysis. Focusing on the incumbent's price adjustment lag, they argue that relaxing that assumption moves the market outcome far from the contestable equilibrium. Of course the model of this section has revealed that perfect contestability does *not* require such a lag. However, this issue is relevant in the case of the absence of sunk costs: an assumption that is necessary for perfect contestability in our current formulation. The moral of the analysis of this section is that models of behaviour under imperfect contestability in which behaviour converges continuously towards that under perfect contestability are possible and can be extremely plausible. In the model discussed above, and no doubt in others as well, where there are almost no sunk costs, markets are almost perfectly contestable.

It should be emphasised that models which support the robustness of contestability analysis follow a relatively long tradition going back at least to the work of J. S. Bain. This tradition holds that increased ease of entry and exit improves the welfare performance of firms and industries. On this subject, the theory of contestability has only sought to contribute insights on the underpinnings of that judgement. Certainly it is a view widely accepted on the basis of casual observation, though compelling empirical testing still remains to be carried out. One step in this direction is the recent empirical work by Ioannis Kessides (1982), which shows that among 4-digit US manufacturing industries, entry increases with the profit levels of incumbents, holding fixed the expected losses from the possibility of exit. These expected losses are greater, Kessides finds, the greater are the sunk costs (as measured by several proxies) that must be committed by an entrant. Sunk costs deter entry and also diminish the rate at which entry responds to incumbents' profits. In Kessides' estimated model, these effects are statistically significant and they behave in a continuous and monotonic manner. They lend some support to the hypothesis that market performance depends continuously on the degree of imperfection in their contestability.

10. A multi-product firm with diseconomies of scope cannot constitute part of a sustainable configuration, by Proposition 5. With strict economies of scope, a configuration comprised solely of single-product firms cannot minimise industry costs and so cannot be sustainable, again by Proposition 5.

11. It is shown as Lemma 7D1 in our book that with decreasing average incremental costs of product i either $C((y_i^a + y_i^b) + y_{N-i}^a) + C(y_{N-i}^b) < C(y^a) + C(y^b)$ or $C((y_i^a + y_i^b) + y_{N-i}^b) + C(y_{N-i}^a) <$

$C(y^a) + C(y^b)$. Thus, no configuration with more than one firm producing good i can minimise industry costs. The price of such a good must exceed marginal cost in PCMs because, by Proposition 3, price cannot be less than average incremental cost, and this is greater than marginal cost, except in the knife's-edge case of a locally unitary degree of product-specific scale economies.

12. See the text of Chapter 8 and its Appendix II in our book for a complete statement, proof, and citations.

13. See Proposition 11D2 in our book.

14. However, in markets that are not contestable, monopoly firms may have incentives to extend their operations into related lines of business in a manner that does not serve the public interest. See J. Ordover and R. Willig (1981).

15. This subsection and part of the next essentially reproduce the discussion in Section 11F and 11G of our book, pp. 329–34.

REFERENCES

Baumol, William J. (1982) 'Contestable Markets: An Uprising in the Theory of Industry Structure', *American Economic Review*, vol. 72, no. 1, Mar., pp. 1–15.

Baumol, William J., Panzar, John C. and Willig, Robert D. (1982) *Contestable Markets and the Theory of Industry Structure* (San Diego: Harcourt Brace and Jovanovich).

——, (1983) 'Comment on the Comments', *American Economic Review*, vol. 73, no. 3, Jun.

Kessides, Ioannis (1982) 'Toward a Testable Model of Entry: A Study of the U.S. Manufacturing Industries', Princeton University, unpublished thesis.

Ordover, Janusz and Willig, Robert (1981) 'An Economic Definition of Predation: Pricing and Product Innovation', *Yale Law Journal*, vol. 90, no. 473, Dec., pp. 1–44.

Schwartz, Marius and Reynolds, Robert (1983) 'Comment', *American Economic Review*, vol. 73, no. 3. Jun.

Weitzman, Martin (1983) 'Contestable Markets: An Uprising in the Theory of Industry Structure: Comment', *American Economic Review*, vol. 73, no. 3, Jun.

[23]

Monopolistic competition with outside goods

Steven C. Salop

Bureau of Economics
Federal Trade Commission

*The Chamberlinian monopolistically competitive equilibrium has been explored
and extended in a number of recent papers. These analyses have paid only
cursory attention to the existence of an industry outside the Chamberlinian
group. In this article I analyze a model of spatial competition in which a second
commodity is explicitly treated. In this two-industry economy, a zero-profit
equilibrium with symmetrically located firms may exhibit rather strange properties. First, demand curves are kinked, although firms make "Nash" conjectures. If equilibrium lies at the kink, the effects of parameter changes are
perverse. In the short run, prices are rigid in the face of small cost changes.
In the long run, increases in costs lower equilibrium prices. Increases in market
size raise prices. The welfare properties are also perverse at a kinked equilibrium.*

1. Introduction

■ The Chamberlinian (1931) zero-profit monopolistically competitive equilibrium has been explored and extended in a number of recent papers. These
analyses have focused on the monopolistically competitive industry and have
paid only cursory attention to the existence of an industry outside the Chamberlinian group. In this paper, a model of spatial competition is analyzed in which
a second commodity is explicitly treated.

In this two-industry economy, a zero-profit equilibrium with symmetrically
located firms may exhibit rather strange properties. First, demand curves are
kinked, even though firms make "Nash" conjectures. If equilibrium is a tangency
solution away from the kink, the short- and long-run responses to parameter changes
are conventional. However, if equilibrium lies at the kink, the effects of parameter changes are perverse. In the short run, prices are rigid in the face of small
cost changes. In the long run, increases in costs lower equilibrium prices.
Interpreting the cost increase as an excise tax, this result states that the incidence
of the tax is negative. Increases in market size raise prices. The welfare prop-

This is a revised version of a survey paper entitled "Monopolistic Competition Reconstituted"
(1976). I am indebted to Don Hester, Lew Johnson, Bob Mackay, Perry Quick, Steve Salant, Joe
Stiglitz, Andy Weiss, the referee and editor, for helpful comments and to Mary Ann Henry for
editing and typing. The remarks in this paper represent only my personal views. They are not
intended to be, and should not be construed as, representative of the views of any other member of
the Federal Trade Commission staff or the individual Commissioners.

142 / THE BELL JOURNAL OF ECONOMICS

erties are also perverse at a kinked equilibrium. Decreases in cost and increases in market size lower both consumer and aggregate welfare.

In the next section the formal model is presented and the symmetric zero-profit Nash equilibrium (SZPE) is defined. Conditions for existence of the SZPE are derived in Section 3. Comparative statics and welfare properties are explored in Sections 4 and 5, respectively. The paper concludes with a short discussion of the deterrence equilibrium concept.

2. The basic model

■ In this section we analyze a variant of the traditional Hotelling (1929) model of spatial competition which is derived from Lerner and Singer (1937). In this variant the economy that is envisioned consists of two industries. The one upon which we focus is monopolistically competitive with differentiated brands and decreasing average costs; the other is a competitive industry producing a homogeneous commodity. Each of L consumers purchases either one unit or none[1] of the differentiated commodity according to preferences, prices, and the distribution of brands in product space. Remaining income is spent on the homogeneous commodity.

Each consumer has a most-preferred brand specification l^*. A brand l different from the most preferred specification is valued lower according to preferences in product space $U(l,l^*)$. The product space of the industry is taken to be an infinite line or the unit-circumference of a circle. While neither assumption is realistic, both allow the "corner" difficulties of the original Hotelling model to be ignored and an industry equilibrium with identical prices by equally-spaced firms to obtain. Eliminating the technical difficulties makes it simpler to analyze the qualitative equilibrium properties of the model. Thus, the model is a benchmark for subsequent analyses with nonuniform preferences across empirically validated product spaces. By eliminating technical problems, this model allows a focus on the essential interactions of firms in an industry.

If there are n brands of the differentiated commodity available at prices p_i and locations l_i, a consumer whose most preferred specification is l^* will purchase one unit from some brand if the maximum surplus of utility less price across brands outweighs the surplus from the homogeneous other good. Denoting that surplus by $\bar{s}$, we have the decision rule: Purchase one unit of the brand satisfying

$$\max_i \ [U(l_i,l^*) - p_i] \geqq \bar{s}. \tag{1}$$

The traditional model of constant transport costs is captured with preferences given by

$$U(l_i,l^*) = u - c\,|l_i - l^*|, \tag{2}$$

where the "distance" $|l_i - l^*|$ refers to the shortest arc length between l_i and l^*. In this case, equation (1) may be rewritten as follows:

$$\max_i \ [v - c\,|l_i - l^*| - p_i] \geqq 0, \tag{3}$$

where the effective reservation price is given by

$$v = u - \bar{s} > 0. \tag{4}$$

---

[1] The model easily generalizes to elastic demands.

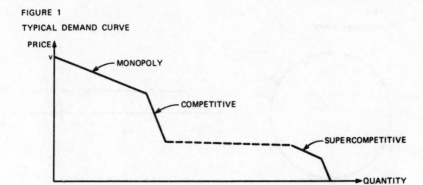

FIGURE 1

TYPICAL DEMAND CURVE

We now explore the existence and properties of a symmetric zero-profit Nash equilibrium (SZPE). By symmetric we mean an equilibrium in which the brands are equally spaced around the circular product space and charge identical prices. By zero profits, we mean an equilibrium in which free entry leads to a situation of each brand earning zero profits. The equilibrium is Nash in that each brand chooses a best price, given a perception that all other brands hold their prices constant. The conclusion discusses the requirement that the number of brands be integer-valued.

The methodology here consists of deriving the perceived demand curve for a single representative brand as a function of other brands' prices and locations and then finding a tangency between that demand curve and the average cost curve. Three regions of the representative brand's demand curve may be distinguished: the "monopoly," "competitive," and "supercompetitive" regions. The "monopoly" region consists of those prices in which the brand's entire market consists of consumers for whom the surplus of no other brand exceeds the surplus of the homogeneous outside good. The "competitive" region is composed of those prices in which customers are attracted who would otherwise purchase some other differentiated brand. The "supercompetitive" region consists of those prices in which all the customers of the closest neighboring brand are captured. These three regions of a typical demand curve are illustrated in Figure 1.

Suppose the representative brand charges price p and its nearest competitors located at distance $1/n$ charge $\bar{p}$, as shown in Figure 2. We derive the regions of the demand curve as follows. In the absence of competition from other differentiated brands, the representative brand captures all consumers living within a distance where the net surplus given in (3) in nonnegative. Denoting the maximum distance by $\hat{x}$ and substituting into (3) we have,

$$\hat{x} = \frac{v - p}{c}. \tag{5}$$

If there are L consumers around the circle, since the brand captures customers within a distance $\hat{x}$ on each side, its monopoly demand q^m is given by

$$q^m = \frac{2L}{c} (v - p). \tag{6}$$

This defines the potential monopoly market of the representative brand.

Industrial Organization

FIGURE 2

THE CIRCULAR MARKET

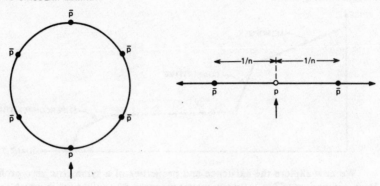

Those consumers residing in the potential monopoly market of two brands purchase from the one offering higher net surplus. If the brands are located a distance apart of $1/n$ and the neighboring brand on one side charges a price $\bar{p}$, then from (3) the representative brand captures all those consumers within a distance x given by

$$v - cx - p \leqq v - c\left(\frac{1}{n} - x\right) - \bar{p}. \tag{7}$$

Denoting by $\bar{x}$, the value for which (7) holds with equality, we have

$$\bar{x} = \frac{1}{2c}(\bar{p} + c/n - p) \tag{8}$$

and hence a firm's competitive demand $q^c = 2L\bar{x}$ is given by

$$q^c = \frac{L}{c}(\bar{p} + c/n - p). \tag{9}$$

Differentiating (6) and (9), the slopes $sl(D)$ of the demand curve in these two regions are given by

$$sl(D^m) = -c/2L \tag{10}$$

$$sl(D^c) = -c/L. \tag{11}$$

Thus, we have the unusual result that demand is more elastic in the monopoly region than in the competitive region. Moreover, as illustrated in Figure 1, the monopoly region comes at higher prices.

The two regions fit together as follows. Suppose the right-side neighbor has a potential monopoly market illustrated in Figure 3. At prices above v, the representative brand obtains no customers. As it begins lowering prices below v, it captures demand from the homogeneous good according to the monopoly

FIGURE 3

MARKET SEGMENTS

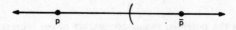

FIGURE 4

MARKET OVERLAP

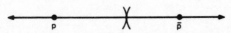

slope $c/2L$. Eventually its price becomes low enough that its monopoly market overlaps the monopoly market of its neighbor as illustrated in Figure 4. Now as it lowers price further, it begins to capture customers from its neighbor according to the steeper competitive slope c/L. At the kink in Figure 2, the monopoly regions just touch. Note that the kink arises here from the existence of the other industry, not from the non-Nash perceptions discussed by Sweezy (1939). It generalizes to higher dimensional spaces.[2]

At some lower price, even those customers residing at the neighbor are indifferent between the representative firm at p and the neighbor at $\bar{p}$ (and additional surplus $c(1/n)$). This price p_z is given by

$$p_z = \bar{p} - c/n. \tag{12}$$

At prices below p_z, the representative firm captures the entire market of its neighbor, for not only are those consumers residing at the neighbor willing to incur the surplus loss c/n for the price differential $\bar{p} - p$, but so are all the customers of the neighbor. Thus the representative brand's demand has a discontinuity at p_z from this "predatory" pricing.

The demand curve in Figure 2 displays the typical shape of these three regions. It shifts according to the prices and locations of the neighboring brands. Since demand can never exceed the monopoly demand, the kink always lies on that monopoly curve, as illustrated in Figure 5 (with supercompetitive regions deleted). Note that the market may be so competitive as to make the kink nonexistent. This occurs when the neighbors' potential monopoly market includes the location of the representative brand.

3. Existence of a symmetric zero profit equilibrium (SZPE)

■ A SZPE is defined as a price p and a number of brands n such that every equally spaced[3] Nash price setter's maximum profit price choice earns zero profits. We ignore the additional requirement that the number of brands must be an integer and discuss it later. In addition, the potential nonexistence of equilibrium arising from the discontinuity in demand is also postponed. If an equilibrium exists, the representative brand's demand curve and average cost curve will be tangent, for then the zero-profit point is surely also one of maximum profits. Three equilibrium configurations are possible, as illustrated in Figure 6, where the monopoly, kinked, and competitive equilibrium prices are denoted by subscripts (m,k,c), respectively.

At the monopoly equilibrium, some consumers lying between two neighboring brands may not purchase the differentiated commodity. Thus, the markets

---

[2] This may be confirmed in a two-dimensional product space. The monopoly market is circular, while competitive markets are polygonal.

[3] This equilibrium concept is static. In a dynamic context, it assumes that firms may costlessly relocate in response to entry and, in fact, do relocate. Thus, equal spacing is maintained. For a discussion of an alternative equilibrium concept, see the conclusions.

Industrial Organization

FIGURE 5

FAMILY OF DEMAND CURVES

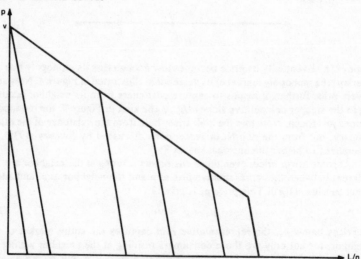

of neighbors may not overlap and each can act as a monopolist, constrained only by the outside commodity. Monopoly equilibria with and without overlap are pictured in Figure 6. At a kinked equilibrium, markets just touch. As illustrated in Figure 6, since the extension of the monopoly demand curve lies above the average cost curve, the monopoly price p_m lies below the kinked equilibrium price p_k. At the competitive equilibrium configuration, monopoly markets completely overlap. However, p_c may be above or below p_m, depending on demand and technologies.

It is easy to show graphically which equilibrium configuration obtains for any set of technology and demand parameters $\{F,m,v,c,L\}$. Simply drawing the average cost curve and the entire family of demand curves, existence of an equilibrium configuration requires maximum profits equal to zero-point E in Figure 7. A zero-profit point like G does not satisfy maximum profits because it is dominated by a point like F.

FIGURE 6

EQUILIBRIUM CONFIGURATIONS

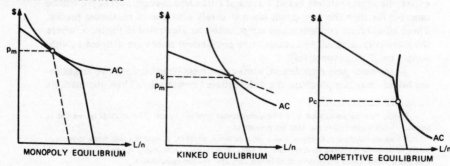

FIGURE 7

EXISTENCE OF EQUILIBRIUM

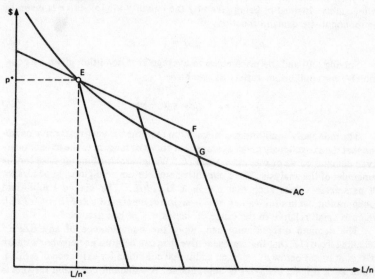

The SZPE satisfies two conditions: marginal revenue (less than or) equal to marginal cost and price equal to average cost. For constant marginal cost m and fixed cost F, the SZPE is given by

$$p + q\,\frac{dp}{dq} \leqq m \qquad (13)$$

$$p = m + F/q, \qquad (14)$$

and from symmetry, if the equilibrium has no gaps,

$$q = L/n. \qquad (15)$$

At the monopoly equilibrium dp/dq is given by $sl(D^m)$ in (10); at the competitive equilibrium by $sl(D^c)$ in (11); and at the kinked equilibrium by a slope between $sl(D^m)$ and $sl(D^c)$. Substituting (15) and (10) into (13) and (14), the monopoly price and number of brands[4] are given by

$$p_m = m + c/2n_m \qquad (16)$$

$$n_m = \frac{1}{\sqrt{2}}\,\sqrt{cL/F}. \qquad (17)$$

Using (11) instead of (10), the competitive equilibrium is given by[5]

$$p_c = m + c/n_c \qquad (18)$$

$$n_c = \sqrt{cL/F}. \qquad (19)$$

---

[4] There may be gaps at a monopoly equilibrium. This calculation yields the maximum number of brands at a monopoly equilibrium.

[5] See Grubel (1963) for a short derivation of the competitive equilibrium.

The values (p_k, n_k) for a kinked equilibrium lie between the values given in (16)–(19). Since there is no tangency at a kinked equilibrium, (13) holds as an inequality. Instead of being given by the equality in (13), price is given by the monopolistic demand function, or

$$p_k = v - (c/L)q = v - c/n. \tag{20}$$

Solving (20) and the price equal to average cost condition given by equation (14) for equilibrium variety n_k, we have

$$\frac{F}{L} n_k + c/n_k = v - m. \tag{21}$$

The monopoly equilibrium configuration requires the very restrictive condition that the exogenously given average cost curve be tangent to the exogenously given demand curve or $v - m = \sqrt{2cF/L}$.[6] We ignore this limiting case for the remainder of the analysis. The competitive equilibrium configuration occurs for all parameter values such that $v - m \geqq \frac{3}{2}\sqrt{cF/L}$.[7] The kinked equilibrium configuration occurs for values of $v - m$ in the interval $[\sqrt{2cF/L}, \frac{3}{2}\sqrt{cF/L}]$, which is small relative to the range of values $v - m$ can assume.[8]

The demand discontinuity can imply the nonexistence of any SZPE.[9] Recalling from (12) that the representative firm can capture its neighbor's entire market at prices below $\bar{p} - c/n$, an additional condition for existence of a SZPE is that such pricing behavior is unprofitable. A sufficient condition for this is that the predatory price $\bar{p} - c/n$ does not exceed marginal cost m, for price equal to or below marginal cost necessarily is a losing strategy in the presence of fixed costs. Referring to (16) and (18), supercompetitive behavior is not profitable, since the equilibrium price is no greater than $m + c/n$. Similarly, if marginal costs are increasing, as with U-shaped AC curves, then the market-capturing price lies below the minimum AC price. However, if marginal costs are decreasing, then such price cuts may be profitable and cause nonexistence of a SZPE.

4. Comparative statics

■ As the exogenous technological or demand parameters $\{F, m, v, c, L\}$ vary, the equilibrium price-variety pair also changes. These changes may be calculated from the equilibrium values in equations (16)–(19).

□ **Competitive equilibria.** The comparative statics at competitive equilibria are straightforward and traditional. Substituting (19) into (18) we have

$$p_c = m + \sqrt{\frac{cF}{L}} \tag{22}$$

$$n_c = \sqrt{\frac{cL}{F}}. \tag{23}$$

---

[6] For the derivation, see the derivation of equation (31) below when profits are zero.

[7] The derivation is as follows. Referring to Figure 6, the equilibrium p_c derived in (18) and (19) must lie below the monopoly portion of the demand curve, or $v - \frac{1}{2}(c/L)(L/n_c) \geqq p_c$. Substituting for p_c and n_c, the stated condition obtains.

[8] This interval may be larger for alternative technological and demand specifications.

[9] See Roberts-Sonnenschein (1977) for examples of discontinuous reaction functions leading to nonexistence of equilibrium.

As fixed costs (F) rise, price rises and equilibrium variety falls. Changes in marginal costs (m) are fully shifted onto consumers; equilibrium variety remains the same. Surprisingly perhaps, changes in the net valuation v have no effect on the equilibrium. The market is competitive enough that aggregate demand is unaffected by changes in this demand price.

As the value of product differentiation (c) falls, prices fall and variety falls. As market size (L) rises, prices fall and variety rises. As c/L decreases, demand becomes more elastic and price moves toward marginal cost. Thus, the ratio c/L is the relevant measure of monopolistic product differentiation in the model. For U-shaped average costs, perfect competition obtains when $c/L = 0$, for then every brand faces a perfectly elastic demand function.

☐ **Kinked equilibria.** The comparative statics at kinked equilibria are all perverse. An increase in either fixed or marginal costs lowers prices. This is illustrated diagrammatically below as a movement from E to E'. Intuitively, cost increases reduce the equilibrium number of brands, allowing the remaining brands to further exploit scale economies. This is a very striking result. If the increase in costs is interpreted as an excise tax levied on the industry, then the incidence of that excise tax is negative at the kinked equilibrium. In terms of consumer welfare, the lower price is offset by the decline in variety, of course. However, it is shown in the next section that consumer welfare does rise from the tax, even if the proceeds of the tax are ignored.

It should be emphasized that this perverse reaction to a cost increase is a long-run response that results from the exit of marginal firms. In the short run, there is no reaction at all. Since the marginal revenue cuₐve is discontinuous at the kinked equilibrium, a small change in marginal costs induces no price response. Thus, the industry responds to a small marginal cost increase as follows. In the short run, prices and quantities do not change, though profits fall below normal (zero). These losses induce some firms to exit, resulting in higher demand for those that remain. This increased demand allows the remaining firms to better exploit scale economies, resulting in decreased long-run prices.

An increase in the valuation (v) raises price and variety, as illustrated by the movement from E to E''. As may be seen from Figure 8, price rises by more than the increase in valuation, as scale economies are lost. As with cost increases, the welfare effect of this increase in valuation is also perverse; it may be shown that consumer welfare falls. Interpreting the increase in valuation as arising from informative advertising and the cost increase as the cost of that informative advertising, the valuation effect lowers welfare, while the cost effect raises welfare.

Decreases in c/L, arising from either an increase in market size (L) or a decrease in the value of product differentiation (c), raise prices in equilibrium, as illustrated in Figure 9 as a movement from E to E'. As with the other comparative statics discussed, this result is the reverse of what occurs in the competitive equilibrium configuration.

5. Welfare analysis

■ **Product selection.** It has been pointed out by Spence (1976) and others that the production of some unprofitable commodities may be optimal and the production of some profitable commodities may be nonoptimal. For the circular

FIGURE 8

COMPARATIVE STATICS OF (v, m, F): KINKED EQUILIBRIUM

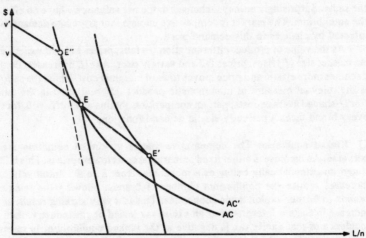

market, this may be tested by comparing the condition under which a segment of the market will be served by a monopolist (the profitability condition) with the condition under which service yields positive net surplus (the optimality condition).

Suppose each brand produces up to the point where the net benefit to the marginal consumer, who is at a distance x^* from the brand serving him, is zero. Then, the net social benefit per brand of serving the entire circular market is:

$$B = 2L \int_0^{x^*} (v - cx - m)dx - F, \qquad (24)$$

FIGURE 9

COMPARATIVE STATICS OF c/L: KINKED EQUILIBRIUM

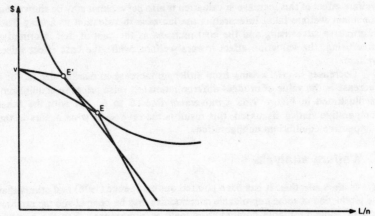

where the marginal consumer's benefit is given by

$$v - cx^* - m = 0. \tag{25}$$

Substituting (25) into (24) and integrating, we have

$$B = \frac{L}{c} (v - m)^2 - F, \tag{26}$$

and this surplus is nonnegative ($B \geq 0$) if and only if the following optimality condition is satisfied:

$$v - m \geq \sqrt{\frac{cF}{L}}. \tag{27}$$

On the other hand, a monopolistic firm will choose to serve any segment of the market only if its profits are nonnegative,[10] where profits for the monopoly portion of the demand function are given by

$$\Pi_m = \left(v - \frac{c}{2L} q - m \right) q - F. \tag{28}$$

Maximizing (28) with respect to q, we have

$$q_m = \frac{L}{c} (v - m). \tag{29}$$

Substituting (29) into (28), profits are given by

$$\Pi_m = \frac{L}{2c} (v - m)^2 - F. \tag{30}$$

Profits are nonnegative ($\Pi_m \geq 0$) if and only if the following profitability condition is satisfied:

$$v - m \geq \sqrt{\frac{2cF}{L}}. \tag{31}$$

Comparing the optimality and profitability conditions, we see that profitability is sufficient but not necessary for optimality. All markets served should be served, but not *vice versa*.

☐ **Optimal vs. equilibrium variety.** Given that the entire circular market should be served, the optimal price-variety pair may be compared with the equilibrium price-variety pair. A tradeoff between price and variety exists because of the scale economies present in production.

If n firms operate and serve the entire unit-circumference market, then the marginal consumer travels a distance $\frac{1}{2}n$ and a consumer located at $x \leq \frac{1}{2}n$ obtains a surplus in excess of marginal cost of $v - m - cx$. Since there are L consumers per unit distance and $2n$ intervals of length $\frac{1}{2}n$, total surplus is given by

$$W = 2n \int_0^{1/2n} (v - m - cx) L dx - nF. \tag{32}$$

---

[10] It should be noted that if one monopolist does not wish to serve one segment, no monopolist will serve any segment since the circular market is symmetric.

Integrating, we have:

$$W = \left(v - m - \frac{1}{4}\frac{c}{n}\right)L - nF. \tag{33}$$

The interpretation of (33) is the following. Since (i) the marginal consumer travels a distance of $\frac{1}{2}n$ in product space, (ii) the consumer who travels the shortest distance (zero) obtains his most preferred brand, and (iii) L consumers are distributed uniformly in product space, the average distance travelled is $\frac{1}{4}n$ at an imputed cost of c per unit. Then the average net surplus per consumer is $v - m - c/4n$. Total fixed costs are nF. Maximizing (33) with respect to the number of brands n to find the optimal price-variety mix, we have

$$n^* = \frac{1}{2}\sqrt{\frac{cL}{F}}. \tag{34}$$

Comparing this optimum to the possible equilibria given by (17), (19), and (21) we have

$$n^* < n_m < n_k < n_c. \tag{35}$$

That is, optimal variety is less than equilibrium variety for this circular market, if the market should be served.

    This result of too many brands is not robust, but rather depends crucially on the distribution of consumers and preferences. As Spence (1976) and others[11] have pointed out, the optimum depends on the difference between the average surplus and the surplus of the marginal consumer relative to fixed costs; the value of adding an extra brand (and respacing the others) effectively converts marginal consumers to average ones, at fixed cost F.[12]

    Graphically, the comparison of the equilibrium with the optimum may be made as follows. The planning problem in (33) is equivalent to maximizing average consumer welfare minus price $W(n,p)$ subject to the price equal to average cost breakeven constraint.[13] Since the average consumer travels a distance $\frac{1}{4}n$ in product space, we have

$$\max W(n,p) = v - p - \frac{1}{4}\frac{c}{n} \tag{36}$$

$$\text{subject to} \quad p = m + \frac{F}{L}n. \tag{37}$$

Equation (36) defines linear indifference curves in $(p, L/n)$ space with slope of $-\frac{1}{4}(c/L)$ while (37) expresses the constraint. As illustrated in Figure 10, a smaller value of S expresses a higher surplus $v - S$. Then, the optimum lies at the point where the average cost has slope equal to $-\frac{1}{4}(c/L)$, whereas equilibrium lies at the point where the average cost curve has slope between $-\frac{1}{2}(c/L)$ (for monopoly equilibrium) and $-c/L$ (for competitive equilibrium).

    A graphical representation of the optimum vs. equilibrium price-variety pair may be used to show the welfare effects of the comparative statics at

---

[11] For example, Dixit and Stiglitz (1977) and Lancaster (1975).

[12] It can be shown that any utility function that is concave in distance will yield excess variety, for a uniform consumer distribution. Convex functions are necessary for deficient variety.

[13] Since consumers have inelastic demands in this example, that price does not equal marginal cost introduces no distortion.

FIGURE 10

EQUILIBRIUM VS. OPTIMAL VARIETY

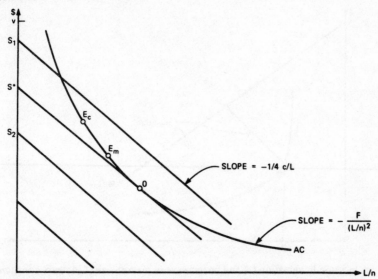

the kinked equilibrium. (See Figure 11.) For example, an increase in costs from AC to AC' that lowers prices will improve welfare, since the slope of the indifference curve $(-\frac{1}{4}c/L)$ is flatter than the slope of the monopoly demand curve $(-\frac{1}{2}c/L)$. Thus, movements down the demand curve represent higher welfare as illustrated below by comparing S to S'. Similar analysis will show that

FIGURE 11

DERIVATION OF OPTIMAL VARIETY

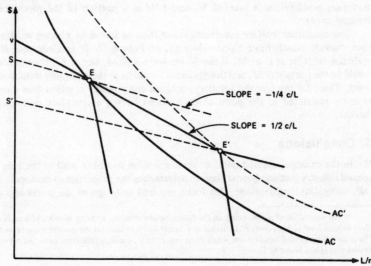

Industrial Organization

FIGURE 12

DERIVATION OF THE p(L/n) FUNCTION

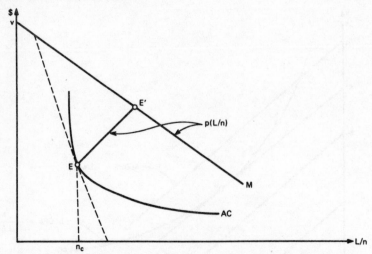

an increase in valuation (v) and an increase in market size (L) lowers consumer welfare.

Finally, we can determine the optimal number of brands given monopolistically competitive pricing. Spence (1976) shows that for his partial equilibrium model, the market solution is optimal. For the circular model studied here, the optimum is either the market equilibrium or complete monopoly. We may prove this as follows. First we derive the Nash equilibrium price for different (exogenously given) numbers of symmetrically spaced brands. We denote this relationship by $p(L/n)$.[14] The $p(L/n)$ function is illustrated in Figure 12 as $EE'M$, where we assume the SZPE (point E) is competitive. The complete monopoly equilibrium is labeled M, and $E'M$ is a portion of the monopoly demand curve.

The consumer welfare maximum could then be found by placing indifference curves, which have slope $-\frac{1}{4}(c/L)$, in Figure 12. It is clear that the optimum must lie at E or M. If the SZPE were kinked, say at E', then $p(L/n)$ would be the portion $E'M$, and the optimum would lie at the complete monopoly point. Thus, for the circular industry, optimal entry policy is either free entry or entry restricted to the point of each brand having a complete monopoly market.

6. Conclusions

■ In the example studied here, explicit attention has been paid to the role a second industry (outside goods) plays in determining the properties of monopolistically competitive equilibrium. This focus required us to ignore the possibility of

---

[14] The derivation of $p(L/n)$ relies on the following observation. For any number of brands n, there exists a level of fixed costs F' such that an n-brand SZPE obtains (or the market is not served). Thus, an n-brand Nash equilibrium, when fixed costs are F, yields equilibrium price $p(L/n)$ and excess profits per brand of $\Pi = F' - F$.

nonuniform preferences across more complicated and realistic product spaces or different technologies across brands.

The major contribution of the approach taken here, which was first noted by Lerner and Singer (1937), is to provide a rationalization of the kinked demand curve in terms of symmetric "Nash" conjectural variations. Previous rationalizations by Sweezy (1939) and others were based upon asymmetric competitive responses to price increases and decreases. This paper goes beyond Lerner and Singer by deriving the industry equilibrium and analyzing its properties.

The industry equilibrium model displays conventional properties when equilibrium occurs at a Chamberlinian tangency away from the kink. On the other hand, the properties of equilibria occurring at the kink are perverse. In the short run, industry prices do not adjust to small cost changes, as noted by Sweezy in his model. It is only through the process of entry and exit that the industry adjusts to cost changes. Moreover, at the kinked equilibrium, the long-run response to a cost increase is exit by some brands followed by a decrease in industry prices, as remaining brands better exploit scale economies.

The short-run price rigidity of the kinked equilibrium accords with casual empiricism. However, the long-run properties are more difficult to confirm or reject, since they depend on longer run entry adjustments. Moreover, the actual symmetric example analyzed entails the abstract and unrealistic assumptions of uniform preferences around a circular product space and identical cost functions and valuations among competing brands. While these assumptions considerably simplify the theoretical analysis, they make empirical confirmation more difficult.

Other shortcomings of the approach taken here are the zero-profit and costless relocation assumptions we have made. Because the technology is characterized by an indivisible fixed cost, the number of brands must be integer-valued. Therefore, free entry need not lead to a zero-profit equilibrium, as originally pointed out by Kaldor (1935) and analyzed by Eaton (1976). An interesting "deterrence" equilibrium concept built on these foundations has been explored for a circular market by Hay (1976) and Schmalensee (1977) and for other spatial markets by Prescott and Visscher (1977). In a deterrence equilibrium sequential entrants locate in such a way that no new entrant wishes to locate in the interval between two firms. As a result, the deterrence equilibrium has half the number of brands as the SZPE.

In the model analyzed here, the deterrence equilibrium configuration is generally that point in the $p(L/n)$ curve with the number of brands n equal to ½ the number at the SZPE.[15] If the SZPE is competitive, the deterrence equilibrium may be competitive, kinked, or at the monopoly point; which equilibrium occurs depends on the particular parameter values. Hay showed that if the deterrence equilibrium is competitive, prices are higher than at the SZPE. However, kinked or monopoly deterrence equilibria may result in lower prices than the competitive SZPE. Finally, if the SZPE is kinked, the deterrence equilibrium lies at the monopoly point and entails lower prices and unserved segments of the circular market.

---

[15] The exception arises when this point on $p(L/n)$ lies below the monopoly point on the monopoly portion of the demand curve. In this case, while the number of brands is still halved, the remaining brands raise price and lower output to the monopoly point. Hence, the deterrence equilibrium entails unserved segments of the circular market.

156 / THE BELL JOURNAL OF ECONOMICS

In closing, it should be reemphasized that the exact results derived here merely reflect the example used. That there is excess variety at equilibrium is not robust. The kink appears robust as the number of dimensions of product space increases. However, as Archibald-Rosenbluth (1975) and Weiss (1977) point out, equilibrium may not exist with higher dimensional product spaces.

References

ARCHIBALD, G.C. AND ROSENBLUTH, G. "The 'New' Theory of Consumer Demand and Monopolistic Competition." *Quarterly Journal of Economics*, Vol. 89 (1975).

CHAMBERLIN, E.H. *The Theory of Monopolistic Competition*. Cambridge, Mass.: Harvard University Press, 1931.

DIXIT, A.K. AND STIGLITZ, J.E. "Monopolistic Competition and Optimum Product Diversity." *The American Economic Review*, Vol. 67 (1977).

EATON, B.C. "Free Entry in One-Dimensional Models: Pure Profits and Multiple Equilibria." *Journal of Regional Science* (1976).

GRUBEL, H.G. "Wastes of Monopolistic Competition." (Based on a lecture by J. Tobin.) Yale University, 1963.

HOTELLING, H. "Stability in Competition," *Economic Journal*, Vol. 39 (1929).

KALDOR, N. "Market Imperfection and Excess Capacity." *Economica NS. 2* (1935).

LANCASTER, K. "Socially Optimal Product Differentiation." *The American Economic Review*, Vol. 65 (1975).

LERNER, A.P. AND SINGER, H.W. "Some Notes on Duopoly and Spatial Competition. *Journal of Political Economy*, Vol. 45 (1937).

PRESCOTT, E. AND VISSCHER, M. "Sequential Location Decisions among Firms with Foresight." *The Bell Journal of Economics*, Vol. 8 (1977).

ROBERTS, J. AND SONNENSCHEIN, H. "On the Foundations of the Theory of Monopolistic Competition." *Econometrica*, Vol. 75 (1977).

SCHMALENSEE, R. "Entry Deterrence in the Ready-to-Eat Breakfast Cereal Industry." *The Bell Journal of Economics*, Vol. 9 (1978).

SPENCE, A.M. "Product Selection, Fixed Costs and Monopolistic Competition." *Review of Economic Studies*, Vol. 43 (1976).

SWEEZY, P.M. "Demand under Conditions of Oligopoly." *Journal of Political Economy*, Vol. 47 (1939).

WEISS, A. "Spatial Competition with Two Dimensions." Unpublished manuscript, Bell Laboratories, 1977.

Name Index